COVID DAYS

A Further Chronicle of Law, Faith & History in the Time of Trump

Rex Grady

Lilburne & Company, LLC

Lilburne & Company, LLC
Santa Rosa, California
lilburneandcompany@gmail.com

Cover: *L'Énigme*, by Gustave Doré, 1870, {{PD-US-expired}}{{PD-Art}}

Covid Days: A Further Chronicle of Law, Faith & History in the Time of Trump/
Rex Grady -- 1st ed.
ISBN 978-0-578-85207-2

To My Father

Jeffrey Osborne Grady

TABLE OF CONTENTS

PROLOGUE

WHEN I commenced writing this second volume of my account of legal and constitutional culture and controversies during the years when Donald Trump was President of the United States, I could not have conceived how strange the times to come would prove to be, nor foreseen how radically the wheel would turn by the end of the President's four-year term. I fully expected that I would be writing a series of chapters on legal and constitutional challenges to the Trump Administration's policy choices, as well addressing the unrelenting critique of the President emanating from nearly every voice in the media, the Democrat Party, the bureaucracy and the intelligentsia.

Impeachment, of course, was predictable, as was its outcome. Accusations of treason against the President were fully consistent with what had come before. Debates over immigration policy, abortion, and control of the federal bureaucracy and the courts were all the stuff for which this book was intended to address. What wasn't expected even remotely was how every topic that could have been conceived of as forming a part of my larger narrative would become more or less changed by and made subject to the tale of a disease of curious origin that arrived on American shores near the start of the year the writing of this volume began. The disease transformed the trajectory of law and politics, our society and economy more quickly even than it physically infected the population. In a far more profound sense, it was a disease not of the body but of the mind, a poison injected into the thinking and rhetoric of the progressive generation and made manifest in actions so unprecedented that only a malignancy of the profoundest kind or outright demonic possession could explain it. Everywhere, shops closed, traffic lightened and our fellow citizens became unrecognizable behind masks they donned either in obedience to the ruler's command or out of sincere terror that a viral death awaited them should they literally show their faces in public.

The mania over the coronavirus generated many symptoms, not least of which was hypocrisy: the President was condemned for not wearing a mask when speaking to the press by people who could see no wrong when progressive governors, legislators and their families flaunted the same rule. No matter what the President did, he was wrong, and not merely wrong, but more wrong than anyone ever could be, and his wrongness would surely be the cause of the death that we were told was closing in around us.

The insanity of those who hated what the President stood for spilled over into violent uprisings around the country, the destruction of civil liberties by public and private actors (often in concert with one another), the abolition of public worship, the burning of private businesses, the beating and killing of police officers and bystanders, and the tearing down of statues commemorating people and causes that no card-carrying progressive could possibly tolerate. In seeking to destroy the President and the governing philosophy he championed, his critics and opponents would destroy the peace of the nation. For them, no price seemed too great for others to pay if it meant achieving the dual overthrow of the commander-in-chief and his commands.

Fear of the disease, both real and feigned, ultimately drove changes in the way we voted that could only lead to fraud and abuse come election day, and though warnings were given of the fate to come, few seemed at all concerned, including judges appointed by the President and legislatures dominated by the President's own party charged by the Constitution with the authority to regulate elections for federal offices.

So much distortion in the mind, so much unrest in society, could only lead to confusion and controversy unlike anything seen in recent years. As this chronicle of the law and our Constitution documents, that's exactly how this story concludes. So much hope for a Constitution restored; so many beneficial results flowing from a return to neglected ways of steering the ship of state, and all of it improbably due to the acumen of a leader who didn't conform in any way to what historically was considered to be the stuff of greatness, or even competence. Whether he was great or not, competent or incompetent, is less important than what he accomplished and tried to accomplish, and how an opposition driven seemingly mindless by their hatred of him and what he strove to achieve, managed to conceive and execute a strategy that overthrew both him and the classical image of the Constitution for which he might well be the last champion.

In the writing of the following pages, I remain grateful to a handful of people whose presence in my life, or the insights they provided, or the careful reading they undertook, made my life and my writing better had they not contributed in the various ways they did. My adversarial friend Walter Rubenstein read nearly every word with care and seldom failed either to provide a contrary opinion or a compliment for my learning and style. Andrew Quinn shared his own insights into many of the issues touched upon in this volume and again carefully read the manuscript and found all but those errors in the typescript I insisted on retaining through my own negligence. Jeffrey Scharfen reviewed the text for any lingering flaws, but informed me that he was too captivated by the subject matter to notice any—a fine compliment, but not very helpful in the detection and removal of defects. My wife Becky provided me with far greater support than she did in the writing of the first volume, if only because after publication of the earlier work she became convinced that I actually was writing, as opposed to simply trying to avoid her. Finally, I am grateful to the journalists and scholars of all philosophical inclinations who have provided me with factual information and scholarly insights that have shaped how I've perceived the topics of which I've written and made it possible for me to have some measure of confidence that my own biases have to some extent been fairly evaluated on the judgment seat of my mind before being fixed more or less forever in print.

January 20, 2021
Santa Rosa, California

"Impeach 45!"

NO fantasy has more animated the thoughts of many on the left since the emergence of Donald J. Trump as a major candidate for the presidency than his impeachment and removal from office. Many months before he won the 2016 contest, many on the left (and some on the right) earnestly speculated about possible routes by which removal might occur should he ever assume office. Impeachment, said a *Politico* correspondent in April of 2016, "is already on the lips of pundits, newspaper editorials, constitutional scholars, and even a few members of Congress."[1] Congressman Alan Grayson predicted that building the much ballyhooed border wall without congressional approval might spark the drafting of impeachment Articles.[2] Yale Law School lecturer Eugene Fidell speculated that any number of policy objectives, from torturing terrorists to killing their families, "if followed through on, would constitute high crimes and misdemeanours."[3]

Trump's victory early in November of 2016 provided impetus to further elaboration on the fantasy. Within a week after the election, *Vanity Fair* identified as many as thirty-seven newspaper headlines bearing the name Trump and variants of the word "impeach."[4] Law Professor Christopher Peterson of the University of Utah recommended impeachment as soon as Trump assumed office.[5] Elizabeth Warren and four of her fellow Senators on the Democrat side of the aisle went so far as to prepare a bill in December requiring the President to divest himself of any assets that "could pose a conflict of interest" and rendering the failure to do so a crime they believed was sufficient to satisfy the criteria for impeachment set forth in the Article II of the Constitution.[6]

---

[1] Darren Samuelsohn, "Could Trump be Impeached Shortly After He Takes Office? It's Highly Improbable, but Law Scholars and Political Junkies are Speculating About it," www.politico.com, April 17, 2016.

[2] Id.

[3] Id.

[4] T.A. Frank, "Will Trump Be Impeached?," www.vanityfair.com, November 14, 2016.

[5] Id.

[6] Emily Jane Fox, "Democrats are Paving the Way to Impeach Donald Trump," www.vanityfair.com, December 15, 2016.

Inauguration Day came and went, yet impeachment never happened, less because the President hadn't done anything impeachable than because those who desired it most were in the minority. The talk of it, however, never ceased. While her constituents wallowed in poverty as old as her decades-long tenure in office, Congresswoman Maxine Waters could speak of impeachment and nothing else, but her reasons for urging so intensely the launching of such an effort were so disconnected from any basis in the Constitution as to be as laughable as her embarrassing chanting of the phrase "Impeach 45" in place of intelligent or even intelligible discourse.

As the Trump University bubble burst with the pin prick of settlement, and Stormy Daniels went from suing the President to suing her own attorney, and the "kids in cages" were exposed as victims of a policy pioneered by President Obama, the reputed "collusion" with Russia to thwart the election of the first female chief executive emerged as the last best hope for ending the Trump presidency. For months, Congressman Adam Schiff had predicted the uncovering of evidence beyond a reasonable doubt of the President's alliance with Putin's Russia and "the real prospect of jail time" for collusion and other alleged offenses, and waited, without baited breath, upon the imminent disclosures contained within the Special Counsel's report. As the report proved a dud, and the special counsel himself even more so when questioned by members of Congress about the results of his year-and-a-half long inquisition, Schiff and his compadres in Congress eagerly searched for other reasons to impeach. What they latched onto was a phone conversation between the President and the leader of Ukraine in which the former asked the latter to consider looking into possible Ukrainian involvement in the 2016 election and the heavy-handed role of Joe Biden in influencing the Ukrainian government to provide favours to himself and his family. A series of secret inquiries at which not a single Republican was allowed to be present culminated in a few public hearings and a rushed vote to impeach on two Articles that would repose for the following three weeks in the vice-like grip of the Speaker of the House, without any hint of when they might be transmitted to the Senate for trial.

More astonishing than the procedure leading to the impeachment were the Articles themselves. The President, the Articles alleged, used his high office to solicit "the interference of a foreign government...through a scheme or course of conduct that included soliciting the Government of Ukraine to publicly announce investigations that would benefit his re-election, and influence the 2020 United States Presidential election to his advantage," and attempted to exert the leverage of congressionally approved foreign aid as an inducement so powerful that Ukraine's President couldn't resist. The scheme not only aimed to benefit the President personally, but "compromised the national security of the United States and undermined the integrity of the United States democratic process." The Articles charged him, too, with resisting the House's effort to investigate the matter of the President's impeachable offenses by instructing executive branch agencies, officers and officials not to comply with the House's subpoenas.

Entitled "Abuse of Power" and "Obstruction of Congress," the Articles are remarkable in that they appeared to target a President for removal from office merely for doing what a President does, which includes negotiation with foreign nations in a manner consistent with his discretion and insistence on the privilege of communications within the executive branch. More significantly, the Articles failed to identify any offense that the Constitution defines as impeachable.

Impeachment is a process derived from the English parliamentary tradition. Parliament reserved for itself the power to check executive authority by impeaching agents of the king when convinced that lawlessness in the execution of official duties had occurred. The result was not merely removal from office, but loss of property and loss of life. The American version of the procedure is found in the Constitution and markedly lacks the penal aspect of its English forerunner. No criminal consequences flow from removal via the impeachment device and are actually expressly prohibited. The basis for impeachment, however, remains commission of a crime. Article II, Section 4 limits impeachment and removal to those civil officers who have committed the felonies of treason and bribery, and "other high crimes and misdemeanours." Each of these terms has a specific meaning. Treason is defined in Article III, Section 3, and entails the levying of "war against the United States, or adhering to their enemies, [or] giving them aid and comfort." Bribery is a common law crime, understood by the Framers to consist of receipt by an official connected with the administration of justice of any undue reward to influence his behaviour in office.[7] "High crimes and misdemeanours" is a much broader basis for impeachment and has often invited the broadest of charges, none of which have ever proven sufficient to justify removal of an impeached official.

Though undefined in the text of the Constitution, the phrase, "other high crimes and misdemeanours" strongly suggests significant felonies on the same level as treason and bribery. When some at the Philadelphia Convention suggested a far more relaxed standard, James Madison argued that anything less than serious crime would invite "the wanton dismissal of meritorious officers" and render the elected President an easy target for impeachment and removal.[8] The settling by the Framers on the phrase "other high crimes and misdemeanours" in place of the term "mal-practice or neglect of duty" hints at general accord among the delegates with Madison's stricter view. Supportive of this conclusion is the conduct and outcome of the impeachment trial of Justice Samuel Chase in 1805. Chase's alleged offense was rudeness toward criminal defendants and their counsel, his imperious way with juries, and his insistence on lecturing everyone in the courthouse with respect to his ideological views. That his animus was reserved almost exclusively to those making common cause with politicians with whom he disagreed hastened an effort to remove him once those self-same politicians rose to power following the general election of 1800. While the managers of the impeachment trial spoke of the purely political nature of impeachment, Justice Chase and his attorneys insisted that removal of a government official could only occur if it was proven at trial that a crime for which an indictment might issue had been committed. According to legal historians Melvin Urofsky and Paul Finkelman, Chase's argument not only won the day at trial, but formed a precedent governing the meaning of the term "high crimes and misdemeanours" that has persisted into modern times.[9]

Chase's position is hardly counter-intuitive. It wouldn't be particularly logical from the standpoint of the principles of construction

---

[7] William Blackstone, *Commentaries on the Laws of England*, Vol. IV (Oxford: Clarendon Press, 1765), at § 17, p. 139.

[8] Legal Information Institute, U.S. Constitution Annotated, Article II, Section IV, Impeachment, www.law.cornell.edu.

[9] Melvin Urofsky & Paul Finkelman, *A March of Liberty: A Constitutional History of the United States*, Volume I (New York: Oxford University Press, 2002), at p. 200.

for a legal document to contain the phrase "high crimes and misdemeanours" without its drafters having intended that actual crimes were what was meant. It isn't without relevance that six decades later, during the impeachment trial of President Andrew Johnson, the President's counsel, former Supreme Court Justice Benjamin Curtis, agreed with Chase's view. "There can be no crime, there can be no misdemeanour," he said, "without a law written or unwritten express or implied. There must be some law, otherwise there is no crime."[10]

President Trump was not impeached for treason or bribery. Instead, he was charged with "abuse of power" and "obstructing Congress." A search of the U.S. Code for either offense comes up empty. "Abuse of Power" is but a phrase connoting political decisions with which a particular beholder disagrees. "Obstructing Congress" bears some resemblance to the statutory crime of Obstructing Congressional or Administrative Proceedings and, perhaps, to the crime of Obstruction of Justice. The resemblance, however, is superficial and imperfect. The offense of obstructing congressional proceedings involves the use of influence, or threats, force or intimidation, not the assertion of executive privilege or challenging the validity of Congress's subpoenas in Court, which are entirely lawful activities. Obstruction of Justice includes destruction of evidence and lying under oath, not the invoking by the head of the federal government of executive rights recognized by every court since John Marshall's time and entirely consistent with the notion of due process. The lack of an actual indictable offense suggests that the impeachment itself was invalid procedurally as well as substantively, and that the President might have been within his rights to bring a motion to quash the Articles or dismiss them on the grounds that the House had exceeded the scope of the impeachment power by failing to limit impeachment to offenses recognized by the Constitution.

The conduct underlying the Articles of Impeachment consists of a conversation with a foreign leader, the alleged withholding of foreign aid, and the President's reliance on executive privilege to resist Congress's inquiries. The first two actions fall within the broad discretionary scope of the President's power over foreign affairs. "In this vast external realm, with its important, complicated, delicate and manifold problems," Justice Sutherland once observed, "the President

---

10 *The Great Impeachment and Trial of Andrew Johnson* (Philadelphia: T.B. Peterson & Brothers, 1868), at p. 110.

alone has the power to speak or listen as a representative of the nation. He makes treaties with the advice and consent of the Senate, but he alone negotiates. Into the field of negotiation the Senate cannot intrude, and Congress itself is powerless to invade it."[11] The responsibility, Sutherland said, was not one granted by an act of the legislature, but flows from the Constitution itself, and the "very delicate, plenary and exclusive power of the President as the sole organ of the federal government in the field of international relations."[12] It was quite apparent, he noted, "that if, in the maintenance of our international relations, embarrassment—perhaps serious embarrassment—is to be avoided and success for our aims achieved, congressional legislation which is to be made effective through negotiation and inquiry within the international field must often accord the President a degree of discretion and freedom from statutory restriction which would not be admissible were domestic affairs alone involved."[13] If it is actually true that the President briefly withheld foreign aid from Ukraine to exert leverage to obtain the desired investigation of someone who happened to be an actual or potential political opponent, the express or implied power of the President to withhold aid to advance what he considers to be the national interest insulates the President from any plausible charge of wrongdoing.

That the President might benefit politically from an executive decision at the expense of a domestic foe is hardly a novel or even controversial proposition; for few Presidents have ever believed that their political interests were inconsistent with the best interests of the nation they led. In this case, the President might not actually be wrong when conflating his interests with the country's. A videotaped admission by Joe Biden while speaking to fellow members of the Council on Foreign Relations that while serving as Vice President he used his power over foreign aid to obtain the discharge of a Ukrainian prosecutor investigating a company in which his family held a financial stake suggests that inquiry into the Democrat presidential hopeful's role in Ukraine might well be warranted.

---

[11] *United States v. Curtiss-Wright Export Corp.* (1936) 299 U.S. 304, 319, 57 S.Ct. 216.

[12] Id., at 320.

[13] Id.

The third of the President's actions forming the basis of the Articles of Impeachment emanates from the assertion of privilege regarding communication with department heads and other members of the executive branch in the especially sensitive area of foreign affairs. The privilege itself is unmentioned in the Constitution but has long been recognized by the Court as flowing naturally from the office, the discretionary nature of intra-branch communications, the principle of the Separation of Powers and a constitutional system designed to generate friction between the organs of government. Hardly a novel principle, it was first identified by John Marshall in his landmark *Marbury* opinion. "The intimate political relation subsisting between the President of the United States and the heads of departments," he noted, "necessarily renders any legal investigation of the acts of one of those high officers peculiarly irksome, as well as delicate; and excites some hesitation with respect to the propriety of entering into such investigation."[14] Any inquiry by the Court into what he called "the prerogatives of the executive" was "an extravagance, so absurd and excessive" that it couldn't be "entertained for a moment."[15] The Court might decide the rights of individuals, but it was prohibited from any probing into "how the executive, or executive officers, perform duties in which they have a discretion."[16] Subsequent Courts confirmed this notion of executive privilege and established that only a compelling purpose, unmatched by any interest of the executive commensurate with the maintenance of confidentiality, could justify a limited piercing of the wall separating discretionary discussions from public or even in camera disclosure. When the interests of criminal justice and the search for evidence of crime in the context of actual criminal prosecutions by prosecuting attorneys vested with that responsibility is resisted only by a general assertion of privilege, the President's sweeping claims might be overcome.[17] When a mere congressional committee without any power to investigate or prosecute crimes, and which cannot even identify a crime that might possibly have occurred, seeks information about the President's negotiation, discussion and exercise of

---

[14] *Marbury v. Madison* (1803) 5 U.S. 137, 169.
[15] Id., at 170.
[16] Id.
[17] *United States v. Nixon* (1974) 418 U.S. 683, 94 S.Ct. 3090.

discretionary power over foreign aid, it isn't likely that the privilege can be surmounted.

Many on both the right and left have argued that impeachment is a political, not a legal process, hence mere policy disputes are fair game and legal formalities need not be followed. "Lack of an impeachable offense is not the relevant impeachment consideration," declared *National Review's* Andrew McCarthy. "Impeachment is political, not legal."[18] As much as I respect Mr. McCarthy, I believe his assessment of the nature of the process is incorrect. The impeachment process is defined in the highest law of all: the Constitution. It is carried out by the Nation's two law-making bodies, the House of Representatives and the Senate. Removal requires first a "trial," which is a legal proceeding. In the case of the President, the trial is to be presided over by a judge: the Chief Justice of the United States. As impeachment is a legal proceeding that is prescribed and governed by the Constitution, it isn't unreasonable to expect that due process and other protections afforded by the Bill of Rights apply, particularly with respect to the person to be tried. Due process requires compliance with governing procedures and adherence to the substantive law. The procedure for impeachment is the charging and then trial of an officer for substantive offenses identified in the Constitution's text. Because the President hasn't been charged with a constitutionally prescribed offense, his impeachment actually violates the Constitution.

Weeks after the House voted to Impeach, the Articles had yet to be transmitted to the Senate. The Speaker of the House handed out twenty-five pens at a celebratory signing ceremony and posed for photos with her colleagues, but not a single manager had yet been appointed to try the matter.[19] The Senate Majority Leader soon signaled that he would proceed without formal transmittal and permit the bringing of dispositive motions. It actually appeared that if trial did proceed without any further action by the House, dismissal either for lack of prosecution or want of an impeachable offense remained a viable prospect. Those who insisted that such an outcome would have been illegitimate failed to recognize the broad discretion the Senate has over the procedure of

---

[18] Andrew C. McCarthy, "What is Impeachment For," www.nationalreview.com, October 12, 2019.

[19] Kerry Picket, "'No One's Giggling Around Here': Democrats Defend Impeachment Ceremony," www.washingtonexaminer.com, January 16, 2020.

the trial once the House votes to impeach.[20] If the House truly was serious about the matter and wasn't interested in mere politics, it really needed to stop the high-fiving and send its managers over to commence the prosecution posthaste. The lack of a sympathetic jury is hardly a reason to hesitate; nor is the certainty of acquittal for the accused.

After a month of inaction by the House, the matter had lingered too long to be defensible and became an absurdity virtually incapable of rehabilitation. And after the actual trial finally commenced, it ended with the proverbial whimper in the wake of a masterful presentation by a galaxy of legal talent on the President's side that included Ken Starr, Robert Ray, Alan Derschowitz, Pam Bondi and Jay Sekulow. Speaker Pelosi blamed Republican Senators for the President's vindication, saying that because of their "betrayal of the Constitution, the President remains an ongoing threat to American democracy."[21] She and the Democrat majority in the House say they did the right thing, though most Americans didn't agree.[22] They might even impeach again—perhaps for the President eliminating Iran's field commander without prior congressional approval, or his disregarding of the House's resolution limiting his ability to protect American interests and troops in a war zone, or for some other, equally dubious reason. Certain to energize a progressive base that defines "unconstitutional" and "treasonous" to be any deviation from the tenets of its irreligious faith, such a move would only further cheapen the exercise of the power and make a mockery of the oath to uphold the Constitution that each member of the House necessarily swore when entering office. Impeachment is a powerful device, designed as a remedy for obvious criminality, but ought to only be employed by those sure of their constitutional righteousness and competent in following through with their initial resolve.

---

[20] See *Nixon v. United States* (1993) 506 U.S. 224, 113 S.Ct. 732.

[21] Philip Ewing, "'Not Guilty'" Trump Acquitted on 2 Articles of Impeachment as Historic Trial Closes," www.npr.com, February 5, 2020.

[22] Jed Graham, "Despite Trump Impeachment Trial, Americans Lean Against President's Removal: IDB/TIPP Poll," www.investors.com, January 31, 2020.

The New Meaning of Treason, and the Old

FEW words are more easily and thoughtlessly expressed in modern political discourse than those screamed by Athaliah when realizing the rightful heir to Judah's crown was about to displace her from her usurped thrown.[1] Much, for instance, has been made by the President's critics of how his attitude and conduct toward Russia either borders on or crosses the line into treason. Former Republican congressman Tom Coleman declared that "Russia's cyber-attack was an act of war. They significantly disrupted and damaged our Constitutional infrastructure in an attempt to undermine the foundation of U.S. democracy.... Clearly, they meet the international criteria of an armed attack and an act of war against the United States."[2] To the question of whether or not Trump assisted Russia in its belligerency, the answer, for Coleman, is a resounding "yes."[3]

The former Director of the CIA, John Brennan, agrees with Coleman, and concludes that the President's conduct "was nothing short of treasonous."[4] Of the President's more recent interaction with the leader of Ukraine, former Massachusetts Governor and GOP challenger William Weld characterized it as "pressuring a foreign country to interfere with and control a US election," and said it wasn't "just undermining democratic institutions...it's treason pure and simple."[5]

In his normally combative way of attempting to flip the narrative, even the President has joined in the casual application of the term, calling Brennan, various Democrat critics and miscellaneous others "traitors" for this or that alleged sin, only to be condemned anew by a largely hostile media for misusing the term in a way that constitutes a breach of his oath to defend the Constitution and grounds for yet

---

1 2 Kings 11:14

2 Tom Coleman, "It's Not a Liberal Fantasy to Ask if Trump Committed Treason," www.thedailybeast.com, May 17, 2018.

3 Id.

4 Grace Panetta, "Former CIA Director John Brennan said Trump's Press Conference with Putin was 'Treasonous'—Here's What Legal Expert's Say," www.businessinsider.com, July 16, 2018.

5 Paul LeBlanc, "GOP Challenger Bill Weld: Trump Committed Treason and 'the Penalty for Treason... is Death,'" www.cnn.com, September 23, 2019.

another Article of Impeachment.[6] Thank goodness for the Framers, noted *The Atlantic's* Colin Friedersdorf, apparently without irony, for including in the Constitution so narrow a definition of treason so as to guard "against the possibility that Americans would one day elect a man so morally weak and corrupt that he would falsely accuse political enemies of treason."[7]

It's doubtful that the Framers were so prescient as to have had Donald Trump in mind when drafting any provision of the Constitution, though the general point is certainly correct—that the Framers were indeed concerned that history might repeat itself in the form of politically motivated accusations, lacking in evidentiary substance, and far attenuated from any procedural protections. "As treason is the most atrocious offense which can be committed against the political body," observed John Marshall, "so it is the charge which is most capable of being employed as the instrument of those malignant and vindictive passions which may rate in the bosom of contending parties struggling for power."[8] The haunting spectre of the great tyrant of England's past and his abominable Treason Act were very much alive within the founding generation's historical memory. That notorious piece of legislation, manufactured for King Henry by a terrorized and docile Parliament, "involved an unprecedented broadening of the concept of treason to encompass all types of 'malicious' attack on the king…or the succession, including those made even orally or in writing."[9] The Act "was designed to root out the seditious 'imps'… and made it treasonable merely "to call the king a heretic, schismatic, tyrant, infidel, or usurper…."[10] To bar the possibility that such a dismal turn of events could ever present itself anew in the new nation, the Framers included a prohibition on mere legislative declarations of guilt, liberated the people from any restraint on their speech, and narrowly defined treason against

[6] Conor Friedersdorf, "A President Falsely Charging 'Treason' is What the Founders Feared: Trump's Accusation Violate his Oath of Office," www.theatlantic.com, April 11, 2019.

[7] Id.

[8] Jean Edward Smith, *John Marshall: Definer of a Nation* (New York: Henry Holt and Company, LLC, 1996), at pp. 359-360.

[9] John Matusiak, *Henry VIII: The Life and rule of England's Nero* (Stroud: The History Press, 2013), at p. 214

[10] Id.

the United States as "levying War against them, or in adhering to their Enemies, giving them Aid and Comfort."[11]

When the Court first addressed the issue of whether the conduct of those accused of treason met the constitutional standard, it confirmed the extreme narrowness of the definition and tightly confined the offense to partaking in arms against the United States, or aiding those who had. For the accused to rightfully be declared a traitor, said Chief Justice Marshall, "war must be actually levied against the United States."[12] Mere conspiracy to take up arms against the nation, however flagrant it might be, "is not treason."[13] One guilty of the offense need not actually lift a weapon in concert with an enemy, but his or her guilt must be predicated on an actual armed attack by those whose efforts the unarmed partisan provided support, assistance, aid or comfort.

Marshall confirmed the necessity of armed assault on the nation in the famous case against former Vice President Aaron Burr. The traitor, he said, must "truly and in fact levy war."[14] He must "perform a part in the prosecution of the war." And this levying of war required "an assemblage in force," and not merely "a secret furtive assemblage without the appearance of force."[15] The gathering "must be such as to prove that [war] is its object."[16] If the alleged treasonous act did not entail "a military assemblage in a condition to make war, it was not a levying of war."[17]

The narrowness of a legal definition curtails the liability of the accused when the principle defined is penal in nature. The result generally, and in the case of the crime of treason, is a downward pressure on the universe of alleged offenders prosecuted and convicted. In the case of the crime of treason, only a handful of people have ever been convicted of the charge. Of these, several were involved in enemy propaganda efforts overseas during World War II. The most significant, constitutionally at least, was the case of Hans Haupt—a naturalized

---

[11] Constitution of the United States, Article I, Section 9, Clause 3; Constitution of the United States, First Amendment; and Constitution of the United States, Article III, Section 4.

[12] *Ex parte Bollman* (1807) 8 U.S. 75, 126.

[13] Id.

[14] Id., at 484.

[15] Id., at 484.

[16] Id., at 486.

[17] Id., at 488.

American citizen born in Germany who enlisted as a clandestine agent of the Nazi regime in 1942. He was captured after being dropped from a German U-Boat off the Florida coast, charged and tried for treason, and executed with a half dozen of his collaborators whose crime was violation of the laws of war. His father suffered conviction as well for numerous overt acts in support of his son's mission. The elder Haupt's unsuccessful appeal did at least provide the Court with further opportunity to review the constitutional standard for treason. "The Law of treason," said Justice Jackson, "makes, and properly makes, conviction difficult, but not impossible."[18] And yet, in Haupt's case, "his overt acts were proved in compliance with the hard test of the Constitution...and the proof leaves no reasonable doubt of the guilt."[19] Haupt didn't raise an armed hand against his adopted country, but the aid and comfort he provided a Nazi saboteur operating in the United States during active armed hostilities was sufficient for the conviction to lie.

The charges by the President's critics obviously fall short of the constitutional standard. Assuming that Putin's Russia did indeed launch cyber-attacks on the Democrat party data bases, hacked into its server and stole information that was then used to undermine the Party's effort to advance its candidates to office in 2016, the effort was obviously an assault on a private organization rather than the state, executed not with the aim of militarily weakening the United States and making it susceptible to actual invasion, but (perhaps) for the purpose of rendering its own defenses against American belligerence emanating from unfriendly Democrats significantly more secure. No arms were raised, nor were the nation's defenses against armed attack targeted. It was just wretched old Hillary and her friends who suffered, not the nation as a whole. This is not to condone or defend any Russian effort to interfere with the American election or a major political party; it is merely to distinguish it from the kind of activity that is a necessary predicate to any charge of treason against those, including the President, who might have benefitted from or in some way assisted the interference. Some crime could have been committed, but it wasn't treason. The same is true of the alleged efforts by intelligence agencies and people in the Obama Administration who abused the FISA process and obtained warrants to

---

[18] *Haupt v. United States* (1947) 330 U.S. 631, 644, 67 S.Ct. 874.
[19] Id.

conduct surveillance of the Trump campaign. A host of laws might have been broken, but the law against treason wasn't one of them.

The necessity of actual armed conflict being established, the recent hostilities between the United States and long-time rival Iran raise an interesting prospect with respect to who may and who may not have committed treason. Few of the current critics of the President thought twice about the killing of an American contractor, or even the siege of our embassy in Iraq by forces aligned with and financed by Iran. It was only when the President sent reinforcements to the embassy and ordered the destruction on Iraqi soil of Iran's military chief and a cadre of Shiite militiamen that an Armageddon-type disaster was said to be in the offing, or at least a repeat of the second Gulf War debacle. *Slate's* Fred Kaplan said "you don't deliberately kill someone like Soleimani unless you're at war with his country, and even then, you want to think long and hard before you do, given the near-certainty of blowback."[20] The killing of Soleimani, he declared, went far beyond a measured or proportionate response to Iranian provocation and constituted "a major, in some ways, unprecedented escalation."[21] Congresswoman Ocasio-Cortez agreed that the President had committed an act of war, and even hinted that it was purchased by Iraqi politicians through their patronage of the Trump hotel in Washington, D.C.[22] Frequent critic Adam Schiff said the President had put the country "on a path to war where we will be at war with Iran."[23] Many other commentators criticized the President for his action, condemned him for starting a war without authorization from Congress, and supported efforts to reign in or hamstring the President from further military action. On January 9, the Democrat controlled House of Representatives passed a resolution that "directs the Trump Administration to immediately halt any military attacks on Iran and Iranian officials that are not separately authorized by Congress."[24]

---

[20] Fred Kaplan, "Trump Just Declared War on Iran," www.slate.com, January 3, 2020.

[21] Id.

[22] Sam Dorman, "AOC Slams Trump, Says Soleimani Strike Risks 'Lives of Millions of Innocent People,'" foxnews.com, January 3, 2020; and "Ocasio-Cortez Suggests 'Powerful People Trying to Bribe' Trump into Iran War," Haaretz.com, January 12, 2020.

[23] James Politi and Katrina Manson, "Democrats Try to Hold Trump to Account Over Iran Strike," www.ft.com, January 6, 2020.

[24] Rachel Oswald, "House Approves Resolution Aimed at Trimming Trump's Power on Iran," www.rollcall.com, January 9, 2020.

"The American people do not want war with Iran," quipped Foreign Affairs Committee Chair Eliot Engel. "With the measure before us today, we are denying the President the authority to wage such a war."[25]

Though it expresses the House majority's attitude toward the President's combative response to Iran's hostile acts, the Resolution is a dubious piece of legislation, both because it purports to impose a bar on the President's discretion as commander-in-chief of the armed forces, and because as much as the Democrats say they wish to avoid war, war with Iran has been with us for decades. The war commenced in 1979 with the Iranian invasion of the American embassy in Tehran in violation of international law and the holding hostage for well over a year of the entire embassy staff. With Iran's leadership and state-controlled press regularly declaring America to be "the Great Satan" whose future defeat at the hands of a messianic imam was foretold of old, Iran's operations against the United States continued following the hostages' release. Former House Speaker Newt Gingrich recently recounted the long history of Iranian violence against the United States, its soldiers and its interests abroad. U.S. Courts, he noted, have found Iran responsible for a Hezbollah truck bomb that killed 63 people in April of 1983 at the U.S. Embassy in Beirut, the truck bombing of the same Embassy that killed 241 American soldiers, and the abduction and torture of U.S. citizens working in Beirut, including journalists, educators and a priest.[26] Over the course of the past several decades, U.S. Courts have "issued some 92 judgments finding the Iranian government and its officials liable for acts of terrorism that claimed American victims," entailing $53 billion in damages, including a billion dollars against Iran's current Supreme Leader.[27] In April of 1988, the Iranians attacked an American vessel with a mine, which in turn prompted the destruction by U.S. forces of most of the Iranian navy. Intelligence reveals that Iranian money has been flowing into the Middle East wherever Iranian-backed militant organizations are active. Iranian backed operatives bombed the U.S. embassies in Kenya and Tanzania, killing 300 people and wounding more than 5,000, and then fatally

[25] Nicholas Wu and Christal Hayes, "House Votes to Limit Trumps Ability to Wage War with Iran After Soleimani Killing," www.usatoday.com, January 9, 2020.

[26] Newt Gingrich, "Iran has been at War with America for 40 Years," www.gingrich360.com, January 8, 2020.

[27] Id.

struck the *U.S.S Cole*. "Syrian proxies," quotes Gingrich, "receive an estimated $6 billion, some of which ends up in the hands of militia organizations. Lebanon, which is of course home to Hezbollah, sees around $700 million of financial support—practically all of which goes to the militant group. Yemen receives $100 million a year. Afghanistan militants get $2 million annually. Various groups in Gaza, including Hamas, get about $100 million a year."[28] This, says Gingrich, "is the scale of activity Soleimani was managing in addition to direct Iranian assets."[29] In light of this history, there can be no mystery over why Iran has been designated a sponsor of terrorism since 1986, nor why no President has altered this designation, including President Trump's predecessor, who believed he might reason with Iran's mullahs and win their hearts through concessions and cash.

The state of war that exists between the United States and Iran, though not always hot, has nevertheless endured. The siege of the embassy in Iraq was but the latest incident in this long war. If not halted it might well have presaged a repeat of the overrunning of the Tehran compound, as well as the catastrophe at Benghazi during the Obama years. With armies in the field and the attack's architect himself present on Iraqi soil not far from the embassy, the lethal strike on him was a discretionary call in wartime by a commander-in-chief whose authority to act was granted by Congress through a joint resolution passed in 2002, broadly governing the advancement of American arms against those who wage conventional and asymmetrical war against the United States. That the President even needed the authorization once American interests and troops were under attack is doubtful. For the President to require a vote by Congress to end a threat to an American embassy and the staff inside is too unreasonable a contention to sustain beyond the issuance of a responsive shush.

The point I am finally getting around to making is that any effort to advance this unsustainable contention, along with all of the condemnation of the President for responding to the latest in a four-decade long series of Iranian attacks, actually far more closely resembles the treason so many have accused the President of committing. Iran is at war with the United States and has been for years. Iran besieged our embassy, which the President then reinforced with a thousand marines.

---

[28] Id.

[29] Id.

When the President attacked and destroyed the enemy's field commander, the response from many in the political party opposing him was to condemn him, and then to actually seek to impair his ability to exercise his constitutional discretion and duty to defend American troops and American facilities in an active war zone and replace that discretion with their own. That the effort could provide cover for further Iranian attacks is as obvious as Iran's widely proclaimed promise to exact its revenge.

Admittedly, it strains reason to insist that the House majority has committed treason, notwithstanding the aid that Congress might have provided to Iran in the latter's effort to outmaneuver the United States militarily. A heated policy dispute in the area of foreign affairs, touching on the issue of whether the United States will be party to an escalation of an existing conflict, isn't quite the Anschluss. Moreover, while no immunity exists for words and deeds expressed outside the halls of Congress, members of the House are protected by the Speech and Debate Clause, which holds that no acts occurring in session, inside the House chamber, can form the basis of any personal liability, including for treasonous words and deeds.[30] It is nevertheless useful in this time of easy accusations of disloyalty to consider what treason actually is and what it isn't, and hopefully to check the precipitate impulse to accuse those with whom one disagrees of the most heinous of motives and a veritable hatred of the nation that extends to them the freedoms they ostensibly hold dear.

Slummin It

EVERYWHERE in the American urban environment they can be found. Dressed in worn clothes, both faded and stained, beards untrimmed in what seems like decades, mouths exhibiting gaps wherever the teeth aren't discoloured, and eyes sunken and old beyond their years, gazing at the world with that special delight so indicative of lunacy, the homeless of America's cities great and small are a class unto themselves, unavoidable, immovable despite their lack of discernible

[30] Constitution of the United States, Article I, Section 6, Clause 1.

roots, and defying all remedy despite the technological prowess of society at large and the compassion of those whose hands hold tight the reins of authority. From city to city, the scenes are but variations on a theme. In Los Angeles, the buildings are but walls for the encampments marked by makeshift and actual tents, piles of garbage bags filled with treasures mined from actual garbage heaps, and what appears to be trash strewn everywhere but which is just as likely to be the belongings and bedding of the 44,000 denizens of the street who shuffle and scream in the roadways, block hundreds of store fronts, and wave cardboard signs scrawled with accounts of hardship stemming from some unspecified war, the bad economy or just plain bad luck, often with an invocation of the blessings of God for those who convey alms. To a growing extent, these behaviours are augmented by open and notorious acts of a sexual nature, practiced without a concern for who might watch or judge. "They are so bizarre and different," says one social worker, "that I don't even feel right describing the behaviours."[1]

Along the Santa Ana storm channel, a leisurely bike ride turns into a tour of a post-apocalyptic landscape, marked by tarp dwellings, garbage piles and hordes of idle souls. Smaller metros like Santa Rosa host tent cities, streets dedicated to car camping and freeway bridges transformed into shelters beneath which loungers can be found asleep at all hours of the day and night. And then there is the great metropolis of the Golden Gate, a dystopia beyond the imagination of most science fiction writers, where police are instructed not to act against actual criminal conduct, where the district attorney refuses to employ the power of prosecution, and where puddles of urine, piles of faeces and stray and bloodstained needles are so prevalent that it's possible to obtain maps of the most affected areas. The city literally stinks, some say worse than the slums of Mumbai and São Paulo, and yet the powers-that-be seem unconcerned, even pleased, with the situation—indifferent to how demoralizing the impact on the people it has become and oblivious to the thoughts of flight beyond this awful fantasy-come-true increasing numbers of San Franciscans are acting upon.[2]

---

[1] Michael Shellenberger, "Why California Keeps Making Homelessness Worse," www.forbes.com, September 12, 2019.

[2] Samantha Raphelson, "San Francisco Squalor: City Streets Strewn with Trash, Needles and Human Feces," www.npr.org, August 1, 2018.

The contrast between the present day's emergence of homeless dystopias and vagrancy in the past could not be more striking. From the earliest days, legislative bodies enacted laws to discourage vagrancy by imposing criminal sanctions. The grand social experiment of democratic government, said the historian Lawrence Friedman, "depended on discipline and self-control," both of which were threatened by the presence of "rootless, normless people" free of the "yoke of conventional morality, the handcuffs of moderate behaviour and self-discipline."[3] Such laws were in keeping with what Connecticut Chief Justice Samuel Church said was "the first object of society and of the law," which was "to protect life, health and property, and the comfortable enjoyment of them."[4] Vagrancy laws took on added importance as large cities rose in the middle of the Nineteenth Century. The waves of epidemic recorded in the chronicles of man in the old world and the new were to be halted by the adoption of regulations to protect the water supply, the food supply and the air from contaminants so dangerous to the health and safety of the population. As the urban demographic expanded, hygiene emerged as a pre-eminent concern of the urban planner—a reaction, said Lewis Mumford, "against the miserably insanitary conditions, the devitalized diet, the constant state of ill-health and enfeeblement, in which the denizens of...Nineteenth Century towns lived."[5] New York City led the way in filling the statute books with public health laws. By 1860, "New York City health regulations filled an entire volume. Provisions included the establishment of a board of health and Marine Hospital, the quarantining of vessels in port, vaccination, the regulation of 'infected places'...the 'cleansing and purifying' of buildings and lots, the removal and destruction of putrid or dangerous cargo, the duties of physicians...street cleaning, dumping, the cleansing of tenement houses, the filling up and draining of land, the regulation of markets and the sale of foodstuffs, garbage, the removal of putrid and unsound meat, privies, sinks, and cesspools, slaughterhouses, the removal of dead animals...the regulation of swill carts, waste water, the washing and drying of clothes,

---

[3] Lawrence M. Friedman, *Crime and Punishment in American History* (New York: Basic Books, 1993), at p. 103.

[4] *Whitney v. Bartholomew* (1851) 21 Conn. 212, 218.

[5] Lewis Mumford, *The Culture of Cities* (New York: Harcourt, Brace and Company, 1938), at p. 422.

the prohibition of stagnant water, burials and cemeteries, the removal of night soil, sewers and drains...and the removal of nuisances generally."[6]

This expansion of law inevitably gave rise to cries of foul from those who preferred an unregulated existence, with some libertarian-minded folks even attempting to take shelter behind the Fourteenth Amendment of the Constitution to resist the imposition upon them of the new hygienic regime. Upon reviewing the argument that public health and a New Orleans law that confined animal slaughtering to a single location must give way to the liberty interests of independent butchers, Justice Samuel Miller noted that "it cannot be denied that the statute under consideration is aptly framed to remove from the more densely populated part of the city the noxious slaughterhouses, and large and offensive collections of animals necessarily incident to the slaughtering business of a large city, and to locate them where the convenience, health, and comfort of the people require they shall be located."[7] Miller was speaking of regulations designed to limit contamination caused by rotting animal entrails, but he could just as well have applied his words to laws outlawing public defecation and camping on the streets.

The conflict between order and those who do not and cannot conform to it has once again reached the courts, and quite incredibly the Supreme Court, when asked to consider whether a Circuit Court finding that the imposition of criminal penalties, however light, on persons sleeping on the public streets and sidewalks violated the Eighth Amendment prohibition against the imposition of cruel and unusual punishment, declined without any explanation the request, leaving in place the lower court's ruling to govern the expansive district covering a third of the territory of the United States.[8] What the hard working butchers of New Orleans were denied by virtue of limits on the rights protected by the Constitution, the toothless, jobless, shiftless and drug addicted hobos of Boise, Idaho, Los Angeles, California, Las Vegas, Nevada and mighty San Francisco have won: a constitutional right, not to pursue a common calling, but to idle around the public places, sleeping, sitting, resting, and presumably pissing and crapping

---

[6] William J. Novak, *The People's Welfare: Law & Regulation in Nineteenth Century America* (Chapel Hill: The University of North Carolina Press, 1996), at p. 198.

[7] *The Slaughterhouse Cases* (1873) 83 U.S. 36, 64.

[8] Robert Barnes, "Supreme Court Won't Review Decisions that Protects Homeless from Tickets," www.washingtonpost.com, December 16, 2019.

whenever they feel so inclined, so long, however, as appropriate facilities for these activities are unavailable.

The case is *Martin v. City of Boise*. It dates back to 2007, when several of the plaintiffs were first arrested for violation of the City's Camping and Disorderly Conduct Ordinances, which prohibited camping or sleeping on public property if the local shelters were not filled to capacity. Repeated arrests and convictions for the same violation culminated in a 2014 lawsuit brought in accordance with 42 U.S.C. § 1983 for damages and injunctive relief against the City for acts constituting cruel and unusual punishment in violation of the Eighth Amendment. The case was initially dismissed for lack of standing and other justiciability flaws, but reinstated following a successful appeal. The case was again dismissed due to application of several rather arcane justiciability doctrines, including the obscure Rooker-Feldman Doctrine, and the principle that a party might only bring an action for relief pursuant to Section 1983 following favourable termination of an underlying criminal matter. The case proceeded to the court of appeals, where it lingered for a time before an opinion was issued in September of 2018. Though Judge Marsha Berzon and her colleagues on the appellate court agreed that the failure of all of the plaintiffs to raise the Eighth Amendment as a defense in the underlying criminal matters precluded Section 1983 relief for past prosecutions, a cause of action had been stated for prospective relief—that is, an order barring the police from ever again arresting anyone for camping in public places. More importantly, the Court opted to consider the merits of the contention that the Eighth Amendment had been violated, and found "that the Eighth Amendment prohibits the imposition of criminal penalties for sitting, sleeping, or lying outside on public property for homeless individuals who cannot obtain shelter."[9]

Ostensibly, the scope of the decision is limited only to those homeless campers unable to find shelter space, and leaves the voluntary homeless unprotected. And yet the decision disregards the ordinance itself, which already exempts campers from prosecution at times when all available shelter space was taken, as well as the police authorities' method of determining whether local shelters were at capacity. Nor did the Court consider any burden by the camper to demonstrate that he or

[9] *Martin v. City of Boise* (2019) 920 F.3d, 584, 616.

she had attempted to find shelter but been denied, or that they were not among the class of homeless who have adopted homelessness as a lifestyle or who otherwise reject the conventions of society, or who are so mentally ill or drug addicted that their willingness or ability to take any steps in the direction of healthier choices is lacking. The Court appears merely to have accepted the premise that anyone who is camping in public space must have no other choice, and assumes they must have sought out shelter unsuccessfully. Consequently, any arrest, charge and conviction of a homeless person for camping in public spaces presumptively violates the Eighth Amendment.

The decision is nothing short of revolutionary. And yet, the opinion is without the heft one would expect from something so far-reaching. Lacking is any discussion of the history of the Amendment, what specifically it sought to prevent, and what the Framers might have thought about its meaning and scope. Nor is there much in the way of discussion of judicial gloss. The Court's position is anchored not to the historical jurisprudence, but to a decision from 1977 in the matter of *Ingraham v. Wright* (1977) 430 U.S. 651, 97 S.Ct. 1401. That decision, said the Court, held that "the Cruel and Unusual Punishments Clause 'circumscribes the criminal process in three ways.' First, it limits the type of punishment the government may impose; second, it proscribes punishment 'grossly disproportionate' to the severity of the crime; and third, it places substantive limits on what the government may criminalize."[10] It was the third factor that Judge Berzon and her colleagues thought was most relevant. The analogous case, they said, was in the matter of *Robinson v. California* (1962) 370 U.S. 660, 82 S.Ct. 1417, where a defendant was charged for violating a statute that criminalized not buying, selling or using drugs, but one's status as a drug addict. Addiction, the *Robinson* Court thought, was an involuntary condition, beyond the addict's control, hence an inappropriate basis for the State to impose sanctions. A subsequent Court explained *Robinson's* rationale more precisely. "The entire thrust of *Robinson's* interpretation of the Cruel and Unusual Punishment Clause is that criminal penalty may be inflicted only if the accused has committed some act, has engaged in some behaviour, which society has an interest in preventing, or...has committed some *actus reus*."[11] Better yet, in Judge Berzon's view,

[10] Id., at 615.
[11] Id., at 616.

was *Powell v. McCormick* (1968) 392 U.S. 514, 88 S.Ct. 2145, wherein five justices held that "criminal penalties may not be inflicted upon a person for being in a condition he is powerless to change."[12] Since sitting, lying, and sleeping are defined as acts or conditions, "they are universal and unavoidable consequences of being human," are "involuntary and inseparable from status," and rooted in the biological reality of the animal form.[13] To criminalize such action is to "criminalize conduct that is an unavoidable consequence of being homeless—namely sitting, lying, or sleeping on the streets."[14]

The homeless of Boise may well be an innocuous lot: humble, respectful and clean, and lacking any association with the trash heap hovels erected along public trails, storm channels and even public streets in the great flesh pots of the west. The population may indeed be among those spoken of by Christ as the poor in spirit and to whom St. Martin gave his cloak, as opposed to the horde of drug ravaged lunatics who wander the urban landscapes of America screaming obscenities, threatening passersby with their words and demeanour, looting small businesses, casting their used hypodermic needles along public pathways, defecating in plain sight against storefronts in commercial districts and running through traffic demanding spare change. Judge Berzon's opinion may be an act of charity, motivated by the higher impulses of humanity and the grand faith traditions of this nation, but it operates so broadly on the reality of modern urban life as to compel only one of two choices: either raise taxes to build massive facilities for a class of people who largely eschew the conventions of human society and lack any respect for public or private property, or suffer the inconvenience and burdens of the presence of the post-apocalyptic herd wherever it might find itself impelled to travel. No thought is given to the condition of individual hobos and whether they wilfully engage in drug use, or prefer the life on the streets to that of the norms embraced by most Americans, or are so mentally impaired for any number of reasons that they are incapable of rational decisions about their welfare and oblivious to the negative impact they have on their fellow man. Nor does the decision account for the multifarious ills the congregants of homeless havens have on the environment, the petty and not so petty criminality

---

12 Id.

13 Id., at 617.

14 Id.

so endemic to the homeless lifestyle, and the breeding ground for vermin and disease they've manage to resurrect after *homo urbanus* so triumphantly extinguished them through thoughtful civic planning and pragmatic and consistent enforcement of the laws.

The historical context of the Eighth Amendment is of some relevance. At the time of the framing of the Amendment and its ratification, an understanding existed of a tradition of heinous punishments inflicted by the Crown for any number of crimes, from the worst of offenses to what are considered to be mere misdemeanours. Without the benefit of procedural protections against state action, or a culture thoroughly committed to fairness, men and women were easily accused of the worst of crimes, convicted and then subjected to unspeakable punishments. The worst consisted of being dragged through the crowded streets, hanged to within an inch of one's life atop a gallows, and dismembered while still living, followed by post-mortal mounting of the convict's disconnected limbs in prominent public places until the natural process of decomposition took its course. Others were burned alive, stretched on racks until their joints separated, or stabbed with hot irons. Some people lost hands, others were whipped. Petty thieves caught and convicted a handful of times for the same class of offense might suffer capital punishment, even when the motivation for the crime was to avoid starvation. "Anyone who stole so much as a silver spoon…could be sent to the gallows."[15] Others still were transported from their native land to serve as slaves, regardless of the whiteness of their skin. It is no wonder that the adoption of the Eighth Amendment corresponded with a movement in the American States to bring criminal codes into conformity with the notion of proportionality.

When the courts began to review the concept of cruel and unusual punishment, they no doubt had an eye to history, but they were not oblivious to the concept that our consciousness as a people might evolve and that changes in society's views of what is either cruel or unusual are relevant in determining the meaning of the terms.[16] Nevertheless, the two words do have some core meaning that cannot be disregarded. "Fines, imprisonment and even execution," said Chief Justice Warren, "may be imposed depending on the enormity of the crime, but any technique outside the bounds of these traditional penalties is

[15] Friedman, op. cit., p. 63.
[16] *Weems v. United States* (1910) 217 U.S. 349, 30 S.Ct. 544.

constitutionally suspect."[17] In the case of *Weems v. United States*, the crime at issue was falsifying a public record in furtherance of a fraud against the government, and the punishment was incarceration for 15 years, during which the defendant was to be chained ankle and wrist to a wall when not performing "hard and painful labour."[18] Though the crime was a felony, the severity of the punishment was so extreme, medieval and disproportionate to the offense that even justices who enshrined Jim Crow for sixty years through the embrace of the principle of "separate but equal" found it unconscionable.

Judge Berzon and her colleagues on the Ninth Circuit appear to have disregarded this tradition. They've decided with little analysis that fines and a few days in jail are both cruel and unusual when, in fact, they are far less exacting on the homeless than punishment for vagrancy in the past. They've accepted uncritically the premise that anyone on the street must be there against their will—a presumption which the State and the people can do little or nothing to rebut. The only options are to tolerate the zombie-like horde, or undertake the expensive construction and maintenance of housing. Whether the masterless men and women of the streets would actually prefer to confine themselves to a government corral, subject to even the most basic of rules governing their conduct, isn't apparently a consideration, nor is the responsibility of any given homeless person for the fate that defines their status. Men and women who've spent their lives rejecting behavioural norms, any sense of right and wrong, any obligation to take responsibility for their own actions, and any notion of courtesy to others are now protected in their most uncivil and obnoxious conducts by a document drafted by men who well understood the need for vagrancy laws and rules aiming to maintain public hygiene lest the plagues that once decimated cities and towns return with all their lethal and tragic results.

There is in the Constitution a principle of balance. In the area of public fora, such as streets, town squares and public parks, it is understood that the people have rights to congregate, and they cannot be denied access capriciously or arbitrarily. Though the government is empowered to balance the needs of multiple users in those spaces, any regulation limiting access must be reasonable and not so restrictive of

---

[17] *Trop v. Dulles* (1958) 356 U.S. 86, 78 S.Ct. 590.
[18] *Weems v. United States*, supra, at 366.

use as to render it meaningless or functionally non-existent. The vagrant has a right to use the public space, as do the men and women who've accepted society's restrictive norms. And yet the vagrant should have no right to impair the latter's access and enjoyment, to discard his trash, his drug paraphernalia, to harass with demands for money and threaten or frighten with terete-like cursing and screaming. Boise and other cities might now be unable to arrest the vagrant for merely sleeping, but these other behaviors may well be fair game, and certainly the city and other jurisdictions might impose a reasonable time, place and manner restriction in the form of public campgrounds in lieu of formal shelters, where camping is allowed indefinitely if necessary, basic facilities are provided, and a permanent law enforcement presence is maintained to keep the peace. Instead of fines and jail for vagrants, perhaps a work release program is in order, whereby the offenders are required to clean up the messes left by themselves and their peers. Certainly, it couldn't be either cruel or unusual for those who would sleep on the streets to be required to apply a little disinfectant to the emissions that attest to their presence. This might be a better option to explore until the Supreme Court finally opts to consider the merits of the Eighth Amendment argument and engages in a balancing of the rights of those unwilling to conform with the mores that much of society still accepts and the needs of that society to enjoy the public space and to be free from behaviors that historically have encouraged crime, vermin, disease and the debasement of civilization as whole.

Then Cometh Also Contempt

PRIOR to the mid-term election of 2018, the Democrats relished the idea of laying siege to the Trump Administration with investigations and subpoenas following their predicted victory. Turn-about, as they say, is fair play. The Republican majorities in the House and Senate, after all, had waylaid the Obama Administration with inquiries into the Fast and Furious gun-running operation, Benghazi and the IRS roadblock to approval of conservative 501c3 organizations. For eager Democrats, "the menu of possibilities from the first two years of the Trump Administration is dizzying," said one observer, "from possible malfeasance with the inauguration fund to the possible illegal use of the military to repel Central American immigrants."[1] If Democrats were able to win a majority of House seats in the November mid-term election, "they wouldn't just get the ability to block the Republicans' legislative agenda, along with the President's. They would also gain control of Congress's oversight authority, which they could use to dig into everything from Trump's possible ties to Russia to his alleged business conflicts-of-interest...."[2] They would, said Congressman Tom Davis, "have the power to go after every executive agency—and it's basically unlimited."[3]

Once the Democrats actually took control of the House in January of 2019, eighty-five targets were quickly identified by subpoena-ready committeemen: the Trump family businesses, the payments to Stormy Daniels, the firing of James Comey, the proposed transgender ban for the military, the travel ban, the family separation policy and the response to Hurricane Maria, to name but a few.[4] Though the targets were many, few observers doubted that the ultimate objective was impeachment of the President and presentation of a compelling case for his removal by the Senate. The House soon set to work dividing the investigative labor among several committees. Adam Schiff's Intelligence Committee ploughed forward with examination of the alleged collusion by the Trump Campaign with the Russian government to subvert the American electoral process. Jerry Nadler would focus on oversight of the Justice Department and ensure that any documents relevant to the ongoing Mueller investigation were produced. And the powerful Oversight Committee of Elijah Cummings would dedicate itself to obtaining the mother lode of evidence of Trump's supposed criminality: the President's tax returns. This three-pronged effort has borne fruit: Schiff's work laid the foundation for the two Articles of Impeachment recently delivered to the Senate; the refusal by Attorney General Barr to respond to subpoenas from Nadler's committee prompted Barr's citation for Contempt of Congress; and a U.S. District

---

[1] Harry Litman, "Congress Can Issue Subpoenas. Will They Matter? Trump Opponents Should Prepare for a Long and Bumpy Road Ahead," *The New York Times*, November 8, 2018.

[2] Alex Seitz-Wald, "Democrats' Agenda: Win House in 2018, Investigate Donald Trump," www.nbcnews.com, May 15, 2017.

[3] Id.

[4] Zachary Basu, "Democratic Hit List: At Least 85 Trump Investigation Targets," www.axios.com, November 12, 2018.

Court and the D.C. Circuit Court of Appeals have each upheld the authority of Congress to obtain copies of the President's tax returns from his accountants. The executive remains defiant in the face of these efforts. Impeachment was stoutly and successfully opposed by a legal team consisting of Alan Derschowitz, Jay Sekulow and Ken Starr. The Contempt citation appears to have died on the vine. And the pending order of the Circuit Court for the District of Columbia is (at the time of the writing of this chapter) stayed at the behest of the Supreme Court pending its review of the substance of the matter. The House is undeterred in its struggle against the White House, though the headway it's making appears to have slowed. Impeachment failed, at least for now, but hope remains that production of inculpatory information will be the result of the orders on the subpoena.

In truth, the road ahead for the House and its subpoena strategy is not particularly promising. Many, many subpoenas have issued from Congress over the years, and uncooperative respondents have been cited for contempt, some have been jailed by court order and otherwise sanctioned, and records and testimony have been compelled. And yet the problem and the question facing the House with respect to its pending subpoena is the same that all Congresses have faced when confronted with witnesses unwilling to provide the requested information: does Congress itself have the authority to act as a judicial body, issue judicial-like orders and enforce compliance? On the face of the text of the Constitution, it would seem that the answer is no. Among the various powers granted to Congress—from the power to tax to the power to establish uniform weights and measures—there is none to issue subpoenas, nor to punish contempts. "This government," said Chief Justice Marshall, "is acknowledged by all to be one of enumerated powers. The principle, that it can exercise only the powers granted to it [is] now universally admitted."[5]

That would seem to be the end of the matter, but not entirely. The same Justice and his colleagues, when asked in the matter of *Anderson v. Dunn* whether Congress could hold certain respondents in contempt for ignoring congressional process and even haul them before the bar of the House or Senate, held that Congress could in fact do so, notwithstanding the absence of any mention of such authority among the powers

[5] *McCulloch v. Maryland* (1819) 17 U.S. 316, 405.

enumerated in the Constitution. "It is certainly true," said Marshall's colleague Justice William Johnson, "that there is no power given by the Constitution to either House to punish for contempts, except when committed by their own members. Nor does the judicial or criminal power given to the United States, in any part, expressly extend to the infliction of punishment for contempt of either House, or any one coordinate branch of the government."[6] Without a reference to authority, but instead in reliance solely on reasoning from premises of his own devising, Johnson noted that "there is not in the whole of that admirable instrument a grant of powers which does not draw after it others, not expressed, but vital to their exercise; not substantive and independent, indeed, but auxiliary and subordinate."[7] The power of Congress drawing behind it the power of contempt was apparently the rather ambiguous power to guard against efforts to bribe members of the House. Without questioning the existence of the underlying power, Johnson explained that to deny the ability to punish contempts "leads to the total annihilation of the power of the House of Representatives...and leaves it exposed to every indignity and interruption that rudeness, caprice, or even conspiracy, may meditate against it."[8]

Similarly, the power to issue subpoenas has been inferred from the text of the Constitution, but was more specifically tied to the Congress's legislative power and the need of Congress to inform itself of facts relevant to potential legislative acts. The earliest Congresses assumed it possessed such power, derived perhaps from the very parliament Americans of the founding generation had rejected. Without much chagrin, the early Congresses served subpoenas for the production of documents relevant to the disastrous St. Claire expedition of 1792 and the negotiation of Jay's Treaty, as well as to the doings of the Secretary of the Treasury, Alexander Hamilton. In 1799, William Duane was ordered to appear before the Senate to answer the charge that he had committed libel against the Senate and one of its committees. When he refused to make an appearance, the Senate held him in contempt, deployed its Sergeant at Arms to arrest him and held him in custody until it was decided that the better course was for Duane to be prosecuted in a court of law. The matter did not pass without some

---

[6] *Anderson v. Dunn* (1821) 19 U.S. 204, 225.
[7] Id., at 226.
[8] Id., at 228.

controversy. A majority of members, however, agreed that while the power was absent from the text of the Constitution, the Senate's power to serve process and cite for contempt "was an inherent right of legislative bodies, derived not specifically from the Constitution, but rather from 'the principle of self-preservation, which results to every public body from necessity and from the nature of the case.'"[9]

The Supreme Court eventually considered the issue of the power of the Congress to serve and enforce subpoenas in the 1871 matter of *Kilbourn v. Thompson*. While it held that Congress did, in fact, possess implied authority to issue subpoenas and punish contempts, it placed on its exercise significant limitations. Samuel Miller, whose views tended to the conservative when confronted with claims of far-reaching government authority, recalled the silence of the text of the Constitution with respect to the alleged power, and then observed that the Fifth Amendment's demand that no "person shall be deprived of life, liberty, or property without due process of law" appears to be "the strongest implication against punishment by order of the legislative body."[10] That Parliament exercised the power was no endorsement of a like authority possessed by the Congress. Parliament was not merely a figment of the medieval world, but also acted, when its two Houses convened together, as both a legislative body and a high court of judicature. Miller acknowledged that each House of Congress possessed authority over its own members and must of necessity possess some power to maintain order among those in attendance, as well as compel persons summoned before it to appear and testify. But when the power was exercised over non-members, Miller was "sure that no person can be punished for contumacy as a witness before either House unless his testimony is required in a matter into which that House has jurisdiction to inquire, and we feel equally sure that neither of these bodies possesses the general power of making inquiry into the private affairs of the citizen."[11] In the case of Mr. Kilbourn, who had been dragged by force back to Washington, D.C. from Ohio, the inquiry Congress was making was into possible financial crimes that were the subject matter of an on-going

---

[9] Todd Garvey, "Congress's Contempt Power and the Enforcement of Congressional Subpoenas," Congressional Research Service Report, May 12, 2017, at p. 6.

[10] *Kilbourn v. Thompson* (1871) 103 U.S. 168, 182.

[11] Id., at 190.

judicial proceeding. Not only did the House disregard any legitimate legislative basis for its subpoena and contempt, it also ran roughshod over the prerogatives of the judicial branch, which had jurisdiction in the matter. Any power Congress had to punish contempts, including for the ignoring or evasion of its subpoenas, must, said Miller, be "very limited."[12]

The scope of whatever power the Congress possessed in this area was further defined in the wake of the Tea Pot Dome scandal, when Mally S. Daugherty successfully convinced a District Court that the power itself was non-existent. On appeal, the Supreme Court reversed. It said that the power did indeed exist, and while it was not expressly identified, could be reasonably inferred from the investment of all legislative authority in the Congress, the role the two different Houses played in the legislative process, and the requirement that the bills they enact be identical if they are to be presented to the President. "In actual legislative practice," said Justice Van Devanter, power to secure needed information by such means has long been treated as an attribute of the power to legislate," and it was a power "both asserted and exerted by the House of Representatives in 1792" and afterward.[13] It was a power defended by one of the great advocates who appeared before the Supreme Court, Senator John J. Crittenden, who said that "the means of carrying into effect by law all the granted powers is given where legislation is applicable and necessary, but there are subordinate matters, not amounting to laws; there are inquiries of the one house or the other house, which each house has a right to conduct, which each has, from the beginning, exercised the power to conduct, and each has, from the beginning summoned witnesses. This has been the practice of the government from the beginning, and if we have a right to summon the witness, all the rest follows as a matter of course."[14] From this, Justice Van Devanter concluded that the power of inquiry, of which the power to issue and enforce subpoenas is a concomitant part, "is an essential and appropriate auxiliary to the legislative function. It was so regarded and employed in American legislatures before the Constitution was framed and ratified," and by its continuous employment by successive Congresses "it falls nothing short of a practical construction, long

[12] Id., at 197.

[13] *McGrain v. Daugherty* (1927) 273 U.S. 135, 161.

[14] Id., at 164.

continued, of the constitutional provisions respecting their powers, and therefore should be taken as fixing the meaning of those provisions, if otherwise doubtful."[15]

Dunn, Kilbourn and *McGrain* are persuasive authority. A power to subpoena and enforce the same when spurned exists and is constitutionally sanctioned. And yet, the power has limits – not only the ones identified in *Kilbourn*, but others arising from the abrading of one branch of government by another. Messrs. Dunn, Kilbourn and Dougherty were each private citizens whose testimony and documents the Congress wished to obtain. No issue of the separation of powers arose in those cases, other than perhaps the invasion by the Congress in *Kilbourn* of the province of the judiciary, and no analysis of the embarrassment the subpoenas posed to other branches of government was undertaken.

In contrast, the actions initiated and presently employed by the House of Representatives are directed at the executive branch and a principle office of the federal government, and additionally seek the personal financial data of the President of the United States held in private hands. The uncertain power of the House in this context is evident, notwithstanding the threat by Speaker Pelosi to arrest the Attorney General for failing to produce the un-redacted Mueller report. General Barr's subsequent public meeting with the Speaker prompted his laughter at the thought of the Sergeant at Arms attempting to effect his arrest in the presence of a heavy guard of Secret Service agents and U.S. Marshalls trained to defend their charge to the death.[16] It was prudence that dictated the alternative course of proffering the citation to the Attorney General's office for presentation to a Grand Jury for possible indictment. The absurdity of the Attorney General actually making the presentment to a Grand Jury is self-evident and highlights the fundamental shortcoming of a hostile House of Congress holding a member of the Executive Branch in contempt. The long-established discretion of prosecutors, including the Attorney General and his staff, stands as an immovable impediment to obtaining what the contempt citation ostensibly aims to secure.

---

[15] Id., at 174.

[16] Ed Mazza, "Bar Jokes About Contempt to Pelosi's Face: 'Did You Bring Your Handcuffs?'", www.huffpost.com, May 16, 2019.

Greater promise exists with respect to the use by the House of Representatives of the statutory provision for judicial enforcement of its subpoena of the President's tax records from the President's accounting firm. In two successive opinions, by the District Court and the D.C. Circuit Court of Appeals, the House's demands were vindicated and the tax records were ordered produced. The D.C. Circuit's opinion relied in part on the long history of Ccngressional subpoenas and the *McGrain* Court's determination that legislative purposes are broad. In the case of the subpoenas at issue, the House had identified four purposes: to inquire into "whether the President may have engaged in illegal conduct before and during his tenure in office"; whether he "has undisclosed conflicts of interest that may impair his ability to make impartial policy decisions"; whether he "is complying with the Emoluments Clauses of the Constitution"; and whether he "has accurately reported his finances to the Office of Government Ethics and other federal entities."[17] Each of these purposes, said Judge David S. Tatel, falls within the broad scope of the legislative power of Congress and involve questions that Congress has a legislative interest in informing itself about as it contemplates possible statutory reforms.

Judge Tatal's decision provides the broadest possible scope for Congress's inquiries. While it examines the objections to the legitimacy of Congress's quest for personal financial data that is ordinarily considered confidential and private for profound public policy reasons, it easily disposes of them. That they actually can be so casually disregarded is an unresolved question, but doubts ought to nag the reasonable mind. The President's alleged illegal conduct would appear to be his filing of tax information that is incorrect, in this case the reimbursement to Michael Cohen of money the latter paid to Stormy Daniels in exchange for her silence during the election campaign. This matter, however, is properly the subject of the IRS and the State of New York's tax agency, neither of which has yet to identify any possible violation of some provision of the rather elaborate and arcane federal and state tax codes, nor has there been any inquiry by the FEC, which is charged with enforcement of campaign finance laws. Congress's effort to second guess executive agencies that have special expertise as well as

[17] *Trump v. Mazars USA, LLP*, No. 19-5142 (D.C. Cir. 2019), at p. 8.

access to all of the documents Congress hopes to obtain is not convincing as a legitimate legislative concern.

Conflicts of interest are ethical and legal in nature, but they appear to be unenforceable against a President, whose qualifications are limited to three, and who is subject to an enormous amount of vetting prior to election to the office. That Congress could impose statutory qualifications on candidates for President in the form of requiring disclosure of possible conflicts of interests is doubtful. Verifying the accuracy of his financial reports has already been done—by the President himself, in compliance with existing law. His accountability (if any) is to the agency charged with collecting that information, not to the Congress. If the President has erred or even intentionally misstated the truth contrary to operative reporting provisions, it would seem that reform is less relevant than enforcement of existing legal standards—something that isn't in Congress's wheelhouse.

The Emoluments issue, is certainly an interesting one, partly because it relates to a clause of the Constitution that has generated virtually no jurisprudence until the year 2017, when the President's overly enthusiastic opponents started suing him for supposed violations in the form of his supposed receipt of income from foreign nationals who've paid money in exchange for the right to stay at his company's hotels. Purchasing a service independent of the office of the President isn't remotely an emolument prohibited by the Constitution. The Foreign Emoluments Clause appears to be self-executing; and acquiescence to it depends in large part on the oath of the office holder. Congress itself has no apparent power to enforce the Clause, at least with respect to any office created by the Constitution itself, hence the power to issue subpoenas to investigate the President's compliance with it is dubious to say the least.

What Congress appears to be doing in serving its subpoenas is either exposing "for the sake of exposure," which the Supreme Court has found to be an illegitimate use of the subpoena and contempt powers, or engaging in an elaborate fishing expedition with the goal of generating fodder for Articles of Impeachment.[18] Why the House hasn't invoked its actual impeachment authority as a justification for the subpoenas is rather curious, given the explicit authority it possesses over

---

[18] *Watkins v. United States* (1957) 354 U.S. 178, 200, 77 S.Ct. 1173.

impeachment. The House certainly hasn't shied away from relying on that power elsewhere. It may be that the House recognizes that the subpoenas based on the House's legislative power are broad and presumptively valid, while any subpoena pursuant to the House's authority over impeachments would, at the very least, be subject to the whole panoply of due process protections traditionally available to the subject of impeachment inquiries. Whether the House could even issue enforceable subpoenas rooted in its impeachment power at all is questionable. When the Senate Select Committee subpoenaed President Nixon's tapes and then attempted to enforce the subpoena, it suffered defeat in court.[19] Who actually did succeed in enforcing a subpoena against the President was the special prosecutor, charged with the responsibility to investigate criminal wrongdoing in the executive branch, and who made a sufficient showing that the interests of criminal justice were sufficient to overcome the President's vague and overly broad objections.[20] The House in the instant case can make no such showing since it hasn't invoked the impeachment power when issuing its subpoenas, and even if it had, it isn't engaged in a criminal prosecution.

As noted, the Supreme Court issued a stay in the matter of the Trump tax returns. It will consider the merits of the case sometime this year, and may or may not reach a decision until after the election, and perhaps not until after the Congress itself that issued the subpoena has dissolved—a development that would essentially moot the case due to the fact that a subpoena endures only so long as the session of the Congress that served it. In the event the Court does review the matter, it will consider anew the purposes advanced by the House to anchor its subpoena to its legislative powers and will ponder whether the House possesses any authority to investigate matters that are in their nature criminal, over which it has no discernable power and which falls to other departments either to prosecute or adjudicate. It may be that the Court will agree with the dissent of Judge Neomi Rao, who expressed grave concern that the Circuit Court had expanded Congress's control over the other branches through the device of "invoking a need for remedial

---

[19] *Senate Select Committee on Presidential Activities v. Nixon* (D.D.C. 1973) 366 F.Supp. 51; and *Senate Select Committee on Presidential Activities v. Nixon* (1974) 498 F.2d 725, 162 U.S.App.D.C. 183.

[20] See *United States v. Nixon* (1974) 418 U.S. 683, 94 S.Ct. 3090.

legislation," without any showing of an actual nexus between the legislative power and the alleged problem at the root of the inquiry.[21] If the Supreme Court finds merit in Judge Rao's view, it may spell the end of decades of Congress's free reign with subpoenas and may even embolden future Presidents in their opposition to congressional oversight that the Executive formerly would have been inclined at least to moderately tolerate. Sometimes, by pushing a prerogative as far as it goes, it gets lost over the edge of the defile.

Razing the Wall

IN January of 2020, the media buzzed with accounts of argument in the Supreme Court over an obscure tax deduction and school funding program coming out of the equally obscure State of Montana. The program at issue permitted tax payers to claim a deduction of not more than $150 when they donated to scholarship funds used to provide tuition to low income families seeking to attend private schools. Montana's Supreme Court held that the State tax agency's rule barring allowance for the deduction or use of the money when the donation was ultimately directed to pay tuition at religious schools was consistent with the State's Constitution, which read that neither the State nor any other public entity could "make any direct or indirect appropriation or payment from any public fund or monies, or any grant of lands or other property for any sectarian purpose or to aid any church, school, academy, seminary, college, university, or other literary or scientific institution, controlled in whole or in part by any church, sect, or denomination."[1] On one side of the case were the representatives of conservative Montana defending the State Supreme Court's ruling, aided by the ACLU; on the other were the penurious claimants, backed by a host of school choice organizations and the Trump Administration.

For those hopeful that religious organizations—particularly conservative Christian ones—can and will be denied money that might otherwise be dedicated to support secular schools where anti-Christian

---

[21] *Trump v. Mazars*, supra, dissent of J. Rao, at p. 8.
[1] Montana Constitution, Art. X, Sec. 6.

values are ascendant and a unionized labour force trends progressive at the polls—the hearing went badly. NBC News reported that the Supreme Court seemed prepared "to rule that States violate the U.S. Constitution if they prevent religious schools from receiving some state benefits."[2] The conservative justices, led by Brett Kavanaugh, indeed seemed poised to lower Thomas Jefferson's vaunted wall of separation standing between a secular nation and an America modelled after *The Handmaid's Tale*. Others saw a ruling favourable to religious proponents as more sinister still. In the wake of such an outcome, public schools and secular values, apparently so withered behind the breached parapets of secularism, would yield to a resurgent racism through the incentives posed by a constitutionally protected right to dedicate public money to private religious schools populated by lilly-white children, attired in crisp and creased uniforms and all but goose stepping their way through their studies. A victory for "school choice," warned Monica Blair in the pages of *The Washington Post*, "would exacerbate school segregation, thanks to the long history of racial segregation within parochial schools"—something she said the justices "largely ignored during oral arguments."[3] The case, intoned the ACLU and other progressive activist organizations, was but "the latest in a disturbing line of cases attacking the very foundations of the separation of church and state," and would likely inure to the detriment of all historically maligned minorities, including lesbian, gay and transgender Americans.[4]

The opposition to the parents of the students desiring to attend a private school in rustic Montana exhibits all the hallmarks of modern progressive statism—the mandatory attendance of the young in institutions of education where progressive values can be presented as the only option, while the alternatives, starved both of funds and credibility, would ultimately wither away like the bourgeois state in the prophetic dreams of Marx and Engels. The sanctified doctrine of separation of church and state and Jefferson's hallowed wall of separation must ever hold, lest racism, sexism and homophobia run

---

[2] Pete Williams, "Supreme Court Appears Likely to Allow Public Funding for Religious Schools," www.nbcnews.com, January 22, 2020.

[3] Monica Kristin Blair, "What the Supreme Court Missed About Wednesday's Religious-Schools Case," www.washingtonpost.com, January 23, 2020.

[4] Katie Reilly, "Supreme Court Weighs Case Over Religious Schools That Could Upend the Line Between Church and State," www.time.com, January 23, 2020.

rampant through the minds of indoctrinated private schoolers and plunge the commonwealth into a new age of right-oriented ideological pogroms. For the parents of the students seeking relief from the discriminatory policies of Montana, however, the desire is merely to obtain some help getting their children into a school they have faith in, where they might learn the fundamentals necessary to be competitive in the job market of the future and perhaps a bit about the faith of their fathers. Sending African Americans back to the plantation, women back to the kitchen and gays back into the closet is likely the furthest thing from their minds. Such misfortunes could certainly come to pass again, but past Supreme Court decisions striking at the ability of private schools to racially discriminate and the existence of public accommodation laws in every State in the Union provide remedy to some if not all discrimination that might emanate from the private sector. The greater threat in our progressive-dominated culture is not a new Jim Crow or a million Mathew Shepards, but the further erosion of religious liberty.

The Free Exercise Clause was the axle on which the recent argument in the Supreme Court turned, not the Establishment Clause and its separation requirement. The case—*Espinoza v. Montana Department of Revenue*—came via an appeal from a decision by the Montana Supreme Court that had completely disregarded the claimant's Free Exercise contentions. Instead, it focused exclusively on the Montana Constitution and the long-recognized principle that while the State might have avoided offending the Establishment Clause by allowing religious schools to benefit from the program, it was within its rights to deny the privilege through more stringent legal standards embodied within the State's own Constitution. The State's version of the Establishment Clause, however, is just as subject to review as the federal version when the State employs it in a way that discriminates against the practitioners of religious faith.

There is no doubt that the State and federal versions of the Establishment Clause prohibit the imposition of special assessments to support religious entities, or any requirement of citizens to attend religious services on pain of punishment. "Neither a State nor the Federal Government can set up a church," said Justice Black.[5] "Neither

[5] *Everson v. Board of Education* (1947) 330 U.S. 1, 15, 67 S.Ct. 504

can pass laws which aid one religion, aid all religions, or prefer one religion over another. Neither can force nor influence a person to go to or to remain away from church against his will or force him to profess a belief or disbelief in any religion. No person can be punished for entertaining or professing religious beliefs or disbeliefs, for church attendance or non-attendance. No tax in any amount, large or small, can be levied to support any religious activities or institutions, whatever they may be called, or whatever form they may adopt to teach or practice religion."[6]

That religion might receive support indirectly is another matter altogether. The expansion of government involvement in funding programs to benefit all of society over the past century has increased the potential that these benign and generally applicable programs would come to the attention of religious organizations interested in enjoying the benefits along with everyone else. When organizations are excluded from benefits available to others on account of a particular or even general religious bent, the Free Exercise Clause is implicated. The Clause not only allows for persons to worship as they see fit, but also prohibits the reliance by the States on religious criteria in the decision to bar people or organizations from receiving benefits created to advance broad social interests.

In the 1940s, the Court considered one such program: a State subsidy to any school, public or private, to support bus transport of students to and from campus. In *Everson v. Board of Education*, objections were raised that the receipt of public money by private religious schools violated the Establishment Clause, which had yet to be incorporated into the Fourteenth Amendment. For the Court's majority, Justice Hugo Black acknowledged the call of the Establishment Clause, which prohibited the contribution of tax money to support churches, but pointed out the existence of other language in the Amendment commanding that a State not "hamper its citizens in the free exercise of their own religion."[7] The result of Black's construction of the two clauses was that the State could not "exclude individual Catholics, Lutherans, Mohammedans, Baptists, Jews, Methodists, Nonbelievers, Presbyter-ians, or the members of any other faith, because of their faith, or lack of it, from receiving the benefits

[6] Id., at 15-16.
[7] Id., at 16.

of public welfare legislation."[8] He found the support religious organizations obtained via the subsidy to be indistinguishable from the benefits churches receive from public police and fire departments and public sewage systems.

In the wake of Black's *Everson* opinion, a steady stream of precedent flowed from the Supreme Court confirming that generally applicable benefits cannot be denied anyone on the basis of their religious status. In *Walz*, the Court permitted churches to receive an exemption from State property taxes along with a host of other organizations dedicated to socially beneficial activities.[9] In *Roemer*, it held that public money could be granted to private religious colleges for construction of facilities to be used in the general education of students.[10] In *Lamb's Chapel*, all organizations, including religious ones, were to be permitted to use public school facilities during off-hours.[11] And in *Zelman*, the State of Ohio was vindicated in allowing the use of vouchers to pay for school tuition at private schools, regardless of religious affiliation.[12] In all but one of these cases, the Court considered the secular purpose of the aid, the neutrality of the State with respect to religion and whether the program at issue gave rise to excessive entanglement between church and state. In none of them was this constitutional standard deemed to bar the receipt of public benefits by religious organizations.

The most recent case dealing with public benefits denied to religious groups is the one the claimants in *Espinoza* most heavily relied on: *Trinity Lutheran Church of Columbia, Inc. v. Comer*. In that case, Trinity Lutheran applied for a public benefit in the form of a rubberized surface for its gravel playground to prevent the youngsters attending its campus from scraping elbows and knees when not in class learning the Three Rs and tales of the Fall of Man, the rebellion of Jeroboam and the resurrection of the Lord Jesus Christ. The state agency in charge of the program denied the request due to an administrative regulation based on its understanding of a prohibition set forth in the State Constitution similar to the one operative in Montana. Trinity then sued on the grounds that

---

[8] Id.

[9] *Walz v. Tax Commission of the City of New York* (1970) 397 U.S. 664, 90 S.Ct. 1409.

[10] *Roemer v. Board of Public Works of Maryland* (1976) 426 U.S. 736, 96 S.Ct. 2337.

[11] *Lamb's Chapel v. Center Moriches Union Free School District* (1993) 508 U.S. 384, 113 S.Ct. 2141.

[12] *Zelman v. Simmons-Harris* (2002) 536 U.S. 639, 122 S.Ct. 2460.

the veto of its application, pursuant to the Department's policy of denying grants to religiously affiliated applicants, violated the Free Exercise Clause of the First Amendment. The lower court dismissed the case as controlled by *Locke v. Davey*, wherein a scholarship applicant was refused public aid due to his intention to use the money to pay for divinity school. The Supreme Court of the United States granted Trinity's writ and then heard argument in the matter.

In evaluating the merits of the case, Chief Justice Roberts stated that the "Free Exercise clause 'protects religious observers against unequal treatment' and subjects to the strictest scrutiny laws that target the religious for 'special disabilities' based on the 'religious status.'"[13] He noted the tradition going back to *Everson* wherein the Court has "confirmed that denying a generally available benefit solely on account of religious identity imposes a penalty on the free exercise of religion that can be justified only by a state interest 'of the highest order.'"[14] The program at issue was not a direct grant of support to churches in their religious mission, nor an endorsement of a church's spiritual message. Instead, the church was but one of numerous parties seeking a benefit available to organizations that applied so long as resources were available. The program itself had an entirely secular purpose. Indeed, it cannot be plausibly asserted that renovating a children's playground served any religious purpose at all. Nor was there any real entanglement between the Church and the State aside from simply sending government contractors to the school grounds to resurface the play area. Where the State's rule was problematic was its lack of neutrality. Rather than view the church as one of many applicants seeking to upgrade their playgrounds, the State was singling out the church for exclusion from the benefit solely on the basis of its religious character. The state interest asserted in defense of the rule—"achieving greater separation of church and state"—was already ensured by the Constitution's prohibition on Establishments, hence redundant and essentially prohibited by the Free Exercise Clause.

The Supreme Court has said that "governments have not always been tolerant of religious activity, and hostility toward religion has taken many shapes and forms—economic, political, and sometimes harshly

---

[13] *Lutheran Church of Columbia, Inc. v. Comer* (2015) 137 S.Ct. 2012, 2019, 198 L.Ed. 2d 551.

[14] Id.

oppressive."[15] From the earliest days of settlement in what became the United States, colonial governments were authorized "to erect religious establishments which all...would be required to support and attend."[16] In the patchwork of colonial American jurisdictions, "Catholics found themselves hounded and proscribed because of their faith; Quakers who followed their conscience went to jail; Baptists were peculiarly obnoxious to certain dominant Protestant sects; men and women of varied faiths who happened to be in a minority in a particular locality were persecuted because they steadfastly persisted in worshipping God only as their own consciences dictated. And all of these dissenters were compelled to pay tithes and taxes to support government-sponsored churches whose ministers preached inflammatory sermons designed to strengthen and consolidate the established faith by generating a burning hatred against dissenters."[17] In the 1830s, the Mormons became the special pariah of Protestant America. Driven from New York, they settled in Missouri, but then were expelled by the State Militia on order of the Governor.[18] When the charter the Church received for a new settlement in neighbouring Illinois was revoked by the Legislature of that State, the Mormons departed for the Far West.[19] Even the desert was too dear a place for many Americans to allow the Mormons to occupy unmolested. War nearly erupted several times between the Mormons and the United States government in the first decades of western settlement. In 1870, President Grant dispatched General James McKean as Chief Justice of the Utah Territory for the purpose of bringing the Mormons to heal. Statehood for Utah was long delayed due entirely to a powerful animus in Congress toward the Mormon population of the place. More expansive than the persecution of the small Mormon population was the official reaction to the Catholic Irish, whose flooding into American ports beginning in the 1840s prompted a wave of State laws prohibiting aid to private schools. More extreme reactions occurred in New Jersey and Massachusetts, where the legislatures passed laws to block Irish Catholics from taking office after prevailing in municipal

---

[15] *Walz v. Tax Commission of the City of New York*, supra, at 673.

[16] *Everson v. Board of Education*, supra, at 9.

[17] Id., at 10.

[18] See William Alexander Linn, *The Story of the Mormons: From the Date of Their Origins to the Year 1901* (New York: The MacMillan Company, 1902), at pp. 195-356.

[19] Id.

elections.[20] It was in this historical moment of religious bigotry that Jefferson's obscure quote about the wall of separation from the text of a letter to a Baptist pastor came into fashion and was affixed to the notion that total separation was an immutable doctrine of Constitutional law.[21]

It was a rather unexpected outcome that a chief proponent of defending America's Protestant hegemony from Catholic subversion would draft an opinion that opened the door to public funding of some aspects of private religious education, notwithstanding his use of Jefferson's wall of separation language. Yet even a man like Justice Black, haunted by youthful commitments to religious bigotry and the Klan, could overcome those innate biases and see the Constitution for what it is: a document designed to maximize liberty by restraining the hand of government and its control by an unforgiving majority, and setting certain types of legislative uses completely beyond regulatory reach. Among those uses are laws that violate religious liberty by withholding certain generally applicable benefits from religious people and the organizations to which they belong simply and solely on account of their religious dimension. That is a wall too high and too strong, and contrary to the natural construction of the First Amendment. The Amendment calls not for complete separation. It requires, said Justice William O. Douglas, merely that "there shall be no concert or union or dependency one on the other."[22] If this were not the case, the State and religion "would be aliens to each other—hostile, suspicious, and even unfriendly. Churches could not be required to pay even property taxes. Municipalities would not be permitted to render police or fire protection to religious groups. Policemen who helped parishioners into their places of worship would violate the Constitution."[23] That the author of these words was one of the most progressive, even extreme, thinkers in the area of individual liberty the Court has ever seen ought to caution those who insist on a barrier both impregnable and infinitely high between the secular and the spiritual.

Justice Douglas didn't believe in so impervious a wall, even as he pressed his brethren to discard the concept of obscenity as an affront to

---

[20] Kirby Miller, *Emigrants and Exiles: Ireland and the Irish Exodus to North America* (New York: Oxford University Press, 1985), at p. 498.

[21] See Philip Hamburger, *Separation of Church and State* (Cambridge: Harvard University Press, 2002).

[22] *Zorach v. Clauson* (1952) 343 U.S. 306, 312, 72 S.Ct. 679.

[23] Id.

free speech and permit draft dodgers jurisdictional standing to challenge the Constitutional validity of overseas conflicts. In light of the jurisprudence he helped refine, it appears likely that the Court will overturn the Montana decision on Free Exercise grounds and permit qualified individuals to use public moneys in the manner of their choosing, consistent with their own beliefs and concept of their best interest. That the use ultimately promotes faith should be of no concern in a nation that was founded on the principle that all persons were endowed by their Creator with certain inalienable rights. Hypocrisy may have been too rich when those words were first published. There's no reason to continue embracing a similar hypocrisy today.

A Public Charge to Keep

EVER since Donald Trump announced to the world his intention to "build the wall and make Mexico pay for it," the die was cast. The forces of American progressivism, committed to the demographic transformation of the country—and with it the termination of the rule of white men and all of its associated evils—would stop at nothing to thwart him. In steady succession challenges came, first to the wall itself through environmental objections, then to the "family separation" policy, followed by the enactment of State laws to prevent local law enforcement from turning alien felons over to INS for deportation, lawsuits to prevent the identification of citizens in the decennial census, opposition to the temporary travel ban, and then the effort to halt the use of emergency powers to re-purpose public funds toward the construction of the hated wall. The latest challenge is now in full blossom. Throughout the nation, lawsuits were filed by States, municipalities and non-profit organizations over the proposed refinement of the so-called "Public Charge Rule" that would expand the definition of a "public charge" to include, for the first time, non-cash public assistance such as Medicaid, Medicare and housing vouchers, and allow the federal government to consider deportation of immigrants who would take advantage of such benefits to make ends meet. As noted by Justice Neil Gorsuch, "these efforts have met with mixed results. The Northern District of California ordered the government not to enforce the new rule within a hodge-podge of jurisdictions – California, Oregon, Maine, Pennsylvania, and the District of Columbia. The Eastern District of Washington entered a similar order, but went much farther geographically, enjoining the government from enforcing its rule globally."[1] Much more modestly, the Court for the Northern District of Illinois enjoined enforcement merely in the territory within the State of Illinois. After a panel of judges in the Ninth Circuit lifted the stay in the west, "a single judge in New York enjoined the government from applying the new definition to anyone, without regard to geography or participation in this or any other lawsuit."[2]

After declaring that the plaintiffs were likely to succeed in their claims against the Trump Administration, Judge George B. Daniels in New York explained the rationale for the injunction. "The Rule is simply a new agency policy of exclusion in search of a justification. It is repugnant to the American Dream of the opportunity for prosperity and success through hard work and upward mobility."[3] Nicole Narea of *Vox* said the Rule was but a riff on the age-old nativist theme of immigrants who "take advantage of public assistance without offering the US anything in return."[4] The theme, she and others say, is false, and has created "an impression that undocumented immigrants and temporary residents are gobbling up public benefits, which they're not because they're generally not eligible," and has the effect of terrifying "those who are eligible, who are primarily permanent residents with green cards,... [into] un-enrolling from programs they are perfectly eligible to take advantage of under the law."[5] The Rule, she and others warn, may cause up to 2.7 million children nationwide to "lose access to food stamps" and deter poor immigrants from accessing health care, or at least divert them from low income clinics to the far more expensive emergency rooms.[6] Dr. Bruce Siegel, president and CEO of America's Essential Hospitals,

---

[1] *Department of Homeland Security, at al. v. New York, et al.* (2020) 140 S.Ct. 599, J. Gorsuch, concurring.

[2] Id.

[3] Laurel Wamsley, Pam Fessler & Richard Gonzales, "Federal Judges in 3 States Block Trump's 'Public Charge' Rule for Green Cards," www.npr.org, October 11, 2019.

[4] Nicole Narea, "Courts Blocked Trump's rule to keep out low-income immigrants," www.vox.com, October 11, 2019.

[5] Id.

[6] Dennis Herrera and Jill Habig, "Local Governments Need to Join the Fight Against Trump's Cruel 'Public Charge' Rule, *Sacramento Bee*, November 14, 2019.

said the expanded definition of Public Charge "worsens the chilling effect that threatens the health of millions of people by making it more likely they forgo care for themselves and their families to avoid putting their legal immigration status at risk."[7] The Rule even threatens the stability of hospitals, "which will sustain higher uncompensated costs as immigrants put off care and seek treatment later, only as a last resort, when they're sicker and more costly to treat," and will in turn, "drive higher costs for taxpayers and the entire health care system."[8] The President's old nemesis, California Attorney General Xavier Becerra, simply called the rule "vile," and said it is but the "latest attack on families and lower income communities of color."[9]

It isn't surprising that the criticism of the change in the Public Charge Rule resolves into an accusation of racism. The rich history of racial animus in America lends itself to use and abuse by those anxious to more radically change American society, preferably through the power of the state. Becerra's charge, though, is but the beginning, not the end. Former State Department employee and immigration attorney Chris Richardson said the Rule's roots in the nation's racist past run deep. "It comes," he says, "from the 1840s and 1850s when the nativist 'Know Nothing Party' used provisions in anti-Catholic States such as New York and Massachusetts to deport poor Irish Catholics because they were 'likely at any time to become a public charge.' By the 1880s, as immigrants from Eastern and Southern Europe started entering the country, these same nativists urged Congress to act in a more forceful fashion."[10] Congress obliged them with the Immigration Act of 1882, which barred entry to "any convict, lunatic, idiot, or any person unable to take care of himself or herself without becoming a public charge."[11] The law augmented the Page Act that barred emigration of Chinese women due to fears that they were likely to be drawn to prostitution, and the Chinese Exclusion Act that barred entry to Chinese men.[12] In the

---

[7] John Commins, "Providers Pan Trump Administration Final Rule on Public Charge," www.healthleadesmedia.com, August 12, 2019.

[8] Id.

[9] Id.

[10] Christopher Richardson, "We Must Abolish the 'Public Charge' Rule," www.thewashingtonpost.com, August 19, 2019.

[11] Id.

[12] Salonee Bhaman, "How President Trump's New Immigration Rule Could Erode the Social Safety Net," www.thewashingtonpost.com, August 14, 2019.

years since, the Rule has been a consistent tool, say the critics, in the white man's war against color, ethnicity and even sexual preference. After employing it as a justification for turning Jewish refugees back upon the mercy of the Nazis in the 1930s, the government "continued using it decades after to bar gay men, lesbians and the disabled from getting visas."[13] From "relatively open borders" prior to 1882, the Rule propelled America into becoming a nation closed to those who didn't conform to the white, Christian, heterosexual majoritarian profile.

Disingenuous it would be, or naïve or dishonest, to deny the potency of race in American law and policy, or to contend that racial animus played no role in immigration policy from 1882 onward. It is equally disingenuous or dishonest to contend that the Public Charge Rule is either racist per se or rooted in racism, and that its deployment brought an end to the era of open borders, or that there ever were open borders in this country. Indeed, history tells a different story. America, both under the British and then in the early years of Independence, was never a place immigrants were free to access. The stinginess of the Crown in permitting immigration was actually one of the grievances enumerated in the Declaration of Independence. Though immigrants were generally welcomed following the advent of the Republic, the States each pursued a course that prohibited the entry or settlement of those deemed deficient in health or the means or ability to fend for themselves. "At the time of independence," notes historian Gerald Neuman, "the states took with them the heritage of the English poor laws, which made the relief of the poor the responsibility of the local community where they were legally 'settled.' These laws gave localities various powers to prevent the settlement of persons who might later require support, and to 'remove' such individuals to the place where they were legally settled."[14] The Articles of Confederation empowered the States to guard against paupers and vagabonds, and while the Constitution eliminated reference to those classes, the Framers and those of that generation tended to view control of entry to a State as a fundamental element of sovereignty not completely ceded to the federal government.[15] Long before the star of the Know Nothings briefly coursed through America's

---

[13] Id.

[14] Gerald L. Neuman, "The Lost Century of American Immigration Law (1776-1875)," 93 Colum. L. Rev. 1833 (1993), at p. 1846.

[15] Id., at pp. 1846-1847.

political skies, Massachusetts and New York led the way, though every State had similar regimes, aimed not at persons of color, but almost exclusively at immigrants from the British Isles and Western Europe—the demographically whitest part of the globe. Pursuant to these laws, immigrants who were liable to becoming a public charge would be subject to removal. Ship captains were required to report the name, origin, age, character and condition of immigrants from foreign parts. In time, security was demanded of ship captains when passengers seemed likely to become paupers. In Massachusetts, they were additionally required to pay two dollars per any alien who was not in the high-risk category. In New York, a Commission of Emigration was created in 1847 to oversee bonding of certain classes of immigrants by captains, as well as to protect immigrants from abuse. The State also imposed a 1 dollar per head fee on every emigrant who crossed a gang plank onto New York soil.

The power of the States to impose restrictions on immigrants whose condition rendered them likely to become public charges during the era of exclusive western European immigration was acknowledge by John Marshall as early as 1819. "Inspection laws, quarantine laws, health laws of every description, as well as laws for regulating the internal commerce of a State, and those which respect turnpike roads, ferries, &c., are component parts" of what Marshall called "that immense mass of legislation which embraces everything within the territory of a State not surrendered to the General government; all of which can be most advantageously exercised by the States themselves."[16] The Taney Court reaffirmed the States' authority to regulate entry of immigrants through State ports, and to protect the peoples of the States from sickness and the expense of public charges. When reviewing New York's public charge provision, the Court observed that the law was designed to address the burden caused by the "influx of persons brought thither by ships, either from foreign countries or from any other of the states," and to allow city authorities "to prevent them from becoming chargeable as paupers."[17] Though there was some impact on interstate and international commerce, Justice Philip Barbour and his brethren concluded that "we think it as competent and as necessary for a State to provide precautionary measures against the moral pestilence of paupers,

[16] *Gibbons v. Ogden* (1822) 22 U.S. 1, 203.
[17] *Mayor of New York v. Miln* (1837) 36 U.S. 102, 133.

vagabonds, and possibly convicts; as it is to guard against the physical pestilence which may arise from unsound and infectious articles imported, or from a ship, the crew of which may be labouring under an infectious disease."[18]

In the same case, the concurring Justice Henry Baldwin thought it absurd that the people of the States "should have adopted a Constitution which has taken from the States the power of regulating pauperism within their territory."[19] Indeed, when vesting with the federal government the power over interstate and international commerce, the People "little thought that...they also granted, as a means, the regulation of internal police."[20] There never would have been a federal government, he said "if there had been a declaration in its frame that Congress could pass poor laws or interfere to revise or control those passed by the States, or that Congress could legislate on any subject of legislation over which no jurisdiction was granted to them and which was reserved to the States or people in the same plenitude as they held it before they surrendered any portion of their power."[21] Even the dissenting Justice Joseph Story conceded (in another case) that "the States have a right to pass health laws and quarantine laws and other police laws not contravening the laws of Congress," and that they "have a right to pass poor laws and laws to prevent the introduction of paupers into the State under the like qualifications."[22] Story reiterated this view several years later when saying that he and the rest of the Court "entertain no doubt whatsoever, that the States, in virtue of their general police power, possess full jurisdiction to arrest and restrain runaway slaves, and remove them from their borders, and otherwise to secure themselves against their depredations and evil example, as they certainly may do in cases of idlers, vagabonds, and paupers."[23]

The Court directly confronted the New York and Massachusetts laws imposing bonding requirements on ship captains and head taxes on all immigrants in *The Passenger Cases*. The great advocates Daniel

---

[18] Id., at 142.

[19] Richard Peters, *Reports of the Cases Argued and Adjudged in the Supreme Court of the United States*, Volume XI (New York: The Banks Law Publishing Company, 1903), at p. 120.

[20] Id.

[21] Id.

[22] *Mayor of New York v. Miln*, supra, at 156.

[23] *Prigg v. Pennsylvania* (1842) 41 U.S. 539, 625.

Webster and Rufus Choate argued that the laws were unconstitutional invasions by the States into the ken of interstate commerce. New York's attorney general, John Van Buren, insisted that the laws were traditional exercises by the States of their long-standing authority to regulate the health of the ports and the settlement or exclusion of immigrants within their bounds. A divided court embraced Webster's arguments with respect to the laws at issue, but its members remained convinced of the general authority of the States to exercise their police powers to govern and even exclude persons liable to become public charges. In his majority opinion, Justice John McLean opined that "except to guard its citizens against diseases and paupers, the municipal power of a state cannot prohibit the introduction of foreigners brought to this country under the authority of Congress. It may deny to them a residence unless they shall give security to indemnify the public should they become paupers."[24] Justice James Wayne affirmed that "the States have the right to turn off paupers, vagabonds, and fugitives from justice."[25] Such people, he said, "never have been subjects of rightful national intercourse, or of commercial regulations, except in the transportation of them to distant colonies to get rid of them, or for punishment as convicts."[26] The States were entitled to "meet such persons upon their arrival in port, and may put them under all proper restraints. They may prevent them from entering their territories, may carry them out or drive them off."[27] The States might have surrendered their power over interstate commerce, but they remained empowered to "remove all persons who are thought dangerous to its welfare, and...to determine who shall enter."[28] Justice Robert Grier contended that the right of a State "to repel from her shores lunatics, idiots, criminals, or paupers, which any foreign country, or even one of her sister states, might endeavour to thrust upon her" had "its foundation in the sacred law of self-defense, which no power granted to Congress can restrain or annul."[29] All "those powers which relate to merely municipal legislation, or what may be more properly called internal police, are not surrendered or restrained; and that it is as competent and necessary for a state to provide

---

[24] *The Passenger Cases* (1849) 48 U.S. 283, at 406.
[25] Id., at 426.
[26] Id.
[27] Id.
[28] Id., at 427.
[29] Id., at 457.

precautionary measures against the moral pestilence of paupers, vagabonds, and convicts, as it is to guard against the physical pestilence which may arise from unsound and infectious articles imported."[30]

The rights of the States to deport immigrants who became public charges was even more forcefully articulated by the dissenters in the matter. The scholarly New Englander Levi Woodbury traced the power of the States in this regard back to the Mayflower and the early colonial charters.[31] Even after Independence the States exercised the power, often with the formal blessing and admonition of the Congress. The steady flow of "voluntary emigrants, or traveling absentees, or refugees in revolutions, party exiles, compulsory victims of power...large bands of convicts, or brigands, or persons with incendiary purposes, or imbecile paupers, or those suffering from infectious diseases, or fanatics with principles and designs more dangerous than either, or under circumstances of great ignorance, as liberated serfs," counselled the exercise of the power, lest these masses pose a substantial financial and even moral burden on the people of the States.[32] Woodbury explained that it "is for the State where the power resides to decide on what is sufficient cause for it, whether municipal or economical, sickness or crime; as, for example, danger of pauperism, danger to health, danger to morals, danger to property, danger to public principles by revolutions and change of government, or danger to religion."[33] Much stronger still was the opinion of the Chief Justice, who believed that if a State "may remove from among its citizens any person or description of persons whom it regards as injurious to their welfare, it follows that it may meet them at the threshold and prevent them from entering. For it will hardly be said that the United States may permit them to enter and compel the State to receive them and that the State may immediately afterwards expel them. There could be no reason of policy or humanity for compelling the States, by the power of Congress, to imbibe the poison, and then leaving them to find a remedy for it by their own exertions and at their own expense."[34] It was entirely up to the States "to determine whether any particular class or description of persons are likely to

[30] Id., at 458.
[31] Id., at 519.
[32] Id., at 525.
[33] Id., at 528.
[34] Id., at 466.

produce discontents or insurrection in its territory, or to taint the morals of its citizens, or to bring among them contagious diseases, or the evils and burdens of a numerous pauper population."[35] In the case at bar, the Chief Justice was convinced that Massachusetts was free to determine that "the introduction into the State from foreign countries [was] likely to produce in the State a numerous pauper population heavily and injuriously burdensome to its citizens.[36] "An individual," he analogized, "may forbid another from digging a ditch through his land to draw off water from the property of the party who desires the permission. Yet he may allow him to do it upon such conditions and terms as, in his judgment, are sufficient to protect his own property from overflow, and for this purpose he may either take a bond and security or he may accept a sum of money in lieu of it and take upon himself the obligation of guarding against the danger." The same principle, he said "must apply to governments which are charged with the duty of protecting their citizens."[37]

The history of the Public Charge Rule, deep as it is, dispels the misconception that its origins lay in the reaction of white America to emigrants of color. It arose at a time when the only immigrants of note were Europeans. The objective informing it was not to exclude poorer races, but to ensure that the white immigrants who settled in the individual states would be productive members of American society. When the federal government finally entered the field of immigration and enacted the first comprehensive immigration law in 1882, the historic functions of the States were effectively pre-empted, but the public charge principle naturally found its way into the statutory scheme. Racist prohibitions and limitations entered the statutes, yes, and entire racial groups were excluded for a period of time, but at no time did the Public Charge Rule ever cease operating against white immigrants. To the extent that any immigrant was allowed into the country, they were subject to the same rule: that they be excluded from American shores if they were unable to care for themselves. Since the role of the States in enforcement of the ancient rule was now pre-empted, the only thing that changed was who would be enforcing it henceforth.

---

[35] Id., at 467.
[36] Id.
[37] Id., at 468-469.

It may be that the new version of the rule is bad policy. As the nation's natural increase has declined, our people depend on the influx of immigrants to maintain the national population. As the economy grows so too does the demand for labor. Not all jobs are skilled jobs, hence poorer, less educated people have a place in the immigration scheme. It isn't so much a matter of importing the poor as importing the class of workers suitable for certain types of employment. Poor workers allowed entry certainly are going to be less likely to afford housing and medical care, particularly in parts of the country like the Bay Area of California where prices are inflated for any number of reasons. Taxes, regulations and basic principles of economics aside, these much-needed less educated and less skilled workers perhaps ought not be denied the privileges that all other lawful residents of the State and nation are entitled to enjoy. There is much sense in what the critics of the current tightening of the Rule have to say. I am not so learned in these things as to be able to express a definitive opinion on that point. What I am a bit more confident in expressing is the opinion that the constant reliance on race and racism to explain away the policies of the Trump Administration is simply tiresome, ignorant and, at times, idiotic. If there is a heavier impact on non-white immigrants than white, it has little to do with racism and almost everything to do with the fact that our immigration policy is less racist than ever if measured by the percentage of non-white people admitted into the country each year. More people of color coming into the United States from countries that tend to be poorer than nations that are predominantly white explains most if not all of the disparity.

Racism hysteria on the left, however, may inadvertently serve one productive function. The reflexive resort by progressives to the courts with accusations of racism and the insistence of sympathetic judges in lone judicial districts on solving all of the nation's problems through nationwide injunctions may well spell the end of the latter practice once and for all when the Supreme Court, under the intellectual dominance of Clarence Thomas and Neil Gorsuch, finally address the merits of the challenge to a rule that undoubtedly will survive their review.

ERA No!

HAVING apparently weathered the controversy of his youthful hijinks donned in blackface and avoided any threat of removal from office and replacement by a lieutenant governor accused of rape, Virginia's chief executive Ralph Northam excitedly watched the election returns in November of 2018 as the grand old party of Slavery and Jim Crow took control of both houses of the State legislature. Locked up for decades by Republican majorities, the Virginia legislature could now take action on Northam's progressive agenda of gun control, abortion rights and sanctuary cities. It could also undo forty years of legislative inaction by ratifying the Equal Rights Amendment. Just the previous year, a resolution to finally ratify the Amendment died in committee without ever reaching a vote.[1] "If we get it to the floor and let people vote," said the Governor, "then it will become law."[2] It would become law, in his view at least, because Virginia would be the thirty-eighth State to ratify the Amendment since it was approved by Congress and sent out to the States for their consideration back in 1972.

Tremendous momentum in the several years following the Amendment's publication by Congress presaged what looked like would be an easy and rapid ratification. A counter-movement, however, stalled the forward progress. "Warning of disastrous consequences if traditional gender roles were eroded," including the drafting of women to serve in combat and mandatory bi-gender public restrooms and shower facilities, its leaders managed to chill enthusiasm for constitutional change.[3] Within a decade, progress stopped altogether, leaving the would-be amendment three States shy of becoming part of the Constitution. The inertia ended in 2017, when the State of Nevada's new Democrat legislature ratified the Amendment, followed by Illinois.

---

[1] "One of These States Could Ratify the Equal Rights Amendment," www.pbs.org, February 26, 2019.

[2] Maggie Astor, "The Equal Rights Amendment May Pass Now. It's Only Been 96 Years," *The New York Times*, November 6, 2019.

[3] Id.; and Molly Olmstead, "Why Virginia's Election Results Mean the Equal Rights Amendment Could Finally Pass," www.slate.com, November 6, 2019.

Inevitably, the Democrat majority in Virginia performed as expected and ratified the Amendment as one of its first legislative acts.[4] The State's attorney general then caucused with his counter-parts in Illinois and Nevada and filed suit in the United States District Court sitting in Washington, D.C., asking for a writ of mandate to force the archivist of the United States "to carry out his statutory duty of recognizing the complete and final adoption of the Twenty-Eight Amendment to the Constitution."[5]

Why a suit is necessary might be perplexing to those who contemplate that attachment of amendments to the Constitution is a matter of the mere operation of law once the constitutional requirements are satisfied. Article V of the Constitution provides that Congress may propose amendments for consideration by the States if three fourths of each House approve, and those amendments are to be attached to the Constitution if and when three quarters of the States ratify them. The catch here is that when Congress proposed the Equal Rights Amendment, it imposed a condition that it only take effect if the requisite number of States took affirmative action within a seven-year time frame. As explained by CNN's Veronica Stracqualursi, opponents of the ERA "argue the deadline to pass the amendment expired decades ago, and point to several states that are among the 38 that rescinded their support before the deadline."[6] Conversely, the Amendment's proponents deny a lapse occurred because the time frame is not included in the Amendment's text and rescission of ratification is "constitutionally unauthorized and without legal effect."[7] The Justice Department has sided with the Amendment's opponents and issued an opinion that "the deadline to ratify the ERA has expired and the matter is no longer pending before the States."[8] It then blocked the archivist from taking action.

The sudden revival of interest in the Equal Rights Amendment and renewed belief that it remains viable run counter to learned and popular

---

[4] Ed Kilgore, "Virginia Could Soon Place the Equal Rights Amendment in the Constitution, https://nymag.com, January 15, 2019.

[5] Veronica Stracqualursi, "Three Democratic Attorneys General Sue to Have Equal Rights Amendment Added to Constitution," www.cnn.com, January 30, 2020.

[6] Id.

[7] Id.

[8] Id.

opinion. Why such an opinion, so widely embraced, should suddenly yield to a new consensus is the function to some extent of desperation over what progressives see as the destruction of the advancements the country has made in the area of sexual equality ever since the election of a President they believe possesses notions regarding the sexes rooted in the Palaeolithic Age and who seems in their view to have set himself the goal of remaking the federal judiciary by installing judges and justices who share his primitive outlook. The hysteria surrounding the Kavanaugh hearings, the co-ordination of an accuser with opponents in the Senate, the dubious accusations nearly four decades old, and the appearance of the legal huckster Michael Avenatti with additional victims of the Judge's youthful sexual rampages, are a milestone of just how far separation of reason from prior consensus has come. Clearer minds, of course, see the tremendous benefit to the progressive cause the Amendment would provide. No longer would advocates for progressive feminism need rely on the imperfect Fourteenth Amendment for relief and social change. With the level of scrutiny set firmly at the intermediate level, far too much inequality for far too long has escaped the chastising hand of the judiciary. The fact that the philosophic profile of so many of the recent additions to the federal courts is classically liberal, if not originalist, further counsels an amendment displaced in time from those backward thinking Framers, and might even compel the court to adopt only the highest standard of scrutiny in reviewing all claims of inequality along sexual lines.[9] The proposed Amendment's enabling clause would expand the powers of Congress to advance and enforce sexual equality, and this power might extend so far as to reach even private action. The shortcomings of the Violence Against Women Act, uncovered by the Supreme Court in the *Morrison* decision, stemming directly from Congress's faulty reliance on the Commerce Power, would never again be possible should the discarded law be revived.[10] Most important of all, the most expansive access to the procedure that destroys life in the womb might be protected for all time

[9] See Alex Dean, "One State Away: The Need for Ratification of the Equal Rights Amendment in a Justice Kavanaugh, Conservative Court Era," 10 Wake Forest J.L & Pol'y 1 (2019); and Helen Hershkoff & Elizabeth M. Schneider, "Symposium: Sex, Trump, and constitutional Change," 35 Const. Commentary 43 (2019), at 125-126.

[10] Alex Dean, supra.

from any abbreviation and even receive the blessing of direct congressional funding.

Without more, these motivations would rest purely on aspirations, not law. What renders the aspirations more than mere vapor is the remarkable and sudden inclusion of the Twenty-Seventh Amendment in the Constitution. On May 18, 1992, the Archivist of the United States announced that the Amendment, first proposed with the original Bill of Rights and written in the hand of James Madison himself, had received sufficient support from the States in the wake of recent ratification by the State of Michigan. The Amendment popped into the Constitution at a time when the national mood had soured on Congress and had the effect of barring its members from receiving self-dealing pay raises until the subsequent election. Some doubted the efficacy of the Archivist's declaration, while others were simply amused. In short order, though, the Congress accepted the Amendment and resolved that it was indeed part of the Constitution. Lack of any court challenge left the issue of congressionally imposed time limits and the continuing viability of an Amendment that had lingered in ratification limbo for so long without definitive answer. Believing it was worth exploring, and seeing the grim reality of Trumpism making mischief throughout the land, a new generation donned the ERA YES button, adopted the white attire of the Nineteenth-Century suffragettes, and lobbied with the legislatures of the States that had not yet ratified to get with the times and take affirmative action.

The only legal authority available to proponents of the continuing viability of the ERA, notwithstanding long expired deadlines, is not particularly helpful to their cause. The first instance in history wherein the Court reviewed the power of Congress to set limits on the time during which ratification could occur, or considered the existence of inherent or implied limitations in Article V itself, was in 1921 in the matter of *Dillon v. Gloss*. A man convicted of violating the National Prohibition Act appealed his conviction on the grounds that the Amendment on which the Act was based was invalid due to a time limit on its ratification imposed by Congress. For a unanimous Court, Justice Willis Van Devanter acknowledged that the text of Article V lacked any express provision on the subject and that it was silent "about the time within which ratification may be had—neither that it shall be unlimited nor that it shall be fixed by Congress."[11] Faced with this silence, the Court felt unrestrained in its ability to seek out any limitations in the nebulous realm of inference and implication. Van Devanter and his colleagues did not believe that the Constitution's silence in the matter was "in itself controlling; for with the Constitution, as with a statute or other written instrument, what is reasonably implied is as much a part of it as what is expressed."[12] The absence of limitations in Article V actually convinced the Court that the Framers "intended to invest Congress with a wide range of power in proposing amendments."[13]

Though such power is implied, some reasonable limits on ratification appeared to be implicit in the text. Article V authorizes Congress to propose amendments "when necessary," which suggested to Van Devanter and his colleagues that the proposals must relate to a particular need of the day. He thought it was reasonable to infer "that when proposed, [amendments] are to be considered as disposed of presently."[14] The act of proposing, followed by ratification by the States, yielded a "fair implication that it must be sufficiently contemporaneous in that number of States to reflect the will of the people in all sections at relatively the same period, which of course ratification scattered through a long series of years would not do."[15] This conclusion was supported by the comment of a treatise writer of the day "that an alteration of the Constitution proposed today has relation to the sentiment and the felt needs of today, and that, if not ratified early while that sentiment may fairly be supposed to exist, it ought to be regarded as waived, and not again to be voted upon, unless a second time proposed by Congress."[16] As a limitation on time to ratify was a reasonable inference drawn from the nature of the amendment process and the peculiar need of the moment that prompted an amendment's proposal, and because Congress's power wasn't expressly limited, the imposition by Congress of a time limit appeared consistent with the Constitution's text.

In the only other authority on point—*Coleman v. Miller*—Chief Justice Hughes affirmed the reasoning and holding of *Dillon*. "It is true that in *Dillon v. Gloss*, the Court said that nothing was found in Article V

---

[11] *Dillon v. Gloss* (1921) 256 U.S. 368, 41 S.Ct. 510, 511.

[12] Id., at 512.

[13] Id.

[14] Id.

[15] Id.

[16] Id.

which suggested that an amendment once proposed was to be open to ratification for all time, or that ratification in some States might be separated from that in others by many years and yet be effective; that there was a strong suggestion to the contrary in that proposal and ratification were but succeeding steps in a single endeavour, that as amendments were deemed to be prompted by necessity, they should be considered and disposed of presently; and that there is a fair implication that ratification must be sufficiently contemporaneous in the required number of States to reflect the will of the people in all sections at relatively the same period; and hence that ratification must be within some reasonable time after the proposal."[17] These considerations, said Hughes, "were cogent reasons for the decision...that the Congress had the power to fix a reasonable time for ratification."[18] And yet, possessing the power as it did, the Congress wasn't obligated to exercise it. Its failure to do so was the reason for the controversy at hand, but, alas, it was one the Court couldn't resolve; for it was one vested expressly with the political departments to determine due to the absence of any "satisfactory criteria for a judicial determination."[19] A reasonable length of time to ratify does exist, and Congress could have imposed one, but having refrained from doing so, the Court was powerless to intervene. The only remedy was for the States to ratify with some celerity, or for Congress to deem an amendment ratified at its own discretion whenever, in its view, the requisite number of States took affirmative action.

The Chief Justice's reasoning was not entirely satisfactory to the rest of the Court. Justice Black thought he was correct to cite with approval the conclusion of *Dillon v. Gloss*, "that the Constitution impliedly requires that a properly submitted amendment must die unless ratified within a 'reasonable time,'" and that Congress possesses authority to prescribe a temporal deadline.[20] His only objection was that the Court bothered to intervene at all. Black agreed with Justice Frankfurter that the litigants themselves had no standing. A State could send the ratified amendment to Congress, and Congress was free to accept or reject it as it saw fit in its role as the judge of whether ratification had occurred, but

---

[17] *Coleman v. Miller* (1939) 307 U.S. 433, 59 S.Ct. 972, 981.
[18] Id.
[19] Id., at 982.
[20] Id., at 984.

no individual had authority to challenge the final decision in court. Not even the dissenters disagreed with the outcome of the case. Both Pierce Butler and James McReynolds were of a mind to oppose the substance of the putative amendment and tended to be highly sceptical of Congress's powers when wielded broadly. Their objection was simply that far from being non-justiciable, the issue of the implicit time limits governing the ratification process lent itself to judicial scrutiny, hence the Court should have determined what length of time was reasonable.

The decision in *Coleman* is remarkable in that it occurred during the waning of the era of hostility to governmental action and scepticism regarding the extent to which Congress could exercise its enumerated powers. It is remarkable, too, in that it was drafted by a Chief Justice usually associated with the conservative wing of the Court and was concurred in by the Court's leading progressives. What all agreed on was that the Congress's authority in the area was vast, might be non-justiciable due to the political nature of the issues involved, and that time limits were either inherent in Article V or subject to prescription by Congress, or both.

Notwithstanding the challenges posed by *Dillon* and *Coleman* to proponents of a revivified ERA, the probability that Congress might exercise power over ratification deadlines, and the hint that a proposed amendment might never lose its viability despite the passage of centuries, has sparked hopes for victory of the Equal Rights Amendment and even inspired its progressive advocates to adopt a strict construction of Congress's power and a singular appreciation for the true intent of Framers they never really appreciated until now. "There is nothing in Article V," said one modern-day progressive strict constructionist, "that suggests or mandates that the succeeding steps" of proposal by Congress and ratification by the States "must be related in time," or contemporaneous.[21] Others have joyfully concluded that as Congress might impose a deadline, it can both extend and revive one after it has expired. Still others contend that the inclusion of the ERA's time limit in a resolving clause that was not actually part of the text of the Amendment both reduces the persuasiveness of an existing limitation and suggests that mere legislative language is as amenable to further

[21] Mason Kalfus, "Why Time Limits On the Ratification of Constitutional Amendments Violate Article V," 66 U.Chi.L.Rev. 437 (1999), at p. 447.

legislative revision as any other bill or statute.[22] More amazing still has been the resort to States Rights—the argument that the Amendment process was designed to empower the States, and that any limitation on their time to ponder the merits of an amendment must be unconstitutional. "With time limits," says Mason Kalfus, "States no longer retain exclusive control over amendments after they have been proposed by Congress.... If Congress can put an expiration date on the amendment, the Constitution's grant of exclusive control to the States is lost."[23]

The hopes of the ERA's supporters fly to the heavens, but like Icarus they likely will return to earth, and not because of the gravitational forces of originalism and male-centered bigotry. The Framers really didn't address the details of how the Constitution was to be amended. They described it in broad language, suggesting that it is up to Congress and the States to promulgate rules and procedures to advance the amendment process. This broad language is the first obstacle to overcoming the Court's rulings in *Dillon* and *Coleman*. Since John Marshall's exposition of the powers of Congress in the *McCulloch* case, it has been understood that Congress's jurisdiction, while confined to the narrow limits of the enumerated powers, nevertheless leaves Congress with expansive authority within the scope of those powers. "We admit," he noted, "as all must admit, that the powers of the Government are limited, and that its limits are not to be transcended. But we think the sound construction of the Constitution must allow to the national legislature that discretion with respect to the means by which the powers it confers are to be carried into execution which will enable that body to perform the high duties assigned to it in the manner most beneficial to the people. Let the end be legitimate, let it be within the scope of the Constitution, and all means which are appropriate, which are plainly adapted to that end, which are not prohibited, but consist with the letter and spirit of the Constitution, are Constitutional."[24] The broad language of Article V obviously leaves Congress with some discretion to establish limits on the time to ratify an amendment if Congress concludes that too long a time would allow the intent and purpose of those who framed it

---

22 Maggie Astor, op. cit..
23 Mason Kalfus, op. cit., at p. 456.
24 *McCulloch v. Maryland* (1819). 17 U.S. 316, 421.

to drift away from the moorings of the circumstances out of which it arose.

The Equal Rights Amendment provides a perfect example of why Congress might think it proper to impose a deadline. When the ERA was drafted, the Court had yet to engage in the application of the Equal Protection Clause to the problem of sex inequality. Those who devised the Amendment and promoted it may well have hoped to solve the basic inequalities women still faced despite gaining the right to vote decades before. Since that time, as many of the Amendment's proponents acknowledge with pleasure, the progressive conception of sex has broadened to embrace homosexuality, non-binary sexuality, transgenderism, and gender fluidity. For many of the contemporary advocates of the Amendment, passage of the ERA at this moment "would draw from a...founding history that acknowledges structural discrimination as a cause of gendered inequality and subordination, recognizes the importance of public goods, and appreciates the role of law in creating, sustaining, and perpetuating social and market relations that disadvantage women," in addition to building "on the Constitution's existing protection for reproductive and marital choice—and move forward from those baselines."[25] Obviously, this isn't your mother's Equal Rights Amendment, though it comes packaged in the original bundle. Its language hasn't changed, but it contains a host of concepts those who drafted and initially supported it likely never remotely contemplated. Acknowledgement of the potential for drift of textual meaning over time during the pendency of a drawn-out process of ratification might well have been a key reason why Congress desired the States to act quickly, or lose their opportunity to alter the Constitution.

The broad language of Article V appears to some ERA proponents to shift too much power from the States to the Congress in violation of the Constitution, but this isn't true at all. Article V does appear to reserve for Congress discretion with respect to the mode of proposing amendments, the content of amendments, and time limits for ratification, but only when Congress itself is availing itself of the discreet authority to engage in the amendment process. The alternative method of amending the Constitution set forth in Article V vests no similar

---

[25] Hershkoff & Schneider, op. cit., at p. 126.

authority with the Congress. Instead, it actually places a similar broad power in the hands of the States meeting at a Constitutional Convention. Though that provision has never been acted upon, a Convention of States would remain outside of Congress's ken and would provide the States themselves with far greater control over the amendment process than Congress enjoys when taking the initiative to propose constitutional change. When acting in Convention, the States command both the proposition of amendments and the process of ratification. For those concerned over a loss of State power to Congress, they need only advocate the Convention route for their concerns to be ameliorated. So long as Congress proposes amendments, its power over that process remains dominant.

It is not without relevance to the outcome of the pending suit that *Dillon* was a unanimous decision. Not a single justice even bothered to offer an alternative rationale, let alone a dissent. It was authored by a justice associated with the so-called Four Horsemen of the Apocalypse, who expressed throughout his 26 year-long Supreme Court career much discomfort and doubt over an expansive view of Congress's power. If even he and his conservative colleagues were untroubled with broad congressional authority to set limits on the time to ratify an amendment, it isn't likely that modern justices will feel any differently. *Coleman* is even more authoritative, in that it was authored by one chief justice and joined in by a second, and failed to achieve unanimity only because one group of justices felt the Court didn't even have a right to review the matter of Congress's choice, while another felt cheated out of an opportunity to rule on what they were confident were inherent temporal limits on the life cycle of any amendment. One of the lawyers arguing the case for Congress's broad power was none other than Robert Jackson, the Solicitor General of the United States and future member of the Court, and he was joined in the effort by a leading authority on the Constitution, Professor Paul Freund. The pedigree of the two cases is simply too distinguished to ignore, and to overcome it would require the kind of creative jurisprudence that is the hallmark of justices who don't presently constitute a majority of the Court's membership.

The last factor that may be of relevance when the Court addresses the claims of Virginia, Illinois and Nevada is not so much constitutional as contractual. When Congress proposes amendments for consideration by the States, it is in essence making an offer, to be accepted by the States in accordance with the terms. The terms themselves are the text of the amendment, in addition to any conditions placed on ratification. Those conditions are not without import. They are no mere precatory statements. They are the result of a bargaining that overcame opposition within the two Houses of Congress and made it possible for three quarters of each House to agree that a particular proposal merited consideration for inclusion in the Constitution. Without the relevant conditions, a given amendment might never have been proposed, hence the conditions must be seen as essential, whether those conditions appear in the text of the amendment itself, as was the case with the amendment considered by the Court in *Dillon*, or in a resolution separate from the text, as is the case with the ERA. As the condition is essential, the hope of the States presently seeking an order that the Archivist declare the Amendment ratified is likely doomed. Any attempt to sever from the Amendment what cannot be severed will result in the Amendment's demise.

There is an alternative to fighting in court over the power of Congress to limit the time for ratification, and that alternative is what some advocates call the "Fresh Start" strategy. Congress can reconsider the Amendment, negotiate revised language and propose to the States what is agreed upon among its two chambers. Given the nature of the discussion of what the ERA means to those presently promoting it, it isn't likely that any successor amendment would be stated so broadly as to make possible the inference that it relates to anything other than men and women as they are biologically determined. That may be disheartening to progressives who aspire to liberate sex and gender from any and all social or biological bias, but it is the truth in a nation that is divided on these issues. The question therefore becomes: just how badly do feminist advocates of equality for women want the equality principle expressly embodied within the Constitution? Are they willing to forego any progress through a compromised text narrow in scope simply because they cannot accept anything less than the immediate fulfillment of their commitment to gender fluidity and unrestricted abortion rights, or will reason prevail? Social progress should seldom be an all-or-nothing proposition, and it should never come at the expense of everyone opposed to it. In a diverse community of ideas, it can never be the case that everyone's view of progress is the same, or that all people believe that "progress" is even necessary. If "progress," however defined, is to be had, small steps are better than none at all. In the wake of the defeat of the effort to revive the lapsed Amendment in Court, perhaps we will see some small steps that most of us agree on.

Indian Giving & Taking

WITHIN two weeks of taking office—after most of the inauguration day rioters had bailed out of jail and were awaiting the roll out of indictments, but before the advent of the long ordeal of the Mueller investigation and the claims about the President's secret alliance with Vladimir Putin to thwart Hillary Clinton's political ambitions—President Trump announced the first and one of the most consequential acts of his term: the nomination of a successor to the late Justice Antonin Scalia. The nomination was expected by everyone, and was especially dreaded by those on the left still feeling cheated by the refusal of the Republican majority in the Senate to act on President Obama's nominee for the position, Merrick Garland—a fine man and excellent judge, who had the misfortune of winning a coveted nomination in an election year, at a time when the Senate was controlled by the nominating lame duck President's opponents. Predictably, the Garland nomination went the way of so many others in like circumstances—John J. Crittenden's in 1829, William C. Micou's in 1853, and Jeremiah Black's eight years later.[1]

The new nominee was a man of similar stature judicially, whom even the left-leaning ABA considered to be supremely qualified for the job. And yet his credentials were marred for those on the left by his well-documented track record as a trend setter in the revival of classical liberal jurisprudence. He attended Harvard and even obtained a doctorate from Oxford University, but his early writings were considered to be "reactionary," and his doctorate was supervised by John Finnis, a leading figure in modern natural law philosophy. It was particularly aggravating for opponents of Neil Gorsuch that he was well mannered and handsome in a Jimmy Stewart kind of way, and was facile

---

[1] See Charles Warren, *The Supreme Court in United States History*, Volume I (Boston: Little, Brown and Company, 1922), at pp. 701-704; and Charles Warren, *The Supreme Court in United States History*, Volume II (Boston: Little, Brown and Company, 1922), at p. 245 and p. 364.

throughout the twenty hours of questioning during his confirmation hearing in the art of saying "nothing of substance" while presenting himself "as a folksy servant of neutral legal principles" who spewed nothing "but canned answers."[2]

Attempts to break the veneer of moderation were not lacking. One Senator read a letter from one the nominee's former law students, alleging that he "used class time to argue that women exploit their employers for maternity benefits 'in order to have a baby and then leave right away,'" while another hammered him for a dissenting opinion in a case of a truck driver fired by his employer after he took a break from his route when he experienced a loss of sensation in his extremities.[3] Others condemned him "as a callous ally of corporate interests who was 'outside the mainstream' and could not be trusted to stand up to the president who nominated him."[4] The critics held that Gorsuch was certain to "benefit wealthy corporations challenging laws that protect workers, consumers, and the environment," and would undoubtedly do everything he could to "tie the government's hands in keeping Americans safe and healthy and let judges strike down common-sense regulations that ensure the nation's air and water are clean."[5] The entire structure of administrative law, overseen by regulatory agencies, was in danger from this throwback to an era when corporations policed themselves and the government was kept at bay by narrow rulings on the scope of the state's power to intervene for the common good. Perhaps worst in the minds of the critics was the nominee's attitude toward religious liberty, and his view that the Free Exercise Clause might be employed to sabotage powerful state interests in protecting the rights of women and various sexual minorities. It was he, after all, who wrote the appellate opinion in the *Hobby Lobby* case that was subsequently upheld by the Supreme Court, holding that federal law could not require private employers to provide health care coverage that

---

[2] Adam Liptak and Matt Flegenheimer, "Neil Gorsuch Confirmed by Senate as Supreme Court Justice," *The New York Times*, April 7, 2017.

[3] Dylan Matthews, "Neil Gorsuch, Donald Trump's Supreme Court Nominee, Explained," www.vox.com, March 20, 2017; and Lauren Gambino, "Senate Confirms Neil Gorsuch to the Supreme Court After Historic Rules Change," www.theguardian.com, April 7, 2017.

[4] Gambino, op. cit..

[5] Billy Corriher, "Neil Gorsuch Would be a Dream Justice for Corporations Suing the Government," americanprogress.org, February 1, 2017.

included provisions for certain types of birth control. For the President of the National Abortion Rights Action League, the decision sent "a chill down my spine," and presaged what she was certain would be an expansion of religious liberty "in a lot of frightening new ways."[6]

Leading the opposition to Gorsuch both inside the Senate and without was Senator Elizabeth Warren, from the very progressive State of Massachusetts. Hitting the talk shows and print media, Warren denounced the frustration of the Garland nomination as the "latest step in [a] campaign to tilt our courts in favour of big corporations and the wealthy," and the product of a scheme by "giant corporations and their right-wing buddies...to keep the Supreme Court seat open so that Donald Trump could fill the vacancy."[7] The tilt in recent decades was bad enough—under the leadership of Rehnquist and Roberts, the Court has issued decisions that had allowed "the scales of justice" to be "weighted further and further in favour of the wealthy and the powerful." Apparently unmindful of the tremendous slur on the distinguished members of the judicial branch and their commitment to the rule of law and the Constitution, Warren credited the high court with decisions that "have let giant corporations that cheated their consumers off the hook, unleashed a flood of secret money into the political process, and made it easier for businesses to abuse and discriminate against their employees." Gorsuch, she admitted, was "charming and intelligent" and possessed "an impressive legal pedigree," but insisted he could not be permitted onto the Court due to his "right-wing, pro-big business views." His outlook on "important social issues like gay marriage, physician-assisted suicide, and school vouchers" tracked alongside his dismissive attitude toward progressives who "are too addicted to the court system." He was a champion of what Warren considered an utter absurdity: a bill of rights that protected fictitious persons rather than real people. His *Hobby Lobby* decision was a case in point. Having to choose between the 'rights' of corporations and the rights of women, "Gorsuch sided with corporations." As extreme as Clarence Thomas and Samuel Alito had proved to be, "Gorsuch would be even worse." The nominee had to be stopped at all costs, lest the nation and its people suffer a most

---

[6] Mattie Kahn, "Elizabeth Warren and NARAL President Illyse Hogue on the Dangers of Neil Gorsuch," www.elle.com, March 28, 2017.

[7] Elizabeth Warren, "Neil Gorsuch Does Not Belong on the Supreme Court," *The Boston Globe*, March 20, 2017.

damaging inversion of the very purpose of the Constitution and a loss of liberty by the people in favour of profit-driven entities utterly unconcerned with the lives and comfort of those who would be forced to slave on their behalf and purchase and consume their overpriced, unhealthy and dangerous goods and services.

Warren's attacks on Gorsuch were consistent with the Senator's progressive populism and the world view embodied within it: a view marked by a belief in an eternal urge by the powerful to transform free men and women into cogs in an industrial system that aims to impoverish over ninety percent of the population for the benefit of the one percent. Warren and her allies consistently present themselves as the champions of the weak and exploited, of women victimized by employers and abusive husbands, workers underpaid and overworked by those who are enriched by their underappreciated labours, and non-white minorities cast into third class status, inferior schools and even prison merely on account of race.

Truly, defense of the weak and those victimized by the powerful is a high obligation for all men. Our nation's religious traditions speak of the wrath of God to come on those who "take advantage of the widow or the fatherless" or fail to pay the wages of the worker "who is poor and needy."[8] Our laws and Constitution, emergent from the Enlightenment, aim to prevent the kind of systematic exploitation that characterized human history in all preceding ages. The commitment of progressives is consistent with this tradition and is admirable, however incorrect or miscalculated the progressives' means to their noble ends might be in the eyes of classic liberals, libertarians and conservatives.

Senator Warren, as the self-appointed leader of the progressives' campaign to defend our society's high values in the face of the reputed threat posed by Neil Gorsuch, might be the least apt person to have filled that role. The woman is the epitome of white privilege, who attended the best schools, won admission to the bar, and then enriched herself in the employ of the very corporations she currently denounces. Hypocrisy, of course, isn't the worst of sins, and one might atone for one's own shortcomings by using the advantage one has gained in a corrupt system to reform it. Warren's approach hasn't quite matched this model. Her defense of minorities is particularly obnoxious in that she

---

[8] Ex. 22:21-24; and Deut. 24:14-15.

claims a special sensitivity as well as entitlement on account of her own reputed descent from abused and exploited Native Americans. Throughout her entire adult life, from her admission to college until her elevation to the United States Senate, Warren claimed the heritage of the Cherokees and Delawares as her own, identified herself in official documents as Native American, submitted recipes alleged to have been passed down in the family for inclusion in a cookbook dedicated to Native American delicacies, and allowed herself to be presented by her employers—the University of Pennsylvania and Harvard University—as a faculty member of Native heritage.

Anyone looking at Elizabeth Warren knows the truth: she's the whitest of the white, without an apparent ounce of non-European blood. The obvious was finally stated by Warren's opponent, Senator Scott Brown, back in 2012, when Warren was challenging the incumbent for re-election. His charge that she lied about her heritage was quickly investigated by friend and foe alike. Officials of the Cherokee Nation confirmed that she had no documented connection with any person listed in the historic records of the tribe that are the touchstone for determining membership.[9] The authoritative New England Historic and Genealogical Society declared that "in her immediate pedigree there is no one who is listing themselves as not white."[10] Even the sympathetic *Atlantic Monthly* concluded that "the progressive consumer advocate has been unable to point to evidence of Native heritage except for an unsubstantiated third hand report that she might be 1/32 Cherokee."[11] Nonplused by these findings, Warren didn't relent in her claims. "These are my family stories," she said. "This is what my brothers and I were told by my mom and my dad, my mammaw and my pappaw." Appearing on CNN, she declared "I'm proud of my Native American heritage… I'm proud of my family." In an interview with *The Boston Herald*, she stated that "being Native American has been part of my story I guess since the day I was born. These are my family stories, I have lived in a family that has talked about Native Americans and talked about tribes since I was a little girl."

---

9 Garance Franke-Ruta, "Is Elizabeth Warren Native American or What?," www.theatlantic.com, May 20, 2012.

10 Id.

11 Id.

Warren's claims are profoundly egregious in light of her actual heritage. A genealogist operating the website *pollysgrandaughter.com* explored at length the Warren family tree with an eye to discovering the truth of the Senator's claims. Using the heritage of the mixed-race Cherokee Chief Bill John Baker as a basis for comparison, she explored nearly 200 years of census records and found that while Chief Baker's ancestors consistently referred to themselves as mixed race and Cherokees, Warren's ancestors consistently reported themselves to be white. Marriage records and other documentation revealed the same degree of consistency. Warren's own tale of her grandparents' elopement due to racist attitudes on the white side of her family proved to be utterly false, right down to the elopement itself. Far worse was the fact that her family exhibited animus of a high degree, not affinity, toward natives. One white ancestor shot an Indian man who had attacked his son. Yet another referred to Natives as "pretty mean," while a cousin whose grandmother was one of Warren's supposedly native ancestors, fretted in a letter to his absent father over the threat posed to him by wild Indians during a trip west. In keeping with Warren's own imposture was the fraudulent claim by a white ancestor to native status in order to obtain a grant of land reserved for native peoples. Further damage to the narrative came when other researchers discovered that rather than taking part as victims on the notorious Trail of Tears, Warren's supposedly Native American ancestors included members of the Tennessee Militia that escorted the Cherokees' along the way.[12] The final blow came when the thin-skinned senator succumbed to the barrage of trolling by the allegedly thin-skinned President and took a DNA test to settle the matter once and for all. The test proved that she had genetic markers suggesting an ancestor ten generations back who might have been a subject of the Spanish Crown living in the conquered provinces of the late Incan Empire.[13] Perhaps she had an infinitesimal amount of native blood, but it was native to Peru, not the United States.

---

[12] "Elizabeth Warren's 'ancestor rounded up Cherokees from their Homes for the Trail of Tears,' but she brushes off the claims," www.dailymail.co.uk, May 9, 2012; and Daniel Moritz-Rabson, "Fox News Guest Says Elizabeth Warren's Ancestors 'Rounded Up Cherokees For the Trail of Tears,'" www.newsweek.com, October 16, 2018.

[13] Chris Francescani, "The Real Problem with Elizabeth Warren's DNA Test: Geneticists," www.abcnews.com, October 18, 2018.

The DNA test results sparked further uproar. The President and his surrogates called it junk science. The Cherokee Nation also discounted its value. A spokesman declared that "using a DNA test to lay claim to any connection to the Cherokee Nation or any tribal nation, even vaguely, is inappropriate and wrong," and "makes a mockery out of DNA tests and its legitimate uses while also dishonouring legitimate tribal governments and their citizens, whose ancestors are well documented and whose heritage is proven."[14] In the Tribe's view, Senator Warren was "undermining tribal interests with her continued claims of tribal heritage."

Warren's false narrative about her ancestry, her misuse and abuse of native identity, and the disrespect that native peoples have formally denounced her for exuding contrasts markedly with the actions of the man she condemned as an enemy of vulnerable minorities, and whose place on the Supreme Court she has declared to be a threat to constitutional liberties. For a decade, Justice Gorsuch served on the Court of Appeals for the Tenth Circuit and reviewed issues on a wide array of subjects. The presence of seventy-eight recognized Indian bands made the Circuit one which considered the claims and defenses of native peoples on a regular basis. The historic attitude of the courts in this country toward native interests hasn't been particularly sympathetic. Though the organic law of the nation required that "the utmost good faith shall always be observed toward the Indians; their land and property shall never be taken from them without their consent; and, in their property, rights, and liberty, they shall never be invaded or disturbed," the nation and its government have fallen considerably short in the treatment of America's first peoples.[15] Even John Marshall, who was sympathetic to the plight of the natives and who ruled in their favour in one of the most significant cases of his long tenure, considered them to be "in a state of pupilage," whose "relation to the United States resembles that of a ward to his guardian."[16] In time, a consensus emerged that federal authority over Indians and Indian affairs "is of a 'plenary' power drawn from the Indian Commerce Clause, the Treaty

---

[14] Asma Khalid, "Warren Apologizes to Cherokee Nation for DNA Test," www.npr.org, February 1, 2019.

[15] Northwest Ordinance (1787), Sec. 14, Art. 3.

[16] *Cherokee Nation v. State of Georgia* (1831) 30 U.S. 1.

Clause, and sources outside the text of the Constitution."[17] From 1886 onward, a series of Supreme Court decisions "synthesized congressional authority over Indian affairs into a nearly unlimited authority based in a guardian-ward relationship as well as 'pre-constitutional powers necessarily inherent in any Federal Government."[18] This approach has ever been objected to by tribal leaders and Indian rights advocates as an expression of power largely disconnected from the Constitution's text. As the relevant case law turned on interpretations of treaties as well as statutes, Gorsuch's commitment to textualism and legislative intent boded well for Natives who insist on both whenever disputes about their rights are before the courts.

While on the appellate bench, Gorsuch did not disappoint. In reviewing Gorsuch's performance from that time, John Dorsey concluded that the Judge's opinions "commonly recognized tribes as sovereign governments and have addressed issues such as state police incursion onto tribal lands, sovereign immunity, religious freedom, accounting for trust funds, exhaustion of tribal remedies, and Indian country criminal jurisdiction."[19] In *Ute Indian Tribe v. State of Utah* (10th Cir. 2015) 790 F.3d 1255, Gorsuch outlined the history of the Federal Government's responsibility to protect tribal sovereignty from trespass by State government and condemned the effort by the State of Utah for its "renewed campaign to undo tribal boundaries." In *Ute Indian Tribe v. Myton* (10th Cir. 2016) 835 F.3d 1000, he ruled against Utah's effort to expand State judicial jurisdiction over crimes committed within reservation boundaries. In yet another case, he reviewed a district court's dismissal of a suit by the Osage Tribe to obtain an accounting from the federal government of trust monies generated by exploitation of natural resources on tribal land. Holding the federal government to the high standard imposed on all trustees, Gorsuch disregarded the long history of deference to the United States as the ward of native peoples and found that an accounting was required. The ambiguities in the treaty and the statutes governing the issue must, he said "be construed for, not against, Native Americans."[20] Finally, his keen appreciation for the

---

[17] John Dorset, "Justice Gorsuch and Federal Indian Law," 43 Human Rights 7 (2017), at p. 9.

[18] Id.

[19] Id.

[20] *Fletcher v. United States* (10th Cir. 2013) 730 F.3d 1206, 1212.

protection afforded all Americans for religious liberty was reflected in his ruling against a federal prison that denied a Native American prisoner his request to access a sweat lodge as part of a religious ritual. "The deference this court must extend to the experience and expertise of prison administrators does not," he said, "extend so far that prison officials may declare a compelling governmental interest by fiat."[21]

Since taking his seat on the Supreme Court, Gorsuch's jurisprudence has remained true to these decisions, even when confronted with opposition from his ideological allies. This became evident in March of 2019, when the Court issued a ruling in the case of *Washington State Department of Licensing v. Couger Den, Inc.* that a tax by the State of Washington upon fuel importers who travel public highways, when imposed on Native importers serving the Yakamas, violated the Treaty between the Yakama Nation and the United States that expressly guaranteed the Yakamas "'the right, in common with citizens of the United States, to travel upon all public highways.'"[22] The Court's four progressive justices—Breyer, Ginsburg, Sotomayor and Kagan—favoured the tribe against the State of Washington. Breaking with his conservative brethren, Gorsuch not only provided the winning fifth vote, but wrote a concurring opinion so persuasive that Justice Ginsburg opted to join it instead of the opinion authored by Justice Breyer. Gorsuch asserted that the task before the Court was a simple one: to adopt "the interpretation most consistent with the treaty's original meaning."[23] In doing so, he noted that precedent required that the Court "give effect to the terms as the Indians themselves would have understood them" at the time the treaty was executed.[24] This rule was not only rooted in the Court's jurisprudence, but was consistent with the canon of contractual construction that "any ambiguities be construed against the drafter—in this case, the government of the United States."[25] The rule was especially applicable here, as the treaty was written in English, which the Yakamas could neither read nor write, and translated into a non-Yakama language for their review. When considering the treaty when it was first presented to them, the Yakamas were repeatedly

[21] *Yellowbear v. Lampert* (10th Cir. 2014) 741 F.3d 48, 59.

[22] *Washington State Department of Licensing v. Couger Den, Inc.* (2019) 139 S.Ct. 1000, 1016, Gorsuch, J. Concurring.

[23] Id.

[24] Id.

[25] Id.

reassured that they would "be allowed to go on the roads to take [their] things to market," and would enjoy the same liberty "to travel with goods free of restriction 'outside the reservation' that the Tribe would enjoy within the new reservation's boundaries."[26] This reliance on the explanations offered by the treaty's drafters was further conclusive of the understanding the Yakamas had when offering their consent.

How the Yakamas understood the treaty was not quite how the State of Washington did a century and a half later. The State's narrow reading of the Yakamas' travel right—confining it to the same right that non-natives had to travel the highways subject to all general laws and regulations, including taxes—was contrary to the ruling of prior courts regarding the Yakamas' understanding of the treaty language, and grossly out of sync with the consideration the Tribe provided in the form of a quarter of the State's current territory. The size of this consideration, noted Gorsuch, "was worth far more than an abject promise that they would not be made prisoners on their reservation."[27]

Gorsuch fortified his opinion with reference to the *Winans* decision from 1905 and the 1942 decision in *Tulee v. Washington*. In those cases, the Court wrestled with the contention by those adverse to the Yakamas that the treaty guaranteed tribal members rights subject to the same regulations as non-Indians. Gorsuch explained that the Court rejected that argument as an "impotent" construction of the treaty, and held instead that the "treaty language prohibited state officials from imposing many non-discriminatory fees and regulations on tribal members."[28] The treaty, he acknowledged, was not fair to the Yakamas, who yielded a veritable empire in exchange for "a handful of modest promises."[29] The State's attempt to erode even these was but "an old and familiar story," rooted in greed. To vigorously defend the few rights the natives received in exchange for so much, concluded Gorsuch, "is the least we can do."[30]

Though condemned by Senator Warren and others as an enemy of the vulnerable and oppressed, who would reflexively rule with the conservative majority, Gorsuch's concurring opinion in *Couger Den*

---

[26] Id., at 1017.
[27] Id., at 1018.
[28] Id.
[29] Id., at 1021.
[30] Id.

indicates the Justice is a far more independent thinker, whose commitment to textualism, original intent, and vested rights recognized by the Constitution takes precedence over any home team loyalty. There is no question that Gorsuch will likely weigh in heavily on the side of undermining administrative law and the massive administrative state that arose in the last century in violation of the separation of powers set forth in the organic structure of the Constitution, and that religious liberty enjoyed by Christians (as well as others) will find a strong defender in his pen. Progressives might yet worry about the changes in the status quo that will result and what impact this might have on the ability of the economically strong to have their way with everyone else. Yet they should not worry that Gorsuch won't listen to honest pleas for redress, rule in a manner consistent with a close reading of the relevant text, and demand that any solutions to the various problems facing people in this country not traceable to violations of existing legal standards flow from the legislature, not the courts. As evidenced by his respectful attitude toward the native peoples of this country, he is a surer friend to the weak, exploited and oppressed than some who scream so loudly of their own solidary with the same and insist so forcefully on a special privilege of speaking on their behalf.

Oh They of Little Faith

THE election of Donald Trump proved so alarming to his opponents and critics that unprecedented agitation became manifest among them in the days and weeks following the President-elect's wry announcement that elections are "complicated business." In the dark days in the aftermath of what many considered the worst moment in history, social media became both an outlet for the left's collective angst and a barometer measuring the popular mood. One person on Twitter summed up the attitude of many with the comment that "this is unutterably horrifying."[1] Another lamented that "a rapist, a bigot, a man who has promised untold pain to so many people in this country is now

[1] John Queally, "WTF USA? Shock and Horror as Donald Trump Wins Presidency," www.commondreams.org, November 9, 2016.

our president."[2] Yet another prophesied that "the fascists he empowers and seeks to legitimize present a terrifying immediate future." Putting her most mature spin on it, activist Linda Sarsour voiced the commitment of many of her compatriots that they were "gonna wake up" the next morning "and organize like we never organized before."[3]

As if on que, prominent persons in the media immediately began describing a new strategy to stop the President-elect. Actor and progressive activist Martin Sheen, who had gained some notoriety playing a progressive President on television, appeared on the small screen reading from the Federalist Papers in support of his contention that "our Founding Fathers built the Electoral College to safeguard the American people from the dangers of a demagogue, and to ensure that the presidency only goes to someone who is 'to an eminent degree, endowed with the requisite qualifications.'"[4] Electoral College member Christine Pelosi (who also happens to be Nancy's daughter) was joined by Colorado colleague Michael Baca and another 80 Democrat electors to demand that they be briefed by the Obama Administration on the state of any investigations into collaboration between the President-elect and the Russian government. They justified their unprecedented demand on the grounds that "the Constitution envisions the Electoral College as a deliberative body that plays a critical role in our system of government—ensuring that the American people elect a president who is constitutionally qualified and fit to serve." Accordingly, they insisted that they be given the tools necessary to engage in "an informed and unrestrained opportunity to fulfil our constitutional role… that is, the ability to investigate, discuss, and deliberate with our colleagues about whom to vote for in the Electoral College."[5] As the date for the casting of votes approached, at least eight of the 538 Electors "indicated that they intend to break ranks with modern tradition and vote against their party in a protest directed squarely against Trump."[6] They would vote against

---

[2] Id.

[3] Id.

[4] Spencer King, "Watch: Celebrities Urge Electoral College to 'Vote Their Conscience,'" www.pastemagazine.com, December 15, 2016.

[5] Christine Pelosi, "Bipartisan Electors Ask James Clapper: Release Facts on Outside Interference in U.S. Election," www.extranewsfeed.com, December 12, 2016.

[6] Ed Pilkington, "'Faithless Electors' Explain Their Last-Ditch Attempt to Stop Donald Trump," www.theguardian.com, December 19, 2016.

the candidate to whom they were formally pledged in the hope that their example might "encourage their Republican fellow Electors to follow suit and rally around a compromise alternative candidate."[7]

The plot to transform the Electoral College from a mechanism of registering the results of voting among the peoples of the several States into a deliberative body possessing absolute discretion as to the selection of the nation's chief executive never advanced beyond the casting of a handful of votes for candidates who hadn't appeared on the November ballot. Looking ahead to the 2020 contest, the plotters reformulated their plan and launched a lawsuit against the State of Colorado for the purpose of obtaining a judicial ruling confirming the reservation in the Constitution for the discretion they insisted members of the College possessed. The aforementioned Michael Baca and two other former members of the Electoral College filed their suit seeking nominal damages for the injury they suffered in violation of their rights as Electors in accordance with Article II of the Constitution. Judge Wiley Daniel of the U.S. District Court for the District of Colorado dismissed the case for lack of standing. Intrigued by the issue, and perhaps hoping to deter further litigation by establishing a record for any appeal, Judge Daniel proceeded to rule on the merits of the claim by denying that a cause of action had been stated. Article II, he said, "does not limit the State's power to attach conditions" to the appointment of Electors. Such conditions can include both the requirement that any Electors cast their vote in favour of the candidate to whom they were pledged, and removal from office and imposition of a fine in the event that the pledge is spurned.[8]

The issue was not exactly one of first impression, though it is true that the courts—particularly the Supreme Court—had not had many occasions to consider the meaning of the language in Article II relating to the workings of the Electoral College. The primary critique of the College over the past several decades has been that it permits a candidate who fails to win a majority or even a plurality of all of the votes cast throughout the nation to nevertheless achieve victory and claim possession of the highest office in the land. The elevation of Donald Trump raised the critique to a new level and prompted, as we have seen, very elaborate efforts to convince enough Electors to discard

---

[7] Id.

[8] *Baca v. Colorado Dept. of State*, Case No. 17-cv-01937-WYD-NYW.

their pledges and consider an alternative to a candidate who had actually stood for election before the People. Article II allocates the responsibility of appointing Electors to the States, and most States have adopted rules that require Electors pledged to a particular candidate to cast their vote in that candidate's favour. The language of Article II, however, suggests to some a lack of any State authority over the substance of an Elector's vote once appointment occurs. Judge Daniel was aware of the sparse textual support for such authority, but was untroubled by it. Absence of any prohibition must be construed, he said, as implying the continuing power of the States to impose whatever conditions they wished on those who were charged with casting the only ballots that mattered in electing the President of the United States. The absence of any case law contrary to this implication further supported his conclusion. The one case decided by the Supreme Court that dealt with the States' control over the appointment of Electors—*Ray v. Blair*—rejected the argument that the Constitution "demands absolute freedom for the Elector to vote his own choice, uninhibited by pledge." The citation by the Plaintiffs to the Federalist Papers was far less persuasive to the Judge than was the actual workings of the Electoral College after ratification. If the Framers actually intended for the members of the College to exercise independent discretion when casting their votes, that intention "never came to pass."

Predictably, Judge Daniel's decision was appealed. Not long ago, a three-judge panel in the Tenth Circuit reversed it, both with respect to the issue of standing and the merits of the contention that Article II authorized Electors to vote their conscience.[9] Admittedly, said the appellate court, the case law was sparse, but the citation to *Ray* by the lower court was simply too narrow a basis to permit so sweeping an outcome in the State's favour. There was no rational basis for the conclusion that the State's power to appoint Electors implies a power to remove an Elector should conditions attached to the appointment not be honoured. The natural analogy, said the Court, was the implied power of the President to remove subordinate officials within the Executive Branch. The analogy, however, was inapposite; for as the President required obedience within the branch over which he presided in order that his policy preferences might be achieved, the State had no similar

---

[9] *Baca v. Colorado Dept. of State* (2019) 935 F.3d 887.

interest. The purpose the Electors were to fulfil once appointed was a federal function, not a State one. The longstanding practice by the States of controlling the votes of Electors was real, but practice was not dispositive of the meaning of the Constitution's text, which provides only that States appoint Electors, not dictate the substance of the votes they were to cast. Moreover, there is, said the Court, "an opposing historical practice at play: a history of anomalous votes, all of which have been counted by Congress." This uninterrupted history of Congress counting every anomalous vote cast by an Elector "weighs against a conclusion that historical practices allow States to enforce Elector pledges by removing faithless Electors from office and nullifying their votes."

The lack of any express textual allocation of power to the States to dictate the choice to be made by Electors once appointed might, said the Court, have rendered the text ambiguous were it not for the record of the opinions of the Framers, as documented in the Federalist Papers. Alexander Hamilton, for instance, proposed that the College was to be made up of men "most capable of analysing the qualities adapted to the station, and acting under circumstances favourable to deliberation, and to a judicious combination of all the reasons and inducements that were proper to govern their choice. A small number of persons, selected by their fellow citizens from the general mass, will be most likely to possess the information and discernment requisite to so complicated an investigation." John Jay wrote that the Electoral College would "in general, be composed of the most enlightened and respectable citizens," and that their attention and their votes would "be directed to those men only who have become the most distinguished by their abilities and virtue, and in whom the people perceive just grounds for confidence." These views, concluded the Court, were "inconsistent with the [State's] argument that the Electors are mere functionaries who can vote only for the candidate dictated by the State. Instead, these contemporaneous interpretations of the federal Constitution support the conclusion that the presidential Electors were to vote in accordance with their best judgment and discernment."

The case is on its way to review by the Supreme Court of the United States, whose opinion may well fixate on whether the Plaintiffs' possess standing to bring the matter, thus disappointing everyone who desires a resolution of the doubts over the extent of the freedom of Electors to disregard the votes of the peoples of the States who appoint them to their office. Not that there aren't a host of problems with the Circuit Court's analysis and its conclusion that the Electoral College is a deliberative body unhinged from any controls that the States might wish to impose. The first of these problems is that the language of the text "permits a broad reading of States' abilities to select Electors, and lacks any express limitation on the scope of the appointment power."[10] Where the powers of the States are expressly limited, the limitations appear in other sections of the Constitution. States, for instance are expressly prohibited from denying the privileges and immunities of citizens of other States, from imposing duties on goods entering State ports, entering into treaties of alliance with other nations, enacting ex post facto laws and bills of attainder and imposing any impairment of obligations on contracts. Lack of any restriction on the power to appoint Electors, in combination with express authorization to the States to determine the mode or manner of appointment, appears to green light a rather wide array of controls States might employ at their discretion.

Additionally, the conclusion that the States have no authority to remove insubordinate Electors due to the supposed lack of any interest in the function the Electors are to fulfil following their appointment is specious. The Electoral College is a federal body, yes, performing a federal function, but as it is federal, it is necessarily one that embodies the interests of each of the States, whose peoples have separately selected delegates to represent their interests in accordance with rules that the Constitution allows the States to enact. The States' representatives in the Electoral College are exactly that—representatives of the State, employed by the State to advance the State's individual interests; and they are even reimbursed by the State for any expenses incurred in the performance of their appointed task.

The "uninterrupted history" of faithless Electors whose votes were counted by the Congress isn't particularly compelling as evidence of the liberty Electors possess to vote as they see fit. There have indeed been instances of such Electors—167 in all over the course of 230 years—but their appearance has always been on the fringe, without even a remote threat that their breach of faith might influence the outcome of a

---

[10] John A. Zadrozny, "The Myth of Discretion: Why Presidential Electors do not Receive First Amendment Protection," 1 Comm.Law Conspectus 165 (2003), at p. 175.

presidential race.[11] A large share of these wayward Electors were actually faithless not because they despaired over the credentials of the candidate to whom they were pledged, but because the candidate for whom they were required to vote had died prior to the meeting of the Electoral College. The trivial extent of the deviation of Electors from their pledges ensured that no litigation ever arose, hence any decision by Congress to count the votes of such Electors can hardly be said to be conclusive of the freedom Electors might have to vote in accordance with their own discretion. Far more persuasive, and overwhelmingly so, is the long and deep history of Electors living by their promise to vote as pledged. It is the norm that dictates the rule, not the exception.

While the Supreme Court of the United States has explored the issue but rarely, a richer mine of material can be found in the reports of State Courts. In *State ex rel. Nebraska Republican State Central Committee v. Wait*, the Nebraska Supreme Court "sided with the State's Republican organization, noting that the Electors were bound by their pledges to vote for the Republican candidate and that their representations in favour of the Progressive Party could be viewed as abdications of their duties as Republican electors."[12] In *Thomas v. Cohen*, the New York Supreme Court considered a petitioner's "contention that he had an absolute constitutional right to vote for Electors rather than the presidential and vice presidential candidates."[13] In rejecting the contention, the Court denied the "claim that Electors are free agents unbound by party labels or general election results."[14] It noted that "the American people have grown to regard the Electoral College as a matter of minor importance," whose members are obligated by the will of the People to vote as they are directed. "So sacred and compelling is that obligation…, so long has its observance been recognized by faithful performance, so unexpected and destructive of order in our land would be its violation, that the trust [given to Electors] has…ripened into a bounded duty—as binding upon them as if it were written into organic law."[15]

---

[11] Zachary J. Shapiro, "The Constitutionality of Methods that Influence a Presidential Elector's Ability to Exercise Personal Judgment," 26 J.L. & Pol'y 395 (2018), at pp. 399-400.

[12] Zadrozny, op. cit., at p. 177.

[13] Id.

[14] Id.

[15] Id., at p. 178.

Professor Akhil Amar—a pronounced progressive—all but laughs off the idea that the Electoral College was intended to be a deliberative body expressing discretion over the choice of the nation's chief executive. The Electoral College, he observes, was not "created and revised to enable wise philosopher-king 'electors' to substitute their superior wisdom for the ignorant preferences of the unwashed masses."[16] The Constitution itself dictates that members of the College were "to meet on a single day, with no real time for genuine deliberation," and the meeting was not to be in a single location, but in as many locations as there were States.[17] He makes the highly salient point that if the Framers truly intended the Electors to vote their conscience, we might see in the historical record of the early Republic some evidence of this. Yet "from the first election in 1788 to the present day, most Electors have simply carried out the will of those who chose them. As a rule, Electors have been potted plants, nobodies from nowhere, instructed or even pledged to vote for a particular candidate."[18] This reality has been accepted by the People at large, hardly ever contested in Court, and suggests that this is how the Framers actually intended the process to work.

The contention that the Electoral College was designed to be a bulwark against the election of an unqualified or unfit President cannot easily be squared with various features of the Constitution designed to control who ascends to the office. Article II prescribes minimum qualifications, and limits a President's actions almost entirely to the mere execution of laws enacted by Congress. What the Congress does not enact, the President cannot execute. The President's term is limited to four years, and it might be curtailed even more through application of the power of the Congress to impeach and remove when the President's conduct breaches certain prescribed standards. The vast powers the President has over foreign affairs and the conduct of war, as well as his discretion in the staffing of his government, is substantially circumscribed by allocation to Congress of the power to declare war and its express right to confirm or reject the President's nominees. Modernly, the People have imposed further limitations on the President's ability to

---

[16] Akhil Reed Amar, "Electoral College Reform, Lincoln-Style," 112 Nw. U.L. Rev. 63 (2017), at p. 67.

[17] Id.

[18] Id.

act in reckless ways by limiting the total number of terms that might be served to two and providing a mechanism in the text of the Twenty-Fifth Amendment for the sidelining of a President unable to perform his or her duties as a result of some form of incapacity. The real textual limitations on Presidents who might prove reckless, intemperate and incompetent are far superior to any speculation between the time of election and inauguration by nearly anonymous members of the Electoral College as to whether the person selected by the Peoples of the several States is fit to serve in an office to which he or she has been duly elected.

Much is made in the Court of Appeal's decision of the words of Hamilton, Madison and Jay in the pages of the Federalist Papers, as if these words were the true and correct gloss on the intent of the Framers when crafting the text of Article II. Though a valuable source from the minds of brilliant men who took part in the debates at the Philadelphia Convention, the Federalist Papers are not legal documents. They were not, like the Constitution itself, authorized by the members of the Convention as a whole. Instead, they were the product of three individuals, not for the purpose of convincing a court of law as to the proper interpretation of the organic law, but of persuading voters in a single State to cast their ballot in favour of ratification. Rather than being legal authority, they are but propaganda, crafted by three of the best lawyers of the age in order to achieve a particular end in a particular State.

Finally, there is the notion that nonentities like Michael Baca, lacking any special background or qualification in law, politics, government, philosophy, ethics or even psychology, are the equivalent of "the most enlightened and respectable citizens" the Framers supposedly expected would form the Electoral College and decide for the entire nation who was best suited to be President of the United States. Almost no one who voted for President in 2016 had any idea who Michael Baca was, nor that they were voting for him when casting their ballots. Baca's credentials and qualifications were never at issue, and no one was ever presented with any choice as to whether Baca or any other Elector was a fit person to decide who the President ought to be. The thought that a completely unknown person, untried and untested in public life, without any discernible or relevant qualifications, would be charged with electing our President on behalf of the People at large, notwithstanding State law and a 200-year-long tradition binding him and all other Electors to the will of the People, is a joke that ought to have been laughed out of court instead of given credence by the distinguished justices of the Tenth Circuit.

The power of the centuries-old tradition of allowing the People to define what the appointment of Electors entails, and of requiring Electors merely to register the will of the majority of the voters in individual States, has been addressed at length by Professor Keith Whittington of Princeton University. Whittington concedes that "the Constitution would seem to leave the presidential Electors unbound in their decision-making. Once appointed to the office in a manner chosen by the state legislature, the presidential Electors are constitutionally free to choose how to cast their ballots."[19] Why the Framers might have envisioned the Electoral College in this manner was due not so much to a distrust of democracy as to a concern that parochial preferences among voters in the individual States might prevent consensus as to a national leader. "In a world in which fewer than a million voters were spread across more than a thousand miles of the Atlantic coast and were more comfortable thinking of themselves as Virginians or New Yorkers than as Americans, the Founders struggled to imagine how the people would settle on a choice for President." Certain figures had local prominence, "but they were much less likely to be equally well-known or beloved in other States and regions.[20] It didn't take long, however, for the presidential selection process to deviate from the Framers' expectations. Indeed, by the election of 1796, most States had moved toward binding Electors to the will of the emergent political parties and the voters who empowered them. "In effect," says Whittington, "a new constitutional rule was established, unwritten and informal, that limited the discretion of the Electors."[21] The relevant text itself was broad and vague enough to permit this kind of informal rule making, and even demanded it so that the gaps in content might be filled with meaning that had the advantage of being generated by practical knowledge gained from real experience.

---

[19] Keith E. Whittington, "Originalism, Constitutional Construction, and the Problem of Faithless Electors," 59 Ariz. L. Rev. 904 (2017), at pp. 920-921.

[20] Id., at p. 925.

[21] Id., at p. 927.

Whittington characterizes this procedure of defining the meaning of the Constitution as a "constitutional construction." Constructions, he notes, "can help resolve textual indeterminacies...[and] can help fill in gaps where a constitutional rule is needed but is not adequately supplied by the constitutional text itself. Such constructions operate in the interstices of the Constitution, providing a richer set of principles, norms, and practices to guide political behaviour and constrain political choice than the bare text can do itself."[22] Ordinarily, it is the courts that construe the meaning of vague terms. The Courts, however, can only act in the context of a case or controversy. Where litigation is absent, judicially engineered constructions have no chance to germinate. In the case of the meaning and scope of the States' power to appoint Electors, the people have intervened and established a rule that Electors are but "instruments for expressing the will of those who selected them," rather than "independent agents authorized to exercise their own judgment."[23]

In the end, Whittington dismisses the originalist-tinged arguments of Baca and the other faithless Electors as a failure to appreciate the historical process that has given meaning to the Constitution's broad and rather indeterminate language. He concludes that if Baca and his compadres had their way, they would upend and abandon "two centuries of political practice and well-settled constitutional norms" and replace the will of the voters in the several States with that of persons whose names never appeared on a ballot and whose identities are almost entirely unknown to the voters.[24] Their preferred outcome would be a rather stunning result, veering far from the alleged motives of those Electors who spoke so respectfully of the Framers' intent and of their desire to honor the will of the majority of the voters who cast ballots in 2016. That these concerns were not truly motivating them at all should come as no surprise. Their originalism was feigned for the moment, as was their abandonment of their normal commitment to the broadest possible reading of the Constitution's text in order to maximize the power of Government over the fortunes of the people. Their adoration of popular votes and majoritarian outcomes was belied by their willingness to cast aside the popular will of the peoples of nearly every State that had long embraced a particular construction of the Elector

[22] Id., at p. 928.
[23] Id., at p. 911.
[24] Id., at pp. 936 and 942.

selection process set forth in Article II and cast their votes not for Electors but for the preferred Presidential candidate whose name actually appeared on a ballot. Baca himself didn't even cast his vote for the winner of the aggregate popular vote. Instead, he and seven others voted for candidates who weren't even on the November ballot. They cast their votes for these candidates not because they were objectively more suited to serve in the office, but simply because they weren't Donald Trump, the winner of the majority of the fifty individual campaigns waged in the fifty States of the Union. Originalism is a great theory, but not in the hands of those who don't believe in it, who use it for narrow political purposes, can't see where originalism must stop and proper construction of the text begins, and who cannot trust the constructions evolved over the stretch of 200 years through the collective action of the People whose will they insist they care so much about. Baca likely won't be an elector in 2020, but no doubt there will be a few like him faithlessly looking for any edge in thwarting the settled workings of our Constitution in order to defeat a candidate they despise.

The Gig is Up

IN May of 1905, in a 5 to 4 decision in the matter of *Lochner v. New York,* the Supreme Court of the United States struck down as unconstitutional a state law prohibiting the employment of bakery workers in excess of ten hours in a single day. The challenge to the law stemmed from two convictions by bakery owner Joseph Lochner following criminal complaints lodged against him by union officials impatient over the slow pace of the law's enforcement. In the majority's view, the law's profile as a device to protect and promote the health of workers employed in the bakery industry was too attenuated from the actual goal and imposed an unreasonable restriction on the right of employers and employees to freely determine the terms of their working relationship. Such freedom, said the Court, was among the sticks in the bundle of liberty protected by the Due Process Clause of the Fourteenth Amendment.

The labour press denounced the decision as the "hardest blow ever dealt by the courts of this country to organized labour," and mocked the

Court for standing pat as "bakery workers died like flies, of consumption, rheumatism and other physical punishments."[1] Labour lawyer Morris Hillquit condemned the Justices for ruling that "it is unconstitutional if legislation provides and takes care of the interests of workingmen; it is unconstitutional if bakery workers demand eight hours a day work; it is unconstitutional if bakery workers ask for a humane existence; if they begin to know their human rights; or demand to be treated like men."[2] Professor Ernst Freund criticized the Court's apparent assumption of the role of censor "of the legislative power," while Sir Frederick Pollock wrote to the decision's famed dissenter, Justice Holmes, that while the majority had doubted the relationship of the law to health, it did so in a state of gross ignorance of the actual working conditions in the State's bakeries.[3] "Legal scholars such as Roscoe Pound...and Learned Hand accused the Lochner majority of engaging in 'mechanical jurisprudence,' or abstract reasoning, instead of relying on modern scientific knowledge about the health effects of long hours on bakers."[4] Far worse was the chilling effect the law would have on "the entire progressive legislative enterprise of enacting labour laws, public health laws, and workplace safety regulations...solely on the basis of its own allegedly common-sense, but in fact woefully uninformed, opinions—opinions that were shaped by class biases and laissez-faire politics, and that flew in the face of actual data and informed legislative judgment."[5]

When progressives seized the moment and the helm of government in the 1930s, they made quick work of the decision by burying it beneath a presumption of legislative validity and a fresh and indelible narrative of the noble savants of the universities and the bureaucracy who possessed at last the tools to end threats to health and safety in the workplace, inequality in the economy and injustice in society as a whole. *Lochner* was relegated with *Dred Scott v. Sandford* and *Plessy v. Ferguson* to the anti-canon of Constitutional law—to serve as an object lesson of

---

[1] David E. Bernstein, "Lochner v. New York: A Centennial Retrospective," 83 Wash. U.L. Rev. 1469 (2005), at p. 1501.

[2] Paul Kens, *Lochner v. New York: Regulation on Trial* (Lawrence: University of Kansas Press, 1998), at p. 144.

[3] Id., at p. 147.

[4] David E. Bernstein, op. cit., at p. 1504.

[5] Thomas B. Colby & Peter J. Smith, "The Return of Lochner," 100 Cornell L. Rev. 527 (2015), at pp. 538-539.

the evil of class bias and how it might be elevated illegitimately from raw principle to inform the highest law of the land.

The decision was not without its flaws, but its soundness in constitutional theory was not one of them. Its roots lay in Eighteenth-Century classical liberal thought, originating in England, then adopted in the colonies on the eve of the Revolution. Typical of the Framers' outlook was the view of James Madison, whose concept of property rights extended to "the free use of the faculties and free choice of the objects on which to employ them."[6] There were, he thought, natural limits on the power of the State to restrict one's rights, and an affirmative duty by the State to avoid "arbitrary restrictions, exemptions, and monopolies" that would "deny to part of its citizens that free use of their faculties, and free choice of their occupations."[7] Justice Samuel Chase spoke of "certain vital principles in our free Republican governments, which will determine and over-rule an apparent and flagrant abuse of legislative power; as to authorize manifest injustice by positive law; or to take away that security for personal liberty, or private property, for the protection whereof the government was established."[8] Among those liberties, he said, was the right of the person to enjoy the fruits of lawful private contracts. Justices Field and Bradley made much of the liberty of contract in their dissenting opinions in *The Slaughterhouse Cases*, and continued to speak of the right afterward. As the States began exercising greater legislative power over the conduct of business, legal commentators began addressing the question of the modern limits of the police power and identifying laws that overstepped the boundaries between the general welfare and the economic liberties of individuals. In 1894, Justice Henry Billings Brown wrote that "the legislature may not, under the guise of protecting the public interests, arbitrarily interfere with private business, or impose unusual and unnecessary restrictions upon lawful occupations."[9] A year later, Justice Field's nephew, David Brewer, declared that "among the inalienable rights of the citizen is that of the liberty of contract."[10] The doctrine was formally

---

[6] James Madison, "Property," *National Gazette*, March 29, 1792.
[7] Id.
[8] *Calder v. Bull* (1798) 3 U.S. 386.
[9] David E. Bernstein, "Lochner Era Revisionism, Revised: Lochner and the Origins of Fundamental Rights Constitutionalism," 92 Geo. L.J. 1 (2003), at pp. 42-43.
[10] Id., at p. 43.

incorporated into a judicial opinion in 1897, when Justice Rufus Peckham announced that the Constitution unequivocally protected "the right of the citizen to be free in the enjoyment of all his faculties; to be free to use them in all lawful ways; to live and work where he will; to earn his livelihood by any lawful calling; to pursue any livelihood or avocation; and for that purpose to enter into all contracts which may be proper, necessary and essential to his carrying out to a successful conclusion of the purposes above mentioned."[11]

It was with this right that the Court held New York's bake shop law unreasonably interfered. The State had authority to regulate the health, safety, welfare and morals of the people, but the nexus between these interests and any law that advanced them must be close, and any infringement of the rights of the people must be utterly unavoidable if the interests were to be promoted. It was not sufficient, said the Court, for the legislature merely to declare a law to be in the furtherance of public health or safety for it to pass constitutional muster – the law must actually advance these important interests. Examples of laws that properly impaired the contractual liberty of the employee and the employer were laws limiting hours in the day miners could dig beneath the earth, or steel workers could spend in the factories smelting raw ore and turning it into usable metal. Where the danger of fatigue was great, and the consequences for the worker and his colleagues possibly lethal, the Constitution provided no hedge between the individual and the power of the State. But here, no such danger could be perceived. "There is no contention," said Justice Peckham, "that bakers as a class are not equal in intelligence and capacity to men in other trades or manual occupations, or that they are able to assert their rights and care for themselves without the protecting arm of the State, interfering with their independence of judgment and of action. They are in no sense wards of the State."[12] There was, he said, "no reasonable foundation for holding this to be necessary or appropriate as a health law to safeguard the public health or the health of the individuals who are following the trade of a baker."[13] If the statute was valid, "there would seem to be no length to which legislation of this nature might not go.... No trade, no occupation, no mode of earning one's living could escape this all-pervading power,

[11] *Allegeyer v. Louisiana* (1897) 165 U.S. 578, 17 S.Ct. 427.

[12] *Lochner v. New York* (1905) 198 U.S. 45, 25 S.Ct. 539.

[13] Id.

and the acts of the legislature in limiting the hours of labor in all employments would be valid although such limitation might seriously cripple the ability of the laborer to support himself and his family."[14] The end result of indulging the State's legislative tinkering would be the State assuming "the position of a supervisor, or *pater familias*, over every act of the individual, its right of governmental interference with his hours of labor, his hours of exercise"—in short, absolute control over every aspect of human existence, private and public.[15]

In retrospect, Justice Harlan's dissenting opinion that the evidence supported a finding that significant health risks posed to bakers working in confined spaces justified limiting their hours of work was not without merit. The majority did indeed seem to ignore the legislative history and the hazards posed by the bread dust-filled air the average baker in the State of New York invariably inhaled in excess of ten hours per day. *Lochner* was subsequently marginalized by other decisions of the Court, which recognized the relevance of legitimate, even compelling, interests the State had in reducing the freedom the employer and employee had to construct the terms of the working relationship. *Lochner*, however, was never forgotten by the legal elite, and when they had their chance, they consigned it to the lowest circle of jural hell, all while denouncing through the ages the principle it represented—the fundamental right of individuals to work free of unreasonable and arbitrary restrictions—as a fiction devised by capitalists and Social Darwinists eager to coat with the patina of justice (however thin) their gross and exploitative ways. The Great Depression provided a crisis deep enough from which to cull a theory as to its origins, traceable to human greed and aided by a generation of judges drawn from the elite class of society. A new Court, in step with the times, made a show of repudiating activism and approving every progressive statute that came its way for review. Congress passed and the Court approved laws that literally put millions of Americans on the government payroll at taxpayer expense, imposed a nation-wide minimum wage, all but mandated private employers paying for their employee's retirement, and even prohibited farmers from feeding their livestock with the grain they grew on their own land. In this new age, it seemed that the State could do what it wanted, that no limitation on the right to contract, nor any liberty in economic life,

---

[14] Id.
[15] Id.

was too extreme or came remotely close to exceeding any limits implied or expressed in the Constitution's text.

That is, until late in the year 2019, when the Legislature of California enacted AB 5 and codified a definition of "independent contractor" that was so difficult to satisfy that nearly anyone receiving pay for work would be legally classified as an employee, subject to all of the rights and obligations that status entails. The new standard, known as the ABC Test, would render all workers presumptively employees unless the putative employer could demonstrate that (A) the worker is free from the control and direction of the hiring entity in connection with the performance of the work, both under the contract and for the performance of the work, and (B) the worker performs work that is outside the usual course of the hiring entity's business, and (C) the worker is customarily engaged in an independently established trade, occupation, or business. The ABC test replaced the far more lenient standard for determining employment status that was derived from a decision of the State Supreme Court in the matter of *S.G. Borello & Sons, Inc. v. Department of Industrial Relations* (1989) 48 Cal.3d 341, 256 Cal.Rptr. 543. The true import of the change in test by which to gauge whether one was an employee or an independent contractor was that hundreds of thousands of workers would suddenly find themselves either enrolled as employees of the enterprise for which they had previously labored as independent contractors, or completely out of a job. Unemployment was a likely prospect given the massive burdens employers would now be under to provide workers compensation coverage, liability insurance, medical benefits, payroll taxes, meal and rest breaks, and premium pay for overtime, among other things.

Such a radical change in industrial relations, impacting employers and workers alike, and eliminating a field of liberty that players in the State's economic life had enjoyed since the beginning of Statehood, inevitably caused a reaction that can only be characterized as explosive. Lawsuits were either filed or planned. In the U.S. District Court in Los Angeles, drivers employed by Uber and Postmates filed one of the first suits, wherein they alleged the law was "an irrational and unconstitutional statute designed to target and stifle workers and companies in the on-demand economy."[16] Freelance writers and

---

[16] Johana Bhuiyan & Suhauna Hussain, "Uber and Postmates Call AB 5 Unconstitutional in New Lawsuit," *The Los Angeles Times*, December 30, 2019.

photographers likewise filed suit, alleging equal protection and other constitutional violations. Speaking of the impact on writers and photographers, attorneys Caleb Trotter and Jim Manley of the Pacific Legal Foundation explained that the law would ruin many companies that "cannot afford to convert contractors into employees even if they wanted to."[17] Freelancers, enjoying the flexibility and independence of their historic status, will find themselves out of work due to the inability of newspaper, journal and magazine publishers to cover the overhead the employee status entails. The labyrinth of exceptions to the ABC Test only made the law worse, not better. "For example, individuals performing certain 'professional services' are exempt from the new three-part test. These professions include marketers, graphic designers, grant writers and fine artists. Journalists and photojournalists weren't so lucky." If they submitted more than a few pieces per year for publication, they were either converted into employees, or lost the gig completely. "These sorts of arbitrary distinctions," said Trotter and Manley, "are unconstitutional under the First Amendment, as well as the Fourteenth Amendment's Equal Protection Clause, which protects against the arbitrary and irrational treatment of professionals seeking to earn a living."[18]

Miriam Raftery of *East County Magazine* in San Diego agreed. The Equal Protection problem outlined by Trotter and Manley pales, however, in proportion to the massive First Amendment violation the law impels. The limitation on the ability of small media outlets such as community newspapers will likely impair the ability of media to gather and report the news and make it much more difficult for contributors to raise their voices in matters of community concern. This, she says, "violates the First Amendment of the Constitution, which guarantees freedom of the press and your freedom of speech."[19] Moreover, for those free lancers induced to become employees, they lose an essential property right in the form of the copyright to the materials they submit for publication. Their independence guaranteed their right to own their

---

[17] Caleb Trotter & Jim Manley, "California Law Unjustly and Unconstitutionally Restricts Freelance Journalists, www.thehill.com, December 23, 2019.

[18] Id.

[19] Miriam Raftery, "AB 5 Silences Your Voices and Violates Constitution Several Ways: Please Help Us Protect a Free Press," *East County Magazine*, February 16, 2020.

intellectual property. Once converted into employees, their property interest in their work vests with their employers. This undermines the rights of creative people to benefit from their creation and the spirit of the laws enacted by Congress in accordance with Article I, Section 8, Clause 8 of the Constitution, to vest "for limited times to authors and inventors the exclusive rights to their writings and discoveries."[20]

The most aggressive in attacking the law have been independent truckers and the companies that employ them. On New Year's Eve, Judge Roger Benitez of the U.S. District Court for the Southern District of California issued a temporary injunction against enforcement of the law pending resolution of the merits of the truckers' claim that the law is pre-empted by an Act of Congress governing the operation of truckers transporting goods in interstate commerce.[21] Far more consequential was the ruling of Judge William Highberger in the Superior Court sitting at Central Civil West in Los Angeles County that a suit by the State of California against a trucking company that had vowed not to heed the law would be governed by the *Borello* standard rather than the ABC Test on account of the obvious conflict of the latter with the Federal Aviation Administration Authorization Act that endorsed the use of non-employee independent contractors, or owner-operators, in the interstate shipment of goods. "Congress's intent to protect the owner-operator business model in the trucking industry," he said, precluded "its replacement by an 'employee-operator' regime."[22] Application of the ABC Test would inevitably lead to the conclusion that owner-operators were employees due to the fact that they were almost never employed outside the scope of the general contractor's ordinary business. This result would not only violate federal law; it would undermine the purpose of the law itself, which was to promote and protect independent truckers as "one of the most efficient movers of goods" by eliminating the "barrier to entry that States had imposed on truckers seeking to enter the motor carrier industry," as well as aid both shippers and consumers by "eliminating the patchwork of state and local regulations that had

---

[20] Id.

[21] Miriam Raftery, "Lawsuits Mount Against New California Labor Law, AB 5," *East County Magazine*, January 6, 2020.

[22] Order Granting in Part Defendants' Motion in Limine Re Preemption and Non-Retroactivity of ABC Worker Classification Test, *People of the State of California v. Cal Cartage Transportation Express, LLC, CCX2931, LLC and Does 1-50*, case no. BC689320.

bogged down the motor carrier industry and increased costs for motor carriers and consumers."[23]

AB 5 has managed to create what might prove to be the perfect storm of constitutional violations that succeeds in resurrecting the defunct right to contract from *Lochner's* long neglected grave. Infringement upon the right of the press to gather and report the news, of writers and photographers to sell and publish their work, of any number of workers to be treated the same as similarly situated workers who happen to benefit from carefully carved out exceptions to a law of general application, impairment of the right of truckers engaged in interstate commerce to be free of state and local regulations that increase costs and inefficiencies and, of course, the freedom of the worker to negotiate the terms of his employment, to select independence over dependence, and to forego certain protections of the law in favor of flexibility, form a great ball of malfeasance that might embolden courts ordinarily committed to stare decisis to consider whether this radical law has actually gone so far as to trounce upon a right so languid that many thought it incapable of violation.

This isn't so remote a possibility. Times have changed considerably since the hegemony of the New Deal Court. They've even advanced quite a ways since Richard Epstein's libertarian voice cried alone in the wilderness that "courts should aggressively protect economic rights" and strive to convince the government to confine its police powers to the protection of "'individual liberty and private property against all manifestations of force and fraud.'"[24] The rise of the Federalist Society's profile in the selection of judges and the reliance by the President on the Society's membership rolls for nominees to federal judicial positions, as well as the general conformity of the President's philosophical outlook with that of the *Lochner* majority, ought to be viewed as an omen of things to come.[25] Lower courts have already moved to embrace the principle of economic liberty and liberty of contract. In *Hettinga v. United States,* Judge Janice Rogers Brown wrote a concurring opinion in support of a decision dismissing a challenge to a statute that regulates the price

---

[23] Id.

[24] Thomas B. Colby & Peter J. Smith, "The Return of Lochner," op. cit., at p. 564.

[25] See Mila Sohoni, "The Trump Administration and the Law of the Lochner Era," 107 Geo. L. J. 1323 (2019), at pp. 1328-1329.

that milk processors and distributors pay to dairy farmers. In it, she stated her dissatisfaction with reliance on the most lenient level of review of regulations impairing economic liberty and declared its use to constitute an abdication of the court's "constitutional duty to protect economic rights completely."[26] She reasoned that "the practical effect of rational basis review of economic regulations is the absence of any check on the group interests that all too often control the democratic process," thereby allowing "the legislature free rein to subjugate the common good and individual liberty to the electoral calculus of politicians, the whim of majorities, or the self-interest of faction." Rational basis review, she concluded, "means property is at the mercy of the pillagers. The constitutional guarantee of liberty deserves more respect—a lot more."[27]

For light in the dark tunnel ahead of us, we might consult the leading eminence of classical liberal legal thought, Justice Thomas. In 1999, he dissented in the matter of *Saenz v. Roe*. In that case, the Court vindicated the claim of a woman who contended that a residency requirement for the receipt of state welfare benefits constituted an impairment of the privileges and immunities of citizenship protected by the Fourteenth Amendment. Taking issue with the majority, Justice Thomas opined that his view of the privileges and immunities alluded to in the Amendment was quite different, and that the meaning of the phrase was easily discoverable in history. "The colonists' repeated assertions that they maintained the rights, privileges, and immunities of persons 'born within the realm of England' and 'natural born' persons suggests that, at the time of the founding, the terms 'privileges' and 'immunities' were understood to refer to those fundamental rights and liberties specifically enjoyed by English citizens and, more broadly, by all persons."[28] Presumably, "members of the Second Continental Congress so understood these terms when they employed them in the Articles of Confederation," and the Framers apparently concurred when including the phrase in Article IV of the Constitution.[29] When a member of the Supreme Court first addressed what these privileges and immunities entailed, Justice Bushrod Washington—nephew of the President of the Philadelphia Convention and of the United States—identified a series of

---

[26] Colby & Smith, op. cit., at p. 575.
[27] Id.
[28] *Saenz v. Roe* (1999) 526 U.S. 489, 524, 119 S.Ct. 1518, Thomas, J., dissenting.
[29] Id.

rights associated with economic activity, productive labor and the enjoyment of the fruits of one's enterprise. Washington's opinion, Thomas noted, was much on the tongue of those drafting, supporting and debating the Fourteenth Amendment and the Privileges and Immunities Clause therein. While he rejected the Court majority's reliance on the Privileges and Immunities Clause to find a right to travel from State-to-State in order to obtain welfare benefits, he noted he "would be open to re-evaluating its meaning in an appropriate case."[30]

The host of constitutional challenges facing AB 5 may well prove to be that very case; where the Court, changed in composition since the *Saenz* decision, finally considers the meaning of the Clause and decides if it was intended by its Framers to protect economic liberties, and whether the law at hand, so destructive to the freedom to prosper through the sweat of one's brow, can withstand scrutiny of the legislature's claim that it is these self-same toilers they aim to protect.

The Iceman Cometh

FROM the diminutive northern California city of Santa Rosa came word that federal immigration agents had arrested at least three people within the curtilage of the hallowed grounds of the Hall of Justice in plain sight of a host of dignitaries whose initial shock soon gave way to outrage that the sacred precincts of the bench and bar—where attorneys routinely exaggerate the merits of their clients' claims and defenses and denounce each other's clients as liars—could be so outrageously violated. Maintaining the dignity of his position through adoption of a measured yet critical statement, Presiding Judge Bradford DeMeo said that "the arrest and detention actions of ICE at courthouses like ours interrupts the judicial process and undermines equal access to justice."[1] Less measured were the comments of the County's District Attorney and Public Defender, Jill Ravitch and Kathleen Pozzi, each of whom condemned the arrests "for undermining public safety and the fragile

[30] Id., at 528.

[1] Julie Johnson, "ICE Agents Arrest 3 at Sonoma County Courthouse," *The Santa Rosa Press Democrat*, February 18, 2020.

yet crucial trust between immigrants and local authorities."[2] Sounding more like the District Attorney than the defender of the accused ever striving to win dismissal of her clients' cases, Ms. Pozzi predicted that "it's now going to put total fear in the community. People aren't going to come to court. Victims will refuse to show up. Witnesses will refuse to show up. Cases will have to get dismissed."[3] County Counsel Bruce Goldstein seemed most upset of all, calling ICE's actions "lawless" in that they were "carried out without judicial warrants and violate recently passed state law prohibiting civil arrests at a courthouse."[4] Fresh from his failed and legally meritless effort to remove from office the President responsible for these outrages, Congressman Mike Thompson expressed fear that "the courthouse arrests run the risk of eroding trust between public safety officials and immigrants" and "putting all of us at risk" by making immigrant witnesses less likely to come forward.[5]

Officials elsewhere were similarly concerned. Taking time from completing his plan to defer prosecutions in favour of reimbursing crime victims the costs of undeterred and unpunished crime, San Francisco's new District Attorney suddenly sounded like an old time prosecutor, worried that ICE's actions would ruin his effort to bring wrongdoers to justice by "deterring undocumented victims and witnesses from cooperating with the justice system."[6] His colleague, the mayor, saw fit to remind the terrified masses of her town that San Francisco was a Sanctuary City and vowed that she and her administration would "continue to do everything we can to support our immigrant communities."[7]

What none of the critics of federal action bothered to mention was that the men apprehended appeared to be in the country illegally, not so much working in productive employment as engaged in a long string of low crimes and misdemeanours: wife beating, drunk driving, driving

---

[2] Id.

[3] Id.

[4] Darrell Smith, "Sonoma County Officials Condemn ICE Arrests. 24 Hours Later, 2 More Were Detained," *The Sacramento Bee*, February 19, 2020.

[5] Id.

[6] Alejandro Serrano & Tatiana Sanchez, "ICE Arrests at Sonoma County Courthouse Infuriate Bay Area Officials, Immigrations Activists," *The San Francisco Chronicle*, February 19, 2020.

[7] Id.

without a license, battery, trespass, witness intimidation, and sundry other offenses. Two of the men had been repeatedly deported, but managed without much difficulty to return just as often to take up their crime sprees where they'd left off.[8] That northern California harboured mayors who welcomed illegal aliens and promised to shield them from removal by federal authorities, and prosecutors who wanted to convert their offices into insurance agencies reimbursing property damage caused by criminals left free to smash and grab with impunity, may well have entered the minds of these two men as they considered where they might enjoy living once they slipped through the unguarded and unfenced international border. These men, and many others, obviously found the State to be a target rich environment, flush with victims, whose peace officers, legislators and judges lacked the will to hold them to account when actually apprehended. The only officials interested in halting their unlawful activities are the ones California's high and mighty have just condemned.

Lying in wait at courthouses is a logical strategy to apprehend the very people federal authorities have placed a priority on removing from the country. Yet it's one that has been adopted only in the wake of the growing resistance of State and local authorities to federal immigration enforcement. At the heart of that resistance in California is the so-called Sanctuary City policy of San Francisco and its counter-part on the State level in the form of the recently enacted SB 54. Sanctuary Cities, of course, antedate the Trump Administration. Indeed, their earliest incarnation appeared during the ante-bellum period, when cities and States in the north refused to cooperate with federal officials in the capture and return of runaway slaves. As early as the 1970s, the City of Los Angeles adopted a policy of non-cooperation with federal officials in the identification of illegal aliens within City limits. A more aggressive commitment to non-cooperation came with the emergence of the current incumbent as a candidate for President, and even more so following his election and inauguration. The President quickly made good on his promise to expand enforcement of the nation's immigration regime by deploying "federal resources to enforce immigration laws" and moving "aggressively to harness the enforcement power of state and local

---

[8] Smith, op. cit.

police."[9] His administration also "reinvigorated the 287(g) program, whereby local and state police agree to be deputized to enforce immigration laws" and act in subordination to federal immigration officials.[10] Information sharing was also expanded via the Secure Communities program, "through which ICE is automatically notified if an individual of interest is booked into a local jail."[11] When the Trump Administration attempted to withhold congressionally authorized grants to municipalities to promote public safety, State and local officials finally rebelled and alleged (quite accurately) that such action violated the Supreme Court's interpretation of Congress's spending power.

Invoking the Tenth Amendment, California and other jurisdictions enacted legislation forbidding local police agencies from any cooperation with federal authorities, whether it be in providing information about the immigration status of arrestees, release dates of convicted criminals, or direct assistance during immigration raids. California went so far as to bar federal officials from government premises for the purpose of arresting illegal aliens unless they came armed with a court issued arrest warrant. New Jersey went further still by requiring state officials to notify convicted criminals in State and local custody of any federal warrants issued for their arrest.[12] The chief executive of King County in the State of Washington even prohibited any contractor with the County's airport from providing any assistance to federal authorities involved in the transport of aliens apprehended by immigration officials, including the fuelling of planes.[13] Not waiting for the legislature to act, Oregon's Chief Justice took matters into her own hands by issuing an order banning ICE from making arrests at State courthouses without "a criminal judicial warrant."[14]

In response, the Trump Administration issued warnings to State officials throughout the nation against interfering with federal

---

[9] Huyen Pham & Pham Hoang Van, "Sub-federal Immigration Regulation and the Trump Effect," 94 N.Y.U.L. 125 (2019), at p. 147

[10] Id.

[11] Id., at p. 148.

[12] Hans A. Von Spakovsky & Lora Ries, "Trump's Counterattack on Sanctuary Cities Has Begun, and It's About Time," www.heritage.org, February 17, 2020.

[13] Id.

[14] Tobias Hoonhout, "Trump Admin Warns Sanctuary States Against Barring ICE Courthouse Arrests in a Letter," www.nationalreview.com, November 22, 2019.

immigration enforcement and defended ICE by noting that "an administrative arrest warrant is all that Congress requires for authorities to make an arrest of an alien inside the United States for violations of federal immigration law."[15] Any interference, whether in the form of State court orders or acts of State legislatures prohibiting execution of such warrants were ineffective to deter federal agents from executing their duty under federal law. "Under the Supremacy Clause of the United States Constitution," explained the Attorney General, "such rules cannot and will not govern the conduct of federal officers acting pursuant to duly-enacted laws passed by Congress when those laws provide the authority to make administrative arrests of removable aliens inside the United States."[16]

Non-cooperation in the States and the success of State officials in invoking the Tenth Amendment and Spending Clause have guided the Administration's decision to deploy its own personnel and resources to places such as courthouses to detect and arrest illegal immigrants whose criminal conduct has made them a priority for deportation. Opponents object even to this, and have continued to rely on the Tenth Amendment in increasingly creative ways. As noted by Sarah Rogerson of Albany Law School, "legal theories advanced in one of the first cases to formally protest courthouse apprehensions by ICE support the position that the practice violates the Tenth Amendment because: (1) the practice interferes with the state's right to form its own government by interfering with state court operations; (2) that by enlisting state court personnel in effectuating apprehensions, the federal government is engaging in unconstitutional commandeering of state resources; and (3) the practice violates individual rights that have been held to be implicated when the state's rights are so violated."[17] Others have suggested that the long neglected Guarantee Clause provides a basis to exclude ICE from the courthouse grounds. Never has the Court relied on the Clause either to uphold federal action in the States or to prohibit the federal government from interfering with the operation of existing State governments. And, yet, it is said by some that since "the state's right to establish and maintain a functioning judiciary is...central to a

---

[15] Id.

[16] Id.

[17] Sarah Rogerson, "Sovereign Resistance to Federal Immigration Enforcement in State Courthouses," 32 Geo. Immigr. L.J. 275 (2018), at p. 299.

state governmental function," and a functioning judicial branch is a fundamental incident of a republican form of government that the Clause is designed to protect, the Guarantee Clause is an appropriate device to shield the States from the federal government's effort to use State court precincts as traps to spring on unwary litigants, witnesses and defendants who happen to be subject to immigration warrants.[18]

Far more interesting is the argument of Professor Christopher Lasch that long-standing common law principles, well accepted by American courts, already provide the protection that immigrant rights advocates seek through more doubtful resort to novel and uncertain arguments based on provisions of the Constitution that current jurisprudence render toothless, if not utterly impotent. The principle Lasch speaks of is the common-law privilege from arrest dating back to the early Fifteenth-Century. "Suitors, witnesses, and other persons, necessarily attending any courts of record upon business, are not to be arrested during their actual attendance, which includes their necessary coming and returning. And no arrest can be made in the King's presence, nor within the verge of his royal palace, nor in any place where the King's justices are actually sitting."[19] Even the Supreme Court of the United States recognized the privilege and explained it as proceeding "upon the ground that the due administration of justice requires that a court shall not permit interference with the process of a cause pending before it, by the service of process in other suits, which would prevent, or the fear of which might tend to discourage, the voluntary attendance of those whose presence is necessary or convenient to the judicial administration in the pending litigation."[20] Violation of the privilege was something remedied by courts in days-gone-by through contempt as well as orders of protection, offering safe passage for those subject to service of process in order to attend court in unrelated matters.

While Lasch is optimistic that the privilege might be available to banish ICE from the courthouse steps, his optimism is best checked by a healthy degree of scepticism. The authorities he cites range from the reign of Henry IV through the first years of the Twentieth Century. The privilege was one designed to protect persons from arrest in civil rather

---

[18] Id., at p. 303.

[19] Christopher Lasch, "A Common Law Privilege to Protect State and Local Courts During the Crimmigration Crisis," 127 Yale L.J. F. 410 (2017), at p. 423.

[20] Id., at p. 427.

than criminal matters, at a time when arrest was the recognized means of initiating civil suits. In the American context, the privilege appeared rather rarely, but when it did it tended merely to shield a person from service of civil process while attending court in a State not one's own. The American sources are confined to very narrow circumstances and almost exclusively lie in State court proceedings. The privilege itself has never been codified, and no modern authorities for it seem to exist.

This isn't to say the privilege isn't still a vital one; it only suggests that its application is narrow, rare and perhaps easily overcome. Even were it a far more robust principle of law, its employment as a shield against federal immigration warrants wielded by armed agents of the Immigration Control Administration isn't likely to survive judicial challenge. This is because of the very well-worn principle embodied in Article VI of the Constitution in the text of the Supremacy Clause, that "this Constitution, and the Laws of the United States which shall be made in Pursuance thereof; and all Treaties made, or which shall be made, under the Authority of the United States, shall be the supreme Law of the Land; and Judges in every State shall be bound thereby, any Thing in the Constitution or Laws of any State to the Contrary notwithstanding." The principle of federal supremacy has been interpreted to mean that should collision exist between a law of Congress and the law of a State, the law of the State "must yield to the law of Congress; and the decision sustaining the privilege they confer, against a right given by a law of the Union, must be erroneous."[21] This is true of laws only inadvertently in conflict with federal authority no less than laws intentionally designed to thwart the workings of federal law as administered by the executive branch. No principle, said John Marshall, "can be admissible, which would defeat the legitimate operations of a supreme government. It is of the very essence of supremacy, to remove all obstacles to its action within its own sphere, and so to modify every power vested in subordinate governments, as to exempt its own operations from their own influence."[22] As the State has sovereignty over only those things that exist by its own authority or is introduced by its permission, its power does not "extend to those means which are employed by Congress to carry into execution powers

[21] *Gibbons v. Ogden* (1824) 22 U.S. 1, 210.
[22] *McCulloch v. Maryland* (1821) 17 U.S. 316, 427.

conferred on that body by the people of the United States."[23] Any attempt to so extend its power "is itself an abuse," and a "usurpation of a power which the people of a single state cannot give."[24]

Efforts by States to exercise control over federal operations, or to render them void, tended historically to be turned back in judicial proceedings, but exceptions occur in the record from time-to-time in the form of executive action against obstructive state officials. In 1807, the Legislature of Pennsylvania enacted a resolution condemning the exercise of federal judicial jurisdiction over cases and controversies involving the State and arising from disputes over land formerly claimed by Pennsylvania but ceded to the United States. The resolution mandated all monies payable to the United States for sale of public lands be paid instead into the State Treasury, and for the Governor "to protect the just rights of the State in respect to the premises, by such means as he may deem necessary for the purpose, and also to protect the person and property" of State officials acting in accordance with the Resolution "from any process whatever which may issue out of the Supreme Court of the United States in consequence of his obedience to the requisition and injunction of this Act."[25] When the Supreme Court responded to this legal insurrection by issuing an order enforcing federal rights contrary to State law, the governor of the State prepared to mobilize the State militia "to prevent any enforcement of the Court's decrees."[26] Federal marshals attempting to execute the Supreme Court's order against the State Treasurer were met with armed resistance by State troops who protectively surrounded the intended target. The end result wasn't victory for the State, but an indictment by a federal grand jury of the militia's commanding officer for resisting the laws of the United States.[27] The General and his chief adjutants were tried and convicted as charged, fined and ordered to the gaol for a term of years. More elaborate resistance was undertaken by the State of South Carolina some years later in opposition to enforcement of the Tariff Acts of 1828 and 1832, which in turn prompted President Jackson to call on the people of the State and its government to "snatch from the archives of your State the

---

[23] Id., at p. 429.

[24] Id., at 430.

[25] Charles Warren, *The Supreme Court in United States History*, Volume I, Rev. ed. (Boston: Little, Brown, and Company, 1926), at p. 373.

[26] Id., p. 377.

[27] Id., at p. 379.

disorganizing edict of its convention" and "bid its members to re-assemble and promulgate the decided expressions of your will to remain in the path which alone can conduct you to safety, prosperity, and honour."[28] Jackson's poorly veiled threat to invade the State and force compliance with federal law met with the expected results. When the State again defied federal authority and seized a federal military installation several decades later, its bluff was called, an invasion was mounted and a forced reduction of State sovereignty secured.

The Supremacy Clause entails not only the pre-emption of State laws in conflict with the operation of federal policy, but also immunity for federal officials carrying out federally mandated duties. When Federal Marshall David B. Neagle was charged with the murder of David Terry on a train in Lothrop, California after Terry assaulted Justice Stephen Field, Neagle's Petition for a Writ of Habeas Corpus was granted on the grounds that a federal officer is immune from state prosecution when performing "an act which he was authorized to do by the law of the United States, which it was his duty to do as a marshal of the United States."[29] Under such circumstances, "he cannot be guilty of a crime under the law of the State of California."[30] The rationale for such immunity was more fully explained by Justice William Strong and the Supreme Court in the matter of *Tennessee v. Davis*. Strong observed that if, "when thus acting, and within the scope of their authority, those officers can be arrested and brought to trial in a state court, for an alleged offense against the law of the state, yet warranted by the federal authority they possess, and if the general government is powerless to interfere at once for their protection...the operations of the general government may at any time be arrested at the will of one of its members."[31] An immunity of this kind flowed naturally from the nature of the relationship between the States and the federal government: in order for the federal government to advance its legitimate purposes, its agents must be free to perform their duties. The immunity is applicable both in criminal prosecutions and civil suits, and has always been

---

[28] *Gen. Jackson's Farewell Address to the People of the United States, Together with the Proclamation to South Carolina* (Harrisburg: J.M.G. Lescure, 1850), at p. 24.

[29] *In Re Neagle* (1890), 135 U.S. 1, 75.

[30] Id.

[31] *Tennessee v. Davis* (1880) 100 U.S. 257, 263.

construed in the broadest of terms.[32] So broad is the immunity that it protects law enforcement officers "even where their actions are unconstitutional," so long as "they might have reasonably thought their actions were permissible."[33]

One has to wonder what's in it for California officials to engage in such massive resistance to the enforcement of federal immigration law. Arguments that the State and municipalities desire to control the allocation of their own resources in keeping with the Tenth Amendment and protect the integrity of the operation of State courts, to secure the cooperation of witnesses and compliance of criminal defendants, certainly sound plausible, but these justifications tend to pale in significance when one contemplates how dependent the States are on federal funds, how much power they have ceded or allowed to be seized by the federal government in nearly every facet of governance, and just how little need for the witnesses and parties supposedly being driven from the courts there would be if the criminal element among the immigrant class were handed over to federal authorities for deportation.

What the leadership of California and other sanctuary jurisdictions really want isn't autonomy and smoothly operating courts. They want to preserve the massive constituency living and working in their jurisdictions that reliably votes them into power and pays all number of State and local excises to fill the public treasury. They say they stand with humanity and in support of the fundamental human rights of those fleeing to this country from elsewhere, but say nothing in criticism of the governments that make the migrants' lives unbearable and cause their flight, and even oppose the federal government when it considers intervening abroad. They decry the rights of victims who are deterred from testifying in court and of parties having their day in court, but have no problem with habitual criminals remaining in this country and continuing their criminal ways, or with laws and policies that bar the police from enforcing even the most basic standards of right and wrong, such as "thou shalt not steal." It's hard to imagine that most people actually support a policy of non-cooperation and opposition to

---

[32] Michael P. Stone & Jeremy Warren, "Supremacy Clause Immunity for Federal Officers and Agents in State Criminal Prosecutions: What Happens When Federal Officers Are Accused of Committing State Crimes While Performing the Federal Duties," https://poracldf.org, October 13, 2013.

[33] Id.

immigration law, even if they are sympathetic to the many good people who have entered this country illegally, live peaceful and productive lives, and ought to be given an opportunity to legalize their presence. The President has said that if he is given support in his efforts to enforce the law, he will cooperate in reviving such policies as DACA and a pathway to citizenship for those who qualify for its benefits. The current government of California – in the hands of extremists who seem bent on turning every norm of governance and administration on its head – can't be relied on to compromise in a manner that would relieve our communities of the bad apples while preserving in the barrel the good ones. As the State's government turns to more and more determined resistance and prompts more heavy-handed federal response, perhaps the State's voters might reconsider their options and encourage their leaders to choose a path forward that strikes a better balance between the interest of the State in maintaining its autonomy and its interest in protecting its people from persons over whom the federal government has exclusive jurisdiction.

In God She Trust

PERHAPS the least favourite exercise for a member of any Administration is the walk across the National Mall up the Capitol steps and down the hallway into a committee room, taking a seat in front a dais occupied by a group divided roughly in two, but whose animosity for one another is exceeded only by their collective sense of self-importance, and then to field questions touching upon one's competence in the conduct of an office that is, in this complex world, nearly impossible to manage. For the Secretary of the Treasury, the ordeal is probably doubly uncomfortable given the nature of the job. Overseeing the collection and distribution of trillions of dollars brings with it the scrutiny of a myriad of agencies, organizations and individuals, whose collective greed for other people's money is so intense as to prompt accusations of misconduct and graft with all the alacrity of a hair trigger. Any fear on the part of the current Secretary that security of the money supply, the relations between the federal government and the Federal Reserve, the debt to GDP ratio, and tax code enforcement might form the most controversial and vexing elements of his cross-examination and give him cause to consider following Reince Preibus, Rex Tillerson, and Anthony Scaramucci into the private sector was relieved when the greatest controversy presented to him focused not on the weighty matter of the fate of the public fisc, but the personage whose visage might grace the nation's currency.

During the last years of the Obama Administration, a decision was reached to replace one of the exclusively masculine faces on the money supply with that of a prominent woman. After a nationwide vote, the decision was made to switch out the face of the slaveholding Indian fighter Andrew Jackson with that of fugitive slave and Underground Railroad conductor Harriet Tubman. When asked by Representative Ayanna Pressley when exactly the new bill would be put into circulation, a confused Secretary struggled to come up with an answer. He was focused, he said, less on whose face appeared on greenbacks than on whether counterfeiters the world over could manufacture passible forgeries. He thought that "the imagery feature will not be an issue that comes up until, most likely, 2026."[1]

Concealing any urge to cry racism—at least too hastily—the late Elijah Cummings said "the Administration's decision to drag their feet" and delay the redesign was "unacceptable" and that "it is far past time that we recognize [Tubman's] place in history."[2] Nancy Pelosi said that it was "an insult to the hopes of millions that the Trump Administration is refusing to honour Harriet Tubman on our $20 bill."[3] Senator Ron Wyden said he thought it was clear that the Secretary had withheld disclosure of the real reason the Tubman bill was spiked. One step behind was Chuck Schumer, who demanded an investigation by the Department's Inspector General.[4]

Beyond Congress, the critics on the left were far more pointed and claimed to know exactly what was going on. Dorothy Brown of CNN said it wasn't the worst thing the President had done "to disrespect a

---

[1] Christina Prignano, "Ayanna Pressley Asked Steven Mnuchin When Harriet Tubman Would Be Put On The $20. He Didn't Know," www.bostonglobe.com, May 22, 2019.

[2] Id.

[3] Tal Axelrod, "Pelosi: Trump Delay on Harriet Tubman $20 is Insult to the Hopes of Millions," www.thehill.com, June 20, 2019.

[4] Dan Mangan, "Treasury Watchdog Will Investigate Trump Administration Delay of $20 Harriet Tubman Bill," www.cnbc.com, June 24, 2019.

source of black pride," but it was typical of the man whose father's company had settled a justice department suit alleging racial discrimination in housing and who himself ran a full page ad in *The New York Times* condemning the Central Park Five.[5] Doreen St. Felix of *The New Yorker* inferred that the President just couldn't "stand to see Jackson's face usurped" by Tubman's, and that this was further evidence that "the symbols of white supremacy are Trump's most powerful currency."[6] Reputed confirmation of the Trump-is-racist narrative came when Trump acolyte turned bitter critic Omarosa published her tell-all memoir of her brief tenure in the White House. The woman who famously can't get along with anyone, including the man who elevated her from anonymity to international fame as a contestant on *The Apprentice*, wrote that the President took one look at the proposed image of Tubman and said "you want to put that face on the twenty-dollar bill?"[7] The obvious implication was that it was distaste for the black-as-night and very African-featured Tubman's appearance that was the basis of the President's objection, and that the distaste was rooted in racial bigotry.

The outline of Tubman's life is reasonably well known, particularly in the wake of the recent biopic for which the actress portraying her received an Oscar nomination. Born into slavery in Maryland, put to work at a young age, cruelly abused by her white "owners" both routinely and when she aided a fellow slave's escape from corporal punishment, she finally flew alone through the Maryland countryside, evading bloodhounds and slave catchers, until reaching free soil in Philadelphia. Overcome by an intense urge to assist her family and others in escaping bondage, she returned many times to the south, alerted bondsmen of her presence, led them through forests, swamps and fields, all while eluding fervent pursuit by armed posses and occasionally forcing her skittish charges to go on at gun point lest their lack of faith in their objective betray them all. Rewards for her capture escalated until the amount reached $40,000, and posters calling for her arrest appeared everywhere with her picture affixed. The dominant class

---

5 Dorothy Brown, "The Real Reason Trump Won't Put Harriet Tubman on the $20 Bill," www.cnn.com, June 14, 2019.

6 Doreen St. Felix, "The Haunted Image of Harriet Tubman on the Twenty-Dollar Bill," *The New Yorker*, June 18, 2019.

7 "Omarosa Claims Donald Trump Mocked Harriet Tubman's Looks: 'That Face on the $20 Bill?,'" www.people.com, August 14, 2019.

deemed her a mortal threat to southern institutions and the social order; the slaves considered her the second coming of the liberator Moses, charged by God Himself with the task of freeing them from thrall to Pharaoh and leading them to the promised land of Canaan. She was acclaimed and celebrated by the great men and women of the day. Secretary of State William Henry Seward said of her that "a nobler, higher spirit, or a truer, seldom dwells in human form."[8] The abolitionist Gerritt Smith said she possessed "a rare discernment, and a deep and sublime philanthropy."[9] The orator Wendell Phillips called her a "fearless and sagacious friend."[10] John Brown consulted with her and called her "the General," while Emerson invited her to live with him and his family for a time.[11] She was, said Thomas Wentworth Higginson, who knew her during the War, quite simply "the greatest heroine of the age."[12] In her own day, she became a symbol not merely of liberty, but of the essence of the Union cause championed by Lincoln and the Republican Party, and the spirit of freedom infused into our nation's Constitution, but tainted like man himself following ingestion of the fruit of the tree with a corruption that only the sacrifice of life might overcome.

It is an odd evolution that has taken Tubman from her firm place in the iconography of freedom associated with the Republican Party and transformed her into a forerunner of the Social Justice Warrior that Ayanna Pressley and the Squad represent. Like most figures of the past, a superficial reading of her commitments and achievements has permitted a projection of the prejudices of the present, and turned her into something not so much different from what she actually was, but something awkwardly incomplete. School children might read accounts of her life drawn from the school library and internet and report to their classmates what they learned, but absent from those accounts is the very thing that defined Tubman, motivated her flight to freedom, and inspired her to heroics that are beyond ordinary human ability, and

[8] Sarah H. Bradford, *Harriet: The Moses of Her People* (New York: George R. Lockwood & Son, 1897), at p. 76.

[9] Id.

[10] Id., at p. 77.

[11] "The Moses of Her People: Proposed Memorial to Harriet Tubman," *The Sun*, May 2, 1909.

[12] Elizabeth Cobbs, "Harriet Tubman, America's Foremost Female Patriot, Belongs on the $20 Bill Now," www.thewashingtonpost.com, May 26, 2019.

indeed, comprehension. Harriet Tubman was as fiery and faithful a Christian as any who ever walked the earth. And it is only in her faith that her life and legacy can be understood.

The faith of the slave has become something of a stereotype in American lore and subject to much ex post facto theorizing. The backwoods scenes of Negro revivals in the South, "grotesque and funny" in appearance said W.E.B. Du Bois, harboured a deeper meaning as "almost 'the only habitual recreation not purely sensual,'...hence slaves poured all their emotions into them 'with an intensity and vehemence almost terrible to witness.'"[13] The natives of the African continent, ripped from their lands of origin, placed into a new setting utterly powerless to exercise any physical autonomy, and presented with a foreign faith, adopted and modified it to their own psychic needs, turning it into an avenue for mental and emotional independence and a device for the expression of the longing for physical freedom. In the mind of the slave, slaves became the Israelites, beloved of God yet fated for servitude; the white race were the Egyptians, proud and unyielding in the face of calls from God's anointed "to let my people go"; cruel plantation foremen, whip in hand, were the task masters charged with overseeing completion of the impossible detail of erecting Pharaoh's monuments and cities; and Moses was the yet unknown agent of collective liberation, offering hope for escape and delivery to a better place, where the product of one's work might be one's own, one's family couldn't be ripped from one's bosom, and the crack of the whip was never to be heard.

For some cynics, like Du Bois, Christianity was less an authentic expression of sincere faith in the Deity, or even a coping mechanism for highly distressed psyches, than a device for the psychological conditioning of the black man to servitude. And certainly, there were many in the days before Fort Sumter who saw it in just this way. Many a slave owner initially balked at introducing slaves to the faith for fear that baptism might mysteriously alter the status of the slave from bondman to free. After colonial legislatures enacted laws expressly providing that conversion would not have this effect, and a theory came to be elaborated that the teachings of Christ might be used to induce

---

[13] Du Bois, *The Souls of Black Folk* (New York: Bantam Books, 1989), at p. 134; and Kenneth M. Stamp, *The Peculiar Institution: Slavery in the Ante-Bellum South* (New York: Vintage Books, 1956), at p. 372.

humility and passivity in the face of oppression, "most masters encouraged Christian proselytizing among their bondsmen, and conversion proceeded rapidly."[14] Greater scrutiny of the expression and practice of the faith by slaves occurred in the wake of notorious slave insurrections and the growth of abolitionist agitation due specifically to fear that "too many of the conspiracies had been planned in religious gatherings and that such groups gave the abolitionists an opportunity to distribute incendiary ideas and literature."[15] But even as white society restricted unsupervised slave congregations and forced slaves to attend the masters' churches, the minds of slaves continued in absolute autonomy to ponder the promises of God the Father and the sacrifice of His Son on the cross, and dreamed of a physical liberty to match the freedom they experienced in their completely internal relationship with the Creator.

Among those who experienced the faith on an intensely personal basis was Harriet Tubman. One can hardly deny the fulfillment through faith of the profound psychic need for autonomy and its use as a psychic devise to cope with physical circumstances that were otherwise intolerable. And yet it is utterly unfair to dismiss her faith as merely this; for through it she did indeed cope with her dismal condition, but also moved the proverbial mountain spoken of by the Redeemer.[16] In her daily routine, the shrewd and highly observant Tubman must have recognized as others did the stark distinction between the condition of the slave and the teachings of the Good Book that she couldn't read, but heard tell about in the meetings of the faithful. In the most rudimentary of the teachings—in the Ten Commandments, the Beatitudes and the Lord's Prayer—the obvious surely became evident: that slavery is contrary to the Will and the Word of God.

Tubman's life and career amply support her likely accord with the views of formally educated Christian opponents of slavery. "Just after the Israelites were emancipated from their bondage in Egypt," wrote the abolitionist Theodore Weld, "while they stood before Sinai to receive the law, as the trumpet waxed louder, and the mount quaked and blazed, God spake the Ten Commandments from the mists of clouds and

---

[14] Stamp, op. cit., at p. 156.

[15] John Hope Franklin, *From Slavery to Freedom: A History of Negro Americans*, 3d Ed. (New York: Vintage Books, 1969), at p. 200.

[16] Matt 17:30; Matt 21:21; and Mark 11:23.

thunderings," and what he spoke dealt "death to slavery."[17] The Eighth Commandment, he said, "presupposes and assumes the right of every man to his powers, and their product. Slavery robs of both."[18] It "forbids the taking of any part of that which belongs to another. Slavery takes the whole."[19] Slaveholding, he declared, was "the highest possible violation of the Eighth Commandment. To take from a man his earnings, is theft. But to take the earner, is a compound, life-long theft -- supreme robbery that vaults up the climax at a leap -- the dread, terrific, giant robbery, that towers among other robberies a solitary horror."[20] In violating the Eighth Commandment, slavers violated the Tenth as well; for "who ever made human beings slaves without coveting them?"[21] By the law that God gave the Israelites, those who stole a man and sold him were condemned to death.[22]

To those who relied on the Bible when arguing the virtues of bondage, who pointed out that Abraham had slaves, that the Law of Moses provided rules governing the employment and treatment of slaves, and that even Christ himself commended slaves to remain loyal to their masters, Weld replied that there could be no comparison between the bondage referenced in the Bible and what was practiced in North America. Servants in the Bible, he explained, "were admitted into covenant with God...statedly instructed in morality and religion... released from their regular labor nearly one half of the whole time protected by law equally with the other members of the community...placed upon a level with their masters in all civil and religious rites" and were presumed the victims of oppression when they fled their service.[23] Most often, they contracted for the status, and in return for work, were entitled to wages; and if the wages were not paid, the heavy sanction of the law fell upon the master. "Let those believe who can," Weld concluded, "that God commissioned his people to rob others of all their rights, while he denounced against them wrath to the

[17] Theodore Dwight Weld, *Bible Against Slavery: An Inquiry into the Patriarchal and Mosaic Systems on the Subject of Human Rights* (New York: American Anti-Slavery Society, 1838), at p. 10.

[18] Id.

[19] Id.

[20] Id., at p. 11.

[21] Id.

[22] Id., at pp. 11-12.

[23] Id., at pp. 25-28

uttermost, if they practiced the far lighter oppression of Egypt."[24] Tubman appears to have reached the same conclusion, and "in her mind, her people were the Israelites in the Land of Egypt, while far away to the north somewhere, was the land of Canaan."[25]

The strength of Tubman's faith appeared early in life. She was, said her friend and biographer Sarah Bradford, "brought up by her parents possessed of strong faith in God," and "she had never known the time...when she did not trust Him, and cling to Him, with an all-abiding confidence. She seemed ever to feel the Divine Presence near, and she talked with God 'as a man talketh with his friend.' Hers was not the religion of a morning and evening prayer at stated times, but when she felt a need, she simply told God of it, and trusted Him to set the matter right."[26] Her faith only intensified in the wake of her recovery from a head injury inadvertently inflicted by a white man attempting to strike an escaping slave. As her injury slowly healed, "a deeper religious spirit seemed to take possession of her than she had ever experienced before. She literally 'prayed without ceasing.'"[27] In a tone of the profoundest pathos and supplication that defied description, Tubman informed Bradford that "pears like, I prayed all de time about my work everywhere; I was always talking to de Lord. When I went through the horse-trough to wash my face, and took up de water in my hands, I said, 'Oh, Lord, wash me, make me clean.' When I took up de towel to wipe my face and hands, I cried, 'Oh, Lord, for Jesus' sake, wipe away all my sins!' When I took up de broom and began to sweep, I groaned, 'Oh, Lord, whatsoebber sin dere be in my heart, sweep it out, Lord, clar and clean."[28]

Those who doubt the objective veracity of the focus of Tubman's faith, even as they accept its subjective reality, might reflect on what she attributed solely to the Lord's intervention. Her one-hundred-mile exodus from bondage was a near impossible feat. The woods and swamps of the ancient south historically provided ample cover for fugitives. Once they made it to a place like Virginia's Great Dismal Swamp, they might disappear forever. "Even during daylight hours, but

---

[24] Id., at p. 64.
[25] Bradford, op. cit., at p. 26.
[26] Id., at p. 23.
[27] Id., at p. 25.
[28] Id., at p. 25.

especially at night, the woods neutralized the advantage slaveholders enjoyed on open land."[29] In the older colonies such as Maryland, the clearing of the land incidental to the expansion of slave-powered agriculture shifted the advantage back to those who might recapture the fugitive and return him to bondage. Underground Railroad conductor John Parker observed that when he first began his work among slaves, the landscape "was still covered with virgin forest, broken here and there by clearings, with many trails and few roads."[30] But as settlement expanded, "the forest gradually disappeared," making "it more difficult for the fugitives to pass through the country successfully."[31] Adding to the difficulty was the emergence of white southern society as a single massive militia, literally charged by law with the task of patrolling the countryside day and night and pursuing all runaways as if a single successful escape might spell the doom of slavery.[32] Despite the challenges posed by the heavily settled and cultivated land and the armed patrols that pursed her, and lacking any personal knowledge of the terrain, Tubman journeyed the hundred miles overland and crossed the Maryland border into Pennsylvania. Tubman herself attributed her success to a vision she had of the landscape prior to her flight, and to "an invisible pillar of cloud by day, and of fire at night, under the guidance of which she journeyed or rested."[33] In later years, as she returned south on nineteen separate occasions to lead 300 slaves to freedom through an increasingly vigilant countryside, with wanted posters covering the land and a bounty on her head, she commonly encountered desperate situations. While those around her despaired of capture, she invariably listened as if to silent voices, abruptly changed course or forded what appeared to be an unfordable river, as if she were the Apostle Peter, accosted by an Angel seen and heard by no one else, admonishing her to be "quick," to "get up," and to "follow me."[34] In the more perilous situations she simply invoked the protection of the living God without any apparent thought for those around her. "Oh Lord!," she would groan, "you've been wid me in six troubles, don't desert me in the

[29] Walter Johnson, *River of Dark Dreams: Slavery and Empire in the Cotton Kingdom* (Cambridge: Belknap Press, 2013), at p. 232-233.

[30] Id., at 221.

[31] Id.

[32] Stamp, op. cit., at pp. 214-215.

[33] Bradford, op. cit., at pp. 29-30.

[34] Id., at pp. 84-85; and Acts 12:7-8.

seventh."[35] On other occasions, the power that inhabited her was exposed to the world, as when she mustered a horse and wagon in broad daylight and like Jehu himself careened toward freedom on the public thoroughfare with her mother and father in tow, or when she seized hold of a captured fugitive in Troy, New York, and though beaten with clubs, never released her grip until the man was safely aboard a boat bound for Canada. The abolitionist Thomas Garrett said he "never met…any person, of any colour, who had more confidence in the voice of God, as spoken direct to her soul."[36] Her faith was absolute, and its power is manifest in the superhuman, nay supernatural, work of her hands.

Her efforts and her success continued even as the world grew darker and the power of slavery closed around those trapped within its net in reaction to acts "not only of individuals, but States…whose gratification is sought in the pursuit of measures, whose inevitable consequence must be the overthrow and destruction of" slavery.[37] When the Fugitive Slave Act and the *Dred Scott* decision emboldened those who would pursue slaves into free territory and reclaim them for servitude, Tubman led her charges not merely across the Mason Dixon Line, but north into Canada, where the long arm of American law could not extend.

The secession of the Southern States and the eruption of war came to her as a summons to further action. "The good Lord has come down to deliver my people, and I must go and help Him.'"[38] Suddenly it was as if there were many Tubmans, so diffuse and diverse were her activities. She headed south to Florida with the Massachusetts Volunteers at the personal request of the State's Governor to lend her aid as a military guide and spy and to act as an emissary to the indentured population. She dined with Colonel Shaw and bade him and the 54th farewell on their march to eternal fame.[39] She crossed enemy lines and obtained helpful intelligence for use in future military operations. She cooked for the troops, tended their wounds and buried those that couldn't be saved. Her skills in treating dysentery, small pox and other ailments became renowned and much in demand. She took to wearing

[35] Bradford, op. cit., at p. 61.

[36] Id., at pp. 83-84.

[37] *Scott v. Emerson* (1852) 15 Mo. 576, 586.

[38] Samuel J. May, *Some Recollections of Our Antislavery Conflict* (Boston: Fields, Osgood, & Co., 1869), at p. 406.

[39] "The Moses of Her People: Proposed Memorial to Harriet Tubman," *The Sun*, May 2, 1909.

trousers and the blue cloak of a soldier and regularly carried a canteen, haversack and musket. When her expert knowledge of the terrain was required to aid in the removal of explosive devices from the Combahee River, the firing of plantations, destruction of railroads and cutting the enemy off from its sources of supply, she joined one of John Brown's former foot soldiers, Col. James Montgomery, on a mission that today seems so improbable as to be more fantasy than fact.[40]

It was said of the original Moses, as it was said of Tubman, that he was the most humble of persons, and yet both rose to the occasion in moments of crises to perform miracles that each would have been scandalized to hear being attributed to their own power and virtue rather than to the Lord's.[41] This great Christian lady—the breaker of chains, the veritable leader of men, and speaker of truth to power who became the greatest heroine of the age—was far more than that. She was arguably the greatest hero our nation has ever known, whose life story cannot be contemplated without awe and even emotion welling within the heart. Even that same President who is said by his critics to be hostile to her has acknowledged that she was indeed "fantastic."[42] Calling him a racist in the face of his public praise for the woman is perhaps more evidence of the standard tactic of the left to discredit their opponents by characterizing them in only the most rancid of terms. Rather than attribute his resistance to honoring the "fantastic" Tubman to a deep-seated affection for the founder of the Democrat Party, whose macho style of leadership, commitment to limited government and proud nationalism are in some ways akin to his own, his critics ascribe it to racism, as they do every single one of his policies and policy objectives. They are right about one thing, though. The President should overcome his apparent apprehension to honor Tubman, follow through on the Obama Administration's plan to put her face on the $20 bill, and place the new notes into circulation. In doing so, he honors the Party of Abraham Lincoln which he presently leads, the nation that long ago was said to have been "conceived in liberty," and the Great God who raised Tubman up in a moment of historic crisis as He did the Judges of old and in whom our currency says we have placed our collective trust.

---

[40] Bradford, op. cit., at p. 99.

[41] Num 12:3.

[42] Perry Bacon, Jr., "For Trump, Tubman on $20 Bill Illustrates Broader American Problem," www.cnbc.com, April 24, 2016.

The Gag Rule

ITS critics call it the "Gag Rule." Others refer to it as "one of the most sweeping federal assaults on abortion providers in decades."[1] Nearly everyone opposed to it considers it to be yet another example of the overreach by the "unqualified ideologues" of the Trump Administration that can only "make it harder for women to access health care."[2] Promulgated last year by the Department of Health & Human Services, the rule precludes the receivers of Title X moneys from either advocating abortion as a method of family planning or referring clients to abortion service providers, and requires a veritable "wall of separation" between a Title X funded program offered by an organization and any programs offered by the same organization taking a more favourable position toward abortion.

Over the years since the implementation of Title X, so intertwined with abortion advocacy have Title X funded programs become that the ability of many fund recipients to segregate resources as strictly as the new rule requires is all but impossible. As the recipient of nearly forty percent of all Title X moneys, Planned Parenthood very quickly contemplated the loss of "as much as $60 million in Title X funding."[3] It ultimately concluded that compliance with the new rule was impossible, cancelled its involvement with Title X and began looking elsewhere for funding, all while planning an elaborate litigation campaign in concert with California's Attorney General and twenty other jurisdictions. Once underway, the litigation scored victories in several District Courts and secured a nationwide preliminary injunction. The entire banc of justices sitting on the increasingly conservative Ninth Circuit Court of Appeals subsequently overruled the lower courts, vacated the injunctions and cleared the way for enforcement of the rule.

Calling the regulation "the Gag Rule" is, of course, calculated by its opponents to create the impression that it represents an attack on the fundamental liberties protected by the Constitution. It is an allusion to

---

[1] Mark Joseph Stern, "Trump's TRAP: The New Federal Gag Rule is Designed to Silence Doctors and Shutter Countless Abortion Clinics. It's Also a Flagrant Violation of the ACA," www.slate.com, March 7, 2019.

[2] Ariana Eunjung Cha, "Trump Administration's Abortion 'Gag Rule' Can Take Effect, Court Rules," www.thewashingtonpost.com, June 20, 2019

[3] Id.

the Gag Rule of old that mandated the tabling by the House of Representatives of all petitions addressing the matter of slavery and the need for its abolition. The name originated in the reaction of John Quincy Adams—then a member of the House—to being cut off during debate over the measure: "am I being gagged or am I not!?"[4] The rule, he shouted above frantic cries by the Speaker of the House for order, was "in direct violation of the Constitution of the United States, of the rules of the House, and of the rights of my constituents."[5] When informed that his colleagues would not permit even the referral of the petitions to the appropriate committee, he vowed to "speak at every possible opportunity about the gag itself, the 'sacred right' of petition, and the right of free speech."[6] Henceforth, every time he took the floor, regardless of the issue, he brought the matter up, even reading from petitions which the House rules forbade be disclosed. For four successive Congresses, spanning nearly eight years, the rule remained in place, as did Adams' guerrilla campaign on the knife edge of contempt. The long and ultimately successful struggle to defeat the rule became legend: the tale of the heroic effort of a lone politician against even his own party, raising him from a despised failed President to the status of a statesman, fearless in opposition to those who threatened him with death should he persist in his challenge.

The allusion to and attempt to connect with this noble history by opponents of the modern-day "Gag Rule" is utterly erroneous. The rule at issue hasn't actually prevented anyone from petitioning Congress for the redress of their grievances, nor from speaking out in favour of abortion. In the legal challenges currently pending, the rule hasn't even been cited as a violation of the First Amendment, let alone of any other provision in the Constitution.

That the rule is not a "gag rule" is evident from its history. Title X itself came into being in 1970, when Congress enacted the Public Health Service Act and authorized the Department of Health and Human Services to make grants to organizations that provide specified family planning services. In so doing, Congress delegated to the Department "broad authority to promulgate regulations to administer the grant

---

[4] Fred Kaplan, *John Quincy Adams: American Visionary* (New York: Harper Perennial, 2014), at pp. 490-491.

[5] Id., at p. 491.

[6] Id.

program, as well as to impose conditions on the grants that HHS 'may determine to be appropriate to assure that such grants will be effectively utilized for the purpose for which made.'" One significant restriction found within the law itself was that "none of the funds appropriated under this subchapter shall be used in programs where abortion is a method of family planning." The first regulations issued pursuant to Title X came in 1981, and included a provision permitting neutral (or "non-directive") counselling regarding abortion, so long as it was requested by the participant. This regulation was eliminated in 1988, when the Department re-evaluated the Act and concluded that Congress "intended to create 'a wall of separation between Title X programs and abortion as a method of family planning." Organizations that received Title X money were subsequently required to ensure that its Title X funded programs remained utterly and absolutely segregated from any programs they sponsored advocating or providing abortion. Any organizations whose principle business was abortion were ineligible to receive Title X funds.

The change prompted aggressive challenge in the matter of *Rust v. Sullivan*, prosecuted by Professors Lawrence Tribe and Kathleen Sullivan, primarily on First and Fifth Amendment grounds. The change in the rule, they argued, violated the First Amendment by impermissibly discriminating on the basis of viewpoint because it "prohibited 'all discussion about abortion as a lawful option—including counselling, referral, and the provision of neutral and accurate information about ending a pregnancy—while compelling the clinic or counsellor to provide information that promotes continuing a pregnancy to term."[7] The First Amendment, they contended, barred the conditioning of grants of federal money on the waiving of one's speech rights.

Heeding the opposing arguments of Solicitor General Kenneth Starr and his chief lieutenant, the future Chief Justice John Roberts, Chief Justice Rehnquist and the majority disagreed. The statute at issue was rooted in Congress's broad power to spend to advance the general welfare. In exercising its power, Congress was permitted to identify particular policy objectives and limit the spending of public money accordingly. "The Government can, without violating the Constitution, selectively fund a program to encourage certain activities it believes to

---

[7] *Rust v. Sullivan* (1991) 500 U.S. 173, 111 S.Ct. 1759.

be in the public interest, without at the same time funding an alternative program which seeks to deal with the problem in another way."[8] When it does so, "the government has not discriminated on the basis of viewpoint; it has merely chosen to fund one activity to the exclusion of the other."[9] To hold that when spending money to advance a particular idea, the government must spend money to advance all competing ideas "would render numerous government programs constitutionally suspect," including the National Endowment for Democracy, which aimed "to encourage other countries to adopt democratic principles."[10] As the government was not required to also use its money to encourage communism and fascism, it wasn't required to use public funds to pay for abortion advocacy or refer patients to abortion providers. Organizations that accepted Title X money, as well as their employees, were hardly prohibited from expressing their own views on their own time, and they could advocate abortion all day long so long as the advocacy did not occur within the context of programs the government funded.

The Court was even less troubled by the contention that the limitation on the use of Title X funds violated a woman's Fifth Amendment right to choose whether to terminate her pregnancy. The Due Process Clauses of the Fifth and Fourteenth Amendments "generally confer no affirmative right to governmental aid, even where such aid may be necessary to secure life, liberty, or property interests of which the government itself may not deprive the individual."[11] Congress opted to fund a program that did not include abortion advocacy or referral. This decision changed nothing with regard to the ability of women to avail themselves of their rights. Nor did it place any "governmental obstacle in the path of a woman who chooses to terminate her pregnancy."[12] Only an outright prohibition on seeking out information about abortion and the services of a professional to perform the procedure would constitute the kind of burden that a court would consider to be a violation of the Constitution.

---

[8] Id., at 193.
[9] Id.
[10] Id., at 194.
[11] Id., at 201.
[12] Id.

The criticism of *Rust* has been harsh and sustained. "The regulations upheld by the Supreme Court," said Dorothy Roberts, "violated the minds and bodies of women," and the violation (or "violence") was all the harsher for women of color.[13] Michael Fitzpatrick and others were concerned more broadly that the decision would allow the government to "'freely use benefits to shift viewpoints in a direction favourable to the existing regime,' thus expanding 'the sphere of state power by exerting moral and social control that it could not constitutionally impose directly.'"[14] Floyd Abrams "criticized the *Rust* majority for upholding the regulations and permitting a 'price-tag for the acceptance of public funds' that amounted to 'nothing less than a forfeiture of First Amendment rights.'"[15] Paula Berg said the decision opened the door to the government "using doctor-patient discourse as a tool for indoctrination" and failed to "protect patients' interest in receiving the information they need to exercise meaningfully their constitutional right to determine the course of their medical treatment."[16]

The criticism no doubt fuelled efforts to modify the underlying statute to cure what the critics saw as the fundamental defect. None of those efforts bore fruit. The statutory prohibition on the use of funds to promote abortion remained. Administrations came and went, and during their tenure the most they accomplished was modification of the subordinate regulation, allowing greater leeway with respect to what could be said about abortion. In time, the wall of separation intended by Congress weakened, and Title X funds—originally designed to promote childbirth—were lost in the fungible waters of organizational budgeting. Title X had become de facto public funding for the promotion of abortion for all purposes.

Few would have imagined that Donald Trump—a man whose political loyalties had long shifted with the wind—would prove such a proponent of classic liberalism that even the dominant figures in his own

---

[13] Dorothy E. Roberts, "Rust v. Sullivan and the Control of Knowledge" (1993). Faculty Scholarship. Paper 1207. http://scholarship.law.upenn.edu/faculty_scholarship/1207.

[14] Michael Fitzpatrick, "Rust Corrodes: The First Amendment Implications of *Rust v. Sullivan*," 45 Stan. L. Rev. 185 (1992), at p. 199.

[15] Id., at p. 200.

[16] Paula Berg, "Toward a First Amendment Theory of Doctor-Patient Discourse and the Right to Receive Unbiased Medical Advice," 74 B.U.L. Rev. 201 (1994), at p. 206.

party began to flinch. Nor was it predictable that a man whose own family relations and commitments were hardly conventional, and who staked out a staunchly pro-choice position as recently as 1999, would emerge as the greatest champion of the pro-life cause ever to occupy the oval office.[17] "The far left," he recently said at the March for Life in Washington, D.C., "is actively working to erase our God-given rights, shut down faith-based charities, ban religious believers from the public square, and silence Americans who believe in the sanctity of life.... They are coming after me because I am fighting for you and we are fighting for those who have no voice."[18] More recently still, he called on Congress to "pass legislation finally banning the late term abortion of babies."[19] The Rule—now known as the Final Rule—actually antedated these remarks. It was promulgated in March of 2019 and took a form almost identical to the 1988 incarnation upheld in *Rust*, with the exception that it permitted "non-directive pregnancy counselling" that included discussion of abortion, but only "so long as the counsellor neither refers for, nor encourages" the procedure.

Once the Final Rule was published, challenges mounted. After a back-and-forth battle for injunctive relief, the district courts in three states in the Ninth Circuit issued preliminary orders enjoining the Department from enforcement after determining that the challengers were likely to prevail on the merits of their claim that the changed rule, though nearly identical to the rule at issue in *Rust*, was contrary to the Department's own policy and was barred by a provision in the Affordable Care Act that prohibited restrictions on what health care providers could discuss with their patients. It was these injunctions that reached the Ninth Circuit Court of Appeals for its review in the consolidated matters of *State of California v. Azar*, *Essential Access Health, Inc. v. Azar*, and *Washington v. Azar*.

Though the Circuit Court was required to review the decision of lower courts in accordance with the highly deferential abuse of discretion standard, it nevertheless was entitled to consider the lower courts' interpretation of the relevant law de novo. A de novo review of

---

[17] Philip Bump, "Donald Trump Took 5 Different Positions on Abortion in 3 Days," www.thewashingtonpost.com, April 3, 2016.

[18] David Smith, "Trump Tells Anti-Abortion Activists at March for Life: 'I am Fighting for You," www.theguardian.com, January 24, 2020.

[19] Carla Hall, "Trump's State of the Union Attack on Abortion Rights was Pathetic— Even for Him," *The Los Angeles Times*, February 5, 2020.

the purely legal issue eliminated the advantage the plaintiffs had going into the hearing of the appeal. The fact that they were challenging the actions of a federal agency meant they were swimming against the current of a channel the progressive movement had cut starting a century before. Piece-by-piece a succession of courts, beginning in the early years of the Twentieth Century, constructed the edifice that is the modern administrative state. At present, a court will defer to an agency's expertise in identifying the appropriate course of action, refrain from substituting its own judgment for that of the agency or second guessing the agency's weighing of the risks and benefits, avoid penalizing it for departing from the inferences and assumptions of its critics, and eschew heightened review of agency decisions even when the agency changes course and replaces an old rule with a new one. Such a change will be deferred to even if the Court believes it is not superior to its predecessor. Conservatives of the libertarian wing of the movement long railed against this deferential approach to governance and dreamed of reversing it, but its deep entrenchment in the governing jurisprudence can't be disregarded in the adjudication of cases and controversies until that change comes to pass. The blade of the administrative state, thus, is now revealed to have more than a single edge.

The provision of the Affordable Care Act singled out as nullifying the prohibition on the distribution of Title X money to organizations dedicated to counselling about and even providing abortion was Section 1554, which provides that the Department "shall not promulgate any regulation that (1) creates any unreasonable barriers to the ability of individuals to obtain appropriate medical care; (2) impedes timely access to health care services; (3) interferes with communications regarding a full range of treatment options between the patient and the provider; (4) restricts the ability of health care providers to provide full disclosure of all relevant information to patients making health care decisions; (5) violates the principle of informed consent and the ethical standards of health care professionals; or (6) limits the availability of health care treatment for the full durations of a patient's medical needs." The Final Rule, said the plaintiffs, violated several of these provisions, by restricting the promotion of "medical care" in the form of abortion.

The Circuit Court disagreed. It disagreed because of the absence of any expression of intent in the ACA to alter the implementation of Congress's decision to allocate money to support some activities, but not others. Were the challenges here to the constitutionality of the government's action, a greater degree of scrutiny might have applied. But all at issue was the supposed conflict between one Act of Congress with another. Unless there is clear and unambiguous evidence that Congress intended to repeal a particular law, or that another law was designed to supersede it, the inference is that Congress intended each to remain in operation, hence they must be construed in a manner that would preserve both. That is exactly what the Court did in this instance. What Congress was doing with the ACA was directing private health care providers as to what they could and could not do. It was not changing its own prior decision to narrowly fund particular activities. Until Congress repealed the older law that limited the ability of health care providers to use money it received from Congress to fund particular activities, the ACA mandate embodied in Section 1554 did not apply in the context of the administration of the older law. Those in need of care beyond the scope of the program were hardly prevented from seeking it. They simply couldn't expect to obtain it from those providers operating in accordance with funds received through Title X. Clients were free to ask about abortion as an option to carrying a pregnancy to term, and once prompted in this way, a health care provider could provide the information in a non-directive, neutral manner. Title X funded providers just couldn't initiate the conversation and couldn't become an advocate once the conversation commenced.

The continuing criticism of *Rust*, and now of the Final Rule, while purporting to prove the roots of conservative opposition to abortion in a callousness toward the poor, a condescension toward women generally, and contempt for women of color in particular, actually reveals far more about the critics. One ought to think back to 1969, before Title X existed, when none of the support provided by the Act had come to be. Certainly, the situation facing the would-be beneficiaries improved in the wake of the law's enactment and remains better to this day notwithstanding the limitations on how the funding might be used. The critics, however, behave as if it is their sincere belief that because the law fails to provide all that they believe is necessary they have gained nothing, and rather than accept compromise on an issue touching upon the most controversial topic in the nation and focus on developing private resources to fill the gap, they cast aspersions on the opposition, litigate and lobby, and hope one way or the other to secure an extreme outcome without a thought for how it might violate the conscience of a large segment of the nation's population.

This attitude is a dishonest one, and finds a companion in the creation by its adherents of false standards that their opponents must live up to if they are to be true to what they supposedly believe in and thereby avoid the egregious sin of hypocrisy. As the merits of the *Azar* case will turn in large part on the Court's application of the traditional deference paid to administrative agencies, these critics expect that conservatives such as Justice Gorsuch, who have long been sceptical of the administrative state, "should have no difficulty striking down the Final Rule as the lawless work of unelected bureaucrats eager to disregard the plain text of a law passed by Congress" -- in this case the ACA.[20] The problem with this expectation, and the chalking up of its potential disappointment to conservative hypocrisy, is that the constitutionality of the administrative state and the deference that have empowered it over time are not at issue in the case. While Gorsuch and others might be prepared to support the reduction of the bureaucracy and the power it exercises, they will only do so in a case wherein the precedents supporting the so-called "fourth branch of government" are in the cross-hairs of the litigants. So long as the precedents girding the administrative state are not challenged, it shouldn't come as any surprise that the textualist Gorsuch will be applying traditional canons of construction, including the principles that repeal by implication is disfavoured and that provisions of a legal texts be interpreted in a way that renders them compatible, not contradictory.[21]

There is some irony in the fact that the harshest critic of the administrative state on the Court might disregard his qualms for the moment in a matter that a stricter standard of review for administrative actions might result in the government's defeat. The irony lies in the critics' ordinary love for the ceding of legislative and executive power to administrative agencies, and how in this case the methodically constructed battery of rules devised by the Supreme Court over the course of a century might be deployed to ensure the survival of a rule aiming to defeat what for many of the critics is an element of their most cherished right. The irony will be all the more pronounced when, in the

---

[20] Stern, op. cit.

[21] Canons of Construction: Adapted from Scalia & Garner, www.law.uh.edu/faculty/adjunct/dstevenson/2018spring.

wake of upholding the Ninth Circuit's recent decision, as direct challenges to the legal foundation of the rule-making authority of administrative agencies come before it, the Court takes the hammer to the very principles employed here in defense of the Final Rule. The so-called Gag Rule will survive unscathed. In the long run, the same may not be true of the bureaucracy that promulgated it.

Who's The Boss?

THE long war against the current Administration's immigration policy began in earnest, when the acting head of the Justice Department, a holdover from the Obama Era, publicly declared her unwillingness to enforce the President's so-called Travel Ban because she was not "convinced that the executive order is lawful."[1] The moment marked the first opportunity the President had to use the catch phrase he'd made famous on television, and certainly not the last. The war continued through many phases, including more recently in the form of a lawsuit by three would-be asylum seekers challenging both the policy of requiring anyone seeking asylum from across the southern border to remain in Mexico while their requests were vetted and the man appointed by the President to administer it. Contending that the policy was invalid because Ken Cuccinelli, the Director of Citizenship and Immigration Services, lacked any governmental authority on account of his appointment being contrary to law, the suitors met with a receptive audience in the person of Judge Randolph Moss of the United States District Court for the District of Columbia. In a fifty-five page opinion, Judge Moss ruled that the official action taken against the plaintiffs was invalid because the Director's appointment was in violation of an Act of Congress governing the temporary succession in executive departments that lose their chief official. The Judge's ruling, declared Immigration activist Anne Harkey, "is a big win that confirms Ken Cuccinelli's installation and service as acting director of USCIS was unlawful. This is

[1] David Smith, Ben Jacobs & Spencer Ackerman, "Sally Yates Fired by Trump After Acting US Attorney General Defied Travel Ban," www.theguardian.com, January 31, 2017.

both a victory for the rule of law and a significant blow to the Trump Administration's xenophobic agenda."[2]

The decision may or may not reach the Supreme Court for review. Cuccinelli has, of course, stated that an appeal is certain.[3] The President has already moved to neutralize the decision by reissuing the policy without Cuccinelli's imprimatur. It likely won't impede the Administration's immigration goals, though it might open the nation's gate wide enough for the few claimants who brought the case to squeeze through. The matter, in truth, is but a blip in the larger scandal of the President's personnel chaos that seems part of the President's brand, yet remarkably incapable of derailing the advancement of the President's agenda. An irritant, however, it remains, and an impediment of some kind to the President's ability to rely on personnel within the executive branch to execute the policies of his choice.

Such problems are hardly unprecedented. The most prominent incident of the kind during the early years of the Republic was Andrew Jackson's failed attempts to compel his own Treasury Secretary to divest national assets from the Bank of the United States. When Jackson fired the Secretary, the Senate retaliated by censuring the President for assuming "the exercise of a power over the treasury of the United States, not granted to him by the Constitution and laws, and dangerous to the liberties of the people."[4] Jackson demurred, and stated in response that because "the whole executive power" was vested by the Constitution in the President, "who is responsible for its exercise," it was "a necessary consequence that he should have a right to employ agents of his own choice to aid him in the performance of his duties, and to discharge them when he is no longer willing to be responsible for their acts."[5] Permitting the Senate "to interfere with this exercise of Executive power," Jackson warned, "would inevitably lead to the complete destruction of executive independence," and would "leave the President as powerless as he

[2] Stephen Dinan, "Judge Rules Cuccinelli Appointment to Citizenship Office was Illegal," *The Washington Times*, March 2, 2020.

[3] Anna Giaritelli, "Cuccinelli Refuses to Leave DHS After Judge Finds He Was Illegally Appointed to His Prior Role There," www.washingtonexaminer.com, March 2, 2020.

[4] Steven G. Calabresi & Christopher S. Yoo, "The Removal Power: The Unitary Executive During the First Half-Century," 47 Case W. Res. 1451 (1997), at p. 1544.

[5] Id., at p. 1548.

would be useless—the shadow of authority after the substance had departed."[6]

President Andrew Johnson's struggle three decades later was far more significant. Jackson's Treasury Secretary dithered; Johnson's War Secretary profusely leaked executive confidences to the President's opponents in Congress and actively worked to undermine the President's authority to execute policy. After Congress enacted the Tenure of Office Act in March of 1867, mandating Senate approval for removal of any official requiring Senate confirmation at the time of appointment, the recalcitrant Secretary became "more open and defiant of the President and 'assumed the task of inspiring in Congress the belief that his chief, the President, was a desperate character, bent on overriding the majority by military force.'"[7] When the President defied the Act and fired the Secretary, Congress went a step further than Andrew Jackson's adversaries by sending Articles of Impeachment to the Senate and prompting a trial that fell short of a conviction by a single vote.

The actions of Presidents Jackson and Johnson were actually less constitutionally controversial than the contemporary uproar suggests. From Washington's time through the various administrations of the early Republic, the general consensus was that the President's authority to take care that the laws be executed extended to the authority to remove an official in whom his confidence was lost. Summing up the relevant history, Chief Justice Taft concluded that "Article II grants to the President the executive power of the Government, i.e., the general administrative control of those executing the laws, including the power of appointment and removal of executive officers—a conclusion confirmed by his obligation to take care that the laws be faithfully executed; that Article II excludes the exercise of legislative power by Congress to provide for appointments and removals, except only as granted therein to Congress in the matter of inferior officers;...that the provisions of the second section of Article II, which blend action by the legislative branch, or by part of it, in the work of the executive, are limitations to be strictly construed and not to be extended by implication; that the President's power of removal is further established

---

[6] Id., at 1551.

[7] Robert W. Winston, *Andrew Johnson: Plebian and Patriot* (New York: Henry Holt and Company, 1928), at p. 417.

as an incident to his specifically enumerated function of appointment by and with the advice of the Senate, but that such incident does not by implication extend to removals...; and finally that to hold otherwise would make it impossible for the President, in case of political or other differences with the Senate or Congress, to take care that the laws be faithfully executed."[8] To permit the Senate or the Congress as a whole to control the removal of an official subordinate to the President, would be, said Taft, to thwart "the Executive in the exercise of his great powers and in the bearing of his great responsibility, by fastening upon him, as subordinate executive officers, men who by their inefficient service under him, by their lack of loyalty to the service, or by their different views of policy, might make his taking care that the laws be faithfully executed most difficult or impossible."[9] For the Senate to exercise even part of the power jointly with the President, would, in the words of James Madison, "abolish at once that great principle of unity and responsibility in the Executive department, which was intended for the security of liberty and the public good."[10]

The removal power is considered a fundamental mechanism whereby the President is able to exert his authority over the executive branch. Without the power to remove, the President lacks any leverage over his subordinates. Absence of the power would release "those who are employed in the execution of the law" from awareness of the "proper situation" and disrupt "the chain of dependence" whereby "the lowest officers, the middle grade, and the highest...depend, as they ought, on the President."[11] In the absence of any consequence for disobedience to the President's directives, agents and employees of the various executive departments would be free to develop their own policy, to execute it, and defy the President's efforts to impose preferences of his own.

Of course, if the President is unable to appoint in the first place, there is no leverage to exercise through use of the threat of removal. Offices would simply sit empty. In the early days of the Republic, this wasn't so terrible a prospect given the diminutive size of the departments and the small number of persons employed. In those days, President Washington and his immediate successors "often exerted their control

---

[8] *Myers v. United States* (1926) 272 U.S. 52, 47 S.Ct. 21, 41.
[9] Id., at 30.
[10] Id., citing 1 Annals of Congress, 499.
[11] Id.

over the execution of the laws and did not hesitate to direct lower-level executive officials."[12] Control extended even to the supervision of the conduct of U.S. attorneys, the determination of what charges to bring, and against whom mercy in the form pardon might be shown. The expansion of the size of government has rendered such scrutiny and control impossible and forced Presidents to rely more heavily on appointees. When the Senate is controlled by a President's political party, the confirmation of a President's nominees goes relatively smoothly. When government is divided, the process tends to be far more challenging. President Obama's nominees to chief positions, for instance, became especially difficult to get confirmed during his second term when the Republican Party thwarted the Democrat majority through procedural mechanisms and then assumed control of the Senate. To overcome the Senate's refusal to confirm his nominees, President Obama took to rather aggressive use of the power to fill vacant positions during Senate recesses. The problem with this strategy to overcome opposition to his personnel preferences was that the Senate hadn't really recessed. It had adjourned temporarily during a pro-forma session that was a session in name only. When the matter came before the Supreme Court, all nine justices agreed that the Senate was the sole judge of when it was in session and when it wasn't, and that its determination on this point controlled whether or not a recess appointment could be made.[13] The only dispute among the justices was whether recesses could occur in the midst of a session, or only at the end of one.

President Trump's travails in this area have been particularly acute. When he won the Presidency against Hillary Clinton and the Democrats, he'd already bulldozed his way through a field of the best and brightest in his own Party and alienated in the process most of the Party's leadership, including Mitch McConnell. The Senate, though controlled by the President's Party, was reticent to give the President too much benefit of the doubt in the confirmation of his nominees. Meanwhile, the departments of government remained under the control of holdovers from the Obama Administration, most of whom were opposed, if not utterly hostile, to the President and the policies he'd promised to

---

[12] Calabresi & Yoo, op. cit., at p. 1561.

[13] *National Labor Relations Board v. Noel Canning* (2014) 573 U.S. 513, 134 S.Ct. 2550.

undertake. The uprising of the execrable Sally Yates, who screamed her defiance of executive orders she erroneously deemed to be illegal, was but the first of a series of open and unprecedented rebellions against the President within the Executive Branch. The rebellions continued even after Yates's termination in the form of the spy ops run by the nation's security agencies, and culminated in the appointment of Special Counsel Mueller to investigate a completely contrived conspiracy by the Trump campaign to undermine American democracy in concert with the Russian government. Repeated disappointment in many of his appointees, manifest in tweeted criticism followed by resignation or termination, created repeated gaps in the leadership of important agencies and led to the designation of "acting secretaries" to avoid the lengthy process of Senate confirmation and the statutory succession plan that too often put yet more Obama holdovers in charge of executing policies they preferred to stymie. Cuccinelli was a special case, disliked by the Republican Senate Majority Leader for support he'd provided to the latter's electoral opponent, and by the caucus generally for his "career in attacking other Republicans."[14]

To overcome the obstacles to placing his preferred man in command of immigration enforcement policy, the President appointed Cuccinelli to the newly minted position of Principal Deputy Director of USCIS five days after the chief position became vacant. The Acting Secretary of Homeland Security then issued a memorandum designating the Principal Deputy Director to be the chief assistant and most senior subordinate, who was to assume command of the department in the event of a vacancy at the top, thereby leaping over the existing senior deputy originally slated to temporarily take the helm. It was a rather ingenious scheme, albeit a patent work-around of the requirement that principal officers of the government receive Senate confirmation and that all other officers be appointed in accordance with rules enacted by Congress. It also ran afoul of the Federal Vacancies Reform Act (FVRA), which provided that vacancies at the top of government agencies be filled by "the first assistant to the office of such officer," who "shall perform the functions and duties of the office temporarily in an acting capacity" until the Senate confirmed a permanent replacement. The President might circumvent this procedure by designating an acting

[14] Jordain Carney, "Republicans Warn Cuccinelli Won't Get Confirmed by GOP Senate," www.thehill.com, June 10, 2019.

department head of his own preference, but only if the person so designated had already served in a senior position in that agency for at least 90 days during the 365-day period preceding the occurrence of the vacancy.

Barring formal nomination followed by Senate confirmation, Cuccinelli's path to remaining in office and exercising authority that would have the binding effect of law was to obtain his position in compliance with the FVRA. The Executive's attempt to manufacture compliance with the Act by appointing Cuccinelli to a new position with an authoritative title, followed by his formal designation as chief in the line of succession, was utterly unconvincing to Judge Moss as a means of cementing the appointment. The fundamental and irrefutable flaw, he said, was that Cuccinelli "did and never will serve in a subordinate role—that is, as an 'assistant' to any other USCIS official."[15] For this reason, he said, the Executive's "contention that his appointment satisfies the FVRA cannot be squared with the text, structure, or purpose" of that law. Cuccinelli was made a Principle Deputy, which implies he was the top assistant, but in truth, he had never served as an assistant to anyone. Instead, he was immediately vested with the sceptre of authority over his department. He didn't "qualify as a 'first assistant' because he was assigned the role of principal on day-one and, by design, he never has served and never will serve 'in a subordinate capacity' to any other official at USCIS." It defied the rationale of the statute for a person to be appointed as the principal assistant after the head position became vacant, and thereby immediately qualify as the acting departmental head. So contrived an elevation simply couldn't be accepted as legitimate, hence the ability of Cuccinelli to issue binding orders was utterly absent and any orders he'd actually issued were ultra vires and without effect on anyone, including the plaintiffs bringing the case.

Judge Moss was undoubtedly correct that Cuccinelli's appointment was contrary to existing law. It didn't conform to the process set forth in Article II of Constitution whereby the President can fill vacancies in the government; nor was it consistent with the statutory method of providing for temporary leadership when departments become leaderless. He is likely incorrect, however, in his assumption that the

[15] "Memorandum Opinion & Order," *L.M.-M et al. v. Kenneth T. Cuccinelli II*, Case No. 1:19-cv-02676.

FVRA is a valid exercise of Congress's power to legislate. Congress only has power to provide for appointment of inferior officers; its power over principal officers consists only of unicameral, Senate confirmation. As the President is vested by the Constitution with all Executive Power, he has the authority to direct the departments as he sees fit. Congress has no authority to mandate who shall temporarily preside over the departments of the President's government. Confirmation of that fact lies in the fate of Sally Yates, who rose to pre-eminence in the Justice Department in accordance with the FVRA, but whose defiance of the President resulted in her immediate termination. She was fired, and there was nothing the Congress could do about it. The President, in fact, could have kept firing officials as they assumed the chief position until he found one to his liking without running afoul of any law. If this assessment isn't true, then there is no substance to the vesting of executive power with the President, nor in the vaunted principle of the separation of powers.

Judge Moss was wrong about something else. He concluded that Cuccinelli's actions as acting head of the department were ultra vires due to his lack of lawful authority. A purely discretionary decision by an improperly appointed agent might in fact be without legal effect. But Cuccinelli's acts in the form of the directives he issued were not of his own devising. They were but the policy preferences of the President himself, and Cuccinelli was but the agent who published them. As the chief of a unified executive, the President might have published the directives personally, but instead he authorized Cuccinelli's department to do so. Cuccinelli exercised no discretion in the matter; he was simply doing the President's bidding. Even were this not the case, the Administration quickly cured the defect following Judge Moss's ruling by reissuing each of the directives struck down by the court.

Cuccinelli, of course, isn't a valid appointee. For a short amount of time he might have been a lawful acting chief of the Department. He ought to have been formally nominated to the office, or someone else should have been, so that his temporary leadership was just that, temporary. No President can long circumvent compliance with Article II and expect that the culture of our Constitution can withstand erosion. In a nation of 350 million people, there ought to be at least one person in whom both the President and the Senate might have confidence to perform competently in a particular position, particularly in light of just how much a cypher executive officers can be and often are in a branch of government over which the President has such constitutionally permissible control. In the end, it really doesn't matter who a President nominates and entrusts with executive branch business. So long as they enforce the President's lawful policy preferences, their job will be secure.

Credit, Where No Credit is Due

THE chronicle of early California is replete with confusion over the Constitution and laws of the State. Uncertainty over language governing the tenure in elected and appointed office bred competing claims for the same position, spawned litigation and occasionally sparked violence between competing candidates. When William Stark Manlove prevailed in an election for the office of Sheriff in Sacramento County, his defeated opponent claimed the law permitted him to continue in office into his successor's term in order to complete unresolved duties.[1] Dr. Samuel Langdon attempted to assume the position as Director of the State Lunatic Asylum, only to be rebuffed by an incumbent who claimed continuing tenure on account of his reading of the law defining tenure in office and the mechanism of appointment.[2] A year later, Langdon himself made similar claims when yet another candidate appeared, expecting to assume his duties in an office the incumbent refused to vacate.[3] Most comical of all was the opening of the Court for the Fourth District in the City of San Francisco in January of 1859, when two incumbents simultaneously arrived to convene the court and call the calendar. Unable to take the bench on account of the presence of a large body of men in support of either candidate, the two self-styled judges each gave a statement explaining their right to the judicial office before retreating to the company of their respective attorneys.[4]

On the federal level there aren't many examples of similar controversies between self-styled incumbents for the same office—until just two years ago, when President Trump appointed former

---

1 *Manlove v. White* (1857) 8 Cal. 376.
2 *People ex rel. Reid* (1856) 6 Cal. 288.
3 *People ex rel. Aylett v. Langdon* (1857) 8 Cal. 1.
4 *The Sacramento Daily Union*, January 11, 1859.

congressman and Director of the Office of Management and Budget to take temporary helm of the Consumer Financial Protection Bureau (or CFPB) following the resignation of its Director, Richard Cordray. The controversy arose when the President's appointee, Mick Mulvaney, found Leandra English occupying the position, claiming the statute creating the office authorized the Department's chief lieutenant to act when the director was "unavailable," and that this very specific statute pre-empted the more generally applicable law governing the filling by the President of temporary vacancies. Finding that rare judge in the District of Columbia unwilling to heed the demands of a progressive litigant battling the Great Satan Trump, English's request for emergency injunctive relief met with disappointment. Her lawsuit only ended when the Administration agreed not to insist on Mulvaney's permanent appointment. It was a small victory for the progressive holdovers of the Obama Era, but essentially meaningless in light of the President's success in scuttling the Bureau by the capture of the only position in it that mattered.

The struggle for control of the office wasn't merely a chapter in the long saga of the American president's power to appoint. It was a front in the war between a particular president who vowed to reduce the scope of the administrative state and those who saw the bureaucracy generally and this office specifically as the guarantor of a long-term commitment to statism in this country. The office was a novel creation, conceived in the immediate wake of the great mortgage melt-down of 2008 that brought to ruin much of the financial sector, the stock and mortgage markets, and enterprise in the United States, and provided the very type of emergency that statists always dream of as a justification for the latest coming of messianic government. With the Toxic Assets Relief Program (TARP) and the Affordable Care Act (ACA), the CFPB was one of a trio of initiatives President Obama and the Democrat majority in Congress enacted in the brief era of undivided progressive government at the beginning of the President's first term. While TARP supposedly aimed to jump-start a stalled economy, but in truth was designed to buy the loyalty of favoured businesses through life-saving subsidies, and the ACA brought the health care industry into closer orbit around the national government, the Dodd-Frank bill of which the CFPB was a part placed tighter controls on the financial industry and streamlined the regulatory processes that permitted the siphoning of wealth to whomever government desired it to go.

The CFPB was to be the enforcement arm of the new financial regime. It was, said Eric Pearson, an agency like no other.[5] The overarching feature of the Bureau was its near complete independence from control by any of the three branches of government. While nominally an executive branch department whose chief was nominated by the President subject to confirmation by the Senate, the Bureau's Director would serve for a term of five years, thus ensuring a tenure that exceeded that of any President who might prove hostile. Executive hostility was further neutered by a prohibition on removal except for objective misconduct. While Congress created the Bureau and the Senate confirmed its Director following nomination by the President, the Bureau's dependence on the Legislature ended there. Instead of being subject to the normal appropriations process originating in the House of Representatives and suffering perpetual threat in the form of budget cuts, the Bureau was formally grafted onto the essentially independent Federal Reserve, with funding drawn directly from the Fed in an amount roughly $400 million per year. Its broad rule-making authority, power to prosecute and discretion in the adjudication of its own prosecutions was expressly subject to the most deferential of standards of judicial review, hence removing much of any threat of interference with its operation by the courts. The accumulation of fines and civil penalties ensured that the money to fund its operations incentivized perpetual motion in litigation and guaranteed an interminable swelling of its budget.

These startling design features, said Hosea Harvey, "were needed, in part, to consolidate regulatory authority and other functions from numerous other federal regulatory agencies," and would allow the Bureau protection "from outside influence" emanating from the other branches of government as it pursued its vital mission, particularly during "turbulent political times."[6] There was a thought, too, to lessen the possibility that the Bureau might suffer the predictable fate of most

---

[5] Eric Pearson, "A Brief Essay on the Constitutionality of the Consumer Financial Protection Bureau," 47 Creighton L. Rev. 99 (2013), at p. 104.

[6] Hosea H. Harvey, "Constitutionalizing Consumer Financial Protection: The Case for the Consumer Financial Protection Bureau," 103 Minn. L. Rev. 2429 (2019), at pp. 2430 and 2434.

bureaucratic agencies of being "captured" by the very industry it was charged with regulating.[7] That, at least, is what some proponents said, but the more likely rationale was not to prevent capture by the financial industry, but by Republican Congresses and Presidents who might pare back its regulatory power to less grandiose proportions and hobble its mission to pick and choose winners in the market place.

It's certainly reasonable for those who support a law and enact it to have sought to protect it from revision or repeal. The better inquiry is whether the features of the CFPB that separate it so remotely from political and judicial control are consistent with the requirements of the Constitution. Certainly, it can be said that the division of sovereignty outlined by the first three Articles of the Constitution suggest that a combination of all three of the respective sovereign powers in a single agency is highly suspect. So too is the vesting of executive, legislative and judicial power in a single office holder whose position falls within the executive branch, under nominal authority of the President, yet who is largely independent from the President's ability to control through the power to remove.

The *Myers* case decided nearly a century ago establishes the President's power to remove any executive branch official due to the President's repose at the apex of the pyramid of the executive branch hierarchy.[8] The novelty of administrative organization, however, wasn't under consideration in *Myers*, hence when the legitimacy of a novel agency was at issue before the Supreme Court some years later in the matter of *Humphrey's Executor v. United States*, the Court hesitated to rely on the *Myers* precedent at all. In a challenge to the power of the President to remove a commissioner serving on the Federal Trade Commission, an aggrieved heir, seeking recovery of his deceased benefactor's unpaid wages, defended Congress's decision to restrict the President's removal power to those situations where misbehaviour justified its exercise. Speaking through the normally conservative Justice George Sutherland, the Court agreed with the heir. The Commission, said Sutherland, was "an administrative body created by Congress to carry into effect legislative policies embodied in the statute in accordance with the legislative standard therein prescribed, and to perform other specified

[7] Pearson, op. cit., at p. 103.

[8] *Myers v. United States* (1926) 272 U.S. 52, 47 S.Ct. 21.

duties as a legislative or as a judicial aid."[9] In prescribing rules to enjoin unfair methods of competition, "the Commission acts in part quasi-legislatively."[10] In acting as a master in chancery to adjudicate violations of the commission's regulations, it acts "in part quasi-judicially."[11] Not being entirely an executive agency, the FTC and its agents and employees could not be said to be a purely executive functionaries, fully under the control of the President. Congress was free to insulate its operation from executive control by minimizing the President's power to remove its personnel. The President might exert control in his own house, but not in the house of another. To allow the President to control the Commission through his general power to remove officers in whom he lacks confidence would threaten "the independence of the Commission which is not only wholly disconnected from the executive department, but which…was created by Congress as a means of carrying into operation legislative and judicial departments."[12]

In retrospect, the decision is utterly dismaying. The ordinarily brilliant and thorough George Sutherland, typically hostile to the delegation of power belonging to one branch to another, and normally committed to the classical vision of the Constitution wherein three branches wielded the power to check one another, inexplicably deviated from the expected analysis, even to the extent of jettisoning his penchant for very thorough exploration and explanation of the legal authorities. Rather than resting on a solid foundation of jurisprudence, case law and analysis, Sutherland's conclusion rests virtually on itself. That Congress even had the power to create administrative agencies that blended elements of all three sovereignties he took for granted, saying merely that the power was one that could not be doubted. Why he acted in so uncharacteristic a fashion is not entirely known, though it could be that his hostility to Franklin Roosevelt and the New Deal offers something of an explanation. He was the intellectual leader of the classically liberal wing of the Court, and became even more so upon Roosevelt's election. He wrote the majority opinions in *Adkins v. Children's Hospital* and *New Ice Co. v. Liebmann* striking down laws that interfered with the rights to

---

[9] *Humphrey's Executor v. United States* (1935) 295 U.S. 602, 55 S.Ct. 869, 874

[10] Id.

[11] Id.

[12] Id., at 875.

contract and pursue a common calling.[13] He dissented powerfully in *Home Building & Loan Assn. v. Blaisdell,* disputing the majority's upholding of a state law altering the rights and remedies of contracting parties.[14] He joined the Chief Justice's majority opinions in *Panama Refining Co. v. Ryan* and *A.L.A. Schechter Poultry Company v. United States,* striking down the N.L.R.A. as an invalid delegation of legislative power to the Executive Branch and private industry, and also wrote the majority opinion in *Carter v. Carter Coal Company,* invalidating the Guffy Act as an invasion by the Congress of the sovereign powers of the States to regulate entirely intrastate commercial and non-commercial activities.[15] The *Humphrey's* case didn't involve the vital principles of federalism, fundamental economic rights or the power of the Congress to delegate legislative and executive powers to administrative agencies. Instead, it involved the narrow issue of the President' authority to control an agency that had been acting defensively against the tide of the New Deal, in a manner consistent with Sutherland's own policy preferences. It makes considerable sense that the decision reflected his desire to thwart the New Deal and preserve in office appointees whose tenure predated Roosevelt's in order that they might continue their resistance, rather than a fundamental difference with *Myers* and the well-crafted opinion in that case by Chief Justice Taft. Indeed, as noted by Professor Paul Moreno, "it looked to many New Dealers that Sutherland and the conservatives on the Court had designed the opinion to spite the President."[16]

Regardless of the reasons why Sutherland and majority so substantially deviated from the *Myers* precedent and so blithely concluded that the President was constrained in his ability to terminate the services of certain Executive Branch officials with whom he disagreed, it proved revolutionary in a way they likely never intended. The conclusive statement by a pre-eminently conservative member of the Court that the restraints imposed by *Myers* didn't apply when

---

[13] *Adkins v. Children's Hospital* (1923) 261 U.S. 525, 43 S.Ct. 394 and *New Ice Co. v. Liebmann* (1932) 285 U.S. 262, 52 S.Ct. 262.

[14] *Home Building & Loan Assn. v. Blaisdell* (1934) 290 U.S. 398, 54 S.Ct. 231.

[15] *Panama Refining Co. v. Ryan* (1935) 293 U.S. 388, 55 S.Ct. 241; *A.L.A. Schechter Poultry Company v. United States* (1935) 295 U.S. 495, 55 S.Ct. 837; and *Carter v. Carter Coal Company* (1936) 298 U.S. 238, 56 S.Ct. 855.

[16] Paul D. Moreno, *The Bureaucrat Kings: The Origins and Underpinnings of America's Bureaucratic State* (Santa Barbara: Praeger, 2017), at p. 94.

administrative agencies blended the powers of all three branches of government hastened the erosion of the principle of the separation of powers. Where a "state" of the kind contemplated by Europeans barely existed prior to the 1930s, America would afterward lead the way in the elaboration of the so-called rechsstaadt. The most enthusiastic champion of this trend was the scholar James M. Landis, who chided the decisions that obstructed the New Deal as "grounded on models of government that were unrealistic in a modern industrial society" and "based on the limited conceptions of government associated with a far less industrialized and less democratic social order than that which early twentieth century Americans were experiencing."[17] If government "was to respond effectively to the new conditions and problems of modern life, the institutions of that government should assume a shape that best enabled them to facilitate that response. Essentialist constitutional conceptions of the branches of government needed to yield, in this context, to pragmatic ones."[18]

As Landis's mentor Felix Frankfurter and other progressive-minded men replaced Sutherland and his more conservative colleagues on the Court, Landis's viewpoint overtook the Court's jurisprudence. The concern over legislative delegation disappeared, as did any substantial concept of economic liberty, and with it went any remaining deference to *Myers*. In its place emerged *Humphrey's Executor* and its principle that Congress might vest executive authority with an executive agency, but nearly completely insulate it from executive control. Instead of looking at the text of the Constitution and the structure of government its text defines as the source of rigid limits on the rights and powers of the respective branches, the Court now tends to balance the power of a particular branch against the encroachment upon that power, and will only invalidate the latter if it unduly burdens the exercise by the branch of its fundamental responsibilities.[19] For the modern Court, flexibility to address what the Congress considers to be compelling social problems has taken precedence over the rather quaint notion of the separation of

---

[17] G. Edward White, *The Constitution and the New Deal* (Cambridge: Harvard University Press, 2000), at pp. 114-115.

[18] Id., at p. 115.

[19] Lee A. Deneen, "Defeating a Wolf Clad as a Wolf: Formalism and Functionalism in Separation-of-Powers Suits Against the Consumer Financial Protection Bureau," 48 Ga. L. Rev. 579 (2014), at p. 586.

powers as the key to guaranteeing a government that is incapable of exploiting the governed.

The foundational principles of the administrative state are currently under siege. The Trump Administration has made it clear that the President intends to reduce its power. He has accomplished much of his goal by cutting administrative regulations by a third and appointing agency heads who are committed to reducing governmental control over private enterprise. A repeat of TARP seems unlikely and unnecessary given the positive response by the economy to substantial reductions in taxes and the recession of the regulatory environment. Obamacare remains in place, but its most obnoxious features, designed to direct Americans into government-controlled health care markets, have been eliminated through reduction and alteration of regulations promulgated by the Department of Health & Human Services and the setting of the notorious "tax" known as the individual mandate to zero. The last man standing of the Obama Era innovations that so dramatically expanded governmental control over the private sector is the CFPB.

The President won the first round in his effort to reduce the Bureau's power by installing his own appointee in the Directorship and reversing the pace of litigation. As for subsequent rounds, it's probable that the administration isn't particularly enthusiastic about defending the Bureau in a variety of challenges that are now working their way through the courts. The law certainly is vulnerable on numerous fronts, including the "(a) agency's broad empowerment; (b) its relative immunity from Congressional oversight, courtesy of the agency's self-funding authority; (c) its relative immunity from executive oversight, courtesy of the Director's removal protections; and (d) its relative immunity from judicial oversight, courtesy of the requirement for courts to review the CFPB's statutory interpretations with high deference."[20] As the Framers "took every reasonable step to assure that no one branch would gain an ascendancy over the others," the combination of elements rendering the CFPB so powerful and independent from political and judicial control "seriously undermines the intended distribution of authority" as set forth in the Constitution.[21] "With respect to the Congress, it can undercut and usurp a legislative priority or the realization of a congressional goal by its unilateral initiatives. It can,

[20] Pearson, op. cit., at p. 104.
[21] Id., at pp. 120 and 121.

without fear of opposition, fundamentally reorder the vast financial sector of the private economy," and all without any say and even contrary to the wishes of the elected officials in the executive and legislative departments.[22]

Most ominous of all for the champions of the administrative state and its manifestation in the form of the CFPB is the President's appointment to the Supreme Court of Brett Kavanaugh. Lambasted and smeared as a sexual predator, but whose entire life belied the claim of the bizarre woman with the baby-like voice from the lunatic fringe of the so-called left coast who walked away from the scandal that her implausible accusations spawned with a pile of cash from anonymous go-fund-me donors never to utter a word afterward outside of the libel-free zone of the Senate's hearing room, Kavanaugh won the President's confidence through his learned and able articulation of the classical liberal position. When offered the chance to review the CFPB as a member of the D.C. Circuit Court of Appeals, Kavanaugh struck it down as a gross violation of the separation of powers. When the entire Court of the D.C. Circuit reversed him, he eloquently defended his original position, explaining that it was the mandate of the Constitution to keep the powers of the state segregated and supreme within their respective branches. *Myers,* not *Humphrey's,* was the salient precedent, and the latter, if it actually was valid authority, stood only for a narrow exception to the rule that the President controls the Executive Branch. The agencies the Supreme Court has previously upheld, starting with the FTC and continuing with the War Claims Commission, tended to have pronounced judicial dimensions, which justified some insularity from the arbitrary power of the President to remove. Other independent agencies winning approval by the Court have at least displayed some further internal restraints in the form of commission leadership, rather than having power vested in a single director. Judge Kavanaugh thought it notable that in the case of the CFPB, "the Director… wields enormous power over American business, American consumers and the overall U.S. economy…, unilaterally implements and enforces 19 federal consumer protection statutes, covering everything from home finance to student loans to credit cards to banking," and "alone may decide what rules to issue… how to enforce, when to enforce, and against whom to

---

[22] Id.

enforce the law,...whether an individual or entity has violated the law" and "what sanctions and penalties to impose."[23] The vesting of all this power in a single unelected and politically unaccountable Director presents a constitutional anomaly in the form of an executive branch figure who "possesses more unilateral authority—that is, authority to take action on one's own, subject to no check—than any single commissioner or board member in any other independent agency in the U.S. Government."[24] Indeed, said Kavanaugh, the Director "enjoys more unilateral authority than any other official in any of the three branches of the U.S. Government" with the exception of the President himself.[25] While many independent agencies might be dubious from an Article II standpoint, they at least have the sanction of the Supreme Court. This particular agency, however, is headed by a single director vested with far too much executive power, hence it violates the purpose, governing text and function of the executive branch.

Few if any of the decisions that have upheld the viability of the CFPB or any other administrative agency ever bothered to discuss the wisdom or the efficacy of such innovations. In the case of the CFPB, its defenders cite such things as the $12 billion in monetary relief to approximately twenty-seven million consumers, the half a billion dollars in civil penalties levied, the scrutiny it provides the operation of 135 banks, credit unions and non-depository mortgage lenders, its regulation of pay day loans, debt collection and overdraft services, the easing of restrictions on borrowing by non-white loan applicants, and the wave of rules that mandate further disclosures, underwriting and other loan origination procedures.[26] What the true impact the CFPB is having on overall economic health isn't as widely touted, let alone studied. Many of its actions appear to be heavy handed: imposing a $100 million fine on an organization that for years had relied on another agency's opinions; cancelling debts incurred by borrowers; and encouraging (if not compelling) the issuing by private lenders of loans to high risk borrowers simply on account of the borrowers' race. There is also the

---

[23] *PHH Corporation, et al. v. Consumer Financial Protection Bureau*, U.S. Court of Appeals for the District of Columbia Circuit, Case No. 15-1177, J. Kavanaugh, dissenting.

[24] Id.

[25] Id.

[26] See Kelly Thompson Cochran, "The CFPB at Five Years: Beyond the Numbers," 21 N.C. Banking Inst. 55 (2017).

formidable interventionist mandate of the Bureau and its interference with the operation of the market. Far from being a collection of big fish preying on the small, the market is but the sum total of all actions aiming to satisfy each market actor's needs. As noted by the economist Ludwig Von Mises, "there is in the operation of the market no compulsion and coercion... Each man is free; nobody is subject to a despot. Of his own accord, the individual integrates himself into the cooperative system. The market directs him and reveals to him in what way he can best promote his own welfare as well as that of other people."[27] The continually changing forces "determining the...state of the market are the value judgments of these individuals" and their actions are directed by those judgments.[28] It is a supremely democratic process, to which all actors in the market contribute. Prices determined by the aggregated actions of market participants "tell the producers what to produce, how to produce, and in what quantity," and result in the direction of the resources of the market along the most efficient of lines.[29] The government bureau, whether it be the ICC, the FTC or the CFPB, presumes to exceed in wisdom the aggregate determinations of a hundred million individual actors, to shift preferences from one channel to another, and to completely foreclose some channels in favour of those preferred by the government, all in the name of higher efficiency, fairness and productivity. That a commission comprised of a handful of people, or a single director, could actually possess the omniscience to make choices superior to that of the market—the sum total of the values and choices of all market participants—is laughable.

Equally laughable is the reputedly noble purpose of a government battling powerful moneyed interests on behalf of everyman. Save when they break the law and subject themselves to penalties long-antedating the CFPB, the moneyed interests only do that which the law allows. Every supposedly immoral or unvirtuous act of money men not cabined by law is committed because the law permits it, whether the law be in the form of special immunities, exceptions, subsidies, caps on damages, limits on attorney fees and impediments to class action proceedings. The

---

[27] Ludwig Von Mises, *Human Action: A Treatise on Economics*, 4th Rev. Ed. (Irvington-on-Hudson, New York: The Foundation for Economic Education, Inc., 1996), at p. 257.

[28] Id.

[29] Id., at p. 258.

very crisis that made possible and even demanded the CFPB's birth was itself the result not of lawlessness by business enterprise but of the regulatory state playing favorites by lawfully promising lenders it would guarantee any loans issued to homebuyers, regardless of how reckless the lenders became as a result of such largess. As it tends to favor Shiva over Brahma, better to permit the consumer the freedom to pursue his or her own remedy than to allow the State to play the deity. The greater efficiency is to be found in freedom, not restraint; the greater prosperity in consensual relations between buyer and seller, not coercion; the greater justice in laws that favor no one save he or she in possession of the evidence to prove their case at trial.

We'll see what the Supreme Court thinks about all this soon enough. It has for the first time agreed to hear a challenge to the constitutionality of the CFPB.[30] We'll see, too, if the Bureau's most prominent critic, the dissenter in the PHH matter and now a member of the High Court, is able to persuade a majority of his brethren of the merits of a view of the Constitution drastically at odds with *Humphrey's*, its progeny and the sweeping authority vested by Congress for a century now in administrative bodies and bureaucratic suzerains not a single voter ever directly endorsed.

Typhoid Trump

IT was, said the biographer Julius Capitolinus, the fate of the Emperor Verus that he appeared in the wake of his triumph over the Parthians "to bring the plague with him into those provinces through which he made his return journey as far as Rome."[1] Rumour spread that the disease sprang from a Babylonian tomb opened and defiled by pillaging Roman soldiers. The stone was broken and a pestilential vapor emitted to "fill the Parthians' land and the world."[2] Others blamed the General Avidius Cassius for incurring divine retribution by breaking faith with the City of Seleucia and allowing it to be sacked in violation of an agreement to permit a peaceful surrender. Whatever its origin, the

[30] "CFPB Constitutionality to Get Early March Supreme Court Hearing," www.bloomberglaw.com, November 27, 2019.

[1] *Lives of the Later Caesars* (New York: Penguin Books, 1976), at p. 144.

[2] Id.

expansion of the plague was fearful. "Spreading misery and death in its progress, it advanced to the Rhine and year after year carried desolation through the peoples of the Empire."[3] Such a pestilence, said Orosius, so "devastated all Italy that everywhere estates, fields, and towns were left deserted, without cultivators or inhabitants, and relapsed into ruins and woodland."[4] Many thousands were carried off. The cemeteries filled to overflowing and gave rise to the heretofore unknown crime of grave appropriation. The Emperor Marcus tried to calm the people and to assuage the obvious dissatisfaction of the gods by summoning priests from all sides to perform foreign religious rites and purify the city in every way. Whichever god was angry, surely one of the rites performed might placate him and stay the hurling of yet another thunderbolt of judgment.

The plague abated, but the Empire's decline never fully reversed. In time, it split asunder, with only the eastern portion surviving beyond the Fifth Century. It, too, suffered its great judgment by Nature or Nature's God when it was visited "by one of those immense but rare calamities in the presence of which human beings could only succumb helpless and resourceless until the science of the Nineteenth-Century began to probe the cause and supply the means of preventing and checking them."[5] Beginning in the summer of A.D. 542 in Pelusium on the Egyptian border, it progressed, said Gibbon, on a double path, spreading "to the East, over Syria, Persia, and the Indies, and penetrated to the West, along the coast of Africa and over the continent of Europe."[6] At the capital of Constantinople and its environs, during a three month period, "five and at length ten thousand persons died each day," many places were left vacant and in several districts "the harvest and the vintage withered on the ground."[7] As the death toll mounted, the ordinary solicitude for the souls of the dead relaxed and eventually was abandoned altogether. "Huge pits were dug at Sycae, on the other side of the Golden Horn, in

---

[3] Wilhelm Weber, "The Antonines," in *The Cambridge Ancient History*, Volume XI (Cambridge: Cambridge University Press, 1954), at p. 349.

[4] Anthony Birley, *Marcus Aurelius* (New York: Barnes & Noble Books, 1996), at p. 149.

[5] J.B. Bury, *History of the Later Roman Empire*, Volume II (New York: Dover Publications, Inc., 1958), at p. 62.

[6] Edward Gibbon, *The Decline and Fall of the Roman Empire*, Volume II (New York: The Modern Library), at p. 665.

[7] Id., at p. 668.

which the bodies were laid in rows and tramped down tightly," but so overwhelming was the task of burying the dead that "the men who were engaged on this work, unable to keep up with the number of the dying, mounted the towers of the wall of the suburb, tore off their roofs, and threw the bodies in."[8] Everywhere, said Procopius, "an evil stench pervaded the city and distressed the inhabitants still more, and especially whenever the wind blew fresh from that quarter."[9] As in the case of Rome centuries before, industry came to a standstill, scarcity abounded and starvation triumphed where the disease failed in its deadly assault upon the family of man.

Epidemic and pandemic diseases did not cease with the setting of the ancient world's sun. Such things were the lot of man in a world filled with microorganisms programmed to attach themselves to a host and drain away its life force as they strove to fulfil the objective of all living things—to survive. In the western world, bubonic plague gave way in prominence to diseases caused by exposure to bacteria in tainted drinking water such as typhoid and cholera, to yellow fever spread by mosquitos in exotic places, and to airborne plagues such as tuberculosis and influenza. Combined, the toll these diseases have taken on humanity is incalculable. Even in the age of medical miracles, beginning with the tracing of the source of disease to opportunistic creatures too small to discern with the naked eye and the development of antibiotics, vaccines and principles of hygiene and public health, diseases once believed to have been defeated have reappeared in mutated form and now threaten mankind anew.

The latest threat comes from COVID-19, also known as the Coronavirus, a variant of the recently discovered SARS that visited our nation in 2004. COVID-19 supposedly first surfaced at a Chinese seafood and poultry market late in 2019. After news spread of dozens of cases of pneumonia in the Wuhan region of China, Chinese researchers announced they had identified a heretofore unknown virus. The first death was reported in January. Soon the virus appeared in Japan, South Korea and Thailand. By the middle of January, the entire State of Wuhan was under a militarily enforced quarantine that cut eleven million people off from the outside world. The World Health Organization declared a global health emergency. The Trump Administration issued

[8] Id.
[9] Id.

a travel advisory to Americans to avoid China, and when the death toll topped 200 there, prohibited all contact with that country. By mid-February the disease made its first appearance in Europe, when a Chinese tourist died of it in a Paris Hospital. A cruise ship full of passengers was quarantined in Japan, while kindergartens, nursing homes, community centres and political rallies were shut down throughout Korea. Confirmed cases of the virus exploded in Iran following the death of two patients there, and rapidly spread from that country to Iraq, Afghanistan, Bahrain, Kuwait, Oman, Lebanon and the United Arab Emirates. A similar outbreak hit Italy. Northern Italy went into lockdown. Soon the whole country was under a rigid quarantine regime and the fatalities mounted. Just as the President asked Congress to allocate $1.25 billion in emergency funds to aid in preparing for the possibility of an epidemic on these shores, the virus surfaced in South America. The first Americans died of the disease in Seattle on February 28, 2020, joined every day or so afterward by one or two more. Daily, the federal government ramped up its response, as did the individual States. On March 3, the Administration lifted all federal restrictions on testing for the disease, but testing kits were scarce and at first defective. Fear grew. Panic crested like a white cap on a wave at sea still far from shore. By mid-March, over 60 Americans were dead, thousands were known to be infected, and the number of infections was expected to rise as testing expanded. States declared emergencies, New York mobilized the National Guard, Louisiana postponed its upcoming primary election, large gatherings were cancelled if not prohibited, the NBA, NFL and Major League Baseball suspended operation and entire school systems and colleges closed. Contemplating a quarantine of the likes never before known, the public rushed the stores, buying up all stocks of hand sanitizer, toilet paper and rice. Meanwhile, the economy took a dive. The stock market was down and entire industries were threatened with temporary (if not permanent) extinction. What the Great Influenza of 1918-1919 failed to do to the national economy and civilization as a whole despite a million fatalities in the United States and 100 million worldwide, the coronavirus, with its still paltry death toll, seemed poised to accomplish.

As with everything that is wrong, going wrong or which could go wrong in the country, most of the press focused its criticism and blame on you-know-who. Regarding a recent press conference held by the

President to discuss the government's handling of the outbreak, *Vox's* Catherine Kim said "Trump did little to help Americans understand the government's response to the virus, instead spreading misinformation while using the public health crisis for self-aggrandizement."[10] Instead of real management of the situation, the President put "science denier" Mike Pence in charge.[11] And now, with test kits and other resources woefully scarce, his cuts to the CDC were proving to have been short-sighted and even deadly.[12] *Wired's* Adam Rogers characterized the President's public statements as "terrifying" and "full of Dear Leader-ish compliments, non-sequitorial defenses of unrelated matters, attacks on an American governor, and—most importantly—misinformation about the virus and the U.S. response."[13]

Not surprisingly, CNN has taken a prominent role in criticizing the President on this topic. CNN's Samantha Vinograd said "we should expect Donald Trump to continue checking off the 'do not do' list when it comes to disaster response, including by spreading misinformation with statements minimizing the extent of the problem and contradicting health officials on the availability of testing kits."[14] "Whether it's sharing his 'hunch' that the coronavirus death rate is lower than 3.4%, saying that the United States had contained the spread of the virus from China back in February, claiming that cases are going down, muddying the waters on vaccine development and more, the President is a walking, talking, tweeting disaster when it comes to the communications strategy required during a complex crisis like this one."[15] The President wasn't merely incompetent, said Daniel Dale and Tara Subramaniam; he and his Administration were liars! The duo claimed to have documented more than 28 lies disseminated by the President and his spokespeople about the disease.[16] Progressive commentator Alex Zeldin traced the

---

[10] Catherine Kim, "Trump's Visit to the CDC Shows Why There's Concern About His Coronavirus Response, www.vox.com, March 7, 2020.

[11] Id.

[12] Id.

[13] Adam Rogers, "Trump's Coronavirus Press Event was Even Worse Than it Looked," www.wired.com, March 7, 2020.

[14] Samantha Vinograd, "On Coronavirus, Trump is a Walking, Talking, Tweeting Disaster," cnn.com, March 9, 2020.

[15] Id.

[16] Daniel Dale and Tara Subramaniam, "Fact Check: A List of 28 Ways President Trump and his Team Have Been Dishonest About the Coronavirus, www.mercurynews.com, March 11, 2020.

Administration's failures in coronavirus management back to its beginning: the President's "obvious shortcomings from day one," his appointment of cabinet officials unprepared and unqualified for office, the regular appeals to racism and xenophobia, the "Muslim ban and cruel deportation policies for Latin Americans seeking refuge in the United States," and now his "fantastic claim that the media is exaggerating the coronavirus crisis" and his attempt to blame the virus's spread to immigrants "rather than a government that was and is unprepared."[17] Summing up the media's critique, a writer with *The New York Times* went so far as to propose renaming of the disease the Trumpvirus.[18]

In reviewing the comments of the Democrat contenders to succeed the President, no one can doubt that the virus has been politicized. Though his hopes of ever obtaining the Democrat Party nomination for the Presidency dim by the day, Senator Bernie Sanders tested out the limits of hyperbole by suggesting that the death toll may exceed that of American service members during World War II.[19] Only Medicare for All, paid sick leave, a moratorium on evictions, and all the other things he's been urging for years, stand as an adequate response to this supposedly non-political disease.[20] Remembering for the moment that he's running for the Presidency and taking a break from plagiarizing the words of others, or claiming he was Nelson Mandela's cell mate, swearing at and insulting his supporters and groping small children, Joe Biden delivered a well-coached, scripted and edited address on how he would handle the crisis as commander-in-chief when, after 77 years on this planet, he finally grew up. Public fears, he said, were being compounded, not by a news media that has switched out the non-stop impeachment narrative in favour of the one featuring the coronavirus, but "by a pervasive lack of trust in this President fuelled by adversarial relationships with the truth that he continues to have."[21]

---

[17] Alex Zeldin, Trump's Presidency Led Straight to America's Epic Coronavirus Failure," https://forward.com, March 10, 2020.

[18] Gail Collins, "Let's Call it Trumpvirus: If You're Feeling Awful, You Know Who to Blame," *The New York Times*, February 26, 2020.

[19] Adam Edelman & Allan Smith, "Biden, Sanders Take Aim at Trump Over Coronavirus: 'Incompetence and Recklessness,'" www.nbcnews.com, March 12, 2020.

[20] Id.

[21] Id.

Taking political advantage of a health crisis is nothing new. Dr. Benjamin Rush sought to promote his concept of "Republican medicine" while attempting to treat the sufferers during the awful Yellow Fever epidemic in Philadelphia during the year 1793. As patients dropped to his left and right in response to his worthless and idiotic treatment regimens, Rush waged a newspaper campaign to prove the merits of his politicized medical theories and trash critics whose motivation he claimed was purely partisan.[22] The British took the politicizing of disease to the logical extreme by turning smallpox into a weapon of war during the Revolution, as did the Confederate States during the Civil War.[23] During the Antebellum Period, local boards of health tended to use the incidence of disease as opportunities to increase "personal and political power which is sure to be abused."[24] When Yellow Fever broke out in 1899, Texas sealed its borders with Louisiana, less to stop the spread of the disease west from New Orleans than to divert commercial shipping traffic from that port to Galveston Bay.[25] San Francisco authorities took advantage of a mere rumor of the outbreak of bubonic plague to cordon off the economically vibrant Chinatown district, much to the pleasure of white merchants throughout the rest of the City.[26] A few years later, during perhaps the last epidemic of the kind, Governor Vardaman of Mississippi equipped a flotilla of boats to cruise upriver in order to drive out Louisiana fishermen and seize control of contested oyster fields, all in the name of preventing the spread of the contagion, but actually to provide an advantage to Mississippi fishermen and Mississippi markets.[27]

The authority to regulate and contain the spread of infectious disease was entirely local during the colonial period, largely due to the relative isolation of each colony from one another and from Mother

---

[22] See Randal Baldwin Clark, "Bleeding, Purges, and Vomits: Dr. Benjamin Rush's Republican Medicine, the Bilious Remitting Yellow-Fever Epidemic of 1793, and the Non-Origin of the Law of Informed Consent," 24 J. Contemp. Health L. & Pol'y 209 (2008).

[23] Laura K. Donohue, "Biodefense and Constitutional Constraints," 4 U. Miami Natl Sec. & Armed Conf. L. Rev. 82 (2013-2014), at pp. 110 and 136.

[24] Id., at 135.

[25] Polly J. Price, "Epidemics, Outsiders, and Local Protection: Federalism Theater in the Era of the Shotgun Quarantine," 19 U. Pa. J. Const. L. 369 (2016), at p. 393.

[26] Id., at p. 401.

[27] Id., at p. 394.

England. The colonial regimes in Massachusetts, New York, Pennsylvania, Delaware, Maryland and Rhode Island "entertained provisions that imposed harsh penalties—such as death without benefit of clergy—on those refusing to abide by the law" when disease became rampant and threatened the health and safety of the people. Quarantine was the primary device employed in such times—the barring of infected ships from the docks and the forcible removal of infected residents from within the town limits, usually to a pest house. The States inherited these powers and expanded upon them by vesting their governors with the authority "to cut off relations with other states and localities."[28] The fact that these laws interfered with interstate and international commerce little impressed most observers, and was disregarded as irrelevant by none less an authority than John Marshall, who considered the power to impose a quarantine for the health and welfare of the people in the States to be a fundamental element of State sovereignty which the States never ceded to the federal government.[29] Such authority lay at the core of a State's police power, and could, said Justice Grier, legitimately "compel mere commercial regulations to submit to their control."[30] To the extent that the federal government involved itself at all in the efforts to combat the spread of pestilence, it merely made itself available to the States in the event the latter desired assistance in enforcing their own quarantine measures in the ports.[31]

It was the politicizing of disease, or its use as a justification to obtain economic or even ideological advantage at a parochial level, that led to calls for a shift from the traditional local and state control of the social response to the pandemic to greater control by the federal government. In 1878, Congress responded to calls throughout the south in particular for more uniformity and impartiality in the imposition of quarantines and other protective measures.[32] A new federal regulatory scheme enacted in that year created criteria for sanitation on board ships, made provision for a federal board of health, mandated the collection by consular officials abroad of information about the status of any communicable diseases in the nations where they were posted,

---

[28] Donohue, op. cit., at p. 113.
[29] *Gibbons v. Ogden* (1824) 22 U.S. 1, at 205-206.
[30] *Thurlow v. Massachusetts* (1847) 46 U.S. 504, 632.
[31] Donohue, op. cit., at p. 126.
[32] Id., at pp. 137-138.

expanded the number of federal quarantine stations, and provided for the transfer of state quarantine facilities to federal control. Rather than pre-empt state and local authority via invocation of the commerce or some other Article I power, the Act modestly called for state and federal cooperation, and for the federal government to assist the localities in the management of precautionary and preventative measures at the latter's invitation. Primary responsibility for responding to possible and actual epidemics remained with the States. Why this was the case was explained by Justice Miller and the Supreme Court in 1882. While the Congress might pre-empt state and local law governing the management of disease effecting interstate or international commerce, it had refrained from doing so, apparently because it "believed that what ought to be done could be better and more wisely done by the authorities of the States who were familiar with the matter."[33] This was in keeping with earlier authority, articulated by Justice Curtis, that though a matter affecting interstate or international commerce might be pre-empted at the discretion of Congress, "the nature of the subject" in the nation's ports "is such as to leave no doubt of the superior fitness and propriety, not to say the absolute necessity, of different systems of regulation, drawn from local knowledge and experience, and conformed to local wants."[34] It made practical sense, too, for the federal government to refrain from occupying the field. Not only did local authorities possess unique knowledge of the peculiar needs of a particular locale, their continuing responsibility to protect the peoples under their jurisdiction relieved the federal government from the obligation of establishing a massive bureaucracy aimed at detecting, monitoring and responding to the presence and advance of infectious diseases.

Today, despite the expansion of federal control everywhere else, management of epidemics, whether introduced through the ports of entry or endemic to the nation, remains vested with State officials. The great statutory innovations since the 1878—the Public Health Service Act of 1944 and the Robert T. Stafford Disaster Relief and Emergency Assistance Act of 1988—vest power with the federal government to impose quarantines at the ports of entry in the event of outbreaks of cholera, diphtheria, tuberculosis, plague, smallpox, yellow fever, viral haemorrhagic fever, influenza and SARS. In the event that it is

---

[33] *Morgan's S.S. Co. v. La. Bd. Of Health* (1886) 118, 455, at 466.

[34] *Cooley v. Board of Wardens* (1851) 53 U.S. 299, at 320.

determined by the Director of the CDC that "local authorities have not taken adequate steps to prevent the spread of the disease," these laws direct the federal government to "take whatever measures may be necessary to prevent the spread of communicable disease from one state to any other state."[35] The latter law in particular allows the President to respond to the request for aid from the States, and to declare national emergencies at his or her own discretion within a narrow band of incidents involving a primary federal responsibility. Once an emergency is declared, federal resources, including personnel and funds, are available to assist the States in managing the crisis, and various regulations and statutes that might ordinarily slow response time can be suspended in order to facilitate more rapid if not immediate remedy of the situation.

In the official response to the coronavirus, we see the several layers of government at work, and the interaction between them. Notwithstanding the many splendored criticism of the President, he was taking action back in December, issuing travel advisories and then prohibiting travel to and from China. As Democrats were impeaching him, the President and his administration were still busy at work. In his State of the Union address—a copy of which the leader of the Democrats so astonishingly ripped up on camera—the President informed the Nation about his plan to combat the virus. His Administration removed all restrictions on States conducting testing, continued to provide financial and personnel support to the States that requested it, and then declared a national emergency in order to mobilize federal resources even more extensively. Even the Governor of California, one of the President's harshest and most consistent critics, noted that in a private conversation "President Trump said everything that I could have hoped for…and every single thing that he said, [he] followed through on."[36] Similar praise came from the mouth of another of the President's leading critics, Governor Cuomo of New York, who thanked the President and the "extraordinarily helpful" Jared Kushner for their assistance and

---

[35] Donohue, op. cit., at pp. 153-154.

[36] Missy Halsey, "'They Followed Through': Gov. Newsom Shocks at Presser with High Marks for Trump Admin's Handling of Coronavirus," www.bizpacreview.com, March 10, 2020.

cooperation in addressing the challenges posed by the viral emergency.[37]

In all of this, the President's response has been in advance of his predecessor's reaction to the Swine Flu that hit the nation in 2009. Indeed, it wasn't until 8 or 9 months after the date of the initial reports of the disease that President Obama declared a State of Emergency, and this only after 1,000 Americans had died. President Obama certainly had his virtues, but a resume indicating a superior degree of competence and relevant life experience wasn't one of them. Nor have his accomplishments in politics, either as a Senator or President, merited the hagiographic praise the man is subject to. His response to the Swine Flu was belated and may well have contributed to the death toll that exceeded 12,000 despite the existence of a vaccine. It is too much, though, to blame any President for the advance of a disease that is the creation of Nature, or of God, or the consequence of the choice our first ancestors made to blaze their own trail in a world not of their making and far more complex than their innate capacity for ignorance could allow them to comprehend. Blame, if there is any, is to be shared. The constitutional and statutory diffusion of authority in preventing and containing the spread of infectious diseases makes this necessarily the case. It is only the disease of the mind and its sequela in the form of excessive bias that impairs the ability to understand this truth; and only the inoculation of reason and a bit of knowledge allows any of us to overcome it.

Gifts From a King

HE was born, improbably, in Shanghai, China, to refugees from Hitler's and Stalin's Europe. He grew up in San Francisco, attended high school there, and then obtained a degree in mathematics at Harvard, followed by a law degree from the same institution. His promise attracted much attention and won him clerkships with Matthew Trobiner of California's Supreme Court and Justice Potter Stewart. His tenure on the faculty at Harvard began in 1968, only two years after graduating, and continues to the present. His law review contributions

[37] Bernadette Hogan & Aaron Feis, "Cuomo Thanks Trump for his 'Cooperation' Amid Coronavirus Response," https://newyorkpost.com, March 25, 2020.

are many, and his book on constitutional law remains a landmark of scholarship and analysis. His protégés include two generations of law professors, leaders of business and government, and the very highest officials in the land. Ted Cruz, Elena Kagan, John Roberts and Barack Obama all consider him a mentor. Over the years, he has lent his powers of advocacy to litigants in a host of cases involving constitutional issues and appeared three dozen times at the bar of the Supreme Court, winning and losing cases of great significance and contributing mightily to the continuing discourse over the meaning of our nation's highest law. Always a partisan, and fiercely so, he nevertheless garners respect from all sides due to his scholarly knowledge, social graces, and willingness to concede points on which he has been bested. If there are giants in the field of law, Laurence Tribe must be counted among them.

As great as he is, he has not proven immune to a condition that afflicts many on the progressive side of things that some have likened to a disease, and even referred to as a discrete syndrome of derangement. Indeed, if Professor Tribe is not actually patient zero in this epidemic, he must be close to the epicentre of infection. Once the most recent presidential election passed, this very vocal advocate for the defeated candidate commenced what amounts to a sustained rant against the President-elect. When he failed to generate much interest in his offer to represent members of the Electoral College who opted to exercise the courage to defy the people of the States who charged them with casting their ballot for the office of President, Tribe began looking for anything that might provide a basis for impeachment as soon as possible.[1] Impeachment of the President "should begin on Inauguration Day," he declared, for abuse of power and "shredding the Constitution more monstrously than any other president in American history."[2] While elections are the usual method of removing an unfit President, Tribe believed that "some leaders are much too dangerous to leave in power."[3]

In Tribe's Trump-addled mind, the list of impeachable offences has grown by the day, from "the 'cruel brand of bigotry' that supposedly

---

[1] William A. Jacobson, "Democrats Follow Harvard Law Prof. Laurence Tribe off the Impeachment Cliff," legalinsurrection.com, December 20, 2019.

[2] Gene Healy, "Laurence Tribe's Impeachment Hysteria," www.cato.org, June 23, 2017.

[3] Jason Lemon, "Trump is 'Dangerous' and 'May Fabricate' Another National Emergency to Remain in Power After 2020, Harvard Law Professor Warns," www.newsweek.com, March 17, 2019.

motivates the travel ban to a State Department blogpost touting the 'winter White House' at Mar-a-Lago," not to mention the President's "claim that Obama had his 'wires tapped' in Trump Tower."[4] He invited Russian assistance, said Tribe, to undermine the candidacy of his rival by calling on that nation to release hacked emails, and when law enforcement attempted to get to the bottom of this particular axis of evil, he brazenly fired the Director of the FBI and created entirely "phony justifications" for doing so.[5] Even if it was unlikely that the Senate would convict, Tribe urged the House to impeach the President anyways, and then to withhold the Articles so that the President might be denied the opportunity to ever formally challenge the allegations, thus leaving impeachment to stand as a perpetual, unresolved taint on his Presidency. Such a strategy had the advantage, he said, of avoiding the Constitution's ban on Bills of Attainder and yet would possess the "deliberately stigmatizing character as a 'Scarlet I' that Trump would have to take with him into his re-election campaign."[6]

These, of course, are the Professor's more lucid thoughts on the President. When not writing editorials decrying the President's supposed criminality or making his case on MSNBC, Tribe is apt to take his campaign of vilification to the twitter-sphere, where he decries the President as a "pathetic coward," a "pathetic schmuck," "shallow jerk," a "f*cking idiot," "batsh*t crazy," and a small-handed "crime boss."[7]

Of the many criticisms Tribe has levelled at the President, one of the earliest and most persistent has been the contention of an alleged violation of an obscure part of the Constitution known as the Foreign Emoluments Clause, which provides that "no Title of Nobility shall be granted by the United States: And no Person holding any Office of Profit or Trust under them, shall, without the Consent of Congress, accept of any present, Emolument, Office, or Title, of any kind whatever, from any

---

[4] Healy, op. cit.

[5] Laurence H. Tribe, "Donald Trump Will Violate the US Constitution on Inauguration Day," www.theguardian.com, December 19, 2016; and Laurence H. Tribe, "Trump Must be Impeached. Here's Why," *The Washington Post*, May 13, 2017.

[6] Laurence H. Tribe, "Impeach Trump. But Don't Necessarily Try Him in the Senate," *The Washington Post*, June 5, 2019.

[7] Bob Brigham, "Harvard Prof. Laurence Tribe calls Trump a 'Compromised,' 'f**king idiot,'" www.salon.com, December 27, 2018.

King, Prince, or foreign State."[8] Even before the President took office, Tribe argued that the President would violate the Clause the moment he took the oath due to his continuing interest in the Trump Organization, which receives a "steady stream of monetary and other benefits from foreign powers."[9] "Foreign interference in the American political system," he explained, "was among the gravest dangers feared by the Founders of our nation and the framers of our Constitution. The United States was a new government, and one that was vulnerable to manipulation by the great and wealthy world powers (which then, as now, included Russia). One common tactic that foreign sovereigns and their agents used to influence our officials was to give them gifts, money, and other things of value."[10] The Clause, he said, applies to gifts to Presidents and monetary support, as well as "ordinary, fair market value transactions with foreign states and their agents that result in any profit or benefit."[11] The President's continuing relationship with his corporate interests guaranteed that he stood "to benefit personally, in innumerable and largely hidden ways, from decisions made daily by foreign governments and their agents."[12] Only a "complete divestment," he concluded, "will ensure adherence to the constitutional guideline set by the framers of the Constitution."[13] Otherwise, Trump would be "a walking, tweeting violation of the Constitution from the moment he takes office."[14]

Tribe didn't merely make the argument, he did something no one in history had ever done before, which was to file suit against the President for violation of the Clause and seek a court order forcing the President to divest himself of his far-flung business interests. In the suit, Tribe alleged that the President's continuing interest in the Trump Hotel in the nation's capital inflicted an actual injury on competing hotels whose

---

[8] *Constitution of the United States*, Art. I, Sec. 9, Cl. 8.

[9] Laurence H. Tribe, "Donald Trump Will Violate the US Constitution on Inauguration Day," www.theguardian.com, December 19, 2016.

[10] Norman Eisen, Richard Painter, and Lawrence H. Tribe, "The Emoluments Clause: Its Text, Meaning, and Application to Donald J. Trump," www.brookings.edu, December 16, 2016.

[11] Tribe, "Donald Trump Will Violate the US Constitution on Inauguration Day," supra.

[12] Id.

[13] Jordyn Phelps, "Everything You Need to Know About the Emoluments Clause," www.abcnews.com, June 12, 2017.

[14] Id.

facilities diplomats and officials from abroad were shunning in order to curry favour with the President by patronizing his business.[15] The filing of the suit quickly inspired two others: one in the federal court for the District of Maryland alleging that the President's violation of the Emoluments Clause impaired the sovereign, quasi-sovereign, proprietary and *parens patriae* interests of the State of Maryland and the District of Columbia; the other in the D.C. District Court brought by members of Congress contending that the President's failure to seek consent for his acceptance of foreign emoluments deprived them of their right to perform a function allocated to them alone.[16]

To date, the courts overseeing these lawsuits have issued rulings on threshold matters. Both the Maryland Court and the District Court in Washington D.C. held that the Clause applies to an extremely broad range of benefits, though the claims of some of the plaintiffs were dismissed for want of standing. Tribe's own suit was dismissed due to an absence of any concrete injury, and because the controversy was found to constitute a non-justiciable political question. On appeal, the matter was restored to the docket and remains pending in New York.[17] The cases that survived the District Courts' initial rulings were also appealed and both have been dismissed following appellate review. Of the case brought by the State of Maryland and the District of Columbia, Judge Paul Niemeyer said the plaintiffs' "interest in enforcing the Emoluments Clause is so attenuated and abstract that their prosecution of this case readily provokes the question of whether this action against the President is an appropriate use of the courts, which were created to resolve real cases and controversies between the parties."[18] Of the lawmakers' suit, a three-judge panel of the Maryland Circuit Court of Appeals unanimously held that while the institution of Congress might possess standing to pursue an institutional injury arising from a violation of the Clause, the individual members of Congress did not.[19]

---

[15] *CREW et al. v. Trump* (S.D.N.Y. Dec. 21, 2017), 276 Supp.3d 174.

[16] *District of Columbia & Maryland v. Trump* (D. Md. 2010) 315 F.Supp.3d 875; and *Blumenthal et al. v. Trump* (D.D.C. 2018) 335 F.Supp.3d 45.

[17] Sharon LaFraniere, "U.S. Appeals Court Reinstates Emoluments Case Against Trump," *The New York Times*, September 13, 2019.

[18] Laurel Wamsley, "Appeals Court Orders Dismissal of Emoluments Lawsuit Against Trump," www.npr.org., July 10, 2019.

[19] Sharon LaFraniere, "Federal Appeals Court Rules for Trump in Emoluments Case," *The New York Times*, February 7, 2020.

This is hardly the end of the matter, since further *en banc* proceedings are in the works and review by the highest court of the land seems inevitable.

Though Tribe rather prematurely and ungraciously said the President's lawyer "wouldn't get a passing grade in constitutional law," the merits of the matter are far from as clear as he insists.[20] All parties are in agreement that the Clause, along with the two other provisions in the Constitution governing Emoluments, were designed as hedges against corruption. "At the Constitutional Convention," notes Michael Foster and Kevin Hickey, "Charles Pinckney of South Carolina introduced the language that became the Foreign Emoluments Clause based on 'the necessity of preserving foreign Ministers & other officers of the U.S. independent of external influence.'"[21] At Virginia's Ratification Convention, Edmund Randolph confirmed Pinkney's view when he explained to his fellow delegates that "the Foreign Emoluments Clause was intended to 'prevent corruption' by 'prohibit[ing] any one in office from receiving or holding any emoluments from foreign states.'"[22]

Beyond this one point, however, agreement appears to end. Since the issue entered litigation shortly after the President's inauguration, disputes emerged as to whether elected officers, including the President, are subject to the Clause, what exactly constitutes an emolument prohibited by the Clause, whether the Clause's prohibition can be litigated civilly by anyone, and even whether Congress has the power to enact legislation to enforce the prohibition. The outcome of the various cases at the district court level indicate a split of authority on these various points, which only increased as the appellate courts weighed in.

There is, no doubt, a meaning to be found, as obscure as it presently appears to be. To find it, it is necessary to proceed back in time to the era that formed the relevant backdrop to the Framers' deliberations: that great period of constitutional ferment from the middle of the Seventeenth Century until the first few years following the termination of the American Revolution. The era was one of the great periods of reform in Western history, animated by the critique spawned by the

---

[20] Jordyn Phelps, op. cit.

[21] Michael A. Foster & Kevin J. Hickey, "The Emoluments Clauses and the Presidency: Background and Recent Developments," crsreports.congress.gov, November 5, 2019.

[22] Id.

Enlightenment and aiming to relieve mankind of the oppression that flowed so predictably from the governing class and the levers of power they controlled. The time was also one of great venality in government. Nearly every office of state was one wherein the compensation came not from a pay check drawing on the national treasury, but from gratuities demanded by the office holder. Distribution of such offices was a means that Kings such as George III employed to forge bonds of loyalty with their ministers and other officials.[23] "Fees and other non-salary payments," notes Professor Breihan, "were familiar forms of official emolument in the Eighteenth Century," formed "a more important source of income for public officials than their salaries," and were "cultivated assiduously in almost every government department."[24] Any time a citizen sought the services of the state, a fee was required, payable not to the government per se, but to the office holder directly. Tax farmers, revenue officers and port officials were among the most notorious beneficiaries of this venal system, and it was one that easily lent itself to abuse.[25] The abuse was all the greater when foreign nations sought to directly influence the decisions of officials in other countries by proffers of gifts of money, land and titles.

Competing claims of loyalty certainly were nothing new on a continent where a landholder might owe obligations to a variety of liege lords. The corrupting influence was bad enough during the preceding Medieval and Early Modern Eras. Its potential for mischief and oppression on the continental or even a global scale only magnified as nation states coalesced behind monarchs eager to expand the scope of influence and control beyond what was inherited from their predecessors. The worst offender in this regard was Louis XIV, whose kingdom was the largest, richest and most powerful of the Age, and whose policy toward England sought to undermine the authority of a Protestant Parliament through clandestine financial support to its King—his own cousin, Charles II. The affinity between the two men was

---

[23] See Robert G. Natelson, "The Original Meaning of 'Emoluments' in the Constitution," 52 Ga. L. Rev. 1 (2017), at p. 20.

[24] John R. Breihan, "William Pitt and the Commission on Fees, 1785-1801," 27 Hist. J. 59 (1984), at pp. 60-61, N1.

[25] A. Goodwin, *The New Cambridge Modern History*, Volume VIII (Cambridge: Cambridge University Press, 1965), at pp. 582-583; and Olwen Hufton, *Europe: Privilege and Protest, 1730-1789* (Ithaca: Cornell University Press, 1980), at p. 41.

great on account of the consanguinity of relationship and the protection and patronage by Louis of Charles and his family during their exile following the Great English Civil War. Anxious for funds but leery of making concessions to a Parliament he found odious and out of step with his own policy preferences, Charles entertained the entreaties of the French, extended through the familiar personage of his sister, the Duchess d'Orleans. The result was the entirely secret Treaty of Dover. The Treaty, said historian Gail Savage, guaranteed Charles's "support to French ambitions for European domination," in return for the "resources to enable him to thwart the power of Parliament over the crown and return England to Catholicism."[26] This preeminent example of the corrupting influence of foreign gifts was alluded to by Charles Pinkney at the Constitutional Convention as proof of the need for a prohibition on emoluments derived from foreign States.[27] What precisely an emolument was, and whether it included every conceivable benefit traceable to a foreign government, including arms-length open market transactions conducted in an official's personal capacity, Pinkney never explained.

Professor Tribe has argued for the widest possible definition of emolument, focusing not on payments or benefits received by virtue of the President's office, but on "any situation in which a federal officeholder receives money, items of value, or services from a foreign state."[28] Under this approach, says Professor Grewal, an American judge of German origin who qualified for a settlement award for the injuries he suffered at the hands of the Nazis, and an American official with a vacation home in Europe, would not be entitled to receive the award, nor a license to renovate the premises.[29] The broad Tribian view of the term, says Professor Natelson, would render "it unconstitutional for almost any government employee to purchase the debt securities of foreign governments," or to sell "goods abroad where they might be purchased by a foreign government," or to purchase "land from an

---

[26] Gail Savage, "Why the Founders Feared Foreign Influence in American Politics," www.thewashingtonpost.com, July 19, 2018.

[27] Id.

[28] Norman L. Eisen, Richard Painter, and Laurence H. Tribe, "The Emoluments Clause: Its Text, Meaning, and Application to Donald J. Trump," www.brookings.edu, at p. 11.

[29] Amadeep S. Grewal, "The Foreign Emoluments Clause and the Chief Executive," 102 Minn. L. Rev. 639 (2017), at pp. 664 & 679.

Indian tribe if that tribe were recognized as a foreign nation," and would discourage "public service by imposing crippling burdens on people involved in foreign commerce (and necessarily engaged in transactions with foreign governments)," and thus "repel some of the very people the Constitution-makers wanted to attract to government service."[30]

Tribe's view rests both on the Framers' unquestionable commitment to preventing corruption by foreign states and statements of participants at the Constitutional Convention and in the *Federalist Papers*. Augmenting his view is that of Professor John Mikhail—a member of his litigation team—who contends that there is "abundant evidence that 'emolument' was often used at the founding in a much wider sense, one that went beyond the duties of an office and included the fruits of ordinary market transactions."[31] This broad use of the term he says can be found in such documents as the Virginia Nonimportation Resolutions of 1770, the Proclamation on Intercourse with British Warships of 1776 (issued by the New York Committee of Safety), James Madison's letter to Thomas Jefferson dated August 12, 1786, the Declaration of the Causes and Necessity of Taking Up Arms drafted by Jefferson and John Dickenson, *The Farmer Refuted* penned by Alexander Hamilton in 1775, John Adams' essay *Novanglus* of the same year, The Virginia Declaration of Rights of 1776, the Constitution of Pennsylvania, and Adams' draft of the Constitution of the State of Massachusetts.[32] Mikhail's reading of Blackstone's discussion of the term confirms the broader definition as being current at the time of the Founding.[33] He further bolsters Tribe's position by noting that any claim that contemporary dictionaries supported a narrow reading of the term was contradicted by his finding that "every English dictionary definition of 'emolument' from 1604 to 1806 relies on one or more of the elements of the broad definition…'profit,' 'advantage,' 'gain,' or 'benefit.'"[34] In ninety-two percent of these dictionaries, he notes, the word is defined "exclusively in these terms, with no reference to 'office' or 'employment.'"[35] The two dictionaries that contain a narrower definition—Barclays from 1774 and

[30] Natelson, op. cit., at p. 52.
[31] John Mikhail, "Emoluments and President Trump," 53 Val. U.L. Rev. 631 (2019), at p. 644.
[32] Id., at pp. 644-648.
[33] Id., at pp. 649-651.
[34] Id., at p. 655.
[35] Id.

Trusler's from 1766—were not known to have been "owned, possessed, or used by the founders," nor to have "had any impact on them or on the American people who debated and ratified the Constitution."[36]

To this seemingly compelling evidence, there is a response. Arguably, the sources identified by Mikhail use the term broadly, but there are numerous contrary authorities of significant weight. As noted by Professor Grewal, "an almost endless number of legal authorities show that when 'emoluments' is used in connection with the description of an office, officer, or employee, it refers to compensation for services performed."[37] This conclusion was recently tested by two legal scholars with a background in linguistics who are involved in the assembly of material included in the soon-to-be launched digital Corpus of Founding Era American English at Brigham Young University. James Phillips and Sara White conducted searches of three massive collections of Founding era documents—The Evans Early American Imprint Series, the National Archives Founders Papers Online, and Hein Online, which consist of legal materials from 1760 to 1799, including statutes, cases, and legislative debate transcripts. The duo conducted searches in accordance with principles of corpus linguistics, or the "empirical study of language that is based on the notion that 'the best way to find out about how language works is by analysing real examples of language as it is used.'"[38] The approach is superior to simply analysing contemporary dictionaries, or to sampling a few incidental uses of a particular term that are not necessarily representative of how the term was more usually or generally employed. Dictionaries, they say, are particularly problematic in that they "lack the ability to handle context or to define phrases," and tend to reflect proper rather than common usage. To the extent that they provide a variety of definitions both proper and common, dictionaries don't necessarily yield any insight into which one applies in a particular context. There, too, is the problem of the idiosyncratic nature of Eighteenth-Century lexicons, reflecting the eccentricities of the authors, who tended to work alone, and the

---

[36] Id.

[37] Id., at p. 651.

[38] James Cleith Phillips & Sara White, "The Meaning of the Three Emoluments Clauses in the U.S. Constitution: A Corpus Linguistic Analysis of American English from 1760-1799," 59 S. Tex. L. Rev. 181 (2017), at p. 197.

proneness of dictionary compilers to plagiarize the work of their predecessors.

In applying the principles of corpus linguistics to the term "emoluments," Phillips and White searched the three databases for all occurrences of the word in the constitutional context. They found that when the term was used to discuss Presidential and Domestic emoluments, the narrow definition applied overwhelmingly. Less conclusive were the results of the search of the word in the context of the Foreign Emoluments Clause, but even here, the reference tended to be to "office-related emolument rather than any kind of emolument in the broad sense of the word."[39]

Whether the term "Emolument" as used in the Foreign Emoluments Clause entails the broad or the narrow definition would be irrelevant if the President isn't even subject to it. This is the argument by the one scholar whose work antedates the interest in the obscure Clause that erupted in the wake of Donald Trump's 2016 election victory. For over a decade, Professor Seth Tillman has argued that the Clause expressly applies only to "officers...under the United States," which do not include any elected federal officials. A significant piece of evidence in support of this view, he says, is a schedule compiled by Alexander Hamilton in 1792 at the request of the Senate listing all "officers under the United States," along with each of their "emoluments." The list took nine months to compile and when completed "included appointed or administrative personnel in each of the three branches of the federal government," but omitted the President, Vice President, and members of Congress.[40] The document casts light "on the original public meaning of the phrase "office...under the United States," and is of especial significance due to its author's prominence as an important participant of the Convention and his role in the ratification debates.

Further support for the position that the President is exempt from the Foreign Emoluments prohibition is found in "historical practice from Washington, Jefferson, Madison, Hamilton, and the First Congress."[41]

---

[39] Id.

[40] Seth Barrett Tillman, "The Foreign Emoluments Clause- Where the Bodies are Buried: 'Idiosyncratic' Legal Positions," 59 Tex. L. Rev., 237 (2017), at p. 252.

[41] Brief for Scholar Seth Barrett Tillman as Amicus Curiae in Support of the Defendant, *Citizens for Responsibility and Ethics in Washington, et al. v. Donald J. Trump*, U.S. Dist. Court for Southern District of New York, Case No. 1:17-cv-00458RA.

Quite openly, President Washington received a portrait of King Louis XVI from the French Ambassador to the United States and a key to the Bastille from the Marquis de Lafayette. President Jefferson received a bust of Czar Alexander I, and President Madison received two pistols from a revolutionary South American government.[42] In none of these cases was Congress's approval sought for receipt of the gifts. It wasn't sought, says Tillman, because it was the understanding of the Founding generation, including Washington, Jefferson, Hamilton and Madison, that the President was not an officer "under the United States" subject to any limitation on emoluments he might receive from foreign nations.

There is some force in Tillman's argument, though not invincible in strength. The inferences from Hamilton's list and the history of executive action during the first thirty years of the nation's existence are certainly salient. That the President might be free to accept gifts and other benefits from foreign nations, however, does seem rather shocking, and even contrary to the Framers' obvious intention to prevent foreign influence of a corrupting nature from the affairs of state. Alternatively, it makes some sense that a President be permitted to accept gifts from foreign ambassadors and leaders in order to facilitate good relations abroad and advance the international interests of the United States. Unlike an ambassador nominated by the President and confirmed by the Senate, a President is subject to a variety of controls on his or her exercise of power. The President is subject to nation-wide approval at election-time and the unending scrutiny and criticism of the press. He or she remains within the often-withering gaze of the Congress, and is perpetually under threat of impeachment for accepting bribes and committing treason. If it is true that the furtive alliance between Charles II and Louis XIV was on the minds of Convention delegates when contemplating the Foreign Emoluments Clause, removal from office for conduct similar to the English Monarch's amounting to treason and bribery find remedy in the Congress's power to impeach and remove.

Whether any of these measures are an adequate safeguard is another matter. If they aren't, an approach superior to litigation that aims to fill the gap in the Framers' intent might be to consider amending the Foreign Emoluments Clause to clarify and extend the prohibition so as to prevent the use of private businesses owned but not directly operated by a

---

[42] Id.

President as avenues for foreign nations to attempt to curry favor with and influence the official actions of our nation's chief executive. The concern harbored by Professor Tribe and others that a far-flung business enterprise, decades in the operation and in which the President retains a stake might provide an opening to corrupting foreign influence is legitimate; but exploiting that concern to judicially impose a meaning on the operative Clause that the Framers never intended is a corruption equally undesirable.

Shelter in Place... Or What?

IN February of 2020, the first of the orders began to appear. Declarations by the elected officials of Cities and Counties, promulgated in accordance with a range of State laws providing municipalities with authority to curb the spread of infectious disease, tipped one by one like dominoes and seemingly triggered the issuance of similar orders in adjacent jurisdictions. Restrictions on the size of public gatherings—voluntary at first—came one after another, followed by proclamations of public emergency mandating more extreme limitations on mobility and work. Santa Clara County's order was first, followed by San Diego's four days later. A lull of ten days in length occurred, then a cluster of orders emanated from San Francisco, Orange, Solano and Placer Counties appeared. On March 4, the Governor of the State declared a state-wide emergency in the wake of California's first death. Its purpose, he said, was to help the State "prepare for and contain the spread of the coronavirus by allowing state agencies to more easily procure equipment and services, share information on patients and alleviate restrictions on the use of state-owned properties and facilities," in addition to combatting price gouging by vendors attempting to take "advantage of people seeking hand sanitizer and other in-demand goods."[1]

On March 13, school districts in San Joaquin, San Luis Obispo, Santa Clara, Solano, Placer, and Contra Costa Counties and the Cities of Los Angeles, Oakland and San Diego closed classroom doors. Three days

[1] "California's Coronavirus State of Emergency," *The Los Angeles Times*, March 5, 2020.

later, after completion of multi-jurisdictional consultations, the Counties of Alameda, Contra Costa, Marin, San Francisco, San Mateo, Santa Clara and Santa Cruz issued formal shelter-in-place orders, restricting all actions outside the home except for those deemed "essential" until April 7. The next day, Monterey, San Benito, Sonoma and Sacramento Counties joined the effort, and other jurisdictions prepared to follow suit. Seeing the widening scope of the epidemic and understanding the need for conformity state-wide, Governor Newsom issued Executive Order N-33-20, invoking the powers set forth in Government Code Sections 8567, 8627 and 8665, and mandating public compliance with a concurrently issued State public health directive that "all individuals living in the State of California…stay home or at their place of residence except as needed to maintain continuity of operations of the federal critical infrastructure sectors" and "practice social distancing" when leaving their homes in order to obtain food and other essentials. It further directed that health care providers "prioritize services to serving those who are the sickest" and place priority on use of resources by those persons "providing direct care to them," and that the Office of Emergency Services "take necessary steps to ensure compliance with this Order." It was not a state of martial law by any measure, but it was the most significant and widespread limitation on freedom the people of the State of California had experienced in generations.

The results were telling. In Sonoma County, the civic concourses became veritable ghost towns, seemingly devoid of human population. "The verdant plazas of Sonoma and Healdsburg were empty," noted writers for *The Press Democrat*, "and Santa Rosa's downtown square was deserted."[2] Where a day before community life appeared to be "routine, reliable, flourishing," all now was "idled, shuttered or closed indefinitely."[3] In those places where business remained open, people assembled, but only at a discrete distance from one another lest they receive or transmit the dreaded contagion. Lines became elongated due to the imperative of separation and shoppers were limited within the confines of grocery stores to only a few dozen at a time. Increasingly, consumers took to the internet, and when they had no choice but to

---

[2] Will Schmitt, Yousef Baig & Mary Callahan, "Sonoma County Shelter-in-Place Orders Spurs Closures, Scaled-back Business and Worry," *The Santa Rosa Press Democrat*, March 18, 2020.

[3] Id.

venture to market, more and more of them donned masks and gloves to avoid accidental exposure to the virus. The fear and the threat of disease were everywhere, or so the people thought, and they passed the hours in constant apprehension of an infection that might change their lives inalterably.

They lived this way yes, but only until it was time to hit the public beaches, the parks and the trails and put aside all their anxieties and trepidations and live as if nothing had changed at all. All the grave seriousness with which Californians approached the need to socially distance from one another dissolved at the parking lot's edge and gave way to a carefree loosening of the restraints dutifully exhibited everywhere else. In Sonoma and Marin Counties, on that first weekend after the shelter-in-place orders came down, the crowds that flocked to the beaches caused "overflowing parking lots and packed stretches of sand."[4] The scene was replicated all along the California coastline, at inland parks, lakes, and on hiking trails everywhere. Stanislaus National Forest's Pine Crest Lake area "'was completely packed" with visitors from as far away as San Francisco; long lines of parked vehicles stretched along the roads in the San Gabriel Canyon area in the midst of the Angeles National Forest; and beaches in Southern California looked no different than they do on a typical summer's day.[5] The utter flaunting of shelter-in-place drew the ire of the Governor himself, who berated the crowds for "thinking it's party time," and admonished them that it was "time to grow up, time to wake up."[6] County after County began closing their parks; the parking lots to public beaches and other recreational areas were padlocked; and even the National Forests shut down. Instead of running campfire programs and pulling swimmers from rip-currents, rangers and lifeguards patrolled with ticket book in hand, on the look-out for trespassers too dense or too daring to act in accordance with the law. Certain public hiking trails and foot and bicycle paths remained open, but only so long as the people using them practiced proper social distancing etiquette.

---

[4] Chantelle Lee, "All Parks Closed in Sonoma County amid Coronavirus Outbreak," *The Santa Rosa Press Democrat*, March 23, 2020.

[5] Rosalio Ahumada, "Recreational Sites Closed at National Forests in California to Slow Coronavirus Spread," *The Sacramento Bee*, March 26, 2020; and Hollie Silverman & Sarah Moon, "Crowds Packed California Beaches Despite Shelter in Place Order," www.cnn.com, March 23, 2020.

[6] Chantelle Lee, op cit..

And so it was that there would be no neutral zone, no place of refuge from the rigors of this contemporary variation on the quarantine of old. The State would exercise its power to limit access to familiar places, and the people would be confined to their homes and a narrow scope of activity outside. Those who tested the resolve of the State would encounter first an understanding voice, interested more in educating them and gaining voluntary compliance than in harshly enforcing the law, but only for a time. San Francisco's police chief, William Scott, promised a "'compassionate, common-sense approach' to the order," followed by enforcement only "as a last resort."[7] Sonoma County's Sheriff's Office said it would dedicate itself to educating the public, but urged residents and business owners "not to 'force' them to take action to enforce the new law."[8] In Petaluma, the police would be "actively patrolling the streets, hoping to maintain a watchful presence," but a spokesman ominously admonished the "people to use common sense when they think about what they want to do."[9] In Alameda, police expected compliance, but announced that "if people are blatantly ignoring the shelter-in-place order, deputies will step in."[10] Where compliance was lacking, said Sergeant Ray Kelley, "the law is giving us the authority to act."[11] San Jose's police chief promised that the general educational approach his department was deploying would change quickly "if people aren't paying attention." The plan, he said, was "to move from an educational stance to an enforcement stance on any business that has been contacted, warned and then reopens again."[12]

Elsewhere, in other States, the story was the same. More aggressive enforcement of this massive infringement on the liberty of the people to move and to work was imminent: citations, arrests, convictions, fines and jail time. Some Governors were mobilizing the National Guard to assist in law enforcement, and rumours spread that soon the President would be invoking some of the more far reaching powers at his disposal

---

[7] Vivian Ho, "What Does 'Shelter in Place' Mean? California Coronavirus Order, Explained," www.theguardian.com, March 16, 2020.

[8] Schmitt, Baig & Callahan, op. cit..

[9] Id.

[10] Katie Nielson, "Police, Sheriffs Hope Enforcement of Shelter-in-Place Order won't be Necessary," http://sanfrancisco.cbslocal.com, March 16, 2020

[11] Id.

[12] "Coronavirus: Dozens violate COVID-19 shelter-in-place order in San Jose," www.abc13.com, March 21, 2020.

via the Warner Act to shut down ordinary interstate traffic and allocate the manpower to enforce it. The nation had not yet become a police state in response to the virus, but signs appeared to point down one possible road in that direction. That so few voices were heard decrying this trend and defending the hallmarks of our constitutional system of government and the liberties it protects was far more remarkable than the unprecedented events that unfolded before us.

There are those who insist, expect and dream of a government that is adequate and capable of responding to every crisis with whatever measures are appropriate at exactly the right moment, and will never deviate from the highest standards nor forget that it is the people it serves, not itself. For such thinkers, liberty can be a nuisance and an impediment to achieving great and necessary objectives, and those who attach themselves so childishly to such notions as entailed by due process and the Bill of Rights are best patronized, but never humoured. Such thinkers really have had their way in the past century and helped transform our understanding of the nature of government from one of self-restriction, to one of nearly unbounded power. "Our constitutional system," said one of the chief theorists of the broader view of governmental power in the Twentieth Century, "contains within itself all that is essential to its own preservation. It is adequate to all the exigencies which may arise."[13] Though many strides were taken this past century toward the full realization of this view and the centralization of the state that statist visionaries thought might operate efficiently in accordance with the dictates of dispassionate experts, the goal remained frustrated by a constitutional system designed to protect individual liberties and check any impulses toward centralized control through the mechanisms of the separation of powers and federalism. These mechanisms contained within them a deep assumption that the threat to individuals from without was no greater than the threat from within, and while the state might defend, it was equally apt to destroy.

In keeping with the traditional or classical theory of the Constitution, any effort to protect the people at large could not come at the people's expense in the form of an erosion (if not outright obliteration) of the people's liberty. A balanced approach was required, even when governmental action for the protection of the people from

---

[13] Charles Fairman, *The Law of Martial Rule*, 2d ed. (Chicago: Callaghan & Company, 1943), at p. 47.

dire threats to health and safety was deemed necessary. The assumption is at least as old as Locke, who championed individual liberties during the Enlightenment, but qualified it with the observation that "the first and fundamental natural law, which is to govern even the legislative itself, is the preservation of the society and (as far as will consist with the public good) of every person in it."[14] The assumptions of Locke were subsequently embedded in the constitutions of the American States following the Revolution—protecting liberty, but also empowering the States to act for the common good when faced with riot, insurrection, natural disaster and epidemic disease. From an early date, State authorities, in keeping with State constitutions and duly enacted statutes, wielded "a wide range of public health powers to quell and lessen the severity of disease outbreaks," including "disease surveillance and reporting requirements, mandatory treatment and inoculation, impounding unsafe or diseased property," and the authority to impose mandatory quarantine and isolation orders.[15] These powers might at times take on a draconian hue and challenge the axiom that the purpose of the constitutional state was to restrict the force of authority and preserve the liberty of individuals. And yet they were wielded not to advance the interests of tyrants, but to protect as many individuals as possible from the real prospect of a wasting death caused by the passage of any number of deadly plagues from one person to the next.

The protective nature of the state's power to overwhelm the rights of individuals in the name of public health, and the balance that must be struck between individual liberty and the public good, is perhaps best exemplified in a case arising from a challenge to a law of the State of Massachusetts permitting the forced inoculation of the adult population in the event of a smallpox epidemic. The defendant in that case argued that "his liberty is invaded when the State subjects him to fine or imprisonment for neglecting or refusing to submit to vaccination; that a compulsory vaccination law is unreasonable, arbitrary and oppressive, and, therefore, hostile to the inherent right of every freeman to care for his own body and health in such way as to him seems best, and that the execution of such a law against one who objects to vaccination, no matter

---

[14] John Locke, *Second Treatise of Government*, at XI.134.

[15] Ernest B. Abbott, "Law, Federalism, the Constitution, and Control of Pandemic Flu," 9 Asian-Pacific L. & Pol'y J. 185 (2008), at p. 195.

for what reason, is nothing short of an assault upon his person."[16] The question posed to the Supreme Court of the United States was whether the statute granting the State the power to compel the defendant's inoculation on pain of criminal punishment was "inconsistent with the liberty which the Constitution...secures to every person against deprivation by the State."[17] In discussing the problem, Justice Harlan the Elder explained the balance that state action to quell the spread of disease and other public disorders must strike. "The liberty secured by the Constitution," he noted, "does not import an absolute right in each person to be, at all times and in all circumstances, wholly freed from restraint. There are manifold restraints to which every person is necessarily subject for the common good. On any other basis, organized society could not exist with safety to its members. Society based on the rule that each one is a law unto himself would soon be confronted with disorder and anarchy. Real liberty for all could not exist under the operation of a principle which recognizes the right of each individual person to use his own, whether in respect of his person or his property, regardless of the injury that may be done to others."[18]

In evaluating the facts of the case, Justice Harlan and all but two of his brethren found the statute reasonable in that it was to be employed only in an emergency, or great threat to public health and safety, and that the localized control of the determination to do so ensured that the power, so closely scrutinized by those against whom it operated, would serve as a deterrent to its abuse. It was in keeping, too, with that "principle of self-defense, of paramount necessity," by which a community "has the right to protect itself from an epidemic of disease which threatens the safety of its members."[19] There was obviously an impairment of liberty that occurs when action was taken in accordance with the law, and the infliction of distress and inconvenience on individuals could well be extreme, but when "nothing more could be reasonably affirmed of the state in question," it was within "the duty of the constituted authorities to keep in view the welfare, comfort and safety of the many, and not permit the interests of the many to be

---

[16] *Jacobson v. Massachusetts* (1905) 197 U.S. 1, 26, 25 S.Ct. 358.
[17] Id., at 24.
[18] Id., at 26.
[19] Id., at 27.

subordinated to the wishes or convenience of the few."[20] Were the individual to prevail in such a case as this it "would practically strip the legislative department of its function to care for the public health and the public safety when endangered by epidemic disease."[21] Harlan and the majority were "not prepared to hold that a minority, residing or remaining in any city or town where smallpox is prevalent, and enjoying the general protection afforded by an organized local government, may thus defy the will of its constituted authorities, acting in good faith for all, under the legislative sanction of the State. If such be the privilege of a minority, then a like privilege would belong to each individual of the community, and the spectacle would be presented of the welfare and safety of an entire population being subordinated to the notions of a single individual."[22] The liberty secured by the Constitution simply could not and did not extend to any given individual "the power to thus dominate the majority when supported in their action by the authority of the State."[23]

The decision of Justice Harlan and the Court's majority was delivered in light of the knowledge of an actual and imminent threat to public health posed by smallpox, lack of any evidence of health risks posed by the vaccine, and properly tailored exceptions to the broad reach of the inoculation order in the case of children whose particular health conditions rendered the vaccine objectively dangerous. The possibility that action by the State in the furtherance of public health might not pass constitutional muster was hardly precluded. Indeed, judges throughout the land were already well-versed in the balance between the obligation of the state to protect the safety of the many and the rights of individuals, and the possibility that the latter might exceed in weight that of the former. Such a case occurred in the Spring of the year 1900, when the San Francisco Board of Health and the chief quarantine officer of the United States in the Port of San Francisco responded to reports of bubonic plague in the City by imposing an order that any and all Chinese residents "submit to inoculation with the serum known as 'Haffkine Prophylactic,'' and confining those who resisted either to the limits of the City or to a jail cell. Some of those effected by

---

[20] Id., at 29.
[21] Id., at 37.
[22] Id., at 37-38.
[23] Id., at 38.

the law contended that it violated their right to travel, the equal protection of the laws and their freedom from unreasonable exposure to the potential health and life-threatening side effects of the vaccine. In reviewing the matter, the Circuit Court for the Northern District of California acknowledged the right and obligation of municipal authorities to take action pursuant to the relevant law in order to protect the City and the State from contagious diseases. Such action that was appropriate and calculated to accomplish the end of protecting the public would not be subject to judicial second guessing. And yet, any measure of this sort, said the Court, "must have some relation to the end in view."[24] Authority exercised "under the mere guise of the police power" cannot be permitted to arbitrarily invade the personal and property rights of individuals. In the case at bar, the Court ultimately held that the order issued by municipal authorities was "not based upon any established distinction in the conditions that are supposed to attend this plague, or the persons exposed to its contagion," but were "boldly directed against the Asiatic or Mongolian race as a class, without regard to the previous condition, habits, exposure to disease, or residence of the individual," and were justified on nothing more than a suggestion, without supporting evidence, "that this particular race is more liable to plague than any other."[25] In short, the action by the Board of Health couldn't be squared with the Constitution because of the lack of sufficient evidence of a threat to public health, was imposed improperly on individuals in a manner that wasn't well tailored to address the supposed threat, and posed significant and unnecessary danger to the health and safety of those against whom it was directed without an offsetting benefit for society as a whole.

The same court reaffirmed its analysis in a case arising out of a similar action by the San Mateo County Board of Health, stating that while decisions of public health authorities are presumptively valid, "there are, of necessity, limits beyond which [government action] cannot rightfully go."[26] If a statute or a governmental action based thereon purports to advance the public's safety and health, but "'has no real or substantial relation to those objects, or is a palpable invasion of rights

[24] *Wong Wai v. Williamson* (1900) 103 F. 1.
[25] Id., at 7.
[26] *Jew Ho v. Williamson* (1900) 103 F. 10, 17.

secured by the fundamental law, it is the duty of the courts to so adjudge, and thereby give effect to the Constitution.'"[27]

In the same era, the Supreme Court of South Carolina noted that the power of the state to protect against threats to public health posed by infectious diseases certainly permitted invasions of liberty essential to that object, but no more. Though the legitimacy of laws allowing for the exercise of broad power to safeguard public health and safety in times of epidemic could be questioned, courts nevertheless were empowered to consider "whether there is any real relations between the preservation of the public health and the legislative enactment, or the regulations and proceedings of boards of health under authority of the state," and to determine if "the statute or the regulations made or the proceedings taken under it are not reasonably appropriate to the end in view."[28] In considering the facts of the particular case – the forcible confinement of an elderly woman suffering from a non-communicable form of leprosy to a foul pest house used primarily for the quarantining of smallpox victims instead of within the confines of her own home – South Carolina's high court held that the limits of the police power had been exceeded due to a failure by the State to tailor its order so as to limit the impairment of liberty no more than necessary under the circumstances.

Despite the gradual emergence of a more exacting standard of review when individual liberties protected by the Constitution are impaired by the state, courts tend to question only the scope of public health directives and focus on determining whether or not the aim they purport to serve has been secured "by means which sweep unnecessarily broadly and thereby invade the area of protected freedom."[29] This very approach was lately recommended by the drafters of the Model State Emergency Health Powers Act (MSEHPA), whose recommendations have been adopted by nearly all jurisdictions in the country.[30] In keeping with this approach, States and municipalities that issue orders impacting the mobility and livelihood of the people must ever respect "the rights of people to liberty…to the fullest extent possible consistent with

---

27 Id., at 18, quoting the Supreme Court in *The Sinking Fund Cases* 99 U.S. 700, 718.

28 *Kirk v. Board of Health* (1909) 65 S.E. 387, 390.

29 *Griswold v. Connecticut* (1965) 381 U.S. 479, 485, 85 S.Ct. 1678.

30 Michelle A. Daubert, "Pandemic Fears and Contemporary Quarantine: Protecting Liberty Through a Continuum of Due Process Rights," 54 Buffalo L. Rev. 1299 (2007), at p. 1337.

maintaining and preserving the public's health and security."[31] This is really no different from the standard articulated more than three hundred years ago by John Locke and incorporated into the constitutions and the laws of the States ever since. And yet it is no easy task to measure the appropriate restriction on liberty when faced with an emergency, particularly one posed by a disease of novel composition with which humanity has little experience. How far the state might go in limiting freedom protected by the Constitution simply cannot be calculated with any degree of certainty, hence the temptation to be better safe than sorry becomes difficult for the conscientious public servant to resist.

In the case of the Coronavirus, the response of the State and Federal Governments to the growing profile of the disease has been both expansive and measured. Restrictions on liberty have issued gradually in proportion to what was currently fathomed of the disease and its progress. Limitations on movement and size of assembly, at first only voluntary, became mandatory as testing indicated a wider spread of the contagion than previously known. When people were ordered to shelter-in-place, exceptions for essential activity, including essential employment, were carved out, and reasonable time, place and manner regulations were adopted to govern any necessary public assemblies, such as at grocery stores, hospitals and gas stations. Police as yet have been more educational than penal in their approach to enforcement, and much of the onus for compliance has been placed on the public spiritedness of the people themselves. And yet, more severe restrictions on work and mobility appear on the near horizon, not to mention the threat of enforcement of a quality less benign than a mere quest for compliance. Such may be necessary in light emerging conditions, but will come with a downside that we fail to contemplate at our peril. We might be saved from a threat of illness and death—or the actual coming to pass of such things—by an aggressive restriction of the liberty protected by the Constitution. What it takes, or what our public officials and the courts deem to be necessary, to achieve this result, may well have consequences that are both longer lasting and detrimental to the freedom to be exercised by the people once the danger has passed. There may come a time when we might find ourselves entertaining feelings of

[31] Id., at p. 1338.

sympathy even for those Texans who wrote discrete provisions "into the fundamental law as direct inhibitions upon the executive" after suffering "under the imposition of martial law, with its suspension of civil authority, and the ousting of the courts during Reconstruction."[32] Those same considerations were certainly in the minds of the Framers of our national Constitution, and they, if not the Framers of Texas' Jim Crow Era document, are entitled to our respect and worthy of our remembrance as the product of the ideations of men who aimed to protect the many from all manner of oppressions, including the oppression of those guided and misguided by desires to help, not hurt.

The downside to protecting the health and safety of the public, and the potential to hurt rather than help, is evident today as the nation's economy shrinks by the minute, jobless claims grow exponentially, and household items long taken for granted haven't been seen on store shelves in weeks. Those dependent on the courts for adjudication of legal disputes are denied access, a speedy trial, and all the other rights associated with the administration of justice, while those awaiting hearings on requests for probation, parole or early release remain in a strange limbo where due process does not exist. The daily casualty reports convey the reality of the danger, but still they are not so voluminous as similar reports during past epidemics, or even contagions that never caught our attention or resolve. The threat is real, as are the bed-ridden, the dying and the dead, but the present magnitude of the threat reasonably provokes doubt as to the deployment of the awesome power of government to solve a problem inherent in all living organisms and addressed in times past merely by a combination of immunity come from exposure, identification, isolation and treatment of the sick, and preventative measures including better sanitary practices, vaccination and immunity boosting regimens.

So drastic and intentional a limitation on human mobility and the ability of people to earn a living has never occurred in this country, and certainly not during the epidemics of the recent past: the Spanish Flu in 1918 that killed a million Americans; the 1968 Hong Kong Flu that left 100,000 Americans dead; and H1N1 in 2009, from which 12,000 in this country perished. Evidence indicates a fatality rate among those contracting the disease that may be as low as 1 percent. If true, says

---

[32] *Sterling v. Constantin* (1932) 287 U.S. 378, 395.

Stanford Epidemiologist John Ioannidis, "locking down the world with potentially tremendous social and financial consequences may be totally irrational."[33] As life-saving medicines and other products become hard to obtain due to the reduction in all links in the chain of production and distribution, and a decreasing store of resources are prioritized for use by those felled by COVID-19, the extreme measures might actually cost more lives than they save. The measures, and what might follow, are potentially irrational in other ways too: namely the adverse impact they are having and may yet have on the constitutional structure of our society that has proven to be relatively successful in limiting the natural tendency of the state and those who control it to manipulate, oppress and even slaughter the people.

A massive deprivation of liberty is occurring at this moment, and the longer it continues the more settled it becomes, the more natural and entrenched. What is intended as a temporary, emergency measure, will come to be seen as a handy mechanism to achieve other ends, and will prove far too lucrative to those who would control it to relinquish it too easily. There is always yet another justification for the use of the state's power, some noble cause to champion, some more efficacious end to pursue. The current justifications for emergency power have within them the forces to effect further erosion of the constitutional checks on government and the liberties of the people our government was designed and empowered to protect. These next few weeks should be telling. If the death rate stabilizes and begins to decline, the spread of infection is contained, and progress occurs with respect to treatments and a vaccine, the limitations on freedom that the people are currently accepting with such an admirable degree of public mindedness will have to be revised in the people's favor. If not, the threat to the constitutional order becomes all the more potent, and the danger increases, both of attempts to render the emergency of longer duration and a reaction by the people that only concessions or further repression can defuse.

[33] Thomas L. Friedman, "A Plan to Get America Back to Work," *The New York Times*, March 22, 2020.

Matters of Life…And Death

AS the fear of the great epidemic of our time spreads, and more and more people became convinced of the need for extreme precautions lest the disease transmit rapidly among the population and cause massive fatalities, those in the business of providing goods and services began to consider what they personally might do to advance the common good. Long touting themselves as providers of "medical services," the staffs at abortion clinics across the land contemplated what measures they could take to protect themselves and their "patients" from harm. Some clinics began "asking women to do as much paperwork as possible online and over the phone to reduce the time they spend in the office," while others "adjusted their patient schedules" and spaced "appointments further apart so there is less overlap."[1] In a nation where the number of abortion clinics is on the decline, concerns arose over growing restrictions on travel that governments at all levels were imposing and the lack of money many "patients" were beginning to experience as shelter-in-place orders prevented large numbers of people from earning a living.[2] And then there was the real scarcity of medical supplies such as gloves and masks and the rededication of the remainder by government order to fight the epidemic. There was no doubt that COVID-19 was about to adversely affect abortion clinics and the practice of abortion in a monumental way through the extinction, at least temporarily, of paying clients.

The challenge faced by abortion providers only worsened as State after State declared that only non-elective medical procedures would be permitted during the emergency. Every other procedure, not aimed at staving off life-threatening conditions or necessary for the preservation of the well-being of the patient from the profoundest health consequences, would be deferred. In States such as Mississippi, Texas, Maryland, Tennessee, Louisiana and Ohio, defenders of abortion rights decried these "extreme" actions and contended that officials were cynically "exploiting the public health crisis to advance a political

---

[1] Melissa Jeltsen, "Abortion Access is Under Threat as Coronavirus Spreads," www.huffpost.com, March 17, 2020.

[2] Id.

agenda."[3] The President of the Center for Reproductive Rights called the bans "an abuse of power" that were part of a long-term effort "to use sham justifications to shut down clinics and make an end-run around *Roe v. Wade*."[4] Delma Catalina Limones of NARAL Pro-Choice Texas said abortion must go on even during the pandemic because "we know that abortion is essential health care. It is a procedure where time is of the essence."[5] Quickly, Planned Parenthood announced that abortion procedures would continue without violation of the emergency decrees, and the American College of Obstetricians and Gynaecologists called on providers not to classify the procedure as "elective and non-urgent."[6] Brushing off criticism that abortion couldn't be non-elective if it truly was the "choice" its advocates had always said it was, clinics in some States remained open in disobedience of public orders.[7] Government notices inevitably began to issue, directing the defiant clinics to comply with the prohibition on all non-essential procedures, and threats were made, including by Texas's Attorney General, that fines of up to $1,000 per violation and 180 days in jail awaited those who continued to flaunt the law.[8]

A counter-offensive wasn't long in coming. In New Jersey, Massachusetts, Virginia and Washington, governors decreed abortion to be an essential need, exempting it from bans on non-essential medical procedures.[9] Iowa's governor agreed with abortion providers to allow surgical abortions "if delaying them would push the patient past the point at which legal abortions were allowed," and in Michigan and Pennsylvania, governors simply left abortion off the lists of prohibited non-essential treatments.[10] Where bans remained in place, abortion clinics took to the courts, seeking orders allowing abortions to continue unrestricted. In Texas, Ohio and Alabama, federal judges promptly

---

[3] Caroline Kelly, "Mississippi, Texas and Ohio Move to Limit Abortion as Part of Coronavirus Response," www.cnn.com, March 25, 2020.

[4] Jennifer Haberkorn, "Amid Coronavirus Outbreak Some Red States Move to Restrict Abortion, Spurring Legal Fight," *The Los Angeles Times*, April 2, 2020.

[5] Paul Strand, "While Some States Abortion Temporarily Ban Abortion as Elective, Others Designate it 'Essential,'" www.1.cbn.com, March 27, 2020.

[6] Id.

[7] Christine Carrega, "Are Abortions Considered 'Essential' Medical Procedures Amid COVID-19 Outbreak?" www.abcnews.com, March 24, 2020.

[8] Kelly, op.cit.

[9] Strand, op. cit.

[10] Jennifer Haberkorn, op. cit.

issued the requested relief, at least until hearings could be conducted via Zoom due to the epidemic-related restrictions on the operation of federal courts currently in effect.[11] Speaking of Alabama's prohibition, Judge Myron Thompson declared that "the State's interest in immediate enforcement…against abortion providers does not…outweigh plaintiff's concerns."[12] Addressing Texas's argument that suspension of protected rights was permitted during emergencies, Judge Lee Yeakel said that he would "not speculate on whether the Supreme Court included a silent 'except-in-a-national-emergency clause' in its previous writings on the issue."[13] Texas's Attorney General denounced the judicial interference with the State's effort to protect the public during the epidemic, and said it had the effect of placing the right to an abortion in a class of rights that could never be impaired, even as the sacred rights to vote, freely assemble, travel and receive due process of law remained subject to infringement to such a marked degree.[14] Just as the Supreme Court in the 1897 case of *Sentell v. New Orleans & C.R. Co.* held that "it is clearly within the power of the State" to order the destruction of private property "in times of epidemic, or whenever they are so exposed as to be deleterious to the public health," it is, argued the Attorney General, just as permissible for the State to temporarily limit other vested interests and other rights, including the right to an abortion.[15]

The agitation over access to abortion clinics during the pandemic is part of a fifty year-long war between "life" and "choice," wherein choice remains largely victorious because its interests remain protected by a right discovered over a hundred years after the ratification of the Fourteenth Amendment to be invisibly embedded beneath or between the black letter of the Constitution's text. The recent action by the courts enjoining the closure of clinics even in the midst of the compelling government interest to curtail the spread of a dangerous virus is reflective of the continuing precedence courts give to so-called abortion

---

[11] Alice Miranda Ollstein, "Judges Block 3 States from Enforcing Abortion Bans Pegged to Pandemic," www.politico.com, March 30, 2020.

[12] Id.

[13] Id.

[14] State Defendants' Response to Plaintiffs' Motion for a Temporary Restraining Order, *Planned Parenthood Center for Choice, et al. v. Greg Abbott, et al.*, Civil Action No. 1:20-cv-00323-LY, at p. 22.

[15] Id., at p. 21.

rights over even those rights of individuals and powers of government expressly set forth in the law.

The solicitous attitude of the courts to abortion during this crisis is part and parcel of what Justice Thomas said is the judiciary's "troubling tendency 'to bend the rules when any effort to limit abortion, or even to speak in opposition to abortion is at issue.'"[16] From the time of *Roe v. Wade* onward, the courts relaxed the ordinary rules of justiciability that require a litigant to have suffered an actual injury that was redressable in a meaningful way by allowing litigants to sue for declaratory and injunctive relief even after the pregnancy had been taken to term. Subsequent decisions of the courts went further by permitting doctors and even abortion clinics to sue on a patient's behalf, in clear violation of the venerable prohibition against third party standing and the principle that the court "not listen to an objection made to the constitutionality of an act by a party whose rights it does not affect and who has therefore no interest in defeating it."[17] The rationale for relaxing the rules governing standing was that the party bringing the action supposedly had "a close relation" to the injured person, who "faced a formidable 'hindrance' to asserting his own rights," and thus was in need of third party assistance if his (or her) rights were to be vindicated.[18] Even this more relaxed qualification for party standing was finally jettisoned when courts simply adopted a rule that permitted third parties to sue to vindicate the rights of women who supposedly desired an abortion. The result, noted Justice Thomas, was the encouragement of abortion providers to sue, even though the only injury such parties suffered was an economic injury to themselves through the loss of paying clients. He found it supremely ironic that "after creating a constitutional right to abortion because it 'involve[s] the most intimate and personal choices a person may make in a lifetime, choices central to personal dignity and autonomy, the Court has created special rules that cede its enforcement to others."[19]

The battle over abortion clinic closures during the coronavirus epidemic will likely resolve as the epidemic itself subsides and life

[16] *Whole Women's Health v. Hellerstedt* (2016) 579 U.S. ___, 136 S.Ct. 2292, at 2321, J. Thomas, dissenting.

[17] Id., at 2322.

[18] Id., at 2322.

[19] Id., at 2323.

returns to normal. Other fronts in the larger war will remain active until finally settled by decisions issuing from the nation's high bench. Those fronts include the ongoing controversy over laws unquestionably designed to promote childbirth and deter abortion by regulating the qualifications of doctors who perform abortions and the imposition of minimum standards of operation in the clinics themselves. A typical law of this kind was enacted in Texas in the past decade and required any physician performing an abortion to possess admitting privileges at a hospital that was situated "not further than 30 miles from the location at which the abortion is performed or induced," and that abortion clinics comply with facility standards that are "equivalent to the minimum standards" mandated for ambulatory surgical centres.[20] The Texas law was challenged not by women seeking abortions, but by actual abortion clinics whose doctors apparently couldn't obtain admitting privileges at area hospitals and whose facilities fell short of the requisite standards. Though it was their own economic interests that were at risk, the clinics alleged that their relationship to women seeking abortion was sufficient to establish standing in accordance with post-*Roe* justiciability principles governing abortion litigation. They prevailed in federal district court after a bench trial, but were then disappointed by the contrary opinion of the court of appeals.

Instead of seeking review by the High Nine, the plaintiffs regrouped and brought an entirely new action alleging yet again that the Texas law imposed an "undue burden" on women seeking an abortion. Rather than dismiss the suit as barred by the principle of res judicata, the District Court heard the case on the merits, as did the Supreme Court when the matter finally reached it. A narrow majority headed by Justice Stephen Breyer agreed with the initial determination of the District Court and struck down the law. The admitting privilege requirement was said by its proponents to have been designed "to help ensure that women have easy access to a hospital should complications arise during an abortion procedure," but in truth didn't advance that end at all because abortion was supposedly extremely safe to begin with.[21] Worse yet, the burden on the right to an abortion was unduly onerous because too many Texas hospitals required that doctors who enjoyed admitting privileges at their facilities actually admit a set number of patients per

---

[20] *Whole Women's Health v. Hellerstedt*, supra, opinion of the Court, at 2300.
[21] Id., at 2311-2312.

year lest the privilege be lost. The lack of any need to admit patients to hospitals due to the absence of any medical reason to do so meant that most abortion doctors couldn't qualify for admitting privileges, hence they couldn't lawfully perform abortions. The subsequent reduction of the number of abortion doctors deprived abortion clinics of medical staff to do the work, which in turn resulted in a decrease in the number of functioning clinics and the imposition on abortion clients of a further burden in the form of extended drive times to reach the few remaining facilities in the State where an abortion could be obtained.

Justice Breyer and the majority also held that the requirement that clinics be outfitted as ambulatory surgical centers imposed an undue burden on the right of women to obtain an abortion by further contributing to clinic closures. The standards governing ambulatory surgical centers included minimum staffing requirements, the presence of a registered nurse and at least two persons trained in basic cardiac life support, and installation of "a full surgical suite with an operating room that has 'a clear floor area of at least 240 square feet' in which '[t]he minimum clear dimension between built-in cabinets, counters, and shelves shall be 14 feet."[22] Compliance with these requirements cost money and tended to place the overhead of most clinics at an unsustainable height. That the requirements supposedly had no effect in enhancing the safety of the procedure or the health of women rendered them not only useless in the majority's view, but unnecessarily obstructive of the constitutionally protected rights of women seeking abortions.

The decision was celebrated as "a major setback for the anti-choice movement," if not the death knell of efforts by States to regulate abortion clinics out of existence through measures "masquerading" as rules to enhance the health and safety of women undergoing the procedure.[23] Even President Obama weighed in, saying he was "pleased to see the Supreme Court protect women's rights and health."[24] Others said that the decision as crafted by the "wonkish" Justice Breyer was destined to make it harder for States attempting to regulate abortion "to meet their

[22] Id., at 2314.

[23] John A. Robertson, "Whole Woman's Health and the Future of Abortion Regulation," blog.petrieflom.law.harvard.edu, July 11, 2016.

[24] "Statement by the President on Whole Woman's Health v. Hellerstedt," https://obamawhitehouse.archives.gov, June 27, 2016.

burden of proof in court."[25] That the report of the demise of such laws was premature became evident when Louisiana enacted a similar statute. An aggressive response to this new law was quickly advanced in *June Medical Services, L.L.C. v. Gee* even before it took effect and resulted in a decision by the District Court that it was essentially no different than its Texas counterpart and must be struck down in accordance with the analysis provided by Justice Breyer. As in Texas, though, the U.S. Circuit Court of Appeals reversed the lower court's decision and upheld the law. That decision is now headed to the Supreme Court for reconsideration.

Though the Louisiana law shares some similarities with its Texas counterpart, there are differences, and certainly the effect on the purported rights of women seeking abortions may well not be the same. The Court of Appeals' starting point in reviewing the law was the standard articulated by the Supreme Court in *Planned Parenthood of Southeastern Pennsylvania v. Casey* that Justice Breyer had relied on in *Whole Women's Health*. This standard prohibits state action that imposes an actual rather than irrelevant restriction constituting a "substantial" or undue burden on the rights of a large fraction of the population seeking an abortion. That burden, said Court of Appeals Judge Jerry E. Smith, must be considered in light of the benefits the law at issue conveys, not in isolation, and must actually be substantial or undue. Any burden that was less than substantial would not rise to the level of a violation of the Constitution. "A minimal burden even on a large fraction of women," he said, "does not undermine the right to abortion."[26] Slight or even moderate burdens will not invalidate a law.

Turning its eye to the substance of the Louisiana law, the Court indicated that unlike its Texas forerunner, evidence appeared at trial of its "minimal benefit."[27] The Texas law requiring abortion doctors to possess hospital admitting privileges was said by Justice Breyer to have had no relationship to ensuring physician competence because the hospitals themselves did nothing to review the substance of a physician's skills and experience. Conversely, in Louisiana, hospitals

---

[25] Amanda Hollis Brusky & Rachel Van Sickle-Ward, "Here Are Two Ways that Breyer's Wonky Opinion in *Whole Women's Health* Could Transform Abortion Politics," www.washingtonpost.com, July 3, 2016.

[26] *June Medical Services, L.L.C. v. Gee* (2018) 905 F. 787, 803.

[27] Id., at 805.

actually followed policies that entailed review of a physician's competency as a condition of a physician obtaining and maintaining admitting privileges.

Having established an actual benefit served by the law, Judge Smith and the majority then considered the alleged burdens on the rights of women seeking abortions the law imposed. The Court in *Whole Women's Health*, Smith observed, identified burdens on the right in the form of "closure of facilities, difficulty in obtaining privileges, driving distances, and clinic capacities." While not necessarily imposing an undue burden individually, each of these discreet factors flowed from the next, commencing with the inability of doctors to obtain admitting privileges due to the safe nature of abortion procedures, and then dominoing one by one until the impermissible substantial or undue burden was achieved.[28] "Had that difficulty not loomed, there would have been no facility closures, no increased driving distances, and no issues regarding clinic capacities."[29] Because of "the high minimum admission requirements at most Texas hospitals, that burden was unavoidable" and logically gave rise to others.[30] A similar burden or set of burdens, however, was not evident on the record under review. Hospitals in Louisiana didn't impose minimum admitting quotas on doctors granted admitting privileges, hence the burden that existed in Texas was non-existent in Louisiana, and didn't similarly cause the chain of burdens that led the Supreme Court to conclude that the Texas law imposed the kind of detriment that violated the Constitution. That doctors performing abortions didn't obtain admitting privileges in Louisiana following passage of the law wasn't particularly meaningful to Judge Smith, in part because the law was never given a chance to take effect, but mostly because the physicians performing abortions weren't particularly diligent in attempting to comply with the requirement. While some made cursory inquiries and a few were actually denied privileges, "the vast majority largely sat on their hands, assuming that they would not qualify."[31] Their inaction, said the Court, "severs the chain of causation" between their failure to obtain admitting privileges

---

[28] Id., at 807.
[29] Id.
[30] Id.
[31] Id.

and the various other burdens that naturally and logically flowed from that fact in the Texas context.[32]

In his dissent against the appellate court's decision to decline *en banc* review, Judge Stephen Higginson insisted that his brethren had misread the relevant precedents, including and especially *Whole Women's Health*. So recent a decision would not, he thought, be easily overcome by justices on the High Court who decided that case. The majority, he suspected, would likely reject the Louisiana law and the Circuit Court opinion that upheld it.[33] Even justice Thomas, he contended, would likely join with a majority in reversing the appellate court because of his stated concern that courts abide "by one set of rules to adjudicate constitutional rights" rather than reduce "Constitutional law to policy-driven value judgments."[34]

Judge Higginson's invocation of support from Justice Thomas, of course, wasn't likely sincere. Rather, it was an attempt to frame the issue as one of formal precedent over a given majority's different understanding of what the Constitution requires. It was also likely calculated either to shame Thomas into acknowledging his past critique of the court or set him up for charges of hypocrisy when he votes to sustain the Louisiana law. Thomas isn't a hypocrite. He is probably the least hypocritical member of the current court. He has long criticized the Court's due process jurisprudence, as well as any deviation from reliance on the original intent of the Framers when interpreting the law. It is hardly a controversial proposition that the Framers' original intent in no ways contemplated a right to destroy life in the womb, and likely extended to condoning the power of States to protect such life through outright bans on the procedure. And that is exactly what lawmakers in the States did once abortion became a remotely viable procedure, to protect women from quacks wielding the proverbial coat hangers, as well as the human life relentlessly growing within them in accordance with the biologically programmed goal of reaching that point of maturity at which birth naturally ensues.

Roe is not under assault in the Louisiana case, and will not be directly threatened if the majority, lacking the contributions of the pro-choice Justice Kennedy, upholds the Louisiana statue as imposing only a slight

---

[32] Id., at 805.

[33] *June Medical Services, L.L.C. v. Gee* (2019) 913 F.3d 573, 585.

[34] Id.

burden on the right. There is little doubt, too, that if ever it came before them, the present Court would uphold the State decrees closing abortion clinics as non-essential in the fight against widening infections by a disease nearly everyone accepts is spread through casual and non-intimate contact, hence easily distributed within the close confines of a clinic's facilities. The right, such as it exists, of women to destroy their children before birth, and of doctors and clinics to line their pockets with the profits from services rendered, are subject, like all other rights, to the real interests of society in protecting itself from the rapid transmission of a potentially deadly contagion. That there are those who disagree, and judges even who are willing to countermand well-tailored limitations on human activity while the threat endures, is indication of just how unreasonable those asserting their rights are, and just how committed they are not to "choice," but to the true antithesis to what their opponents advocate— not life, but death.

The Cult of Ruth

AS news spread from the confines of the exclusive hunting lodge in a remote part of Texas of the death of 79-year-old Justice Antonin Scalia, the encomiums began to take shape in the minds of friends and admirers, and would appear over the course of the next several days in many of the publications and broadcasts of note. For a completely positive spin to find expression at such a time was an impossibility given the prominent place Scalia played in the framing and adjudication of the most fundamental legal issues in the country for the past three decades, and his role in defining modern conservativism and the judicial philosophy of originalism that came to pose such an obstacle to those who preferred expediency in the pursuit of policy at the expense of respect for the basic formalities of black letter text. The outright glee as well as hatred expressed for Scalia upon his passing, however, was shocking both in its extent and how profoundly contrary it was to historic norms governing the tone of commentary to be struck when speaking of the recently departed. Admitting her understanding that her delight contradicted traditional decorum in such circumstances, Barnstable County Commissioner Sheila Lyons nevertheless went on to justify her elated state of mind by referencing Scalia's orchestration of "tremendous power to benefit the powerful who have controlled the message to the American people."[1] Disregarding any concern over respect for the dead, journalist Michelangelo Signorile celebrated Scalia's demise as the first impulse presaging a release of "a right-wing, conservative homophobic, racist, misogynistic grip that held the court tightly for decades."[2] For his own part, the noted author and legal thinker Stephen Carter registered discomfort when many of his friends and followers filled his Twitter feed with hate—"not disagreement or disrespect—actual hate."[3] "He was an ignorant waste of flesh," read one tweet, while another said "his death was the best news in decades." Several Twitter users were so inspired by the unexpected windfall that they ventured to hope that "Clarence Thomas would die next."[4] "As a proud liberal, I'm happy he's gone," exclaimed *Huffington Post* Senior Editor Gabriel Arana.[5] One lesser known tweetist said they would feel guilty about being so happy over Scalia's death if he wasn't so "unashamedly evil."[6] Another urged people to pay an appropriate homage to the man by shitting on his grave.[7]

No doubt there are those on the other side of the ideological spectrum who would react the same way to the death of, say, Ruth Bader Ginsburg, though we will have to wait for that day to know for sure. So far, the only prominent people on the Right who have even hinted at her death are a Senator whose own expiration not long afterward was noted with satisfaction by Ginsburg herself, and more recently, a Congressman who dispelled a rumour that he had "asked for a joint meeting with Justice Ginsburg" after he had been exposed to the Coronavirus.[8] In bad taste yes, but not quite the visceral and ghoulish glee of the celebrants of

---

[1] Joan Vennochi, "Antonin Scalia, Death and Due Restraint," *The Boston Globe*, February 17, 2016.

[2] Id.

[3] Stephen Carter, "Scalia's Grave-Dancers Deserve a Harsh Verdict," *The Chicago Tribune*, February 16, 2016.

[4] Id.

[5] Becket Adams, "Some in Media Revel in Scalia's Death," www.washingtonexaminer.com, February 16, 2016.

[6] Kyle Olson, "'Burn in hell': Leftists Cheer Death of Antonin Scalia," www.theamericanmirror.com, February 13, 2016.

[7] Id.

[8] Erin Vanderhoof, "Ruth Bader Ginsburg is Proud to Have Outlived a Senator Once Called 'Too Mean and Weird for the GOP,'" Vanity Fair, July 24, 2019; and Matt Naham, "Self-Quarantining GOP Lawmaker Jokes About Meeting with Ruth Bader Ginsburg," www.msn.com, March 11, 2020.

the death of Ginsburg's good friend Justice Scalia, some of whom might well have been among the ranks of those who quickly retaliated against the Coronavirus jokester by denouncing him as "a monster," wondered if he had been "born this vile," and suggested that this was but a reflection of the "culture of cruelty that early fascism creates."[9] One commentator summed up the Congressman's statement as "an offensive partisan jest designed to elicit chuckles among GOP ghouls lusting for another Supreme Court seat to hand Trump to fill from the Federalist Society's list of approved reactionaries."[10]

The quick and hard-hitting defense of Justice Ginsberg is a function in part of the fact that she occupies a place in the ideological pantheon of the left analogous to that which the late Justice Scalia occupied for those on the right. As Scalia was a conservative icon and thought leader, Ginsburg is the progressive voice of the living Constitution and the champion of those who have longed for a resumption of the New Deal or the Warren Court, so that the promise of a "fair and just" America be stymied no longer by the dead hand of Framers whose commitments to slavery, racism and the subjugation of women hardly recommend them as authorities to follow when determining the meaning of our nation's highest law. But unlike the devotion to Scalia on the right, the left's sentiments regarding Ginsburg have found expression in ways unprecedented and at times strange. In even the briefest tour of merchandise available on-line one encounters the many fangled manifestations of Ruthmania: socks embroidered with her picture, wine glasses, shower curtains, pillow cases, a coffee cup inscribed with the word "Dissent" accompanied by an image of the Justice holding up both middle fingers, and even a waffle iron. There are mints (called "Judgmints"), earrings, T-shirts, plush dolls, calendars, posters, coloring books, bobble heads, and even a six-inch tall "action figure" that allows the possessor to "take the fire of the notorious supreme court justice anywhere." Stephanie Mencimer claims to have visited a store in Washington D.C. dedicated almost exclusively to Ruth merch, including yoga mats, water bottles, magnets and other items bearing her image, as

---

[9] Travis Gettys, "Self-Quarantined GOP 'Monster' Blasted for Joking About Giving Justice Ginsburg Coronavirus," www.alternet.org, March 11, 2020.

[10] "Self-Quarantined Republican Jokes About Deliberately Infecting Supreme Justice Ginsburg With Virus," https://occupydemocrats.com, March 11, 2020.

well as pins designed to look like Ginsburg's famous lace "dissent collar."[11]

And there are the books. Scalia, of course, has been the subject of biographers, but the most prominent—Joan Biskupic and Bruce Alan Murphy—were respectful critics, not hagiographers. In contrast, the entries in the biographical bibliography of Ruth Bader Ginsburg might be better classified with the lives of saints than with the chronicles of the achievements of members of the bench. In addition to the collection of her own writings—*In Defense of Justice, My Own Words* and *You Can't Spell the Truth Without Ruth*, there are Jeffrey Rosen's interviews with the Justice, entitled *Conversations with RBG*, Teri Kanefield's *Free to Be Ruth Bader Ginsburg: The Story of Women and the Law*, and the friendly and admiring biography by Jane Sherron de Hart and Suzanne Toren entitled simply *Ruth Bader Ginsburg: A Life*, as well as the over-the-top love fest that is Antonia Felix and Mimi Leder's *The Unstoppable Ruth Bader Ginsburg*. A series of children's books, aiming to instil post-modernist feminism in the minds of young girls, has also dampened the printing press: *Who is Ruth Bader Ginsburg* by Patricia Brennan Demuth, Debby Levy's *Becoming RBG: Ruth Bader Ginsburg's Journey to Justice*, Jonah Winter's and Stacy Innerst's *Ruth Bader Ginsburg: The Case of R.B.G. vs. Inequality*, *Dissenting on the Bench: Ruth Bader Ginsburg's Life & Work* by Victoria Ortiz, and the volume by Anna Membrino and Fatti Burke entitled *I Look Up To... Ruth Bader Ginsburg*. Setting the pace for all of these volumes celebrating the Justice's life is literally the earliest and most notorious of all: *Notorious RBG*, by Irin Carmon and Shana Knizhnik, in which the brainy, bespectacled, and purse wielding Justice is presented as a hard core badass with an attitude and the fighting chops to back it up. She ain't old, she ain't finished, and she sure as hell ain't takin no for an answer.

Though diminutive in physical proportions, Ginsburg's intellect is monumental. Searing on paper when expressing her profound disagreement with her colleagues, she is nevertheless in person the epitome of civility and class. Her work ethic is legendary as is her pre-judicial career, during which she took the lead in challenging traditional narrow views of the protections afforded by the Fifth and Fourteenth Amendments and advocated successfully for the constitutionalizing of

---

[11] Stephanie Mencimer, "What the Cult of Ruth Bader Ginsburg Got Wrong," *Mother Jones*, November 24, 2018.

gender equality.[12] She was notable enough for her contributions to the law to gain the attention of President Carter, who appointed her to the D.C Circuit Court of Appeals as a counterpoint to Conservative giant Robert Bork. Her elevation by President Clinton to the High Court in 1993 put her on the path to consolidating and preserving her achievements as a litigator and perhaps exceeding them.[13]

Because the Court has remained resistant to many of the impulses that motivate the political left, Ginsburg's chief service to the cause has been as a forceful voice of the opposition, a critic of the majority's allegedly incorrect or short-sighted or biased reading of the Constitution, and a worthy successor to that tradition of dissent originating with William Johnson and continuing through the ages in the lives and careers of Justices Harlan the Elder and Oliver Wendell Holmes. Over the years, she has been praised for her "blistering dissenting opinion" in *Lily Ledbetter v. Goodyear Tire & Rubber Co.*, castigating the majority for making it easier, she thought, for employers to win pay discrimination claims, and for her dissent in *Board of Education of Independent School District No. 92 of Pottawatomie County v. Earls*, in which she spoke "powerfully for the civil liberties of the youngest Americans in the context of school drug testing."[14] In *Burwell v. Hobby Lobby*, she was credited with "destroying the thin arguments of Justice Alito in a 35-page opinion that should be required reading for anyone who still cares about the rule of law in America."[15] She rejected the majority's reasoning in *Masterpiece Cakeshop v. Colorado Civil Rights Commission* as permitting and promoting discrimination on the basis of sexual orientation.[16] In *Shelby County v. Holder*, she defended the continuing need for Civil Rights Era protections for voting rights of

---

[12] See *Reed v. Reed* (1971) 404 U.S. 71, 92 S.Ct. 251; *Frontiero v. Richardson* (1973) 411 U.S. 677, 93 S.Ct. 1764; *Wiesenfeld v. Wiesenfeld* (1975) 420 U.S. 636, 95 S.Ct. 1225; *Craig v. Boren* (1976) 429 U.S. 190, 97 S.Ct. 451; and *Duren v. Missouri* (1979) 439 U.S. 357, 99 S.Ct. 664.

[13] See, for instance, *United States v. Virginia* (1996) 518 U.S. 515, 116 S.Ct. 2264.

[14] See "Justice Ruth Bader Ginsburg: Dissenting for Democracy," www.pfaw.org, July 2014, as well as *Lily Ledbetter v. Goodyear Tire & Rubber Co.* (2007) 550 U.S. 618, 127 S.Ct. 2162, and *Board of Education of Independent School District No. 92 of Pottawatomie County v. Earls* (2002) 537 U.S. 822, 122 S.Ct. 2559.

[15] "Justice Ruth Bader Ginsburg: Dissenting for Democracy," supra, and *Burwell v. Hobby Lobby* (2014) 273 U.S. 682, 134 S.Ct. 2751.

[16] *Masterpiece Cakeshop v. Colorado Civil Rights Commission* (2018) 584 U.S. ___, 138 S.Ct. 1719.

African Americans and federal supervision of voting in various parts of the country decades after the end of Jim Crow.[17] In her most recent dissent, she lamented the Court's prohibition in the State of Wisconsin on further submission of absentee ballots as likely to "result in massive disenfranchisement" due to the inability of people to physically reach polling places closed by the State's Shelter-in-Place order in the midst of the epidemic.[18]

Perhaps her finest contribution to advancing the principle that progressive results matter more than formal constitutional restraints was her dissenting opinion in *National Federation of Independent Business v. Sebelius*.[19] Though her side won the larger argument that the Affordable Care Act's individual mandate was lawful, she took the time to address the majority's rejection of the ACA as a legitimate exercise of the commerce power, and all but declared that the relevant clause comprised no outward limit save the very democratic process the Constitution was designed to keep in check.

For Progressives, Ginsburg is the conscience of the Court, who witnesses loudly for the ages in opposition to the "rampage against the constitutional, reproductive, and civil rights of the American people" by the Roberts Court, and "carefully spells out a path for corrective legislative action and for the elaboration of a principled jurisprudence in the future."[20] Her's is a much-needed tonic in a dangerous time, an "alternative vision of democracy and the Constitution" that challenges the majority's defense of "corporate and government power over individual rights and liberties" and the discarding of "federal and state laws that seek to promote democracy and the common good."[21]

Though her most prominent role has been in dissent, she has nevertheless done much to hold the line against a more conservative regime on the high bench. Her efforts to hold back a very non-progressive flood, however, did not immunize her from gentle suggestions that she leave the court to allow a progressive President to

---

[17] *Shelby County v. Holder* (2013) 570 U.S. 529, 133 S.Ct. 2612.

[18] Colin Kalmbacher, "Ruth Bader Ginsburg Goes off on Conservative Majority Jeopardizing Voters' Safety Amid Pandemic," https://lawandcrime.com, April 6, 2020.

[19] *National Federation of Independent Business v. Sebelius* (2012) 567 U.S. ___, 132 S.Ct. 2566.

[20] People for the American Way Foundation, op. cit.

[21] Id.

appoint a successor, lest the progressive movement suffer the unthinkable blow of a conservative President making the selection and nominating someone more like Clarence and less like Ruth. Her still very agile mind and vivid pen tend to mitigate some of the concerns about her age. The reality of her physical health, however, remains unchecked by any similar offsetting factors.

Her health indeed has followed a perilous path. She had a serious bout with cancer in 1999, and another a decade later. Radiation apparently proved successful in turning the tide of those threats to her life, yet she grows increasingly frail, visibly fatigued and unable at times even to move. Lack of cameras while the Court is in session obscures this fact from the general public, though those who are able to be physically present and remain after the conclusion of arguments have observed the difficulty she has in getting out of her chair or descending a single step without assistance.[22] Her dozing off for 15 minutes during oral arguments back in 2006 was certainly the most prolonged period of deep relaxation while the Court was hearing its calendar, though it was eclipsed in notoriety when she napped during the 2015 State of the Union Address—a faux pas she later attributed to sharing a bottle of wine with Anthony Kennedy before-hand.[23]

The near universal belief that Hillary Rodham Clinton would succeed Barack Obama as President may have formed a significant variable in Justice Ginsburg's calculus when she decided to remain on the Court beyond 2016. That, at least, is what some have theorized. In any event, the outcome of the 2016 election utterly frustrated any hope that she might retire without sacrificing her seat to the opposition. The adoration of her by progressives has nevertheless continued, but even more so has the reporting on her health and the hair trigger reassurance by much in the press that she remains in exceptional shape and expects to continue on in her role as a member of the Court for the foreseeable future. Speculation during the first two years of the Trump Administration that she was prepared to retire was quickly disproven by the Justice herself when she said "she will continue to serve as long

---

[22] Mencimer, op. cit.

[23] Jake Miller, "Ruth Bader Ginsburg: 'I Wasn't 100 Percent Sober' During State of the Union," www.cbsnews.com, February 13, 2015.

as she has the 'full steam' necessary for the job."[24] A fall at her office in the Supreme Court building caused fractures in three ribs and a stint in the hospital, though the press reassured the public that she didn't initially seek out medical aid and all she required was mere "observation and treatment."[25] Ginsburg's biographer Irin Carmon reminded her fellow stressed-out liberals to "remember that the Justice is TAN… She's tough as nails. You think three ribs are going to stop Justice?"[26] The doctors treating the rib fractures, however, apparently uncovered evidence of cancerous growths on her lungs, requiring surgical intervention. Worse news came when it was revealed that her long dormant pancreatic cancer had returned. She underwent three weeks of radiation to reverse the spread of the disease and quite incredibly (as is her penchant) bounced back to speak at the Library of Congress Book Festival, where she confirmed, "I am alive. And I'm on my way to being very well."[27] The Court vouched for her recovery by announcing "the tumor was treated definitively and there is no evidence of disease elsewhere in the body."[28] When the Court returned to session the following month, Ginsburg vowed to be there.[29] She didn't quite make it due to what was reported to be "a stomach bug," followed by another visit to the hospital for treatment of "chills and fever."[30] Her condition appeared alarming when news came that Johns Hopkins received the Justice for "further evaluation and treatment of any possible infection" after initial admittance to Sibley Memorial Hospital in Washington, D.C. News stories appeared here and there of her presence at public events. In January, it was reported that she was at last "cancer free."[31]

---

[24] Amir Tibon, "At D.C. Synagogue, Ruth Bader Ginsburg Says She'll Continue to Serve with 'Full Steam Ahead,'" www.haaretz.com, March 2, 2018.

[25] Camila Domonoske & Nina Totenerg, "Justice Ruth Bader Ginsburg Hospitalized After Falling, Fracturing 3 Ribs," www.npr.com, November 8, 2018.

[26] Mencimer, op. cit.

[27] Ben Hooper, "Ruth Bader Ginsburg on Her Way 'to Being Very Well,'" www.upi.com, August 31, 2019.

[28] Id.

[29] Id.

[30] "Supreme Court Says Ginsburg Home Sick With Stomach Bug," www.dailyherald.com, November 13, 2019; and "Ginsburg Hospitalized for Treatment of Chills and Fever," www.kold.com, November 23, 2019.

[31] "Ruth Bader Ginsburg Says She's Cancer-Free," www.kiro7.com, January 8, 2020.

The most interesting aspect of the phenomenon that is the Cult of Ruth is the intense focus on and promotion of her workouts. The intensity has only grown as the years pass and her health has become more questionable. Unlike the professional athlete, whose prowess is well known to decline steadily as the seasons pile up, Ginsburg appears more physically fit than ever, notwithstanding four bouts with cancer, numerous stints in her arteries, many falls and a number of broken ribs. In 2017, reports circulated in the left-friendly media that she was staying in top physical condition via rigorous workouts designed and overseen by a man whose former career was training Navy Seals. *Politico* journalist Ben Schreckinger even made it his mission to try the octogenarian Justice's workout. After doing so he reported he had "barely lived to tell the tale."[32] "Forget aqua-aerobics and nursing home dance cardio—Ginsburg's workout would make a solid addition to your regimen too—if you can make it through."[33] The reporter breathlessly told of how the spry Justice warmed up with a run on the elliptical and a round of stretches, then moved without pause through a series of exercises: machine chest presses, "leg curls to hit her hammies," wide grip pull-downs, seat rows, the butterfly press, standing cable row, one legged squats, push-ups without reliance on the knees, planks, step-ups, dumbbell curls, wall squats and on and on and on. Talk show host Stephen Colbert came to run with the Justice through her paces, and reportedly failed miserably.[34] Even during the Coronavirus shut-down, Ginsburg was "continuing with her workout routine," despite the fact that "many gyms across the country have been shuttered to curb the outbreak."[35] To isolate "the liberal icon" from germs, her trainer carefully wiped down "every piece of equipment she will be using during her routine, then washes his hands."[36] Otherwise, her trainer simply observed as the Justice ran through the exercises in her typically self-disciplined and spritely way. "All I have to do is set it up and she just automatically knows what I want to do. It doesn't require me to grab

---

[32] Lauren Mazzo, "This Ruth Bader Ginsberg Workout Will Totally Crush You," www.shape.com, January 13, 2019.

[33] Id.

[34] Erin Jensen, "'The Late Show': Ruth Bader Ginsburg Shows up Stephen Colbert During Their Workout," www.usatoday.com, March 22, 2018.

[35] Tamar Lapin, "Coronavirus Outbreak Isn't Stopping Ruth Bader Ginsburg's Workouts," *The New York Post*, March 31, 2020.

[36] Lapin, op. cit.

her, hold her, get up close and personal." In other words, she's not forgetting the routine from one session to the next, she's not so frail that she can't stand on her own, and the trainer is keeping her safe from disease so that her work on the Court can continue.

The portrayal of Ruth Bader Ginsburg is reminiscent of so much else in our popular culture where progressives are controlling the narrative. Traditional genders roles are jettisoned. Women are no longer the damsels in distress or even those who patiently and stoically hold down the home front. They are commanders, warriors and even the saviors of the universe whom even strong men cower behind. So many are the movies and television shows in recent years in which women punch harder, kick faster, spring with more agility, think quicker on their feet and solve more daunting scientific problems than any and every man, despite the fact that women, for all of their many superior virtues, are on average physically slower and weaker and less inclined to pursue the study of STEM subjects than men. The women who excel physically and intellectually in traditionally male dominated fields are real, and they are proper role models for young men and women alike, not to mention path finders (we can only hope) to a more equitable future. But the woman who will defeat the strongest and fastest man in a physical contest is a fantasy that is fun to indulge periodically but absurd when the indulgence is the rule rather than the exception.

Ruth Bader Ginsburg isn't a superhero, nor is she ready to take on Floyd Mayweather in the ring. What she actually is is impressive enough without embellishment or embroidery designed to hide the truth: a brilliant yet increasingly frail person whose energies are waning in the face of age and an originalist gale. As a lawyer she won repeatedly in the Supreme Court; as a judge she issued landmark decisions and brilliant though at times erroneous dissents. In her close friendship with Justice Scalia she shamed all those who contend they cannot respect, let alone be friendly, with someone whose beliefs about the proper organizing of society are so different from their own. And she often enough in her career got it right. She has been a sceptic of the State in the prosecution of those accused of crime and a friend to those seeking to challenge corporations in private actions based on both common and positive law. She memorably agreed with both Scalia and Chief Justice Rehnquist when dissenting against the majority's conclusion reducing a jury's award of punitive damages, saying that the Court "unnecessarily and unwisely ventures into territory traditionally within the State's domain."[37] In fact, she and Scalia agreed a surprising seventy percent of the time.[38] And then there is her majority opinion for the ages in the matter of *Timbs v. Indiana*, incorporating the Excessive Fines Clause into the meaning of due process as that term appears in the Fourteenth Amendment.[39]

If one were to have a hero, Justice Ginsburg is an admirable choice, especially if the hero one seeks is a champion of progressivism. Even the best of heroes, though, have ever been disappointing as they tend to receive the psychological projections of their admirers, complete with all the shortcomings the latter seek refuge from in their homage to someone or something outside themselves. And they've always had their own infirmities quite apart from those saddled on them by others. Brave Achilles suffered a wound in the tendon; and the Philistines dissevered Samson from his Nazirite locks. Justice Ginsburg, too, yields her share of shortcomings, the most obvious of which is that she is "a mere mortal," whom the actuarial table does not favor.[40] There is, says the very progressive Stephanie Mencimer, a "real possibility Ginsburg will not outlast the Trump Administration or live long enough for a Democrat to replace her."[41] This thought is terrifying to progressives, many of whom see the nation as a sinkhole of corporate corruption, raging sexism, intolerable homophobia and incurable racism that only the cutting edge of progressive thinking and judicial activism can alter for the better. This terror explains in part the progressive movement's abetting of the Cult of Ruth and the desperate hope if not delusion that so long as she trains with the Navy Seals she will outlive this dark age.

Her potential departure from the public stage ahead of the current President does indeed present the GOP with the prospect of achieving objectives "that have eluded Republican presidents for over six decades."[42] Certainly the President has not been idle in acting on the

---

[37] *BMW of North America, Inc. v. Gore* (1996) 517 U.S. 559, 116 S.Ct. 1589, Ginsburg, J. dissenting.

[38] Jeremy Bowers, Adam Liptak and Derek Willis, "Which Supreme Court Justice Vote Together Most and Least Often," *The New York Times*, July 3, 2014.

[39] *Tyson Timbs v. State of Indiana* (2019) 586 U.S. ___, 139 S.Ct. 682.

[40] Mencimer, op. cit.

[41] Id.

[42] Jonathan Turley, "Ginsburg Gambled to Stay and Now She May Lose Her Legacy," www.thehill.com, April 10, 2017.

power at his disposal by filling the large number of vacancies that remained unfilled at the time of his inauguration or have subsequently appeared. In the past three years, 190 judicial vacancies have been staffed with the likes of Don Willett, Chad Andrew Readler, James C. Ho, Mark Norris, Neomi Rao, Stuart Kyle Duncan, and Amy Coney Barrett, not to mention the successful nomination of the son of a hated former head of the EPA and "the rapist" Kavanaugh to empty seats on the Supreme Court.[43] Filling a vacancy in Ginsburg's seat while this President remains in office will crown the conservative judicial strategy with its greatest victory and may well lead to a marked recalibration of the law as interpreted by the courts that will stand for decades to come. Should that future come to pass, Justice Ginsburg will remain relevant as an able member of the court, the leading representative of a particular school of constitutional jurisprudence during her era, and a hero to many, though her aspirations and those of her admirers will track far in advance of her actual and lasting achievements.

Fraud in Absentia

IT is a terror subtle in execution, insidious in its advance, with little trace of blood or carnage, and yet so potent in its ability to still the manifold norms of human society. Restaurants remain shuttered, schools are vacant, and the public parks are silent save for the rustling of the wind and the gradual swell of the orchestration of birds who appear to be enjoying a heightened level of comfort in the deserted fora constructed by men. The so-called essential business of life, however, continues: grocery shopping, certain trades, public services, and even, here and there throughout the country, primary electoral contests. The dirty, dingy and germ filled precincts hosting public elections have nevertheless struck horror in the hearts of a certain faction of the masses as polling day in any given locale approaches. Others cynically cry that the polls must be closed in the name of public health and the elections conducted entirely by mail.

---

[43] Elie Mystal, "How the 45th President Has Packed the Courts with Ultraconservatives—and Reshaped the Judiciary for a Generation," www.thenation.com, July 15, 2019.

The drama over pending elections in the days of the modern plague reached an extreme in Wisconsin, where the Democrat Party actually went to court to obtain an order to extend the time for the receipt of absentee ballots in order to accommodate the voting needs of a populace affrighted at the thought of venturing into the contagion-rich environment of the voting booth. With only days to go before the election, a federal district court in Madison enjoined the enforcement of a long-standing state law requiring the receipt of completed absentee ballots by the close of business on election day, extended voting by mail an additional week in defiance of the statutory date, and even suspended the few ballot security rules governing voting by mail as impediments to the fundamental right to vote. The opposing party sought immediate stay of the injunction by the Supreme Court pending a broader appeal. Justice Kavanaugh forwarded the request to the entire bench and a ruling striking down the lower court's injunction resulted. "By changing the election rules so close to the election date and by affording relief that the plaintiffs themselves did not ask for in their preliminary injunction motions," said the Court, "the District Court contravened this Court's precedents and erred by ordering such relief."[1] Because the Supreme Court had "repeatedly emphasized that lower federal courts should ordinarily not alter the election rules on the eve of an election," the eleventh-and-half-hour contravention of the law setting the deadline for the receipt of absentee ballots could not stand.[2]

The loser in the bid for a last moment judicial amendment of the statutory date of the election decried the Supreme Court's decision as a partisan hatchet job in what was dubbed "one of the most politically freighted voting-rights cases since *Bush v. Gore*."[3] One "election law expert" characterized the decision as "a very bad sign for November that the Court could not come together and find some form of compromise here in the midst of a global pandemic unlike anything we have seen in our lifetimes."[4] Marge Baker of the left-leaning People for the American Way denounced the decision as "outrageous," and said it constituted a

---

[1] *Republican National Committee et al. v. Democratic National Committee* (2020) 589 U.S. ___.

[2] Id.

[3] Jim Rutenberg & Nick Corasaniti, *The New York Times*, April 13, 2020.

[4] Robert Barnes, "Supreme Court rules for Republicans over Wisconsin Vote, Highlighting Partisan Divide Before November Poll," www.thewashingtonpost.com, April 7, 2020.

placing not merely of a thumb, but an "entire fist, on the scale in favor of making it harder for people to vote."[5] The practical result of the decision, said *The New York Times*, was the disenfranchisement of thousands of voters," the forcing of "several thousand more to endanger their lives at polls," and the burdening of "already strained state health officials with a grim new task: tracking the extent to which in-person voting contributed to the virus's spread in the State, a federal disaster area."[6] A writer for *The Atlantic Monthly* attacked the Supreme Court for forcing "Wisconsin residents to choose between voting and staying safe."[7] The better choice—recommended by "experts and advocates"—would be "to move to a system of voting by mail for the upcoming general election. Doing so would ensure that people can exercise their franchise and that America remains a representative democracy without threatening millions of lives."[8] Congress, opined one such expert, can act in accordance with its power under Article I, Section 4 to modify the time, place and manner of voting in the States via a uniform law mandating mail-in ballots in time of the November election.[9] Any objection to this proposal due to the potential for fraud, he said, is utterly specious. "If serious, systematic problems with voting by mail existed, they would have already presented in Washington, Oregon, and California, where the option is available to a combined 50 million residents."[10] Without relief along these lines, the supposed experts agree, the nation's health is imperilled, and so is the fundamental right to vote.

In such criticism, the cynic can discern the makings of a narrative and the use of the epidemic to advance a long-desired partisan political objective, which is to permit voting in every jurisdiction for both state and federal elections in the least regulated and most permissive manner possible. The cynic's doubts are easily bolstered by the observation that no one was actually prevented from going to the polls or submitting an absentee ballot in Wisconsin in a timely fashion, and that the epidemic itself was at yet no worse in its impact than the annual flu season and

---

5 Id.

6 Rutenberg & Corasaniti, op. cit.

7 Leah Litman, "The Supreme Court's Wisconsin Decision is a Terrible Sign for November," www.theatlantic.com, April 7, 2020.

8 Id.

9 Ronald J. Krotoszynski, "Vote-by-Mail Can Save the 2020 Election," www.theatlantic.com, March 27, 2020.

10 Id.

was already abating in much of the country. The cry for so drastic a change in the manner of voting under such dubious circumstances is easily disregarded when first hearing it, and yet the cry continues to the point that one must either plug one's ears or address the source directly so that it might be allayed. The right to vote, of course, is precious, as all agree. But the security of the ballot is the flip side of the concern that voting be accessible. So free a vote inevitably creates the risk, if not the reality, that legitimate votes cast are diluted in value entirely through the ease by which fraud is perpetrated. Casual denial that the risk is real, or that fraud occurs, disregards the history of voting generally, as well as its present milieu.

Though the right to vote is not identified in the Constitution, it is nonetheless protected from impairments based on age, gender and race, and subject to strict scrutiny when a law places obstacles in the path to the voting booth for one class of voters, but not another. Such impairments are generally improper because voting is regarded as "a fundamental right…preservative of all rights."[11] The Constitution, said Congressman John Churchill during debates over the Force Act of 1871, quite clearly conveys "the principle that government depends upon the will of the governed; in other words, that the will of the majority… when that will can be ascertained, is the proper law of the country."[12] The will of the governed can only be discerned through voting, hence Chief Justice Warren's observation that "as long as ours is a representative form of government, and our legislatures are those instruments of government elected directly by and directly representative of the people, the right to elect legislators in a free and unimpaired fashion is a bedrock of our political system."[13]

These thoughts are true enough and rest atop a deeper strata of republican theory derived not during profound imaginings within the comfort of an armchair situated close to a crackling fire in a warm den but from wisdom acquired through the often violent rumblings of political life during the middle and late stages of the Enlightenment in Europe and what became the United States. "The idea that voting was a

---

[11] *Yick Wo v. Hopkins* (1886) 118 U.S. 356, 370, 6 S.Ct. 1064.

[12] James A. Gardner, "Consent, Legitimacy and Elections—Implementing Popular Sovereignty Under the Lockean Constitution," 52 U. Pitt. L. Rev. 189 (1990), at p. 240.

[13] *Reynolds v. Sims* (1964) 377 U.S. 533, 562, 84 S.Ct. 1362.

right, even a natural right," says historian Alexander Keyssar, "had become increasingly widespread in the eighteenth century...and was embraced by many small farmers and artisans, as well as by the most radical leaders of the Revolution, such as Franklin, Thomas Young of Pennsylvania, and Ethan Allen of Vermont."[14] The proposition that voting was a natural right "meshed well with the Lockean political theory popular in eighteenth-century America."[15] Though hardly the first to have stumbled upon the idea, John Locke summed up the general notion that any government, if it is to be legitimate, must be the result of free and willing consent, that the waiver of any rights one had prior to its formation must be both knowing and executed in exchange for the continuing opportunity to consent to the restrictions the state places on liberty. The principle was one wholeheartedly shared by the signatories of the Declaration of Independence and subsequently provided "a comprehensive rationale not only for the American Revolution, which the Declaration sought to justify, but also for the founding of the new nation."[16] The Constitution that emerged in the wake of the Revolution "merely consummated the triumph of Lockean ideology, by putting the ideas contained in the Declaration into a practical form, suitable for establishing and guiding a government."[17] Any flaw in the electoral process that registers the people's continuing consent to our Constitutional system—any break down in the security and integrity of the vote—"can, according to the Lockean theory of popular sovereignty, undermine the legitimacy both of the apparent winner of an election and the government in which he or she serves."[18] A discrepancy in the process, said Professor James Gardner, "has the potential to transform an apparently successful candidate into a usurper whose actions are invalid and whose laws need not be obeyed."[19]

As elections became the means by which the governed consented to the regulations impinging upon their liberty, some thought was expended over the proper mechanism whereby they might be carried out. Utterly transparent voting was deemed appropriate when the votes

[14] Alexander Keyssar, *The Right to Vote: The Contested History of Democracy in the United States* (New York: Basic Books, 2000), at p. 12.

[15] Id.

[16] Gardner, op. cit., at p. 193.

[17] Id.

[18] Id., at p. 222.

[19] Id.

cast were those of elected officials. More discrete expressions of preference, with some protection against fraud or duress, came to be preferred in elections characterized by broad participation. On the eve of the Jacksonian Era expansion of voting rights, and decades before the great amplification of the franchise that occurred in the wake of the Civil War, the influential thinker Jeremy Bentham considered the potential for fraud in mass elections and prescribed secrecy of the vote as a useful and necessary tonic. Vote buying and intimidation were evident even in his time. Secrecy impeded both of these mechanisms of election abuse because—with respect to vote buying at least—"the buyer cannot observe whether the voter followed through on the contract."[20] Thinking the potential reforms through, Bentham considered "the most detrimental arrangement" to be any form of virtual or remote voting, because "individuals would thus be exposed, in all their votes, to every seductive influence, and would be withdrawn from the principle tutelary influence," including poll watchers and election judges.[21] Such a system, he said, would be one which "would secure punishment to probity, and reward to prevarication."[22] His fellow Utilitarian, John Stewart Mill, thought that any vote from home—"allowing the voting papers to be filled up at the voter's own residence, and sent by the post"—should be regarded "as fatal."[23] The corrupt purchaser of the vote might, "in the shelter of privacy, behold with his own eyes his bargain fulfilled, and the intimidator could see the extorted obedience rendered irrevocably on the spot; while the beneficent counterinfluence of the presence of those who knew the voter's real sentiments, and the inspiring effect of sympathy of those of one's own party or opinion, would be shut out."[24]

The populace in American localities where elections occurred in the early Republic didn't at first pay much heed to the reflections of British public intellectuals. The people were far too busy organizing political action through party politics and seeking advantage for their respective sides at the polls. The greatest elaboration on the party apparatus was in the cities, where veritable political machines, once successful in

[20] Allison R. Hayward, "Bentham & Ballots: Tradeoffs Between Secrecy and Accountability in How We Vote," 26 J.L. & Politics 39 (2010), at p. 46.

[21] Id., at pp. 46-47.

[22] Id.

[23] Id., at p. 48.

[24] Id.

elevating members of the party to political prominence, essentially ran civic government. Parties printed their own ballots for the faithful to fill out, and even completed them before hand to remove any doubt about the candidate for whom the voter would be supporting. The lack of secrecy in the balloting process contributed to a well-known mid-century culture of urban corruption. The machines that controlled political life in the cities would "condition jobs on the submission of the proper ballot, or they might pay money for the confirmed deposit" of the same.[25] It was this kind of abuse that spawned the first significant demands for election reform and regulation. At the same time that Congress moved to ensure the ability of former slaves to vote in local, state and national elections, state legislatures entertained and ultimately adopted the so-called Australian Reform, entailing written ballots, sealed up and cast without public disclosure at sanctioned polling places, overseen and administered by neutral officials. By many accounts, the reform effected an immediate change for the better. In Massachusetts, one observer noted in the wake of the first election following adoption of Australian balloting that "it is an undeniable fact that in the late election there was, except in one place, no corruption successful, and but little attempted, and that with this evidence of its successful working the chances have greatly lessened that bribery will be tried."[26] Even the reduction in the aggregate number of votes cast was seen as a positive reflection on the reform's merits, and proof positive that fraud, duress and ballot box stuffing had been significantly curtailed.[27]

The Australian Reform ran counter to the modern impulse to expand voting through the very non-secret and largely unregulated method of mail-in or absentee voting. And it was a reform that occurred with full knowledge of both the supposed benefit and drawbacks of such an alternative means of casting a ballot. Indeed, it had only been a few decades before that the nation had experimented with absentee voting. The Civil War necessarily separated military voters from their homes and deprived them of the opportunity to cast ballots for candidates

---

[25] John C. Fortier & Norman J. Ornstein, "The Absentee Ballot and the Secret Ballot: Challenges for Election Reform," 36 U. Mich. J.L. Reform 483 (2003), at p. 488.

[26] Id., at p. 491.

[27] Id.

seeking local, state and federal office. Both of the leading political parties favoured permitting absentee voting by soldiers in the field, and contributed with varying degrees of enthusiasm toward the successful effort in many States to amend their election laws. The knowledge of the corruption of man and the great temptation presented by the prize to be won through electoral contests stimulated some discussion about the prudence of such changes, even as it was conceded that men placing their lives at risk for the nation ought not be disenfranchised in the process. Some wondered how the voting in places far removed from their own State's boundaries might be conducted in compliance with the State laws designed to guard against fraud. Indeed, no compliance could ever be enforced due to the lack of jurisdiction State election officials had beyond a State's borders.[28] A Michigan legislative committee asked what power or authority there was "to prevent...persons who are not qualified voters, from coming forward and offering to vote, and if objected to, from swearing their votes in?"[29] As the power to enforce the laws outside the State did not exist, "the ballot boxes might be stuffed or destroyed by a disorderly rabble, either of soldiers or of people, in the towns through which the commissioner would have to pass on his return to this State."[30] In New York, Governor Horatio Seymour actually vetoed a law authorizing absentee voting by soldiers due to his concern that "the ballot could be seen or tampered with by a number of intermediaries who transported the ballot from the field to the poling place."[31] Scandals indeed did occur, and two men were actually convicted and sentenced to life in prison for their acts of "falsely personating and representing officers and soldiers in the United States service, and with falsely and fraudulently signing and forging names of such officers and soldiers...for the purpose of transmitting the votes of the soldiers to be used at the general election."[32] In light of actual abuses and the contradiction between such laws and expressed anti-fraud provisions in State Constitutions requiring that votes be cast by the voters themselves in the locales within the State where they resided, a number of State Supreme Courts struck these Civil War Era absentee

---

[28] Id., at p. 494.
[29] Id.
[30] Id.
[31] Id., at p. 495.
[32] Id., at p. 496.

voting laws down.[33] Those laws that remained on the books at the time of Lee's surrender, were quietly repealed soon afterward.

For reasons not entirely clear, absentee voting laws made a comeback during the Progressive Era in the early years of the Twentieth Century. The populist atmosphere of the time perhaps contributed to a feeling that men (and later women) of good will ought to be provided with as many options as possible to ensure their ability to cast their ballots and register their voice. The first such law came onto the books in 1912, followed by others in quick succession until, in 1924, only three States lacked any absentee voting provisions.[34] In every State where they took effect, the laws remained limited in scope. They offered absentee voting options to travelling salesmen, soldiers deployed away from home, and persons suffering some physical incapacitation barring their physical appearance at a voting booth. In every case, a requirement existed that an affidavit be sworn out, notarized and witnessed before a ballot could issue, and no third parties were permitted to deliver the same back to the election authorities. In some instances, States enacting the laws amended their constitutions to permit voting in this manner, but always in this early period some thought was given to ensuring that the well-known abuses in voting be avoided.

Unlike in the aftermath of the Civil War, the early Twentieth Century laws permitting absentee voting were not repealed. Instead, they were expanded, and most of the provisions designed to guard against fraud, coercion and abuse were eventually eliminated. Consequently, absentee voting has opened "the door to elector fraud and political manipulation of the voting process, which can distort election outcomes and undermine the integrity of the elector system."[35] Many have expressed concern that "absentee voting is much more susceptible to illegal activity than voting in person at the polling place' because absentee ballots are cast in private. While election officials are able to monitor ballots cast in person, in the presence of many observers, absentee ballots are cast at various times without the same physical

---

[33] Id., at 498.

[34] Id., at p. 504.

[35] Edward B. Moreton, Jr., "Voting by Mail," 58 S. Cal. L. Rev. 1261 (1985), at p. 1261.

accountability, making it harder to detect fraudulent conduct."[36] No barriers exist to prevent an employer, church, union, club, or family from viewing the voter's ballot. Historically barred from invading the sanctum of the polling place, political parties have exploited absentee voting laws to evade the remaining in-person regulations designed to prevent abuse and have adopted absentee balloting as a preferred means of registering support for their candidates.[37] Lacking any meaningful features to confirm the identity of the voter, absentee ballots are easily completed by persons loyal to particular parties and particular candidates using the name of an actual person listed on the voting rolls. And tampering with the ballots while in transit to election authorities, as occurred during the Civil War, is relatively simple to perform. "Unlike ballots cast in person, which are in the hands of election officials only for a matter of hours until they are counted, and then usually in the presence of observers from both parties, absentee ballot applications and absentee ballots are in the physical possession of local election officials, often partisans themselves, for weeks or months and are out of the physical view of any outsiders."[38] Then-mayor Diane Feinstein summed up these concerns well when she observed that "ballot by mail abandons the protection of the neighbourhood polling place. It can be abused in the hands of political manipulators…and can give inordinate advantage to well-organized special interests."[39]

Critics of those who worry about absentee voting compromising the integrity of the voting system typically insist on the paucity of evidence of fraud and abuse. In their defense of reliance on absentee voting during the coronavirus epidemic, Jim Rutenberg and Nick Corasaniti of *The New York Times* have dismissed any actual fraud as "vanishingly rare in American elections."[40] Ronald J. Krotoszynski notes that no fraud has occurred at all in the far west where vote by mail is the freest and most widely used in the country.[41] While they seem in earnest, these boosters for the Democrat Party's agenda of universal absentee voting are best

---

[36] Sal. H. Lee, "Judicial Review of Absentee Voting Laws: How Courts Should Balance State Interests Against the Fundamental Right to Vote Going Forward," 105 Iowa L. Rev. 799 (2020).

[37] Fortier & Ornstein, op. cit., at p. 512.

[38] Id., at pp. 512-513.

[39] Moreton, op. cit., at p. 1276.

[40] Rutenberg & Corasaniti, op. cit.

[41] Krotoszynski, op. cit.

taken with a measure of scepticism. So long as the electoral spoils to be won in a nation with a 4 trillion-dollar budget remain so vast, there will be those who seek shortcuts to possessing them. And so long as the States of California, Oregon and Washington remain in the control of single party-machines that have mastered the art of ballot harvesting via absentee ballots, the likelihood of serious investigation and prosecution of mail-in ballot offenses in those places is essentially non-existent.

History is the best guide to understanding the problem, and recent history provides ample evidence of the kind of abuse the prohibitions against (and later strict controls imposed on) absentee voting were once intended to prevent. The segregationist Byrd Organization in Virginia was a notorious master of the many nuances of election fraud using absentee ballots. Through the practice known as "black satchelin," teams consisting of a registrar and notary public would deploy to the homes of voters, present them with already completed ballots and notarize the voter's signature, whereupon the ballot would be placed directly into an election board member's "black satchel."[42] Filling out absentee ballots for voters known to be dead but still on the voting rolls was common as well. The fraud was so bad that a federal grand jury indicted ten conspirators for their part in absentee fraud in 1968.[43] In Pennsylvania in 1993, William Stinson came from behind to win a seat in the State Senate on the strength of absentee ballots. The election was later overturned by court order and the loser declared the victor after proof was presented that the Stinson campaign peddled ballots directly to voters and completed ballots themselves and forged the signatures.[44] A similar result occurred in Florida, Alabama, Connecticut, Indiana, New York and elsewhere in Pennsylvania a few years later, after "many absentee ballots were shown to be forged, coerced, stolen from mailboxes, or fraudulently obtained."[45] More recently, there was the great scandal that was the congressional election in Bladenboro, North Carolina, where the Election Board refused to certify the results after learning that the winning candidate's campaign had employed agents to present absentee ballots to voters and deliver them directly to the polls after being filled

[42] Hayward, op. cit., at p. 58.

[43] Id., at 59.

[44] Michelle L. Robertson, "Winning at All Costs: Election Fraud in the Third Circuit—Marks v. Stinson," 40 Vill. L. Rev. 869 (1995), at pp. 903-904.

[45] Id., at p. 513.

out. Worse yet was the discarding by these agents of ballots believed to be in favour of the opposing candidate. "I'm not surprised this happened in Bladenboro," said one voter, "but I wouldn't be surprised if this happened anywhere."[46]

Those who dismiss concern over protecting elections from fraud perpetrated through absentee ballots are either blind to history or willfully denying a truth to advance a political objective that depends for its success on a system of voting lacking in features aimed at defeating dishonest tactics and illegal conduct. Voting rights indeed are precious. Real deterrents to voting serving no compelling purpose must be eliminated. The evils of the past in the form of laws designed to thwart voter participation ought never be allowed to flourish again. Too much blood and treasure has been expended in eliminating them. Unfortunately, so many of those who sincerely fear vote suppression and prescribe as a cure elimination of any regulations governing the electoral process fail to appreciate that their prescription is an open invitation to cheating that has the very same effect that outright vote suppression does—it cancels out the choice of bona fide voters and thereby deprives them of their own precious right to vote.

There is some irony in the fact that so many of those advocating lack of regulation in voting take the opposite stance with respect to big business, and fail to apply a similar logic in both instances. Irony, too, exists with respect to proponents of deregulation of economic life, who often enough favor strong election laws. As with much in life, a balance is desirable. Absentee voting is certainly a salutary option for those genuinely unable to attend the polls and cast their vote in person on election day. A strictly regulated absentee system would go far in ensuring every eligible and willing voters' preference is accurately expressed. Strict regulation will ensure participation of qualified voters, without reasonable fear of a dilution of the rights of those voters able to more publicly participate in the election, who trust that their vote will not be canceled out by one of dubious provenance, and that their consent to the existing political order, win or lose, will not be stolen from them by those whose chief aim lies not in honest and intelligent political dialogue, but in victory at the cost of political and constitutional legitimacy.

---

[46] Khushbu Shah, "Absentee-Ballot Fraud Scandal Speaks to Wider Issue of Racism in North Carolina," www.theguardian.com, December 12, 2018.

This is Our Freedom Now

WHEN the notice appeared at posting sites throughout San Leandro, five days were given to those effected to depart the coastal region of the State of California known as Zone 1 and report to what was called an "Assembly Center." Instead of obedience to the government's dictate, Fred Korematsu travelled to San Francisco and paid what money he had to a surgeon of doubtful skill to transform his features so as to appear less obviously Asiatic.[1] A flophouse in Oakland became his refuge and a Spanish Hawaiian named Clyde Sarah his ostensible identity. A suspicious police officer arrested him for vagrancy while he was awaiting the arrival of a girlfriend on the public sidewalk, and when taken to the station, an acquaintance employed there recognized him. He was ultimately convicted of violating the order to evacuate, notwithstanding his argument that he posed no threat to his country, was being victimized by racially discriminatory state action, and was given no prior opportunity to challenge the application of the order as to him. Lost on the jury that tried him was any concern that the order subjected him to indefinite incarceration far from home and without means of earning a living, denied him free mixture with friends and associates and travel from place to place within the country, and deprived him even of the right to attend religious services that might be occurring outside the boundaries of his confinement. When reviewing the case, the Supreme Court agreed that "all restrictions which curtail the civil rights of a single racial group are immediately suspect," but held that "public necessity may sometimes justify the existence of such restrictions."[2] Military necessity certainly posed a sufficient reason generally for such a sweeping curtailment of constitutional liberties, and here, said the Court, "exclusion of those of Japanese origin was deemed necessary because of the presence of an unascertained number of disloyal members of the group."[3]

Unnoticed to some extent in the subsequent ink spilled condemning the decision was the spirited dissent of Justice Murphy, outlining the

---

[1] Roger Daniels, *The Japanese American Cases: The Rule of Law in Time of War* (Lawrence: University of Kansas Press, 2013), at p. 35.

[2] *Korematsu v. United States* (1944) 323 U.S. 214, 216, 65 S.Ct. 193.

[3] Id.

range of violations the government's order committed: the deprivation "of all those within its scope of the equal protection of the laws," excommunication "without benefit of a hearing contrary to due process," and denial of the "rights to live and work where [one] will, to establish a home where they choose and to move about freely."[4] It was, said Murphy, "one of the most sweeping and complete deprivations of constitutional rights in the history of this nation in the absence of martial law."[5]

It is a truism of the law that no right, however vital and precious, is absolute. Speech conveying state secrets in war time might be stifled, contractual remedies might be stayed and even the writ of habeas corpus suspended if the emergency is sufficiently acute.[6] Notwithstanding his own dissent in the Korematsu matter, Justice Owen Roberts admitted that "the liberty of every American citizen freely to come and to go must frequently, in the face of sudden danger, be temporarily limited or suspended."[7] Citizens on occasion might be excluded from a locality, fire lines in case of a conflagration might be drawn, and persons "from an area where a pestilence has broken out" might be removed.[8] For Roberts, for Murphy and many others since that time until the present, what is disputed is often not the justification for the impairment of liberty, upon which all agree, but the impairment's scope. Only the most extreme of circumstances would justify, if at all, the total suspension of the Bill of Rights, and even then an honest court, if not an honest legislature or executive, would be forced to consider whether any less broad a limitation were possible without sacrificing the great goal for which liberty, albeit temporarily, is to be sacrificed.

This debate over the scope of liberty's truncation is the very one occurring at present in nearly every State in the Union, as advocates of safety insist on the most stringent and long lasting of controls on human freedom, and libertarians demand, at the very least, more reasonable and well-tailored limitations. The many orders restricting human action are of a piece, paring down lawful commercial and communal activity

---

[4] Id., at 235, Murphy, J., dissenting.

[5] *Korematsu v. United States*, supra, at 231, Roberts, J., dissenting.

[6] *Near v. Minnesota ex rel. Olson* (1931) 283 U.S. 697, 51 S.Ct. 625; *Home Building & Loan Association v. Blaisdell* (1934) 290 U.S. 398, 54 S.Ct. 231; and The Constitution of the United States, Art. I, Sec. 9, Cl. 2.

[7] *Korematsu v. United States*, supra, at 231, Roberts, J., dissenting.

[8] Id.

to a set of essential functions, to be performed by individuals at a distance from their fellows, often adorned with face masks and even gloves. Massive numbers of businesses have gone dormant, millions are out of a job, schools operate via zoom and religious congregations must watch a podcast if their members are to commune with one another and hear the words of wisdom of their spiritual leaders. Some States are more conservative in imposing emergency measures; others less so. Orders in Alabama, Arizona, Colorado, Georgia, Hawaii, Illinois, Indiana, Iowa, Louisiana, Maine, Nevada, North and South Carolina, Tennessee, Texas and West Virginia are scheduled to expire at the end of April.[9] The orders in Alaska, Idaho, Kansas, Massachusetts, Michigan, Minnesota, Missouri, New Hampshire, North Dakota, Pennsylvania, Ohio, Oklahoma, Rhode Island, Utah, and Washington will expire early in May. Government decrees limiting freedom in Connecticut, Delaware, New York, Vermont, and Wisconsin will be lifted later that month, while Governors in California, Kentucky, Maryland, New Jersey and Oregon have set no termination date. In all of the States, the situation remains fluid. Some Governors hint at an extension of the scheduled end to the shut-down, though they appear reticent to reveal their hand too soon lest the public outcry prematurely still their plans.

And the outcry is growing. In all but a hand-full of States, lack of work has translated into a lack of income, an inability to purchase basic necessities, the draining away of savings, the foregoing of plans for both recreation and medical interventions, the curtailing of social visitation and the breaking off of family ties. Subjected to forced inaction and confinement within the four walls of finite spaces, arguments grow heated, anger percolates and violence at times erupts. The self-worth that comes with work and play, exercise and friendship, diminishes on a state-wide (even national) scale, and the country becomes poorer not only in its pocketbook, but in its spirit as well. The innate hostility in much of the media to any let up of the pressure on the people, a liberation of their bodies and their energies, is palpable. The hostility is evident in the drumbeat of stories about new waves of infection to come should the orders be lifted too soon, the opinions that our lives may now be fundamentally changed for all time, and, in California, applause for the promulgation of a difficult-to-satisfy multi-factor set of criteria that

---

9 Alicia Cohn, "Here's When all 50 States Plan to Reopen After Coronavirus Restrictions," www.thehill.com, April 20, 2020.

must be met before the people can return to a semblance of normalcy.[10] During the lulls in the media accolades we hear California's Governor say that even then, should such a day come, life will be anything but normal. "People might need to wear face coverings in public for months...and mass gatherings could be cancelled for the foreseeable future, until the State reaches 'herd immunity'—the point at which enough people have been exposed to the virus to prevent its transmission—and scientists develop a vaccine."[11] We are, it seems, at war with Eastasia for the long haul. Democracy for the time being is impossible, the Governor and his Party are the guardians of our freedom, and one day, when the long campaign at last is over, we will all smoke victory cigarettes and give praise to Big Brother.

In the past, when disease transmission was thought to be a function of unseen miasmas, evil spirits or the Devil himself, the dread of the unknown might have justified so extreme a retreat from ordinary life. In modern times, when the scientific method supposedly prevails, open-ended restrictions on basic human activity are hard to justify, and harder still when the statistics such as they are show a lack of growth of fatalities in certain locales, a concentration of death in certain States and cities, an admission by health authorities that cause of death is attributed to the virus even when other ailments predominated, and money continues to flow from federal and state spigots so long as the crisis endures. The need for an economy-crushing event cheers the thoughts of some, who see the economic success of the nation during the past few years as an insurmountable barrier to defeating the hated incumbent President. Some on the political left have openly expressed their desire for a recession in order "to get rid of Trump."[12] Bill Maher is said to long on a weekly basis "for economic pain and suffering." In fact, he's "hoping for it because one way you get rid of Trump is a crashing economy."[13] And now, hopeful commentators are abuzz over an economic tailwind that "might turn into a headwind" that could in turn translate into "a one-

---

[10] Alexei Koseff & Erin Allday, "California's Coronavirus Reopening: Gavin Newsom's Six-Point Plan Will Alter Daily Life," *The San Francisco Chronicle*, April 15, 2020.

[11] Id.

[12] Stephen Moore, "Democrats Rooting for Recession: The Drumbeat for an Economic Contraction is Non-Stop," *The Washington Times*, August 25, 2019.

[13] Mairead McArdle, "Bill Maher: 'Bring on the Recession' if it Will Remove Trump," www.nationalreview.com, June 11, 2018.

term Trump presidency."[14] Reaching beyond simple hopes that Orange Man will lose his throne, more thoughtful progressives grasp at the prospect that the virus provides an opportunity to achieve goals that the structure of the separation of powers, federalism and the Bill of Rights ordinarily prohibit. Lacking any opposition press, or any reasonable fear that his political prospects in California might be threatened by too loose a tongue, Gavin Newsom recently admitted to the possibility of using "the coronavirus outbreak to usher in new progressive policies in his state and elsewhere in the country."[15] Democrats packed early drafts of the gargantuan stimulus bill with giveaways to favoured groups, and Democrat leader James Clyburn expressed supreme satisfaction to his partisan allies over the "tremendous opportunity to restructure things to fit our vision."[16]

The use of a crisis to justify the exercise of power to achieve ends utterly unrelated to the defeat of the danger at hand constitutes a grave offense against the trust a people must have in its government to act wisely and honestly. The threat that government might exceed the scope of its power, or misuse it, is the very reason the Framers drafted a Constitution and created a structure of government designed to limit government's ability to act in any but very constrained ways, with numerous checks upon its power, both in the form of organic contradictions and outright prohibitions. Everywhere we see these limitations on power falling away. The shelter-in-place orders might be justified for a moment, but they cannot endure long without leaving our instrument of government, our Constitution, and the scheme it outlines an utter shambles. Those who fear the threat of a virus they have never directly experienced, who greedily lap up the fare presented by corporate media that seems inordinately tied to one political party or ideology, stand by impassively, perhaps at times approvingly, as those who question authority are castigated as virus deniers instead of being praised as necessary voices standing witness to the freedom that formerly seemed so deeply embedded in the American psyche.

---

[14] James Pethokoukis, A Coronavirus Recession Would Likely End Trump's Presidency," www.theweek.com, February 28, 2020.

[15] Michael Ruiz, "California's Newsom Says Coronavirus Provides 'Opportunity' to Push Progressive Agenda," www.foxnews.com, April 2, 2020.

[16] James S. Robbins, "Democrats Try to Hijack Coronavirus Stimulus for Liberal Christmas in March," www.usatoday.com, March 23, 2020.

The freedoms we have lost, at least temporarily, include the most essential in what the Supreme Court has oft described as our system of ordered liberty: First Amendment speech, assembly, press, petition and free exercise rights; the equal protection of the laws, due process and even less esteemed rights, such as the right to keep and bear arms, the right to contract and other economic liberties. Of the rights impaired, those protected by the First Amendment are the most obvious. While the Constitution is silent as to the policy supporting the prohibition on government's impairment of expressive liberty, the commentators have been far less reticent. Many of these policy rationales fall within the camp of the progressives, or what used to be. The great progressive justices of a century ago—Holmes and Brandeis—cast the initial gloss that progressives once heartily cheered: "that we should be eternally vigilant against attempts to check the expression of opinions that we loath and believe to be fraught with death, unless they so imminently threaten immediate interference with the lawful and pressing purposes of the law that an immediate check is required to save the country;" that speech might "result in some violence or in destruction of property is not enough to justify its suppression," because "the ultimate good desired is better reached by free trade in ideas—that the best test of truth is the power of the thought to get itself accepted in the competition of the market;" that "freedom to think as you will and to speak as you think are means indispensable to the discovery and spread of political truth; that without free speech and assembly discussion would be futile; that with them, discussion affords ordinarily adequate protection against the dissemination of noxious doctrine; that the greatest menace to freedom is an inert people; that public discussion is a political duty" and hazard inheres to the discouragement of "thought, hope and imagination."[17] Freedom of expression has been said to be "essential as a means of assuring individual self-fulfilment," of "advancing knowledge and discovering truth," ensuring "participation in decision making by all members of society," and "achieving a more adaptable and hence a more stable community."[18] Suppression of discussion, said Thomas Emerson, "makes a rational judgment impossible, substituting force for reason;

---

[17] See *Abrams v. United States* (1919) 250 U.S. 616, 40 S.Ct. 17; and *Whitney v. California* (1927) 274 U.S. 357, 47 S.Ct. 641.

[18] Thomas I. Emerson, *The System of Freedom of Expression* (New York: Vintage Books, 1970), at pp. 6-7.

because suppression promotes inflexibility and stultification, preventing society from adjusting to changing circumstances or developing new ideas; and because suppression conceals the real problems confronting a society, diverting public attention from the critical issues."[19]

Many might doubt First Amendment liberty has been curtailed at all during the current crisis, or that any curtailment that has occurred is disproportionate to the threat posed to public health by "inaccurate" information. The former view is unreasonable, if not a lie; the latter is increasingly difficult to sustain as time elapses and the so-called curve that the suppression of human freedom was designed to flatten becomes flatter without any commensurate thickening of freedom. Everywhere restrictions on the right to assemble, petition, to speak and to act as members of the press or obtain vital information have tightened without any thought about whether the restrictions are so extreme as to terminate meaningful exercise of the same. Churches might meet online, or members might read the Bible, but in-person congregations are prohibited, even if social distancing remains a viable option. Religious services at a drive-in were recently broken up by police, despite the sequestering of the congregation in their cars as the pastor delivered his sermon from a distance near the outdoor screen.[20] In one instance, recording of choral presentations for the benefit of zooming congregants was banned as dangerous to public health.[21] Having filed a suit for violations of First Amendment freedoms, attorney Harmeet Dhillon said that "the state and localities have granted sweeping exceptions to the shutdown orders for favoured businesses and professions, while specifically targeting people of faith and decreeing to religious institutions that it is 'good enough' that they be allowed to offer streaming video services."[22] A similar lawsuit proceeds in Kansas, where the Governor vowed to defend her restrictions on public worship after a

---

[19] Id., at p. 7.

[20] Natasha Anderson, "Mississippi Police Issue $500 Tickets to Drive-in Church Service Attendees," https://fox8.com, April 12, 2020.

[21] Caleb Parke, "California County's Order Criticized for Limiting Online Worship: 'No Singing,'" www.foxnews.com, April 15, 2020.

[22] Jason Lemon, "Pastors Sue California Governor for Coronavirus Restrictions 'Criminalizing the Free Exercise of Religion,'" www.newsweek.com, April 14, 2020.

court found them to be violative of the Free Exercise Clause.[23] Once the most traditional of public forums, where demonstrations for and against principles and ideas that might help or hurt the community have flourished from time immemorial, the capitol malls in Washington and California are closed to any expressive activity at all and those who resort to them, either for expressive or non-expressive purposes, find themselves subject to penalty.[24] Certain officially favored activities might be engaged in, but others, including protest *against* various factions and "rights," such as the right to terminate a pregnancy, can only be pursued on pain of punishment.

When frustrated citizens organized and engaged in public protests around the country, wearing masks and practicing social distancing, but demanding an easing of restrictions on personal liberty and economic activity, a chorus of condemnation in sync with the preferences of state governors and local officials flooded the media, as if the media—ostensibly a privately held concern—was an agency of the state, whose purpose was either to propagandize the people with the government's message and persuade them of the merits of a particular governmental agenda, or shame the few dissenters into submission through unending criticism and ridicule. The same media springs with alacrity to condemn those officials, particularly at the federal level, who suggest the need for an easing of sanctions in the States where partisans of a particular political party hold sway. Some media even accuse the protestors of the very kind of collusion with political authority they themselves are guilty of—in the protestors' case, a nefarious connection with the election campaign of an allegedly incompetent and evil President who puts profits above lives. It is a veritable symbiotic relationship, or "sufficiently close nexus," between government and private actors that makes it possible to characterize the actions of the later as if they belonged to the former.[25] Progressive and Democrat leaning Facebook and YouTube engage in the removal of content critical of the extreme

---

[23] Daniel Politi, "Federal Judge Blocks Kansas Rule Limiting Religious Gatherings Amid Coronavirus Outbreak," www.slate.com, April 19, 2020.

[24] Rolf Boone, "Capital Mall in West Olympia Will Close Because of Coronavirus," www.msn.com, March 24, 2020; and Sam Stanton, "CHP Bans Protests at State Capital After Rally Against Newsom's Stay-at-Home Order," *The Sacramento Bee*, April 22, 2020.

[25] See *Burton v. Wilmington Parking Authority* (1961) 365 U.S. 715, 81 S.Ct. 856; and *Jackson v. Metropolitan Edison Co.* (1974) 419 U.S. 345, 95 S.Ct. 449.

measures.[26] Facebook did so only after discussing the matter with officials in California and other Democrat-controlled States, and now is even policing its forum for evidence of anti-shut-down organizing and removing the offending posts to ensure that protests challenging government controls do not go forward.[27] By becoming a willing agent of the government, Facebook is the government, and its actions violate the people's right to organize, to assemble, consult, learn and dissent. Progressives and Democrats are constantly warning of fascism. Somehow they've missed this overtly fascist development.

What people are protesting the loss of is far more than the loss of the ability to protest. The lockdown has thrown tens of millions out of work and effected a monumental drop in the average person's income. Long ago, the Supreme Court ruled that mere economic liberty received only the barest of protections. The government's ability to regulate for the common good was not to be impeded by antique notions of individual liberty. An outright ban on work, however, far exceeds mere regulation. Mandating wage and hour rules, work place safety practices and fuel emission standards, though they place a drag on job creation, cannot compare with an edict denying a man or woman the ability to adhere to the commandment of God Himself that they earn their bread through the sweat of their brow. The malignant consequences of such a mandate cascade through the days and weeks since first promulgated. Household budgets are trimmed, bills are deferred, some go entirely into arrears, mortgages and credit card debts are delayed in exchange for the racking up of interest and penalties. The moratorium by the state on payment of taxes is a helpful nod to the real life consequences of state action, though the long term cost of government benefits, from stays on eviction from public housing to bail outs and interest free loans, is hastening the day of reckoning our political leaders have traditionally delayed through debt ceiling elevation and the borrowing of non-existent dollars from a bank that their own legislative power first invented. The government has purportedly helped, too, by extending the time to file suits, to serve process, to answer complaints, to bring cases to trial, but justice delayed

---

[26] Holly Yan, "Protests Erupt Over Coronavirus Shelter-in-Place Orders—Here's Why Some Governor Aren't Budging," www.cnn.com, April 20, 2020.

[27] Id.; and Kim Coulter, "Facebook is Trying to Prevent In-person Anti-Lockdown Gatherings, but There Are Too Many Posts to Delete," www.nationalfile.com, April 23, 2020.

in this regard is, as they say, justice denied. Courthouse doors remain locked, as are most government offices. The right to petition goes fallow; the right to inform oneself of the conduct of the people's business is obstructed. Libraries and universities are silent and the archives in State capitals cannot be entered. Those government operations that do continue, do so remotely, and the pace of action, long a complaint of the citizen, has slackened considerably. These are all real results of the sheltering-in-place imposed on us by our governmental representatives. They take an oath to uphold our Constitution, then violate it in the most obvious of ways, all while being applauded by those who love the idea of the state directing human action, human thought and human conscience. Where once we robustly defended freedom of the press, speech, assembly and petition, we sheepishly wait at present for our rulers to unlock our cages. This might not be what we once considered to be freedom, but it is our freedom now.

Of all the freedoms lost, the one we feel most acutely is not one even expressly identified in our higher law. It is evident, though, in the interstices between expressed limitations on state power and overtly identified privileges and immunities of the people. There is a premium rightfully placed on those freedoms articulated in the law itself—set forth in black letter text—and criticism, if not opprobrium, for those rights inferred by courts where no distinct language is to be found and no history of the rights' exercise exists. Seemingly unclear to us, privileges and immunities of citizens as understood by the Framers and by others in the early republic was no vague concept. They were civil liberties protected by the common law, the law of the land, by due process, and involved those activities that made it possible for a person to survive and even flourish through his or her own efforts, unimpeded by unreasonable restraints pulled tight by state actors.[28] In the familiar litany of these civil rights—the ability to buy and sell, to take to market, to convey for a price and receive in exchange for payment, to seek out work and perform it for hire—there is a common denominator of mobility, a thing that must itself be a right if any other right dependent thereon is to be exercised. This right of mobility, or the right to travel within and beyond individual States of the Union, was said by Justice Douglas to be "part of the 'liberty' of which the citizen cannot be

[28] See Rex Grady, *What is this Freedom: Law, Faith & History in the Time of Trump* (Santa Rosa: Lilburne & Company, LLC, 2019), at pp. 406-410.

deprived without due process of law under the Fifth Amendment."[29] The freedom to move "across frontiers in either direction, and inside frontiers as well, was a part of our heritage. Travel abroad, like travel within the country, may be necessary for a livelihood. It may be as close to the heart of the individual as the choice of what he eats, or wears, or reads. Freedom of movement is basic in our scheme of values… Freedom of travel is indeed an important aspect of the citizen's 'liberty.'"[30]

This freedom is one existing of old. It was expressly recognized as a fundamental feature of human existence even under the tyrants who ruled England before the Enlightenment. Blackstone said the right of movement embraced "the power of locomotion, of changing situation, or of moving one's person to whatsoever place one's inclination may direct without imprisonment or restraint, unless by due process of law."[31] The Constitution itself came into being in part to ensure intercourse between the States. It manifests a number of provisions supporting the right of the people to move freely: the Privileges and Immunities Clause, the Commerce Clause and the Fourteenth Amendment, which prohibits States from impairing the Privileges and Immunities of American citizens. Without any deep analysis of the precise constitutional supports for the right, Antebellum courts acknowledged that citizens of the United States, "as members of the community, must have the right to pass and repass through every part of it without interruption, as freely as in our own States."[32] That the Fourteenth Amendment protects the right of the people to move locally is evident from the concern of its Framers to moor the Civil Rights Act of 1866 in a discreet power of Congress to bar the States from making it illegal for black men and women to travel from town to town in search of work, or simply to lounge about with nothing to do.

Periodically, reference to the right surfaced in Twentieth Century opinions of the Supreme Court. In 1900, Chief Justice Fuller declared that "the right of locomotion, the right to remove from one place to another according to inclination, is an attribute of personal liberty, and the right, ordinarily, of free transit from or through the territory of any State is a

---

[29] *Kent v. Dulles* (1958) 357 U.S. 116, 125, 78 S.Ct. 1113.

[30] Id., at 126.

[31] Sheldon Elliot Steinbach, "Constitutional Protection for Freedom of Movement: A Time for Decision," 57 Ky. L.J. 417 (1969), at 419.

[32] *The Passenger Cases* (1849) 48 U.S. 283, 292.

right secured by the Fourteenth Amendment and by other provisions of the Constitution."[33] Fuller closely linked the right to others associated with the Privileges and Immunities of old: "the right of the citizen to be free in the enjoyment of all his faculties; to be free to use them in all lawful ways; to live and work where he will; to earn his livelihood by any lawful calling."[34] His successor as Chief Justice, Edward White, concurred in this view two decades later, when he noted that "in all the States from the beginning down to the adoption of the Articles of Confederation, the citizens thereof possessed the fundamental right, inherent in citizens of all free governments, peacefully to dwell within the limits of their respective States, to move from place to place therein, to have free ingress thereto and egress therefrom, with a consequent authority in the States to punish violations of this fundamental right."[35]

The Court never felt entirely comfortable with the right. Even as the Warren Court expanded protections for the criminally accused, there were moments with it granted permission to the police to restrict the free movement of those subject to the "reasonable" suspicions of law enforcement. Warren himself said of the freedom of movement that it didn't mean "that areas ravaged by flood, fire or pestilence cannot be quarantined when it can be demonstrated that unlimited travel to the area would directly and materially interfere with the safety and welfare of the area or the nation as a whole."[36] Rebelling against such open-ended concessions to state power to restrict freedom, the libertarian Douglas explained that the right was not merely about movement, but about what rights required movement if the exercise of the same was to occur. "Freedom of movement, at home and abroad, is important for job and business opportunities—for cultural, political and social activities—for all the commingling which gregarious man enjoys," and its consanguinity with other freedoms, such as assembly and association, could hardly be denied.[37] "Like the right of assembly and the right of association, it often makes all other rights meaningful—knowing, studying, arguing, exploring, conversing, observing and even thinking. Once the right to travel is curtailed, all other rights suffer, just as when

---

33 *Williams v. Fears* (1900) 179 U.S. 270, 274.
34 Id.
35 *United States v. Wheeler* (1920) 254 U.S. 281, 293, 41 S.Ct. 133.
36 *Zemel v. Rusk* (1965) 381 U.S. 1, 15, 85 S.Ct. 1271.
37 *Aptheker v. Secretary of State* (1964) 378 U.S. 500, 519-520, 84 S.Ct. 1659.

curfew or home detention is placed on a person."[38] Douglas's viewpoint contributed eight years later to the overthrow of an overly broad and vague vagrancy law. Because his own reasoning wasn't entirely adopted by the majority, he took the opportunity to explain that walking about in public is "historically part of the amenities of life as we have known them."[39] Unmentioned in the Constitution, yes, that was true; these amenities had nevertheless contributed mightily to instilling in "our people the feeling of independence and self-confidence, the feeling of creativity," have "dignified the right of dissent," and condoned and encouraged "the right to be nonconformists and the right to defy submissiveness."[40]

The tendency of Douglas's thought and aspirations to fly beyond the limits of text and history is evident in this rather attenuated defense of a right nowhere mentioned in the Constitution. His mad streak, however, ought not discount the value of his gloss on what federal courts for two centuries have considered to be a right within the imagination of the Framers. It was this very right that Fred Korematsu yearned to exercise when changing his face through surgery and hiding out in an East Bay flophouse. It was the same right that Gordon Hirabayashi defiantly flaunted when brazenly walking past a police station until noticed by the officers inside.[41] It was the right fought for and won by Mitsuye Endo, of whom the Court declared that "under the Constitution she should be free to come and go as she pleased."[42]

It is a right, with other rights, protected by the First Amendment, the Fourteenth Amendment and Article IV, that we are all now doing without by action of the government, purportedly attempting to stay the spread of a virus not unlike the flu in its impact on human health and mortality, but perhaps doing more harm than good in the process. Some physicians claim shelter-in-place is actually contrary to best health practices, that social distancing and hand washing undermine the onset

---

[38] Id., at 520.

[39] *Papachristou v. City of Jacksonville* (1972) 405 U.S. 156, 164, 92 S.Ct. 839.

[40] Id.

[41] *Hirabayashi v. United States* (1943) 320 U.S. 81, 63 S.Ct. 1375.

[42] *Ex parte Endo* (1944) 323 U.S. 283, 65 S.Ct. 208.

of herd immunity.[43] Economists suggest that inducing recession as our government has done might actually take a toll in lives of up to 37,000 for every percentage point added to the ranks of the unemployed, thus eclipsing the likely number of deaths caused by the virus itself.[44] Andrew McCarthy points to the tradeoff between those who might be saved and the destruction of "additional trillions of dollars in wealth...surges of suicides, drug addiction, divorce, broken families, and other social disasters," and the unsustainable nature of a strategy of combatting disease "by ordering communal and commercial activity to cease, then trying to compensate increasingly destitute citizens by borrowing and printing money to throw at them."[45] And then there are the statistical models on which the lock-down strategy was initially based—models that were only as good as the guesses of the modelers, who simply lacked the foresight of the Prophets, yet have so far escaped the Mosaic decree respecting those whose predictions fail the test of time.[46] These are but policy matters, medical matters and the stuff of mathematicians. When looking at the problem from the standpoint of the law and a Constitution that was intended to be a hedge against the errors of wise men and women and the overreach of those with access to power, we might agree that so extreme a pruning of its flanks comes with a cost so dear that it's best avoided like the plague.

Pass the Ammunition

IN the primordial State of Nature, it was said by certain scholars during the Enlightenment, that each man was the equal to his fellow,

[43] See Marta Paterlini, "'Closing Borders is Ridiculous': The Epidemiologist Behind Sweden's Controversial Coronavirus Strategy," www.nature.com, April 21, 2020; and "Bakersfield Doctors Dispute Need for Stay-at-Home Order," www.bakersfieldnow.com, April 22, 2020.

[44] See Barry Bluestone, Bennett Harrison & Lawrence Baker, Corporate Flight: *The Causes and Consequences of Economic Dislocation*.

[45] Andrew C. McCarthy, "COVID-19 and the Limits of the Law," www.nationalreview.com, March 21, 2020.

[46] Seth Borenstein & Carla A. Johnson, "Modeling Coronavirus: 'Uncertainty is the Only Certainty,'" https://apnews.com, April 7, 2020; and Hannah Osborne, "Why the COVID-19 Death Forecasts Are Wrong," www.newsweek.com, April 21, 2020.

possessing an equal share of power that comes with the sojourning of a soul within a living carcass, and could claim by virtue of inherent worth no title to any of the riches of the earth to a degree greater than anyone else. The absence of a government to judge between competing claimants for the same ground, the same seed, the same fruit bearing tree, or the same mate, quite naturally led to a conflict "of every man, against every man," as violent as it was predictable. It was entirely natural in that state, as Thomas Hobbes observed, for two men who "desire the same thing, which nevertheless they cannot both enjoy, [to] become enemies; and in the way to their End, endeavour to destroy, or subdue one another," and that "if one plant, sow, build, or possesse a convenient Seat, others may probably be expected to come prepared with forces united, to dispossesse, and deprive him, not only of the fruit of his labour, but also of his life, or liberty."[1] In such a condition of existence there is, he said, "no place for industry; because the fruit thereof is uncertain; and consequently no Culture of the Earth; no Navigation, nor use of the commodities that may be imported by Sea; no commodious Building; no Instruments of moving, and removing such things as require much force; no Knowledge of the face of the Earth; no account of Time; no Arts; no Letters; no Society; and which is worst of all, continuall feare, and danger of violent death."[2] It was the fate of such a man, dwelling in Nature's domain, that "he armes himselfe, and seeks to go well accompanied; when going to sleep, he locks his dores; when even in his house he locks his chests."[3] So it was in the original State of Nature; so it becomes when the government that emerged from that lawless condition either adopts the savagery of the natural world or recedes from the scene on account of emergent chaos, lack of will, or a dedication of its energies to address only a few of the threats to public order on account of a diminishing of resources in the face of broadening catastrophe that its own oppression or indifference encouraged in the first place. The apocalyptic thrillers and dystopian epics of print and screen tell the same story: a world descending into barbarism in the aftermath of a natural terrestrial disaster, alien invasion, an unthinkable nuclear exchange, or a worldwide epidemic.

---

[1] Thomas Hobbes, *Leviathan, or the Matter, Forme & Power of a Commonwealth, Ecclesiasticall and Civill* (Cambridge: Cambridge University Press, 1904), at p. 82.

[2] Id., at p. 84.

[3] Id.

We have not quite witnessed a denouement so distressing in the extreme as to place our society on the level of Hobbes's State of Nature. Government yet strives to maintain order, even as the people react, sometimes irrationally, by pursuing bizarre fads such as the quest to pack their garages with shrink-wrapped bundles of toilette paper, or loading up their pantries with products like oat milk which they'd never heard of prior to first learning of the ensuing plague. Many of the wave of consumers that swept the nation's gun shops in response to the tremors of information telling of an approaching biologic scourge may not have acted entirely without reason. Many didn't already own firearms, yet were motivated by announcements that some convicted criminals would be released, or that local police would be focusing on only the most serious of offenses. Others acted on a nagging concern that "the pandemic's ripple effect may cause a breakdown of societal norms."[4] With gun purchase and background check numbers off the chart, the inference is strong in the minds of some that a degree of "panic buying," as opposed to self-defensive prudence, is really what's at play.[5] A bloodbath of violence flowing from untrained hands, unbalanced minds and ready access to a new cachet of weapons presents itself to the troubadours of a disarmed society as the raw material for a song of lament and a call for action to prevent the pending disaster. "What really has me concerned," says Chelsea Parsons of the Center for American Progress, "is that people who are choosing to buy guns right now, particularly people who are first-time gun buyers, are making that decision from a place of anxiety and fear."[6] More guns means more children who will play with stray and errantly loaded pistols, more depressives ending their torment by swallowing a muzzle, and more gun-related violence due to "a breakdown of law and order, and the cognitive stress of social isolation."[7] "Adding more guns to more homes during a time of more anxiety could lead to more deaths," said John

---

[4] Allie Volpe, "A Legacy of the COVID-19 Pandemic Will be that Even More Americans Own Guns," www.rollingstone.com, April 8, 2020.

[5] Lois Beckett, "Americans Purchasing Record-Breaking Numbers of Guns Amid Coronavirus," www.theguardian.com, April 1, 2020.

[6] Volpe, op. cit.

[7] Id.

Feinblatt, President of Everytown for Gun Safety.[8] "And that's the last thing we need when our hospitals are already bursting at the seams."[9]

Sensing the moment was here for a remedy to the age-old problem of an armed America too violent and immature for its own good, government officials have issued orders confiscating weapons and closing gun shops, and enacted legislation imposing far more expansive impediments to gun ownership than ever before. Pennsylvania's Governor Thom Wolf, for instance, "issued an order on March 19 mandating the closure of the physical locations of 'all non-life-sustaining business,' including gun shops."[10] Governor Cuomo in New York likewise left gun shops off the list of essential businesses. Los Angeles County Sheriff Alex Villanueve affirmatively announced he would close down all firearms retailers in the County while the epidemic lasted. These moves and others like them throughout the country quickly prompted litigation by plaintiffs asserting violation of the Second Amendment. As the people cannot be denied the right to vote or express their opinion publicly, so too they cannot be prevented from obtaining a weapon the Constitution assures is their right to own.

While some authorities have backed off the restrictions, others hold firm. Even the President has weighed in on the matter by issuing guidelines identifying gun shops as essential businesses that are best allowed by State officials to remain open. As with everything the President does, his usual critics immediately suspected collusion with some nefarious source—in this case the NRA—and demanded disclosure of correspondence detailing how the decision to ensure public access to firearms came to pass.[11]

The struggle to maintain or to subvert Second Amendment liberties is nothing new. This step-child of constitutional rights had already been the subject of sneers, insults and outright attacks from those who would tell you they possess a more refined sense of morality and justice than the ordinary mortal. For them, the right to resist tyranny or defend

---

[8] Lawrence Hurley, "Trump Coronavirus Guidance on Keeping Gun Stores Open Draws Criticism," www.reuters.com, March 30, 2020.

[9] Id.

[10] Adam Edelman, "Buckling to Pressure, Many States Deem Gun Stores 'Essential,' Allow them to Remain Open During Pandemic," www.nbcnews.com, April 7, 2020.

[11] Rebecca Falconer, "Trump Administration Deems Gun Stores Essential Amid Coronavirus Outbreak," www.axios.com, March 31, 2020.

hearth and home is an affront to human liberty that should have been forever terminated upon formation of the social compact. Hobbes, not Locke, is their guiding light, and the man or woman who even harbors the thought that a person might lawfully lift a weapon to defend oneself or another, their home or family, is actually an offender against the public good as much as any felon intent on unprovoked rapine. They equate the proponent of defensive violence with the home invader and strong-arm assailant, and insist that only those concurrently condemned as the legalized oppressors of ethnic minorities be authorized to raise or discharge a firearm.

In California, on the frontier of the struggle between an armed populace and a condescending elite, the tide of regulation has been in full flood, washing over consumer and retailer alike, and leaving the citizen with less recourse to the tools of self-defense than in years past. The network of current regulation is both intricate and ingenious: "a universal background check for firearms, an 'assault weapon' ban, a ban on magazines holding more than 10 rounds, a gun registry, firearm confiscation orders, a minimum gun purchase age of 21 years, a limit of one firearm purchase per month, a requirement that would-be gun buyers first earn a safety certificate, a 10-day waiting period on gun purchases even for persons who already own a firearm, a ban on campus carry for self-defense, a ban on K-12 teachers being armed for self-defense, a ban on openly carrying a firearm, a highly restrictive concealed carry law, and a moribund roster of handguns permitted for retail sale."[12] If these restrictions were not enough of a deterrent to gun purchase and gun ownership, the State enacted a further hurdle in the form of Proposition 63—a requirement that ammunition purchasers first prove their identity via presentation of a so-called "Real I.D." and undergo a background check similar to that reserved for gun purchasers. Any impulse to evade the background check by purchasing ammo in another State, in person or by mail, was simultaneously extinguished by the *coupe de gras* of regulations: an actual ban on importation of ammunition direct to the consumer from other States.

The law is analogous to a ridiculous enactment to require purchasers of ink for use in printing presses to prove their identity and lack of history as a libeler, and barring any interstate shipments of ink from

---

12 Order Granting Plaintiff's Motion for Preliminary Injunction, *Kim Rhode, et al. v. Xavier Becerra*, Case No.: 18-cv-802-BEN, at pp. 38-40.

alighting on the printer's doorstep. While such a fantastic law would be readily understood to constitute a constitutionally repugnant prior restraint, highly chilling to expressive freedom and a text book example of a fatal trigger of the dormant commerce clause, California's latest attempt to disarm the people, in its proponents' view, is just another example of progressives sagely ignoring limitations on government power in the name of a cause that is righteous beyond dispute.

When this last law took effect, it wasn't immediately challenged as a violation of the Second Amendment. Instead, gun dealers and consumers attempted to work within the law's strictures, only to find that the possession of a Real I.D. was far more difficult to come by than initially thought. Without such a document, the background check could not proceed. While many were able to obtain the required document relatively quickly, others struggled due to lack of an ability to confirm basic facts through no fault of their own. The end result was the barring of an unknown number of people from even getting through the law's front door, where the background check could then proceed. The broad sweep of the background checks that did occur inaccurately flagged a hundred thousand persons as ineligible to purchase ammunition without informing them of the reason for the snag, forcing them to undergo a diligent search for the error and then to correct it before trying again. The detection of two hundred persons actually ineligible to purchase a gun because of criminal prohibitions hardly matched the broad and unnecessary impairment of what is actually a constitutional right.

That we might stop one criminal from obtaining a gun and using it to commit a crime or even killing someone was well worth it to the supporters of this onerous regulation of firearms, but never was any thought given to the lives lost because a gun wasn't available, or the uneasiness that keeps one awake at night in high crime neighbourhoods and causes him or her to wonder if the sound heard outside was resonating from a burglar, rapist or kidnapper attempting to breach the curtilage of the home. Nor do superior progressive minds ever comprehend the dangers that come from a generous berth granted by the courts to other elements of the Bill of Rights—the right to be free from unreasonable searches and seizures, the right to remain silent, the right to counsel, a trial by jury, and due process—dangers such as those that proceed from violent criminals who go free on account of these liberties only to rob, main and kill again. We tend to think of the threat to be avoided as one coming from the weapon when a weapon is at issue, but forget all about the human intelligence controlling the weapon and the context in which it is wielded when the one who wielded it for a criminal purpose is finally at the mercy of police and prosecutors. The criminal who shoots and kills is less vile than the artefact that serves as a convenient vehicle for the crime, and while the criminal might win his freedom through a scrupulous application of the Bill of Rights, the gun that might save a life in another context is beyond the power of the Bill of Rights to redeem.

When the challenges to the law came, they came with a demand that enforcement be enjoined until a trial of the substantive claims and defenses could be had. The contention was that the law impaired protected liberty interests so obviously, and the prejudice to the afflicted in the meantime was so great, that the law need not be fully and finally determined to be invalid before restraints on its enforcers were placed. In considering the issue of an injunction, the rumination of Presiding Judge Roger Benitez in the Federal District Court in San Diego focused first on the standing of the parties and the standard of review to apply, then whether ammunition was protected by the Second Amendment and, if it was, whether the law at issue actually restricted the right in a manner contrary to the Constitution.

The plaintiffs included arms dealers, in addition to consumers. The former sued because their right to sell weapons shrivelled under the withering heat of the law, indirectly affecting the right to keep and bear arm enjoyed by the latter. The normal death blow to tertiary standing launched by the Attorney General was successfully parried with the shield of a special relationship normally reserved for physicians who might perform an abortion. Feeling first the forehand of the application of the exception to first party standing ordinarily justified in privacy cases, the Attorney General then took a backhand in the form of the Judge's holding that the right to keep and bear arms did indeed extend protective cover to both the firing mechanism and its missile. "Citizens of the United States have a constitutional right to keep and bear firearms and the ammunition which makes a firearm useful."[13] The Second Amendment, he continued, "protects firearms and ammunition, though

[13] Id., at p. 33.

admittedly, the Amendment didn't "explicitly mention ammunition." An absence of bullets, he reasoned, renders a gun inert, and without bullets, the right at issue "would be meaningless." Any regulation, such as Proposition 63, that eliminates "a person's ability to obtain or use ammunition could thereby make it impossible to use firearms for their core purpose."

The State actually conceded the relevance of the Second Amendment. Its primary substantive defense was that the law was presumptively valid due to its reasonable relationship to a legitimate governmental interest. Finding the contention too rich to partake in, and so utterly inconsistent with the traditional approach to any right enumerated in the Bill of Rights, Judge Benitez batted it aside and addressed the State's fallback position that intermediate scrutiny ought to apply. The argument made some sense in light of the jurisprudence governing the Ninth Circuit. Courts in the Circuit, even the appellate bench as a whole, tend to uphold firearms regulations if they are "a reasonable fit to achieve the State's legitimate safety interests."[14] Doubting the relevance of any standard other than the one relied on by the Supreme Court in *District of Columbia v. Heller*, Judge Benitez humoured the Attorney General by analysing the law in accordance with the far more lenient standard.

The interest informing the law was, of course, legitimate: "to keep aliens illegally or unlawfully present, felons, and other prohibited persons from obtaining ammunition." That the statutory means of achieving this laudable goal was a "good fit," or a regulation that tends to promote the goal more effectively than would be possible in its absence, he found far more problematic. The burden of establishing this fact remained with the government," and the burden could only be met by demonstrating through actual evidence that "the recited harms are real, not merely conjectural, and that the regulation will in fact alleviate these harms in a direct and material way."[15]

With respect to the law at issue, Judge Benitez noted that the evidence supporting the claim that the law actually advanced the State's interest and was a "good fit" was thin, even shoddy.[16] The primary evidence was the text of the law itself, passed by the people of the State,

---

[14] Id., at p. 50.
[15] Id., at p. 62.
[16] Id., at pp. 67 and p. 72.

announcing that "voters declared that 'we should require background checks for ammunition sales just like gun sales, and stop both from getting into the hands of dangerous people.'" Such findings are not evidence at all, but ipse dixit, lacking even the support of legislative committee reports, or any indication that the people themselves, when casting their vote, even considered the merits of the law's inherent conclusions. For a court to trust the conclusive boiler plate of a ballot measure has in fact never been done, and is especially improper when the law itself infringes on the Bill of Rights – a feature of the Constitution designed to protect individuals from majoritarian bulldozing.

Three studies undertaken by other jurisdictions were also presented in support of the law, but the Judge considered these to be in essence valueless since they didn't even address an actual working ammunition registry – something that no State jurisdiction other than California had ever instituted. Far more persuasive was the evidence presented by the plaintiffs, including the report of an investigation by federal authorities in two regulatory agencies that had experimented with a registry and their conclusion that ammunition recordkeeping had no substantial law enforcement value. Further evidence indicated that the very people the law is ostensibly designed to prevent from obtaining ammunition to use in crime were more inclined to and actually did evade the law by purchasing firearms and ammunition illegally. Though he acknowledged that discovery may turn up evidence of a different nature, the evidence that existed at present suggested the law itself, to the extent that it had been tried at the federal level years before, was a failure. Failed measures, he concluded, could never be the basis for a finding by a court that the government's regulation of a fundamental right bore a substantial relationship to an important government interest.

In contrast to the lack of evidence that the law advanced the State's laudable goals was the evidence that the law unnecessarily impaired the Second Amendment rights of honest citizens. Premised on an intention "to stop persons from acquiring weapons in violation of federal law," Prop 63 disproportionately stopped eligible people from acquiring weapons, thus stripping them of an important constitutional right. The federal law at issue was the Real I.D. requirement, designed in part to restrict the freedom of persons illegally in the country. Only identification documents that satisfy strict federal standards were to be presented to licensed dealers of ammunition at the outset of the transaction, prior to the actual background check. Aside from the absurdity of the Sanctuary State of California insisting on presentation of documents aimed at thwarting the freedom of illegal aliens, the law itself creates a presumption that anyone attempting to buy a gun is illegally in the country. It is up to the would-be purchaser to prove that he isn't, not the State to prove that he is. An alternative is provided in the form of proving one's identity through presentation of a U.S. Passport or a certified birth certificate, neither of which is easily or inexpensively obtainable if one doesn't already have one or both. The much-lamented onus of presenting a driver's license when voting in some States is nothing compared to the burden imposed on Second Amendment rights by Prop 63's far more stringent identification requirement.

Judge Benitez didn't think it was a close call. The incongruity between the supposed purpose of the law with its actual results likely doomed it once the merits of the case were vetted. The continuing harm to Californians desirous of availing themselves of their Second Amendment rights wasn't merely slight, it was profound and irreparable, especially in these uncertain times. "Schools, parks, beaches, and countless non-essential businesses are closed. Courts are limping by while police make arrests for only the more serious crimes."[17] The people are entitled to protect themselves, and if the police are unavailable, the full burden of that responsibility should rest not on armless shoulders, but on the confidence that violent criminal force will be met with a counter force possessing the full backing of the Second Amendment.

With the fall of the background check requirement, the rationale for the importation ban was weakened. No more would the State need to head off at the State line those unwilling to submit to a background check before purchasing ammunition. Yet it remained a formidable restriction due to the fact that ammunition manufacturing occurred primarily in other States. So long as the barrier stood, ammunition supplies would quickly dwindle and guns would be firing blanks. Remarkably, this particular provision wasn't attacked as a violation of the Second Amendment. Instead, the Commerce Power was the bludgeon raised by the plaintiffs against it. The allocation of control over

---

[17] Id., at pp. 117-118.

interstate commerce to Congress was long ago said to have deprived the States of much of their authority to enact laws that directly or indirectly interfered with the flow of goods and services across State lines. The States might enact laws to promote the health, safety, welfare and good morals of the people, and might even do so in a way that impacted interstate commerce, but when the impact is palpable or severe, doubts abound as to the legitimacy of the regulation, even in the absence of any contrary action by Congress. Congress might prohibit articles of interstate trade for entirely moral reasons (e.g. lottery tickets), not because of its power to legislate the morals of the people, but because it possesses plenary authority over the channels of interstate commerce.

The States, of course, can regulate the morals of the people directly, and even prohibit particular products and pastimes, but if the prohibition interferes with the transport and sale across State lines of goods generally accepted as lawful, the dormant aspect of the commerce power will intervene. Justice John Catron once observed that the prohibition against sale of one State's products within another State's territory would be to make commerce subordinate to a State's police power, and if permitted would allow a State to ban "any article of consumption that a State might wish to exclude, whether it belonged to that which was drunk, or to food and clothing."[18] Justice Stanley Matthews noted that a State could ban products within its own boundaries, but couldn't shut the door to lawful commerce in the same products with other States. If it were otherwise, it would be left "to each State, according to its own caprice and arbitrary will, to discriminate for or against every article grown, produced, manufactured or sold in any State and sought to be introduced as an article of commerce into any other."[19] If one State, for instance, "may prohibit the importation of intoxicating liquors from all other States, it may also include tobacco, or any other article, the use or abuse of which it may deem deleterious."[20] Local peculiarities, it is true, might be exempt from the reach of Dormant Commerce: "harbor pilotage," said Justice Field, "the improvement of harbors, the establishment of beacons and buoys to guide vessels in and out of port, the construction of bridges over navigable rivers, the erection of wharves, piers and docks, and the like," at least until Congress sees

[18] *The License Cases* (1847) 5 How. 504, 599.
[19] *Bowman v. Chicago & Northwestern Railway Co.* (1888) 125 U.S. 465, 493.
[20] Id.

fit to pre-empt local regulation with a uniform law.[21] Wherever "the subject is national in its character, and admits and requires uniformity of regulation, affecting alike all the States, such as transportation between the States, including the importation of goods from one State into another, Congress can alone act upon it and provide the needed regulations."[22] With these views Chief Justice Fuller concurred, noting that "whenever the law of the State amounts essentially to a regulation of commerce with foreign nations or among the States, as it does when it inhibits, directly or indirectly, the receipt of an imported commodity…it comes in conflict with a power which, in this particular, has been exclusively vested in the general government, and is therefore void."[23] Ammunition being a lawful commodity, even in the State of California, the State is without power to prevent its importation for sale.

These venerable authorities, long forgotten by most, also escaped the notice of Judge Benitez, whose analysis was rather cursory, but nevertheless correct. "Under Proposition 63," he noted, "the single fact of residence in another state forecloses a vendor of ammunition from selling directly to California residents."[24] Non-residence, however, can't "foreclose a producer in one State from access to markets in other States." Citing *Hughes v. Oklahoma*, he reminded the parties that it was the purpose of the Constitution as a whole, and the Commerce Clause more specifically, "to avoid the tendencies toward economic Balkanization that had plagued relations among the Colonies and later among the States under the Articles of Confederation."[25] What the Constitution makes lawful, and every State and Congress permit—interstate trafficking of ammunition—California now criminalizes. The only way around the prohibition is for an out-of-state vendor to incorporate in the State and open a store-front in every county where it wished to sell its wares. Any benefits of the law, whatever they might be, are so outweighed by the burdens on interstate commerce that the law simply could never pass constitutional muster.

---

[21] Id., 507.
[22] Id.
[23] *Leisy v. Hardin* (1890) 135 U.S. 100, 123.
[24] Order Granting Plaintiff's Motion for Preliminary Injunction, supra, at p. 98.
[25] Id.

The Attorney General immediately sought a stay of the Judge's order, but it was denied.[26] Within hours, though, he received one from a friendly judge on the Ninth Circuit bench.[27] The decision is destined for en banc review and no doubt a visit to the Supreme Court of the United States. Those arrayed on either side of the issue will continue their snarling, and the governor in California, and governors elsewhere, will forge ahead in the name of making it harder for a citizen to exercise a right the Framers placed second in the list of enumerated rights. Why someone who has no criminal record ought to be denied either guns or ammunition remains a difficult question to answer. It couldn't be simply because the safety of the community depends on it; for the safety of the community is threatened by far greater dangers. The outlawing of ladders, for instance, might make a dent in the 6,000 fatal falls that occur each year in American homes. Removal of any and all toxic substances from medicine cabinets and tool sheds would undoubtedly reduce the number of poisoning annually from 5,000 to some smaller number. Fire, burns and drownings could be prevented by banning matches, candles, electricity and swimming pools. And then there are the tens of thousands of deaths in automobile accidents every year, and the smaller number killed by trains. No one seriously suggests eliminating the causes of any of these unfortunate deaths due to the dangers they pose because nearly everyone understands there is certain degree of risk involved in living, and a degree of due care everyone must exercise if they are to stay safe. Government officials and activists for social improvement likely refrain from recommending so sweeping a set of prohibitions on everyday articles for far more cynical reasons as well—no one has ever resisted the coercive power of the state with a candle, a ladder or a match; swimming pools hardly impede the advance of a swat team and an automobile cannot withstand a tank.

As those who operate the government lose their affinity with the compact from which the government was born, they wax more akin to the actors in Hobbes' State of Nature, and the people become more not less entitled to retain the means of protection, not for the purpose of waging war against every man, but of overpowering the governors and

---

[26] "Order Denying Ex Parte Motion for Stay," April 24, 2020, *Kim Rhode et al v. Attorney General*, Case 3:18-cv-00802-BEN-JLB.

[27] "Court Reinstates California Ammunition Purchase Law," www.usnews.com, April 25, 2020.

doing what Hobbes' younger contemporary Locke said was their right: "to remove or alter the Legislative, when they find the legislative act contrary to the trust reposed in them."[28] A radical thought yes, but one thoroughly embraced by the Framers who placed the Second Amendment into the pantheon of constitutional liberties, to be valued especially today in times such as these by a people worried that the unprecedented impositions of the State on their liberty will make unavoidable a crisis of confidence in public authorities and require them, like the founding generation in times past, to take the law into their own hands.

Citizenship... What Good is It?

THE recent announcement by the President of $1,500 payments to millions of Americans forced out of their jobs due to the many shelter-in-place orders in effect throughout the country proved highly disappointing to advocates for the nation's "undocumented" community. With federal and State laws barring receipt of any unemployment-type cash benefits by persons illegally in the country, advocates turned to the States as a source of relief for workers whose lack of legal residence within the United States bore no direct relationship to their temporary inability to work.[1] Entreaties for aid to jobless aliens ineligible to receive what many were calling Trumpbux soon found a sympathetic ear in the great sanctuary state of California. Within two days of issuing a state-wide Shelter-in-Place Order, Governor Newsom signed Senate Bill 89, appropriating $500,000,000 for use in mitigating the economic impact of the shut-down on the State and its citizens. Unable to use any of this money to aid illegal aliens, the Governor explored an entirely novel arrangement, which he called a "public-private partnership," to provide $75,000,000 to private organizations to "support undocumented Californians impacted by COVID-19 who are ineligible for unemployment insurance benefits and

[28] John Locke, *Second Treatise of Government*, § 149.
[1] See *Cal. Unemployment Insurance Code* § 1264; and 26 U.S.C. § 3304.

disaster relief...due to their immigration status."[2] In keeping with this plan, he anticipated that "approximately 150,000 undocumented adult Californians will receive a one-time cash benefit of $500 per adult with a cap of $1,000 per household to deal with the specific needs arising from the COVID-19 pandemic."[3]

It wasn't long before Harmeet Dhillon, the gadfly of California' one-party state, filed a lawsuit alleging that the appropriation violated the State Constitution's prohibition on drawing money from the State Treasury "for the purpose or benefit of any corporation, association, asylum, hospital, or any other institution not under the exclusive management and control of the State as a State institution."[4] Dhillon's lawsuit sought an injunction on payment of any benefits on the grounds that they are unsupported by a "legitimate public purpose" due to conflict with Article XVI, Section 3 of the State Constitution. As sweeping as the Governor's power during the crises is, his authority remains subject to the Constitution's firm limits and the rights of the people that the treasury not be dedicated to objectives not supported by the law. If he's going to provide cash benefits to non-citizens illegally in the country, he will have to come up with another way of doing so.

Citizenship, said Hugo Black, "is no light trifle."[5] It comes with a bundle of rights, distinguishing it from other status categories, entitling the holder to far more than mere nominal honor. It was the mere invocation of citizenship that preserved the Apostle Paul from torment and execution and delivered him to a forum where due process distinct from summary procedure was more likely to result in a somewhat more impartial disposition.[6] There are those—supporters of the Governor's policy perhaps—who contend that such things as borders, governments and citizenship are arbitrary by nature, reflective no doubt of biases so old and unexamined that they bear no relationship to current needs, and that what is important is not the status of a person in a country but their actual presence there and the real contributions they are making to the benefit of the whole. Laws are rigid and they apply harshly, especially so in harsh times. Intervention by equity, that old friend and sometime

---

[2] "Governor Newsome Announces New Initiatives to Support California Workers Impacted by COVID-19," www.gov.ca.gov., April 15, 2020.

[3] Id.

[4] Emergency Petition for Writ of Mandate, at ¶ 7, *Benitez et al. v. Newsom et al.*

[5] *Afroyim v. Rusk* (1867) 387 U.S. 253, 87 S.Ct. 1660, 1668.

[6] Acts 22:22-29.

adversary of justice, is needed to remedy an outcome inconsistent with all the humane impulses that surely must be our guide through the rough terrain that is our world. The emotional appeal of this position is great: people are preeminent over imaginary lines on the earth; living souls over empty categories that capriciously split apart people whose interests truly are one. And like much that is emotionally based, it disregards reason and the reasons why seemingly arbitrary categories were devised and permits the belief to flourish that these categories can be easily jettisoned without harm to the social structure and polity.

As long as nations have existed, definitions of who is entitled to membership and for whom a nation is intended to benefit have been drawn. In all times and places, those who first formed a national community have ranked as citizens, obligated to submit themselves to the political authority of the nation's government, yet also entitled to certain privileges denied to all those outside the community's fold. While some citizens might possess greater privileges or rights than others, all citizens regardless of their rank exercised privileges that persons from outside the community lacked. The latter might be citizens of other nations; but with respect to the nation at hand, they were aliens, thus entitled to no more rights than the nation gratuitously extended. Newcomers might acquire citizenship and add to the nation's strength, but typically eligibility would flow only upon demonstration of the candidate's loyalty and potential for positive contribution. In colonial America, aliens had no rights to enter the community, no right to trade with the community's members, and could be excluded at any time. An alien "was not fully entitled, as a matter of equal right, to travel or reside within the…territories,…was not permitted to purchase, convey, or hold real property for his own use, nor was he able to inherit or transmit by inheritance such property," he was forbidden to work "at certain trades" and "unable to hold any public office."[7] All privileges granted to an alien—including the "acquisition of personal property, the use of real property, protection of his person, and the ability to reside…were merely concessions that could be withdrawn, especially if war turned a

[7] David Upham, "Corfield v. Coryell and the Privileges and Immunities of American Citizenship," 83 Tex. L. Rev. 1483 (2005), at p. 1493.

friendly nation into an enemy."[8]

What were denied aliens as a matter of right were the very things extended to citizens of the States as they emerged from colonial servitude. The Articles of Confederation guaranteed that the citizens of the several States, unlike aliens, would be free to enter and exit any other State, and to engage in "all the privileges of trade and commerce, subject to the same duties, impositions, and restrictions as the inhabitants thereof respectively."[9] When the Articles gave way to a new organic law, the same principle found incorporation in the new Constitution's Fourth Article in slightly abbreviated form. Judicial gloss on the meaning of the provision was rare during the early Republic, though not unknown. In the first decade after the Constitution's ratification, Judge Jeremiah Chase in Maryland curtly said that the privileges and immunities of citizens included "the peculiar advantage of acquiring and holding real as well as personal property, and that such property shall be protected and secured by the laws of the State, in the same manner as the property of the citizens of the State is protected."[10] More famous was the exposition of Justice Bushrod Washington while riding the circuit, wherein he explained that the privileges and immunities of citizenship were those "in their nature, fundamental; which belong, of right, to the citizens of all free governments; and which have, at all times, been enjoyed by the citizens of the several States which compose this Union."[11] The privileges of citizenship included "protection by the Government; the enjoyment of life and liberty, with the right to acquire and possess property of every kind, and to pursue and obtain happiness and safety; subject nevertheless to such restraints as the Government must justly prescribe for the general good of the whole," in addition to "the right of a citizen of one State to pass through, or to reside in any other State, for purposes of trade, agriculture, professional pursuits, or otherwise; to claim the benefits of the writ of habeas corpus; to institute and maintain actions of any kind in the courts of the State; to take, hold and dispose of property, either real or personal; and an exemption from

[8] David Bogen, "The Transformation of the Fourteenth Amendment: Reflections From the Admission of Maryland's First Black Lawyers," 44 Md. L. Rev. 939 (1985), at pp. 948-949.

[9] *Articles of Confederation*, Article IV.

[10] Bogen, op. cit., at pp. 952-953.

[11] *Corfield v. Coryell* (1821) 6 F. Case. 546, 551.

higher taxes or impositions…."[12]

The right to speak, assemble and petition for redress of grievances were likely considered by Washington and others at the time to be rights of citizens that couldn't be denied anyone on account of their ordinary residence in a sister State. This was certainly the view of Washington's law teacher and predecessor on the Court, James Wilson, who noted that "the citizen under a free government has a right to think, to speak, to write, to print, and to publish freely, but with decency and truth, concerning public men, public bodies, public measures."[13] Similarly, Chancellor Kent argued that "because the freedoms of speech and press were so essential to that 'control over their rulers, which resides in the free people of these United States' that it has 'become a constitutional principle in this country, that 'every citizen may freely speak, write, and publish his sentiments, on all subjects, being responsible for the abuse of that right, and that no law can rightfully be passed to restrain or abridge the freedom of speech, or of the press.'"[14] Justice Washington, like many others who considered the problem at the time, acknowledged that the right to vote was also a privilege of citizenship, but that it was constrained by a State's interest in setting qualifications so as to prevent mere transients from participating in elections that might impose obligations on those who actually would live permanently within the jurisdiction, and thereby deprive actual residents of some fraction of their sovereign authority.

Ironically, it was the controversy over slavery and whether a free black man could be considered a citizen that clarified beyond doubt the privileges of citizenship comprehended by the Framers of the Constitution. Optimism that American independence portended universal freedom contributed to a wave of manumissions in northern States and even on an individual basis in the South. George Washington famously liberated his slaves, as did New Yorker John Jay, and southern courts adopted a presumption of liberty when contests arose over testamentary intent in the disposition of human property. Racial prejudice, however, could not abide the presence of free blacks, for they

---

[12] Id., at 551-552.

[13] David R. Upham, "Corfield v. Coryell and the Privileges and Immunities of American Citizenship," supra, at p. 1523.

[14] David R. Upham, "The Meanings of the 'Privileges and Immunities of Citizens' on the Eve of the Civil War," 91 Notre Dame L. Rev. 1117 (2016), at pp. 1137-1138.

unsettled the population still in bondage and prompted white fears of insurrection stirred by the living example of bondmen made free. Harsh laws governing the freedom of the freedmen made life untenable in places where slavery remained, hence immigration offered hope for a better future. The free States where former slaves migrated were not always welcoming. As more black Americans crossed the Mason Dixon Line in search of opportunities under freedom's protective wing, white populations turned to the law to provide discriminatory shelter from a demographic they might love, but only at a distance. Missouri was the first State to propose an outright ban on free black migrants settling within its borders. Senator James Burrill of Rhode Island declared the proposal to be "entirely repugnant to the Constitution of the United States," in that it prohibited "a very large class of persons from entering the State."[15] That Congress acquiesced in the admission of the State with a Constitution containing the offensive provision suggested to many that Article IV didn't apply because the population denied the privileges and immunities of citizenship were not citizens at all, but a permanent sub-class trapped within the geographic limits of the United States.

This position was sadly constitutionalized in the Supreme Court's dreadful *Dred Scott* decision. Speaking for the majority, Chief Justice Taney explained that if free blacks were citizens, they would possess "the right to enter every other State whenever they please, singly or in companies, without pass or passport, and without obstruction, to sojourn there as long as they pleased, to go where they pleased at every hour of the day or night without molestation, unless they committed some violation of the law for which a white man would be punished; and it would give them the full liberty of speech in public and in private upon all subjects upon which its own citizens might speak; to hold public meetings upon political affairs, and to keep and carry arms wherever they went."[16] Even the dissenting Justice Curtis agreed with this, though he doubted that free black citizens would necessarily be entitled to full political rights even if they possessed privileges and immunities, including the right to vote or to serve in elected office. Such exalted privileges, being among "the chiefest attributes" and "decisive evidence of citizenship," were privileges the State was entitled to ration

---

[15] Philip Hamburger, "Privileges or Immunities," 105 Nw. U.L. Rev. 61 (2011), at p. 85.

[16] *Dred Scott v. Sandford* (1857) 60 U.S. 393, 416-417.

based on heightened qualifications designed to advance the best interests of the State.[17]

The tragic decision of the Court to exclude African Americans from citizenship and the possession of citizenship's various privileges yielded, with other sectional stressors, the great and lethal Civil War, yet also permitted in the aftermath a moment when a convergence of political, ideological and moral impulses could direct a solid majority in the Congress to promote both freedom and citizenship for the historically excluded class, complete with all of the privileges and immunities historically enjoyed by white citizens. Understanding that freedom for the former slave didn't necessarily convey citizenship, the Congress enacted the Civil Rights Act of 1866 and contemplated a companion bill known as the Privileges and Immunities Act. The former declared that all people "shall have the same right, in every State and Territory of the United States, to make and enforce contracts, to sue, be parties, and give evidence, to inherit, purchase, lease, sell, hold, and convey real and personal property, and to full and equal benefit of all laws and proceedings for the security of person and property, as is enjoyed by white citizens," while the latter provided "that every person, being a citizen of the United States shall, in right of such citizenship, be entitled, freely and without hindrance or molestation, to go from the State, Territory, or District of his or her residence, and to pass into and through and to sojourn, remain and take permanent abode within each of the several States, Territories, and Districts of the United States, and therein to acquire, own, control, enjoy and dispose of property, realty, personal and mixed; and to do and transact business, and to have full and speedy redress in the courts for all rights of person and property, as fully as such rights and privileges are held and enjoyed by the other citizens of such State, Territory, or District; and, moreover, therein to have, enjoy, and demand the same immunities and exemptions from high or excessive impositions, assessments, and taxation as are enjoyed by such other citizens under the law or usages of such State, Territory, or District, and to have, demand, and enjoy all other privileges and immunities which the citizens of the same State, Territory, or District would be entitled to under the like circumstances." The former law ensured that no State could prevent its own citizens from enjoying the

[17] Id., at 581, Curtis, J., dissenting.

privileges of citizenship; the later provided a remedy for citizens of one State being denied the privileges of citizenship anywhere else. That the latter bill wasn't enacted was due only to the veto of the former, and the recognition by majorities in Congress that only a constitutional amendment protecting the privileges of citizenship would absolutely ensure that they would not be eroded or otherwise undermined by action of the States.[18]

In debating the meaning of the Privileges and Immunities Clause of the proposed amendment, speakers made it clear what they entailed. They included not only the familiar litany of privileges identified by Bushrod Washington and others, but other rights expressly stated in the Constitution itself. Senator Henry Wilson of Massachusetts explained that the privileges of citizenship protected were "the rights of personal security, personal liberty, and the right to acquire and enjoy property, including the rights of contract and access to courts essential to secure property."[19] Congressman John Broomal said they were "the right of speech, the right of transit, the right of domicile, the right to sue, the writ of habeas corpus, and the right of petition."[20] William Lawrence of Ohio opined that the protected privileges were "the rights to life and personal security, and the right to acquire and enjoy property...to make and enforce contracts...and to share the benefit of laws for the security of person and property.[21] Andrew Rogers of New Jersey said the Clause protected "all the rights we have under the laws of the country—the right to vote, to marry, to contract, to be a judge or a juror."[22] Senator Jacob Howard of Michigan said Article IV and the new Amendment were the same, except that the latter also protected "the personal rights guaranteed and secured by the first eight Amendments of the Constitution."[23]

Some dispute remained after ratification of the Fourteenth Amendment as to the nature and extent of the privileges protected. When first asked to address the meaning of the privileges of U.S. citizenship, a narrow majority of the Supreme Court denied they

[18] Hamburger, op. cit., at p. 123.

[19] Bogen, op. cit., at 996.

[20] Id.

[21] Douglas G. Smith, "A Lockean Analysis of Section One of the Fourteenth Amendment," 25 Harv. J.L. & Pub. Pol'y 1095 (2002), at p. 1111.

[22] Bogen, op. cit., at p. 1001.

[23] Id., at p. 1002.

encompassed any of the privileges protected by Article IV, and declared instead that they included "the right of the citizen of this great country, protected by implied guarantees of its Constitution, to come to the seat of government to assert any claim he may have upon that government, to transact any business he may have with it, to seek its protection, to share its offices, to engage in administrating its functions," in addition to "the right of free access to its seaports, through which all operations of foreign commerce are conducted, to the subtreasuries, land offices, and courts of justice in the several States,...to demand the care and protection of the Federal government over his life, liberty, and property when on the high seas or within the jurisdiction of a foreign government, and finally, "the right to peaceably assemble and petition for redress of grievances, the privileges of the writ of habeas corpus...[and] the right to use the navigable waters of the United States, however they may penetrate the territory of the several States."[24] This declaration by the Court hardly diminished the rights of citizenship—if anything it added to them, though the procedural mechanism whereby any given right could be vindicated was hobbled by the Court's failure to equate the two clauses and to understand that they were intended to protect the same rights of citizenship regardless of which government—State or federal—impaired them.

There remains to this day some confusion in the matter of the privileges and immunities of citizenship. Objection might be made that except for the Second Amendment and several elements of the First Amendment, jurists and statesmen largely omitted any reference to the Bill of Rights as the birthright of any citizen. It would indeed be incorrect to deny that these rights belong to citizens alone, but a bare admission that they do distorts the broader view that they were not reserved by the Framers exclusively for the citizens' enjoyment. They are, instead, the right of all persons, not merely of citizens, and they are afforded to alien and citizen alike because they are fundamental checks on the power of the government that the Framers distrusted so profoundly. No government can avoid the corruption that comes with license by the state to invade the people's privacy by saddling them with the obligation to board soldiers in peace time or suffer warrantless searches of their persons and papers, or in the denial to the criminally accused of any of

[24] *The Slaughterhouse Cases* (1873) 83 U.S. 36, 79.

the rights of procedure set forth in the Fifth, Sixth, and Eighth Amendments. A government allowed to deny essential rights of due process to some, can be expected to develop a habit hard to break when contemplating the nature of its relationship with everyone else.

Confusion abounds also in the gradual expansion of rights afforded to non-citizens through application of the Equal Protection Clause. For many years, "the governing doctrine permitted States to exclude aliens from various activities when the restriction pertained to 'the regulation or distribution of the public domain, or of the common property or resources of the people of the State."[25] This changed during the course of the second half of the Twentieth Century, as courts applied a stricter standard of scrutiny to classifications relying on alienage, and held invalid statutes preventing aliens from entering a State's classified civil service, practicing law, working as an engineer and receiving state educational benefits. The limit beyond which no alien may pass, however, remained marked by the need "to preserve the basic conception of a political community."[26] As citizens define who the political community is, it is entirely appropriate for the state to exert its preservative power over "the qualifications of voters, but also to persons holding state elective or important nonelective executive, legislative, and judicial positions, for officers who participate directly in the formulation, execution, or review of broad public policy perform functions that go to the heart of representative government."[27] A political community that permits non-members to vote, execute important government policies such as law enforcement and hold elective and appointive office is a community that has ceased to be a coherent one, composed of and serving the interests of its members, and only integrating non-members after a probationary period during which their fitness, loyalty and ability to contribute had been evaluated and ultimately found to be satisfactory.

What the state might do is not necessarily what the state can do. Though the Supreme Court has spoken of the obligation of the government to preserve the basic conception of a political community, others insist that the Constitution imposes no strictures on the power of the state to explode the privileges of citizenship by awarding them to

---

[25] *Ambach v. Norwick* (1979) 441 U.S. 68, 72-73, 99 S.Ct. 1589, citations omitted.
[26] Id., at 74.
[27] Id.

non-citizens, including non-citizens illegally in the country. Such people, the story goes, are "teachers and students, physicians and nurses, musicians and construction workers. They pay taxes, raise their families, send their kids to schools, and make countless social and cultural contributions every day."[28] And yet they "are barred from entering the polling booth. While they live under the same policies set by legislative bodies, they have little ability to influence and select the representatives making those laws."[29] For some, this exclusion "is a fundamental violation of…self-determination—an affront to one of [the] most basic, inviolable rights. It turns millions of people into political subordinates, undermining the vitality of democratic life and making a mockery of American democracy."[30] So prevalent is this view among those on the progressive side of things that more progressive communities around the country have gone so far as to extend voting rights to non-citizen immigrant residents. New York and Chicago were among the first jurisdictions to permit limited voting by aliens. The phenomenon "is most common in Maryland: ten municipalities allow it in all local elections," and "in 2016, the same day Trump was elected, San Franciscans passed a ballot measure opening the franchise to noncitizen parents."[31] Many of these immigrants already enjoy many of the privileges of citizenship protected by Article IV either due to statutory enactments or rulings of the Supreme Court applying the emergent principles of Equal Protection. Others have obtained them clandestinely, either through collusion with the governing authorities, as when they vote in electoral systems that intentionally lack any measures designed to protect citizen voting rights, or outright favouritism of a kind unprecedented in history: sanctuary cities that refuse cooperation with authorities charged with removing illegal residents from the country, and lawless judicial action in the form of dubious rulings that prohibit enforcement of long-standing laws protecting citizens from suffering the disorderly introduction of immigrants lacking any accountability to the existing social structure and existing societal norms.

There is an anxiety almost palpable on the part of those pushing these

---

28 Ron Hayduk, "Why Non-Citizens Should be Allowed to Vote, https://Jacobin.com, November 6, 2018.

29 Id.

30 Id.

31 Id.

remarkable innovations forward: an intense dislocation of the mind that threatens even further break if the most radical of subventions of legal norms governing citizenship are not advanced and any concept that those norms might be enforced and preserved obliterated. It is a form of political warfare being waged from within society's ranks, by persons who've lost faith in any reasonable notion of citizenship and long to destroy it by rendering its definitive privileges the possession of anyone who can cross the nation's threshold and evade expulsion by legal authorities that entire State governments dedicate themselves to undermining. It appears in the guise of a gesture of benevolence, like Caracalla's *Constitutio Antoniniana*, granting the most precious rights to strangers without exacting a price in return, and ruining any of the incentives to earn the benefits that come with full membership in society from a society that apparently values them so little as to give them away for free. A citizenship lacking distinction between the rightfully privileged and all others is a citizenship utterly degraded, and having been granted so freely, contributes nothing to the building of the solidarity of citizen with citizen that makes for a nation unified on the basis of a status that its members share. The nation, in fact, ceases to be the nation at all, and the rights that adhere to citizenship of old become the plaything of the state rather than the heritage of the people who once were considered the state's *raison d'etre* in the first place.

Good Evening, Welcome to Fake News

IN the midst of the Watergate scandal and the steady revelations of the questionable use of government power by the Nixon Administration, rumors spread of an unholy relationship between the nation's intelligence gathering agencies and American media and academic institutions. The Senate Intelligence Committee commenced an investigation, thwarted at many turns by the CIA and its then director, George H.W. Bush, and his still very influential predecessors William Colby and John McCone. Despite access to only summaries of the more detailed files, the Committee's chief investigator discovered that "the sheer number of covert relationships with journalists was far greater than the CIA had ever hinted; and that the Agency's use of reporters and news executives was an intelligence asset of the first magnitude."[1] During the 1950s, 60s and even early 70s, the CIA had "concentrated its relationship with journalists in the most prominent sectors of the American press corps, including four or five of the largest newspapers in the country, the broadcast networks and the two major newsweekly magazines."[2] As later revealed during public hearings conducted by the Committee and investigative work performed by reporters such as Carl Bernstein, it wasn't just low and mid-ranking members of the news corps who collaborated with the CIA; the top executives of the most prestigious journalistic institutions did as well: William Paley of CBS, Henry Luce of Time, Inc., Arthur Hays Sulzberger of *The New York Times*, Barry Bingham, Sr. of *The Louisville Courier-Journal*, and James Copley of the Copley News Service. ABC, NBC, the Associated Press, United Press International, Reuters, the Hearst and Scripps-Howard syndicates, *Newsweek*, the Mutual Broadcasting System, *The Miami Herald, The Saturday Evening Post* and *The New York Herald-Tribune* all worked hand-in-glove with an agency that had regularly exceeded the scope of its legitimate mission abroad by focusing its surveillance activities upon the doings of Americans here at home, contrary to statutory parameters and in likely violation of the "rights of Americans to engage in political activity free from government surveillance."[3]

Of course, the relationship between the government and the media during the Cold War was nothing unique to that era. From the beginning of the Republic, top officials in the executive and legislative branches, in the States and the nation's capital, bankrolled newspapers in order to give themselves favorable press and advance their particular agendas. Thomas Jefferson subsidized James Callender, Alexander Hamilton founded and published *The New York Post*, and Senator David Broderick patronized seven different journals in order to undermine support for the Vigilance movement in San Francisco in 1856. But a turn to the sinister began during the Progressive Era, when Woodrow Wilson created the Committee of Public Information, employing a host of

[1] Carl Bernstein, "The CIA and the Media," *Rolling Stone*, October 20, 1977.

[2] Id.

[3] Foreign and Military Intelligence, Book 1, Final Report of the Select Committee to Study Governmental Operations with Respect to Intelligence Activities, United States Senate (Washington, D.C.: U.S. Government Printing Office, 1976), at p. 136.

writers, editors, artists, actors and speakers who churned "out patriotic pamphlets, books, films, and speakers for the American public," all for the purpose of convincing a reluctant nation to go "all in" for a war waged on a continent separated from the United States by a vast ocean in order to achieve objectives difficult to comprehend even today with the benefit of hindsight.[4] Franklin Roosevelt followed in Wilson's footsteps by putting regiments of writers to work propagandizing on behalf of his social and economic revolution and creating the first revolving door between service in the media and public service. Later, when the nation entered another war across the oceans, actors, filmmakers and reporters eagerly collaborated to sell the effort to a nation starved for heroes and quite literally starving. In the subsequent decades, while the CIA busied itself compromising the supposed independence of the American media and using it to deceive the nation and the world, President Johnson authorized the creation of a permanent public propaganda network to broadcast "education" to the masses, but spewing statist indoctrination just as often.

It seems implausible that the nation's intelligence agencies, whoever they work for, would have ceased their interest in maintaining their alliance with big media, or that media itself, now controlled by massive global corporations with little allegiance to the United States, would be uninterested in leveraging their wealth and power to influence in order to gain access to information that sophisticated surveillance agencies have at their disposal, and that the two together wouldn't continue to attempt to shape the perception of reality through the presentation of what purports to be news. It only takes a cursory view of the recent past to observe the continuing alliance: intelligence agencies continually leaking to the media their "conclusions" about the relationship of the President and his former campaign with the Russian government and breathless reporting of the details by the very same journalistic institutions that colluded with the CIA during the Cold War. Openly employing former members of the intelligence community as "contributors" and "commentators," these institutions are actively engaged in exposing the supposed work-product of Russian intelligence—fake news—and aggressively debunking the myriad alleged falsehoods planted on the world wide web and elsewhere by

---

[4] Thomas Fleming, *The Illusion of Victory: America in World War I* (New York: Basic Books, 2003), at p. 117.

Russian agents and promoted by their supposed ally, the President, via an unrelenting barrage of "fact checking." The President himself appears in their view at the center of a "fake news" conspiracy, distracting attention from Russia, and attempting with counter charges of "fake news" of his own to discredit and delegitimize the media truth tellers who stand between him and the destruction of democracy's faithful media watchdog. That, at least, is the media's narrative. And it's a narrative that appears to be deployed in support of ongoing efforts to regulate speech so as to prevent a vulnerable and gullible public from being exposed to the corrupting influence of what the media and its allies characterize as falsity.

The prevalence of speech some denounce as false, or which actually is false, is a function of our constitutional system generally, and more specifically the First Amendment. The command that "Congress shall make no law...abridging the freedom of speech, or of the press" being so unqualified, the ability of the government to halt or interfere with the dissemination of information, whether true or not, is self-evidently minimal, if not non-existent. The enduring strength of the limitation owes much to its express nature, as well as its place at the head of the Bill of Rights. The policy rationale informing the Amendment cannot be discounted either, particularly when articulated by some of the High Court's most distinguished members. Reflecting on his experience as a young man in the Civil War, whose ardor for violence to preserve the Union and end slavery waned in accordance with the degree of violent death he witnessed on the field of battle, Justice Holmes observed that "when men have realized that time has upset many fighting faiths, they may come to believe even more than they believe the very foundations of their own conduct that the ultimate good desired is better reached by free trade in ideas—that the best test of truth is the power of the thought to get itself accepted in the competition of the market, and that truth is the only ground upon which their wishes safely can be carried out."[5] Justice Brandeis elaborated on this theme eight years later, noting that the Framers "believed that freedom to think as you will and to speak as you think are means indispensable to the discovery and spread of

---

[5] *Abrams v. United States* (1919) 250 U.S. 616, 630 50 S.Ct. 17, 22, Holmes, J., dissenting.

political truth."[6] How committed either of these justices were to an actual free market of ideas is doubtful given their consistent opposition to the then prevailing view of the Court that due process imposed limits on the regulatory power of the state. More likely, the metaphor they selected was designed to embarrass the Court's majority who desired to regulate speech but not the economy, notwithstanding abuses occurring in either field. Whether cynical or not, their particular framing of the right protected by the Constitution gained currency over time, even as the Court and society as a whole warmed to the idea of restricting economic liberty in order to promote what those in power claimed would be broader prosperity and a sure mechanism to avoid unfairness and injustice.

For decades, progressives remained enthusiastic over the theory, despite its kinship and conceptual similarity with the libertarian approach to economics. Discontented with the remaining and still very compelling vestiges of tradition, progressives saw freedom of expression as the means to advance their broad critique of American society and culture. Without majoritarian impediments, only private barriers to critical expression could exist, and these weakened steadily as public schools and universities succumbed to progressive ideology and began indoctrinating student bodies. In time, Moses, Jesus, Locke and Emerson yielded in influence to Freud, Marx and Darwin, and the ideology of liberty fell under a withering attack inspired by progressive intellectuals from Charles Beard to John Dewey and their intellectual progeny. By the end the Twentieth Century, progressives commanded the heights in culture, education, the media and, increasingly, government. The election of Barack Obama was for them a watershed, the beginning of new era of progressivism when the progressive project a century in the making would finally become complete. It didn't quite turn out that way. The troglodytic Neanderthal of their nightmares became President and the scheduled deadline for completion of the project suffered an extremely aggravating delay. Hardly a lone voice, his uppity criticism of the progressive status quo emboldened many others in a way not seen since at least the 1980s. It was hardly surprising then that calls for control of the marketplace of ideas rose above the din of verbal controversy. Campus speech codes popped up around the

---

[6] *Whitney v. California* (1927) 274 U.S. 357, 375, 47 S.Ct. 641, Brandeis, J., concurring.

country, and everywhere there was condemnation of the prevalence of "fake news"—a term made familiar by the President in his own critique of the relentless opposition of the same media institutions that collaborated with the CIA during the Cold War, but subverted by them and applied to much of the speech that supported the President. The market wasn't safe, and like the actual market, it had to be protected from hucksters, confidence men and snake oil salesmen. Having once adored free speech when it challenged a status quo they despised, progressives condemned it when it threatened the status quo of their own making.

The market, the progressive critique goes, is no longer the thing known to Holmes and Brandies. "The prevailing marketplace for speech in their time centered around speakers on soapboxes and printed works like newspapers, journals, and leaflets like those tossed by the *Abrams* defendants from the upper floor of buildings in an attempt to widely disseminate their ideas."[7] These fora for expression constituting the market place of old "provide a sharp contrast to the online marketplaces for speech characteristic of today, in which Russian troll farms create false online accounts on Twitter and Facebook to widely disseminate false news stories at a staggering level of magnitude to sabotage the democratic process in the United States."[8] The Holmes and Brandeis opinions, and many other seminal ones touching upon the freedoms of speech and the press—handed down "before the advent of the Internet, social media, and big data"—simply "do not transplant perfectly onto today's social media environment."[9] As the economy experienced market failure when it became more advanced, sophisticated and cosmopolitan, so too, the story goes, has the market place for speech and ideas. The traditional media, the critics say, formerly served a high and laudable purpose. Its cadre of professionals, guided by experience and training, a code of journalistic ethics and resources to fact check and edit, historically ensured that the information supplied to the public was reliable. This older media "enabled the public to form reasoned opinions

---

[7] Dawn Carla Nunziato, "The Marketplace of Ideas Online," 94 Notre Dame L. Rev. 1519 (2019), at p. 1526.

[8] Id., at pp. 1526-1527.

[9] Jill I. Goldenziel & Manal Cheema, "The New Fighting Words?: How U.S. Law Hampers the Fight Against Information Warfare," 22 U. Pa. J. Const. L. 81 (2019), at p. 96.

that, in turn, informed government action and oversight."[10] Changes in technology, however, have affected the relative prominence of legitimate versus false news, diminished the gatekeeping barriers that traditionally curtailed the production and dissemination of false information, increased the ability of those producing false news to target those most likely to be receptive to and affected by it, diminished the likelihood of consumers being exposed to accurate news that counteracts news that is false, contracted the ability of consumers to distinguish between true and false stories, and enhanced the speed at which false news travels.[11] Research into the human mind has begun to prove, they say, how devastating and dangerous fake news is. There are "fundamental human tendencies that can lead to the acceptance of false information over accurate information."[12] Researchers into the phenomenon "have uncovered various cognitive biases that have been identified correlating with people's susceptibility to 'fake news.'"[13] They have found that "people prefer information that confirms their preexisting attitudes (selective exposure)," that they "view information consistent with their pre-existing beliefs as more persuasive than dissonant information (confirmation bias), and are inclined to accept information that pleases them (desirability bias)."[14]

The concerns over the persuasive power of fake news is rather labored. The media has always been a tool of larger interests, spinning information to influence the formation of public opinion along preferred lines. Media has long embraced persuasive messaging, sometimes true, at other times exaggerated, all for the purpose of promoting the goods and services of its advertisers. And media, too, particularly big media, has been known to employ techniques designed to alter the thinking of news consumers in order to keep them consuming: sensationalism, sex and adorable little animals. The real concern isn't so much about the

---

[10] Daniela Manzi, "Managing the Misinformation Marketplace: The First Amendment and the First Against Fake News," 87 Fordham L. Rev. 2623 (2019), at p. 2627.

[11] Philip M. Napoli, "What if More Speech is No Longer the Solution? First Amendment Theory Meets Fake News and the Filter Bubble," 70 Fed. Comm. L. J. 55 (2018), at p. 59.

[12] Id., at p. 66.

[13] Lili Levi, "'Fake News,' and Fake 'Fake News'" 16 First Amend. L. Rev. 232 (2017), at p. 241.

[14] Goldenziel & Cheema, op. cit., at p. 105.

falsity of the news as it is over the privileged place of the traditional media itself, the threat alternative sources pose, and the desire to diminish the power of contrary voices that now, with the aid of social media and the internet, are able to make themselves heard. Fearful lest a monopoly is lost, the media and its backers demand reforms not unlike those that progressives advocated when they claimed the economic market had failed to deliver economic equity and justice.

The mildest form of regulation is that which comes from the actors in an industry itself: self-imposed criteria for membership and conduct. Consistent with this soft regulatory approach, legal scholar Daniela Manzi advocates the licensing of journalists similar to licensing for doctors, lawyers, plumbers and hairstylists.[15] Litigator Ryan Walters calls for laws "to encourage social media companies to monitor fake news and other problem content online."[16] Professor Dawn Nunziato goes much further in openly praising Germany's heavy handed and highly punitive regulatory approach that is rather reminiscent of central Europe's post-Weimar regime. Admitting that the current configuration of the First Amendment might pose too great a bar to the implementation of this more preferred remedy, she expresses her approval for the adoption by the leading social media companies of measures "to address problems in the online marketplace of ideas, including by enabling the flagging of false news for verification by independent third-party fact-checkers, commissioning the development of counter-speech in response to false news, providing contextual information about purveyors of news-related posts, and removing fake sites and purveyors of false news from their platforms."[17] Some regulatory dreamers, of course, dream of an entirely new Supreme Court, composed of justice with "personal experience and contact with modern facts and circumstances under which average men have to live and work," possessing no doubt about their premises or their power, who might "sweep away all opposition" and overthrow the long-standing limitations on the government's authority to abridge speech. And just about everyone believes that pushing back against the President, every day at his press conferences and everywhere else, is

---

[15] Manzi, op. cit., at pp. 2649-2651.

[16] Ryan Walters, "How to Tell a Fake: Fighting back Against Fake Newson the Front Lines of Social Media," 23 Tex. Rev. Law & Pol. 111 (2018), at p. 170.

[17] Nunziato, op. cit., at p. 1522.

vitally necessary lest his delegitimizing of the traditional media and advancement of an anti-progressive agenda that must be inherently false and immoral gain further traction in the public mind.

These solutions, of course, are all problematic. All apparently avoid any direct involvement by the government, hence a confrontation with the First Amendment. Yet the indirect relationship of licensed practitioners and the state and any positive response to legally based incentives to act in a particular fashion do not completely immunize private censors either from the possibility that the regulatory activity they engage in is repugnant to the Constitution, or that it becomes indistinguishable from fascism. The anti-trust implications certainly raise an eyebrow when the private regulatory activity is to be performed by existing monopolistic entities. The proposed solutions beg questions, too, about whether the danger to be averted really is so dangerous as the proponents say, whether the President and his supporters are really so in need of relentless debunking, and whether the market place of ideas—the market place where the messaging of the new media and the old compete—really requires any intervention at all.

Most agree that a definition of the term "fake news" is both elusive and essential before any remedies can be devised. Some insist that a degree of scienter is required.[18] Others, like Ryan Walters, say this unnecessarily constrains the definition and impairs the fashioning of a remedy. He proposes that "fake news" should be defined as "(1) a piece holding itself out as a news piece (2) that is objectively false."[19] How objective a truth can be, however, is not necessarily easy to discern. Most insist on what they believe is true, while falsity is everything they disown. From one's own perspective everything seems so clear, so obvious and so just. Any offense one suffers couldn't possibly be the result of one's own error; it must be the fault of someone else. In life, we suffer routine disputes of fact. Two people observe the same event, and yet each describes it differently. The phenomenon is no more pronounced than when it enters a court of law, and rival witnesses, each under threat of the penalty of perjury, offer contradictory versions of the truth. With respect to political truth, the possibility of finding it is even rarer than the success of juries in reaching a perfect solution to the dilemma presented for its consideration. Notwithstanding the view of

---

[18] Levi, op. cit., at p. 245.
[19] Walters, op. cit., at p. 141.

Holmes and Brandeis that political truth is the goal of the First Amendment, there really is no such thing. Politics is purely preferential, and while it might be true, for instance, that lower taxes and less regulation lead to greater prosperity in the aggregate, it might also be true that unfairness to some if not many in that approach is unavoidable. How a media corporation, or even a government regulator might sort out the truth and falsity of news stories, especially those supporting or criticizing particular policy preferences, defies understanding. In the law, when truth is to be found, an elaborate system of rules governs what evidence might be admissible, and to what extent and for what purpose. The parties, the court and jurors are ever on the lookout for prejudice to any and all of the participants, and hearings will occur before any disputed point of fact, document or testimony is allowed into evidence for consideration by the trier of fact. It can't be believed that any fact-checker or regulator of "fake news" will be bound by so elaborate a system to detect and prevent bias from entering into the calculus, or that the fact checkers themselves will be so bereft of bias that they would be able to make an entirely righteous determination. The certified fact-checking organizations actually retained by social media to the great applause of progressive supporters—the Associated Press, FactCheck.org., Lead Stories, PolitiFact and (before it folded) the Trump hating neo-conservative *Weekly Standard*—only confirm that the doubt is well placed.

These organizations have been fairly consistent in hostility to the President and his unorthodoxly conservative agenda. The Associated Press has been particularly aggressive in debunking the alleged untruths and outright lies of the President and his Administration. A single entry in its fact-check series is typical enough: the President "offered a highly selective account of the testimony of a damning witness and misrepresented the facts of a phone call with Ukraine at the heart of the constitutional showdown"; he "falsely credited his daughter with creating 14 million jobs when it's not clear she's created any"; he falsely claimed "that he was deprived of a chance to be heard in the House Judiciary Committee hearings"; he "routinely tries to take credit for his predecessor's VA achievement" and is "wrong in saying the U.S. economy is the best ever"; and while the President contended he had committed no crime and thus didn't warrant impeachment, "the constitutional grounds for impeachment do not require a statutory crime to have been committed."[20]

Most if not all of supposed lies or untruths enumerated by the AP are hardly objectively determinable, but that isn't so important as the outright untruths so much of the media peddles about a President it despises. While it condemns the President for calling it "fake news" and attempting to cast doubt on its coverage as a whole, the media's track record of error about him is breathtaking in its scope. Former CBS News anchor and correspondent Sharyl Attkisson reports how the *New York Times, Washington Post, USA Today, New York Post* and an array of other big media outlets have consistently provided reports about a host of supposed facts all later exposed as untrue. These press outlets, she says, falsely reported Trump's wife's illegal entry into the country, Trump's failure to pay taxes for 18 years, that Trump's path to victory in November 2016 was "non-existent," that Nancy Sinatra was unhappy with one of her father's songs being used at the inauguration, that the President removed a bust of Martin Luther King, Jr. from the oval office, that the Justice Department had no input on Trump's immigration executive order, that Trump threatened the President of Mexico with invasion to get rid of "bad hombres," that Trump's campaign staff met with senior Russian intelligence officials, that his nominee to head the CIA waterboarded a captured terrorist 83 times in a single month and mocked the prisoner's suffering, that James Comey was fired after he asked for additional resources to investigate Russian interference in the election, that particular thoughts and feelings were Trump's own when in fact they were invented by reporters, that the President only pretended to listen to the translation of a speech by the Italian Prime Minister, that Vladimir Putin told Megyn Kelly that he had compromising information about Trump, that Comey would refute Trump's contention that Comey told Trump three times that the President was not under investigation, that Congress was investigating a Russian investment fund with ties to Trump officials, that General Flynn would testify that Trump had directed him to contact the Russians, that Poland's First Lady refused to shake Trump's hand, that 17 American intelligence agencies had concluded that Russia orchestrated election year attacks to help get Trump elected, that Trump lied when he said Trump Tower had been "wiretapped," that Trump

[20] Hope Yen, Christopher Rugaber & Ellen Knickmeyer, Associated Press, as reported at https://sentinelcolorado.com, December 16, 2019.

impatiently dumped a box of fish food into water while feeding fish with the Japanese Prime Minister, that Robert Mueller had subpoenaed Trump's bank records, that Donald Trump, Jr. had conspired with Wikileaks in advance of the publication of the Democrat Party and Clinton campaign emails, that the President was abandoning his vow to build the wall, that the Steele Dossier was initially funded by a conservative publication, that a Trump advisory board official had been a Miss America contestant who had killed a rare black rhinoceros, that Trump had ended a program to admit foreign entrepreneurs, that he had referred to immigrants as "animals," that photos of immigrant children in cages were taken during the Trump rather than the Obama Administration, that a Honduran child shown crying in the presence of immigration agents had been separated from her mother, that Trump had banned the Red Cross from visiting children separated from their illegal immigrant parents, that a mass shooter dropped a MAGA hat on the ground before opening fire, that Trump praised Confederate General Robert E. Lee, that Trump failed to visit troops at Christmas time, that Anti-Trump activist Nathan Phillips fought in Vietnam, that MAGA hat-wearing racists assaulted actor Jussie Smollett, that the Mueller Report would prove collusion between Trump and Russia's President Putin, that only a tiny crowd showed up to Trump's Fourth of July celebration on the Capitol Mall, that Trump had loans with Russian co-signers, that the CIA removed a top spy from Russia because of concern over Trump's handling of classified information, that a Russian bank server had been illicitly communicating with Trump Tower, that Trump said he had been a 9/11 First Responder, that Trump asked the President of Ukraine in a phone call eight times to investigate Hunter Biden, that the so-called "government whistleblower" was under federal protection because of fears over his safety, that more than 100,000 children were being held in migration-related detention, that Trump was spending Thanksgiving golfing in Florida at Mar-a-Lago (instead of serving dinner to U.S. troops in Afghanistan), that he was a cheap tipper, that he had spoken about "exterminating Latinos," that Mark Graham regretted voting for Trump (when in fact he never voted for him in the first place), that Trump cut the budget for the Centers for Disease Control on the eve of the Coronavirus epidemic, that the President called the Coronavirus a "hoax," that hundreds of millions of voters were supporting Joe Biden, that Trump attempted to bribe a German coronavirus vaccine maker and wanted to hoard the vaccine so that only Americans would have it, that the United States was short at least 800,000 ventilators and that millions would be needed, that coronavirus stimulus checks would be delayed because Trump wanted to sign them, that Trump owes the Bank of China tens of millions of dollars in loans coming due in 2022, and that Trump called hydoxychloroquine a "miracle cure."[21]

It may be that these reports and many others were mere mistakes, but the odds that they are couldn't be that favorable due to the fact that the journalists who reported them work for the most distinguished media in the country and are themselves likely at the top in their field, employed by corporations that themselves are affiliates or subsidiaries of even larger entities that have far too much at stake to permit such consistent brand defeating lapses in accuracy. Repeated errors arising from incompetence simply couldn't be tolerated if truth was actually valued. Deliberate deception and a commitment at the highest levels of the media that the deception continues as long as the current presidency endures are the more likely explanations.

To his credit, the President hasn't threated to shut down big media for all of these falsehoods. He's only done what they do: exercise his First Amendment right to express his views in the market place of ideas. Big media says his comments are fake news; he says their's are. The media's errors and outright lies are protected by the First Amendment, and so are the President's. "The Constitutional protection," said Justice Brennan, "does not turn upon 'the truth, popularity, or social utility of the ideas and beliefs which are offered.'"[22] Some false and deceitful speech is unprotected, but only if tangible harm proximately results, such as a loss of reputation or other interest, dispossession of property due to reliance on false statements, or some severe degree of emotional distress because of the nature of the words uttered. The champions of regulation, of course, would argue that the harm is great when the President attacks the media, or when Russia launches false news accounts. The reputation of the media declines, and with it its ability to keep a check on the manipulation of the public by society's rulers. The people, too, are misled in ways that distort the political process and results in improper election outcomes (such as the elevation of Trump

---

[21] See "Media Mistakes in the Trump Era: The Definitive List," https://sharylattakisson.com, May 11, 2020.

[22] *New York Times v. Sullivan* (1974) 376 U.S. 254, 271, 84 S.Ct. 710.

over the most qualified candidate in history!). It causes conflict in society, too, manifest in violence and loss of life, or could result in these things if restraint isn't applied.

Whether the critique is accurate or not doesn't really matter, for the First Amendment is what it is, and far from being designed to keep the peace, the Amendment is actually intended to foster dispute and to guarantee that dispute continues perpetually. "I come not to bring peace," said a wise man, "but a sword."[23] The sword the Amendment carries is the sword of discord, disquiet and debate. No one is entitled to peace save the timorous who stay at home, or those who refuse to engage with their fellows in the topics of the day.

To believe that any one person could properly identify what is true and what is false, and what is harmful in some cosmic sense to democracy or the faith we have in it, is to believe a fantasy that many in the past, to their great misfortune, have experienced in reality. The majority of Representatives who controlled the 5th Congress of the United States felt they understood what constituted harmful speech and they outlawed it despite the obvious prohibition of the First Amendment. They believed, said the historian Leonard Levy, "that the true freedom of the press would benefit if truth—their truth—were the measure of freedom."[24] They were thoroughly convinced "that anyone whose opinion differed must be a criminal subversive."[25] Men subsequently went to jail simply because they criticized the policy preferences of the government, or demeaned the President on a personal basis. The Antebellum legislatures of the South expressed a similar belief that they understood the proper nature and scope of harmful speech in the wake of the publication in 1829 of David Walker's *Appeal in Four Articles Together with a Preamble to the Colored Citizens of the World*. Finding the tract to treat "in the most inflammatory terms...the condition of the slaves in the Southern States, exaggerating their sufferings, magnifying their physical strength and underrating the power of the whites, containing an open appeal to their natural love of liberty" and "expressing sentiments totally subversive of all subordination in our slaves," the legislature of Georgia banned it, and authorized police

23 Matt. 10:34.

24 Leonard W. Levy, *Emergence of a Free Press* (New York: Oxford University Press, 1985), at p. 297.

25 Id., at p. 299.

authorities to seize and destroy all copies of the pamphlet and others like it.[26] A few years later, following the most significant servile revolt in the history of American slavery, Virginia enacted a law that "provided severe punishment for any member or agent of an abolition society who should come into the State and maintain 'that the owners of slaves have no property in the same, or advocate or advise the abolition of slavery," and similar punishments for the publication of any book advancing like sentiments.[27] Nearly identical laws appeared on the books in every other slave State. In States both north and south where abolitionists were attacked and killed or their printing presses and literature destroyed, seldom were the offenders brought to justice on account of the consensus that dangerous words, upsetting to popular attitudes and fears, were best left unsaid, and if actually uttered, were properly suppressed by the direct action of a righteously indignant people. We understand slavery to be a great evil today, but not everyone in the age when it flourished saw it so clearly, and some believed it to be an institution beneficial to white and black alike. Others were conflicted and thought that quiet meditation on the problem and its solution was the best approach. Few believed open discussion was always advised due to the violent emotions the issue generated.

No one today would support silence in the face of what we now agree was contrary to humanity, justice and fairness, and certainly an issue like slavery appears so stark in its vileness. Speakers should have been protected; the government should have brought its power behind those who would address the issue and punished those who violated the norms of civilization. Fake news and the competing allegations that speakers are liars or grossly misinformed might not appear to be so valuable as the speech of the abolitionists of old, but who are we to make exceptions based on our current perception of the importance of particular content and viewpoints, the rights of particular speakers, and the medium by which they would express themselves?

Whenever the cry is heard that speech must be controlled, it means those raising the cry don't like what they're hearing. They attempt to justify their appeal to terminate the noise with the argument that the market place of speech is broken, that the First Amendment's purpose

---

[26] Clement Eaton, *The Freedom-of-Thought Struggle in the Old South*, Revised and Enlarged Ed. (New York: Harper & Row, 1964), at pp. 121-125.

[27] Id., at p. 127.

of ensuring the discovery of truth is being thwarted by a confusing melee of dishonest messages, and that the truth itself is being obscured to the detriment of the Republic. Modern technology, the latest exponents of regulation say, is the cause of the distortion today. Not reasonably within the scope of even the wildest imaginations of the Eighteenth-Century, it can only be assumed (they say) that the Framers would surely have modified the absolutist call of the text of the First Amendment had they foreseen the challenges our generation faces. Perhaps the ease of entry to the online marketplace of ideas by purveyors of so-called fake news is a problem, but it is one uniquely our own, distinct from the other manifold vexations that have faced our people since the founding. Widespread illiteracy, marginal education, the limited number of sources of information in existence in bygone eras, the ease by which erroneous data might circulate without any confrontation by contrary input, the broad dispersal of ignorant notions deeply engrained and nearly impossible to unroot in a pre-scientific age, superstition and a host of unexamined prejudices grew like weeds in a garden that choked the life out of the flowers of truth. The news media of the earliest day tended to be the handmaid of political parties and the level of discourse reflected in the typesetting, viewable today of all places in on-line archives, would make even Trump himself blush with embarrassment.

Such challenges, then and now, are in truth a sign not that the market is broken, but that it is functioning as intended. Intervention to ensure that information is accurate can only proceed in accordance with criteria that is rooted in the prejudices of the intervenor, and will end only in the distortion of the market uniquely tailored to those solitary biases, without the salutary influence of equally biased alternatives. "What is truth" a cynical man once asked.[28] Short of God Himself descending from the clouds to straighten the crooked path of our perceptions, the answer can only be that it lies somewhere amidst the competing prejudices of the market place, available for us to find if we can, hopefully hand-in-hand with some measure of skepticism that any inquiry into veracity must accompany if even a flicker of the truth is to be discovered.

---

[28] John 18:38.

Friends Like These

ON August 5, 1948, a wan, debonair, and intellectually pedigreed witness entered the chamber where the House Unamerican Activities Committee was holding extended hearings, in order to swear an oath to tell the truth about his alleged activity as a Soviet Agent during the 1930s and early 1940s. Days before, the journalist Whittaker Chambers had testified to his own involvement as a Soviet agent and of his close relations with numerous New Deal officials, including the man taking the oath, Alger Hiss. "Urbane, smiling, and patronizing," recalled William F. Buckley, "Hiss took the stand and read as categorical a statement as the Committee had ever heard."[1] After giving an account of his career at Harvard, clerkship with Oliver Wendell Holmes, service in several New Deal agencies, and his organizing of the Yalta Conference, Hiss denied he had ever been a member of the Communist Party, that any of his friends had ever been associated with the Party, and that he had even heard of Chambers until the year previous when several FBI agents mentioned his name.[2] Though Hiss appeared confident and many of those present were almost embarrassed that so distinguished a man had been forced to attest his innocence, others were unconvinced. In subsequent testimony, Chambers described very precise and intimate details about Hiss and the entire Hiss family that could not possibly have been within his knowledge unless he actually was on close terms with the man. When Hiss was again confronted with Chambers' testimony, he repeated his earlier denials. Finding both men credible, Congressman Felix Hebert declared that "whichever one of you is lying is the greatest actor that America has ever produced."[3]

To prove that the thespian skills of his accuser were far superior to his own, Hiss initiated a libel suit shortly after Chambers repeated his accusation on *Meet the Press* without the shield of privilege that protected his sworn testimony before the Committee.[4] The suit collapsed when

---

[1] William F. Buckley, *The Committee and its Critics: A Calm Review of the House Committee on Un-American Activities* (New York: G.P. Putnam's Sons, 1961), at p. 149.

[2] Id.

[3] Whittaker Chambers, *Witness* (New York: Random House, 1952), at p. 590.

[4] Ralph de Toledano & Victor Lasky, *Seeds of Treason: The True Story of the Hiss-Chambers Tragedy* (New York: Funk & Wagnalls Company, 1950), at p. 211.

Chambers produced microfilm of documents he had obtained from Hiss when he was Hiss's contact person for transmission of classified government information to the Soviet Union. The documents were subsequently proven to have been typed on the same typewriter Hiss's wife used to draft personal correspondence. Hiss was subsequently indicted, tried and convicted of perjury for his false testimony before the House Committee. After his death, discoveries in the archives of the former Soviet Union proved his formal enlistment as an agent of that government and his receipt of the Order of Red Star for his valuable services to Mother Russia.[5]

The case against Hiss was among the most famous of its kind during the Cold War, and undoubtedly must be characterized as a political prosecution, aiming to score a political point, not merely against the Soviet Union, but also against its apologists in the United States. Seventy-five years later, another man—General Michael Flynn—was accused of being a Russian agent working contrary to the interests of his own country, and of lying to investigators about communications between himself and Russia's ambassador to the United States. The matter had always been questionable and appeared more an effort to gain leverage over potential witnesses in a case to be made against the President that he colluded with the Russians to "sabotage democracy," set him up for impeachment and removal, and perhaps even prosecution for treason or some other serious crime. Ignoring traditional protocols when the FBI seeks to question a member of the government, two anti-Trump agents at Director James Comey's behest called Flynn directly and asked if they could speak with him. Without telling him why, or that he was the target of an investigation, they subsequently inquired if he had ever sought to convince the Russian Ambassador not to escalate tensions with the United States over sanctions imposed by the Obama Administration, or if he had asked Russia to veto a U.N. Security Council resolution that condemned Israel's settlements in the West Bank. Based on his answers, the General was eventually charged with the crime of misleading the investigators. After threats were made to pursue a case against his son in connection with overseas lobbying activity, he agreed to enter a guilty plea and attested that there was a factual basis for the charge that he misled the FBI. It was a political prosecution for sure,

---

[5] G. Edward White, *Alger Hiss's Looking-Glass Wars: The Covert Life of a Soviet Spy* (New York: Oxford University Press, 2004), at p. 226.

designed to advance a larger cause to undermine President Trump and his Administration, but unlike the matter involving Alger Hiss, Flynn wasn't a spy, wasn't loyal to Russia and hadn't committed perjury to cover his misdeeds. He had merely withheld information from persons he wasn't aware were conducting an investigation – information that he felt was best kept confidential lest his ability to maintain candid relations with a major nation's ambassador were compromised.

It wasn't long after the entry of the guilty plea that the prosecution's case began to unravel. Flynn's phone conversations had been monitored, as were the conversations of others associated with the Trump campaign. The warrants to authorize the eaves-dropping were based in part on allegations contained in the so-called Steele Dossier of possible ties between Trump campaign officials and the Russian government – a document even then known by investigators to be a fraud, loaded with false and highly suspect information, and derived, ultimately, from sources in the employ of the President's opponent, Hillary Clinton. When the Inspector General issued his highly critical report on the conduct of the FBI in the context of the Russian Collusion investigation, Flynn retained the fearless Sidney Powell as new counsel. Powell quickly moved to withdraw the guilty plea and made demand for documents she contended should have been disclosed much earlier during the litigation. The Department of Justice went in search of the documents, some of which the prosecuting attorneys previously asserted couldn't be located. When an assistant to the Attorney General found them, they revealed the agents who interviewed Flynn thought he was being honest and displayed none of the normal physical tics indicative of an intent to deceive. They revealed, too, the FBI's motive in pursuing Flynn, which was to get him to lie. With the legitimacy of the investigation into collusion between the Trump campaign and the Russian government already in doubt, the doubts of the investigators themselves about Flynn's guilt removed much of the case's remaining viability. Citing lack of a "legitimate investigative purpose" for the FBI to have interviewed Flynn in the first place, the Department of Justice moved the Court to dismiss the case.

If the entire Russian collusion election narrative truly was contrived by operatives of the Democrat Party as a means to undermine President Trump, touted by a Media long-affiliated with the nation's intelligence gathering agencies and then executed from within the government by holdovers from the Obama Administration, the survival of the Flynn prosecution was vital lest a crucial element of the narrative's plausibility was lost. With the collapse of the case, much of the remaining impetus behind the effort to advance the continuing plan to secure the President's impeachment would go the way of the dodo. One possible strategy to revive it didn't even require that the case be salvaged; it needed only a modicum of active resistance by those supposedly outraged by the alleged politicized actions of a Department of Justice that was less concerned with the rule of law than with saving friends and allies of the President. If the resistance to the effort to drop the case was stout enough, it might create an impression that a sinister spirit animated the Administration and enabled it to so poison the well of justice that even those with a considerable immunity to its effects withered when exposed to the taint. With justice compromised, only the Congress could save the Republic, and if first it did not succeed back in February of 2020, try again it might through the mechanism of impeachment to alert a locked-down nation to the continuing threat posed by the President.

Former President Obama's comment that General Flynn must have committed perjury when he swore that his original plea was truthful well supports this new narrative.[6] So, too, do the 2,000 supposed former Justice Department employees who so quickly attached their names to an open letter to presiding Judge Emmett Sullivan, urging him "to closely examine the Department's stated rationale for dismissing the charges."[7] These alumni of the DOJ suggested that the Judge had the power to hold hearings with live witness testimony and move forward to sentence Flynn despite the prosecutor's reticence. Admitting the rarity of a court denying a prosecutor's request to dismiss an indictment, the alumni explained that "repeated actions to use the Department to further President Trump's personal and political interest have undermined any claim to the deference that courts usually apply to the Department's decision about whether or not to prosecute a case," hence the court's close scrutiny was necessary.[8] Congress, too, ought to act, they added, by demanding the Attorney General appear before the House Judiciary Committee to answer for his abuses of power, and also

---

[6] Glenn Thrush and Michael Crowley, "Obama Warns that Dropped Charges Against Flynn Put 'Rule of Law' at Risk," *The New York Times*, May 9, 2020.

[7] DOJ Alumni Statement on Flynn Case, https://medium.com, May 11, 2020.

[8] Id.

to censure him for "his repeated assaults on the rule of law in doing the President's personal bidding rather than acting in the public interest."[9] Yet another salvo advancing the new narrative came from retired Judge John Gleeson, who opined in *The Washington Post* that the Judge had the power to impose a sentence over the prosecutor's objection, especially as here, when the effort to dismiss "reeks of improper political influence."[10]

Meanwhile, a group headed by Richard Ben-Veniste going by the name "Watergate prosecutors" presented a ready-made notice of intent to file an amicus brief, arguing that "courts have exercised their authority under Rule 48(a) of the Federal Rules of Criminal Procedure when "it appears that the assigned reason for the dismissal has no basis in fact."[11] Citing the DOJ Alumni Statement that was really nothing but a conclusory political attack on Attorney General Barr and an article from the *Times* reporting criticism of Barr's decision to drop the case, the brief stated that there are "substantial questions as to whether factual representations in the Motion are accurate and whether the Motion is made in good faith and consistent with the public interest."[12] The case, they argued, was also not one in a posture to dismiss. A guilty plea had already been entered and accepted by the court, hence Flynn had essentially already been convicted, and was merely awaiting imposition of a sentence. The attempt to end the case, thus, was really an attack on the court in that it aimed to divest the court of its sentencing authority in violation of Article III and the separation of powers. As the parties themselves are unsuited to address the potential impropriety of dismissal, a friend of the court ought to be allowed to intervene. Being veterans of the Department of Justice, with significant experience in investigating and combatting executive branch deviousness, they lauded themselves for being "uniquely suited to help ensure a fair presentation of the issues raised by the Government's motion, which

[9] Id.

[10] John Gleeson, David O'Neail and Marshall Miller, "The Flynn Case Isn't Over Until the Judge Says it's Over," www.thewashingtonpost.com, May 11, 2020.

[11] Notice of Intent of Watergate Prosecutors to File Motion for Leave to File Brief as Amicus Curiae or Application Under Local Rule 57.6, *United States v. Michael T. Flynn*, Crim. No. 17-232 (EGS), United States District Court for the District of Columbia.

[12] Id.

include, without limitation, the accuracy of the facts and law presented in the motion, the significance of the Defendant's prior admissions of guilt and this Court's orders to date, the Trump Administration's opposition to the prosecution of the Defendant, and whether the Government's change of position reflects improper political influence undermining determinations made by the Special Counsel's Office."[13]

The brief was undoubtedly calculated to provide a friendly judge, already on record as unsympathetic to the Defendant, with a basis to consider legal arguments from persons with no right otherwise to intervene and whose political objectives the continuing prosecution served. Without much of a pause, the Judge announced that he would indeed invite argument by Amicus Curiae, or "friends of the court," on the issue of the propriety of dismissing the case, and that none other than Judge Gleeson would act as a kind of special prosecutor to address Flynn's possible perjury and whether the General should face an action for contempt.[14]

The appointment of Amicus Curiae in the Flynn matter might not appear so remarkable to superficial watchers of legal matters as they have evolved in recent times. During the Early Modern period in England, before legal knowledge was widely available in printed form, "the amicus was a neutral lawyer physically present in the courtroom who would engage in an impromptu 'oral sheparding,' [or] the bringing up of cases not known to the judge.'"[15] Since then, Amicus Curiae have become common players in the most prominent cases in the country and appear with a great deal of frequency at oral argument in front of the Supreme Court. At the Supreme Court's invitation, and with the frequent blessing of the parties, amicus "make or reiterate a legal argument, ...flag implications of a law for an industry, ...weigh in and show consensus on a policy debate, or...ask the Court to steer clear of an issue altogether."[16] More often than not they supplement the record with facts not previously presented. Political scientists often praise the "educating" role of amicus as a cost-effective method of providing information to judges and "a critical 'tool to surpass the limitations

---

[13] Id.

[14] Amita Kelly, "Court Appoints Retired Judge to Oppose Justice Department in Michael Flynn Case," www.npr.com, May 13, 2020.

[15] Allison Orr Larsen, "The Trouble with Amicus Facts," 100 Va. L. Rev. 1757 (2014), at p. 1765.

[16] Id., at p. 1758.

placed on the court by an adversary system.'"[17] Members of the High Court likewise praise the role played by amicus "in educating judges on potentially relevant technical matters, helping to make us not experts but educated lay persons and thereby helping to improve the quality of our decisions,'" and providing "'important assistance to the court... [by] collecting background or factual references that merit judicial notice.'"[18] Amicus are admitted on occasion when a party to a case subject to review fails to submit a brief or appear on the record, to brief the court on the issue of its own jurisdiction, and to defend appellate court decisions that an interested party no longer has an interest in sustaining. Less frequently, they are appointed to stake out positions the court itself believes are vital to the outcome of the case, but usually they enter the case as allies of one side or another, seeking to interject entirely new facts and arguments and shape the attitude and outlook of the justices.

The prominence of amicus at the apex of the nation's legal culture belies the rarity of their presence elsewhere. Though the relevant rules permit appointment of amicus for any number of reasons by district and appellate courts, there remain strong impediments to overly free access by amicus to legal matters that involve two or a mere handful of parties, and most courts aside from the Supreme Court strictly limit their involvement. "Our system," Justice Ginsburg once said, "rests on a principle of party presentation."[19] Party presentation entails the engagement in a process to resolve actual disputes between adversaries with very different interests, each possessing a vested stake in the outcome. The issues and the evidence to be presented to the neutral deciders of fact and law are the responsibility of the parties to develop, and this responsibility places a high degree of accountability on litigants, who are trusted to find the strongest foundation for their respective legal positions, and are empowered to do so.

In this system defined by party presentation, the courts themselves "are essentially passive instruments of government," that "do not, or should not, sally forth each day looking for wrongs to right."[20] A considerable amount of efficiency is to be gained by this approach, and

[17] Id., at p. 1760.

[18] Id., at p. 1761.

[19] See Brian P. Goldman, "Should the Supreme Court Stop Inviting Amici Curiae to Defend Abandoned Lower Court Decisions," 63 Stan. L. Rev. 907 (2011), at p. 909.

[20] *United States v. Samuels* (CA8 1987) 808 F.2d 1298, 1301.

a tribute is paid to the notion of due process and the principle that a person is entitled both to notice of the legal issues effecting his or her rights and interests, as well as an opportunity to be heard. The neutrality of the court is essential to the smooth operation of this system of adjudication of disputes, and is required by our Constitution. A judge, whether in the state or federal system, typically hears matters brought to court by litigants and is constrained from introducing issues unrelated to the concerns of the parties. Ordinarily, when a party fails to raise an issue, it is considered waived, and if facts are not developed and disclosed prior to trial, they are excluded. Basic principles of standing further support the party presentation principle. No one may obtain a remedy for an alleged wrong unless they themselves suffered injury or are able to satisfy the court that they are an adequate representative of a third party whose injuries are attributable to the alleged misconduct of someone else. Absence of an injury transforms a legal matter into a mere theoretical discussion and renders any opinion of the court purely advisory. Aside from not qualifying as an actual legal case or controversy, such a matter, if acted on by a court, becomes a vehicle for the transformation of courts into "organs of political theories" and the invasion of territory reserved for the legislative and executive branches in violation of the fundamental principal of the separation of powers.[21]

The appointment by a trial court judge of amicus is not unheard of. But for a trial judge to appoint amicus to argue against the resolution of a matter by the parties who've litigated it for years is highly questionable. When the matter at issue is a criminal case, in which the presumption of innocence heavily favours the accused, the appointment steps so far over the line of propriety as to become outrageous. Rather than take the parties' word for it that they no longer are in dispute and that the interests of justice require dismissal, Judge Sullivan has taken upon himself the duty of sustaining the litigation against the parties' wishes and even of creating an entirely new issue in the form of a potential perjury charge.

The action of the court seems improper on its face, but delving a bit further below the surface, it's likely illegal. The Judge is subject not only to the rules of court, the statutes and Constitution, but also to the decisions of the court of appeals presiding over his District, and the

---

[21] Erwin Chemerinsky, *Federal Jurisdiction* (2007, 5th Ed.) § 2.3, at p. 59.

Supreme Court of the United States. Only four years ago, the Court of Appeals for the District of Columbia announced that the "Constitution allocates primacy in criminal charging decisions to the executive branch."[22] The executive's "charging authority embraces decisions about whether to initiate charges, whom to prosecute, which charges to bring, and whether to dismiss charges once brought."[23] The executive's authority is derived, it said, from the Take Care and Pardon authority vested exclusively with the executive branch by Article II. Discretion in making "decisions to initiate charges, or to dismiss charges once brought, 'lie at the core of the executive's duty to see to the faithful execution of the laws.'"[24] As these matters are delegated to the executive branch, separation of powers doctrine precludes virtually any judicial involvement. The judiciary "generally is not 'competent to undertake' that sort of inquiry," in part because "'few subjects are less adopted to judicial review than the exercise by the executive of his discretion in deciding when and whether to institute criminal proceedings, or what precise charge shall be made, or whether to dismiss a proceeding once brought.'"[25] The power granted to a court to review requests to dismiss a criminal case pursuant to Rule 48 (a) of the Federal Rules of Criminal Procedure—providing that dismissal proceed in accordance with "leave of court"—hardly invites any court to adjudge the merits of a charging decision and substitute its preference in place of the prosecutor's discretion. Instead, the "leave of court" allowance is designed simply "to guard against the prospect that dismissal is part of a scheme of 'prosecutorial harassment' of the defendant through repeated efforts to bring—and then dismiss—charges."[26] To construe "leave of court" as a potential bar to relieving a defendant of the prospect of going to jail is utterly inconsistent with the court's actual authority.

To appoint amicus to argue against the prosecutor's decision to dismiss a case only compounds the judge's error. Reiterating the judiciary's commitment to the principle of party presentation, Justice Ginsburg recently reminded the country that "in both civil and criminal cases, in the first instance and on appeal..., we rely on the parties to

[22] *United States v. Fokker Services B.V.* (2016) 818 F.3d 733, 737.
[23] Id.
[24] Id., at 741.
[25] Id.
[26] Id., at 742.

frame the issues for decision and assign to courts the role of neutral arbiter of matters the parties present."[27] Only the voluntary absence of counsel for a pro se defendant justifies the appearance of amicus, not to argue against either party, but "'to protect a pro se litigant's rights.'"[28] Speaking for a unanimous court, Justice Ginsburg chided an appellate panel of the Ninth Circuit Court of Appeals for appointing three amicus curiae to brief it on issues either previously rejected by the trial court or never raised in the first place, and at odds with defense counsel's presentation of the case at trial. The appeal was against a conviction of a defendant for violation of a statute prohibiting the inducing of aliens to come to the United State with knowledge or reckless disregard of the fact that such could be contrary to law. The amici appointed were organizations actively involved in promoting the interests of illegal immigrants, anxious to convince the court that their agenda was either consistent with existing law, or ought to pre-empt it. Ginsburg and the Court found an absence of any "extraordinary circumstances" to justify the panel's takeover of the appeal, hence the panel's decision to broaden the front of the case through appointment of amicus curiae could not stand.

Judge Sullivan's concern about perjury by General Flynn also does not justify either his rejection of the prosecution's motion to dismiss the case, or his decision to allow the intervention of Judge Gleeson and other amici. Perjury is a legitimate threat to be guarded against in a forum where veracity is at a premium. Only outcomes based on truthful testimony and true and accurate documents possess any currency in a system ruled by due process and designed to vindicate claims for recovery for an actual injury from those to whom the injury can be traced. The elaborate system of rules, not to mention many provisions of the Bill of Rights, are intended to minimize if not eliminate the possibility that triers of fact would be influenced by the deceit of parties and witnesses. And yet to say that General Flynn committed perjury stretches the meaning of the term. The General entered a plea of guilty in exchange for the charge of a lesser offense, potentially entailing a lighter sentence. The entire system of criminal justice is based on the flexibility of the parties to compromise and thereby relieve judges, juries and court administrators of the task of trying every single charge ever

---

[27] *United States v. Sineneng-Smith* (2020) 590 U.S. ___.
[28] Id.

brought against a defendant. To the extent that Flynn lied about being guilty of the charge to which he agreed to plea, the prosecutor is equally a liar and deserves no less rebuke than the defendant with whom he supposedly colluded. The entire system of criminal justice likely would collapse through inertia if defendants who entered guilty pleas, whether subsequently withdrawn or not, were charged and prosecuted for perjury because the offense was other than one they actually committed. Here, however, the withdrawal by Flynn of his plea easily avoids any concern that he lied about his guilt over misleading persons conducting a "legitimate" investigation. His position is that he was mistaken as to the investigation's legitimacy. It wasn't until the internal documents the FBI and the U.S. Attorney had long withheld from him became public that it was clear to him that the investigation wasn't legitimate at all. Clearly, if the investigation wasn't legitimate, there was nothing criminal about misleading the alleged investigators by withholding candid responses to their questions.

There is an even more fundamental problem with the Judge's inquiry into possible perjury by General Flynn. It is true that the court has the power to punish contempts, and if it finds that criminal contempt has occurred, it can request the prosecutor to bring an action against the responsible party.[29] Moreover, if the prosecutor declines to seek and obtain an indictment, the judge is empowered to appoint an independent counsel—a kind of friend of the court—to do so in the prosecutor's place.[30] The problem with the Court's inquiry into possible perjury by General Flynn is that the Supreme Court has long held that perjury is not ordinarily a contempt of court and isn't subject to the court's power to initiate an action against the accused. Over a hundred years ago, a writ of habeas corpus was sought by a trial witness after being confined for a perjury-based contempt citation. Writing for the majority, Chief Justice White acknowledged that perjury could be considered a contempt of court, and that it might, "when exceptional conditions so justify, be the subject matter of a punishment for contempt."[31] However, as contempt constituted "an obstruction to the performance of judicial duty," any perjury punished as contempt of court must be clearly shown in every case both to satisfy the elements of

---

[29] Rule 42, Federal Rules of Criminal Procedure.

[30] Id.

[31] *Ex Parte Hudgings* (1919) 249 U.S. 378, 382, 39 S.Ct. 337.

perjury, and be an "obstruction to the court in the performance of its duty."[32] The lower court erred in simply adjudging the witness as guilty of perjury, hence of contempt, without any examination into whether the court's performance of its judicial obligations had been obstructed. The witness merely claimed he couldn't remember ever seeing the handwriting of one of the parties, which the judge found lacking in credibility. Obviously, the credibility of the witness was a consideration for the jury, not the judge, and might be weighed when deliberating over the merits of the case as a whole. There was no obstruction of the judge's duty, as when a witness, party or visitor to the court engages in disruptive behaviour, or threatens the judge or others in the court, or fails to answer a subpoena, or refuses on the stand to answer the interrogator. In the Flynn matter, it is all but impossible to consider how entering a guilty plea pursuant to a plea deal with the prosecutor impaired the judge's exercise of his judicial function. His duty was merely to accept the plea or reject it.

The lack of any plausible legal foundation for Judge Sullivan's decision to appoint amicus curiae to argue against dismissal of the Flynn prosecution and in favor of the bringing of a perjury charge against Flynn, suggests that law is less a motivating factor than politics. There is a strong hint of a partisan taint on the Judge's decision, evident in its alignment with the same forces that invented the case against Flynn in the first place and its empowerment of political opponents of the President to use the courts as a forum for weakening public support for him. This kind of partisanship by courts was a reason why the judiciary was established as a separate and independent branch of government, the Bill of Rights focuses so heavily on procedural protections, and the courts are given jurisdiction only over actual cases and controversies brought to it by interested parties. Occasionally courts have abused their power, overstepped their bounds and unfairly inflicted either benefits or burdens on people who came seeking justice. Occasionally good might result from such overstepping, such as when the Supreme Court introduced sua sponte the issue of whether the Due Process Clause of the Fourteenth Amendment incorporated the exclusionary rule when evidence is obtained by police in violation of the Fourth Amendment, or

---

32 Id., at 383.

when it struck down a statute designed to circumvent Miranda.[33] But, as legal Scholar Brian Goldman notes, more often than not, "history suggests that courts engaging in this form of overreaching might do so to advance their own agendas, which is precisely the threat that the adversary system and case or controversy doctrine seeks to mitigate."[34] History will undoubtedly weigh Judge Sullivan and his unusual decision, and, in this matter at least, will likely find him wanting on the scales.

A Different Kind of Pandemic

THE stories circulated widely and few doubted their veracity. He was a lothario whose marriage did nothing to deter, and might have actually encouraged, his wandering appetites. Only an ambition to become President burned hotter in his soul, but even that particular passion yielded, at least for a time, to the obstacle posed by his lust for sexual conquest. His initial foray into presidential campaigning nearly ran aground on the disclosure by a former paramour of their long-running intimate relationship. Nevertheless, Bill Clinton overcame, continued in the race, won his Party's nomination, and then achieved victory with the aid of a strong third-party insurgency that siphoned votes away from his principal opponent. Still, his reputation for philandery followed him, and once again erupted into public view when several news publications reported on the use by the then Governor of Arkansas of state troopers to discreetly procure a steady flow of sexual partners. Disclosure of the first name of one of the alleged women and various details about her interaction with Clinton were sufficient for the woman to realize the reports referred to her. When the President's aids tarred the woman as trailer trash while denying the story's accuracy, the woman—Paula Jones—did something utterly unprecedented: she sued a sitting President of the United States for an array of harms arising from his words and deeds both before and during his Presidency. Lower

---

[33] *Mapp v. Ohio* (1961) 367 U.S. 643, 81 S.Ct. 1684; and *U.S. National Bank of Oregon v. Independent Insurance Agents of America, Inc.* (1993) 508 U.S. 439, 113 S.Ct. 2173.

[34] Goldman, op. cit., 960.

courts upheld her right to proceed toward trial despite the strenuous objections of the President's counsel and the horrific opprobrium directed her way by most of the media, celebrity culture and wayward husbands everywhere.

When the matter reached the Supreme Court, the President's counsel contended that "the potential additional litigation that an affirmance of the court of appeal's judgment might spawn – may impose an unacceptable burden on the President's time and energy, and thereby impair the effective performance of his office."[1] The Court, however, wasn't persuaded. It found the President's prediction of a wave of additional litigation to have "little support in either history or the relatively narrow compass of the issues raised in this particular case."[2] Indeed, "in the more than 200-year history of the Republic, only three sitting Presidents have been subjected to suits for their private actions. If the past is any indicator, it seems unlikely that a deluge of such litigation will ever engulf the President."[3] There really appeared little risk that requiring the President to respond to civil process would "generate a large volume of politically motivated harassing and frivolous litigation."[4] Most frivolous litigation would be defeated at the pleading stage or on summary judgment, "with little if any personal involvement" by the President. The threat of sanctions, too, would likely keep less than sincere litigators at bay. The odd civil case that might find its way beyond the threshold of the court would hardly tax the President's time or impair his ability to perform in office. "Sitting Presidents have responded to court orders to provide testimony and other information with sufficient frequency that such interactions between the Judicial and Executive Branches can scarcely be thought a novelty."[5] President Monroe responded to written interrogatories, President Nixon produced the infamous tapes, President Ford gave a deposition in a criminal matter, and Clinton himself testified in Whitewater-related criminal proceedings. If a case actually survived various procedural obstacles, there was "no reason to assume that the District Courts will be either unable to accommodate the President's

---

[1] *Clinton v. Jones* (1997) 520 U.S. 681, 701-702, 117 S.Ct. 1636.
[2] Id., at 702.
[3] Id.
[4] Id., at 708.
[5] Id., at 704.

needs or unfaithful to the tradition—especially in matters involving national security—of giving 'the utmost deference to Presidential responsibilities.'"[6] Chiming in with his support for the Court's ruling, law professor Erwin Chemerinsky agreed that there was no "reason to think that there would be more than the occasional suit."[7] The paltry history of civil litigation against Presidents for pre-inaugural acts and omissions was "hardly a history that supports the fear that Presidents will be deluged with lawsuits...."[8]

Justice Breyer agreed with the majority, but wrote separately to express his concern that too little deference had been paid to the President, and that the door had been left too far ajar to discourage others from walking through it. No absolute immunity existed, he agreed, but the nature of the President's office supported the principle that judges hearing a private civil damages action against a sitting President be prohibited from issuing "orders that could significantly distract a President from his official duties."[9] Even earlier case law that acknowledged the right of private litigants to sue the President for injuries occurring prior to the President's inauguration recognized that "'the sheer prominence of the President's office' could make him 'an easily identifiable target for suits for civil damages," and that such suits "'could distract a President from his public duties, to the detriment of not only the President and his office but also the Nation that the Presidency was designed to serve.'"[10] With respect to the Majority's confidence that future civil actions against Presidents would be as sparse as they had been in the past, and the expectation that the threat of sanctions would discourage such litigation in the future, Breyer was "less sanguine."[11]

Many were angry that the Supreme Court allowed the Jones suit to continue, but few had deep principled convictions that the President was even temporarily immune to legal process. Most commentators appear to have agreed that litigation naming the President had been virtually non-existent and likely always would be. The passage of more than

---

[6] Id., at 709.

[7] Erwin Chemerinsky, "Justice Delayed is Justice Denied," 2 Nexus J. Op. 24 (1997), at p. 37.

[8] Id.

[9] *Clinton v. Jones*, supra, Breyer, J., Concurring, at 719.

[10] Id., at 719-720.

[11] Id., 722.

twenty years and a veritable pandemic of litigation against the current President has placed that original consensus into question. President Trump has been sued by persons seeking to be unblocked from his Twitter feed, by New York and other States as well as a number of private organizations to force him to restore DACA, and by Jim Acosta and CNN to recover Acosta's press pass after Acosta's bad behaviour at a press briefing caused his temporary expulsion from the White House Press Corps. He has been sued by transsexuals upset over his ban on transgender service in the armed forces, and law professors, Senators and Washington, D.C. itself over his alleged foreign emoluments. Various sanctuary cities have sued him because of his decision to withhold federal money, numerous illegal aliens claiming asylum have brought actions against him over the allegedly discriminatory nature of his border closure, and the State of Hawaii sued because his temporary ban on travel from countries closely associated with terrorism was supposedly racist. He was sued by the ACLU and the NAACP to enjoin him from investigating nationwide election fraud, and by anti-Trump protestors who blame him for being roughed up outside of Trump Tower. Other anti-Trump protestors have sued for the hurt feelings they suffered when receiving insults from persons leaving one of the President's rallies, and others filed suit over the President's alleged suppression of any competition within the Republican Party during the 2019 primary season. The League of Conservation Voters sued the President for opening up Alaska to oil and gas drilling, while an anonymous man has sued him for withholding coronavirus stimulus check money on account of his "undocumented status." Katie Johnson sued Trump for forcibly raping, imprisoning and assaulting her in concert with Jeffrey Epstein; Alva Johnson sued him for forcibly kissing her at a Florida Rally; an adult film actress sued when Trump supposedly defamed her when he denied he paid her to keep quiet about a sexual liaison; and a woman named E. Jean Carroll, who once photobombed a picture of Trump, sued when the President denied he joined her in an "exciting" rape encounter in a department store dressing room some thirty years in the past. Finally, there are several suits aiming to obtain the President's tax returns and compensation for alleged defamation. This slew of legal actions naming the President personally and seeking relief for a host of alleged wrongs committed by him in his official and unofficial capacities isn't anything any sitting President has ever faced, and obviously isn't at all what a majority of the Supreme Court foresaw two decades ago when it ruled against President Clinton's request for a stay of proceedings in the Jones suit until the end of the President's term in office.

At least two of the aforementioned cases present an issue identified by the Court in the Jones matter, but only as a theoretical possibility outside the scope of its review. The cases are *Zervos v. Trump* and *Trump v. Vance,* wherein a New York State court and a New York grand jury have called for the President to submit to discovery. The former case involves Summer Zervos, a one-time contestant on Trump's television show, The Apprentice, who alleges that Trump forced himself on her without her consent at a hotel in Los Angeles, and now is suing him for characterizing her report as false. The *Vance* case arose when Trump brought an action in federal court to quash a state grand jury subpoena issued to his accountants for the purpose of obtaining his tax returns that could then be searched for possible illegality in connection with his business enterprise and the so-called "hush money" pay-off to Stormy Daniels (whose own defamation lawsuit against Trump was summarily dismissed). In denying the President's request for relief in *Vance,* Judge Victor Marrero concluded that so absolute an immunity as asserted by the President, "unqualified and boundless in its reach..., cuts across the grain of... constitutional precedents," and "would tread upon principles of federalism and comity that form essential components of our constitutional structure and the federal/state balance of governmental powers and functions."[12] A constitutional domain exists in this country, he declared, "in which not only the President, but, derivatively, relatives and persons and business entities associated with him in potentially unlawful private activities," are subject to the law.[13] In the *Zervos* matter, Judge Jennifer Schecter concluded that "no one is above the law. It is settled that the President of the United States has no immunity and is 'subject to the laws' for purely private acts."[14] She explained that "nothing in the Supremacy Clause of the United States Constitution even suggests that the President cannot be called to account before a state court for wrongful conduct that bears no relationship to any federal executive responsibility," that "there is no risk that a state will

---

[12] *Trump v. Vance* (2019) 395 F.Supp. 3d 283, 290.

[13] Id.

[14] *Zervos v. Trump* (2018) 59 Misc.3d 790, 795.

improperly encroach on powers given to the federal government by interfering with the manner in which the President performs federal functions," and that no legitimate fear exists "of local prejudice in state court when the actions under review bear no relationship to federal duties."[15]

In *Clinton v. Jones,* the historic non-existence of lawsuits against sitting Presidents for their acts and omissions prior to assuming office undoubtedly coloured the view of the Supreme Court's majority with respect to the oppressive power of civil litigation and its potentially deleterious effect on the President's ability to function in office. This attitude is one obviously shared by the *Zervos* and *Vance* courts, which appear to act as if the two cases before them are the only ones to have arisen against a sitting President since Paula Jones made her fateful walk to the office of the clerk to file her suit. They somehow managed to overlook the novel weight of litigation naming the President as defendant that has accumulated since Inauguration Day in 2017, and failed to recognize any subjective motive by the plaintiffs to use the facade of litigation to accomplish illegitimate ends, including the infliction of political harm.

The Courts, of course, could not possibly be so naïve. Summer Zervos's attorney at the time of the *Zervos* ruling was Gloria Allred, an intimate of Trump's 2016 Democrat opponent who cast her ballot for Hillary Clinton as a delegate at the Democrat National Convention. She was present in down town Los Angeles at an election night party intending to celebrate a Clinton victory, which turned instead into a wake. When asked by sobbing partiers what could be done to undo the astonishing results of the election, she was at first at a loss for words, but soon came up with a solution: "to sue the President-elect."[16] When asked if the Zervos lawsuit aimed to trigger an impeachment effort similar to what happened in the Jones matter after Clinton was caught lying under oath about his relationship with Monica Lewinsky, she smiled and said she looked forward to taking his deposition. "If he's not truthful about a material fact, and he knows he's not being truthful about a material fact—then that would constitute perjury, a high crime or misdemeanour

[15] Id., at 796-797.

[16] Jia Tolention, "Gloria Allred's Crusade: The Attorney Takes on Bill Cosby, Rape Law, and Donald Trump," *The New Yorker*, September 25, 2017.

for which he could be impeached."[17] The man leading the charge in *Vance* – District Attorney Cyrus Vance – is as big a partisan as Allred: the son of a Democrat Secretary of the Army and Secretary of State, who won endorsements from a who's who of New York political players when he moved from Seattle to make a run at replacing Robert Morgenthau as District Attorney for the Borough of Manhattan. He might be quiet himself regarding his views about Trump, but his many colleagues in state office – from the Governor to the Attorney General – more than make up for his reticence.

It is a remarkable statistic that within the first two years of the Trump Administration New York initiated 200 lawsuits against the President and his government. The current Attorney General herself all but campaigned on a platform of suing Trump all of the time. To the applause of her supporters on election night in 2018, she "declared war against Trump" in her announcement that she would "be shining a bright light into every dark corner of his real estate dealings,... demanding truthfulness at every turn."[18] As if she had no other legal matters to tend to, she indicated that she would be looking into "any potential illegalities involving Trump's real estate holdings in New York,... the June 2016 Trump Tower meeting with a Russian official,.. government subsidies Trump received,... possible "violation of the Emoluments Clause in the U.S. Constitution through his New York businesses," and state law charges against anyone the President pardons for federal law convictions for crimes that occurred in New York.[19] Bringing Obama's former Attorney General onto her legal team gives her obvious vendetta a profoundly political dimension by allying it with the policies and interests of the President's very progressive and very Democratic predecessor. Her hope of aiding the misbegotten Mueller investigation was no secret before its collapse, as her praise for him was lavish and her confidence high that he was "closing in on the President," whose days, she predicted, "are going to be coming to an end shortly."[20]

---

[17] Id.

[18] Kristine Phillips, "New York's Next Attorney General Targeted Slumlords. Now She's Going After Trump," www.thewashingtonpost.com, December 19, 2018.

[19] Allan Smith, "Incoming New York Attorney General Plans Wide-Ranging Investigations of Trump and Family," www.nbcnews.com. December 12, 2018.

[20] Id.

In *Clinton v. Jones*, when pondering whether "federalism and comity concerns, as well as the interests of protecting federal officials from possible local prejudice that underlies the authority to remove certain cases brought against federal officers from a state to a federal court," the Supreme Court couldn't say a more compelling case for presidential immunity in a civil suit arising from non-official conduct would be present.[21] Certainly, a primary reason why federal courts were created in the first place was to provide a more neutral forum for litigation bearing upon federal concerns. State courts were and continue to be arms of parochial government, staffed with judges and juries who share unique local prejudices. It was originally feared that state courts might become agents in formal efforts to stifle the operation of the federal government, hence the availability of alternative fora for the adjudication of claims against federal agencies and their officials would stand as a powerful dike against the reassertion by the States of the sovereignty lost on account of the Constitution's ratification. This was exactly the danger that arose in the famous case of *McCulloch v. Maryland*, when a State's judiciary used its authority to thwart national power as manifest in the Bank of the United States. In overruling the State court, John Marshall observed that "States have no power, by taxation or otherwise, to retard, impede, burden, or in any manner control the operations of the constitutional laws enacted by Congress to carry into execution the powers vested in the General Government."[22] Otherwise, it would be possible to arrest "all the measures of the government, and of prostrating it at the foot of the States."[23]

The President is not the Congress, but Marshall might have thought that the limitation on the States' power to retard, impede, burden, or in any manner control...the powers vested in the General Government" extended to the nation's chief executive as well. Some years earlier he had addressed the power of the courts generally to compel the President's response to legal process in matters not directly concerning the President. As trial judge in the Burr treason case, he upheld a subpoena of the President issued by Burr's counsel, seeking potentially exculpatory documents.[24] His rationale had less to do with any lack of

---

[21] *Clinton v Jones*, supra, at 691.

[22] *McCulloch v. Maryland* (1819) 17 U.S. 316, 434.

[23] Id., at 432.

[24] *United States v. Burr* (C.C.D. Va. 1807) 25 F. Cas. 30.

immunity or privilege on the President's part than on the fundamental right of an accused to obtain compulsory process to use in furtherance of a defense against criminal charges. Nevertheless, Marshall noted that the President might still lawfully resist a subpoena or other court order if equipped with "sufficient motives for declining to produce a particular paper," and that the President was entitled to challenge the materiality of any documents or other information sought.[25]

Marshall's position seems reasonable, and yet is hardly so far reaching as the outcome in the *Jones* case, and far less ambitious than the decisions in *Zervos* and *Vance*. He touched only upon the issue of subpoenas arising in criminal matters, wherein the accused sought exculpatory evidence available nowhere else than in filing cabinets situated in the Oval Office. With respect to the broader issue of the President being subject to legal process and civil and criminal prosecution in either State or federal court for acts and omissions committed outside the scope of his official duties, Marshall was silent. His contemporaries, however, did manage to express themselves on the topic from time to time. President John Adams and Chief Justice Oliver Ellsworth opined that the President "personally, was not the subject to any process whatever; could have no action whatever brought against him; was above the power of all judges, justice, etc."[26] For Adams, even a murderous President remained immune to criminal liability during his tenure in office. Only when he left office, after his term concluded, or was forcibly removed by action of the Congress, could he be held to account for his alleged misdeeds. Supreme Court Justice James Iredel expressed the view that "no man is better than his fellow citizens, nor can pretend to any superiority over the meanest man in the country," hence the President, "if he commits any crime…is punishable by the laws of his country, and in capital cases may be deprived of his life," but he didn't quite say that the President was subject to prosecution during his incumbency, either in State or federal court.[27] Iredel's colleague on the Supreme Court, James Wilson, also believed that the President was amenable to the laws "in his private character as a citizen, and in his

---

[25] Laura Krugman Ray, "From Prerogative to Accountability: the Amenability of the President to Suit," 80 Ky. L.J. 739 (1992), at pp. 751-752.

[26] Jonathan Turley, "'From Pillar to Post': The Prosecution of American Presidents," 37 A. Crim. L. Rev. 1049 (2000), at pp. 1064-1065.

[27] Id., at p. 1071.

public character by impeachment," but like Iredel was unclear on whether the President remained privileged from arrest or prosecution during his term in office.[28] Ordinarily a strict constructionist, Thomas Jefferson felt that any submission while in office would tend to "leave the nation without an executive branch, whose agency, nevertheless, is understood to be so constantly necessary that it is the sole branch which the Constitution requires to be always in function."[29] Justice Joseph Story later summarized what seemed to be the consensus—that among the incidental powers of the executive is "the power to perform them, without any obstruction or impediment whatsoever."[30] The President could not, he continued, "be liable to arrest, imprisonment, or detention, while he is in the discharge of the duties of his office; and for this purpose his person must be deemed, in civil cases at least, to possess an official inviolability."[31]

It is true that the Constitution offers no textual commitment of privilege by the President from either civil or criminal process. Yet for some scholars the inference is both obvious and rational. If the President "is indicted or compelled to appear at a hearing," noted Professor Joseph Isenbergh, "the entire executive power may be impaired, or at least constrained in some degree."[32] "If it were possible for another part of the government to act against the President in this way—which would make the United States fundamentally different from any other sovereign nation of the late eighteenth century—one would expect it to be clearly stated in the Constitution."[33] The impeachment provision, he said, strongly implies an understanding of the President's immunity to ordinary process during the four-year term of office. The attitudes of Adams, Ellsworth, Jefferson and Story appear to confirm this view of the inviolability of the President to any judicial demand that he answer in court for his acts and omissions, and seems utterly vindicated by the

---

[28] Id.

[29] 10 Works of Thomas Jefferson, at 401 (letter of June 17, 1807, from Thomas Jefferson to George Hay, as cited by Justice Breyer in his concurring opinion in *Clinton v. Jones*, supra, at 717).

[30] 3 J. Story, *Commentaries on the Constitution of the United States* 1563, pp. 418-419.

[31] Id.

[32] Joseph Isenbergh, "Impeachment and Presidential Immunity from Judicial Process," 18 Yale L. & Pol'y Rev. 53 (1999), at p. 56.

[33] Id.

1838 decision of the Supreme Court that the Postmaster General was subject to an order requiring him to perform mundane administrative tasks within the scope of his official duty. In reaching that decision, Justice Smith Thompson made it clear that the Postmaster General, though receiving his authority from the President, enjoyed none of the superior official's privileges or immunities. To the extent that the President's executive powers "are derived from the Constitution, he is beyond the reach of any other department, except in the mode prescribed by the Constitution through the impeaching power."[34]

Watergate marked a clean break with historical precedent. The open and obvious dearth of lawsuits against a sitting President for his unofficial acts appears to confirm the earlier regime of Presidential privileges and immunities. Only the shock of Watergate shook this earlier regime and provided an opening to subject Presidents to the compulsive power of a court order.[35] But even that development tracked well with historic precedent in that it arose in the context of an ongoing criminal prosecution of a third party and was subsequently corralled by the Supreme Court's decision that a President could not be sued for alleged injuries arising from his performance of his official duties, which were to be very broadly construed.[36] The *Jones* decision created a far larger gap between the modern sensibility of holding a President accountable legally and the original consensus. The *Zervos* and *Vance* decisions, albeit subject to ultimate review by the Supreme Court, significantly widen that gap by permitting State courts to exercise authority over a sitting President in the context of legal actions undertaken by private citizens and county prosecutors seeking to prove that the President, prior to taking office, committed some form of wrongdoing.

It has been said that hard cases make bad law. This is certainly true here. Professor Isenburgh notes that "a lawsuit against the President...brings out the ghouls."[37] In fact, it is the ghouls who initiate them. President Clinton likely committed some impropriety with Paula Jones in his hotel room in 1991. It was consistent with the plethora of information about the then-Governor's sexual proclivities at that time

---

[34] *Kendall v. United States* (1838) 37 U.S. 524, 610.
[35] *United States v. Nixon* (1974) 418 U.S. 683, 94 S.Ct. 3090.
[36] *Fitzgerald v. Nixon* (1982) 457 U.S. 731, 102 S.Ct. 2690.
[37] Isenburgh, op. cit., at pp. 100-101.

and his use of state troopers to procure women to satisfy his personal sexual impulses. And yet rather than proceed independent of political machinations, Jones and her backers revealed highly political reasons for bringing and then continuing her lawsuit. "From the very beginning," observed Carol Andrews, "Ms. Jones sought out the advice of lawyers and other advisors who were associated with conservative, Republican, or anti-Clinton causes."[38] Before she even filed suit, her initial attorney "conferred with Cliff Jackson, who had a reputation in Arkansas for his continued and ardent opposition to Bill Clinton, and then announced her suit at the annual meeting of the Conservative Political Action Conference, "which has been described as a gathering of 'the hard core of the right wing of the Republican Party."[39] Similarly, Ms. Zervos sought out as primary counsel a high profile critic of the President and partisan of his principle foe during the 2016 election campaign, while Vance himself is a highly partisan elected official in a State run by a political party that has aggressively deployed the powers of State government in the service of personal and political opposition to a sitting President, and is aiming his "investigation" at achieving one of the unfulfilled objectives of the 2016 campaign, which is to obtain copies of the President's tax returns.

For some, the idea that a State or its officials might use State power to directly inquire into the official and unofficial acts of a sitting President is monstrous. Long before the election of the current incumbent, Professor Akhil Amar strongly condemned the prospect of a State prosecution of a President "as a dangerous and unconstitutional deprivation of independent federal authority."[40] Prosecution and indictment of "a sitting President would allow a local prosecutor to harass a President or even incarcerate him at a critical juncture of governance."[41] Jonathan Turley disputed Amar's view as resting on "the implausible assumption that an entire state court system could allow a baseless criminal charge to go to trial."[42] The State courts, he observed, are multi-levelled and are empowered to enforce numerous due process protections in both civil and criminal proceedings. He saw "no reason to

---

38 Carol Rice Andrews, "Jones v. Clinton: a Study in Politically Motivated Suits, Rule 11, and the First Amendment," 2001 B.Y.U.L. Rev. 1 (2001), at p. 11.

39 Id., at pp. 11-12.

40 See Turley, op. cit., at p. 1093.

41 Id.

42 Id., at p. 1094.

believe that an entire state system would lack the judicial deference and fairness shown in the federal system during the crisis," or that a state law case "would be any immediate threat to the President."[43] Professor Isenburgh, in turn, doubted Turley's confidence in the imperviousness of a State's judicial process to partiality or abuse in the service to purely political objectives. "Compulsory legal process can be mobilized without any degree of consensus," he said.[44] That makes it, when directed at the President, "a ready-made apparatus for political actors and ideologues of all stripes."[45] It really takes no stretch of the imagination to understand the likelihood of a State harnessing its judiciary to purely political and entirely illegal objectives. The history of Jim Crow is evidence of exactly that.

The concerns of Amar and Isenburgh were dismissed by much of the academic community two decades ago when the debate sparked by the many Clinton-related investigations and prosecutions still raged. At that time, the *Nixon* and *Jones* precedents were far too compelling to overcome. The lack of virtually any litigation naming a sitting president confirmed the High Court's view that the flood gates of litigation were in no danger of opening in the event a president were declared to be subject to ordinary process when the matter involved a president's unofficial conduct. As past is often prologue, no one save a few pariahs crying in the wilderness foresaw the current situation, wherein a President so disruptive of political and policy norms, so aggressive and often ingenious in combatting his critics and successful in thwarting so many of their own treasured agenda items, generated such animosity among his opponents that they would bow to no precedent legal or political in their effort to resist and even overthrow the object of their hatred. The astronomical number of suits filed against the current Administration and naming the President personally—many of which have been dismissed for lack of merit—is evidence of this remarkable change in legal and political culture. Litigation has replaced elections and lawfare has supplanted warfare as the vehicle for achieving political objectives.

The *Vance* and *Zervos* actions are themselves laden with political connotations, hence are highly questionable. In the *Nixon* case, a special

---

[43] Id.

[44] Isenburgh, op. cit., at p. 103.

[45] Id.

prosecutor was actually engaged in the formal prosecution of executive branch officials and sought evidence of the crimes known to be in the possession of the President. Conversely, Manhattan's District Attorney hasn't charged anyone with any of the crimes he is supposedly investigating; he merely seeks private information from the President that might support speculation engaged in by the anti-Trump *New York Times* and other opposition media. Though lower federal courts have upheld his use of grand jury subpoenas to obtain the President's personal information, the lack of an actual prosecution strongly suggests a high degree of impropriety and implicates the very concerns that inform the probable cause requirement of the Fourth Amendment. Unable to satisfy the requirements for a warrant, Vance shouldn't be able to use a more procedurally lax method of obtaining confidential documents belonging to someone who isn't even an announced target of an investigation into a specified crime, let alone an actual criminal prosecution. The *Zervos* matter is far more absurd, in that it arises not from the President's gratuitous false statement against an innocent person, but from his denial of her entirely unsolicited and voluntary contention that he misbehaved with her during a meeting she admittedly solicited over a decade ago. This is a far cry from the *Jones* situation, where Ms. Jones found herself quite against her will the subject of media claims that she willingly engaged in a sexual tryst with a man who eventually became President of the United States. As the Zervos accusation arose during a political campaign and was voluntarily uttered by the accuser for the express purpose of allowing voters to consider its substance before voting, it was campaign speech, which renders (or should render) candidate Trump's response utterly protected by the First Amendment.

These thoughts are as potent medicine against the onslaught of litigation directed at the President as were the criticisms of the High Court's *Jones* decision and the concurrent warnings of Justice Breyer. The steady accumulation of actions, not likely to abate, and all but guaranteed to multiply exponentially in the event of the President's re-election, might well give the Supreme Court pause on some future occasion to consider whether its *Jones* decision was shortsighted. As the President becomes more oppressed with litigation, as his focus on official duties wanes in order to address the demands of his own and opposing attorneys, and more State courts are added to the fora where lawsuits and other proceedings aimed at the President in his so-called personal or unofficial capacity, the older view of the President's privileges and immunities may well appear far more reasonable than the unbounded principle that no man, even a President, is above the law. That principle is a true one, and consistent with what John Marshall called "a government of laws, and not of men," but in order to permit the functioning of our government and the ability of the chosen representative of the People to perform his duties as chief executive, moderation in the form of temporary immunity, may well be the wiser option.

Insurrection American Style

ONE'S memory strains to recall events seemingly removed from all familiarity due to so radical a subsequent modification of circumstances. Outwardly, much hasn't changed. Men and women, citizens and residents of the United States, endowed by their Creator with certain inalienable rights, deny the power of the state to silence their voices of protest against what they contend are much more profound restrictions on human liberty. Yet significant differences abound. For one, the older voices, echoing more faintly as the past recedes, sounded in the ears of opinion makers far more shrilly than the voices of today. The speakers from antiquity were denounced as menaces to the public health, motivated by concerns for personal financial gain, the uncomfortable presence of brown skinned immigrants within the nation's borders, their right to bear as many arms as their arms could hold, and full of disdain for the liberty of women to exercise choice over their sexual lives and sexuality. They bore signs all but screaming "Liberate Minnesota, Michigan and Virginia," "Fear is the Real Virus" and the "Cure is Deadlier than Covid."[1] Any claims that they were acting in accordance with higher values flowing from the Constitution were dismissed as "so much bullshit" and "hogwash."[2] Far from being legitimate protestors against restrictions on their rights, they were "the same people who have

[1] Emma Grey Ellis, "The Anti-Quarantine Protests Aren't About Covid-19," www.wired.com, April 27, 2020.
[2] Id.

been showing up for street brawls with antifascists...in places like Charlottesville, Berkeley, Portland, and Seattle," hopelessly "prone to paranoid conspiracy theories, all peculiarly immune to logic, facts, or reason, all of them eager consumers of far-right propaganda."[3] When a group of these agitators "stormed" the Michigan state house—after going through metal detectors, having their temperatures taken by security personnel and donning masks in compliance with social distancing regulations—word spread that a second Beer Hall Putsch was in the works. The invasion of the capitol building, one State Senator said, "wasn't about the stay-at-home order, it was an opportunity for a small group of folks...to show off their swastika posters, confederate flags, nooses hanging from cars and signs calling for murder."[4] The Mayor of Lansing expressed sorrow over the presence of so many people in one place, wondered about the impact it might have on the transmission of the great plague sweeping the nation, but acknowledged, somewhat regretfully, that the people still had sanction to "exercise their First Amendment right to freedom of speech."[5] When one protestor pushed another outside the building, a riot was declared by critics of the dubious assembly, and some legislators expressed fear for their safety. One even donned a bullet proof vest out of concern that a right-wing anti-government type, in the spirt of the moment, might aim for the heart and pull the trigger.[6]

The characterization that these protests were in essence the equivalent of a "poor man's Trump rally," replacing the twenty-thousand person crowds the President famously drew prior to the pandemic of shut-down orders, only became more pronounced when the President began tweeting his support. The menace the President posed to the nation suddenly replaced fears over the puny cries of a few disaffected rabble rousers here and there across the country. A commentator on MSNBC said the Trump tweets signaled the nation's entry into "an extremely dangerous phase, primarily because Trump

---

[3] David Neiwert, "Anti-lockdown Protesters Are Just the Authoritarian Foot Soldiers Trump Orders," www.dailykos.com, April 21, 2020.

[4] Lois Beckett, "Armed Protesters Demonstrate Against Covid-19 Lockdown at Michigan Capital," www.theguardian.com, April 30, 2020.

[5] Id.

[6] David Neiwert, "Anti-lockdown Protesters Are Just the Authoritarian Foot Soldiers Trump Orders," www.dailykos.com, April 21, 2020.

appears to be deliberately encouraging this behavior."[7] The Governor of Washington denounced the President for "fomenting domestic rebellion and spreading lies even while his own administration says the virus is real and is deadly, and that we have a long way to go before restrictions can be lifted."[8] Condemning the President's hardly discreet support for opponents of the lock down as "dangerous," he further explained that "it could inspire people to ignore things that could save lives."[9] Unable to hold his Nuremburg style hate-fests where he might bask in the adulation of his moronic and racist following, the President was said to be subverting his own stated policies, contributing to the spread of a deadly disease and transforming these few disaffected voices into the vanguard of his reelection campaign. Trump was determined to get re-elected, said his critics, even if he had to kill us all to do so.

This narrative was doing fine until more and more States lifted restrictions on human action, the so-called curve of infection couldn't get any flatter and a new scandal implicated the Democrat Governor of New York for sending vulnerable elderly persons to nursing homes, where they contracted the virus in large numbers and died. Even as dire warnings of an upward spike in the infection rate and strange new ailments affecting children circulated, a video of a police officer in the Democrat run city of Minneapolis, in the Democrat run State of Minnesota, apparently placing his knee on the neck of a black man went viral. The incident arose from a report by a merchant of an attempt by a man named George Floyd to pay for merchandise with what was suspected to be a counterfeit $20 bill. The merchant called the police and they responded with numbers quite out of proportion to the alleged offense. When Floyd died in the wake of the officer's use of force, all hell broke loose. Once said to guarantee spread of the coronavirus, public gatherings suddenly became the greatest expression of civil liberty in a generation. Far from being condemned as reckless grinders of agendas who held public health and safety in contempt, the new batch of protestors were lauded as the natural successors of Martin Luther King, Jr. and those who followed the great man in Birmingham, Montgomery and Selma. The juxtaposition of the George Floyd protestors and that earlier era's civil rights marchers was especially odd given the lack of

---

[7] Id.

[8] Id.

[9] Id.

any opinion favoring the police, any criticism of Floyd, or any insistence by anyone that racial discrimination ought to be promoted, let alone enshrined in the law. No cadre of citizens was meeting the protestors with bricks, guns or sneers; no one in the halls of power was advocating defense of a segregationist regime. Indeed, even the Mayor and Governor moved rather quickly to condemn the wrongdoers and commenced legal action. Everyone but the police officers seem to have acted correctly, and yet still a riot couldn't be stayed.

Far greater a contrast between the non-violent protesters of yesterday, inspired by the Christian martyrs of the early church, and the street protestors of today was the close relationship of violence with the latter. Cars were torched, a police station was razed by fire and its officers chased through the streets, and looting of private businesses on a grand scale commenced. The spirit of destruction quickly spread from town to town, from State to State, until nearly every larger community in the country was the site of similar protests, many of which rapidly devolved into large-scale pillaging. Warehouses, jewelry and big box stores and shoe shops were all fair game. While the pillagers were mostly black—even in downtown Santa Monica—many white men and women appeared in the massive crowds, taunting the few police officers on scene and largely watching with tremendous satisfaction as merchants innocent of any wrongdoing suffered a loss of business already damaged by the recent and still ongoing shelter-in-place orders, all the while ignoring the fact that in many of the riot zones it was black Americans, once the smoke cleared and crowds dispersed, who would be left to experience the consequences of all the destruction.

The arm chair pundits tended to conclude that the riots had nothing to do with the pent up frustrations generated by the largest violation of civil rights since the incarceration of Japanese Americans during the Second World War, nothing at all to do with the policies of Democrat politicians who have ruled America's largest cities for decades, and no relation whatsoever to radicals seizing upon an apparent crime against George Floyd the authorities were fully capable of remedying via existing laws in order to take to the streets and create a massive police response that could then be declared to be proof of the fascist nature of modern America. Democrat politicians who had contributed much to the problems of modern urban America—just as they had created the discriminatory Black Codes, poll taxes, segregation and the Ku Klux

Klan of old—went silent as the carnage grew. Rather than display force to quell the destructive riots, Democrat mayors and governors verbally affirmed the racist nature of America, expressed their understanding for all the rage and even made promises to disband local police forces so that nothing like the death of George Floyd could ever happen again. The police who were on the ground were outnumbered as well as hesitant to use appropriate force lest they, too, be brought up on charges. After months of public health-related lock-downs, the lack of enthusiasm for public safety was astounding and suggested a tremendous amount of official sympathy for the rioters and their efforts both to take what wasn't theirs and to prove that racism and fascism were alive and well in the country.

America's cities had become veritable no-go zones for the police and modern-day versions of the bad lands where outlaws were free to rob, steal and kill without fear of consequences from a law that was spread far too thin to take notice of any particular crime. Riot had become a new pastime, an essential activity of the high minded, and an acceptable response to a social order that was for some reason so utterly inconsistent with the vision of those who acted as if they battled against the grain of public opinion when denouncing the killing of a black man by police. Plenty of Americans, however, disagreed with the resort to violence, including the President. On June 1, 2020, after watching the riots spread virtually unchecked, the President announced to the nation that he had sworn an oath to uphold the laws of the country and was prepared to make good on that promise. Recognizing amidst the rioters many authentic demonstrators committed to peaceful protest and demands for change, the President asserted that "we cannot allow the righteous cries and peaceful protestors to be drowned out by an angry mob."[10] Blaming "professional anarchists, violent mobs, arsonists, looters, criminals, rioters, Antifa and others" for the massive destruction, and highlighting the inadequacy of the response of state and local governments, he called the riots what they were: "acts of domestic terror," and "an offense to humanity and a crime against God."[11] He urged the nation's governors to call out the National Guard to restore order, and warned that if they didn't, he would intervene. "If a city or a state refuses to take the actions that are necessary to defend the life and

[10] Statement by the President, June 1, 2020, www.whitehouse.gov.
[11] Id.

property of their residents, then I will deploy the United State military and quickly solve the problem for them."[12] Among those most afflicted, he said, were "peace-loving citizens in our poorest communities."[13] As their President, and as the President of the entire nation, he vowed he would protect them.

One of the most remarkable elements of this entire incident is the breaking of the spell of passivity on the part of Democrat mayors and governors that the President's announcement effected. While some moved to bolster police presence and mobilized their State's National Guard, others raised their voices in vigorous protest against the President. Ignoring the flames incinerating churches and big box stores, and the deaths and injuries among police officers and members of the public, Senator Ron Wyden of Oregon interrupted his own silence to denounce "the fascist speech Donald Trump just delivered," and called it "a declaration of war against American citizens."[14] Senator Kamala Harris, who had joined protestors at Lafayette Park, said that "these are not the words of a President. They are the words of a dictator."[15] Even as his own church lay in ruins across the street from the Whitehouse, the Episcopal Bishop of Washington, D.C., charged with tending the flock of a Saviour who admonished all men to obey Caesar, trashed the President's words as "antithetical to the teachings of Jesus and everything our churches stand for."[16] The Governor of Illinois, whose lock down orders restricting First, Second, Fourth, Fifth and Fourteenth Amendment rights were among the most strict in the country, denied the President had the authority to send federal troops into his State, or any other.[17] The President's former Defense Secretary, General James Mattis, stated that he never dreamed that when he took an oath as a young soldier to defend the Constitution he would have been "ordered under any circumstance to violate the constitutional rights of…fellow

---

[12] Id.

[13] Id.

[14] "Trump says he's 'President of Law and Order,' Declares Aggressive Action on Violent Protests," cbsnews.com, June 2, 2020.

[15] Id.

[16] Id.

[17] Kathleen Ronanyne, "Democrat Governors Reject Trump's Call to Send in Military," www.startribune.com, June 2, 2020.

citizens."[18] The President's old adversaries, Chuck and Nancy, offered their two cents—noting that "at a time when our country cries out for unification, this President is ripping it apart."[19] Calling the President's "continued fanning of the flames of discord, bigotry and violence" a dangerous mixture of cowardice and infirmity, they urged "law enforcement and all entrusted with responsibility to respect the dignity and rights of all Americans."[20] Like General Mattis, America's soldiers had taken an oath to defend the Constitution. It was their duty apparently to resist the Commander-in-Chief in his pending invasion of America.

So as America burns, those who have always hated the President wish to prevent him from putting out the flames. They contend that the Constitution demands in situations like this the absence of energy in the national executive. The States are quite capable of handling the crisis, and if their preference is to allow the ravaging of the cities, so be it. It is the balance the Framers struck in order to prevent the type of tyranny that even they would have recognized in the atrocious rhetoric and exploits of President Trump. Some might sincerely believe this; others might advance the argument with cynical motives, including the desire to prove a narrative of racism, white violence and problems so profound that only the most radical and violent solutions will overcome them. Either way, the argument is incorrect. The President's call for order, his demand that the governors bring the street violence to an end, and his plan to deploy U.S. troops if the violence continues fall within the scope of Presidential power, and must be considered an affirmative obligation in the face of such unprecedented rioting lest the laws of the United States, the safety and rights of the citizens, and the stability of State governments are lost.

The critique of the President's promise to mobilize federal forces rests on a rather cramped reading of Article IV. This largely neglected passage of the Constitution provides in part that the government of the United States shall protect the States against invasion, "and on Application of the Legislature, or of the Executive (when the Legislature

---

[18] Jeffrey Goldberg, "James Mattis Denounces President Trump, Describes him as a Threat to the Constitution," www.theatlantic.com, June 3, 2020.

[19] "Pelosi, Schumer Joint Statement on Trump Press Conference & Photo Op," www.speaker.gov, June 1, 2020.

[20] Id.

cannot be convened) against domestic violence." The President might act unilaterally in the event of a foreign invasion; he may only intervene to suppress "domestic violence" when solicitations for aid emanate from the afflicted locale. There was some support for this interpretation at the Philadelphia Convention and at various State ratifying conventions, but much of it must be inferred from more general concerns expressed by the Framers about the dangers of a standing federal army and the promotion of State militias as the primary defenders of the nation. Some modern critics of unilateral military intervention in the States also see a very narrow definition of the term "domestic violence" as a limitation on federal license in this area. Mere protests, even riots, are not sufficient to justify such intervention; only the presence of "'violent factions, flying to arms, and tearing a State to pieces,'" or an outright 'insurrection, will do.[21]

The narrow reading of the Clause, no doubt embraced by Blue State governors at the present moment, cannot easily be sustained on deeper analysis. The Clause is part of a larger provision designed to protect the internal integrity of the several States, whose powers were significantly diminished by the creation of a parallel and in some ways supreme national government. It falls within the larger Guarantee Clause, which mandates that the federal government ensure that each State be preserved as individual entities governed by republican institutions. The Clause also seems to have no bearing on the federal government's power or obligation to protect its own interests, the citizens of the United States, and federal law and liberties. Under the original Constitution, the Congress had a separate power "to provide for the calling forth of the Militia, to execute the laws of the Union, suppress insurrections and repel invasions."[22] The Congress's power was further augmented by a separate authorization to raise armies and naval forces, presumably to protect the interests of the nation from internal and external threat.[23] When the people of the United States ratified the Fourteenth Amendment, they vested with the Congress further authority to enact laws to protect individual liberties, and this authority Congress acted on

---

[21] William C. Banks, "Providing 'Supplemental Security': The Insurrection Act and the Military Role in Responding to Domestic Crises," 3 J. Nat'l Security L. & Pol'y 39 (2009), at p. 54.

[22] *Constitution of the United States*, Article I, Section 8, Clause 15.

[23] Id., at Clauses 12-14.

in passing not only the Civil Rights Acts of 1866 and 1871, but the Reconstruction Acts that placed the States of the conquered South under the rule of military governors, whose duty was to ensure that the rights of former slaves were protected, and that republican institutions that might in the long run sustain those rights be nurtured in their infancy.

The power of the federal government in accordance with the so-called Calling Forth Clause to deploy its forces along with State militias for the purpose of suppressing insurrections, repelling invasions, and other objectives was confirmed by the Supreme Court over a hundred years ago, when men drafted for service in World War I denied the constitutionality of the government's calling them forth into any capacity save as a member of a State militia.[24] The result, says Professor Stephen Vladeck, was a firm rejection of the claim, and the revelation by the Court of an absence of any "structural constitutional limitations on the domestic use of the military."[25]

This analysis makes tremendous sense, not only textually, but also logically. Article IV was designed to provide the States with a guarantee of their survival in the event of a catastrophe. If the federal government was reluctant to intervene to protect the State, the State could mandate intervention simply by making a formal request for assistance. Under the Constitution, even a reluctant federal government could not resist the obligation to intervene. To hold that the federal government cannot act until a request is made, provides little guarantee that the union as a whole might survive in the event of widespread rioting of a kind that threatens the stability of the union or its constituent parts. No less an opponent of a strong central government than Patrick Henry made this very point at his State's ratification convention when he observed that if the President must await a request for aid from a State suffering from domestic tumult, federal aid might prove too late in coming.[26] This insight supports a construction of the Clause that holds that the federal government remains free to intervene when the States themselves are reluctant or unable to ask for aid or are actively engaged in promoting violence at the forefront of an insurrection against federal authority.

---

[24] See *Selective Draft Law Cases* (1918) 245 U.S. 366, 38 S.Ct. 159; and *Cox v. Wood* (1918) 247 U.S. 3, 38 S.Ct. 421.

[25] Stephen Vladeck, "The Calling Forth Clause and the Domestic Commander-in-Chief," 29 Cardozo L. Rev. 1091 (2008), at p. 1103.

[26] Banks, op. cit., at p. 54.

Some today insist that President Lincoln had no right to send troops to Maryland without a request by that State's government, or even to invade the Southern States, but such viewpoints hardly square with the larger purpose of the Constitution, which is to ensure the formation and continuation of a union among the States. The federal government had every right to protect its interests, the interests of its Citizens within Maryland, and to preserve the constitutional order from unilateral disruption. As was the case in 1861, it remains true today.

Some others might question the analysis as irrelevant in light of the Posse Commitatus Act and its prohibition on use of U.S. troops in the States to enforce the laws of the United States. Aside from being a relic of a time when racist Democrats in the South gained ascendancy in Congress and sought to prevent a return of Reconstruction, the law is riddled with exceptions, including that Congress is permitted to separately authorize intervention. At the time the Act took effect, there already were various statutes on the books that allowed for domestic use of the military. These statutes included the so-called Militia Acts of 1792 and 1795, the Insurrection Act of 1807, and the Militia Act of 1862. Together, these laws continue to provide the federal government with "a vast reservoir of military force to use in responding to domestic crises."[27] They were "enacted largely pursuant to Congress's authority under the First Militia Clause" and "delegated broad swaths of emergency power to the President, especially the power to impose martial law and suspend the writ of habeas corpus during serious internal crises."[28] The earliest of the laws provided that "whenever the laws of the United States shall be opposed, or the execution thereof obstructed, in any State, by combinations too powerful to be suppressed by the ordinary course of judicial proceedings, or by the powers vested in the marshals by this Act, the same being notified to the President of the United States, by an Associate Justice or the District Judge, it shall be lawful for the President of the United States to call forth the militia of such State to suppress such combinations, and to cause the laws to be duly executed." The 1795 statute was a mere reauthorization of the earlier law, and a vesting of far greater discretion to act on the part of the President. The 1807 Act remains somewhat mysterious due to a lack of

[27] Vladeck, op. cit., at p. 1106; and Vladeck, "Emergency Power and the Militia Acts," 114 Yale L.J. 149 (2004), at p. 152.

[28] Id., at p. 153.

any legislative history; but it nevertheless represents a further removal of checks on the President's power to protect the States and the interests of the nation. Instead of being dependent on State militias, the President now was free to mobilize federal troops to suppress insurrection and enforce the execution of the nation's law.[29] Hardly a deviation from the power under the Constitution to call forth the Militia, the 1807 law took effect pursuant to additional war powers set forth in Article I.[30]

When reviewing the statutes and the scope of authority provided to the President in executing them, the Supreme Court found them to be well within the power of Congress to enact. Speaking specifically of the 1795 Act, Justice Joseph Story stated that "we are of the opinion, that the authority to decide whether the exigency has arisen, belongs exclusively to the President, and that his decision is conclusive upon all other persons."[31] This construction of the law, he said, "necessarily results from the nature of the power itself, and from the manifest object contemplated by the act of Congress."[32] If it was to be exercised, the power could only be "upon sudden emergencies, upon great occasions of state, and under circumstances which may be vital to the existence of the Union. A prompt and unhesitating obedience to orders is indispensable to the complete attainment of the object. The service is a military service, and the command of a military nature; and in such cases, every delay, and every obstacle to an efficient and immediate compliance, necessarily tend to jeopardize the public interests."[33] As the law authorizes military action, the power to discern the necessity of mobilizing troops can only reside with a military commander—in this case, the Commander-in-Chief, or President of the United States. He alone, said Story, was "necessarily constituted the judge of the existence of the exigency in the first instance, and is bound to act according to his belief of the facts."[34] No one—not another civil officer, not a State governor, not even the Court—possessed the right or the jurisdiction "to review his decision, and in effect defeat it."[35] When the Court again

[29] Vladeck, "The Field Theory: Martial Law, the Suspension Power, and the Insurrection Act," 80 Temp. L. Rev. 391 (2007), at p. 419.

[30] Vladeck, "Emergency Power and the Militia Acts," supra, at p. 165.

[31] *Martin v. Mott* (1827) 25 U.S. 19, 30.

[32] Id.

[33] Id.

[34] Id.

[35] Id.

interpreted the power of the President to initiate domestic military action in light of the various Militia Acts, it reaffirmed the President's power to commit federal forces "to suppress insurrection against the government of a State or of the United States," and held that presidential action in this regard wasn't merely a function of the President's discretion; it was obligatory.[36] When ordered by the President to proceed in defense of the States and their peoples, any soldier serving under his command, whether it be General Mattis or the greenest private, possesses no choice but to comply. This, and only this, is what the law, the Constitution and the Oath to defend it demand.

It is probable that the promise to use federal troops was more a prod to compel the States to pick up the slack by mobilizing greater manpower in response to the riots. Though the President probably meant what he said, it's likely he hoped direct federal response wouldn't be necessary. The governments of the States possess the primary obligation to the peoples living there, while the federal duty to protect the people is only supplemental. If the States can be cajoled into protecting the lives and property of their peoples, so much the better. More likely than not, the threat will prove sufficient in most States and federal forces will never touch ground.

The smoke of the fires lit by the rioters, the scars of the wounds inflicted by them on the innocent, in time will dissipate, and any military personnel keeping the peace will withdraw, but what will remain are the emotions of the moment and the challenges that remain for our communities to overcome defects in police procedures. Likely the latter will never be fully eradicated. Procedures at bottom are really no better than the personnel who apply and follow them. As all men and women are less than perfect, are subject to any number of biases or flaws in their ability to assess a given situation, or are too weak not to be provoked by annoyances and threats both great and small, men like George Floyd will continue to be subjected to excessive force and perhaps even die as a result. Racism might play a factor, but the nature of police work must not be overlooked as a cause. An officer of the law isn't unlike General Mattis, sworn to defend the Constitution, including the Fourteenth Amendment. Only a minority of officers likely approach their jobs as a license to abuse people on the basis of race. Seeing a white officer kneel

---

[36] *The Prize Cases* (1863) 67 U.S. 635, 668.

on the neck of a black man, however, is a compelling image, easy to interpret in light of the optics alone as racially motivated. The officers involved will have their day in court, where they will answer the charges against them, and will have a right to defend themselves and even explain what it was they were trying to accomplish. Meanwhile, Mr. Floyd's family will sue for wrongful death and the federal government may bring civil rights charges. We have an array of remedies for criminality, committed by private citizens and officers of the law, and we shouldn't lose faith in them simply because men remain sinners in need of salvation. Our law, said Paul the Apostle, is a sign of our continuing commitment to sin, and so long as the law endures, so too will our shortcomings when measured against it.

A New American Inquisition

THAT modern innovation of the free market known as social media guaranteed that a video captured on a pedestrian's smart phone depicting a white police officer pressing his knee on the neck of a handcuffed black man lying on the pavement of a public street would go viral. When the handcuffed man subsequently died, the outrage generated by the optics of the situation exploded nearly beyond comprehension. Protestors rightfully took to the streets to express their anger, demand reform in police practices in cities around the nation where abuse of black citizens has been pronounced, and call for an expansion of national consciousness on the issue of racial justice. The lack of any necessity in using the force evident in the video by the officer was so obvious, and the expression on the officer's face so hideously defiant toward a crowd that pleaded with him to relent in the pressure on the poor man's neck, may well have contributed to the far-reaching scope of the initial protests and the enduring demands for change. The unsettling nature of the video has shaken millions of white Americans from indifference or complacency, and led many to respond positively to the message appearing on signs at protests and spreading virally in memes across the world-wide-web that "white silence is violence."

The prominence of white people in the protest movement is notable as a "major difference in these protests, compared to others in the past

30 years," noted criminologist Candace McCoy.[1] Organizations and movements like Black Lives Matter have received a major boost in membership and funding, and have been joined by similar organizations focusing on "helping white people detect and combat insidious forms of racism."[2] Phoenix school teacher, Meredith Parets, joined such a group and explained that while she had always defined white supremacy as inextricably associated with neo-Nazis and the KKK, the death of George Floyd made her realize "how much of the world is constructed so that white people feel safe all the time."[3] A white journalist with *The Daily Kos* declared that he was adding his voice to the cries of black men and women that "centuries of systematic oppression must stop now."[4] Racism, he announced, was violence, and the quiescence of white people is violence as well.[5] Any failure to acknowledge the problem faced by African Americans, any reluctance to condemn it, constitutes a statement "that we are fine with this, that the status quo being upheld is in our favour and that we like that it has hidden and non-hidden benefits to us. We enable the continued oppression of our sisters and brothers by saying nothing, by doing nothing."[6] White people, he insisted, "have a moral imperative to not be silent any longer, to help our sisters and brothers feel that they are not alone, with the life being slowly crushed out of them by a society that will never see them as equals. We have a moral imperative to show those who by default we have kept down—by using our words and actions to demonstrate over and over that they are equals, that we are all family, that their lives and experiences matter personally to us, that we will stand with them to erase the wrongs of history and create a new justice for all."[7] Anything short of full commitment to the cause of ending the system of racial oppression and violence renders whites "the oppressor in full force. White silence is violence. There is no middle ground here."[8]

---

1 Catherine Triomphe, "Silence is 'Complicity,' Say Many White Protestors," news.yahoo.com, June 7, 2020.

2 Id.

3 Id.

4 Bill Kerman, "White Silence is Violence," www.dailykos.com, May 30, 2020.

5 Id.

6 Id.

7 Id.

8 Id.

The ability of the Black Lives Matter movement to gain traction in white society and motivate whites to take to the streets to in essence protest themselves is a remarkable social and even political phenomenon. The movement itself began in the wake of the death of Trayvon Martin and the acquittal of his killer after an exhaustive vetting of the evidence during a long jury trial. It received greater impetus following the death of Eric Garner while being restrained by New York police after he was apprehended for selling cigarettes in a manner that evaded payment and collection of state and municipal taxes. Its greatest boost came with the vile "rough ride" homicide of Freddie Grey in the back of a recklessly operated paddy wagon and the shooting of Michael Brown by police, supposedly while he was placing his hands in the air and begging the officers not to shoot. The riots that resulted from these last two incidents shocked the nation and prompted the Obama Administration to launch an investigation headed by Attorney General Holder. The results of the investigation were condemned by many of the more progressive commentators as limped, superficial and less focused on root causes than on preserving the status quo, or "a mode of governance that relies on criminal law enforcement to deal with a broad set of deep-seated social problems, and to rules and authorities that are historically and functionally oppressive."[9] For these commentators, no amount of training for police officers is capable of preventing further violence in black communities aimed at African Americans and perpetrated by the police. For them, policing is a fundamental fixture of a larger system designed to repress, oppress, exploit and control black populations. It is, says Moritz College of Law Professor Amna Akbar, "a historical and violent force in black communities underpinning a system of racial capitalism and limiting the possibilities of Black life."[10] The law itself, including the Constitution, she notes, is "central to the shape and legitimation of this racialized violence and inequality."[11] As such, the conclusions of the Obama Justice Department, that if police departments "followed the letter of the law, such brutality and inequality would not happen, are patently false, and will never solve the larger, more

---

[9] Amna A. Akbar, "Toward a Radical Imagination of Law," 93 N.Y.U.L. 405 (2018), at pp. 410-411.

[10] Id., at p. 405.

[11] Id.

profound problem lying at the base, at the heart, of the American system.[12]

It's impossible not to recognize that this critique is highly ideological and infused with Marxist principles. As the green movement transposes the environment in place of the proletariat, BLM replaces the latter with the nation's African American population. America, the proponents of the critique say, was founded on racism. From the beginning, racism served the larger goals of the masters of the capitalist economy. Born and bred in white Europe, these men employed veritable armies to kidnap African men, women and children from their villages and homelands and transport them across the Atlantic to work in the most dehumanizing of environments, under the most savage of conditions. Literally chained to the yoke of slavery, these men and women cleared the land, planted the crops, tilled the soil, laid the tracks of the railways, built the factories and laboured at the wheel of whatever industrial mechanisms churned out the products destined to be enjoyed by the white masses in a land expressly intended to benefit them alone. Over time, say the critics, white society saw the need for police authorities to maintain the subordination of the black population, keep it compliant, and, if not employed in remunerative activity, confined to ghettos where the only harm that would come to society would come to black society, not white. "The rise of mass incarceration, over-criminalization, and zero tolerance or broken windows policing," they say, are "seen as an evolution of the regime of control, exclusion, and exploitation that began with slavery, convict leasing, the Black Codes, and segregation."[13] In modern America, "the primary role of the state is to 'set up those military, defense, police and legal structures' required for the stability of private property, free trade, and markets.'"[14] Deregulation of the market place and reductions in social spending over the past several decades have contributed to an increase in reliance on "policing, surveillance, court cases and incarceration" as "fundamental tools" in the "state's management of 'surplus populations.'"[15] Instead of "addressing directly the underlying social, economic, and political problems, we police, cage,

[12] Id., at pp. 437-438.
[13] Id., at p. 449.
[14] Id., at p. 451.
[15] Id.

and throw away people who struggle through them."[16] Police don't serve the common interests of society, they serve only white society, hence the disproportionate focus on detention, arrest, prosecution and imprisonment of African Americans. Not surprisingly, when the laws that purportedly protect all Americans from violence by government authorities are broken and the victims are black, the law too often is disregarded by juries entrusted with the task of determining whether the facts of a given situation sustain an allegation. For white and black Americans, the law, the Constitution, and the Bill of Rights mean two entirely different things.

The loss of faith in the law, including the Constitution, marks a dramatic break with past movements for social and political justice. From the Revolution onward, such movements focused on the law as it was and the need to enhance the existing protections emanating from it in order to expand the benefits of the social order to a broader proportion of the population. In the demands for an end to slavery and the expansion of voting rights to free blacks before the Civil War by persons such as Salmon P. Chase, and the efforts of Congress afterward to engineer a legal infrastructure to sustain political and social equality, reformers saw the constitutional framework as capable of accommodating the needs of everyone, and retained their faith in the system it governed. The early feminist movement and the crusade for Civil Rights advanced by the NAACP and the Southern Christian Leadership Conference likewise embraced traditional American principles of justice and fairness and saw the Constitution as a necessary scaffolding on which an expansion of these principles was to find support. The modern reformers currently out in the streets demanding an end to "systemic racism" lack any similar faith in this traditional scaffolding. For them, "the law is political, constructed and subjective, dedicated to the status quo and subject to manipulation," the "core function" of which "is to make raced and gendered power distribution and social domination look rational, neutral, and just—to make it seem outside of and before politics, and therefore objectively valid."[17] So tainted is our system of laws that the only solution is a radical transformation. Policing in society must end or be drastically diminished. Political, social and economic institutions that promote and

[16] Id., at p. 452
[17] Id., at p. 444

protect white supremacy must be undermined. Resources in society must be shifted from the "primary governance of Black people—criminalization—into other social programs, including housing, health care, education, and jobs."[18] The ultimate goal of these modern crusaders for racial justice is "fundamental, structural reform that moves beyond constitutional rights, reconceiving the proper relationship between state, market, and society."[19]

There is much to sympathize in the critique of the challenges facing African Americans. The great tragedy of American civilization was the introduction of slavery, defined exclusively on the basis of race. The tragedy expanded as the white majority itself wrestled with the contradiction between the principles of freedom the American system was founded upon and the continuing dehumanizing of the black population. Antebellum abolitionist literature is replete with tales of the atrocities committed against a permanently enslaved race. Those who attempted to protest the continuing exploitation of African American slaves were beaten by angry white mobs and even imprisoned by the government. In the South, the rudimentary municipal police authorities took shape in the form of slave patrols consisting of all free white men of a certain age, empowered to roam the countryside, apprehend wandering black men and women, punish them for any deviation from the Slave Codes that governed white and black relations, and even to corporally chastise white slave owners who allowed their slaves more autonomy than the integrity of the slave system could withstand. Black soldiers who enlisted in the Army to liberate their people suffered far worse indignities when captured than their white counterparts. Many Southern commanders summarily executed any black man caught in arms against the Confederacy. Lynching, arson, beatings and acts of terrifying intimidation raged like fire across the South after the war, and even the intervention of Congress and the Union Army couldn't repress it entirely. The end of Reconstruction saw the erection of a new system of social control in the South in place of slavery, and a pale counterpart took shape in the North, where acts of private discrimination were tolerated and protected by the law. Race riots were not infrequent, leaving black communities much the worse for wear. The Civil Rights movement of the 1960s, committed to Christian and constitutional

---

[18] Id., at p. 460.
[19] Id., at p. 415.

principles and insistent on non-violence, provoked yet another violent reaction in the form of burnings, beatings and assassinations. Instead of shaming the opponents of equality, non-violence seemed to embolden and enrage them.

The tragic element of race and the painful effort to achieve racial equality in America, however, is only part of the story. Many White men and women before the Civil War decried slavery, risked their lives and fortunes both to rescue human beings from bondage and spread word of the merits of abolition throughout the South. Statesmen such as Joshua Giddings and Salmon P. Chase laboured to build a political movement combining abolition with civil rights for all. As a Senator, Chase opposed the expansion of slavery and the Fugitive Slave law; as Governor of Ohio, he engineered the repeal of racially discriminatory laws. He aspired to the Presidency, but settled for the Treasury Department, where his creative currency and funding policies financed the war that destroyed the Confederacy and ended any political support for human bondage. As Chief Justice during Reconstruction, he ruled against those who discriminated against former slaves and sought the broadest construction of the Fourteenth Amendment. Lincoln declared slaves in the South free and Union generals spread freedom to whatever ground the feet of their soldiers trod. The Freedmen's Bureau provided economic assistance to liberated slaves, land and rudimentary tools, while the military oversaw a system of tribunals where black men and women might find justice when it was lacking in the southern white-man's courts. In Congress, a series of laws were enacted, permitting private and public enforcement of civil rights, outlawing conspiracies to deprive persons of their liberties on the basis of race, and empowering the federal government to hound terrorist organizations like the Ku Klux Klan out of existence. Private fortunes were dedicated to the establishment of colleges where black men and later black women could receive a higher education, and throughout the North in particular schools began admitting black children on an equal footing with white. Even in the South, education was provided, though segregation on racial lines long remained the rule. The first litigator employed by the NAACP was a white man. White Presidents from Grant to Taft employed black men in the federal civil service, and black communities freer than any ever known in the country formed as a result of large-scale migration from the South to cities like New York, Chicago and Detroit. As a result of opportunities made possible by the American capitalist economy, poverty among African Americans steadily fell during the Twentieth Century. By 1970, only 30 percent of African Americans lived below the poverty line.[20] The history of race in America tending to get all the attention these days is largely negative, but the truth is that the first hundred years after the ratification of the Thirteenth Amendment was a time of steady advance in the education, economic success and social status of descendants of American slaves.

This steady advance suggests that Capitalism isn't the source of the disadvantages currently burdening African Americans. Indeed, everything that contributes to enduring poverty and social regress in Black America is the result of restrictions on economic life, not its liberation. Critics of Capitalism seem to be ignorant of the fact that Capitalism started as a reaction to the highly regulated economies in Europe during the Early Modern and Modern periods. It arose from a critique of centralized control that impaired investment, enterprise, and the kind of success that incentivizes further expansion of the economy. By deregulating the market, the market was set free, individual actors in the market were able to negotiate the terms of their relations, and actual demand for goods and services was able to drive rewards in the form of prices to be paid for labour and raw materials. Capitalism made possible the elimination of so many of the impediments to efficiency and wider prosperity inherent in the older systems of economic life. When diligence and speed translate into greater rewards for individuals, those qualities become commonplace in the market. Slavery had no place for such qualities and was incapable of fostering them. The historian Kenneth Stamp once observed the tendency of slaves in the South to discover the proper balance between minimal exertion and punishment for slacking.[21] Lack of reward for exceptional work and the knowledge that high productivity, should it "become known to the master, might lead him to require the same amount every day," exerted a constant downward pressure on both the quality and quantity of labour by slaves.[22] "It appears," noted Adam Smith—the founding father of

---

[20] David Hogberg, "Thomas Sowell Talks About Discrimination, Race, and Social Justice," https://thefederalist.com, June 13, 2019.

[21] Kenneth M. Stamp, *The Peculiar Institution: Slavery in the Ante-Bellum South* (New York: Vintage Books, 1956), at pp. 97-101.

[22] Id., at 101.

Capitalist theory—"from the experience of all ages and nations...that work done by freemen comes cheaper in the end than that performed by slaves. It is found to do so even at Boston, New York, and Philadelphia, where the wages of common labour are so very high."[23] The innovations in industrial techniques that exploded during the Nineteenth Century and continued at an extraordinary pace beyond that time were only made possible by the knowledge in the minds of innovators that their ideas might bring them material gain. The observations of laborers working at the loom or other industrial mechanisms were worthless and incapable of translation into more efficient processes when made by bondmen, for any proposal to improve production through better techniques would be very apt to be considered by the master "as the suggestion of laziness, and of a desire to save his own labour at this master's expense. The poor slave, instead of reward would probably meet with much abuse, perhaps some with punishment."[24] The consequence of these impediments to efficiency, said Smith, was that "more labour must generally have been employed to execute the same quantity of work, than in those carried on by freemen."[25] As more labour was employed in the performance of tasks than was actually necessary, too much labour was diverted from activities that might have grown the economy, distributed wealth more widely, and benefitted society more fully.

Necessary to the success of a Capitalist system is a system of law that aims to protect the employer and the employed in enjoying the fruits of their investment and labour. Slavery was so obviously inconsistent with Capitalism that it is a wonder anyone believes it was capitalistic even in the slightest. The restrictions on black economic enterprise that Congress sought to lift via the Fourteenth Amendment and the Civil Rights Act of 1866 returned following the end of Reconstruction, and the restored pre-capitalistic system, called Jim Crow, proved nearly as hostile to a free economy as slavery was before it. The ability of African Americans to flourish in a free economy was the primary reason why Southern racists

---

[23] Adam Smith, *Inquiry Into the Nature and Causes of the Wealth of Nations* (London: T. Nelson and Sons, 1852), at p. 34.

[24] Id., at p. 284.

[25] Id.

long conducted "a relentless war against the free-market system," both before the Civil War, and afterward.[26]

Capitalism isn't rooted in race and race consciousness; it's indifferent to it. Years ago, the economist Thomas Sowell noted that during the time the black community was forming in Harlem in the early years of the Twentieth Century, white landlords were an excessively racist lot. There was initial reluctance by white landowners to rent property to black immigrants from the South or anywhere else. And yet somehow, African Americans found a home in Harlem, despite the pronounced racial animus of the white propertied class. Sowell observed that "if every single realtor in Harlem had stood firm on not letting Blacks in Harlem, then Harlem might not be Black today. But even racists, who prefer one race to another by definition, tend to prefer themselves most of all. So, if a landlord has a building where he is having trouble finding tenants at the prices he wants to charge, but he can find Blacks willing to pay those prices, then he is not going to pass up that money. Most people would not. And once that process starts, it becomes costlier and costlier for the holdouts among landlords and realtors to continue holding out."[27] A similar process is what led to the destruction of the power of restrictive covenants to keep African Americans out of communities established as exclusive enclaves of white settlement. Once white owners seeking to sell their properties saw the money offered by black families in exchange for their land, they completely disregarded the color of the buyer's skin. When racist residents who had relied on the restrictions to maintain the racial purity of their neighbourhoods sought to enforce the covenants in court, the very laws that progressives now claim are so useless in protecting the interests of America's black population were used to render the covenants unenforceable.[28] And who doesn't know the story of Jackie Robinson breaking the so-called color barrier. As soon as Branch Rickey signed the great ball player from the Negro Leagues, his rival owners followed suit. In truth, Capitalism, the Constitution and the laws have been instrumental in breaking down the systemic racism of the past and providing African Americans with opportunities to flourish and excel.

---

[26] Andrew Bernstein, "Black Innovators and Entrepreneurs Under Capitalism: Capitalism is the Bigot's Worst Enemy," https://fee.org, October 1, 2001/

[27] Hogberg, op. cit.

[28] *Shelley v. Kraemer* (1948) 334 U.S. 1, 68 S.Ct. 836.

One of the great shames of America is the continuing poverty of largely black cities throughout the country. While the upward climb of African Americans economically has continued, the pace slowed following the enactment of the social policies embodied in the legislative agenda known as the Great Society and the War on Poverty. The sudden influx of cash and in-kind assistance made poverty more amenable, and those on poverty's edge came to be seduced by the lure of money for nothing. Even before the massive expansion of the ranks of African Americans on the welfare rolls of the late 1960s and early 1970s, the data revealed that "the new generous War on Poverty welfare benefits actually encouraged men not work, adding to the ranks of the unemployed."[29] After finding that the average family welfare check was between $177 and $238 a month, and wages at $220, a federal commission studying the causes of the Watts Riot and urban discontent among African Americans "concluded that 'the financial incentive to find work may be either negative or non-existent."[30] The construction of hideous looking housing projects to house poor black people, whose rent would be subsidized by vouchers provided by the federal government, stifled the natural feelings of intimacy and the tendency of residents to invest moral value into their homes. Inefficient government, which predictably proved unresponsive to the needs of tenants, contributed to the deterioration of the projects, as did the arrival of a male population who preyed on the growing ranks of single mothers receiving federal and state money. Urban deterioration in cities that once hosted industries that subsequently relocated oversees advanced like so much rot, crime rose, and jobs were replaced by heroin, cocaine and crack. Employment of black men fell dramatically just a few years into the Great Society era, and black youth employment even more so. Prior to the Great Society, black labour force participation was slightly lower than labour force participation by whites. From 1965 to 1976, it was 271 percent smaller.[31] To the extent that poverty among the black community is systemic, the system is a government one, supposedly intended to protect the community, but hampering, demeaning and

---

[29] Amity Shlaes, *The Great Society: A New History* (New York: Harper Collins, 2019), at p. 201.

[30] Id.

[31] Charles Murray, *Losing Ground: American Social Policy, 1950-1980* (New York: Basic Books, 1984), at p. 76.

impoverishing it instead. The rage of black men and women in the cities evident in the recent riots, and the glee expressed while taking what can't easily be purchased due to lack of employment are real, but they are more the product of frustration caused by the benevolent effort to uplift African Americans than any racism endemic to Capitalism, the law, or law enforcement.

It is true that Black Americans are subject to a disproportionate amount of arrest, prosecution, conviction and imprisonment in this country. The mere fact that a higher percentage of Blacks encounter law enforcement and the penal system is considered to be proof positive of the existence of systemic racism, and a justification for the radical Black Lives Matter project of fundamentally transforming America's constitutional order. The connection of one with the other, however, is logically flawed and legally insufficient to satisfy the high bar the law places on those who would use legal processes to provide benefits to one race as opposed to another. "Disproportionate impact is not irrelevant," said the Supreme Court, "but it is not the sole touchstone of an invidious racial discrimination...."[32] If it were true that African Americans committed few crimes, yet were arrested anyway—as they were in the Jim Crow South that rejected Capitalism, Civil Rights and the Constitution—systemic racism would be difficult to deny. But African Americans do indeed commit a far larger proportion of crime than do whites, notwithstanding their smaller demographic footprint. Most of this crime committed is against other African Americans. Indeed, African Americans are more likely to be murdered or otherwise victimized by persons of their own race than they are by white men, or the police. Using the example of driving in excess of the posted speed limit, Thomas Sowell noted the existence of studies "of people who are speeding on the highway, and they show that blacks speed more than whites. Therefore, it is not at all surprising if the cops pull over more black motorists than white motorists. So, the whole argument that cops are discriminating against blacks falls apart when you put facts into the equation."[33] A far more data-driven approach appeared in the pages of a study by James Q. Wilson and Richard Herrnstein. In their exhaustive account of the causes of crimes, they concluded that while racial bias accounted for some portion of the disproportionate numbers of blacks

---

[32] *Washington v. Davis* (1976) 426 U.S. 229, 242, 96 S.Ct. 2040.
[33] Hogberg, op. cit.

convicted of crime, the portion was miniscule.[34] Surveys among black crime victims indicate that the overwhelming percentage of perpetrators are black.[35] A greater proportion of blacks than whites are arrested, charged and convicted of crimes because they commit more crimes, and most of those crimes are against their fellow African Americans. Wilson's and Herrnstein's conclusion suggests that calls for reduction in black arrests and prosecutions are not only misguided, but will, if heeded, leave black victims of crime without redress and without the deterrent of law enforcement to reduce the incidence of further victimization. In all their clamour in support of black persons accused of crime, those chanting the Black Lives Matter mantra appear to have completely forgotten black crime victims.

Those who appear most amnesiac about the black victims of the crimes BLM says ought to go unpunished are the elected officials who have presided over municipal police departments that have perpetrated the offenses that have galvanized so many of those presently demanding change. Baltimore, where Freddie Grey was killed, has been run by Democrats since 1967, and six of its last seven mayors have been black. George Floyd's adopted home town of Minneapolis has been run by Democrat mayors since 1974, and almost entirely by Democrats since 1945, when the champion of the Great Society, Hubert Humphrey, took office prior to his service as a Senator and Vice President of the United States. Chicago hasn't had a Republican mayor since the Great Depression. Atlanta's mayors have been exclusively a Democrat lot since Rutherford B. Hayes was President, and every mayor since 1974 has been black. With the exception of Rudy Giuliani, New York has been a Democrat town for most of its modern history. Other than Giuliani, the so-called Republicans who have served as mayor weren't truly Republican at all. Fiorello La Guardia was a New Deal liberal, John Lindsey actually switched parties mid-tenure, and whatever Republican street cred Michael Bloomberg might once have possessed ended when he walked onto a debate stage with other candidates for the Democrat Party's nomination for the Presidency. One could go on. The fact is, big city America is liberal, progressive and Democrat. It is run by liberals

---

[34] James Q. Wilson & Richard J. Herrnstein, *Crime & Human Nature: The Definitive Study of the Causes of Crime* (New York: Simon & Schuster, 1985), at p. 462.

[35] Id., at p. 463.

and progressives who insist they aren't racists, condemn their opponents as hopelessly racist, and still manage to preside over the worst instances of police violence by municipal police. In truth, they haven't cared a whit about the souls of black folks. The police departments they oversee are just one more cog in the municipal government-labour union industrial complex that keeps big cities perpetually blue. Those police who've been let off the hook unjustly no doubt had the full support of unions to whom city politicians are indebted for their electoral success. In some cities, including Minneapolis, Democrat leaders actually ceded the power to discipline police to the unions themselves in exchange for political support.[36] That Democrat politicians are now lining up in support of the BLM movement isn't all that surprising. Blaming their own failures to restrain police departments and deliver racial justice on America's "systemic racism" evades a designation of culpability that is richly deserved.

The laws might be amended, but the scope of change BLM activists demand far exceeds the limits on the law-making power imposed by the Constitution. To achieve the goals of the movement, the Constitution must necessarily be ignored, re-interpreted or drastically amended. As the latter two options take time and may be impossible to achieve, the first option is the one more likely preferred. The insistence on the Constitution's role in maintaining racial inequality bolsters confidence that disregarding it is not merely appropriate, but necessary. This attitude is a dangerous one, for it justifies any and all opposition to the alleged status quo, and any crime as measured by the existing laws. There is great irony in this. We see protestors filling the streets, burning buildings, looting businesses, and assaulting policemen with fists, rocks and skateboards. They insist on their constitutional right to assemble and speak, and yet they violate the Constitution by attempting to monopolize the public forum that is designed to serve the needs of all persons, not merely protestors. They insist on the right of due process and habeas corpus even as they file from the police stations they desire to close back to the front lines of their entirely unpermitted, unlawful assemblies. They insist on strict adherence to constitutional norms as they work to destroy those norms and replace them with a system of law and order limited by nothing save their impassioned notions of justice.

---

36 See Steven Malanga, "Why Can't Big-City Democrats Reform the Police?," www.city-journal.org, June 12, 2020.

The attitude is one that disregards the wisdom of the Framers. While exclusively male and white, they were at least students of history, who were aware of the power of the state to restrict human liberty, and opted to restrict the state instead. The critics of racial inequality make some good and valid points, but they appear to believe that by discarding historical limits on state power they will eliminate the power of the state to oppress some of the people. In fact, what they will achieve is the oppression of all, which is hardly an improvement over the situation they decry.

Assuming constitutional limits on power were not an issue, the aims of those demanding change run aground on other shallows. So revolutionary a movement can only be achieved if the revolutionaries possess the power to enforce their objectives. They demand an end to the traditional institutions of enforcement—the police and the military—and yet without either they could never hope to establish their version of a perfect social order. Revolutions in all nations teach the students of history one especially salient lesson: only force can render any radical change in the social order more or less permanent. As police departments are disbanded and resources are directed elsewhere in society, there will be those who resist the claims of the new order, who will attack those who promote it, and who will refuse to cooperate when it is their resources, their interests and their property that is condemned for the greater good. Those who direct the great change will have no choice but to re-establish the mechanism of compliance—modern reformulations of the much-maligned municipal police forces. As the traditional limits on state power set forth in the Constitution no longer remain viable and have been disregarded in order to establish justice for the marginalized, the state will suffer no check on its power to enforce its goals. Those who oppose the new order, who criticize it, or advocate for change to correct its flaws and abuses, will be subject to summary procedures, and the courts and prisons that served to oppress the unprivileged of old, will experience a renaissance without the protections for the accused represented by the Bill of Rights. That which the reformers hate is exactly what they and the society they oversee will become.

What they demand is nothing short of a revolution in American law and society, a transformation of both, along with the economy, into a system designed to deliver benefits to blacks and traditionally marginalized populations that necessarily must take from the historically privileged, if necessary (and most likely) through a show of force that can only be applied by some new cadre of armed enforcers, whose effectiveness in achieving their mission will be unhampered by any of the legal or constitutional principles that the police of today so imperfectly uphold.

The most insidiously harmful aspect of the Black Lives Matter movement is the insistence of its most extreme adherents that white people declare their solidarity by openly and publicly acknowledging that "Black Lives Matter," to recite the names of those killed by peace officers, to speak out against racism lest their silence be construed as "violence," and to demand the most radical of changes to the fabric of American society. Demands that citizens speak up in support of a particular cause have a long history in our country and elsewhere in the world. In totalitarian nations during the Twentieth Century, those who did not turn out in support of the dictator at public celebrations of his greatness were singled out as potential or actual enemies of the state. Those falling beneath the shade of such a cloud suffered social ostracism, very public humiliation, termination of employment, invasive investigation and even loss of liberty and life. In Fascist Italy and Nazi Germany, dictators mandated that all teachers, all professors, swear an oath of allegiance, not simply to ensure their loyalty, but to destroy the credibility of any one of them who might subsequently express criticism of the regime and "to humiliate or to destroy them."[37] Orwell's vision of a totalitarian future included the daily ritual of the Two Minutes Hate, when all workers were simultaneously shown the image of a putative enemy of the people and required to scream obscenities until the image was removed.[38]

Compelled statements in the form of oaths are not foreign to our higher tradition of law. The Constitution itself prescribes two oaths: one to be sworn by incoming Presidents "to faithfully execute the office" and "to the best of my ability, preserve, protect and defend the Constitution of the United States"; the other by members of Congress and State officials simply "to support the Constitution."[39] The two oaths are mere

---

[37] *First Unitarian Church of Los Angeles v. County of Los Angeles* (1958) 48 Cal.2d 419, 455, 311 P.2 508.

[38] George Orwell, *1984* (New York: Signet Classic, 1983), at pp. 13-17.

[39] *Constitution of the United States*, Article II, Section 1; and Article VI, Clause 3.

affirmations of the sincerity of those to whom affairs of national and state concern were to be entrusted, and serve as reassurance to the electorate of the trustworthiness of those who would exercise power. The two oaths establish no objective criteria of competence or zeal, and hardly constitute standards of duty that might be enforced when breached. They are a far cry from the kinds of oaths the Framers themselves appear to have rejected: those statements of loyalty and faithfulness that officials and private citizens were compelled to swear on pain of punishment, torment, and death, and constituted, in the words of Thomas Jefferson, a "form of tyranny over the mind of man."[40] Well known to the Framers were the oaths of allegiance to Church and State that England's monstrous Henry VIII required all English men and women to swear on pain of penalty of treason, that James I required of all ministers of the Christian faith, and that Oliver Cromwell imposed on voters as testament of their intention to accept the outcome of an election he fully intended to rig in his favour. A wave of loyalty oaths prescribed by new state governments during the Revolution, and another wave in the aftermath of the Civil War, and a third wave during the so-called American Inquisition designed to root out communist influence in federal, state and local government, successively hit America's constitutional shores, seeking to coerce and control the minds of men. During all of these periods of time, liberty survived, said Justice Black, "because there were influential men and powerful organized groups bold enough to champion the undiluted right of individuals to publish and argue for their beliefs however unorthodox or loathsome."[41]

Test oaths, designed to psychologically condition those who utter them, truly are anathema in the American tradition. Justice Thurgood Marshall noted that such "oaths do not have a very pleasant history in this country" due to their use as instruments "of thought control and a means of enforcing complete political conformity."[42] Justices Douglas and Black said they are "abhorrent to our tradition" because of "the supremacy of conscience in our constitutional scheme."[43] Alexander Hamilton said they violated due process because the need for proof of

---

[40] Letter to Benjamin Rush, September 23, 1800, in Adrienne Koch & William Peden, *The Life and Selected Writings of Thomas Jefferson* (New York: The Modern Library, 1944), at p. 558.

[41] *Wieman v. Updegraff* (1952) 344 U.S. 183, 192, 73 S.Ct. 215.

[42] *Cole v. Richardson*, supra, at 698, J. Marshall, dissenting.

[43] See *First Unitarian Church of L.A. v. County of Los Angeles*, supra, at 548.

substantive disloyalty was eliminated and replaced by determinations of guilt simply through reliance on the conscientious objector's refusal to swear.[44] Speaking of the post-Civil War test oaths imposed on those in the Southern States seeking admission to the legal profession, or to the clergy, Justice Field observed that they "subvert the presumption of innocence, and alter the rules of evidence, which heretofore, under the universally recognized principles of common law, have been supposed to be fundamental and unchangeable." Such oaths, he said, "assume that the parties are guilty; they call upon the parties to establish their innocence; and they declare that such innocence can be shown only in one way—by an inquisition, in the form of an expurgatory oath, into the consciences of the parties."[45] Justices Douglas and Black agreed, saying that "the State by the device of the loyalty oath places the burden of proving loyalty on the citizen," which "goes against the grain of our constitutional system and presumption that every man and woman is "innocent until guilt is established."[46]

The Supreme Court has long embraced the need for full and free discussion, and its importance in keeping "society from becoming stagnant and unprepared for the stresses and strains that work to tear all civilization apart."[47] Freedom of discussion and of opinion, said Justice Douglas, "has indeed been the first article of our faith. We have founded our political system on it. It has been the safeguard of every religious, political, philosophical, economic, and racial group amongst us. We have counted on it to keep us from embracing what is cheap and false; we have trusted the common sense of our people to choose the doctrine true to our genius and to reject the rest. This has been the one single outstanding tenet that has made our institutions the symbol of freedom and equality. We have deemed it more costly to liberty to suppress a despised minority than to let them vent their spleen. We have above all else feared the political censor."[48] Speaking of Marxists who would conspire together to spark a revolution, launch acts of terror, and assassinate American leaders, Douglas expressed no doubt that the public must be protected and the speech directly incident to the

[44] 4 *The Works of Alexander Hamilton* (Fed. Ed 1904), at pp. 269-270.

[45] *Cummings v. Missouri* (1867) 71 U.S. 277, 328.

[46] *Speiser v. Randall* (1958) 357 U.S. 513, 532-533, 78 S.Ct. 1332.

[47] *Dennis v. United States* (1951) 341 U.S. 494, 71 S.Ct. 857, 584, J. Douglas, dissenting.

[48] Id., at 584-585.

conspiracy targeted as evidence of the crime. Ironically, it is Marxists today who light our cities on fire, throw Molotov Cocktails at police officers and their vehicles, and pound police with skate boards who insist most strenuously on their right to speak. And it is they, and those they've convinced to believe that silence is violence, who recite their oath in the form of the Black Lives Matter mantra and demand of all others that they follow suit. How appropriate that it is Marxists who do this, and yet how contrary to the American tradition of liberty of speech, liberty of conscience and the right to remain silent, to withhold one's opinion, and to rely on words of one's own devising to express ideas reflective of one's own understanding of the truth.

It may be that the majority of people, the majority of African Americans, see the phrase "Black Lives Matter" not as a test oath to be recited to prove commitment to a far reaching, far leftist assault on the American constitutional order, but as a simple acknowledgment of the need to find a way to end abusive police practices and hold police who act lawlessly accountable in accordance with existing legal standards. Assuming that to be the case, this would leave in the minority of proponents of the phrase those who insist that any white person who doesn't articulate it and fails to lend their support to the most radical restructuring of the social order in our history, and who would impose ideological conformity through bullying efforts to compel adoption of slogans and with it a set of policy initiatives to shift power in society into hands controlled by brains filled with contempt for the Constitution.

Morality and our commitment to justice demand that all Americans resist oppression by the state and by those who would empower the state to oppress. The same morality and commitment to justice requires us to blame only the culprits, not the innocent. The victims of police violence are victims of the state, not of private citizens. The violence against them is violence by the state, not by private citizens. The radicals who applaud and excuse the looting and destruction of private enterprise that serves black and white alike include both extremists and liars, who blame the excess of government not on government but on a white population that shares with African Americans the burden of being over-regulated and saddled with expanding costs of government that are less dedicated to providing services to privileged whites than benefits for retired workers serving no one but themselves. The great privilege of qualified immunity enjoyed by police officers and other agents of the state only encourages irresponsible governance, while inflated budgets, mostly to fund pensions, only encourage a lack of accountability by the governors to the governed. Some restructuring of government is certainly in order; a restructuring of all of society isn't. Focusing on the actual problem allows for a more perfect solution; focusing on far left progressive and Marxist objectives that have nothing to do with the problem will result only in the opposite—more government, less restraints on abuse of all citizens, and even less accountability by the abusers to their victims. Black lives do matter. So does the health and safety of the larger society in which free black men, women and children are to live. That health and safety can only be promoted by more not less freedom from government, reliable law enforcement to protect black citizens from criminals, and constitutional restraints to protect them from government agents and ensure accountability for all who violate legal and constitutional norms. Black Lives Matter, the movement and its radical leftist adherents, furiously disagree with this view, and they will raze the necessary foundation for the freedom, prosperity and hopes of all Americans, black and white, if they have their way.

Sex and the Transsexual Undertaker

IN contemplating a period of solitude and reflection away from the stresses of ordinary life in the midst of a confused and confusing human mob, Henry David Thoreau thought he might overcome the quiet desperation that plagued both himself and his fellow man in the much quieter precincts of the New England woods. The result was a series of reflections on life and nature, drafted with remarkable sensitivity in an ineluctable style, and considered even in our jaded age a literary classic and a masterpiece of American creativity. Subsequent biographers tended not to delve too deeply into Thoreau's desperation, save to note a hopeless love for a nameless woman who rejected his advances. An undercurrent of a peculiar sentimentality in his prose and poetry continued to perplex critics and biographers, who treated certain affected passages within Thoreau's oeuvre in the same manner as awkward elements of the poet Whitman's writing. A moment of catharsis came to a leading expert on the subject while revising an earlier edition of a biographical monograph in 1961. To a hardly surprised literary world, he announced that on further reflection he had "become convinced that there is evidence of a strong homoerotic element in Thoreau's personality."[1] Unable to document any actual instance of homosexual activity on Thoreau's part, the biographer nevertheless believed that the strain of homoeroticism helped "explain a number of curious facts about his life and facets of his personality and even suggests in the tensions growing out of the conflict between his sexuality and the repressive attitudes of the society in which he lived a possible source of some of his creativity."[2] Were he actually gay, his art might well be an example of what Freud called sublimation, and an explanation more precisely of why the desperation he referred to could never be openly identified. Modernly, Thoreau is a prototype of many who came later, struggling with identity, conflicted over expectations of family, the call of social norms and religious instruction, and seeking ways to come to terms with the pain of daily living with secrets too big to persistently dissimulate.

Among the modern ranks of the quietly desperate was a person we now know as Aimee Stephens. Identifying late in life as a woman, Aimee had been born Anthony, into a religious family in North Carolina in the 1950s. From age five, a sense that all was not right gender-wise became evident, and this in time gave way to a discomfort with her own natural sex and gender identity. Uncomfortable with an understanding of reality so unconventional, and lacking confidence in public acceptance of a consciousness of identity in conflict with formal biology, accommodation was made to the dictates of normalcy. Aimee lived life as a man, engaged in activities traditionally associated with boys, dated women, and ultimately married. Nevertheless, the struggle between the interior world and the external continued. It culminated in the admission to wife Donna that he had been living a lie, that he experienced deep unease over the male identity, and felt profoundly that he was in fact a she. Rather than reject the admission, Donna embraced it. She supported Aimee in her new identity, manifest first only in intimate settings at home and with trusted friends. At work as a Funeral

---

[1] See Paula Ivaska Robbins, "The Natural Thoreau," *Gay and Lesbian Review*, September 1, 2011.

[2] Id.

Director at the R.G. & G.R. Harris Funeral Home, Aimee continued to present as the same man her employer had always known her to be. A near suicide in November of 2012 convinced Aimee to terminate her schizophrenic existence by informing the world of the reality of her inner self. In a letter to her employer and co-workers, she explained that she had "a gender identity disorder that I have struggled with my entire life," and which she'd managed to hide "very well all these years."[3] Acknowledging that "some of you may have trouble understanding this," she said she didn't fully understand it herself. She noted that she hoped she could continue with her employment with the funeral home, where she had always done her best, but just couldn't continue living a dual life any longer. "As distressing as this is sure to be to my friends and some of my family, I need to do this for myself and for my own peace of mind and to end the agony in my soul."[4]

The result wasn't the acceptance that greeted her when revealing the secret to Donna. Instead, the employer informed her that "this isn't going to work."[5] She was terminated, but offered three month's severance on condition that she sign a release of all claims and a non-disclosure agreement. Having made the decision to live openly and honestly with the identity she felt reflected her true self, she declined to agree to keep quiet about anything related to it, especially for something so miniscule as a half dozen pay checks.[6] With the help of the ACLU, she filed a claim with the EEOC alleging that her termination on account of her sexual identity was a form of workplace discrimination on the basis of sex prohibited by Title VII of the Civil Rights Act of 1964. She prevailed, but was forced to defend her position on appeal in the District Court. Admitting that the firing was on the basis of the change in Aimee's sexual identity, the employer presented a rather implausible argument that the application of Title VII violated the employer's religious liberty, in that "it would be violating God's commands if he were to permit an employee who was born a biological male to dress in

---

[3] Masha Gessen, "Remembering Aimee Stephens, Who Lost and Found Her Purpose: The Woman at the Center of the First Transgender-Rights Case to Come Before the Supreme Court Died Before a Decision was Handed Down," *The New Yorker*, May 20, 2020.

[4] Id.

[5] *Bostock v. Clayton County* (2020) 590 U.S. ___.

[6] Trudy Ring, "Aimee Stephens, Fired for Being Trans, Decided to Live and Fight Back," *Advocate*, October 1, 2019.

a traditionally female skirt-suit at one of his funeral homes because doing so would support the idea that sex is a changeable construct rather than an immutable God-given gift."[7] Despite the fact that retaining Aimee as an employee required neither a change of belief nor participation in any activity that actually violated the employer's religious faith, such as an animal sacrifice to Divine Caesar or preparation of a cake celebrating the nuptials of a gay couple, the Court scolded the employer for not being very nice, but ruled in his favour anyway.[8] By the time the case reached the Supreme Court, it had been consolidated with two others, and Aimee herself had developed total kidney failure and was undergoing daily dialysis.[9] She was dead before the Supreme Court published Justice Neil Gorsuch's opinion vindicating her right to bring a Title VII claim for workplace discrimination on the basis of her status as a biological male who identifies as female.

The decision is rightfully celebrated by the LGBT community as a landmark, signifying not only an expansion of our understanding of the scope of a significant remedial statute, but of the fuller acceptance of the community within the larger American polity. The path toward the decision met major headwinds from a majority heterosexual population whose attitudes continue to be influenced by values derived from the nation's Judeo-Christian religious and common law heritage. From the Old Testament to the New, the Bible speaks of the Divine design of man and woman for one another, both sexually and spiritually.[10] Homosexuality bearing a certain violent form of expression was said to have been a cause of the great cry that reached the ear of God and led to the judgment of heaven that destroyed the ancient cities of Sodom and Gomorrah.[11] The law given to Moses on Mt. Sinai included the command to "not have sexual relations with a man as one does with a woman" and for men and women to dress themselves in gender-appropriate attire.[12] In corrupt times during the period of the dual monarchies, kings and priests incorporated the religious practices of the Canaanites, including sexual rituals involving homosexual acts and male priests dressed as women. These practices were condemned by the prophets and

---

[7] Id.
[8] Id.
[9] Id.
[10] Gen. 2:20-25; and Mark 10:6-9.
[11] Gen. 18-19.
[12] 1 Cor. 4:51 Cor. 4:5.

periodically rooted out by traditionalist monarchs.[13] Christ himself never addressed the issue of homosexuality, let alone transgenderism. His message was limited to general principles of spiritual and practical life. His disciples, however, occasionally did. Paul spoke critically of the historicized corruption of man, of how men "abandoned natural relations with women and were inflamed with lust for one another."[14]

Much more has been recorded of the disapproval of homosexuality than transgenderism. Justices Byron White and Chief Justice Warren Burger noted that the "proscriptions against that conduct have ancient roots" and that "decisions of individuals relating to homosexual conduct have been subject to state intervention throughout the history of Western civilization."[15] The historically disfavoured status of homosexuals derived not merely from the Judeo-Christian tradition, but from the classical world. Plato encouraged laws against homosexuality due to his belief that it "undermined the important Greek values of masculinity and procreation."[16] Homosexual sodomy, said the Chief Justice, was "a capital crime under Roman law."[17] Ecclesiastical courts in England punished such conduct, and when the judicial powers of those fora were transferred to the King's jurisdiction, Parliament enacted the first criminal sodomy statutes, making "the detestable and abominable vice of buggery committed with mankind or beast punishable by death."[18] Blackstone "described 'the infamous crime against nature' as an offense of 'deeper malignity' than rape, a heinous act 'the very mention of which is a disgrace to human nature,' and 'a crime not fit to be named.'"[19]

When Englishmen came to the New World, they brought the law with them, including the legal prohibitions on homosexual behaviour. The laws of the original thirteen States at the time of the ratification of the Bill of Rights each embraced criminal sanctions for homosexual

---

[13] 1 Kings 15:12.

[14] Romans 1:27.

[15] *Bowers v. Hardwick* (1986) 478 U.S. 186, 106 S.Ct. 2841.

[16] Yao Apasu-Gbotsu, Robert J. Arnold, Paul DiBella, Kevin Dorse, and Elisa L. Fuller, "Survey on the Constitutional Right to Privacy in the Context of Homosexual Activity," 40 U. Miami L. Rev. 521 (1986), at p. 525.

[17] *Bowers v. Hardwick*, supra, at 196, Burger, C.J., concurring.

[18] William N. Eskridge, Jr., "Law and the Construction of the Closet: American Regulation of Same-Sex Intimacy, 1880-1946," 82 Iowa L.Rev. 1007 (1997), at p. 1012.

[19] *Bowers v. Hardwick*, supra, at 196-197, Burger, C.J., concurring.

sodomy.[20] Only five of the thirty-seven States of the Union at the time of the ratification of the Fourteenth Amendment lacked criminal sodomy laws. Until 1961, "all 50 States outlawed sodomy," and by the mid-80s, laws could still be found on the books in half of them.[21] Conversely, no prohibitions on cross-dressing existed in the country prior to 1848, when Columbus, Ohio was the first to enact an ordinance outlawing a person appearing in public in a dress not belonging to his or her own sex. Similar laws entered municipal codes in Toledo, Saint Louis, San Francisco, Atlanta, Nashville, Memphis, Dallas, Oakland, San Jose, Tucson, Butte, Denver, Salt Lake City, Santa Barbara, Los Angeles, Minneapolis, Sioux City, Sioux Falls, Peoria, Omaha, Cedar Rapids and elsewhere.[22]

That these laws were seldom enforced is undoubtedly true, largely because the nature of the behaviour at the time encouraged shelter from prying eyes. When they were enforced, the focus was usually on "men assaulting women or minors during coercive encounters."[23] There was, said Professor Lawrence Friedman, "never any systematic crackdown."[24] So rare were the prosecutions that in 1880 only sixty-three prisoners were "then incarcerated for crimes against nature in the entire country."[25] In fact, not once in the Nineteenth-Century was anyone actually imprisoned for having consensual sexual intercourse with someone of the same sex.[26] Even after the turn of the century, when many communities focused more heavily on policing the morals of the people, arrests, prosecutions and convictions for sodomy and cross-dressing remained rare.[27] Prostitution and obscenity were the primary vices to be addressed and the primary focus of police authorities in the States.

The deviation of human behaviour from accepted or imposed social and moral norms lends itself to clinical diagnosis. Such was the case with homosexuality and what was formerly called "inversion" or

---

[20] Id., at 193-194

[21] Id., at 194.

[22] Eskridge, op. cit., at p. 1040.

[23] Id., at p. 1010.

[24] Lawrence M. Friedman, *Crime and Punishment in American History* (New York: Basic Books, 1993), at p. 344.

[25] Eskridge, op. cit., at p. 1015.

[26] Id.

[27] Id., at p. 1016

"transvestism." Seeking answers to the question of why some people feel compelled to act in ways at odds with what was considered normal, clinicians in the latter Nineteenth-Century and the first half of the Twentieth tended to lump homosexuality and transvestism together with every other sexual activity that "fail of any possible biologic goal": masturbation, sadomasochism, fetishism, exhibitionism, voyeurism, zoophilia, necrophilia, and obscenity.[28] Richard von Krafft-Ebing considered "inversion" to be "a leading sexual pathology reflecting a broader mental or physical 'degeneration,' or reversion to a prior evolutionary status."[29] The nation's leading enforcer of morals, Anthony Comstock, called "inverts" unfit "to live with the rest of mankind" and properly subject to the branding upon their forehead of the word "unclean,' and as lepers of old," forced to "cry 'Unlcean, Unclean!' as they go about," if not imprisoned for life.[30] American sexologist George Beard attributed any deviation of sexual identity from human biology to a hatred of the opposite sex and a love of one's own.[31] Homosexuality was seen by professionals as "a sign of retarded emotional development," while homosexuals were considered to be "compulsive-obsessional neurotics."[32] It was, said one psychologist, "an expression of abnormal personality.[33]

In attempting to explain it, various theorists postulated "seduction in youth, enforced discipline on a sexual level, resulting in displacement of sexual objects, hostility or excessive affection for the mother, hostility for the father or identification with a weak father; lack of effective males, rebellion against an aggressive father, continual emotional stress, [and] broken homes."[34] The etiology among homosexual women, or lesbians, was "believed to parallel that in men: rejection by one parent with consequent running to the other."[35] Much of the analysis tracked purely Freudian lines. The more assertive homosexual was said to identify "himself with his mother and loves himself in the person of his partner

---

[28] Benjamin Karpman, *The Sexual Offender and His Offenses: Etiology, Pathology, Psychodynamics and Treatment* (New York: Julian Press, 1954), at p. 348.

[29] Eskridge, op. cit., at p. 1023.

[30] Id., at p. 1025.

[31] Id.

[32] Karpman, op. cit., at pp. 609 and 148.

[33] Id., at p. 151.

[34] Id., at p. 609.

[35] Id.

as he had wanted his mother to love him"; while the more passive sort identified his "partner with his mother and enjoys receiving from him the affection which he failed to receive from his mother as a child."[36] The Freudian psychotherapist Otto Fenichel generally agreed with this evaluation, noting that "the homosexual man replaces his love for his mother by an identification with her."[37] The male transvestite, he said, presented a more complex Freudian problem. His castration anxiety is obvious, and he solves it first by fantasizing that a woman actually has a penis, and then imagines that he is such a woman, "under whose cloths a penis is hidden."[38] In the end, the source of the crisis for transvestites and homosexual males was the same: a fixation with the mother and a means of coping with the innately problematic mother-child relationship.

The identification of those who deviated from sexual norms with the morally and psychologically deficient often entailed a rather laboured effort. The short sighted and the self-righteous might define a homosexual as objectively "bad" and a heterosexual as objectively "good," only because their biased outlook made them "prone to forget that in the heterosexual field an individual can be just as reprehensible and disgusting as in the homosexual."[39] Freud himself observed that while some were embarrassed by sexual deviance, it was "nothing to be ashamed of, no vice, no degradation, [and] cannot be classified as an illness."[40] Though homosexuality was in his view a sign of arrested sexual development, "many highly respectable individuals of ancient and modern times have been homosexuals, several of the greatest among them."[41] Professor Karpman asserted that "homosexuality does not in itself invest [the homosexual] with other undesirable characteristics."[42] Nor was he convinced that modern moral sentiments ought to remain free of any re-evaluation of attitudes toward homosexuals and others who deviated from the sexual norm.[43] Freud

---

[36] Id., at p. 303.
[37] Id., at p. 313.
[38] Id.
[39] Id., at p. 349.
[40] Ernest Jones, *The Life and Work of Sigmund Freud, Volume III: The Last Phase, 1919-1939* (New York: Basic Books, 1957), at p. 195.
[41] Id.
[42] Karpman, op. cit., at p. 611.
[43] Id.

thought it "a great injustice to persecute homosexuality as a crime, and cruelty too."[44] Citing various scientific studies that found homosexual conduct to be neither "'unnatural' nor socially harmful," the American Law Institute proposed a revision of the Model Penal Code that decriminalized adult, consensual, private sexual conduct.[45] Illinois adopted the provision in 1961, followed by Connecticut in 1969 and twenty other States in the 1970s.[46] It wasn't long before courts began striking down sodomy laws and other statutes that criminalized private, consensual sexuality. The Supreme Court refused the challenge to strike down the remainder of such laws in the 1980s, but did rule that a constitutional amendment to prohibit a State's legislature from enacting laws to protect the civil liberties of gays and lesbians violated equal protection and the fundamental right of Americans to engage in the political process.[47] Sodomy laws were finally declared to be unconstitutional in 2003, though the dissenters rightfully pointed out the inconsistency of a decision based on the meaning of the Due Process Clause with the Court's historic approach to discerning constitutionally protected rights by comparing alleged rights with those that are "deeply rooted in our Nation's history and tradition."[48] What some thought was the final frontier of full constitutional acceptance was conquered in 2015 when the Court held that marriage was a relationship the State could not limit to couples comprised exclusively of one male and one female.[49] Other frontiers, however, remained untamed, including the workplace and federal law designed to protect workers from discrimination on the basis of inherent and individualized traits.

Conservatives tend to advocate work in favour of welfare, self-reliance in lieu of dependence. The theme is one that echoes in various maxims of our civilization—none but those who work are entitled to eat; earn your keep; and there's no such thing as a free lunch—and finds religious sanction in the punishment of Adam for violating the command of God to avoid the fruit of the Tree of the Knowledge of Good and Evil. The Founders considered work a fundamental right that

---

[44] Jones, op cit., at p. 502.

[45] Yao, et al., op. cit., at p. 526.

[46] Id.

[47] *Bowers v. Hardwick*, supra; and *Romer v. Evans* (1996) 517 U.S. 620, 116 S.Ct. 1620.

[48] *Lawrence v. Texas* (2003) 539 U.S. 558, 123 S.Ct. 2472.

[49] *Obergefell v. Hodges* (2015) 576 U.S. 644, 135 S.Ct. 2584.

government treat gingerly lest the righteous anger of the people be aroused. When the Congress contemplated the essential attributes of freedom at the close of the Civil War, the consensus was that they included the liberty to work, to contract, to travel in search of work, and to buy and sell goods, services and land. The Civil Rights Act of 1866 expressly protected these rights, and the Fourteenth Amendment was ratified in order to ensure that the power of Congress to protect those rights was beyond question. The retreat by the courts, the Congress and the executive during the Gilded Age, the Progressive Era, the Roaring Twenties, the Great Depression, the War Years and the first years of the Cold War came to an end in the 1950s, when the Supreme Court struck down segregated public schools and the armed forces were deployed to enforce desegregation. By 1964, Congress revisited the Civil Rights Act of old, and in keeping with the broad scope of the rights the Framers of the Fourteenth Amendment intended to protect, it inserted a remedial provision to provide those most likely to be subject to arbitrary and capricious mistreatment on the job with the means to protect their ability to earn their keep, buy their own lunch, and obtain this day their daily bread.

The decision in Aimee Stephens's case continues to be excoriated by conservatives. They repeat the same arguments the losing defendants presented in Court, which the conservative dissenters warmed over in their long dissenting opinions. The majority decision, however, wasn't a progressive one. It did not turn on an overly broad conception of the rights protected by the Due Process Clauses found in the Constitution, nor on the intent of the Legislature in enacting it. Nor did the Court weigh the competing claims of the litigants in order to determine if discrimination in the context of the statute was permissible under the circumstances. It turned instead on the plain text of the law itself, and the most fundamental and basic of the canons of statutory construction: where the language is clear, no investigation of what the legislature intended is necessary. As the somewhat conservative Chief Justice joined the majority, he exercised the privilege of either writing the opinion himself or assigning it to the justice of his choice. The selection of the textualist Neil Gorsuch was a clear indication that the decision wasn't progressive, that it was the language of the law that mattered, not abstract rights and the secret intentions of the Congress.

The principle term at issue was "sex." On its meaning turned the outcome of the case. Justice Gorsuch noted that the traditional approach is to interpret the terms in a statute in keeping with the ordinary public meaning at the time when the statute was enacted.[50] The term "sex" related to biology in 1964, and to types of persons, either male or female. The defendants argued that the term "sex" was understood narrowly in 1964—that it was limited only to men and women who expressed particular gender traits that society characterized as male and female respectively. Gorsuch and the majority didn't necessarily disagree. Gays, lesbians, and transsexuals might not have been in the mind of the Congress when it enacted the law, but, in the end, it didn't matter, for it couldn't be more clear that "it is impossible to discriminate against a person for being homosexual or transgender without discriminating against that individual based on sex."[51] Whether homosexual or transgender, one's status is "inextricably bound up with sex, not because homosexuality or transgender status are related to sex in some vague sense or because discrimination on these bases has some disparate impact on one sex or another, but because to discriminate on these grounds requires an employer to intentionally treat individual employees differently because of their sex."[52]

The defendant claimed that it wasn't sex that was the basis of the discrimination in the cases before the court, but sexual orientation, which falls outside the statute's scope. Gorsuch dismissed the distinction as irrelevant. Pondering the situation where a person applying for a job is asked to check a box best matching his or her orientation, he noted that "there is no way for an applicant to decide whether to check the homosexual or transgender box without considering sex... Try writing out instructions for who should check the box without using the words man, woman, or sex... It can't be done. Likewise, there is no way an employer can discriminate against those who check the homosexual or transgender box without discriminating in part because of an applicant's sex."[53] Sexual orientation isn't mentioned in the statute, true, but discrimination based on homosexual or transgender orientation simply can't occur without considering the employee's sex. The gay man who is

---

[50] *Bostock v. Clayton County*, supra, at p. 4.
[51] Id., at p. 9.
[52] Id., at p. 10.
[53] Id.

fired because he is not sufficiently man-like in the eyes of the employer and the transsexual who rejects his or her biological sex are obviously fired because of sex—because of the employer's concept of what a particular sex entails and how the employee's sexual identification deviates from that concept.

Other objections were raised, but Gorsuch swatted each of them down in turn. For one, the Congress's failure to include sexual orientation among the list of protected classes doesn't create an implied exception to a patently broad statute. "[W]hen Congress chooses not to include any exceptions to a broad rule, courts apply the broad rule."[54] Congress's inclusion of the term "sexual orientation" in subsequent laws wasn't an indication of the meaning of the unamended statute, for what one Congress does with a particular law has no bearing on what another Congress did with an entirely different one. To hold otherwise "offers a 'particularly dangerous' basis on which to rest an interpretation of an existing law a different and earlier Congress did adopt."[55] The lack of expectation in 1964 that Title VII would apply to discrimination against homosexual and transgender persons was of no matter; for the Court had long held that novel situations, unanticipated by the law's framers, nevertheless invite a remedy. "To be sure, the statute's application in these cases reaches 'beyond the principal evil' legislators may have intended or expected to address. But 'the fact that [a statute] has been applied in situations not expressly anticipated by Congress' does not demonstrate ambiguity; instead, it simply 'demonstrates [the] breadth' of a legislative command."[56] Men, for instance, were not the expected beneficiaries of the law when it enacted, and yet the Court subsequently held that the law protected them when fired due to their sex and when they were sexually harassed on the job. "If we applied Title VII's plain text only to applications to some (yet to be determined) group expected in 1964, we'd have more than a little law to overturn."[57] Finally, he noted that even if legislative history and legislative intent were relevant, "certainly nothing in the meagre legislative history of this provision suggests it was meant to be read narrowly." The assertion that the law's sponsor introduced the broad language in the hope of scuttling the law

---

[54] Id., at p. 19.
[55] Id., at p. 20.
[56] Id., at p. 24.
[57] Id., at p. 28.

may or may not be true, but if it is, it would seem that the Congress as a whole had no problem with the proposed text's breadth.

Gorsuch acknowledged the potential for future litigation following the broadening of the Court's construction of the operative statutory term. Church employers might now worry that their refusal to hire homosexual and transsexual persons will bring them liability not previously contemplated. Many women and parents might fear that men who identify as women will insist on showering and changing in women's locker rooms, or competing as women in athletic competitions despite their obvious genetic differences and physical advantages. Gorsuch's concerns with respect to these issues were far less pronounced. The First Amendment's Free Exercise Clause, the Religious Freedom Restoration Act and an exception built right into Title VII itself would tend to provide significant protection against church employers being required to embrace employees whose sexual identities run counter to the message of the faith, that God created man and woman, that sexual relations are reserved for opposite sex couples, and that men not dress themselves in women's attire.[58] The other issues were not really issues at all. Bathrooms, locker rooms and athletics are not within the scope of Title VII. Claims involving those facets of life will likely come, but they will involve other statutes and other rights and will turn not on the ordinary meaning of the text, but on such things as privacy, the emotional well-being of women and girls forcibly exposed in their most vulnerable state to biological men whose biologic identity is all too plain to see when standing in the shower, and whether transgender men or women are similarly situated to men or women possessing bonafide genetic credentials. Gorsuch's opinion doesn't presume to rule on those issues, and Gorsuch himself can't be relied on to take a position that would advance the interests of those who would introduce them to the High Court. What his opinion has done is vindicate an important right—the right to work—and extend the scope of Congress's effort to protect that right and thereby ensure that persons whose sexual identity does not align with the majority won't be cast from the job market and deprived of the means to fend for themselves.

The conservative reaction has been overwrought, if not apocalyptic. Rod Dreher of *The American Conservative* said "it is hard to overstate the

---

[58] Id., at p. 32.

magnitude of this decision, and the size of the loss to religious and social conservatives."[59] Terry Schilling of The American Principle Project called the decision "terrible" and a "reckless power grab" by the Supreme Court.[60] Professor Andrew T. Walker of the Southern Baptist Theological Seminary said the decision "treats men and women as nothing more than conglomerations of stereotypes" and "engages in a politically correct form of erasure."[61] *The Federalist's* Joy Pullman's view was the most hysterical of all. "The ruling," she wrote, "will lead to a tsunami of polarizing court cases and further degradation of Americans' natural right to free speech, to free association, and to worshipping God as their consciences require. All this in the name of 'equality,' a word that has become a totalitarian weapon."[62] It was, she said, "a disgrace to these bedrocks of Western civilization, our nation built upon them, the voters who vote for them" and the honour of the Framers.[63]

Western civilization and the nation, too, however, were built on many things, not all of them laudable. The best of stones that form the foundation of each counsel restraint in judgment, magnanimity in victory and defeat alike, and charity toward all, including adversaries. Our nation came into being during a fit of prolonged protest. In that struggle, men sought liberty to do as they will, to worship God in the manner contrary to what the state prescribed, and to work in a profession and on the terms of their own choosing. Our Constitution comprises a compact among us to allow one another what God gave each of us in equal measure, and if some fail in the eyes of their fellow man to take full advantage of that gift, spurn the Creator's testament and act contrary to His prescription for living, even then God advises us to withhold our judgment, to forgive those perceived as sinners and, if nothing else, be a lamp whose light remains uncovered for all the world to see by.[64] The days of the Judges and the Levites are over. The Mosaic

---

[59] Rod Dreher, "SCOTUS Routes Conservatives, Again," www.theamericanconservative.com, June 15, 2020.

[60] Michael Gryboski, "'Devastating for Religious Liberty': 5 Reactions to Supreme Court LGBT Discrimination Decision," www.christianpost.com, June 16, 2020.

[61] Id.

[62] Joy Pullman, "SCOTUS's Transgender Ruling Firebombs the Constitution, www.thefederalist.com, June 16, 2020.

[63] Id.

[64] Mat 6:14-15; Mat. 7:1; and Mat. 5:15.

Law is not enforceable by the state. We who follow the Way, though we be Americans, remain situated in a world not of our own making, are despised by it, and look elsewhere for our hope. If there is a transgression, we do not punish it; we only ask that God might remove the plank from our eyes so that we might see clearer and seek mercy for ourselves and others in prayer.[65] God knows what the sin of world is, and if there is Judgment, it belongs to Him, and only in the fullness of time.[66] "Nothing in all the world," said the Apostle Paul, "can be hidden from God. Everything is clear and lies open before Him, and to Him we must explain the way we have lived."[67] He it is "who will bring to light the things now hidden in darkness and will disclose the purposes of the heart."[68] In the meantime, we sinners live under the curse of Adam, "to eat bread by the sweat our face."[69] We do a disservice to God and man when we make it harder for our fellow sinners to do the same.

Half Sunk, A Shattered Visage Lies

ONLY two weeks out from New Bedford on an extended world tour, the whaling vessel *Virginia* cruised the North Atlantic, south of Newfoundland and the Grand Banks. The primary goal of obtaining whale oil to fill the lamps of New England at the moment rested second on the list of priorities—well behind coming about far enough east to hit the prevailing winds and making the long reach to Cape Horn without coming under the notice of the *C.S.S. Alabama* and its adroit commander, Captain Raphael Semmes. Since the outbreak of the Civil War, the Union Navy under Admiral Farragut had locked up the southern ports in an effort to starve the Confederacy into submission. The blockade was largely successful, notwithstanding the actions of blockade runners operating on the margins of the Union strategy. Servicing itself in neutral and friendly ports around the Atlantic rim, the *Alabama* had no need ever to return to the Confederate States. Over the course of a year and a half,

---

[65] Mat. 7:5; Luke 6:28; and Deut. 9:18-19.
[66] Mat. 7:1; and Heb. 9:27.
[67] Heb. 4:13.
[68] 1 Cor. 4:5.
[69] Gen. 3:19.

the *Alabama* had nearly destroyed New England's whaling industry, and had done further damage to the carrying trade. The Confederate Raider knew the shipping lanes. It could appear at any moment, full steam in the direction of a largely defenseless whaler, delivering fire and Confederate fury.

The sight of a plume of smoke on the far horizon was the first sign that the *Virginia's* voyage would end badly. The presence of the English flag atop the approaching steamer's mast lulled any worries about the ship's identity only until it became clear that the banner flew as a means of deception. Faced with a fully armed and battle-hardened fighting vessel, the *Virginia's* captain surrendered without a fight. He and the crew were placed in double irons on the *Alabama's* deck, from whence they watched, some in tears, as their vessel burned to the waterline.[1] Storms came. Water filled the deck. Tarps were hung, but provided only partial shelter for the enchained men. At some point, Semmes freed one of the prisoners—the cook, Antonio Pereira—and charged him with finding fish and other provisions sufficient to feed his shipmates. A native of the Portuguese Azores and likely a descendant of Sephardic Jews and Berbers who were compelled to convert and emigrate to the Western Isles by intolerant monarchs on the mainland, Pereira proved so resourceful and the food so well prepared that Semmes offered the man a purse full of gold to join his crew as ship's cook.[2] Pereira declined. He wouldn't leave his friends, nor fight for the Confederacy.

Pereira and his shipmates were eventually transferred to a passing vessel bound for England and transported to Liverpool, where Consul Thomas Haines Dudley and Ambassador Charles Francis Adams arranged for their return home. Almost as soon as Pereira set foot on American soil in New York City, in January of 1863, he enlisted in the Union Navy. All the resentment over his captivity at the mercy of the militant defenders of the slave power he channeled to defeat his former captors and assist in the freeing of the men and women held in bondage by people on whose behalf the *Alabama* had terrorized the high seas. He was one of the many heroes of our civilization, and he was my great, great grandfather.

As the storms of war receded, only memories of the horror and the

---

[1] Raphael Semmes, *Memoirs of Service Afloat, During the War Between the States* (Baltimore: Kelly, Piet & Co., 1869), at pp. 446-447.

[2] "Captured by Alabama," *The Boston Globe*, April 28, 1912.

glory of battle remained. In the North, veterans like Pereira organized a great veterans' organization, part social club, part political lobby, known as the Grand Army of the Republic. Though defeated in battle and humiliated during Reconstruction, the white survivors of the war in the former Confederacy rallied and formed their own version of the GAR. Like their northern counterparts, they pooled their money to fund what they considered to be fitting memorials of their sacrifice to what increasingly came to be known as "the lost cause." A women's auxiliary, known as the United Daughters of the Confederacy, took the lead in contracting for the construction of monuments all across the South.[3] For northerners, the zeal for memorials reflected both pride in victory and relief by the former soldier over the fact that he had survived the disease and carnage of the long conflict. In the South, the motivation was different. There was, said W.J. Cash, a profound "need to justify itself in the eyes of the world and in its own and to assert its pride as against the Yankee," as well as "a great aversion on the part of the individuals who made up the master class to surrender the glory which had been theirs under the ancient regime."[4] In segregated schools across the South throughout the reign of Jim Crow the white schoolboy would have "continually before his eyes the vision...of a glorious swashbuckler, compounded of Jeb Stuart, the golden locked Pickett, and the sudden and terrible Forrest, forever charging the cannon's mouth with the Southern battle flag."[5] Monuments would serve as a constant que for this vision, and a not-so-subtle warning to the nominally enfranchised black population of the attitude toward them held by much of the white majority.

As the turn of the century neared, in towns across the South, usually following the lead of the United Confederate Veterans or the United Daughters of the Confederacy, southern whites laid the groundwork for the erection of increasingly large statues commemorating the war and the soldiers who fought it. The Muldoon Company of Louisville, the Franch Teich Company of Llano, Texas and the McNeel Marble Company out of Marietta, Georgia competed in a steadily expanding market, manufacturing often crude, occasionally impressive, statues,

---

[3] C. Van Woodward, *The Origins of the New South, 1877-1913* (Baton Rouge: Louisiana State University Press, 1971), at p. 156.

[4] W.J. Cash, *The Mind of the South* (New York: Vintage, 1969), at p. 127.

[5] Id., at p. 124.

sometimes of noteworthy leaders of the cause, usually of anonymous soldiers, ever looking northward, as if ready even in a state of obvious weariness to return to the field and fight the war anew, perhaps with an outcome more fitting of the bravery and genius displayed at Manassas, Chancellorsville and Chickamagua.[6] Perhaps most impressive was the massive equestrian statue of the noblest Confederate of them all, Robert E. Lee, standing in the midst of an avenue of heroes in the former capital of the Confederacy, at Richmond, Virginia. "Nine thousand whites of all ages, occupations, and genders dragged, by rope and hand" the great monument, and "over a hundred thousand people attended the unveiling three weeks later—the largest ceremony attendant to any Confederate monument."[7]

The shrines to the lost cause of Southern nationalism, slave power and the men who died in the terrible conflict brought on by slavery were not universally popular when first erected. African Americans could not gaze upon the ubiquitous Confederate monoliths without a mix of resentment and fear. Even some whites felt unease over their proliferation. Northerners certainly must have chaffed at the thought of memorials to those who took aim at and killed their friends and family during the many battles of the conflict. Any criticism for the next century or more, however, remained muted. Perhaps it is no coincidence that the criticism became more pronounced after the party of Abraham Lincoln displaced the Democrats in popularity in the South and calls for removal of public allusions to Dixie increased in number and volume. Resistance to removal of the tangible indicia of the past both good and bad delayed any significant expunging from the nation of such monuments, at least for a time. The rise of a new radicalism among leftists of a largely white variety, inspired by opportunities to propel a larger Marxist-Leninist agenda and encouraged by Democrats attempting to hide their own culpability in the historic offenses against justice and humanity, led to the adoption by progressives of the cause of monument removal and transformed it into a centerpiece of protests against a social and legal order they insist is organized on principles of white privilege, white greed and white crime.

The recent protests in the wake of the death of George Floyd

---

[6] Edward L. Ayers, *The Promise of the New South: Life After Reconstruction*, 15th Anniversary ed. (Oxford: Oxford University Press, 2007), at pp. 334-335.

[7] Id., at p. 335.

unleashed a wave of attacks on monuments around the country. While most have proceeded through official channels and resulted in official decisions to remove the memorials from town squares and other public property—often to museums—others have exhibited a far more militant guise. Gangs of radicals, often wearing masks more to disguise their features to escape arrest than to guard against spread of the conveniently forgotten coronavirus, have vandalized monuments with graffiti, slash marks and blood-hued spray paint, decapitated some statues, and even fastened ropes from many angles and toppled monuments to the ground. In cities where radical politics are most pronounced, the attacks have been more numerous and extreme. Seeing the man memorialized as a symbol of all of the horrors brought to the New World by white Christian men, radicals in San Francisco repeatedly vandalized a statue of Christopher Columbus located at Coit Tower. When flyers surfaced calling for sustained efforts to topple the statue and throw it into the Bay, the City removed it.[8] At about the same time, an enraged horde of radicals swept through Golden Gate Park and pulled down the statues of Junipero Serra, Francis Scott Key, and President Grant.[9] Reflecting the spirit of the times, lawmakers around California removed or made plans to remove other monuments to Columbus, Serra and even John Sutter—a pioneer from Germany prior to the Mexican War who became prominent in California afterward.[10] Confederate soldier statues soon began to fall like dominoes across the South, as did statues all over the country commemorating Captain James Cook, Robert E. Lee, William Henry Seward, Thomas Jefferson, Roger B. Taney, John C. Calhoun, Josephus Daniels, Phillip Schuyler, Teddy Roosevelt, George Washington, the poet Walt Whitman and even Captain Semmes in Mobile—all because of some distinct connection with the exploitation of African Americans or some generalized relationship to the grand Christian-Capitalist conspiracy to oppress everyone who wasn't white, male and Christian.[11]

Emboldened by these successes, a well-organized mob attempted to

---

[8] Kellie Hwang, "These are the California Statues Being Removed Amid Calls for Racial Justice," *San Francisco Chronicle*, June 25, 2020.

[9] Id.

[10] Id.

[11] Erik Ortiz & Kaleigh O' Boyle, "The Next Wave of Statue Removals is Afoot. See Where They're Being Taken Down Across the U.S.," www.nbcnews.com, June 12, 2020.

demolish the famed equestrian statue of Andrew Jackson just outside the White House in Lafayette Park but was dispersed before their efforts advanced very far.[12] More surprising were calls for the removal of a monument celebrating Emancipation featuring Abraham Lincoln and a squatting, ill attired and bewildered looking black man, the desecration in Boston of a memorial to Robert Gould Shaw and the 54th Massachusetts Volunteers, and the vandalizing of a life-size image of Founding Mother Abigail Adams. The critics say the image of Lincoln is overly paternalistic, that of the freed slave overly subservient, and the work as a whole dismissive of the role played by the black man in opposing slavery and securing his own liberation.[13] No one has criticized Shaw, but the rioters obviously despise him despite his commitment to freedom and equality and his role as commander of the Union Army's first black regiment. Lack of integrated ranks and absence of any black officers perhaps is the reason for the attack. More likely, the desecration of the monument proceeds from sheer irrational rage over grievances the rioters themselves have never experienced save in the pages of Howard Zinn's simplistic and deceptive Marxist history of America. God knows why the Adams statue was targeted, though likely it was merely collateral damage, or the work of an unusually ignorant group of vandals.

Such mania directed at mute stones is nothing new. Historically, such incidents proceed from profound religious or ideological impulses and mark moments of transition from one age to the next. The conquest of Canaan entailed the erasure of all evidence of the pagan culture that existed there. The periodic lapses from strict adherence to the command that the Israelites were to have "no other gods before thee" gave way to attempts to cleanse the land of any idols dedicated to Chemosh, Dagon, Moloch and Baal.[14] The transition of the ancient world from pagan to Christian following the great persecutions of the faithful of Christ proceeded relatively peacefully, at least at first. The great monuments of Greece and Rome, dedicated to the deities of many nations, "continued

---

[12] Morgan Winsor, "Protesters Try to Topple Andrew Jackson Statue Near White House," www. abcnews.com, June 23, 2020.

[13] Hannah Natanson, Joe Heim, Michael E. Miller & Peter Jamison, "Protesters Denounces Abraham Lincoln Statue in D.C., Urge Removal of Emancipation Memorial," www.thewashingtonpost.com, June 26, 2020.

[14] Judges 6:25-32; 1 Samuel 7:4; 2 Kings 10:18-25; 2 Kings 11:18; 2 Kings 23:4-5; 2 Chronicles 23:17; 2 Chronicles 29:16; and 2 Chronicles 34:6-7.

to be visited, and they were respected as public monuments by cultivated townsmen, pagan and Christian alike, rather like the beautiful Cathedrals of some Communist states."[15] The fanatics among the faithful eventually had their way, first in the more radical enclaves of the Empire, where they roved the countryside in search of memorials to the gods of old and destroying them wherever found.[16] Deaf to the pleas of the orator Symmachus and his appeal to the power of tradition, the Emperor Gratian bowed to popular prejudice by ordering removal from the Senate chamber of the statue of Nike—"a majestic female standing on a globe," said Gibbon, "with flowing garments, expanded wings, and a crown of laurel in her outstretched hand."[17] The campaign to remove statuary reminders of the earlier age quickened during the reign of Theodosius. Special commissioners were appointed in the capital "to seize or destroy the instruments of idolatry, to abolish the privileges of the priests, and to confiscate the consecrated property for the benefit of the emperor, of the church, or of the army."[18] Great zeal became evident outside the imperial city. "In almost every Province of the Roman world, an army of fanatics, without authority and without discipline, invaded the peaceful inhabitants, and destroyed the idols and other memorials of the pagans."[19] The greatest assault came in Alexandria, where a massive Christian mob led by monks and with the blessing of the Bishop, laid siege to the temple complex dedicated to the god Serapis. The monumental figure of the god himself defied destruction until "an intrepid soldier, animated by zeal, and armed with a weighty battle axe, ascended the ladder…aimed a vigorous stroke against the cheek of Serapis," followed by many others, until "the huge idol was overthrown and broken to pieces," dragged through the streets of Alexandria and set afire in the public amphitheater.[20] One by one the great statues of the ancient world were removed from places of honor, destroyed or otherwise disappeared: the Samian Hera of Lysippus, the Cnidian

---

[15] Peter Brown, *The World of Late Antiquity* (New York, W.W. Norton & Company, 1971), at p. 103.

[16] J.B. Bury, *History of the Later Roman Empire from the Death of Theodosius I to the Death of Justinian*, Volume I (New York: Dover Publications, Inc., 1958), at p. 367.

[17] Edward Gibbon, *The Decline and Fall of the Roman Empire*, Volume II (New York: Modern Library), at p. 49.

[18] Id., at p. 54.

[19] Id., at p. 56.

[20] Id., at pp. 59-60.

Aphrodite of Praxiteles, the Athena of Lindos and, finally, the great golden Athena crafted by Pheidias that once graced the Acropolis.[21]

Nearly every subsequent revolution sported similar scenes. Whatever remaining idols and other statues that survived the Christian rampage in the Eastern and Southern Mediterranean were finished off by the iconoclastic followers of Muhammad. Protestant zealots gleefully ransacked the monasteries and churches of England following the repudiation of the Catholic Church and its Christianized version of idolatry. Revolutionaries in France cast down images of former monarchs, as did the opponents of the Tsars in Russia more than a century later. Those who survived the Communist regimes in Eastern Europe also enjoyed a spree of toppling statues honoring their fallen oppressors. And, now, primarily white college students, college graduates, Starbucks baristas and left-leaning tech geeks with far too much time on their hands, protesting non-existent oppression in the wake of an atrocity against a black man that no one is excusing or justifying, follow suit in their quest to overthrow a society far more free and tolerant, with more real potential for improvement, than most any that has ever existed.

Sympathy must lie with those aggrieved over the residual evidence of Jim Crow in the form of Confederate soldier memorials. Many of these have either come down already or are in the process of removal. Few tears are shed for the fall of the statue of arch traitor Jefferson Davis, or of the idol of the South General Beauregard, or of various celebrated sons of the South who championed the cause of the Confederacy with sword in hand. The statue of racist Democrat Woodrow Wilson's racist Secretary of the Navy, Josephus Daniels, is far too late in coming down. Not only did he call for the firing of a university professor who listed Booker T. Washington second only to Robert E. Lee in the South's Hall of Fame, but he also traveled to Louisiana to study the first Jim Crow laws and made favorable report back to his native North Carolina, which quickly adopted a similar statutory scheme.[22] The case of Philip Schuyler is a bit more perplexing. He was a slaveholder, but he served his country well as a military commander during the Revolution. While acting as a member of the New York State legislature he vocally supported ratification of the Constitution that became so great an engine of liberty

---

[21] Bury, op. cit., at p. 370.
[22] Cash, op. cit., at p. 331; and Ayers, op. cit. at pp. 334-335.

on this Continent. Perhaps it is appropriate for New York to remove it from the capitol grounds, but equally appropriate that the town named after him take custody. As for Chief Justice Taney, though he made many admirable and lasting contributions to our understanding of the Constitution, he justly earned the removal of his statue. The only regret is that it came so long after his execrable *Dred Scott* decision and his various ignoble efforts to thwart the labors of President Lincoln to preserve the Union and end slavery.

Mixed emotions naturally greet efforts to dismantle the many tributes to General Lee. True, he owned slaves and led the Confederacy in defense of slavery, but there are few nobler figures in the annals of human kind. Duty to his State rather than to an institution he repudiated when he manumitted his own slaves impelled him to leave the federal service and take up a commission in the Confederate military. Following the war, his call for loyalty and reconciliation aided the Nation's transition from war to peace. That a God sitting in judgment over a nation awash in the sin of slavery could not have created a more effective instrument of his will than the brilliant mind and indefatigable constitution of Robert E. Lee, one of the most gifted of the great captains of history, gives further pause to any thought to remove the man's various commemorations. His familial ties with George Washington and other of the Founding Fathers render him a particularly tragic figure—a man who would undo what was wrought by the forefathers he venerated—and one we shouldn't forget lest we once again tread the tragic ground of his era, without the edifying counsel of his conflicted life and ambiguous example to divert our path from the germination of an even greater ruin.

It is possible to view even the most offensive statues as humbling monuments to folly, or to a moment in history that turned on many indecipherable factors, and to the results of a fate too mysterious to comprehend. The sad visages of the anonymous Confederates, rifle in hand, looking almost longingly north, instruct as much as offend, remind us of that terrible conflict that left well over 600,000 soldiers dead, and teach us that even in the bitterest time reconciliation is possible. The hearts and minds of white southerners carried a torch for the Old South for more than a hundred years, but no longer. The Democracy is overthrown and the party of Lincoln prevails. Racism exists, but it's much harder to discern, and little of it emanates from official government action thanks to widespread embrace of a Constitution and Civil Rights laws southerners long held at bay. But few make these arguments, or want to. Times change and so do the values of the people. The past will be buried, or relegated to museums. There are some monuments, however—to Washington, Jefferson, Lincoln, Shaw, William Henry Seward, Abigail Adams and the poet Whitman, among others—that no principled or honest case can be made in support of removal. Those who would tear them down obviously think less of the offenses rooted in race than they do of a flawed system they would wholly replace with a Marxist-Leninist scheme that history proves is destined to perpetuate far greater evil than is embodied within their hallucinations about the original, all-corrupting sin that is America.

Though Chairman Mao looked to George Washington as an inspiration, our first President's most radical detractors in this country consider him to be a symbol of everything that is wrong with the nation and its founding: a white slave-owner who waged war to protect his financial interests and used his power and influence to maintain human bondage in the South so that he could continue to benefit from the compelled labor of slaves. This progressive pastiche, however, doesn't withstand scholarly scrutiny. The man was complex and far from the perfect soul depicted by early hagiographers. His voluminous papers clearly document a discomfort with slavery that grew as he aged. The paranoid slaveholder within him initially opposed enlistment of free blacks in the Continental Army. The specter of servile revolts that haunted the southern colonies couldn't be shaken so easily even by his mature and robust mind. New England's desegregated troops and the heroism of black men like Peter Salem at the Battle of Bunker Hill later convinced him to demand that the Continental Congress permit the enlistment of African Americans.[23] A Hessian officer subsequently observed that no regiment among the Americans "is to be seen in which there are not Negros in abundance; and among them there are abled bodied, strong and brave fellows."[24] Ultimately, 5,000 free Blacks served in the Continental forces, contributing to the cause of liberty even though most of those whose forebears originated in Africa wouldn't

---

[23] Ron Chernow, *Washington: A Life* (New York: Penguin Books, 2010), at p. 213.

[24] Matthew T. Mellon, *Early American Views on Negro Slavery* (New York: Mentor Books, 1969), at p. 43.

immediately enjoy the results.[25] But for Washington, the Constitutional Convention might have failed and the Constitution never ratified. Without a Constitution, there could have been no Bill of Rights, no Thirteenth and Fourteenth Amendments, and no Civil Rights Acts of 1866 and 1964.

Late in life, Washington's views on the issue had become quite extreme. In a letter to a friend, he concluded that "nothing but the rooting out of slavery can perpetuate the existence of our Union, by consolidating it in a common bond of principle."[26] His legacy to his slaves upon his death was freedom; for the elderly, perpetual care by his estate. In tribute to and acknowledgment of what was owed to the General, Booker T. Washington and so many others freed through the action of the Union Army and the people of the United States assumed the great man's surname.

Thomas Jefferson's flaws are well known: his vanity, pretension and hypocrisy, his exploitation of his late wife's slave half-sister, and his inability to relent in the many grudges he formed over the course of his long life. He was nevertheless too intelligent a man not to comprehend the evil of an institution on which his own prosperity depended. "Who can endure toil, famine, stripes, imprisonment or death itself in vindication of his own liberty," he asked a friend, "and the next moment...inflict on his fellow men a bondage, one hour of which is fraught with more misery than ages of that which he rose in rebellion to oppose."[27] His initial draft of the Declaration of Independence contained a rousing condemnation of slavery and the slave trade, and his *Notes on the State of Virginia* are quite honest in the assessment of the immorality and evil of the institution. While he could not bring himself to free his slaves even in death, he supported and ultimately signed an act of Congress outlawing the importation of slaves, thus dealing a massive blow to the world-wide market for human flesh. His racist views cannot be denied. His many thousands of pages of writings leave too indelible a trace. His eloquent statement of the natural right of all men to freedom, however, transcends his own limitations, inspired the abolitionists, the former slaves who fought and died in the Civil War, and the Reverend

---

[25] Chernow, op. cit., at p. 213.

[26] Id., at p. 800.

[27] Dumas Malone, *The Sage of Monticello* (Boston: Little, Brown & Company, 1981), at pp. 316-317.

Martin Luther King, Jr. He was not perfect. He does not conform to the values we embrace today. And yet if not for the small steps he made, which were massive in his own time, and his contributions as a thinker and magistrate to the creation of a framework for liberty in the form our constitutional system, our modern consciousness of liberty as the birthright of all Americans might not have come to be. The easy morality and moral judgment of the progressives today, so far removed from the reality of a past they are so comfortable criticizing, really is only possible because of the pioneering path of flawed yet courageous men like Thomas Jefferson.

Demands to remove Lincoln's monuments turn the stomach. The man who saw halting the spread of slavery into new parts of the country as the key to eliminating the institution, who condemned the *Dred Scott* decision as a flagrant contradiction of the Declaration of Independence, and who saved the Union and won liberty for men and women in chains may be one of the few for whom no amount of memorials would be too many. Like Washington and Jefferson he was not perfect, though Sandberg's hagiographic portrait of the man makes it possible to argue otherwise. The statue in Washington, D.C. the radicals find so offensive was actually commissioned by former slaves and paid for with their earnings. When it was unveiled, Frederick Douglas spoke of its importance. The mere fact that a gathering of so many African Americans in so public a place without the "opening upon us all the flood-gates of wrath and violence" was proof enough of the "gratifying and glorious change which has come both to our white fellow-citizens and ourselves" due, in part, to the efforts of the late President.[28] "Let it be told in every part of the Republic," he declaimed, "let men of all parties and opinions hear it; let those who despise us, not less than those who respect us, know that now and here, in the spirit of liberty, loyalty, and gratitude, let it be known everywhere, and by everybody who takes an interest in human progress and in the amelioration of the condition of mankind, that, in the presence and with the approval of the members of the American House of Representatives, reflecting the general

[28] Frederick Douglas, "Oration in Memory of Abraham Lincoln, delivered at the unveiling of the Freedmen's Monument in Memory of Abraham Lincoln, in Lincoln Park, Washington, D.C., April 14, 1876," *Inaugural Ceremonies of the Freedmen's Memorial Monument to Abraham Lincoln, Washington City, April 14, 1876* (St. Louis, 1876).

sentiment of the country; that in the presence of that august body, the American Senate, representing the highest intelligence and the calmest judgment of the country; in the presence of the Supreme Court and Chief-Justice of the United States, to whose decisions we all patriotically bow; in the presence and under the steady eye of the honored and trusted President of the United States, with the members of his wise and patriotic Cabinet, we, the colored people, newly emancipated and rejoicing in our blood-bought freedom, near the close of the first century in the life of this Republic, have now and here unveiled, set apart, and dedicated a monument of enduring granite and bronze, in every line, feature, and figure of which the men of this generation may read, and those of after coming generations may read, something of the exalted character and great works of Abraham Lincoln, the first martyr President of the United States."[29] Though he understood Lincoln to be primarily a white man's president, "ready and willing at any time during the first years of his administration to deny, postpone, and sacrifice the rights of humanity in the colored people to promote the welfare of the white people of this country," and even to return escaped slaves to bondage pursuant to Article IV and the Fugitive Slave Act of 1850, he nonetheless praised him to the heavens for having "delivered us from a bondage, according to Jefferson, one hour of which was worse than ages of the oppression your fathers rose in rebellion to oppose."[30] After so much hesitation in the cause of freedom, after placing the salvation of the Union ahead of universal liberty for so long, "under his wise and beneficent rule, and by measures approved and vigorously pressed by him, we saw that the hand-writing of ages, in the form of prejudice and proscription, was rapidly fading away from the face of our whole country; under his rule, and in due time, about as soon after all as the country could tolerate the strange spectacle, we saw our brave sons and brothers laying off the rags of bondage, and being clothed all over in the blue uniforms of the soldiers of the United States; under his rule we saw two hundred thousand of our dark and dusky people responding to the call of Abraham Lincoln, and with muskets on their shoulders, and eagles on their buttons, timing their high footsteps to liberty and union under the nation's flag; under his rule we saw the independence of the black republic of Haiti, the special object of slave-

[29] Id.
[30] Id.

holding aversion and horror, fully recognized, and her minister, a colored gentleman, duly received here in the city of Washington; under his rule we saw the internal slave-trade, which so long disgraced the nation, abolished, and slavery abolished in the District of Columbia; under his rule we saw for the first time the law enforced against the foreign slave trade, and the first slave-trader hanged like any other pirate or murderer; under his rule, assisted by the greatest captain of our age, and his inspiration, we saw the Confederate States, based upon the idea that our race must be slaves, and slaves forever, battered to pieces and scattered to the four winds; under his rule, and in the fullness of time, we saw Abraham Lincoln, after giving the slave-holders three months' grace in which to save their hateful slave system, penning the immortal paper, which, though special in its language, was general in its principles and effect, making slavery forever impossible in the United States."[31] Like I said, talk of removing his statue turns the stomach. What an insult to the ancestors of the black men and women who sacrificed their earnings to pay for it, and what monumental disrespect to Douglas, one of the greatest citizens our Republic has ever seen -- called by Justice Harlan the Elder a remarkable man with no equal as a public speaker -- whose words cannot be read by an honest man or woman, even after the passage of a century and half since uttered, without the reader experiencing a wave of the profoundest emotion.[32]

As nausea-inducing as the calls for removal of the Lincoln monument are, far worse are the acts of vandalism against the monument dedicated to the memory of Robert Gould Shaw and the 54th Volunteer Regiment. Shaw was a young idealist, from a family of abolitionists, who fought at Antietam beside Oliver Wendell Holmes and then was given command of the first black infantry regiment of the War.[33] Frederick Douglas entrusted two of his sons to Gould's command, aided in recruitment and then saw them off at the harbor, praying for their success and hopeful that their example might encourage the Congress to open the ranks of fighting men to those of his beleaguered race. Of the many heroes of that Regiment, none perhaps

---

31 Id.

32 See Tinsley E. Yarbrough, *Judicial Enigma: The First Justice Harlan* (New York: Oxford University Press, 1995), at pp. 80 and 84.

33 See Peter Burchard, *One Gallant Rush: Robert Gould Shaw and his Brave Black Regiment* (New York: St. Martin's Press, 1965).

was as audacious as Sergeant William Harvey Carney of New Bedford, who carried the Stars and Stripes to the enemy's works, and then, with wounds in his chest, arms and leg, carried it back to his own lines, with the flag never touching the ground.[34] Watching the men of the 54th fight from the parapet of Fort Wagner, Confederate Lieutenant Iredel Jones commented that the "negroes fought gallantly, and were headed by as brave a colonel as ever lived."[35] The fighting abilities of the 54th set aside any doubts that Black men could aid the cause of the Union, and did indeed lead to the enlistment of the many thousands referred to by Douglas in his speech commemorating Lincoln.

That anyone wants to remove William Henry Seward's statue seems odd. The man was an abolitionist, one of only two in the Senate in the late 1840s. He won the eternal enmity of the South when he referred to the issue of slavery as "an irrepressible conflict." And he nearly died from a knife wound delivered by Booth's co-conspirator on the same night Lincoln was shot. Apparently, it isn't BLM activists who want him gone. Instead, its two Democrat politicians who see the statue of the first Republican Secretary of State as "a symbol of white, patriarchal authority and the disenfranchisement of Alaska Natives."[36] That reason alone is proof of the idiocy of leftist agitators on the issue of alleged offensiveness of national monuments. Native Alaskans were not enfranchised before the annexation of Alaska occurred, and they are not disenfranchised today. Being natural born citizens of the United States, they enjoy all the rights of citizenship, including the right to vote.

The vandalizing of the statue of Abigail Adams is equally mystifying. The woman utterly despised slavery. Writing to her husband while he was attending the Continental Congress, she thought the revolution "a most iniquitous scheme," so long as Americans continued "daily robbing and plundering from those who have as good a right to freedom as we have."[37] She wondered whether "the agonies of pestilence and war could be God's punishment for the sin of slavery," and mocked the "true republicanism that drive the slaves half fed, and

---

[34] Id., at p. 141.

[35] Id., at p. 143.

[36] "Petition Seeks Removal of Statue of Alaska Purchase Official," *U.S. News and World Report*, June 23, 2020.

[37] David McCullough, *John Adams* (New York: Simon & Schuster, 2001), at p. 104.

destitute of clothing...whilst an owner walks about idle."[38] Her influence on her husband is well known; her impact in shaping the mind and attitudes of her brilliant son, John Quincy, is unquestionable. It was the latter who defeated the Gag Rule that prohibited the receipt of abolitionist petitions in Congress, and who convinced the pro-slavery Supreme Court to find in favor of the *Amistad* litigants. And it was her grandson, Charles Francis, who rescued my ancestor after his term of captivity at the hands of the slave power and delivered him back to the United States.

Attacks on Whitman's statue might be the most curious of all. Without providing any detail, the petition for removal of the statue from the Camden, New Jersey campus of Rutgers University says he "stood for white supremacy and racism against Black and indigenous Americans."[39] In truth, Whitman's only actual sin might be his reluctance to call for abolition as early as the 1840s. He corrected this defect by later quitting the Democrat Party over its enthusiasm for slavery. His advocacy for the Wilmot Proviso and a halt to slavery's expansion across the continent led to his termination as editor of the *Brooklyn Eagle*.[40] Later he denounced the return to captivity by U.S. Marshalls of the fugitive slave Anthony Burns and endorsed the abolitionist John C. Fremont for President.[41] When war came he joined the Sanitary Commission in New York, but was later transferred to the Nation's capital. In his three years of service, he saved untold numbers of men, and eased the final suffering of many others, wounded in the great battles of the war that saw the end of the hated institution and the amending of our great Constitution to ensure that slavery never again blighted American soil. That America's eternal poet laureate, whose non-conforming sexual identity makes him a hero of the LGBT community, could be a villain in the eyes of post-modern radicals is actually quite offensive.

In February of 1993, in Mobile, Alabama, I stood beneath a pedestal atop which rested the larger-than-life bronze figure of a Confederate soldier of old, largely forgotten by the denizens of the town in the

---

[38] Id., at pp. 134 and 553.

[39] "Remove Racist Walt Whitman Statue from Rutgers-Camden Campus," www.change.org.

[40] See Gay Wilson Allen, *The Solitary Singer: A Critical Biography of Walt Whitman* (New York: Grove Press, Inc., 1965).

[41] Id., at pp. 146 and 197.

precinct of which I was present for only a few short hours during a trip across the southland. The figure stood looking slightly off to the side, as if posing for the artist. It was a sight I had navigated my way through Mardi Gras celebrants to gaze upon, not in tribute to the man depicted, but to the man he once held in chains: my great, great grandfather. Their histories remained entwined even after they parted ways. After enlisting in the U.S. Navy in New York, Antonio Pereira was assigned to the blockade fleet under the command of David Farragut. At one point he was aboard the picket boat *Dolphin* off Mobile, the home town of the dreaded Semmes. When Farragut gave the command to storm the Bay, Antone was there and became one of the victors of that engagement. He later returned north to Portsmouth, New Hampshire, where he was assigned to the Navy Yard. There, some months before, shipwrights and engineers designed a ship to be especially tasked with the hunting and destruction of Semmes and his vessel. Off the port city of Cherbourg, France, on June 19, 1864, the *U.S.S. Kearsarge* found its quarry. A well-wrought skirt of iron installed in port in Pereira's homeland of the Azores protected the warship from the *Alabama's* deadly canon. As the iron shot of the enemy bounced harmlessly into the sea, the *Kearsarge* opened fired with an impressive arsenal of guns manned by a crew of flawless Union artillerymen. The engagement was over within minutes. Semmes abandoned his sinking ship and was rescued by admiring Frenchmen who had gathered to watch the exchange. After his return home, he served briefly in the Army, but surrendered to General Sherman. Only the clemency of the victorious federal government saved him from long imprisonment and possible execution for treason and various offenses in violation of the laws of war.[42] The English ultimately agreed to compensate his victims. In his memoirs, he lambasted Pereira's captain for his formal complaints over the treatment of the *Virginia's* crew. He'd treated captain and crew well, he said, and had even let Pereira have the freedom of the deck to prepare what he described as quite sumptuous meals.[43] Though the loss of his ship and the war were far more grievous, there was, it seems, some amount of resentment remaining over the loss of so good a cook.

It was odd gazing upon the great statue. Semmes was a criminal,

---

[42] Warren E. Spencer, *Raphael Semmes: The Philosophical Mariner* (Tuscaloosa: University of Alabama Press, 1997), at pp. 185-194.

[43] Semmes, op. cit., at p. 447.

who waged war against civilians. He ought to have been imprisoned for many years, and yet, here, in Alabama, a beautifully crafted statue commemorated him. I wasn't offended. I was grateful for the tangible evidence of his life and career. Knowing the fuller story, I was hardly impressed by the apparent grandeur of his presentation. He was a figure of history, beloved once by the white people of his native Mobile, but now a symbol not of the glorious deeds of true born southern white men, but of the victory of a cause Semmes made clear in his memoirs he despised. Seeing his statue in the middle of a traffic circle, it was as if he was condemned for eternity to look across the land and observe everywhere the loss of what in life he held so dear: slavery, black servitude, and an overt, virulent white supremacy. I am equally unoffended by most other statues, though I understand why others are, and concede the removal of many of them on account of the view now current that certain historical figures are best not commemorated so publicly, if only to prevent anyone from getting the wrong idea about where we as a people stand on issues of great importance like race and the history of slavery. The North won the war. Slavery was defeated. The Amendments and the Civil Rights Acts and the actions of countless citizens transformed the nation. Those that say it hasn't changed at all, or has only gotten worse, are either liars or imbeciles, and they insult the memory and legacy of patriots like my ancestor who knew chains himself in the grip of a notorious Confederate pirate, and so many others—Frederick Douglas, Booker T. Washington, the brave men of the 54th—white, black, brown, Native American and Jew, who fought to end inequality and the system that made it possible. Semmes' statue is gone now, as are many others. May the future bring a wiser perspective, a respect for the winners and losers of history, and a sense of maturity when facing what we might reflexively respond to as an insult.

Who Is Running the Asylum?

FOR months, immigration activists awaited a decision. The case of a Sri Lankan national who contended that current rules governing the granting of asylum had in essence deprived him of due process and the benefit of habeas corpus had become the latest vehicle for leveling the legal wall erected by the Trump Administration to obstruct the illegal entry into the United States by peoples from the world over. In March of 2019, a three-judge panel of the Ninth Circuit Court of Appeals sitting in San Francisco held that expedited removal procedures relied on by immigration authorities unlawfully suspended the Great Writ. As the decision for the first time permitted judges to question the factual findings of immigration officials, it provided a green light for litigation in the district courts and beyond, and the widening of the front against which open-border advocates might slow the entire immigration enforcement system to a near halt. At the time, Lee Gelernt of the ACLU said that the panel's decision reaffirmed "the right to habeas corpus applies to citizens and noncitizens, regardless of how long they have been in the U.S."[1]

The Supreme Court ultimately accepted the case for review, in part to resolve a split among circuits. Many, of course, hoped that the majority might take the invitation to expand the application of the Suspension Clause from the plight of those accused of being unlawful combatants sitting indefinitely in Guantanamo Bay to migrants held in U.S. custody after gaining unlawful entry to the United States. If those alleged to be enemies of the nation are entitled to an opportunity to challenge the legality of their detention, why not civilian migrants whose only offense was not having the nation's permission when crossing the border? Hopes for such an outcome ended on June 25, when seven members of the Court held that persons who are unable to persuade immigration authorities of their eligibility to receive asylum lack any right to challenge their expedited removal from the United States in federal court.[2] The nation's political authorities, said the Court, possessed plenary power in the area of foreign affairs and immigration, hence the judiciary lacked jurisdiction to second guess factual findings reached by authorized agents of the federal government. Gelernt, among others, lamented that the decision failed "to live up to the Constitution's bedrock principle that individuals deprived of their liberty have their day in court."[3] Others fashionably ascribed the decision to the systemic racism of American law and American society. The plenary power

---

[1] Maura Dolan, "Immigrants Rejected for Asylum May Appeal Removal Orders, 9th Circuit Rules," www.latimes.com, March 7, 2019.

[2] *Department of Homeland Security, et al. v. Vijayakumar Thuraissigiam* (2020) 140 S.Ct. 1959.

[3] Richard Wolf, "Supreme Court Allows Removal of Asylum-Seekers," www.usatoday.com, June 25, 2020.

doctrine itself, they cried, was rooted in the anti-Asian racism of the late Nineteenth-Century and judicial precedent "dripping in bigotry."[4] Critics predicted that the Court's decision was destined to encourage and ultimately permit the government to expeditiously exclude and deport both recent arrivals and those whose tenure in the nation was more longstanding. Professor Kari Hong of Boston College feared that Trump's ICE would soon stray north from the border and begin "stopping anyone at any time on any suspicion that they have committed an immigration violation and deport them."[5]

Those unhappy with the Court's performance in the matter tend to be of the sort who elevate the rights of those outside the country, or those with no legal authority to be within it, above the rights of those lawfully entitled to be here, either by birth, naturalization or lawful immigration. They demand that those already here make room for those who aren't, with little or no consideration for any of the procedures created over time to provide for the orderly admission of aliens. There is only so much room on a bus, or in a tenement, and only so much strain the roads, bridges, water system and the environment as a whole can tolerate without more elaborate planning and a more gradual accommodation of a growing human population. The immigration system presently in place is designed to provide just this kind of order. The human tide that has in the past several decades swept over our borders and inundated the country violates not only the orderly process the system provides, but the ability of the nation to properly accommodate newcomers. Admittedly, asylees are a special case. They represent not merely persons desirous of settling in the United States in order to take advantage of the opportunities available on our soil; they are also victims of oppression, persecution and sundry other mistreatments in their countries of origin. Their presence at our doorstep is an act of desperation, and their admission through the gates a demonstration of our humanity.

The act of seeking asylum from a nation not one's own is hardly a novelty. It is as old as recorded history. The world's first murderer

---

[4] Aaron Reichlin-Melnick, "Congress Needs to Fix Its Bigoted Immigration Law: The Supreme Court Won't Protect Asylum-seekers so it's up to Congress to Fix its Past Mistakes," www.slate.com, July 1, 2020.

[5] Nicole Narea, "The Supreme Court Just Allowed Trump's Expansion of Deportations to go Unchecked," www.vox.com, June 25, 2020.

sought asylum with God himself and received a mark notifying the world of the divine protection he subsequently enjoyed. David fled Saul's wrath to the kingdom of Achish, and remained there until he could claim Saul's crown. The rebel Jeroboam found refuge with a friendly Pharaoh in Egypt, followed centuries later by Christ Himself and his family. In Classical Greece, frequent were the flights of political leaders in the City States: Cimon to the Chersonese, Themisticles to Argos, and Alcibiades to Sparta. Rome repeatedly granted asylum to foreign princes, and nearly as often backed their return to their native countries as vassal monarchs. Her leaders pursued their fallen enemy Hannibal from one asylum state to another until they drove the man to suicide. In later times, Charles II received asylum from his cousin, the King of France, as did his brother a lifetime later following his flight from his rebellious subjects.

Modern advocates of a broad policy of asylum insist that it is a fundamental human right. Most of these persons tend to be critical, if not dismissive, of the ancient source of such rights, and ascribe its origin instead to some coda of human conduct of their own devising, consistent with their political objective that persons unlike the majority in this country be admitted in the hopes of transforming both the demographics and the politics of the same. That much criticized and dismissed source is natural law, with influences from the Judeo-Christian, Reformation and Enlightenment traditions. The Israelites claimed that God himself ordained that they receive the alien with kindness and hospitality, and provide places of refuge for those subject to persecution for alleged crimes. It was assumed among them "that there were areas which stood under the special protection of divine authority and upon which human beings must therefore not infringe."[6] The practice of the ancient Romans was likely related to religious sentiments as well. Those fleeing persecution, including abused slaves, found refuge in Roman temples—a practice continued by Christians during Late Antiquity and the Middle Ages. The sense that asylum was both a God-given right to be asserted by worthy individuals and a duty owed by the state began to emerge during the early Enlightenment, in the wake of the terrible wars of religion waged primarily in France, Germany and the Netherlands. Religious principles continued to influence in this regard. Men had

---

[6] Lucas Kowalczyk & Mila Versteeg, "The Political Economy of the Constitutional Right to Asylum," 102 Cornell L. Rev. 1219 (2017), at p. 1233.

rights, including a right to be free from state oppression. Those rights were the product of a Creator God, who vested in men a sociability that naturally encouraged, if not guaranteed, a striving for justice, fairness and mercy. The Calvinist Grotius recast a long tradition of scholastic and humanist natural law thinking into a system that he contended was valid whether God existed or not, if only to establish a religious neutrality that would permit Catholic and Protestant alike to appreciate it without prejudice.[7] Seeing the grant of asylum to refugees from a rival nation as a potential cause of armed strife, he thought asylum ought not be granted except "for the benefit of those who suffer from undeserved enmity, not those who have done something that is injurious to human society or to other men."[8] Asylum, thus, was "a defense to extradition, through which fugitives are given immunity against the wrongful exercise of authority by their state."[9] Asylum was to be available to all innocent people "who are beaten down by the hard and oppressive strokes of ill fortune."[10] More religious and liberal was the opinion of Samuel Pufendorf, "who admitted the law of nature to be derived from God."[11] In sync with the ancient Israelites, he considered asylum to be a function of the duty of humanity to "admit strangers, as well as...kindly provide travelers with shelter and hospitality."[12] The duty was not absolute; it had to be tempered by concern for what the asylee might offer the country in return for safe harbor—his industry and skills, and tendency to "disturb neither our religious faith nor our institutions."[13]

These thinkers, in addition to Christian Wolff and Emerick de Vattel, each influenced the men who created the United States and its institutions toward the end of the Eighteenth Century. Though the Framers vested the Congress with power to enact a uniform rule of naturalization, and presumably to establish rules whereby aliens might enter the country, no statutory scheme governing immigration and

---

[7] See Richard Tuck, *Natural Rights Theories: Their Origin and Development* (Cambridge: Cambridge University Press, 1979), at p. 76.

[8] Matthew E. Price, "Politics or Humanitarianism? Recovering the Political Roots of Asylum," 19 Geo. Immigr. L.J. 277 (2004), at p. 293.

[9] Id.

[10] Id., at pp. 293-294.

[11] Arthur Nussbaum, *A Concise History of the Law of Nations*, Revised Edition (New York: The MacMillan Company, 1962), at p. 148.

[12] Price, op. cit., at p. 296.

[13] Id., at p. 297.

asylum appeared during the early Republic. The borders were, in essence, wide open, save for any discretion exercised by the States in identifying and excluding those who might pose a danger or a burden to the people already living within their bounds. As virtually anyone could enter the country, a formal request for asylum was hardly necessary. Only with the proffering of demands by other nations for extradition of their wayward nationals might a dilemma arise. It was in such situations that Thomas Jefferson suggested a wide grant of asylum, even for fugitives and wrongdoers, but only when "a gap existed between free countries and despotic regimes in terms of the crimes for which one could be punished, the due process required to convict and the kinds of punishment exacted."[14] Those who took refuge in the United States after taking up arms against their own countries when those nations were in need of reform he thought were suitable candidates for asylum. "The unsuccessful strugglers against tyranny have been the chief martyrs of treason laws in all countries," he said.[15] "We should not wish, then, to give up to the executioner the patriot who fails and flees to us."[16]

The optimism of the natural law thinkers and others sporting a broad view of asylum at some point has always hit the wall of reality. Whenever a gift is made, those who observe the giving consider how they might become the next recipient. The many temples offering asylum in ancient Rome became so "crowded by the most abandoned slaves," debtors screening themselves from their creditors and criminals fleeing justice that any ability to enforce the laws became constrained "under a mask of piety."[17] In time, the Emperor and the Senate required proof of a temple's right to grant asylum under the authority of the state, leading to a great reduction in the number of asylia. Similar increases in abuse of asylum available in Christian churches occurred during the Middle Ages. The English Parliament eliminated the privilege of church asylum in 1625, while monarchs elsewhere "began to consider the individual's reasons for requesting asylum rather than simply guaranteeing protection to anyone who had managed to enter a

---

[14] Id., at p. 303.
[15] Id., at p. 306.
[16] Id., at p. 307.
[17] Id., at p. 285.

sanctuary."[18] Concern that asylum was too easily established to discourage fraudulent claims, the Congress during the 1990s drafted and President Clinton signed an amendment to the Immigration and Naturalization Act making it easier to weed "out patently meritless claims and expeditiously [remove] the aliens making such claims from the country," thereby eliminating "an unacceptable burden on our immigration system."[19] The primary mechanism whereby these goals were to be attained were the requirement that the asylum seeker demonstrate a credible fear of persecution should he be returned to his homeland and an absence of any judicial review of the government's decision to grant or reject an asylee's request.

The efforts of the federal government over the past several years to limit the flow of illegal immigrants across the nation's borders have met with enough success to encourage the ordinary migrant to claim the privilege of asylum based on some threat of persecution in their home country. The army of immigration attorneys paid by non-government organizations have likely encouraged this trend, as it by-passes (at least temporarily) the expedited removal procedures that would ordinarily apply. In 2018 alone, there were 99,035 asylum claims, each of which had to be individually evaluated.[20] There can be little doubt that not all persons claiming asylum have been forthright in the claim. Vijaykumar Thuraissigiam's own account is suggestive of a narrative that suffered amendment for the purpose of avoiding a hasty expulsion from the United States. Initially claiming that he was abducted and beaten for no apparent reason by a group of men he didn't know, his recollection of a racial and political motivation for the attack surfaced in the wake of being informed that his asylum claim had been rejected due to lack of a credible fear of persecution if he was forcibly returned to Sri Lanka.

Mr. Thuraissigiam's attorneys creatively alleged that the procedure for determining the credible fear of persecution itself was too limited to satisfy due process, and that the lack of any ability to appeal a negative finding by the government constituted a suspension of the Writ of Habeas Corpus in violation of the Suspension Clause set forth in Article I, Section 9. Not all artistry, however, is either beautiful or true. The

---

[18] Id., at p. 292.

[19] *Department of Homeland Security, et al. v. Vijayakumar Thuraissigiam*, supra, at p. 6.

[20] Id., at 8.

claimant himself made it no further than 25 yards into the country. He was essentially at the gates, hence hardly a fit subject for the kind of protection afforded by the Constitution to those dwelling within the nation's borders. Someone in the process of entering hasn't really entered, and the claims of those whose entry was illegal are more dubious still. That a man must travel half way across the world to find asylum stretches credulity even more, and suggests a deceit that cannot but be a contempt of the very due process one claims to have been denied.

That the Great Writ applies, even some of the more illegal immigrant-friendly justices could not agree. Speaking for his brethren, Justice Alito noted that Habeas Corpus "has traditionally been a means to secure release from unlawful detention, but respondent invokes the Writ to achieve an entirely different end, namely, to obtain additional administrative review of his asylum claim and ultimately to obtain authorization to stay in this country."[21] Such a use of the Writ, he noted, would have been "unrecognizable" to the Framers.[22] Even if the Writ were available, and Mr. Thuraissigiam were able to use it to gain release from custody within the United States, it wouldn't solve his dilemma; for he would remain subject to removal due to the fact that his non-compliance with the nation's immigration laws disqualify him from staying. So long as he remains an undocumented alien, he is eligible for expedited removal.[23] Thuraissigiam, of course, would have the Court set him free in accordance with a de novo finding of fact that he possessed the requisite fear of persecution, but courts have never exercised this kind of authority in immigration matters, and even if they did, they would likely apply the highly deferential substantial evidence test applicable throughout administrative law.

The Court was unimpressed with the precedent Mr. Thuraissigiam's lawyers cited. The celebrated anti-slavery decision of Lord Mansfield in the case of *Somerset v. Stewart*, it said, was irrelevant. While sitting in custody after fleeing his so-called "master," Somerset sought a Writ of Habeas Corpus on the grounds that though a slave, his presence in England where slavery did not exist rendered him a free man by operation of law. His request was granted, but his right to remain on

---

[21] Id., at p. 2.
[22] Id.
[23] Id., at p. 14.

English soil was not a function of the Writ itself, but of the fact that he was now free, not a slave, and entitled to come and go as he saw fit under the laws of England. Certain Nineteenth Century cases were inapposite as well due to the fact that immigrants who won release from custodians seeking their deportation were not subject to any restriction on immigration due to the absence of any statutes mandating it. The immigrants in question were entitled to release and continued residence in the United States because they were, in fact, lawfully present. Finally, the cases cited from the era following the enactment of the Naturalization Act of 1891 in which habeas review was available obtained it not on account of any appeal to the inherent right flowing from the Suspension Clause, but from a particular statute enacted by Congress that provided immigrants with that particular remedy. In all of American history, and every time until the remedy sought by Mr. Thuraissigiam was filed, no court "ever held that the Suspension Clause imposed any limit on the authority of Congress to restrict the issuance of Writs of Habeas Corpus in immigration matters."[24] Even the case of *Boumediene v. Bush* was unhelpful, despite heavy reliance on it by Mr. Thuraissigiam's attorneys. Boumediene, after all, was never in the United States and was not seeking release within or entry into the country. Instead, he was seeking to be released abroad through a challenge of the government's designation of him as an enemy combatant who could be detained indefinitely. Mr. Thuraissigiam only had detention in common with Boumediene. Unlike the latter, he was actually resisting being returned to his country of origin.

American law in the area of asylum is actually consistent both with historic norms and current practice. The availability of asylum to worthy refugees who establish a credible fear of persecution if returned to their home countries is actually relatively uniform around the world, based on a United Nation's Convention from 1951. The United States has been fairly generous in allowing people to cross its borders. Indeed, said Eleanor Acer and Tara Magner, "there is no question that the United States is a global leader in welcoming refugees and offering them the opportunity to build new lives, free from the persecution that forced

[24] Id., at p. 27.

them to flee from their home nations."[25] This remains true even during the time of Trump. Immigrants from the world over continue to enter the country as permanent residents, destined most likely for citizenship, with not a thought by anyone of barring their entry. Such entrants are good candidates for citizenship in that they respect the laws and procedures governing their admission and are likely to show similar respect for all other laws operative within the nation's jurisdiction. Their first act on our soil, in fact, is to enter in conformity with the law, not in violation of it, and as lawful entrants, they possess no incentive to live underground, to work without a permit, to obtain lodging and vehicles through fraud and subterfuge, to avoid the payment of taxes, and even to vote in our elections and effect the rights of Americans against whom their votes are cast. Among them are righteous seekers of asylum, able to present a credible picture of the fear they harbor that impelled their flight from home. Their place must ever be preserved by close scrutiny of all claims of persecution, and rigorous testing of the same. Mercy is a feature that our law should demonstrate, and it does. But it cannot yield to an indiscriminate benevolence that requires little or nothing from the claimant, or lead to a cheapening of the value of entry, to the discredit of our nation and disregard of the true victims of oppression. The loose standard to qualify for entry to the country simply encourages fraud, and ready access to the federal courts invites abusive litigation the country shouldn't be saddled with.

Within days of the issuance of the Court's decision, a district judge in Washington State issued a new injunction, preventing application of a Trump era rule that asylum be granted to no one who failed to seek asylum in the first country they entered following their flight from their homeland. The Judge—a Trump appointee—explained that the Administration implemented the rule despite "failing to show it was in the public interest to stealthily implement the change and bypass the Administrative Procedure Act."[26] The government's rule, however, was in conformity with international law and disregarded the notice and public comment requirements of the APA in order to avoid a triggering

---

[25] Eleanor Acer & Tara Magner, "Restoring America's Commitment to Refugees and Humanitarian Protection," 27 Geo. Immigr. L.J. 445 (2013), at p. 484.

[26] Spencer S. Hsu, "Federal Judge Strikes Down Trump Asylum Rule Targeting Central Americans," www.thewashingtonpost.com, July 1, 2020.

of "a surge of aliens who would have strong incentives to seek to cross the border" while the effective date of the rule was pending.[27] This reason, and the fact that immigration falls within the plenary authority of the political branches of government, were sufficient in the view of the government to exempt the rule change from the scope of the APA.[28] The Washington District Court decision was followed by another, containing the same general reasoning. The effect of the decisions isn't particularly pronounced given the general moratorium on immigration during the coronavirus scare. But they are indicative of the enthusiasm of a certain element of the population for removing any inhibition to entry into the country by anyone who can make it to our borders. It is a sign of the chaos that is presently being sowed everywhere in our country with the goal of making it ungovernable, if only to justify a radical recasting of all of our ways of doing business and living our lives. Why the judges are inclined to cater to this strategy of disruption may be a result of personal preference, ideological pleasure or fear of being denounced by an angry mob who may soon be as apt to tear actual people down as they presently are their statuesque effigies. There is a belief, as well, among some of the judicial class, that their power extends to all issues, including purely political ones, and that they are far more competent to run the asylum from afar than the political authorities selected by the people to perform this very task. Who knows how the Supreme Court will ultimately rule on this issue; but until it does, more chaos on the border and elsewhere is sure to follow.

Reparations "R" Us

THE narrative is well established: a President whose worldly life experience belies a hopeless intellectual myopia, whose frequent verbal ejaculations are limited to vulgarities when not incomprehensible and incoherent, and whose concept of courtship is to "grab'em by the pussies!" Though unrelenting in the telling, the narrative failed to overcome either the many objections to the global consolidation and

[27] Decision of Judge Timothy J. Kelley, *Capital Area Immigrants Rights Coalition, et al. v. Donald J. Trump et al.*, Case 1:19-cv-02117-TJK, at p. 8.
[28] Id.

economic stagnation of the Obama years, or the widespread distaste for an alternative whose lust for power and greed for material gain was matched in intensity only by her husband's legendary concupiscence. Its usefulness as a stumbling block in the fall of 2020 might have endured had it not been for the emergence of an opponent whose many vices and shortcomings match, if not exceed, those of the current incumbent. Watching the obviously addled Democrat navigate his way through the campaign actually inspires sympathy for a man whose career is riddled with notorious moments of bullying and the most outrageous instances of deceitful self-promotion. When the President touts his wealth and success in business, he's arguably telling the truth; Joe Biden's claim to have been a triple major in college who graduated at the top of his class and to have been arrested while challenging South African Apartheid are just plain sad. In debate after debate, he took hit after unguarded hit from each of his far lesser known, less experienced opponents. Elizabeth Warren scoffed at his attempts to take credit for Obama era successes. Kamala Harris all but called him a racist. Julian Castro pointed out his rapidly deteriorating memory. And Mayor Pete simply said it's time to turn the page. When the dust of the nation's first primary settled, the communist Bernie Sanders prevailed, followed closely by the engaging Mayor, with the former Vice President coming in a distant fifth.

Bizarrely, the candidacy of the apparently washed up former Vice President found renewed life as most Democrats realized every alternative candidate advocated policies that promised historic defeat come November. The strange coronation that followed, with each opponent abandoning vibrant campaigns in favor of a man they'd humiliated on the debate stage, presaged a series of gaffs that have already entered into the annals of politics—rambling talk of leg hair that turned golden in the sun while being twisted by small black children who bounced on his lap, the tale of a near slug fest with a bad dude named Corn Pop, calling out a union laborer as a "horse's ass," challenging a hefty man he called "fat" to a push-up contest, asking voters to support him in his run for the U.S. Senate, thinking he was in Vermont when he was actually in New Hampshire, suggesting anyone not happy with him ought to vote for the "other Biden," announcing that the cure for the coronavirus must be worse than the disease, proclaiming he favored truth over facts and ending a failed attempt to recite a well-known passage from the *Declaration of Independence* with the words "you know, the thing." So hapless was the man that his elderly wife had to physically fend off a crazed protester who suddenly charged the podium during a campaign event. The coronavirus probably saved his candidacy from utter disintegration by justifying his retreat to his Wilmington basement. But even there, in occasional appearances on hyper-friendly news programs, his mental deterioration was all too clear. Once, while sharing the screen with CNN medical expert Sanjay Gupta, he stumbled so painfully that the doctor, a neurosurgeon by profession, visibly winced. And then there is the groping. The President bragged in private in his typical exaggerated fashion about reciprocating the desire of women hopeful of snagging a billionaire. Biden's whip-fast, overly familiar and very public grabbing of women and girls he'd never met before, breast cupping, hair sniffing and refusal to let go even as those in his clutches struggled to avoid his obviously loathsome touch became the subject of numerous photo montages zipping across social media. Only Secret Service protection likely prevented him from either arrest or being punched in the chops by an irate husband or father.

In the search for issues to overcome his obvious shortcomings as a candidate, Joe Biden has focused on cracking traditional progressive chestnuts: expanded access to education and health care, easier methods of voting, immigration reform and "environmental justice." He's also embraced an ambitious racial agenda that now includes consideration for the first time in his career of reparations to African Americans for the injuries arising from slavery and historic discrimination in the United States. Once firmly of the opinion that he wasn't "responsible for the sins of my father and grandfather," and was unwilling "to pay for what happened 300 years ago," Biden now evinces a qualified support for what surely would amount to the largest transfer of wealth in the history of the nation.[1] Early in July, he joined his former primary opponent Bernie Sanders in proposing a "commission to examine the impact of slavery and Jim Crow with the end goal of recommending 'remedies,' or reparations."[2] The commission they envisioned would constitute a "building block to begin to redress the harms committed against African

---

[1] Jason Lemon, "Will Joe Biden Change His Stance on Reparations," www.newsweek.com, June 2, 2020.

[2] Hannah Bleau, "Biden-Sanders Unity Plan Includes Commission to Study and 'Recommend' Reparations," www.brietbart.com, July 9, 2020.

Americans."[3] While supportive of the announcement, a number of far-left members of the Congress called for more extreme measures: "reparations for mass criminalization—including the War on Drugs, the criminalization of prostitution, and police violence; border violence; and the systemic violation of the U.S. Government's treaty obligations to tribal nations."[4] It seems that when talk turns to reparations, just about everyone discovers a grievance to be remedied.

Though touted for several decades as the ultimate demulcent to what the progressive left decries as the systemic racism of American civilization, reparations have come into vogue in the wake of the death of George Floyd and the riots that supposedly expressed pent up rage by African Americans over their long-time mistreatment at the hands of white America. Though a general consensus on the left is emerging, some disagreement remains as to what reparations are and how they ought to be paid. According to Eric Posner and Adrian Vermeule, "they typically refer to schemes that (1) provide payment (in cash or in kind) to a large group of claimants, (2) on the basis of wrongs that were substantively permissible under the prevailing law when committed, (3) in which current law bars a compulsory remedy for the past wrong (by virtue of sovereign immunity, statutes of limitations, or similar rules), and (4) in which the payment is justified on backward-looking grounds of corrective justice, rather than forward-looking grounds such as the deterrence of future wrongdoing."[5] Advocates of reparations say they are owed to African Americans as a whole for "the stolen labor and lives of the millions enslaved until 1865, the stolen labor and lives of those legally segregated from the early 1880s to the late 1960s, and the continuing theft of labor and lives of those who face much racial discrimination today."[6] That white Americans and the nation as a whole are obligated to pay them is due to "many millions of white Americans [who] have been involved, individually and collectively, in the exploitation and oppression of African Americans...for nearly four

---

[3] Id.

[4] Id.

[5] Eric A. Posner & Adrian Vermeule, "Reparations for Slavery and Other Historical Injustices," 103 Colum. L. Rev. 689 (2003), at p. 691.

[6] Joe R. Feagin, "Documenting the Costs of Slavery, Segregation, and Contemporary Racism: Why Reparations Are in Order for African Americans," 20 Harv. Blackletter J. 49 (2004), at pp. 49-50.

centuries."[7] From the foundation of white settlement in North America, says sociologist Joe Feagin, "most whites, as individuals and families, have benefited handsomely from anti-black oppression and the transmission of ill-gotten wealth and privilege from one generation to the next."[8] The longer life expectancies and higher standard of living of white Americans, he asserts, "are significantly rooted in centuries of exploitation and impoverishment of African Americans and other Americans of color."[9] Every "new generation of Americans has inherited this persisting framework of racial inequality and privilege. From at least the early 1700s to the mid-1800s, much of the surplus capital and wealth of the country's white families and communities came directly, or by means of economic multiplier effects, from the African slave trade and the slave plantations and related enterprises."[10] So much wealth was generated by exploitation of black labor, he says, that "it seems unlikely that there would have been a successful British and United States textile industry, which depended heavily on slave-produced cotton." Restrictions on earning a living and investing in land and other enterprise, first by slavery and then by Jim Crow, created a "long-term white/black gap in income" that persists to the present day.[11]

The call for reparations for the harms caused by slavery are hardly new. As early as 1830, David Walker published an address "to the Colored Citizens of the World, but in Particular, and Very Expressly, to those of the United States of America," discussing the need for emancipation and reparations.[12] In 1854, black abolitionists "called for 'a national indemnity' as 'redress of our grievances for the unparalleled wrongs...which we suffered at the hands of this American people.'"[13] Reparations in a broad sense were actually paid during and immediately after the Civil War. Responding to the exigency of tens of thousands of former slaves clamoring for assistance in the final months of the War, General Sherman ordered the distribution of 40-acre parcels along the

---

[7] Id., at p. 50.

[8] Id.

[9] Id.

[10] Id., at p. 52.

[11] Id., at p. 56.

[12] Adjoa A. Aiyetoro and Adrienne D. Davis, "Historic and Modern Social Movements for Reparations: The Nation Coalition of Blacks for Reparations in America and its Antecedents," 16 Tex. Wesleyan L. Rev. 687 (2010), at p. 693.

[13] Id.

Atlantic Coast.[14] Elsewhere, former slaves had been permitted to occupy and farm abandoned land throughout the occupied south.[15] While much of the land distributed by the military was eventually returned to the original owners, other efforts to assist former slaves transition from slavery to freedom followed. Thaddeus Stevens endorsed a plan to transfer 400 million acres of land from former slaveholders to former slaves, as did Senator Charles Sumner.[16] More substantial relief came in the form of the Freedmen's Bureau, charged with feeding and clothing former slaves, coordinating freedman education with private organizations, distributing federal lands, and providing financial assistance in the form of loans.

The limited scope of relief provided by the Freedman's Bureau—due in part to the end of Reconstruction and the emergence of Jim Crow—gave rise to continued agitation for compensation to former slaves for the hardship of bondage and the continuing challenges of daily life in a far from color-blind nation. Abolitionist and proto-feminist Sojourner Truth "circulated a petition urging the federal government to redistribute land to freed Blacks as redress for centuries of coerced uncompensated labor and as a means to independence and freedom from slavery.[17] Walter Vaughn made some waves in 1890 when he unsuccessfully lobbied Congress to pass a pension bill to benefit former slaves, as did Callie House and the Rev. Isaiah Dickerson later in the decade.[18] A lawsuit initiated by Dickerson in 1915 more aggressively sought dedication of the proceeds of a federal cotton tax to the needs of former slaves whose labor had actually harvested the crop.[19] More recently, Queen Mother Audley Moore presented the Kennedy Administration with a petition containing a million signatures seeking payment "for what the white man owes us…for the damages committed against our families, our homes, and our people."[20] The petition asserted that without reparations, "our people can never be on equal terms with the white sons of our former slave-masters who continue to reap the abundant benefits of the wealth created by our fore-parents through

---

[14] Id., at pp. 694-695.
[15] Id., at p. 695.
[16] Feagin, op. cit., at p. 67.
[17] Aiyetoro & Davis, op.cit., at p. 693.
[18] Id., at pp. 698-699.
[19] Id., at p. 703.
[20] Id., at p. 707.

their centuries of unrequited labor."[21] The effort was revived in the 1980s, with the formation of the National Coalition of Blacks for Reparations in America and the publicity campaign of historians and activists such as Ta-Nehisi Coates.[22]

Advocates for reparations cite to this historic tradition, as well as to other compensation schemes evident in the historical record. The first occurred in the 1690s, when the government of Massachusetts compensated families (including my own) for the terror inflicted upon them by false witnesses and prejudiced magistrates during the Salem witchcraft hysteria.[23] A formal program of reparations was initiated by Congress in 1946 "in order to redress a wide range of claims pressed by Indian tribes, including violations of treaties for which a judicial remedy was denied, and the loss of lands under treaties signed under duress."[24] A more narrowly tailored program was created to indemnify Alaskan native peoples for the loss of their land beginning upon their entry into the Union.[25] After years of debate and long-acknowledged deferred justice, Congress set aside over a billion dollars to compensate the survivors of the Roosevelt Administration's internment program victimizing Japanese Americans during the Second World War.[26] Within a decade, the State of Florida created a similar program to benefit the survivors and heirs of the victims of the infamous Rosewood Massacre.[27] A similar effort stalled in Oklahoma to compensate the victims of the horrendous Tulsa race riot of 1921. Various other reparation schemes are evident from around the world: the payment of France to Germany for harms caused by the Franco-Prussian War; of Germany to France and other nations following World War I; of Germany to the Soviet Union after World War II; of Germany to Israel in recognition of the Holocaust; and the many compensation procedures established throughout eastern Europe to provide relief for the victims of communism during the Cold

---

[21] Id., at p. 698.

[22] See Ta-Nehisi Coates, "The Case for Reparations," www.thealtantic.com, June 2014.

[23] Alfred L. Brophy, "Reconsidering Reparations," 81 Ind. L. J. 811 (2006), at p. 817.

[24] Posner & Vermeule, op. cit., at p. 695.

[25] Brophy, op. cit., at p. 819.

[26] Feagin, op. cit., at p. 65.

[27] Id., at p. 72.

War.[28]

These programs, however, are quite distinguishable from what the current advocates of reparations envision. Rather than compensation paid directly to the victims of harm targeting them personally, they insist that payment be made for all the victims of slavery and its aftermath from the beginning of American civilization four centuries ago onward. The broad sweep of such a scheme prompts obvious objections. In our system of justice, only harms legally cognizable are compensable. When the first slave became ensnared in the slavecatcher's net, no law save the law of nature and of the Creator prohibited it. Indeed, the laws of the colonies and later of many States, not to mention the legal systems of the entire globe, endorsed and protected slavery. Consequently, the duty of the slaveholder to the slave for harm arising from slavery, for compensation for labor and the loss of consortium, mobility and conscience did not exist, hence his conduct couldn't form the basis of a legally actionable claim. The state itself tended to be immune to claims against it for any role in the promotion of slavery. The harms, too, extend into the distant past. No living man or woman can claim to have suffered under the task master's whip, the castrator's knife or the executioner's rope. Our system of justice requires standing for the assertion of claims: an injury caused by another in violation of a known legal standard and redressable by a court. When a person dies, their personal injury dies with them. The estate may be able to recover property losses, but only if the proper representative steps forward within a limited period of time. Statutes of limitation, rooted in the concept that stale claims make for uncertain justice, designate discrete windows of opportunity to bring claims depending on the type of injury asserted. No statute of limitation extends claims for a century or more, and such would likely violate due process if they did. Aside from due process concerns, the Constitution also cautions against certain types of legal actions, whether remedial or not. Race based legislation, including reparations paid on the basis of inclusion in a racial group, would be subject to the most searching scrutiny, requiring a compelling purpose and an extremely narrow focus so as to avoid more discrimination against non-beneficiaries than necessary. Awards of money by the government, or any other benefit, simply on the basis of race, might be justifiable pursuant to a compelling

[28] Posner & Vermeule, op. cit., at pp. 694-695.

purpose, but few could predict a court would actually uphold race-based awards payable out of the public fisc to persons whose connection with the harm to be remedied is separated by a gap of a century and a half. The more vague contention that African Americans are owed compensation for more recent examples of racial oppression face similar obstacles. Harm, again, must be proven and an untangling of various alternative causes from the alleged racist source must be undertaken before any award can be determined. That certainly is the burden to be carried by those alleging violation of civil rights laws, long on the books as a remedy for the harms caused by those who disdain fairness and civility simply on account of the superficial quality of skin color. Strict scrutiny requires no less a burden be met when contemplating legislative grants to compensate for injustice past and present.

The problems facing any legislative effort to compensate the victims of slavery and racial injustice are evident in two significant law cases seeking damages for such things. In *Cato v. United States,* a group of African Americans brought suit against the federal government for recovery of one hundred million dollars due to "forced, ancestral indoctrination into a foreign society; kidnapping of ancestors from Africa; forced labor; breakup of families; removal of traditional values; deprivations of freedom; and imposition of oppression, intimidation, miseducation and lack of information about various aspects of their indigenous character."[29] Though the court agreed that "discrimination and bigotry of any type is intolerable, and the enslavement of Africans by this county inexcusable," it was "unable to identify any legally cognizable basis upon which plaintiff's claims may proceed against the United States."[30] The primary obstacle to the action was the doctrine of sovereign immunity and the fact that any waiver of the same was limited to claims arising after the enactment of the Federal Tort Claims Act in 1946. Beyond that mere threshold issue, the court noted the existence of a severe statute of limitations problem. The damages sought were for harms arising hundreds of years before, hence unrecoverable even if the most generous statute of limitations on the books applied. An attempt to overcome the statute problem by analogizing the claimants to native tribes who sued for ancient injuries fell short due to the corporate status of the tribes and the existence of a continuous and unbroken relationship

---

[29] *Cato et al. v. United States* (1995) 70 F.3d 1103, 1106.
[30] Id., at 1105.

between the parties as trustee and beneficiary. An alternative approach in the form of an assertion that the statute of limitations didn't apply because the injuries were ongoing was similarly rejected due to lack of a single justiciable claim. The plaintiffs attempted to overcome the lack of justiciability by insisting that the Thirteenth Amendment itself provided an implied right of action for redress when the government failed to ensure elimination of the vestiges of slavery. Even if such a cause existed, the assertion by the plaintiffs of a "generalized, class-based grievance," rather than a specific injury each of them sustained arising from a breach of a specific legal duty, traceable to a particular statute and perpetrated by a particular agent or agents of the federal government doomed the theory to defeat. The closest the plaintiffs came to identifying a breach of duty was failure by the Congress to enact remedial legislation—a contention the Court rejected on account of the purely discretionary nature of legislative power.

A similar outcome occurred in the *African American Slave Descendants Litigation,* where numerous parties brought actions against private defendants implicated either directly or through a corporate predecessor in the slave trade or the institution of slavery. Aside from the fatal statute of limitations problem, Judge Richard Posner noted the fact that the injury predated both the Thirteenth Amendment and the federal law by which the plaintiffs pursued a remedy. State law-based claims similarly faced defects despite being traceable to statutes enacted prior to the Civil War. "It is," said Judge Posner, "highly unlikely that antebellum laws in northern states were intended to confer financial benefits on twenty-first century descendants of slaves."[31] Even were this not the case, the injury alleged wasn't one the court thought was easily remediable. The larger difficulty consisted of the impossibility "by methods of litigation to connect the defendants' alleged misconduct with the financial and emotional harm that the plaintiffs claim to have suffered as a result of that conduct."[32] An alternative theory—"that had the defendants refused to violate their own States' laws by doing business with slaveholders, there would have been less slavery because the refusal would have been tantamount to subjecting the slave-owners to a partial boycott"—required a causal chain too long and too weak in its links "for a court to be able to find that the defendants' conduct harmed the

---

[31] *In re African-American Slave Descendants Litigation* (2006) 471 F.3d 754, 758.
[32] Id., at 759.

plaintiffs at all, let alone in an amount that could be estimated without the wildest speculation."[33] Even if it could be established that compliance with the aforementioned laws would have curtailed slavery and resulted in the freedom of a particular plaintiff's remote ancestor, Judge Posner wondered how "the wages that the ancestor would have earned as a free laborer [could] be shown to have influenced the wealth of this remote descendant." Though economists are able to study aggregate effects in intergenerational mobility, "there is no way to determine that a given black American today is worse off by a specific, calculable sum of money (or monetized emotional harm) as a result of the conduct of one or more of the defendants."[34] Finally, to the extent that the plaintiffs were seeking redress for harms suffered by third parties, their status as alleged descendants hardly authorized them to act in a representative capacity.

Those seeking reparations don't really care much for logical and legal obstacles to obtaining them. Their argument, say reparation attorneys Aiyetoro and Davis, "rejects legal institutions as illegitimate or hegemonic," or as mere epiphenomena of the "greater structural forces of capitalism and racial oppression," and more harmful than helpful in obtaining ultimate justice.[35] Justice, as we know it, is a product of a long tradition dating back to the ancient near east, Classical Greece and the centuries of Scholastic and Enlightenment thought that proceeded the drafting of our Constitution and laws. At its root lies the concept of a Creator and Judge, measuring all men and women against a standard of right and wrong immutable and unchangeable for all time. Our ability to comprehend this standard might be impaired by our own imperfections, but it remains a standard our civilization in the aggregate has aimed to embrace. That theory of justice, rejected by those who enslaved other human beings, who in the words of John Marshall waged a veritable war against the law of nature, is similarly rejected by those

[33] Id.

[34] Id., at 760.

[35] Aiyetoro & Davis, op. cit., at p. 722.

who would so belatedly seek a remedy for its shortcomings.[36] The justice of the reparations movement is based on one factor alone, and that is race, and it depends for its life not on persuasion, but on access to legislative and executive power, or on judges willing to disregard all legal precedent and principles of law to achieve a desired end. Might makes right is the adage that best describes this principle of justice and it isn't just at all. It was the basis of slavery itself and the racist regimes that succeeded it in the aftermath of emancipation. It reflects not timeless principles applicable to all mankind, but a selfish desire to achieve benefits at the expense of others. It is merely a variation on the theory of Charles Darwin, embraced by progressives over a century ago in its social form, and useful in justifying and protecting the success of society's winners, regardless of the strategies employed to prevail.

More unfortunate still, the insistence on race as the criterion for justice suffers from the same sin as those its advocates condemn. It singles out the factor of race as determinative of virtue and disgrace, of what is reproachable and what is worthy of reward. It contains echoes of the words of those advocates of racism and slavery past who saw the black man as the son of Ham, cursed by Noah to be a servant to this brother for all time, or of Cain, marked by God in some indelible way as a sign to all that he would be forever tainted and deserving of condemnation.[37] Where once blackness "was loaded with intense meaning," conveying a sense of being "deeply stained with dirt; soiled, dirty, foul....having dark or deadly purposes, malignant; pertaining to or involving death, deadly; baneful, disastrous, sinister...foul, iniquitous, atrocious, horrible, wicked,'" now whiteness carries those connotations, symbolizing "baseness and evil, a sign of danger and repulsion."[38] The sins of whiteness, like the sinfulness associated with blackness long ago, is seen as "not confined to the skin, but pervad[ing],

---

36 See *In Re the Antelope* (1825) 23 U.S. 66, at 120-121, as well as the comments of John C. Calhoun and Alexander Stephens expressly rejecting natural law in their justifications of slavery, as quoted in and Eric L. McKitrick, *Slavery Defended: The View of the Old South* (Englewood Cliffs: Prentice-Hall, 1963), at p. 11, and George M. Frederickson, *White Supremacy: A Comparative Study in American & South African History* (Oxford: Oxford University Press, 1981), at pp. 161-162.

37 See Winthrop Jordan, *White Over Black: American Attitudes Toward the Negro – 1550-1812* (Baltimore: Penguin Books, 1969), at p. 17.

38 Id., at p. 7.

in a great or less degree, the whole inward man down to the bones themselves."[39] As leading theorists of slavery saw subordination as the place of the black man, so the leading theorists of reparations would forever subordinate the white man to the consequences of his deficiencies real and imagined, and require him to pay tribute for all time to the putative descendants of those members of a race so cruelly victimized.[40] It's a vile thing, regardless of which race embraces such a theory, and fundamentally unjust for the simple fact that only some white men and women were involved in the subordination of African Americans, and that many more fought to eradicate it and ultimately supported the removal of de jure limitations on the freedom of African Americans to pursue the happiness that God ordained for them. In the fight to end the evil of slavery and racism, many white men laid down their lives, and yet their sacrifice, with consequences cascading through the generations, are rudely disregarded. Those who seek justice would be more honest, and more fruitful, to look for it against the identifiable living person or persons who committed some harm, and then attempt to prove the extent of the injury and obtain a remedy tailored to make the victim whole. Anything but this is a travesty of justice and a violation of the only system of remediation that comes closest in this imperfect world to approximating it.

A Promise Made is a Debt Finally Paid

ON July 9, 2020, the news services of the nation, in print and on line, breathlessly reported a decision of the Supreme Court in a case brought by a Native American man held in prison for twenty years following conviction by the State of Oklahoma for the crime of child-rape. The man's somewhat belated contention was that the State's power to prosecute him for a crime that allegedly occurred on the Creek Indian reservation was preempted by federal jurisdiction. In reporting the criminal defendant's victory, *Reuters* declared that the Supreme Court had in the process "recognized about half of Oklahoma as Native

[39] McKitrick, op. cit., at p. 143.
[40] See Frederickson, op. cit., at p. 162.

American reservation land."[1] CNBC described the ruling as rendering "a huge swath of Oklahoma" Indian Country.[2] Describing the outcome as "a stunning blow to Oklahoma's state government," the *Huffington Post* also reported that much of Eastern Oklahoma was now "located on an Indian reservation."[3] Yet another commentator noted that while the implications were yet to be sorted out, what was clear was that "nearly 2 million people went to sleep Wednesday evening in the State of Oklahoma," but when they woke up, "they did so on an Indian reservation, even though their physical locations had not changed."[4]

Dissenting in the matter, Chief Justice John Roberts noted more precisely that the reservation the majority had "rediscovered" encompassed "the entire eastern half of the State—19 million acres that are home to 1.8 million people, only 10%-15% of whom are Indians."[5] The repercussions, he warned, would be profound. "The decision today creates significant uncertainty for the State's continuing authority over any area that touches Indian affairs, ranging from zoning and taxation to family and environmental law."[6] Lawyers for the oil industry, operating extensively in eastern Oklahoma, quickly expressed concern over the ruling's impact on existing oil franchises. New taxes imposed by native tribes, additional regulations enacted by the Bureau of Indian Affairs and other federal agencies, and rights of way for existing pipelines were now suddenly at issue.[7] There were other critics as well. Republican Senator Ted Cruz mocked the decision by wondering if the Court would give Manhattan away next.[8] Conservative commentator Mike Cernovich sarcastically called Neil Gorsuch—the opinion's author—a "cool conservative" for writing "an opinion freeing a

---

1 Lawrence Hurley, "U.S. Supreme Court Deems Half of Oklahoma a Native American Reservation," www.reuters.com, July 9, 2020.

2 Tucker Higgins & Dan Mangan, "Supreme Court Says Eastern Half of Oklahoma is Native American Land," www.cnbc.com, July 9, 2020.

3 Brooklyn Wayland & Nina Golgowski, "Supreme Court Rules Eastern Oklahoma Land is an Indian Reservation," www.huffpost.com, July 9, 2020.

4 Zack Smith, "Supreme Court Decides Half of Oklahoma has been an Indian Reservation for Past 113 Years," www.dailysignal.com, July 10, 2020.

5 *McGirt v. Oklahoma*, Dissenting Opinion of Roberts, C.J., at p. 1.

6 Id., at pp. 1-2.

7 Dino Grandoni, "Supreme Court Decision Declaring Half of Oklahoma Indian Land Raises Big Questions for Oil Drillers," *The Washington Post*, July 20, 2020.

8 Graham Dockery, "With Half the State Now Deemed a Native Reservation, is a Crime Wave Coming to Oklahoma?" www.rt.com, July 10, 2020.

pedophile who raped a four-year-old" and giving "half of Oklahoma away."[9] Oklahoma officials expressed fear that the decision "opens the door for 155 murderers, 113 rapists and more than 200 child abusers to challenge their sentences."[10] The first of the predicted flood of liberated convicts left state prison a free man only hours later: a gentleman hailing from the Creek Tribe, convicted of pulling his girlfriend's husband from his car, slashing his throat, cutting off his genitals and leaving him on the side of the road to die.

Native leaders and supporters of the decision celebrated the outcome as a long-awaited vindication of the long-abused rights of Indian tribes. The triumphant Defendant's attorney, Ian Gershengorn, declared that "the Supreme Court reaffirmed today that when the United States makes promises, the courts will keep those promises."[11] "Congress," he said, "persuaded the Creek Nation to walk the Trail of Tears with promises of a reservation—and the Court today correctly recognized that this reservation endures."[12] The lawyer for the Creek Tribe, Riyaz Anji, called the decision a "ringing endorsement that the 'rule of law' should prevail over the 'rule of the strong,' and that promises made to Tribes cannot be diminished by claims of disruption or convenience, or by narratives grounded in a course of illegal action over time."[13] A commentator on NPR spoke of "an emotional reaction to seeing the Supreme Court say...what tribes and tribal advocates have been saying for a long time, which is that these promises that were made in these treaties had meaning," and referred to the outcome as "a profound win" for Native Americans that "will give them greater leverage with States on environmental issues like protecting land and water resources."[14] Others were less expansive in their predictions. Oklahoma officials foresaw cooperation between the State and native tribes in reaching an agreement on shared jurisdiction over a variety of matters "that will preserve sovereign interests and rights to self-government while affirming jurisdictional understandings, procedures,

[9] Id.

[10] Id.

[11] Higgins & Mangan, op. cit.

[12] Id.

[13] Jordan S. Rubin, "Supreme Court Tribal Treaty Decision Praised as Game Changer," https://news.bloomberglaw.com, July 9, 2020.

[14] "Supreme Court Ruling Has Being Implications for Native Sovereignty," www.npr.org, July 10, 2020.

laws and regulations that support public safety, our economy and private property rights."[15] Even tribal officials were saying that the jurisdictional problems identified by the Chief Justice were "exaggerated," and only held water to the extent that "both executive branch and state officials actively sought to undermine Congress's determination that the [Creek] Nation's government and territory would endure."[16]

There is no question that the States and federal government long conspired to thwart the rights of Native Americans, including the Creek or Muskogee people of Oklahoma. "There is not among these three hundred bands of Indians one which has not suffered cruelly at the hands either of the Government or of white settlers," said Helen Hunt Jackson nearly a century and a half ago.[17] It really made no difference, she wrote, "where one opens the record of the history of the Indians; every page and every year has its dark stain. The story of one tribe is the story of all, varied only by differences of time and place; but neither time nor place makes any difference in the main facts."[18] For the Creeks, the story was different only in that it began more or less with the promise of a better outcome. The first treaty between the Tribe and the United States memorialized a loss of sovereignty over some of the lands historically controlled by their confederacy, but there was contemplation by Congress, too, that many tribes might eventually "be combined and would live as equal members of the federal union."[19] President Washington's view that the native peoples were equal to the white man in all but civilization fueled a policy of encouraging tribes like the Creeks "to adopt a national organization for police purposes" and "to introduce ploughs, to learn cotton-spinning, and raise crops."[20] As far back as 1800, the so-called Civilized Tribes of the South-East "had begun the manufacture of cotton cloth, and in 1820 there was scarcely a family in

---

[15] Hurley, op. cit.

[16] Higgins & Mangan, op. cit.

[17] Helen Hunt Jackson, *A Century of Dishonor: A Sketch of the United States Government's Dealings with Some of the Indian Tribes* (New York: Indian Head Books, 1993), at p. 337.

[18] Id.

[19] Id., at 263; and Daniel J. Boorstin, *The Americans: The National Experience* (New York: Vintage Books, 1965), at p. 261.

[20] Henry Adams, *History of the United States of America During the Administration of James Madison* (New York: Library of America), at p. 771.

that part of the nation living east of the Mississippi but that understood the use of the card and spinning wheel. Every family had its farm under cultivation."[21] Politically, these tribes began to resemble neighboring Alabama, with the organization of districts, complete "with a council-house, a judge, and a marshal," a national legislature and governing council, schools and printing presses.[22] And at the forefront of it all was the church. "Missions of several sects were established in their country, and a large number of them had professed Christianity, and were living exemplary lives."[23] There was simply "no instance," observed Ms. Jackson, "in all of history of a race of people passing in so short a space of time from the barbarous stage to the agricultural and civilized."[24]

This more or less laudable federal policy eventually changed. Relations were never entirely perfect between the Creeks and other Tribes and the United States. Far more concerning, though, were the ambitions of the States of Mississippi, Alabama, and Georgia, each of which harbored designs on native territory. Until the 1820s, the federal government had actually provided a buffer between the natives and State governments that sought to exert sovereignty over lands nominally within their territorial bounds. Three events contributed to the change: the ratification by the Cherokee of a national constitution, their declaration of a nation-state within the State of Georgia, and the rise of Andrew Jackson to the Presidency. Georgia acted immediately to declare the Cherokee's act of sovereignty illegal, while Jackson, once he took the oath of office, advised the Cherokee and other tribes in the region to submit to State law or leave.[25] Though the constitutional relationship of the natives to State governments wasn't clear at the time, Jackson was of the mind that any purely internal matter was subject to State control, hence the States were within their rights to regulate the native peoples in all matters save commercial relations.[26] He also saw the ability of the southern States to prosper, including through the expansion of plantation slavery, perpetually stymied by the presence of the self-

---

[21] Jackson, op cit., at p. 270.

[22] Id.

[23] Id., at p. 271

[24] Id.

[25] Jon Meacham, *American Lion: Andrew Jackson in the White House* (New York: Random House, 2008), at p. 91.

[26] Ethan Davis, "An Administrative Trail of Tears: Indian Removal," 50 Am. J. Legal Hist. 49 (2010), at 56.

governing native peoples. In exchange for their departure, he offered land in the west, where "your white brothers will not trouble you…and you can live upon it, you and all your children, as long as the grass grows or the water runs, in peace and plenty. It will be yours forever."[27]

It has been said of Andrew Jackson that he was "a man who probably inflicted more pain, suffering, loss, and death upon Indian peoples than any American of the nineteenth century."[28] His high-handed manner in effecting the removal of the Creeks and other tribes from the southeastern portion of the United States certainly doesn't mitigate or modify this judgment. It was he who advocated hardest for a Removal Act, and used his tremendous influence with his party in the Congress to see it enacted. It didn't mandate removal; instead it provided congressional authorization for the President to negotiate treaties with the Creeks and other peoples to vacate their lands and move west. Every single treaty entered into, however, resulted from the same basic tactics: threats to allow the States to run roughshod over Indian rights, outright bribes to influential native leaders, and promises of aid in removing to lands further west reserved for their permanent occupation. The Creeks were the only people who resisted the effort. The tribe never agreed to a corporate transfer. Instead, individuals were allowed to make their choice, and those who remained behind would be deeded portions of the Creek homeland, to occupy as citizens of the States of Alabama and Georgia. The States' enactment of laws stripping natives of civil liberties all but guaranteed the allotments wouldn't be respected, that Indians would be persecuted and rendered no better than slaves. Consequently, most of the Creeks ended up departing for the west and enduring what has justly been described as a trail of tears.

The trail wasn't tearful so much because of an intention to inflict harm on the migrants as they traveled. It was instead the result of poor planning for such a nearly unprecedented transhumance. Nothing like it had occurred in the history of North America. The closet approximation was the evacuation of East Florida and New York City by the Loyalists and their settlement in the West Indies and the Maritime Provinces in modern day Canada. The Loyalists had the advantage of

---

[27] Meacham, op. cit., at p. 92.

[28] Richard White, "How Andrew Jackson Saved the Cherokees: Robert V. Remini, Andrew Jackson and his Indian Wars," 5 Green Bag 2d 443 (2002), at pp. 443-444.

evacuating by sea and of going to places where the British had already settled. The great disadvantage facing the Creeks and other tribes was the fact that the land over which they would travel and to which they journeyed was a waste howling wilderness, covered in swamps, dense forests, and debris-filled and nearly unnavigable streams swarming with hostile insects. Bad timing caused a collision between the migrants and "terrible snowstorms, freezing temperatures, and cholera epidemics" that created a level of "misery that no amount of human regulation could prevent."[29] The actual administration of the migration by federal authorities, though well-intended, proved to be "haphazard, inexperienced, assembled on an ad hoc basis, and insufficiently instructed. At every level, confusion reigned supreme."[30] And when the migrants finally reached their destination, the promises that had induced their migration proved soft in the interpretation by the government and irrelevant to white settlers who eventually formed a state government nearly as unsympathetic to native rights as the governments of Georgia and Alabama.

The natives, of course, are not simply victims of history. Their fate was not the well-known one suffered by the virtuous yet weak throughout time. The Cherokee, for instance, were invaders themselves of the region from which they were expelled. Their language indicates an Iroquoisan origin; their traditions speak of a migration south from the Great Lakes, perhaps in the Fifteenth Century, whereupon they pushed the neighboring Creeks, Choctaws and Chickasaws aside and settled into a balance of power punctuated on a regular basis by raid and counter-raid. The French appeared in the north not long after the Cherokee settlement in the South East, and what they discovered of Iroquois culture was terrifying even to blood soaked veterans of the European wars of religion that wracked the western hemisphere during the preceding century. They found the region already awash in conflict.[31] A 1642 Iroquois attack on an Algonquin village upstream from Montreal was typical. Attacking at night with war clubs and war whoops, Iroquois warriors bound their "prisoners hand and foot, rekindled the fire, slung the kettles, cut the bodies of the slain to pieces, and boiled and devoured

[29] Davis, op. cit., at pp. 99-100.

[30] Id., at p. 84.

[31] See Alan Taylor, *American Colonies: The Settling of North America* (New York: Penguin Books, 2001), at pp. 102-105.

them before the eyes of the wretched survivors."[32] They seized infants from their enslaved mothers, "tied them to wooden spits, placed them to die slowly before a fire, and feasted on them before the eyes of the agonized mothers, whose shrieks, supplications, and frantic efforts to break the cords that bound them were met with mockery and laughter."[33] Other captives the captors verbally tormented by calling them "dead already" and "bound for the land of souls," soon to be followed by "all the rest of your nation."[34] At the captors' home village, the entire populace joyously met the captive train, "singing at the top of their throats," and nearly all partaking in tortures "designed to cause all possible suffering without touching life" in the form of "blows with sticks and cudgels, gashing their limbs with knives, cutting off their fingers with clam-shells, scorching them with firebrands, and other indescribable torments."[35] The final celebration occurred on a scaffold, where women were forced to torture and kill their husbands, and all captives in the end met their fate horribly. One rather stoic man, who taunted his tormentors by saying that were they in his place they would "screech like babies," so enraged them that they swarmed the man with knives and firebrands, "tore out his heart and devoured it; then hacked him in pieces, and made their feast of triumph on his mangled limbs."[36] Survivors of such raids were typically enslaved and forcibly assimilated into the Iroquois nation. Such reports might appear dubious in the eyes of those convinced of the deceit and greater crime of the white man, but they are confirmed by various sources, as well as archeology.[37]

Though not so bloodthirsty as their northern kin, and quite admirable in many ways, the Cherokee were hardly a peaceful and peace-loving people. Even the great admiration of Helen Hunt Jackson and her sympathy for their travails at the hands of white Americans could not cloud her sight to the atrocities they were known to commit.[38] Competing for influence in the Appalachian Mountains with the white settlers of North and South Carolina, the Cherokee joined the British in

---

32 Francis Parkman, *The Jesuits in North America* (Boston: Little, Brown, and Company, 1899), at p. 342.

33 Id., at 343.

34 Id., at 342.

35 Id., at 344.

36 Id., at 345.

37 See Taylor, op. cit., at p. 103.

38 Jackson, op. cit., at p. 261.

opposition to the American Revolution, as did the Creeks.[39] They were not adverse to the tactical and strategic advice of British soldiers, who "had no compunction about inciting the Indians to massacres."[40] Rather than exterminate these enemies who had every incentive to continue to conspire with the British, French and Spanish, General Washington and his peers made peace, and as noted, contemplated elevation of the native to equal status within the new American union.

A significant portion of the Creeks, however, didn't desire peace, peaceful coexistence, or inclusion within the United States. As Britain revealed hostile designs on land and sea, murmur of a continent-wide alliance of native peoples, affiliated with the English, spread across the frontier. Shawnee chieftain Tecumseh (who was part-Creek himself) and his shaman brother preached benevolence to American officials, but violence toward Americans when addressing fellow natives. Among their listeners were delegates from the Creek faction known as the Red Sticks. Enthused by Tecumseh's rhetoric, they attacked a white settlement far from their own tribal territory, murdered two children and took the rest of the survivors captive in order to serve as slaves.[41] Not long afterward, the Red Sticks laid siege to a federal military base where hundreds of civilians had taken refuge. "Once blood was let, the Red Sticks' fever increased, man-to-man combat began, fires were set to the buildings, women cried out, children screamed, and in the sea of emotion both whites and mixed-bloods were killed, and more than five hundred people died."[42] The bodies of the dead, said historian John Ehle, "were scalped and in other ways mutilated, left for dogs and buzzards, exposed to rot in the Alabama sun."[43]

The massacre at Fort Mims was the true beginning of Andrew Jackson's commitment to Indian Removal. As the leading military figure in the State of Tennessee, and subject to the command of Congress and the President, Jackson quickly led a force of 2,500 men down the Mississippi, and then marched to present-day Huntsville. Several other forces converged on Creek territory, but all but Jackson's were deterred by Creek resistance and logistical obstacles. In time, Jackson tracked the

---

[39] Id., at p. 262.

[40] Id.

[41] Adams, op. cit., at p. 777.

[42] John Ehle, *Trail of Tears: The Rise and Fall of the Cherokee Nation* (New York: Anchor Books, 1988), at p. 105.

[43] Id., at p. 105

main Red Stick body to a fortress on the Tallapoosa River known as Horseshoe Bend.[44] With the aid of six hundred friendly Indians from the Creek and Cherokee tribes, Jackson's lieutenant John Coffee led an assault that proved decisive. Rather than slaughter the women and children as had the Red Sticks, Jackson took over 500 non-combatants prisoner, and even lamented that "two or three women and children were killed by accident."[45] And yet, rather than destroy the Creeks or drive them out, the United States merely reduced the size of their territory and continued to encourage their progress in the ways of white civilization. The same was true when the Creeks broke faith with the United States and joined the Confederacy in defense of slavery and disunion. Rather than consider the treaty void at the end of the war, the United States "restated its commitment that the remaining land would 'be forever set apart as a home for said Creek Nation.'"[46]

Nor is it true than in attacking the rights of the native peoples and their possession of their lands, all whites and all Americans partook. Many today who look to Christianity as a source of hegemonic thinking by Americans of European descent might be surprised to learn that it was Christian missionaries who were at the forefront of the opposition. One leading missionary, Jeremiah Evarts, "penned a pamphlet condemning removal that was the most widely read political work since Thomas Paine's *Common Sense*."[47] A leading publication documenting missionary work among the native peoples even attempted to rally support for the natives by declaring that "now is the time when every Christian, every philanthropist and every person in the United States ought to be exerting themselves to save a persecuted and defenseless people from ruin.'"[48] When Andrew Jackson's allies proposed the Removal Bill, opposition was led by an evangelical Christian member of the Senate, Theodore Frelinghuysen, who called the Bill "a stain upon our national character."[49] He was joined by others, including Alamo defender Davy Crockett and a host of others who would become

[44] Adams, op. cit., at p. 797.

[45] Id.

[46] *McGirt v. Oklahoma*, at p. 5.

[47] Gerard N. Magliacocca, "The Cherokee Removal and the Fourteenth Amendment," 53 Duke L. Rev. 875 (2003), at p. 890.

[48] Id., at 891.

[49] Davis, op. cit., at p. 54.

prominent in the struggle against slavery.[50] Even the great compromiser, Henry Clay, sounded off against the effort to remove the Creeks and other natives.[51] He condemned the State of Georgia for "violating the treaties, abolishing the Cherokee government, dividing and surveying the Cherokee lands, distributing the land by lottery to Georgia citizens, and forbidding Indians from testifying in the 'courts of the white man.'"[52] Soon to take a seat in the House of Representatives, ex-president John Quincy Adams opposed the Bill, but recognizing that those in favor of it were at present in the majority, conceded that "there was nothing left for the minority to do but to record the exposure of perfidy and tyranny of which the Indians are to be made the victims, and to leave the punishment of it to Heaven."[53]

The greatest opposition of all was provided not by members of Congress, but by the Supreme Court, led by John Marshall. In reviewing the conviction of a missionary for entering Indian country without the State of Georgia's approval, Marshall held the law by which the man had suffered imprisonment to be preempted by federal treaty with the natives, hence void. Joining him in the majority was John McLean, one of two later dissenters in the *Dred Scott* matter, who wrote separately to state that "so long as treaties and laws remain in full force, and apply to Indian nations, exercising the right of self-government, within the limits of a State, the judicial power can exercise no discretion in refusing to give effect to those laws, when questions arise under them, unless they shall be deemed unconstitutional."[54] The decision was disregarded by the State of Georgia, as well as the Jackson Administration, which continued to work to persuade the Creeks and other tribes to cede their lands and accept new territories in the west, on the assurance that "the United States will forever secure and guaranty to them...the country so exchanged with them."[55]

For those who hoped the Supreme Court of the United States would at last right the many wrongs that John Marshall and his brethren were powerless to mitigate, mild disappointment must have been the emotion that overcame them when the Court announced its decision in *McGirt v.*

---

[50] Jackson, op. cit., at p. 277.
[51] Meacham, op. cit., at p. 94.
[52] Davis, op. cit., at p. 64.
[53] Id., at p. 94.
[54] *Worcester v. State of Georgia* (1832) 31 U.S. 515, 593.
[55] See *McGirt v. Oklahoma*, at p. 4.

Oklahoma. Far from determining the justice of Indian Removal or holding the federal government or the State of Georgia to account for their respective roles in the dispossession of the native peoples of the old South West, the Court's task was significantly more modest, as were the results of the case itself. As noted earlier, at issue was the conviction of the petitioner, Jimcy McGirt, twenty years before in a State court for a sex crime against a child. He and his lawyers contended that the original conviction was invalid due to the fact that State law did not apply in the location where the crime occurred. Because the location of the crime was land historically part of the territory reserved by treaty for the Creeks, State law was preempted by the law of the United States, including the Major Crimes Act (MCA). The State, for its part, contended that while the United States had promised the land at issue to the Creeks forever, Congress retained the right to circumscribe the promise, to limit the scope of the grant, or even to disestablish the reservation completely. The Court agreed that Congress did hold such power, but was highly skeptical of the morality of its exercise. "While there can be no question that Congress established a reservation for the Creek Nation," said Justice Gorsuch, "it's equally clear that Congress has since broken more than a few of its promises to the Tribe."[56] The violation of the promise to guarantee the land to the Creeks is best demonstrated by Congress's authorization that land within the reservation could be broken up into alienable parcels, which could then be sold by the fee holders to whomever they wished, regardless of the purchaser's status with respect to the Tribe. The fragmentation of the physical reserve suggested obliteration of the Tribe's jurisdiction, but this the Court doubted, as no evidence could be found of any intent by Congress to reduce the authority of the Tribe to the land granted by treaty.

Whether Congress actually did reduce the Tribe's authority can only be determined by review of the U.S. Code. Such things as momentous as abrogation of a treaty don't happen by mere implication. Congress must, instead, affirmatively act and explain its motive when doing so. Such a requirement is consistent with the law of contract, particularly when control of land is at issue. When Congress has deprived tribes of their rights over land otherwise granted by treaty, it has always articulated its purpose. Congress, for instance, "might speak of a reservation as being

[56] Id., at p. 6.

'discontinued,' 'abolished,' or vacated.'"[57] Though disestablishment has "'never required any particular form of words,'"...it does require that Congress clearly express its intent to do so, '[c]ommonl[ly with an] '[e]xplicit reference to cession or other language evidencing the present and total surrender of all tribal interests.'"[58] The closest Justice Gorsuch said the Congress came to doing this was during the so-called Allotment Era, when "Congress charged the Dawes Commission with negotiating changes to the Creek Reservation."[59] Those negotiations bore fruit in 1901, when the Commission reached an agreement with the Creeks establishing "procedures for allotting 160-acre parcels to individual Tribe members who could not sell, transfer, or otherwise encumber their allotments for a number of years."[60] The allotment agreement is what led to the partial disintegration of the original reservation, but not its extinction, and so long as the reservation exists, certain rights and privileges possessed by the Tribe continue even on the alienated lands.

It is true, as well, said Gorsuch, that Congress undermined the Creeks in other ways. "For example, just a few years before the 1901 Creek Allotment Agreement, and perhaps in an effort to pressure the Tribe to the negotiating table, Congress abolished the Creeks' tribal courts and transferred all pending civil and criminal cases to the U.S. Courts of the Indian Territory."[61] This and other limitations nevertheless "left the Tribe with significant sovereign functions over the lands in question," including "the power to collect taxes, operate schools, legislate through tribal ordinances, and, soon, oversee the federally mandated allotment process."[62] Serious though they were, "these congressional intrusions on pre-existing treaty rights fell short of eliminating all tribal interests in the land."[63] More telling still, after further restrictions on tribal autonomy, "Congress expressly recognized the Creeks' 'tribal existence and present tribal governmen[t]' and 'continued [them] in full force and effect for all purposes authorized by law.'"[64] When Congress actually addressed the issue of disestablishing

[57] Id., at 8.
[58] Id.
[59] Id., at 9.
[60] Id.
[61] Id.
[62] Id., at 14.
[63] Id.
[64] Id., at 15.

the tribe in 1906, it hesitated, then left the status quo in place.

The best argument the State asserted in support of its position was that historical practices and demographics have so substantially changed in the past century that any pretensions that the native reserve continues to exist are rendered absurd. These changes support the inference that Congress must have intended a disestablishment. The argument, however, failed in everything save provoking the textualist in Justice Gorsuch to fully assert itself. "When interpreting Congress's work in this arena, no less than any other, our charge is usually to ascertain and follow the original meaning of the law before us."[65] It's only when the law is ambiguous that a court is permitted to go beyond the statutory language and seek to discern the actual intent of the Congress in enacting the law. Oklahoma's failure to "point to any ambiguous language in any of the relevant statutes that could plausibly be read as an Act of disestablishing" effectively forestalled the propriety of the Court going beyond any black letter text.[66] The only role extra-textual materials "can properly play is to help 'clear up...not create' ambiguity about a statute's original meaning."[67]

Assuming for argument's sake that the canons of statutory construction were no obstacle to considering the State's contention, Gorsuch didn't find the latter particularly compelling. Prosecution by the State of natives on ground no one disputed was reservation land for years was eventually disavowed by the State, hence its historical occurrence cannot serve as precedent for prosecution of natives on lands within a reservation that have been alienated to non-natives. The Creeks' own understanding that their tribal status was under threat during the late Nineteenth and Twentieth Centuries hardly amounts to a waiver of the rights they had prior to a disestablishment that never actually occurred. Even the federal government's own impulse at one time to terminate the Tribe's status is unhelpful because, as noted, the Congress never acted on that impulse. And, of course, the long period of time the State prosecuted major crimes that occurred on reservation land can never alone be sufficient to effectively disestablish the Tribe. That, he said, "would be the rule of the strong, not the rule of law."[68]

---

[65] Id., at 14

[66] Id.

[67] Id., at 20.

[68] Id., at 28.

The most audacious and ultimately the stupidest argument of the State was not that a disestablishment occurred, but that a reservation was never established in the first place. A "dependent Indian community" is what the Creeks have always been, not a tribe in possession of a federally recognized reservation. The evidence cited—"some stray language from a statute that does not control here, a piece of congressional testimony there, and the scattered opinions of agency officials everywhere in between"—Gorsuch retorted, pales in comparison to "the treaties and statutes that promised the land to the Tribe in the first place."[69] Those promises, though often modified, if not breached, continue to matter. Simply because the price of keeping them is now too great in the eyes of some, is no justification for their repudiation. Congress might actually do exactly what the State argued it must have done at some time in the past, but Congress must explain itself in clear language leaving no doubt as to its purpose. Since that never occurred, the promises remain, and the reservation, now encompassing much of the eastern half of the State, including the City of Tulsa, is exempt from any effort by the State to prosecute major crimes committed there by native peoples.

Though much harm on both sides has occurred, with the natives ultimately suffering the worst due to their defeat in various armed conflicts, the decision authored by Justice Gorsuch does go some distance in resetting the balance between the sovereign nations that our government has long recognized and the States in which their tribal lands are found. Conservatives and classical liberals might bemoan the erosion of States' rights, but only because they forget the moment of the Founding, when sovereign Indian nations surrounded the new republic and the Framers vested with the federal government alone the power to negotiate and ratify treaties and to regulate commerce with the Indians, both within and without the nation's boundaries. The rights of the States, in matters involving truly national concerns, were ever intended to be subordinate to the power of the federal government. Speaking with a single voice in such matters was understood to be superior to thirteen or fifty discordant voices, and much better calculated to avoid conflict. That vision didn't exactly find verification in subsequent events, not because the Framers' eye sight was shoddy, but because those who gained

[69] Id., at 31.

control of the federal government, and those in charge in the States, forgot the wisdom of the founding, disregarded the sovereign and treaty rights of the natives, and combined their powers to overcome all resistance. The rule of the strong fortunately has yielded at last to the rule of law, and the Court, as the guardian of our rights and obligations, as individuals and as a people, has vindicated in some measure the judicious outlook of John Marshall, John McLean and the wise men and women of an earlier age.

Bedtime for Bolton

IN a society in which the phrase "why can't Johnny read" is a long-standing indictment of the quality of public schools, the torrent of books published in America each year is an odd counterpoint. The number of authors is exceeded only by the dizzying array of topics, but none seem so favored these days as those touching upon the alleged unfitness for office of the 45th President of the United States. One of the latest, but not the last by far, is a tome hastily published by John Bolton, the President's late and unlamented National Security Advisor. Notorious for his hawkish views as much as for his walrus-like pilosity, Bolton penned a much-anticipated account of the chaos of a White-House run by someone he concludes is inept and incoherent, who begged the Chinese dictator for aid in his re-election effort after praising China's mass-internment policy, thinks Finland is part of Russia, imagined the "coolness" of invading Venezuela, and is routinely mocked behind his back by top staff.[1] The book is said to have become a hit—at least according to the leading metric-keepers at Amazon and *The New York Times*, both of whom make no secret of despising the President and longing for his removal.

The critics, however, have been less impressed with the quality of Bolton's work product, probably for what it doesn't contain. Disappointed in the hope that Bolton's insider account would deliver confirmation of crimes heretofore hidden in the President's tax returns, or proof of indenture to Vladimir Putin, or frequent use of the N-word

---

[1] Max Benwell, "John Bolton's Bombshell Trump Book: Eight of its Most Stunning Claims," www.theguardian.com, June 17, 2020.

when describing African Americans, the critics' have repaid the memoirist with all the ruthlessness they could summon. Even while the book ranked high on *The New York Times* best-seller list, the paper's own columnist Jennifer Szalai condemned it as "bloated with self-importance," "exceedingly tedious" and "slightly unhinged," with "little discernable attention to style and narrative form" and filled "with minute and often extraneous details, including the time and length of routine meetings and, even, at one point, a nap."[2] Bolton's account of the phone call that launched the most inane impeachment effort in American history she calls "weird, circuitous and generally confounding," replete with the author's "usual small-bore detail" as "the sentences get windy and conspicuously opaque," and ultimately, with everything else, leaving the reader with the impression of the "lavishly bewhiskered figure" as "an unlikely hybrid of Ned Flanders and Yosemite Sam."[3] Peter Conrad of *The Observer* even more ferociously attacked Bolton's physical appearance before assaulting his prose—referring to "that walrus brush, which looks like a grizzled version of the cow-catching guard-rails on an ancient locomotive."[4] Failing to deliver the goods that might have vindicated the House impeachment effort he so publicly dodged reminded Conrad of Bolton's earlier dodging of the Vietnam-era draft and subsequent enthusiasm for sending young American lads to fight and die overseas in wars Bolton never ceased planning and endorsing. *The Chicago Tribune's* John Warner said Bolton's reliance on a title drawn from the hit musical *Hamilton* made him "sick to his stomach," and ended his review by telling readers not to bother buying or even reading the book since the only noteworthy parts had already been reported in papers like his own.[5]

As a bit of revenge for his own failure to become a long-term and historic fixture in a White House occupied by a President the author clearly believes to be his inferior, the book is more bark than bite. His criticisms of his former boss tend to rely on stereotypes coined four years

---

[2] Jennifer Szalai, "Bolton's Bloated Book Lacks Focus and Insight," *The New York Times*, June 24, 2020.

[3] Id.

[4] Peter Conrad, "a Monument to his Own Grandiosity: The Inevitable Fallout Between the President and his National Security Adviser Makes for a Punchy but Self-Aggrandizing Memoir," *The Observer*, June 28, 2020.

[5] John Warner, "Read the Newspaper, Not John Bolton's 'The Room Where it Happened,'" *Chicago Tribune Online*, June 19, 2020.

before during the lead-up to the 2016 election and copiously reused ever since. His own status as a hated man in the demons gallery of the right has ultimately overshadowed whatever merit his account might have in the eyes of a public who has long been informed of Bolton's neo-con obsessions, his rabid lust for dropping bombs on brown people, and even his friendship with supposed race-traitor Clarence Thomas while attending Yale Law School. The larger and more enduring downside to Bolton's performance, however, is the lawsuit the book's publication has provoked. The lawsuit comes not directly from the President, nor from some third-party claiming libel, but the United States government itself, for breaching an agreement that Bolton wouldn't publish any account of his time as an agent of the United States without the employer's approval. Bolton's attorneys, with the aid of his publisher's legal counsel, turned aside an emergency injunction, but failed so far in dismissing the larger suit that seeks the disgorgement of all Bolton's profits.

Some critics, including impeachment cheerleader Noah Feldman, have already concluded the lawsuit is a sham, as if they were fully privy to all of the evidence, all the facts and testimony, before any of it has been vetted in discovery and presented to a jury. Bolton, says Feldman, submitted "his manuscript for an extraordinarily lengthy and detailed review," made "thousands of editorial" changes, and then was given the run-around by the President's political appointees.[6] The book itself, he assures us, doesn't contain classified information, hence hasn't breached the pre-clearance requirement, and even if it did, such content is *de minimis*, meaning that the remedy is equally so, rendering the lawsuit essentially frivolous, and worse still, so grievous "an assault on established law and on the First Amendment" that the government's lawyers "ought to be ashamed."[7]

Bolton's book itself will soon be forgotten. The baggage of its author, his obvious sour grapes, the hostility of the critics and the book's literary flaws condemn it to oblivion. The host of other books of similar theme make it even less likely to be resorted to by historians of the future on the hunt for insight, memorable quotes and readable dirt to recycle in their own accounts of the life and times of the Trump Administration.

---

[6] Noah Feldman, "Trump Lawsuit Against John Bolton is Beyond Frivolous," www.bloomberg.com, June 17, 2020.

[7] Id.

Such books, of course, are par for the course during any presidency. No one against whom tens of millions of people voted is going to be immune to criticism, nor to the interest of hostile consumers anxious for confirmation of their bias against the incumbent. In earlier days, newspapers with obvious editorial slants filled the demand by citizens opposed to a given president for critical political prose. More recently, the book publishing industry has emerged to supplement, if not replace, the traditional medium. FDR generated perhaps the first sizeable array of books critical of his presidency and policies. Nixon was lambasted in hard and softcover alike. In Reagan's time the cottage industry of critical books expanded markedly. But nothing compares to the present moment, when every week virtually a new book containing scathing indictments of the President's personality, character defects, speech patterns, intelligence and general animus to anyone not wholeheartedly on his side finds friendly review in the news of the day. Occasionally, these books even discuss the substance of the President's policies and take aim at their various real and alleged demerits. Taken as a whole, says one critic who claims to have read many of them, the books "paint a damning portrait of the 45th President of the United States" that is so consistent over the untold thousands of pages dedicated to documenting the same set of shortcomings that a reader's "attention is in danger of wandering."[8] The various authors portray the President "as a flamboyantly mean and intemperately indiscreet boss, wrong-footing and humiliating cabinet members and aides with constant criticism, sometimes to their faces, sometimes behind their backs."[9] He "meanders from topic to topic, loops back around, adds new topics, repeats himself, boasts, mixes facts with fake facts, throws in his latest obsession, continuing on and on according to some labyrinthine stream-of-consciousness impulse in which whatever is on his mind is worthy of public utterance."[10] Trump "rarely reads, gets bored easily, is irritable and distracted, has trouble remembering complicated things, has no intellectual curiosity and is ignorant not just about his job but about things generally considered common knowledge."[11] Possessing a "short

---

[8] Sarah Lyall, "In Trumpworld, the Grown-Ups in the Room all Left, and Got Book Deals," *The New York Times*, August 1, 2020.

[9] Id.

[10] Id.

[11] Id.

attention span, he is averse to learning anything at briefings if he finds the information difficult to follow, boring, or in contravention of what he already thinks."[12]

Perhaps the most revealing statement the aforementioned critic makes is that the picture the various authors invariably paint of their protagonist "is so outrageous that if they were fiction they would be dismissed as too broad, too much of a caricature."[13] The statement is revealing in that it suggests the consistency of the authors either proves they are singularly honest and accurate in portraying the true nature and traits of their subject, or are simply following a script they know will find resonance with a particular audience and guarantee them a payday. While many insist the President is whatever a critic says he is and agree that he is an incoherent boor among other things, the portrayal of him in popular non-fiction is in striking contrast to the depiction of this remarkably famous man that was presented for decades prior to his announcement that he was running to become the nation's commander-in-chief from the conservative side of the aisle. Though much criticized over the years for his various marriages, his financial ups and downs, his endless self-promotion, Trump was also an admired figure not just in this country but the world over. His name was synonymous with success and the American Dream. He was the friend and confident of many of his current critics, a favorite of Hollywood and the media, and he even appeared on *Saturday Night Live* more than once—a program that has lost much of its remaining edge due to the tiredness of its current anti-Trump shtick. Prior to 2015, Donald Trump wasn't a bigoted boor of limited mental capacity, but a successful and popular author, a master of finance and the financial comeback, the toast of Hollywood, a favorite on the now hopelessly hostile *The View*, and a hero who helped the people of New York recover from bad management and terrorist attacks. Photos readily available through the internet show him in happy pose with a host of people who now claim to despite him, including Hillary and Bill Clinton. In light of a history that many choose now to forgot, the current portrayal of Trump in books by those who claim to know the man intimately is highly suspect in its intense negativity and the consistency of one account with all the rest. It is as if the script has been flipped and the many authors publishing their memoirs are simply

---

[12] Id.
[13] Id.

running with a new narrative contrived for the moment in order to achieve a particular end.

Some clue as to the origin of the discrepancy between the pre and post 2016 election treatment of the President can be found in the modern nature of the publishing world. A century ago, publishers were family owned for the most part, confined in their scope to particular markets and particular nations. Book publishers in New York tended to direct their sales to Americans, as did publishers elsewhere in the United States. In the past several decades, globalism has trended in economic life, with companies consolidating across national lines and seeking not merely local and nation-state markets, but markets throughout the world. Energy companies, financial institutions and car manufacturers led this trend many decades ago. Media has followed suit, particularly with the rise of the internet and various electronic technologies. The uniformity of presentation of issues and a consistent editorial slant in newspapers and news rooms, and now in books, reflect the attitudes of those who own and operate media outlets and the massive stake those individuals have in globalization. Donald Trump always offered mild criticism for those who would sell out American workers and American industry. He agreed with many on the left who wished to put American workers first and viewed the shipping of jobs overseas as a sell-out of the working class by greedy corporations. Once he rose to prominence as a leading candidate for the Republican nomination for president, and then as an actual candidate in the general election, his criticism became both more pronounced and more of a threat to global interests. Not surprisingly, the media owned by heavily diversified global entities has aligned itself against him and continues to pummel him day in and day out through newspapers, magazines, broadcast and cable television and a myriad of affiliated publishing houses.

Like the print and electronic media, book publishers have undergone considerable consolidation beneath the umbrella of international corporations. In the English-speaking world, 60 percent of books are produced by a total of five publishing houses: Penguin Random House, Hachette, Harper Collins, Simon & Schuster, and Macmillan. Each of these publishers is actually a branch of much larger global entities, some of which are controlled from foreign capitals, and all of whom are heavily invested in publishing elsewhere in the world, including and especially the growing Chinese market. Penguin Random

House is owned by publishing giant Bertelsman, a German company that rose to prominence during the Third Reich through its support of the Nazi regime. In addition to Penguin Random House, it owns BMG, the most prominent Book-of-the Month clubs, Alfred A. Knopf, Anchor Books, Ballentine, Doubleday and Vintage. Hachette is based in Paris and is owned by Lagardere. Under its publishing umbrella can be found Little, Brown and Company, Virago Press, Orion, Perseus, Orbit, and many other publishing houses operating throughout the world. Harper Collins is an arm of the Murdoch family's News Corp, which also owns *The Wall Street Journal*, *The New York Post*, Fox, and Sky News. Simon & Shuster is one of the many holdings of National Amusements, controlled by the Democrat Redstone family, along with Viacom, CBS, BET, MTV, Comedy Central, Paramount Pictures, and Dreamworks. The last of the so-called Big Five publishers, Macmillan, is but a cog in the global corporate wheel of Holzbrink. Like Bertelsman, Macmillan's parent company is a former friend and ally of National Socialism, whose current owner is the son of an actual Nazi.[14] Macmillan's subsidiaries include Flatiron Books, Henry Holt, Farrar, Straus & Giroux, St. Martin's Press, and Darwinism and climate change promoter, *Scientific American*.

Of these publishers, only one—News Corp—is identified as falling upon the right side of the ideological spectrum. But even this is rather misleading as its leadership has waged periodic war against the Trump Administration, attempted to ruin the President's prospects through the agency of former Fox News anchor Megyn Kelly and is now under the lead of the progressive-oriented sons of its founder. In any event, the inventory of books these five publishers have produced includes virtually all of the leading accounts of the alleged misfunction and dysfunction of Donald Trump and his administration, as well as its wonderful and sinless progressive alternatives. Harper Collins, for instance, has published many glowing accounts of President Obama and the Obama White House, including *Thanks Obama: My Hopey, Changy White House Years* by David Litt, and David Garrow's *Rising Star: The Making of Barack Obama*. Other titles include Joy-Ann Reid's *The Man who Sold America: Trump and the Unraveling of the American Story*, Never

---

[14] See Mark Landler, "Another German Publisher Mulls its Wartime Past," *The New York Times*, October 14, 2002; and Patrick Howley, "Biden's Book Publisher is Owned by Company Founded by a Nazi," https://nationalfile.com, July 23, 2020.

Trumper David Frum's *Trumpocracy: The Corruption of the American Republic,* and even an autobiography of one of the radical leaders of the opposition, Ilhan Omar: *This is What America Looks Like: My Journey from Refugee to Congresswoman.*

Penguin Random House and its affiliates have published Kamala Harris' *The Truth We Hold,* Michelle Obama's *Becoming, The World as it Is: A Memoir of the Obama White House* by Ben Rhodes, Jeanne Marie Laskas's *To Obama: With Love, Joy, Anger and Hope,* Trump-hating gun control advocate David Hogg's *#Never Again: A New Generation Draws the Line,* literary and environmental wunderkind Greta Thunberg's *No One is Too Small to Make a Difference* and *Our House is on Fire,* Philip Rucker and Carol Leonnig's *A Very Stable Genius: Donald J. Trump's Testing of America,* Glenn Simpson and Peter Fritsch's fantastical *Crime in Progress: Inside the Steele Dossier and the Fusion GPS Investigation of Donald Trump,* various books by members of the Emanuel Family (Rahm and Ezekiel), Chelsea Clinton's Nobel and Pulitzer Prize worthy children's books, Michiko Kakutani's *The Death of Truth,* Norman Eisen's belated impeachment brief entitled *A Case for the American People: The United States v. Donald J. Trump,* and Andrew Shaffer's ludicrous fan fantasy series starring fictionalized versions of Barack Obama and Joe Biden as the successors to Scooby and the gang, battling the many monsters inhabiting Trump's America.

Simon & Schuster is responsible for John Bolton's masterpiece, Mary Trump, Ph.D.'s reputed psychoanalysis of her uncle and entire family, drama-queen Omorosa Manigault's *Unhinged: An Insider's Account of the Trump White House, Border Wars: Inside Trump's Assault on Immigration* by Julie Hirscheld Davis and Michael D. Shear, *The Book of Gutsy Women: Favorite Stories of Courage and Resilience* by Hillary and Chelsea Clinton, and the autobiography of potential VP candidate Susan Rice—*Tough Love: My Story and the Things Worth Fighting For.*

Macmillan and its subsidiaries and affiliates have published James Comey's failed impeachment memorandum, *A Higher Loyalty,* Barack Obama's *Dreams of my Father* and *The Audacity of Hope,* Joe Biden's several pre-campaign tomes, including *Promise Me, Dad,* the notoriously inaccurate and largely unsourced *Fire and Fury* penned by Michael Wolff, Elizabeth Warren's multi-volume attack on capitalism and Trump, Stacy Abrams' *Lead From the Outside,* Bernie Sanders' twin manifestos *Our Revolution* and *Where We Go From Here,* Russia-hoax advocate Andrew McCabe's *The Threat: How the FBI Protects America in the Age of Terror and Trump*, and a loving biography of progressive pin-up Alexandria Ocasio Cortez by Lynda Lopez, entitled *AOC: The Fearless Rise and Powerful Resonance of Alexandria Ocasio-Cortez*.

There is, of course, an actual market for such books, but the overwhelming flood of titles promoting one set of views and attacking a President who embodies another set suggest there is far more than markets forces at work here. Bernie Sanders and Elizabeth Warren would probably gladly sign their names to outright communist propaganda if presented with it, whether for pay or not, because it is consistent with their belief structure. Joe Biden wouldn't think twice about allowing his name to appear on any book, regardless of the content, in large part because of the absence of any independent or non-mercenary thought, especially now that he appears to be in the early stages of dementia. Some authors might not be so willing to give the store away and would require compensation for the effort. Others appear to be so infuriated by disappointment, both personal and professional, they are quite prepared to put pen to page and follow the outline presented by editors employed by the global entities that oppose Trump's nationalism. The embittered Mary Trump, Ph.D., appears to be settling scores arising from her father's shortcomings and perhaps her own. John Bolton wanted another foreign war, so he's settled for a war of words against the man from whom he couldn't get satisfaction. But, certainly, the paycheck further incentivizes those who might ordinarily be restrained in their criticism by a sense of honor, loyalty to country, or a desire not be perceived as a snitch, tattle tale or someone who will, post-publication, go down in history as a vintner of sour grapes.

And then there is the possibility that book contracts are not so much payment for pages published as a payoff for more discrete services rendered. A mere bribe is a rather distasteful gift to receive, hard to stomach even by the more venal among us, hence some clever guise is devised that the recipient can easily deceive themselves into believing is a legitimate transaction. Former Speaker of the House Jim Wright took money from labor unions and others in exchange for the purchase of the entire run of a pathetic pamphlet he purportedly wrote. Baltimore Mayor Katherine Pugh did something similar with regard to a children's book she claims to have written. Money was paid despite the fact that no one really bought or read the books and both authors suffered the consequences: Wright resigned from office; Pugh entered a federal prison last June to commence a three-year term. The advances these high-profile political memoirs generate often seem suspiciously high. The brain-numbed Joe Biden received $8 million for a three-book deal for books no one believes he actually wrote or will write. The famously venal Bill and Hillary Clinton, who brazenly accepted donations from Chinese military sources while in office and successfully negotiated the rapids of the Whitewater scandal that landed their fellow-investors in the penitentiary, accepted eight figures for their multiple ghostwritten volumes. About the only memorable passage from any of them was Hillary Clinton's terse, tongue-in-cheek three-page account of the Monica Lewinsky incident, wherein she implausibly claimed "I could hardly breath. Gulping for air, I started crying and yelling at him, 'what do you mean? What are you saying? Why did you lie to me?" Bill Clinton's successor, the ostensibly conservative George W. Bush, embraced much of the globalist agenda, waged two wars to make the world safe for the international oil industry and received a $15 million dollar advance for his memoir. And now the Obamas have obtained a combined $65 million for their memoirs after eight years of using executive orders to green light a veritable invasion of America by millions of foreign nationals to fill whatever menial jobs weren't shipped overseas to China and elsewhere.[15] Maybe these paydays are merited, but for people who don't actually write their books or do much other than stand around accepting the congratulations, it all seems a bit contrived, not to mention suspicious.

The pending election seems to have increased the flow of scandalous accounts of the Trump presidency and encouraged those penning and publishing them to cut corners to achieve their symbiotic goals. The demand for Bolton's book in the wake of an impeachment effort that bombed and promises of yet another go at it by the Democrat-controlled House of Representatives prior to the November election may well have prompted both Bolton and his publisher to forego final approval by the National Security Administration and publish the book anyways. Victory over the Trump Administration in its effort to enjoin publication, was achieved, but not because of the demands of the First Amendment, which wasn't really at issue at all. Instead, the Court concluded that an

---

[15] Constance Grady, "What the Obamas $65 Million Book Advance Actually Means," www.vox.com, March 2, 2017.

injunction wouldn't have done any good given the large number of copies that had already been distributed to members of the global media. By the looks of it, said Judge Royce Lamberth, "the horse is not just out of the barn—it is out of the country."[16] As for the government's claim that publication prior to final approval violated the terms of Bolton's employment, the Judge wasn't unsympathetic. Ordinarily, the First Amendment would bar the government from punishing someone for the utterance of true statements, but Bolton, being a government employee entrusted with many state secrets, was contractually bound to remain silent unless his employer permitted his disclosure of what he knew. He actually agreed to remit to the government any profits generated by an unauthorized and uncleared statement. That such an agreement is no infringement on the First Amendment is well established. In 1980, the Supreme Court considered the defense of Frank Snepp, a former CIA official who was sued for publishing an account of his experience in South East Asia without prior clearance. The Court concluded that the pre-clearance requirement of Snepp's contract was no violation of the First Amendment and that disgorgement of the profits flowing from publication was "the most appropriate remedy" for the official's wrongful conduct.[17]

Though it was mere dicta, Judge Lamberth expressed his conviction that the government would ultimately win its case, that Bolton had "exposed his country to harm and himself to civil (and potentially criminal) liability."[18] When the time comes, Bolton might well argue that the review was being delayed unreasonably and that no classified material was actually contained in his published account, hence he was within his rights to go forward with publication. The argument, however, will be a hard sell given the short period of time Bolton took in composing his memoir, his publisher's intense interest in releasing the book as close to impeachment as possible, and the fact that virtually any information drawn from confidential communications with a President is subject to a very broad executive privilege. Bolton may well lose the case, and when he does, it will be he that suffers the consequences, not his publisher, nor his publisher's globally-oriented Trump hating

---

16 Adam Shaw, "Judge Allows Bolton Book to be Released, But Says He 'Gambled with National Security,'" www.foxnews.com, June 20, 2020.

17 *Snepp v. United States* (1980) 444 U.S. 507, 100 S.Ct. 763.

18 Shaw, op cit.

owners. It is fitting perhaps that the man who would use the young men of America as cannon fodder in endless foreign wars would himself be sacrificed as cannon fodder by those who would exploit their immense power over the media to defeat his erstwhile employer.

Natural Born Something

THE first great, unforgivable sin of Donald Trump wasn't defeating Hillary Clinton for the presidency, or jokingly asking Vladimir Putin to locate her missing emails, or suggesting that thousands of Arab Americans celebrated the destruction of the Twin Towers on rooftops and in the streets, or even panning Rosie O'Donnell for being a disgusting slob. No. His first great, unforgivable sin was using the weight of his tremendous celebrity and easy access to the media to question the whereabouts of President's Obama's birth certificate following a string of unsuccessful lawsuits by others aimed at establishing whether the President was a "natural born citizen," hence constitutionally qualified to serve as the nation's Commander-in-Chief. He wondered why a man with nothing to hide would spend two million dollars resisting efforts to force him to disclose his birth certificate instead of just releasing a copy and being done with it.[1] He later told Anderson Cooper during an interview on CNN that he'd been informed that "the birth certificate was missing…or it doesn't exist. And if that's the case, it's a big problem."[2] When the Governor of Hawaii claimed that he remembered when Obama was born at a hospital in Honolulu, Trump guffawed and attributed this unlikely report to the Governor's desire to cover for his friend and party leader.[3] For six weeks, Trump kept it up, even claiming he had investigators at work in Hawaii to solve the mystery. His foray into so-called birtherism came to an end when the President finally released a digital copy of his long-form Certificate of Live Birth. Though the document facially established Obama's Hawaiian

---

[1] Glenn Kessler, "A Look at Trump's 'Birther' Statements," www.thewashingtonpost.com, April 28, 2011.

[2] Id.

[3] Michael Falcone, "Donald Trump Steps up Calls for Obama to Release his Birth Certificate," www.abcnews.com, March 26, 2011.

birth place and put the birther agitation to rest, Trump characteristically claimed victory—crowing that only he was capable of forcing the disclosure of what an army of lawyers in the President's employ had savagely fought to keep under raps.[4]

As with nearly everything else the left is criticized for, it didn't take long for the counter charge of racism to be directed at the critic. Temperamentally incapable of taking a slight against their savior at face value and simply addressing its merits, defenders of President Obama reflexively charged that Trump and his supporters were engaging in "racist ploys intended to delegitimize the nation's first black president."[5] Jessie Jackson accused Trump of "appealing to the President's detractors with 'coded and covert rhetoric for stirring up racial fears.'"[6] Historian Nell Painter thought Trump's inquiry regarding the birth certificate was reflective of a larger foundational premise, originating during the colonial period and continuing through Nixon's Southern Strategy, that black people were not supposed to be powerful.[7] Khalil Gibran Muhammad of Harvard University explained that if the birther lie about Obama was true "we would have elected someone who had no right to run for president, let alone to become the first African American president of this country, but more particularly it expresses the illegitimacy of a person of African descent as a true American, as someone truly endowed with the capacity to govern this great nation," which is a lie, of course, but "foundational for everything else that flows from Donald Trump's lips."[8] Government Professor Phillip Klinkner thought it was fascinating that "here we have the first African-American president, and here was an attempt to sort of delegitimize him in a very overt way as not actually being American."[9] Others saw Trump's embrace of birtherism not so much a reflection of his own racism, but as evidence of his sly recognition of "an opportunity to connect with the electorate over an issue many considered taboo: the discomfort, in some

---

[4] Ashly Parker & Steve Eder, "Inside the Six Weeks Donald Trump was a Nonstop 'Birther,'" *The New York Times*, July 2, 2016.

[5] Gregory Krieg, "14 of Trump's Most Outrageous 'Birther' Claims From after 2011," www.cnn.com, September 16, 2016.

[6] Parker & Eder, op. cit.

[7] Bill Moyers, "Never Forget—Trump Rode to Power on the Wings of a Dark Lie," www.rawstory.com, August 17, 2020.

[8] Id.

[9] Id.

quarters of American society, with the election of the nation's first black president."[10]

Nearly a decade later, the cycle continues: Chapman University law professor John Eastman publishes an essay in *Newsweek* casting doubt on a non-white vice presidential candidate's eligibility for office, President Trump suggests that maybe there's something to it, and the progressive world and its media allies erupt in condemnation of the "obvious" racism of Eastman, Trump and anyone who would give their noxious attempt at narrative-building even the slightest credence. Eastman didn't actually assert that Democrat vice presidential candidate Kamala Harris wasn't born in the United States, or that she wasn't a citizen; he simply noted that because her "father was (and is) a Jamaican national, her mother was from India, and neither was a naturalized U.S. citizen at the time of Harris' birth in 1964," she might not qualify as a "natural born citizen," in which case she would be ineligible to serve as Vice President, or to assume the chief role should Joe Biden exit the stage.[11] He said she might be eligible, but only if both her parents were permanent residents at the time of her birth, as opposed to temporary visitors attending school in the United States on student visas.[12]

The heat from left-leaning readers and others quickly grew so intense that *Newsweek* apologized for the use of the essay "by some as a tool to perpetrate racism and xenophobia," but nevertheless defended the piece as a legitimate "minority" viewpoint on an important constitutional issue.[13] Disregarding both Eastman and any possible scholarly merit in his essay, Biden campaign spokesman Andrew Bates immediately attacked the President as "the national leader of the grotesque, racist birther movement with respect to President Obama," who "has sought to fuel racism and tear our nation apart on every single day of his presidency."[14] Bates said it was "unsurprising, but no less abhorrent that as Trump makes a fool of himself straining to distract the

---

[10] Parker & Eder, op. cit.

[11] John C. Eastman, "Some Questions for Kamala Harris About Eligibility," www.newsweek.com, August 12, 2020.

[12] Id.

[13] Nancy Cooper & Josh Hammer, "Editor's Note: Eastman's Newsweek Column Has Nothing to do with Racist Birtherism," www.newsweek.com, August 13, 2020; and "Editor's Note, 8/14" appended to the foregoing note.

[14] Franco Ordonez, "Trump and his Campaign Amplify Untrue 'Birther' Conspiracy Against Kamala Harris," www.npr.com, August 13, 2020.

American people from the horrific toll of his failed coronavirus response that his campaign and their allies would resort to wretched, demonstrably false lies in their pathetic desperation."[15] Using less purple language than Bates, noted constitutional scholar Erwin Chemerinsky called the notion that Harris might not be a natural born citizen "a truly silly argument" on account of the fact that she was born in the United States, and the first sentence of the Fourteenth Amendment provides that all persons born in the United States and subject to the jurisdiction thereof are American citizens.[16] While Eastman and a few others think more is required to be president than mere birth within the country, Chemerinsky said they were "clearly wrong under the language of the 14th Amendment and under Supreme Court precedent."[17] Jasmine Wright of CNN echoed the good dean's argument, stating that "the United States grants citizenship to anyone born in the country, regardless of their parents' status."[18] Harris herself said of the controversy that it was "the same thing they did to Barack. This is not new to us and so I think that we know what they are trying to do."[19]

Even some on the right were dismissive of Eastman's position. Professor Eugene Volokh explained that the term "'natural born citizen' is an adaptation of the British term 'natural-born subject'—with the final word changed to reflect that the U.S. is a republic rather than a monarchy—and 'English law defined natural-born based on birth (with some narrow exceptions), not on the parents' citizenship.'"[20] *National Review's* Robert Vergruggen conceded that perhaps there was "an academic debate to be had...but if the 14th Amendment wasn't supposed to give citizenship to kids who are born in the U.S. to foreign students and then live here for more than a decade, we've been doing it wrong for a long time, and the courts are not going to change their mind

---

[15] Id.

[16] Melissa Quinn, "Trump Weighs in After Campaign Adviser Floats False Birther Theory About Harris' Eligibility to be Vice President," www.cbsnews.com, August 14, 2020.

[17] Id.

[18] Jasmine Wright, "Kamala Harris Responds to Trump's Birther Attacks: 'They're Going to Engage in Lies,'" www.cnn.com, August 17, 2020.

[19] Id.

[20] Eugene Volokh, "Yes, Kamala Harris is Eligible to be Vice President," www.newsweek.com, August 13, 2020.

just in time to keep Harris out of Joe Biden's White House."[21]

Those defending first Obama and now Harris tend to disregard the nuance of the issue—the distinction between the citizenship protected by the Fourteenth Amendment and natural born citizenship which is a distinct qualification to be President of the United States. They assume that because someone was born in the United States, they are necessarily a natural born citizen. They also assume that any inquiry into a black or non-white candidate's citizenship must be rooted in racial animus, and that no such indignity would ever be inflicted upon a candidate of lighter complexion. With regard to the latter issue, they are patently in error. Just four years ago, there was much discussion of Ted Cruz's eligibility due to the fact that he was born in Canada to an American mother and a Cuban father. John McCain was actually subject to a formal legal challenge to his eligibility to serve as President due to his birth in the Panama Canal Zone. Republicans Barry Goldwater and George Romney were also questioned over their eligibility: Goldwater because he was born in a U.S. territory not yet part of an actual State; Romney because he was born in Mexico. President Chester Allan Arthur bore the brunt of numerous accusations that he wasn't a natural born citizen because he was supposedly born in Canada. The issue really isn't a candidate's race or even place of birth, but whether a citizen who entered life on American soil or abroad qualifies as someone whose citizenship is "natural born."

The academic debate over the meaning of the term "natural-born citizen" has entailed some quite remarkable claims. Several scholars who reviewed the relevant language—that only "a natural born citizen, or a citizen of the United States, at the time the adoption of this Constitution, shall be eligible to the Office of President"—reached the rather surprising conclusion that George Washington was an illegitimate president because his birth antedated the creation of the United States and he himself was never subsequently naturalized.[22] Sanford Levinson and others went a step further in stating that the proper textual read of the qualification clause demands the verdict that no president born or

---

[21] Robert Vergruggen, "The Distraction over Whether Kamala Harris is a 'Natural-Born Citizen,'" www.nationalreview.com, August 13, 2020.

[22] "Contest: Was George Washington Constitutional?," 12 Const. Commentary 137.

naturalized after the time of ratification could be counted as legitimate.[23] "There has," he said, "been no legitimate president of the United States since Zachary Taylor.... [T]he constitutional text clearly limits presidential eligibility to those who were citizens of the United States at the time of the Constitution's adoption in 1788. No one else could (and can) serve in that office, at least without further amendment of the document."[24] These claims can hardly be taken seriously. Levinson all but admits his own arguments were a form of parody, presented in mockery of originalist thinking on the Constitution. It's certainly not plausible to contend or believe that the Framers did not consider that any person born in the colonies who was alive at the time of ratification was not a citizen of the United States, or that no one would have pointed out so glaring a deficiency in the Constitution's text during the first two centuries following Washington's inauguration. It's equally implausible that the same Framers who sought to create an instrument of government to last in perpetuity would have intended that the office of President could only be filled so long as the generation alive at the time of ratification endured.

More serious commentators present more serious concerns. The great legal historian Lawrence Friedman accepted that the clause continues to govern qualifications, notwithstanding Levinson's criticism. The clause, however, he thought vague, anachronistic and inconsistent with modern concepts of citizenship emergent in the wake of the ratification of the Fourteenth Amendment. "It prevents over 12.8 million Americans from being eligible for the presidency... including...former Secretaries of State Madeleine Albright and Henry Kissinger...and over 700 Medal of Honor Winners."[25] The "natural born citizen" requirement, he continued, "appears to disqualify (on a bi-partisan basis) prospective candidates such as California's Republican Governor Arnold Schwarzenegger (born in Austria) and Michigan's Democratic Governor Jennifer Granholm (born in Canada)," jeopardizes

---

[23] Jordan Steiker, Sanford Levinson & J.M. Balkin, "Taking Text and Structure Really Seriously: Constitutional Interpretation and the Crisis of Presidential Eligibility," 74 Tex. L. Rev. 237 (1995).

[24] Id., at 244.

[25] Lawrence M. Friedman, "An Idea Whose Time Has Come—The Curious History, Uncertain Effect, and Need for Amendment of the 'Natural Born Citizen' Requirement for the Presidency," 52 St. Louis L.J. 137 (2007), at pp. 138-139.

the eligibility of Arizona Senator John McCain...who was born in the Panama Canal Zone to American citizen parents," and might well exclude all Native Americans due to the fact that they "are technically considered naturalized rather than natural born."[26] He thought the requirement "an anachronism" no longer relevant today, and unfair in that it "denies to some of our citizens the opportunity to aspire to the nation's highest offices" and disregards "the historic contributions made in all fields of endeavor by foreign-born citizens since the time the Republic was founded."[27]

Professor Lawrence Solum opined that small help in deciphering the term could be found in the historical record, where the original public meaning cannot be discerned from the available source material.[28] Attorneys Paul Clement and Neal Katyal, often on opposing sides in the great constitutional questions of the day, agree that the simplest solution is to recognize that "the relevant materials clearly indicate that a 'natural born citizen' means a citizen from birth with no need to go through naturalization proceedings."[29] They hold that the Supreme Court itself "has long recognized that two particularly useful sources in understanding constitutional terms are British common law and enactments of the First Congress," and that these sources "confirm that the original meaning of the phrase 'natural born Citizen' includes persons born abroad who are citizens from birth based on the citizenship of a parent."[30]

The obvious source of a solution to any uncertainty about the meaning of the term is the Supreme Court. The Court did opine long ago about the term's meaning, but not in the context of a dispute involving the one clause in the Constitution where it appears, but in a larger discussion of the privileges and immunities protected by the Fourteenth Amendment.[31] Lawrence Friedman admits that the High Court has never interpreted the phrase, as does Judge Jill Pryor. "Whether a person

---

[26] Id., at p. 139.

[27] Id., at 150.

[28] Lawrence B. Solum, "Originalism and the Natural Born Citizen Clauses," 107 Mich. L. Rev. First Impressions 22 (2008).

[29] Paul Clement & Neal Katyal, "On the Meaning of 'Natural Born Citizen,'" 128 Harv. L. Rev.F. 161 (2015), at p. 161.

[30] Id.

[31] See *Minor v. Happersett* (1874) 88 U.S. 162 and *United States v. Wong Kim Ark* (1898) 169 U.S. 649, 18 S.Ct. 456.

born abroad of American parents," she noted, "or of one American and one alien parent, qualifies as a natural born has never been resolved."[32] Pryor's own solution to the problem is both complex and novel. The term, she said, "can only be properly understood if we appreciate the interplay" of the clause where it appears "with the naturalization powers clause of Article I, as modified by section one of the Fourteenth Amendment."[33] Congress, she argued, has always exercised power over the naturalization of citizens. "Current immigration and naturalization statutes," for example, "make certain classes of foreign-born children citizens at birth, as have naturalization statutes since the first naturalization act in 1790."[34] When the Fourteenth Amendment entered the Constitution with its definition of citizenship, it must, she said, have implicitly included "natural born" within its protective scope, for otherwise so important a notion of citizenship, fundamental to the qualifications of the nation's chief executive, "would be outside of constitutionally defined and protected citizenship."[35] Natural born, she said, "must be either synonymous with "native born" or be included as a subset of "naturalized." She, Paul Clement, Neal Katyal, Professor Michael Ramsey and Akhil Reed Amar agree that Congress's power to establish a uniform rule of naturalization "encompasses the power to establish birthright citizenship for presidential eligibility purposes" —if not before the ratification of the Fourteenth Amendment, certainly afterward.[36] Congress, then, can solve the dilemma simply by passing a statute declaring who a natural born citizen is.

The argument that because natural born citizenship must be protected by the First Sentence of the Fourteenth Amendment and also subject to Congress's legislative power is more emotional than either logical or historical. Congress simply never discussed natural born citizenship during the debates over the wording of the Amendment, and certainly never enacted legislation afterward defining the term. It is true that if natural born citizens were not protected by the Fourteenth

---

[32] Jill A. Pryor, "The Natural-Born Citizen Clause and Presidential Eligibility: An Approach for Resolving Two Hundred Years of Uncertainty," 97 Yale L.J. 881 (1988), at pp. 881-882.

[33] Id., at 883.

[34] Id., at 891.

[35] Id., at 892-893.

[36] Thomas H. Lee, "Natural Born Citizen," 67 Am. U.L. Rev. 327 (2017), at p. 334.

Amendment it might be possible to strip them of their citizenship per se, but this hardly necessarily impacts their qualification to serve as President of the United States. It is entirely possible that a person who isn't a citizen of the United States either through birth in the United States or naturalization is still qualified and eligible to be President.

The better place to look for the term's meaning isn't post-Fourteenth Amendment theory or the wishful thinking of modern jurists, but in the common understanding of legal terms during the era of the founding. Professor Mary McManamon of Widener Law School suggests that the term "natural born citizen" was derived by the Framers from the body of the common law of England, along with such terms as "ex post facto," "writ of habeas corpus," and "bill of attainder."[37] The term, she says, is but a variation on the older term "natural born subject"—a person, to use Blackstone's words, "born within the dominions of the Crown of England, that is, within the ligeance, or as it is generally called, the allegiance of the king."[38] Persons not owing allegiance to the Crown, but born on English soil, were not natural born subjects. Instead, they might be children of hostile occupying forces, or of foreign ambassadors serving their nations' interests abroad. Natural born citizens also did not apparently include the children of English subjects born abroad. This fact, she says, is evident in the series of special laws and statutes enacted by Parliament beginning in 1350 conveying English citizenship on such children, allowing them to enjoy in England the rights of Englishmen, including the right to inherit property. When the Framers considered the issue, they included the phrase "natural born citizen" in Article II with virtually no debate, indicating an absence of controversy over its meaning. Natural born citizens, eligible to serve as President, were simply persons born in the United States who were not the children of foreign diplomats or foreign occupying soldiers. The terms "natural born" and "native born" are in essence synonymous.

Judge Pryor's view is untenable for the reason that MacManamon states—that only an expressed amendment of a particular provision can alter the meaning of the Constitution—and MacManamon's is suspect because it leads to the conclusion that the children of U.S. citizens born abroad while on business or holiday are not natural born, and that such

---

[37] Mary Brigid McManamon, "The Natural Born Citizen Clause as Originally Understood," 64 Cath. U.L. Rev. 317 (2015), at p. 320.

[38] Id.

persons as the late John McCain—the son and grandson of U.S. naval officers born on an overseas military base—are not eligible for the presidency, while a child of transient visitors to the U.S. or even persons illegally in the country are. Addressing that issue more squarely was Fordham Law Professor Thomas H. Lee. In studying English common law carefully from 1350 until the early part of the Eighteenth Century, Lee found that English naturalization statutes "yield three basic principles that can inform our understanding of the meaning of 'natural born Citizen' in Article II."[39] He noted, first "an unbroken four-hundred-year-old rule…that the children of English fathers or mothers sent abroad in government service were natural born subjects without any disability as to rights to inherit, hold property, sue in English Courts, hold high office, or receive the Crown's largesse."[40] Next is the "rule…that children born to English merchant fathers abroad were natural born subjects, similarly without impediments."[41] Finally, "there were mercantilist statutes minted for the first time in the Eighteenth Century that deemed persons 'natural born subjects' based on religion, military, or nautical service, and an Englishman as paternal grandfather," so long, however, as the statutory beneficiary was willing to take a loyalty oath and accepted the condition they would be barred from public office.[42] From an early time, hundreds of years before the founding of the American republic, the English conceived of the status of natural born subject as being a function of birth within the English realm or birth to a father serving or doing business abroad. That early American commentators emphasized only the first category, not the second, was a reflection, Lee says, of "the geographical separation of the United States from Europe and the geopolitical realities of the new republic's military and economic weakness" that rendered operation of citizenship acquired by children of U.S. citizens born abroad "a small concern as compared to the magnitude of the issue for the British Empire."[43] Lee's conclusion was that "the Americans who adopted the Constitution likely considered three categories of persons as natural born citizens: (1) persons born within the United States; (2) persons born

---

[39] Lee, op. cit., at p. 381.
[40] Id.
[41] Id.
[42] Id., at p. 382.
[43] Id., at p. 388.

outside of the United States to U.S. citizens in government service; and (3) persons born abroad to U.S. citizen fathers who had resided in the United States but went abroad temporarily for a private purpose, like merchants."[44]

Lee's analysis goes much further than the common law, and far beyond where other commentators have rested in their analysis. The American Republic being a renegade of sorts that rejected principles rooted in feudalism, not to mention the doctrine of the divine right of kings, its leaders sought an alternative legitimating principle. They found it in the shifting of ultimate sovereign authority from the Crown to the People, governed by a written rather than unwritten organic and fundamental law.[45] In making this shift, the subject became a citizen, equal in theory if not in fact to all other citizens and eligible, if natural born, for the highest office in the land. As the regnant political philosophy of the new Republic was based in natural law, the term "natural born citizen" obviously evokes that tradition, and strongly suggests that any search for a meaning of the term not be confined to the English common law alone, but extend also to the writings of the leading natural law theorists of the day. Of these, one of the most significant was Emerich de Vattel, whose treatise, *Law of Nations, or Principles of the Law of Nature, Applied to the Conduct and Affairs of Nations and Sovereigns*, was obtained for use by the Continental Congress prior to the drafting of the Declaration of Independence.

Speaking of those who reside in a given country, Vattel noted that "by the law of nature alone, children follow the condition of their fathers, and enter into all their rights; the place of birth produces no change in this particular, and cannot, of itself, furnish any reason for taking from a child what nature has given him."[46] From this, Lee concludes that reliance on place of birth alone is inconsistent with the Framers' own reliance on natural law theory. The child of a transient visitor could not be considered a natural born citizen due to the parents' existing allegiance to a foreign polity; while children born abroad to parents travelling on business or pleasure, or serving the interests of the United States, can be nothing but natural born American citizens.

---

[44] Id., at p. 335.
[45] See, for example, R.R. Palmer, *The Age of Democratic Revolution*, Volume I (Princeton: Princeton University Press, 1959), at pp. 214-215.
[46] Lee, op. cit., at p. 391.

Lee isn't the only one to have concluded that natural born citizenship can only be understood in the context of the body of natural law principles generally embraced by the Framers. John Ira Jones, then a law student, wrote that "Vattel's treatment of the topic is unequivocal, unambiguous and clear," leaving "little to be desired by way of definition. Natural born citizens are those born in the country of parents who are citizens."[47] The term, he explained, was clearly a term of art, evident in both natural law and common law, and could only have been employed as such by the Framers, who tended to use "accepted, established terms to convey meanings in ways that would not be subject to later arbitrary revision."[48] As such, the conflation of the terms "native born" and "natural born" is entirely erroneous. "A natural born-citizen is a person born to two citizen parents within American territory, whereas a person born to anyone within American territory is a citizen."[49] The native born is entitled to all the privileges and immunities of citizenship, though he or she might not also be entitled to serve as President or Vice President. To hold otherwise defies both the contemporary understanding of a precise term of art and the Framers' objective when adopting natural born citizenship as a qualification of office designed to avoid the "risk of dual allegiances."

The failure of the Framers to precisely define the term has created grounds for debate and some degree of uncertainty. The Supreme Court's evasion of the issue for nearly two and a half centuries hasn't been helpful either, though some hint that Vattel's view is the operative one is evident in Chief Justice Waite's dicta in *Minor v. Happersett* that "it was never doubted that all children born in a country of parents who were its citizens became themselves, upon their birth, citizens also," and that such children were "natural-born citizens."[50] Without more precise guidance from the text of the Constitution or unequivocal ratio decidendi, we are left to find our way to the Framers' intent by a less direct route. It is well known that the Framers feared that foreign princes might immigrate to America, seek high office, and drag the nation into foreign conflict contrary to the best interests of the people, or that

---

4747 John Ira Jones, IV, "Natural Born Shenanigans: How the Birther Movement Exacerbated Confusion over the Constitution's Natural Born Citizen Requirement," 27 Regent U.L. Rev. 155 (2014), at p. 161.

48 Id., at p. 162.

49 Id., at p. 161.

50 *Minor v. Happersett*, supra, at 167.

newcomers to America might obtain the Presidency without shedding themselves of prior loyalties and compromise their adopted country's fortunes. It is, of course, true that many immigrants become zealous for America once obtaining citizenship and will fight and die for their adopted country even against their former countrymen. But this is not a universal sentiment, and many are the examples in the annals of history of nationals of one state obtaining power in another and then subverting the latter to become the thrall to the former. Ferdinand of Habsburg won election to the throne of Bohemia in 1526 only to transform the country into a subordinate subdivision of the Austrian Empire. His nephew, Phillip II of Spain, was similarly elected king in Portugal in 1580 after faithlessly promising to respect the rights of the country. Mihai the Brave of Wallachia received the crown of neighboring Transylvania from its nobility and then transformed the country into a tax farm to pay for his war against the Turks. Most poignant of all was the gift of the English Crown by Parliament to William III of the Netherlands and that monarch's subsequent appropriation of British men, guns and money to fight Louis XIV on land and sea. It seems hardly counter-intuitive that a person whose only citizenship is American because both parents are Americans would be less inclined to sacrifice American interests to the ambitions of foreigners and foreign states than a person who holds multiple citizenships.

The Framers' concern over the possibility of divided or weakened loyalty among those chosen to lead our great nation is facially remote from racial considerations, and those who hold and express it today can't be presumed to be racist. Racism probably didn't motivate those who condemned President Arthur for not being eligible for the Presidency, nor those opposed to John McCain taking office in the event he won election. There may have been racists who latched onto so-called birtherism as a vehicle for the delegitimizing of President Obama, but the fact remains—according to the view of Vattel and likely the Framers—President Obama wasn't and isn't a natural born citizen, nor is Kamala Harris, Ted Cruz or, indeed, Chester Allan Arthur. Obama's father was a temporary visitor in the United States who eventually returned to Kenya; neither of Kamala Harris's parents were citizens of the United States when she was born and one of them even left the country with young Kamala in tow; Ted Cruz was born in Canada to an American mother and Cuban father; and President Arthur's father was a British citizen at the time of the President's birth. This conclusion, this message, might outrage the faithful adherents of each of these distinguished Americans, but in any response to it they ought to address its substance rather than accuse the messenger of grave sins. They ought to consider, too, that in a nation of 350 million souls, finding a candidate to be President or Vice President who shares one's outlook yet who is actually eligible to serve in accordance with the requirements of the Constitution shouldn't be so difficult. It's far better to find a qualified candidate than to accept an unqualified one and spend so much energy defending the erroneous and unlawful choice.

Vigilantibus Jura Auxilio

IT was the three shots heard round the world: a 17-year-old Illinois native, attached to an ad hoc para-military band confronting Antifa and BLM rioters, opened fire, wounded one and killed two others. Much of the media went into immediate overdrive to shape the narrative and establish a base line that favored a particular ideological viewpoint. *The Washington Post* said the boy "seemingly idolized…the police… shadowed local law enforcement" and filled "his social media feeds with posts declaring 'Blue Lives Matter' and photos of himself posing with guns."[1] A reputed "neighbor" referred to him as "a high school drop-out who viewed law enforcement officers as his personal heroes."[2] "Maybe he thought he was doing the right thing," he continued, "but you don't kill somebody. That's not your business to kill someone for messing with someone else's business. That's for the cops to deal with."[3] Wisconsin's Lieutenant Governor denounced the shooter as part of an armed band with "no connection to…the state," accountable to no one, and whose ability to "walk away from the scene" without being arrested was utterly

[1] Teo Armus, Mark Berman and Griff Witte, "Before a Fatal Shooting, Teenage Kenosha Suspect Idolized the Police," www.thewashingtonpost.com, August 27, 2020.

[2] Id.

[3] Id.

"ridiculous."[4] The Daily Show host Trevor Noah opined that the only reason the kid had a gun was to shoot someone. "That's the only reason people like him join these gangs in the first place."[5] This wasn't "the battle of Yorktown," he said, "it's just a bunch of dudes threatening people with guns."[6] Representative Ayanna Pressley summed up the emergent narrative best by bluntly denouncing the young man as a "17-year-old white supremacist domestic terrorist" who drove across state lines, armed with an AR 15," and "shot and killed 2 people who had assembled to affirm the value, dignity, and worth of black lives."[7]

The apparent indifference of the police to the shooter's actions, even as he stood in front of them with his gun still slung from his shoulder waving to get their attention, was in stark contrast, many thought, to the police response to Jacob Blake—a black man whose shooting by police only days before had sparked the Kenosha unrest. "The fundamental unfairness of those linked tragedies in one Wisconsin city over the course of three days," said one commentator, "should be enough for even the most stubborn white Americans to understand why people are marching to assert and rightfully demand that black lives matter. The clear-as-glass unfairness of it all should be enough."[8] Blake's father told CNN that the "17-year-old Caucasian" who "shot and killed two people and blew another man's arm off…got to go home. He got water, they gave that guy water, and a high five."[9] Others focused their ire on the President, blaming him for the escalation of violence by supporters whose alleged racism and commitment to armed violence he consistently fails to condemn.[10]

All across the wide range of critical opinion one term in particular

---

[4] Stacey Baca, Rob Elgas and Alexis McAdams, "Antioch Kyle Rittenhouse Appears in Court on Murder Charges for Kenosha Protest Shooting, Lawyers Say he Acted in Self-Defense," http://abc7chicago.com, August 28, 2020.

[5] Poppy Noor, "Vigilante, Volunteer, Terrorist, How the U.S. Media Covers Kyle Rittenhouse, www.theguardian.com, August 29, 2020.

[6] Id.

[7] Id.

[8] Rex Huppke, "Jacob Blake, Kyle Rittenhouse and Kenosha's vivid Example of American Racism," *The Chicago Tribune*, August 27, 2020.

[9] Tom McCarthy, A Tale of Two Videos: Jacob Blake, Kyle Rittenhouse and Two Types of Policing, www.theguardian.com, August 29, 2020

[10] Marlow Stern, "John Oliver Rips Tucker Carlson, Trump, and the McCloskeys Over Kenosha Shooting Suspect Kyle Rittenhouse," www.thedailybeast.com, August 31, 2020.

continued to appear: "vigilante." *The New York Post* called the shooter "a gun-toting vigilante."[11] *The Daily Beast* used the term "teen vigilante" to describe the boy, while the alleged comedian John Oliver referred to him as a "17-year-old vigilante with a rifle."[12] One on-line news source called him a "trump loving vigilante" and a "MAGA vigilante," while another said he even bragged about being one.[13]

As the portrayal of Kyle Rittenhouse took on a dark and critical hue, that of the men he shot soared into the higher reaches of the heavens. Joseph Rosenbaum, the first man killed, was referred to as "a 36-year old father" residing in Kenosha, who was "survived by his fiancée and 2-year-old daughter."[14] He was "known by friends and family as 'Jo-Jo,' was a jokester" and "loved his daughter very much."[15] The second man killed, Anthony Huber, was characterized as a "talented skateboarder" and "hero" who "decided to use his voice and stand up for a cause that meant something," yet died after he broke away from "peaceful protesting" to "selflessly" aid "in taking down an attacker."[16] He was a protest regular, ever there to help wipe the tear-gas from the eyes of his fellow protestors. He and Rosenbaum were apparently quite chummy and were recalled as "the sweetest hearts" and "sweet guys."[17] The third man, who survived despite a significant loss to his right bicep, was Gaige Grosskreutz, "an activist who volunteered as a medic during the Kenosha demonstrations."[18] He was a college student, a river guide and,

---

[11] See Noor, op. cit.

[12] Rachel Olding, Pilar Melendez & Jonathan Ballew, "Teen Vigilante Killed Unarmed Kenosha Protestor Who Threw a Plastic Bag at Him: Court Docs," www.thedailybeast.com, August 28, 2020; and Stern, op. cit.

[13] Bernard Beanz Smalls, "Trump-Loving Vigilante Kyle Rittenhouse Looking at Life in Prison After Being Charged with Murder," https://hiphopwired.com, August 28, 2020; and Karen Ruis & Emily Crane, "Police-Obsessed Gunman, 17, Who is Charged with Murder of Two BLM Protestors During Kenosha Riots Sat Front Row at a Trump MAGA Rally as video Interview Emerges of Him Bragging About Being a Vigilante Before the Mayhem Unfolded," www.dailymail.co.uk, August 26, 2020.

[14] Sarah Rulz-Grossman, "These are the Victims of Kenosha Protest Shooting," www.huffpost.com, August 27, 2020.

[15] Id.

[16] Kunal Dey, "Anthony Huber: Who Was Kenosha Shooter Kyle Rittenhouse's 26-Year-Old Victim?" meaww.com, August 27, 2020.

[17] Stephen Groves & Scott Bauer, "Victims of Kenosha Protest Shooting Suspect Tried to Disarm Kyle Rittenhouse: Reports," https://abc7ny.com, August 28, 2020.

[18] Id.

like Huber, "a hero."[19]

The narrative of saintly social justice demonstrators verses the evil white right-wing racist vigilante began unravelling nearly the same moment it took shape. Sleuths in the amateur journalist community of the internet quickly discovered that Rosenbaum was a violent and perverted felon who had served a decade in prison for raping a child, with added time for disorderly behavior behind bars.[20] His defiant mug shot and sex offender registry page soon dashed across the world wide web, along with the record of his several returns to jail due to repeated violations of the terms of his probation. Huber was found to have been repeatedly charged with serious and lesser crimes, and had a felony conviction for "strangulation" and "repeat domestic abuse." The soon-to-be left hand dominant survivor, Gaige Grosskreutz, proved to be the tamest of the bunch, with convictions for nothing worse than being "intoxicated & armed w/a gun."[21]

A more objective view of Rittenhouse's action emerged through the magic of modern technology and the surfacing of but a handful of likely dozens of cell phone video images of the events that unfolded in Kenosha on the night of August 25. The so-called militia that Rittenhouse joined was there at the request of property owners whose property had already been seriously damaged and even destroyed the previous night by radical insurgents operating under the umbrella of Antifa and BLM. Though he lived just across the State line, Rittenhouse himself worked in Kenosha as a lifeguard, and had friends in town. Together they joined the armed group, using weapons that belonged not to Rittenhouse but to a Wisconsin friend. Whether he was within the law to wield a weapon remains uncertain, but if he wasn't, the crime is but a misdemeanour. He was obviously experienced in the use of AR-15s, as social media images and his own performance under fire attest. Prior to the shootings, the radicals had marched onto one of the properties the armed men were guarding, undeterred by their weapons and angry over the obstacle they posed to further rampage. At one point, Rosenbaum started screaming at several of the defenders, repeatedly daring them to shoot him and strangely calling them a name that is usually employed as a derogatory

---

19 Id.

20 "Sex Offender Joseph Rosenbaum Taunted Armed Civilians: 'Shoot Me, N—r!,'" https://theothermccain.

21 Id.

racial epithet—not something one would expect from an anti-racism demonstrator. Next to him was standing Huber, as well as a tall, bearded man later identified as Joshua Ziminski. This scene was only minutes before the events captured on a second video showing the armed Rittenhouse fleeing from the pursuing child rapist Rosenbaum, who throws an object at his prey a second before Ziminski fires a pistol in the air. Rittenhouse turns a few steps later and Rosembaum is right on top of him reaching for the gun. Several shots ring out off camera, then several others from another gun, before Rittenhouse emerges from behind an obscuring car. He appears to make a phone call and starts running in the direction from which he came.

Numerous other videos captured the next scene. Together what they depict is Rittenhouse running up the street pursued by numerous masked men, all apparently associated with the rioting. One man in a white shirt runs behind him and strikes him in the back of the head, knocking off the teen's hat. Gaige Grosskreutz is seen passing one videographer as he reaches behind him and pulls something with his right hand from his waist band… no doubt the gun he later aims at Rittenhouse. Yet another man is seen rapidly approaching Rittenhouse from behind and appears to hit him a second time. A few steps later Rittenhouse tumbles to the ground, but quickly rights himself and points his gun forward. As Rittenhouse focuses on the white-shirted man and at least one other pursuer, yet another rioter runs at him and kicks him in the head, knocking the teenager onto his back as he himself flies forward and falls to the ground. Just then, Huber lunges with his skate board and hits Rittenhouse in the head or shoulder. As he's carried over Rittenhouse by his own momentum, a struggle ensues for control of the gun. Rittenhouse's sling gives him an advantage and he is able hold on to the gun as Huber attempts to pull it along with him as he starts to move away. Rittenhouse fires, the approaching crowd including Grosskreutz suddenly comes to a half and backs off, and Huber, taking a step or two, grasps his chest, drops his skate board and collapses to the ground. He was probably dead within seconds from a bullet through the heart. Just then, Grosskreutz appears to be confronted with a decision: back off for good or attempt to take down the teen, who has him in his sights, but is holding his fire. After hesitating a moment, Grosskreutz moved forward and was immediately shot. A red plume consisting of the blood and tissue that composed much of Grosskruetz's right bicep exploded. Grosskreutz did what appeared to be a gig, ran a few steps away, took a knee and started screaming for a "medic." The gun he had just pointed at Rittenhouse, seemingly soldered to his limp hand, dangled toward the ground.

It is a strange time indeed when supposedly reputable news outlets and print journalists can venture to present obvious criminal rioters as upholders of justice and a young man who volunteered to defend the peace from disruption by the same rioters as a criminal vigilante. It is stranger still when much of the media has agreed to become the mouth piece for calls to defund and abolish the very authorities to whom vigilantes are traditionally chided for failing to defer. The term vigilante itself is treated as if it were taboo, out of step with any notion of law or justice. The negative connotation of the term is but an example of the kind of forced drift of the language that has occurred in the past half century so that it might accord better with the objectives of those applying the force. While operating outside of existing legal structures, vigilantism has actually played a largely positive role in our nation's history and can be credited in part with the pacification of lawless regions absolutely necessary if any system of law and order were ever to take root. "It arose," said the historian Daniel Boorstin, "not to circumvent courts, but to provide them… not to neutralize institutions already there, but to fill a vacuum."[22]

Vigilantism bears a close relationship with another discounted term, the militia. The singular distinction between the two terms and the concepts they represent is the militia's organizational structure and formal legal status. Early understanding of the militia was of the complete body of adult male citizens capable of bearing arms in the defence of the community.[23] In time, it came to be integrated into the constitutional structures of the States and the federal government. Occasionally, it acted independent of other political authority, transforming its members into vigilantes, as when Chief Justice Marshall helped to organized and lead an ad hoc committee of vigilance in Virginia's capital during the War of 1812 to plan for resistance to the

---

[22] Daniel J. Boorstin, *The Americans: The National Experience* (New York: Vintage Books, 1965), at p. 81.

[23] *District of Columbia v. Heller* (2008) 554 U.S. 570, 128 S.Ct. 2783.

British should the latter advance south from Chesapeake Bay.[24] The Underground Railroad was a type of vigilance movement, as were the committees that formed along the border in northern States beginning in the 1820s to intercept slave catchers operating from south of the Mason Dixon Line in pursuit of fugitive slaves.

We tend to think of vigilantism in the context of nascent communities, often on the frontier, attempting to address problems of lawlessness arising in part from a lack of settled political and social organization, and the opportunism of lawless men to capitalize on unsettled and unregulated conditions by taking from others what they'd prefer not to honestly earn. There seemed always to be an element in early American and frontier society that "wanted to burst their subordinate bounds and take over the new communities," who "rejected the respectable values of life and property and wished to upset the social structure."[25] As the frontier attracted those who refused to conform to societal norms in more settled parts of the country, and law enforcement if not law itself remained at best rudimentary, there was ever a "danger of a takeover of newly settled areas by the alienated, outcast elements of society."[26] Lack of any tradition of law and the tendency of base men to encourage one another in their sins, contributed to the ease such men had in acting to corrupt the earliest phases of development of systems of justice. "Whenever possible," noted the historian Richard Maxwell Brown, "outlaws would obtain false witnesses in their behalf, pack juries, bribe officials, and in extreme cases intimidate the entire system; judges, juries, and law enforcement officials."[27] The ultimate authority in many new communities was the violent and lawless mob of armed men, which citizens good and bad dared not oppose. Early Stockton, California was typical of such places. "Courts were a mockery," said its first historian. "Judges and juries were bribed, or threatened with vengeance if they dare oppose the mandates of the ruling power. Knives and pistols were often drawn in open court, and the leader, pistol in

---

[24] Jean Edward Smith, *John Marshall: Definer of a Nation* (New York: Henry Holt and Company, 1996), at p. 415-416.

[25] Richard Maxwell Brown, *Strain of Violence: Historical Studies of American Violence and Vigilantism* (New York: Oxford University Press, 1975), at p. 105.

[26] Id.

[27] Id., at p. 113.

hand, and jumping upon a desk, would defy the law to take its course."[28]

In these primitive times and places, as those yearning for peace and order grew restless under the regime of terror, there emerged what Brown calls a "philosophy of vigilantism," exhibiting three components: "self-preservation, the right of revolution, and popular sovereignty."[29] Not surprisingly, the philosophy owed much to the ideas of John Locke that had previously inspired the Founders. As Locke touted the liberty of the people to rise up when government "neglects and abandons that charge, so that the laws already made can no longer be put in execution" and thereby "reduces all to anarchy," so one Nineteenth Century defender of vigilante justice exclaimed that "the right of the people to take care of themselves if the law does not is an indisputable right."[30] In Butler, Kansas, one group of vigilantes, "invoking 'self-preservation' as 'the first law of nature,'" asserted that "'however much we deplore the further use of violence in order to secure life and property…we shall not hesitate to do justice to all the guilty if it is necessary.'"[31]

As the frontier moved west so did vigilantism. There were 210 vigilante movements in the west from 1849 to 1902. Some movements were well organized, like the San Francisco incarnations, while others were instant in nature, not formally organized and focused on addressing a single act of lawlessness. The more organized movements had command structures, bylaws, and even courts to try offenders. The San Francisco Committee during the year 1856 is perhaps the most famous, and probably the most organized and efficient, of American vigilante movements. After a series of notorious day light murders that were in part politically motivated, a group of residents headed by prominent members of the business class organized a committee and set at once to forming an armed force. In short time, they had taken control of the jail and seized the murderers. The prisoners were tried, found guilty and then executed. Other ne're-do-wells were apprehended and sentenced to flogging and banishment. When State Supreme Court Justice David Terry entered the City on the Governor's authority with a small posse to serve a writ of habeas corpus on the Committee and

---

28 George H. Tinkham, *A History of Stockton* (San Francisco: W.M. Hinton & Co., 1880), at pp. 155-156.

29 Brown, op. cit., at p. 115.

30 Id., at p. 117; and John Locke, *Second Treatise of Government*, at § 219.

31 Brown, op. cit., at p. 107.

attempt to quell the vigilance uprising, an agent of the Committee attempted to arrest one of his men, with the result that Terry nearly killed him with a Bowie Knife. The vigilante militia mobilized at once, arrested Terry and virtually the entire San Francisco branch of the State militia and put the Judge on trial for his life. He was discharged without a capital sentence, after which the Committee completed its work and then disbanded. Many similar committees would rise over the course of the next half century, most of them serving as what Brown calls "a transitional movement between the old and the new," and paving the way for a society where law was generally obeyed and judicial officers and the courts were mostly respected.[32]

The pejorative reference to Kyle Rittenhouse as a vigilante parallels the attempts to characterize those who would arm themselves in the face of criminal rioters associated with Antifa and BLM as white supremacist successors-in-interest to the Ku Klux Klan. The historian George C. Rable supports this characterization, saying that "the Klan developed as part of an American vigilante tradition" and that Klan violence "was squarely within the tradition of American mob behavior."[33] But, as Rable himself makes clear, the Klan was hardly an organization dedicated to the upholding of the law in the absence of any lawful authority willing to do so. Instead, the Klan was a terrorist guerilla movement composed of veterans of the defeated Confederate military, whose fundamental goal was resistance to the triumphant Union, defiance of the Thirteenth Amendment, and thwarting the ability by Black Americans to enjoy any modicum of liberty or political power. Having lost the war and been compelled to embrace the political equality of the races, Confederate partisans adopted a different strategy. Everywhere, black leaders were beaten and killed. Even whites who supported the Constitution were targeted. "Klansmen," said historian Eric Foner, "murdered three scalawag members of the Georgia legislature and drove ten others from their homes."[34] In Calhoun County, Alabama, white men who voted the wrong way were "ostracized and cursed and…in some instances their houses have been surrounded by disguised bands in the night time,

---

[32] Id., at p. 94.

[33] George C. Rable, *And There Was No Peace: The Role of Violence in the Politics of Reconstruction* (Athens: The University of Georgia Press, 2007), at pp. 92 and 96.

[34] Eric Foner, *Reconstruction: America's Unfinished Revolution – 1863-1877* (New York: Harper & Row, 1988), at p. 427.

threatening their lives if they do not desist in their political course."[35] The Klan put negro schools and churches to the torch, attacked teachers, and roamed the countryside kidnapping black laborers who had opted to quit their jobs because the pay wasn't sufficient and forced them to continue work with their former employers under pain of the whip.[36] In the North Carolina Piedmont, a judge counted twelve murders, nine rapes, fourteen cases of arson, and over 700 beatings committed by the Klan, while in Jackson, Florida, "where Satan has his seat," 150 people were murdered.[37]

Vigilantism is often equated with lynching as well, hence a subtext of racism and racially motivated violence is appended to the term. Though far more white men were lynched than black, it is the all-too-true image of the howling white mob tearing a falsely accused black man from a jail cell or from his bed at home and stringing him up to the nearest tree that excites the American memory. Lynching, however, is hardly consistent with the American vigilante tradition that sought to supplement and support law, not violate it. The lynchings that occurred during Reconstruction and afterward were acts of terror designed to control the black population, often with the full cooperation or tacit consent of elected officials who resented the fall of slavery and ratification of the Thirteenth and Fourteenth Amendments.[38] Guilt or innocence didn't matter as much as sending the black population a strongly worded message. In contrast, the executions performed by vigilantes tended to follow actual trials and were based on evidence of direct witnesses rather than hearsay or pure circumstance. The executions of James Casey and Charles Cora and others by the San Francisco Vigilance Committee in 1856 and the punishment of Judge Terry and others occurred only after a full trial, where witnesses testified and opportunities to cross examine and to introduce evidence were provided to the accused. Lynching was not an example of the people exercising their sovereign authority to override corrupt law enforcement officials to ensure that justice was done. It was, instead, said Justice Joseph Bradley, "the prostration of all law and government; a defiance of laws; a resort to the methods of vengeance of those who recognize no

[35] Id.
[36] Id., at pp. 428-429.
[37] Id., at pp. 430-431.
[38] Brown, op. cit., at p. 161.

law, no society, no government" and "a gross want of fealty to the law and repudiation of legal government."[39]

As traditional vigilantism in this country attempted to fill a gap in ill-formed and immature social structures that lacked law or a legal tradition, and constituted a transition from the state of nature to the state of society governed by law and the rule of law, this modern incarnation, in the form of Kyle Rittenhouse and those whose party he joined that fateful night, is something quite different: a response to the very opposite trend, the dissolution of the rule of law and the attempt by radicals to tear it down so they might replace it with a revolutionary regime designed to correct the many systemic defects they wildly contend plague and oppress our society. These radicals claim they are the true patriots, the true lovers of justice, but who can believe it when instead of seeking out individual malefactors who are causing injustice and oppression and the corrupt officials who permit injustice to flourish, they burn down private businesses, attack anyone seeking to stand in the breach, and commandeer possession of the public forum so that no one else may enjoy its use. They scream obscenities, scrawl their hideous graffiti everywhere and threaten mayhem in places yet untouched by their violence. They have no narrow focus as the vigilantes of old, just ruination in mind, and seek not to establish order, but to destroy it so that anarchy might reign.

In truth, they are more like the Klan than the militia and the vigilantes they equate it to, and are its natural heirs. Even the organization that benefits from their antics is the same that enjoyed and encouraged the Klan's rampage. The very progressive and very fine historian Eric Foner said of the Klan that it was "in effect…a military force serving the interests of the Democratic party."[40] "Its purposes were political, but political in the broadest sense, for it sought to affect power relations, both public and private."[41] Its target was black men and women who might exercise autonomy, but it aimed, too, "to destroy the Republican Party's infrastructure" so that any institutional opposition to the Democrats' political ambition might be rendered null and void.[42] Like Democrat party leaders of old, "who put up bail for arrested

[39] *Ex parte Wall* (1883) 107 U.S. 265, 274.
[40] Foner, op. cit., at p. 425.
[41] Id.
[42] Id., at p. 426.

Klansmen, spoke of the 'good' the organization accomplished despite its 'excesses,' and strongly opposed federal intervention," Democrats today like Kamala Harris and members of the Biden campaign team contribute money to bail out those arrested for rioting across the county, falsely hail the rioters as "peaceful protestors" and condemn the President as a tyrant when he merely dispatched federal agents to protect a federal courthouse under siege in the Democrat bastion of Seattle.[43] As prominent Democrats of yesteryear would rather minimize the Klan's activities or offer "thinly disguised rationalizations for them" than dissociate themselves from the Klan's campaign of terror, Democrats today justify Antifa violence as provoked or instigated by aggressive "white nationalists" and BLM looting as a form of reparations for past injustice and unfairness.[44] While some Democrats of old even "denied the organization's existence altogether," some Democrats and men and women of the left today accuse the President himself of conspiracy theories when he speaks of clandestine organizers who hide in the "dark shadows" and entire plane loads of black clad insurgents travelling from riot to riot.[45] And as the Klan rode throughout the election cycle of 1870 and contributed to the Democrat Party victories in North Carolina, Alabama and Georgia, so some Democrats, like Kamala Harris, seem intent that the "protests" continue through election day.[46] The President's opponent has even declared that people are fools to think that the rioting will stop if the President is re-elected.[47] The message is clear: vote Democrat or face the wrath.

What we face today in many cities across the land is not a vacuum

---

[43] Id., at p. 434; Boris Epshteyn, "Democrats' Hypocrisy on Riots Reveals Political Nature of Coronavirus Lockdowns," www.newsweek.com, June 12, 2020; and "Joe Biden Says Federal Officers are Using 'Egregious Tactics' in Portland," https://katu.com, July 21, 2020.

[44] Foner, op. cit., at p. 434; Dustin J. Seibert, "White Supremacists Infiltrating George Floyd Protests Have a Different Agenda," www.bet.com, June 1, 2020; and Lee Brown, "BLM Organizer Who Called Looting 'Reparations' Dismisses Peaceful Protesting," https://nypost.com, August 13, 2020.

[45] Foner, op. cit., at 434; and David Smith, "Donald Trump Makes Baseless Claim that 'Dark Shadows' are Controlling Joe Biden," www.theguardian.com, September 1, 2020.

[46] Katherine Schaffstall, "Kamala Harris Says Protests Won't Stop Despite Lack of News Coverage," www.hollywoodreporter.com, June 18, 2020.

[47] Laura Clawson, "Biden: 'Does Anyone Believe There Will be Less Violence in America if Donald Trump is Reelected,'" www.dailykos.com, August 31, 2020.

where political and social order ought to abide. Everywhere the legal and political structures are so elaborate that most municipalities often can barely afford them. Those who hold positions of authority at the municipal and State levels are vested with considerable power to control and eliminate expressions of violence and disturbances of the peace, and yet in many places around the country they not only fail to exercise the power, they refuse to. Minnesota's Governor watched as the city of Minneapolis burned, while the mayor himself joined the rioters in the streets. Portland's mayor also refused to act, and even seemed to encourage the construction of a lawless zone in the city center controlled at gun point by insurgents whose efforts to loot and burn and even murder went seemingly unchecked. The mayor claimed they were merely exercising their constitutional rights and then demanded that the President, who'd offered to assist in quelling the disturbance, "'stay the hell out of the way." It was the President who needed to be stopped, he said, not the rioters who seemed to have taken control of his city. In city after city, police refuse to intervene, and when they do Democrat district attorneys refuse to prosecute or simply dismiss any charges. The situation is almost perfectly analogous to the Reconstruction South, where civic leaders either looked the other way or participated in acts of violence, and is an even more perfect fit with Locke's vision of a government that "neglects and abandons" its charge to execute the law, and allows the birth of a condition where effectively law does not exist and becomes that "mystery in politicks, unconceivable to humane capacity" which he called "a government without laws."[48]

It was into this state of acquiescence by government to lawlessness that young Kyle Rittenhouse stepped. On the verge of his majority, already considering himself a citizen defender of law and order, he fled from a gang of insurgents led by a trio of armed felons and only fired when physically attacked, remaining cool headed enough not to indiscriminately spray bullets, and wounding the last of his assailants only when the pistol wielding man visibly chose to proceed in the face of a pointed rifle barrel. The young man chided for being too young to answer the call to arms is now charged as an adult by a Democrat district attorney, facing punishment for the hastily filed crime of first-degree murder and sundry other offenses. He's fortunate that Antifa instructs

[48] Locke, supra, at § 219.

its more passive members to film all its campaigns while the more aggressive ones challenge the police, loot private businesses and burn down buildings; for video from so many angles appears to establish a perfect defense to the most serious charges. Ideology blinds many; but even a blind man or woman can see that Rittenhouse wasn't an aggressor. He was literally running away from a gang of aggressors even as he held a deadly weapon in hand—a weapon he obviously didn't want to use unless a threat against him became far too close for comfort. When his trial might actually take place is anyone's guess—he remains at this writing in Illinois fighting extradition after turning himself in to authorities there. Meanwhile, others undoubtedly have already stepped forward to assume his place in the line of defense, in Kenosha and elsewhere. As the insurgents who despise peace and order continue their rampage unabated by any action by Democrat mayors and district attorneys, it's only a matter of time before more shots are fired. If vigilantism is to be avoided, the authorities simply need to do their jobs.

The Great Tribulation

HE looked, and there before him was a door standing open, and a voice commanding him to come and see what must take place in later times. On a scroll written on either side, clenched within the hand of He who held it, and sealed with seven seals, was writ the message of the ages. "Who," asked the voice, "is worthy to break the seals," to open and to read that the world may know what is fated to come? In all of that great host that crowded about the precinct where that voice was uttered, no one save a lamb could answer the challenge. Undoing one seal after another, many wonders were disclosed: the darkening of the skies at midday, the reddening of the moon, the boiling of the sea, and the approach of four riders atop white, flaming red, black and pale mounts, bringing sword, famine and plague, and laying waste the earth. The kings of the four quarters, the generals, the rich and mighty, and every man free and slave, revealed the scroll, would take to the hills and rocks and hide from the wrath to come, hoping that the stones themselves would fall upon them and shield them from the catastrophe. There among the masses of a panicked humanity would be those marked indelibly above their eyes, robed in white, wielding palm branches in their hands, and crying out in a voice that filled the heavens that salvation belonged to He who sits upon the Throne, and to the lamb. Yet from the sea would come a destroyer, to wreck what remained of the world, to cut down all who would not bear his imprint and fall in worship of his glory, resisted only by those clothed in sackcloth, with the power to deliver fire with their words and devour all those who would raise their hands against them, until they themselves were slain by the destroyer, commander of a legion of armoured locusts, uttering proud words and blasphemies, slandering the Author of creation and exercising authority over every tribe, people, language and nation.

Today, across the country, sword, famine and plague leave their terrible imprimatur upon the land. A terrifying disease, more fearsome in the mind than it is in the body, convenient in its ability to deliver a justification for the subjugation of mankind and the dictation of the terms by which all life is to be lived, shrinks the economy, eliminates many prospects for remunerative work and causes many to fear a terrible death and the loss of all means of earning one's daily bread. Unrest embroils our cities, authority is resisted even by authority itself, and fires burn across the west, consuming the works of man and driving a helpless humanity from homes to which many will not return. In the face of this disorder, the faithful can no longer abide by the laws that require them to hide within their homes and address one another only by means of technological marvels that we now know fall far short of what it means to actually commune and communicate. In Minnesota, the faithful filed a lawsuit in federal court challenging the riot-friendly Governor's executive order requiring social distancing and the wearing of masks during worship services.[1] In Palmetto, Florida, the Reverend Joel Tillis of the Suncoast Baptist Church brought suit to overturn a Manatee County mask mandate on the grounds that it hinders prayer and the free exercise of religion.[2] In June, a federal judge blocked New York State from enforcing restrictions on indoor religious gatherings in excess of 25 percent capacity when other events were permitted to occur at a capacity twice that size. In Kentucky, a federal court of appeals upheld a lower court's issuance of an injunction, freeing the churches of

---

[1] David Crary, "More US Churches Sue to Challenge COVID-19 Restrictions," *St. Louis Post-Dispatch*, August 14, 2020

[2] Id.

that State from total bans on in-person worship.[3] Other States, including Illinois, buckled to the onslaught of litigation and eased up on similar restrictions. In Nevada, after failing to prevail before the U.S. Supreme Court in a challenge to orders that banned religious services but permitted casinos to operate, the faithful took heart from the dissenting words of Justice Gorsuch that "there is no world in which the Constitution permits Nevada to favor Caesar's Palace over Calvary Chapel," and simply moved their meetings to a casino and proceeded to worship as if nothing were amiss.[4] Everywhere, it seems, fire flows from the words of the believer, and none can cause him harm.

Everywhere, perhaps, except in progressive, left-of-center, dystopian California. Early during the so-called Pandemic, county authorities and the Governor issued sweeping orders limiting a broad range of endeavours deemed to be non-essential. Among the deprecated activities were worship and prayer gatherings protected by the First Amendment. Churches tended in those early days to render unto Caesar, concerned as they were to promote brotherly love and the wellbeing of saint and sinner alike. The duration of the restrictions only began to irritate as doubts regarding the true threat posed by the disease emerged and the government showed increasing favour to activities and operations believers considered to be less essential than what the Constitution expressly protects. By the end of the summer, rebellion erupted. In Santa Clara County, a pastor repeatedly refused to follow restrictions on in-person worship services and willingly accepted the consequences in the form of fines totalling $15,000.[5] Outdoor services were an option he accepted in the early phases of the lock-down, but when fires generated thickening smoke and threatened the health of his parishioners far more greatly than the extremely scarce virus, he could no longer obey the County's rules.

To the south, in Ventura, the District Attorney hauled Pastor Rob McCoy into court to hold him to account for his repeated violation of a prior order to cease and desist from holding in-person services. Though represented by counsel, Pastor McCoy ably explained to Judge Vincent

---

3 "Court Halts Ban on Mass Gatherings at Kentucky Churches," https://apnews.com, May 9, 2020.

4 Blake Fussell, "Evangelicals for Trump Bypass Nev. Restrictions by Holding Rally at Las Vegas Casino," www.christianpost.com, August 8, 2020.

5 Meghan Roos, "California Church Fined Thousands for Holding Indoor Services: 'If I Perish, I Perish,'" www.newsweek.com, August 28, 2020.

O'Neill that while he would like to comply with the order, he could not do so in light of the spiritual needs of his parishioners. Though some churches were able to conduct their worship meeting outdoors, his church lacked adequate outdoor facilities. Steaming summer temperatures also posed special dangers to numerous of his older flock. The extremely low incidence of COVID-19 in the zip code where his church was situated and the absence of a single COVID case among his parishioners further mitigated the need for so broad a restriction on religious liberty.[6] The strictures on life and in-person contact were causing profound injury to many in his pastoral care. "There's been family issues, substance abuse issues, suicide concerns, it's affected our fellowship like it has the entire community, it's been devastating since the shutdown started."[7] When asked why he violated the Judge's order, McCoy respectfully replied that "I had to. The church is essential. People need to fellowship in a time of pandemic. God is critical."[8]

Similar trial faced Pastor John MacArthur of Grace Community Church in Los Angeles County. Not content to resist the authority of the County when it impairs the rights of his people to worship their God, MacArthur took his case directly to and against the Governor himself, saying that he had "overstepped his executive privileges with 'draconian' restrictions by shutting down churches and telling believers they cannot worship during the coronavirus pandemic."[9] Though warned by County authorities that he could face fines and arrest for defying the Governor's order by hosting indoor services, he threw open the cathedral doors and summoned the faithful to gather. "We feel like we are the most essential reality in the world," he said. The governor is but a man, and Jesus is Lord, and the latter's command possesses supremacy over the words of any mere man. "The Constitution doesn't give them the power to do that, and they don't certainly have the spiritual power to do that, to usurp the place that only Jesus Christ has

---

[6] Kathleen Wilson, "Judge Holds Godspeak Chapel and Pastor Rob McCoy in Contempt, Orders Fine," *Ventura County Star*, August 22, 2020.

[7] "Godspeak Calvary Chapel Fined $3,000 for Holding Indoor Gatherings," https://christiannewsnow.com, August 21, 2020.

[8] Id.

[9] Caleb Parke, "California Pastor Defies Coronavirus Orders Despite Threat of Arrest: Newsom 'Not the Head of the Church," www.foxnews.com, August 4, 2020.

over his church."[10] It should "shock the conscience of every Christian that churches are coming under assault from our government simply for holding church."[11] His lawyer added that the broad scope of State and local orders restricting in-person and indoor church activities has "gone now far past rational or reasonable and are firmly in the territory of tyranny and discrimination."[12] Far from being about health, orders that permit many less essential activities to carry on and are enforced by authorities who exhibit remarkable passivity in the face of very public and very violent political demonstrations are actually just "blatantly targeting churches."[13] Beating back four successive efforts to enjoin further indoor services, MacArthur failed on the fifth. Outside the courthouse, he vowed to continue meeting with his parishioners in defiance of the State.[14]

Legal pundits and experts on the Constitution predictably scoff at claims by MacArthur and other believers that the government's restriction of religious rights is too broad and unmoored in a compelling purpose. The CDC's own data tells a different story: less than 10,000 deaths can be attributed to COVID-19 alone; the rest were the product of age, obesity and multiple preexisting morbidities.[15] Knee jerk classification of any person who died with the disease as someone who died from it, the evidence of up to a third of all positive tests being false, and the reality that the disease is little distinguishable from the flu (save with regard to how fatalities are counted) undermine the contention that a compelling purpose is served by shutting down not only churches and schools but a significant portion of our economy.[16] The incongruous exceptions to restrictions favoring sex clubs and casinos hardly bode

---

[10] Id.

[11] "Judge Rejects Fourth LA County Bid for Restraining Order Against Grace Community Church," https://losangles.cbslocal.com, August 25, 2020.

[12] David Crary, op. cit.

[13] Id.

[14] Michael Hernandez, "LA Superior Court Rules Against Grace Community Pastor John MacArthur; Orders Church to Close," www.citizensjournal.com, September 10, 2020.

[15] Amanda Woods, "94% of Americans who Died from COVID-19 had Contributing Conditions: CDC," www.nypost.com, August 31, 2020.

[16] Timothy Allen & John R. Lott, Jr., U.S. Covid-19 Death Toll is Inflated," www.realclearpolitics.com, May 29, 2020; Chuck Dinerstein & Charles Geshekter, "Rethinking COVID-19 Mortality Statistics," www.asch.org, May 27, 2020; and Carl Heneghan, "how Many Covid Diagnoses are False Positives?," www.spectator.com.uk, July 20, 2020.

well for any unbiased assessment of the propriety of extending those restrictions to activities as fundamental as the free exercise of religion. When considering these details in light of the fact that so many of those promoting the reining in of our social and economic commerce are the same who express casual hostility to Christianity, it isn't so unreasonable to conclude that the ban on indoor church service is but a pretext for a new age of religious persecution.

Persecution of the faith, of course, is nothing new. From the day Christ read from the Book of Isaiah in the synagogue at Capernaum and pronounced the prophesy to have been fulfilled, a shudder of indefinable revulsion has rippled outward into the world.[17] The Roman soldiers who flayed and mocked Him, drove thorns into His head and spikes into His limbs were but the first who would lay their hands on any who professed the new faith. Saul persecuted and Paul was persecuted, and both he and Peter supposedly met their end in the manner of their Lord. In a fit of madness, or to hide his own culpability for the destruction of Rome, the Emperor Nero condemned the early Christians for the crime. "They died in torments," wrote Gibbon, "and their torments were embittered by insult and derision. Some were nailed on crosses; others sewn up in the skins of wild beasts, and exposed to the fury of dogs; others again, smeared over with combustible materials, were used as torches to illuminate the darkness of the night."[18]

The insistence of Christians on a singular moral vision and the exclusion of any other god before them, extending even to the civic deities and sacred rituals of the government, brought with it a stigma that marked them in the eyes of the state as potential liabilities and sources of discord and disloyalty in good times and bad. "Pagan civilization," said the historian Durant, "was founded upon the state, Christian civilization upon religion. To a Roman his religion was part of the structure and ceremony of government, and his morality culminated in patriotism; to a Christian his religion was something apart from and superior to political society; his highest allegiance belonged not to Caesar but to Christ."[19] The whole body of Christians, said Gibbon,

---

[17] Luke 4:16-4:21.

[18] Edward Gibbon, *The Decline and Fall of the Roman Empire*, Volume I (New York: The Modern Library), at p. 457.

[19] Will Durant, *Caesar and Christ: A History of Roman Civilization and of Christianity from their Beginnings to A.D. 325* (New York: Simon & Schuster, 1944), at p. 647.

"unanimously refused to hold any communion with the gods of Rome, of the empire, and of mankind."[20] Since the gods of Rome became in time "so intimately linked with the State, their worship was part of the duties of a loyal citizen; and since the Christians so pointedly denied them this worship, the antagonism inevitably became a political matter."[21] Men who followed a faith that claimed "the whole man" could not possibly be relied upon to be loyal to emperor and imperium, hence the terrors of death were necessary to deter and punish. Having "dissolved the sacred ties of custom and education, violated the religious institutions of their country, and presumptuously despised whatever their fathers had believed as true or had reverenced as sacred," Christians "incurred the supposed guilt of an unnatural and unpardonable offense."[22] Over the centuries, waves of persecution came and went, and while terrors were inflicted and the faithful fell dead from the torments, the relenting by authorities as the passions of the moment and the need for scapegoats waned became as certain as yet another wave was inevitable.

The greatest and one of the last of these periodic tribulations came in the wake of the Emperor Diocletian's attempted revival of Roman institutions through renewed commitment to the putative father of both gods and men. If Diocletian's restoration of the Empire depended upon the supremacy of and universal homage to great Jupiter, the state's duty was to "ruthlessly suppress the one serious rival creed which throughout the empire was daily gaining ground."[23] In February of A.D. 303, Diocletian "decreed the destruction of all Christian churches, the burning of Christian books, the dissolution of Christian congregations, the confiscation of their property, the exclusion of Christians from public office, and the punishment of death for Christians detected in religious assembly."[24] Through adherence to this remorseless policy it was thought that the broad mass of Christians "would gradually find life so onerous they would eventually make their peace with the state," and if they expressed any hesitation, the offer of sacrifices before an alter on

[20] Gibbon, op. cit., at p. 448.

[21] Stephen Williams, *Diocletian and the Roman Recovery* (New York: Methuen, Inc., 1985), at p. 174.

[22] Gibbon, op. cit., at p. 448.

[23] N.H. Baynes, "The Great Persecution," in *The Imperial Crisis and Recovery: A.D. 193-324*, Volume XII of The Cambridge Ancient History (Cambridge: The University Press, 1956), at p. 668.

[24] Durant, op. cit., at p. 651.

the brink of a capital trial would provide one final incentive.[25] Those who would not worship the gods of the state were to be "subjected to every torture known to Rome."[26] Throughout the Empire, then, "men were flogged till the flesh hung from their bones, or their flesh was scraped to the bone with shells; salt or vinegar was poured upon the wounds; the flesh was cut off bit by bit and fed to waiting animals; or bound to crosses, men were eaten piecemeal by starved beasts."[27] Some, said Durant, "had their fingers pierced with sharp reeds under the nails; some had their eyes gouged out; some were suspended by a hand or a foot; some had molten lead poured down their throats; some were beheaded, or crucified, or beaten to death with clubs; some were torn apart by being tied to the momentarily bent branches of trees."[28]

The persecution of Christian by non-Christian eased in proportion to how less pagan and more Christian the Empire became, and ended for good with the death of the apostate Emperor Julian in A.D. 363. The faith of the Apostles that had sustained the sufferers for so long, however, did not universally preside in the churches that succeeded the temples of old. The lamb who claimed the throne was a lamb in its outward attire alone, and his prey would be not pagans, but fellow believers whose dogma and doctrine were supposedly unsound. Christians tended to treat non-Christians somewhat better—slaughtering whole communities of Jews from time to time, yes, or raising the cross of Crusade, but saving most of their blood lust for those whose beliefs differed only on points so narrow that a single angel couldn't dance atop them. As terrible as were the wars of religion of the Early Modern Era, the greatest persecutions were actually yet to come, as Christendom decayed and older doubts—fortified now by novel techniques of observation—captured the imagination first of the learned and then, through processes of public indoctrination in state supported schools, the minds of most everyone else. Science told us that man wasn't created by God; he evolved from other life forms. It instructed that the world wasn't made in six days; it resulted from processes extending untold billions of years. And man, far from being the chosen of God, was but a complex of biological functions and societal induced

---

25 Williams, op. cit., at p. 176.

26 Durant, op. cit., at p. 651.

27 Id., at pp. 651-652.

28 Id., at p. 652.

traumas that rendered him a neurotic mess that only so-called reason, not non-existent divine intervention, could unravel and overcome. Religion generally, and Christianity in particular, was but an illusion serving the dual purpose of sublimating and repressing unsocial natural impulses and distracting men from the truth of just how exploited they were by persons more powerful.

For Karl Marx, a leading critic of Christendom and a crucial architect of the post-modern world, religion buttressed "the established order by sanctifying it and by suggesting that the political order is somehow ordained by divine authority," and consoled "the oppressed and exploited by offering them in heaven what they are denied upon earth."[29] At best, religion held before the subject masses "a vision of what they are denied," thereby playing "at least partly a progressive role in that it gives the common people some idea of what a better order would be."[30] As society progresses from one stage of evolution to the next, alienation between mankind's view of its world through the filter of religion and the world as it actually is becomes increasingly pronounced. This alienation, said the erstwhile Marxist Thomas Sowell, was "not simply a general malaise but more specifically a misconception of reality growing out of thwarted development—an inversion in which human reality and human needs are made subservient to artificially created things, to the imaginary gods of religion or to the financial institutions of capitalism."[31] Religion itself wasn't fundamentally false; instead it reflected a distorted "projection of unfulfilled human ideals and longings."[32] Marx thought in time that religion wouldn't so much disappear as yield to redefinition. The illusions crafted during earlier stages of human development would be shed in place of more direct ways of satisfying the aspirations that the religious mind exuded. Once a new stage of existence was reached, the conditions in which religious illusions flourished would yield to a new environment where those illusions would be transformed into something real. Bondage to work, to factory, to employer, capitalist, and formal religion and to the notion that a deity oversaw a moral world that not coincidentally reinforced a

[29] Alasdair MacIntyre, "Marxism and Religion," churchlifejournal.nd.edu, January 25, 2019.

[30] Id.

[31] Thomas Sowell, *Marxism: Philosophy and Economics* (New York: William Morrow, 1985), at p. 34.

[32] Id., at p. 43.

political and economic one, would end with the advent of a new order and be replaced by a realization "that man is the highest essence of man."[33]

It is no surprise that when Marxists came to power in places like Russia, disdain for religion became a hallmark of public policy and contributed to a phase of persecution hardly comparable to the far more moderate and inconsistent expressions of intolerance present in the age of the early church. Lenin himself "considered religion in any form as 'stupefaction' and 'stultification,' like individual housekeeping and other 'wasteful' forms of human activity."[34] No mere benevolent force that aroused and organized socially constructive impulses, God, in his view, was instead "always at the center of a world that subjected, impoverished, and oppressed."[35] The Marxist Bolsheviks, said the historian Daniel Peris, "promised to sweep away all that was old in Russian society and to create an entirely new civilization."[36] As the church and the belief structure it promoted were foundational elements of Russian society, there was no question that destruction was to be their fate. How this might come to pass was a subject of no little importance to the Marxists themselves. Marx thought religion would wither along with the state as the people's welfare preempted all other interests. Trotsky was optimistic that "religion would be eradicated over time by education and new diversions, particularly the cinema."[37] Nikolai Bukaharin thought that science would slowly but surely undermine religious authority. Anatolii Lunarcharskii agreed, and expressed confidence that religious superstition and ignorance "would be overcome in the schools through the teaching of science and history."[38]

The majority of Marx's followers weren't so patient to await something that in a nation of over 100 million adherents of a highly organized church containing 40,000 functioning parish establishments and over 100,000 parish priests might take as long as the Second Coming, so they considered how they might lend the destiny of man and the

---

33 Id., at p. 44.

34 Richard Stites, *Revolutionary Dreams: Utopian Vision and Experimental Life in the Russian Revolution* (New York: Oxford University Press, 1989), at p. 103.

35 Id.

36 Daniel Peris, *Storming the Heavens: The Soviet League of the Militant Godless* (Ithaca: Cornell University Press, 1998), at p. 1.

37 Id., at p. 23.

38 Id.

masterplan of history a helping hand. In the first weeks after they seized power, the Bolsheviks assumed control of all Church-run educational institutions and nationalized all Church property. Teaching of religion was banned everywhere but inside the home, and "the clergy were classified as second-class citizens, the same category as 'capitalists, merchants, former members of the police, criminals, and imbeciles.'"[39] The Church's tenacity in surviving in the face of such severe state action convinced Bolsheviks that more drastic measures were required if the Church and its believers were to be extinguished. During the famine of 1921, when the Church was active in humanitarian relief efforts, the government suddenly "ordered the seizure of all Church valuables, including sacramental items."[40] Popular resistance to this attack on Christian material culture prompted Lenin to command "the arrest and execution of many clergy and active laity," including the Metropolitan of Leningrad.[41] After arresting the priests or driving them out of their parishes and chasing parishioners out of the church and into collectivized fields, the state took the wrecking ball to thousands of onion domes across Russia. Disdain for the faith never permitted any admission of the actual reason for the destruction. It was always in the name of progress, to remove an obstacle to the widening of the streets, or because of the need to expand a nearby factory or school or troop garrison, "or for some other reason thought up by local officials."[42] And what the wrecking ball spared, predatory taxation managed to finish off. A final indignity came with the formation of the League of the Godless to harass believers and convince all those intransigently clinging to their faith to embrace atheism for the good of society.

Modern progressives have generally agreed with and embraced Marx's view regarding religion. They deny God created man and insist that natural processes are the cause. They reject the existence of any ingrained tendencies, or a human nature, even though they claim all life results from ingrained changes in the form of genetic mutation, aided by the process of natural selection. They contend that men and women aren't born free, but are slave or free depending on their membership in a particular class based on arbitrary or even superficial criteria. Instead

---

[39] Id., at p. 25.
[40] Id., at p. 26.
[41] Id.
[42] Id., at p. 125.

of God, they trumpet the state as supreme, and instead of faith's role in the improvement of the human soul, they see in the state itself the prospect for "the perfection of humanity, the civilization of the world; the perfect development of the human reason and its attainment to universal command over individualism; the apotheosis of man."[43] The recent emergence of militant atheism has been largely enabled by the progressive movement, and the writings of men like Christopher Hitchens have become its scripture. With Hitchens, progressives believe that the teachings of religion about the origins of the universe and development of living organisms contradict science, that the enormity of human suffering is contrary to belief in a deity who reputedly cares for a humanity he allegedly created, that the holy books of the faithful amount to nonsensical myths and fables, internally contradictory and unmoored in confirmatory sources, that religion is patriarchal and degrades women, encourages intolerance and inhumanity, denies sexual identity and sexual diversity, falsely impresses sinfulness on the mind and psychologically tortures its adherents from cradle to grave. While elevating the state, progressives strangely elevate the human personality as well, contending that religion destroys what is unique about each individual, and psychologically transforms men and women into "groveling, abandoned serfs" who accept a permanent supervision from the moment of birth for all of eternity, pay constant adoration leading to the "dissolution of the personality" and happily embrace a fate, said Hitchens, "worse than hell."[44]

If religion isn't to be overtly confronted through bloody persecution, the wall of separation between society and religion must be thickened and heightened: no teaching of faith in the public schools, no public prayers, no strong religious beliefs by judges appointed to the court or officials executing the laws, and no exercise of religious objections to serving the interests of others in purely private transactions. The First Amendment represents no sacred restriction on the state's power, no guarantee of liberty for all in the face of majoritarian hostility. It is instead but a highly inconvenient obstacle to more direct attacks on a faith that rejects the principle tenets of progressivism. The appearance of

---

43 William A. Schambra & Thomas West, "The Progressive Movement and the Transformation of American Politics," www.heritage.org, July 18, 2007.

44 "'Worse than Hell': Christopher Hitchens on the Religious Mind," www.beliefnet.com.

a novel disease said to be nothing less than the second coming of the bubonic plague in its ability to lay waste the population of the earth presented a remarkable remedy to a constitutional problem previously considered intractable. Faith might not be driven from the heart of man, but church might be closed so as to halt the spread of the deadly contagion...religious teaching that is, not the coronavirus. The faithful who resist can in turn be shamed for not really being so brotherly in their love, not so willing to render unto Caesar, nor mindful of the admonition to tend to the poor and to the sick. The church doors must shut and its bells must be silenced. No singing, no communal prayer, no filing of the faithful into the pews lest the unseen killer opportunistically spreads from person to person and contributes to yet another flare-up of positive tests and the steady march towards the magic 200,000th death that oddly seems so vital a goal to be reached prior to November's election. With church attendance so goes church donations, and with a decline in revenue, the churches shrink in their mission, fail in their outreach to mold the minds of children, and find it increasingly difficult to pay their rents, heating and air-conditioning bills and other expenses incurred when advancing the calling of the Apostles and serving the needs of their members. Like the flu and other common germs, COVID kills the old, the infirm and the obese, but the measures that dubiously aim to restrict its spread achieve a far grander objective dear to the heart of progressives: the ruination of the faithful through the destruction of their infrastructure.

The faithful, however, can take heart. He over whose body the multitude will gloat, will once more inhale the breath of life and strike terror into those who see him risen as if from death, and those whose robes gain color in the slaughter of the innocent shall don white again through the blood of the lamb. The four angels bound at the river will be released, the two hundred million mounted soldiers, bearing blue, yellow and fiery red on their breasts, their horses resembling lions with smoke and sulfur steaming from their nostrils, will ride from the four quarters, and a seventh angel will blow his trumpet, but the faithful shall suffer and abide with patient endurance. The Church of ancient times survived the many persecutions inflicted upon it by Rome's leadership. The Church in Russia, though it was subjected to crueler assaults, emerged from the darkness of Lenin's rule and once again openly prayed for the nation. And now, overseas, in California, its exiled children gather in gratitude for the land that embraced them in their flight from the tyranny of Lenin and decry a governor whose decrees are all too reminiscent of what their own fathers and mothers fled. Though they steadfastly followed the recommendations imposed by local authorities even at the expense of the authenticity of their rituals, they now cannot accept the restrictions in light of the fact "that mass protests are held, which violate absolutely all precautions."[45] This, said the Orthodox Archbishop in San Francisco, is "a clear discrimination, hypocrisy and infringement of our religious rights, reminding us of the times of godless persecution in the U.S.S.R."[46] It is. And like the persecutions of old, it too shall be overcome.

Hatch Act Hysterics

NEVER in the history of the United States had something so unheard of occurred. The threat of a disease that leaves all but a fraction of a percent gravely ill or worse justified in the minds of policy makers the closure of most American businesses, all of its schools and even many of its beaches and parks. The command of the Constitution that public officials swear to uphold and defend the right of the people to speak, assemble, travel, worship and work notwithstanding, these restrictions prompted little initial opposition, so convincing was the prediction of the viral slaughter to come. Time has mellowed some of the alarm, and with it the restrictions on liberty in places where herd immunity to the power of propaganda and fear has managed to acquire a foothold. Six months into the so-called pandemic attitudes toward it exhibit a distinctly political dimension. Those who tend to fear a die-off of humanity insist on a new extremity in the severity of restraints on liberty and tend to align with the political left; those who don't, make their home on the opposite side of the spectrum. Wearing a mask at all events, including riotous gatherings of the leftist faithful in deep blue Portland and Seattle, is presently an unequivocal statement of political allegiance, and those who refrain from doing so even when outdoors

[45] Archbishop of San Francisco and West American, to Governor Gavin Newsome," http_synod.com, July 9, 2020.

[46] Id.

and more than six feet apart simply while taking a walk or riding a bicycle are deemed the enemy of mankind.

The corona litmus test extends to the candidates for the highest office in this very political year and to the conventions their respective political parties threw for the sake of promoting their case for electoral success in November. Limitations on gathering indoors and displaying droplet-spreading exuberance in support of one's candidate, however, posed a unique challenge. The Democrats' response was to stream one speaker after another, with no fanfare, no cheering and barely a clap. The talented Jennifer Hudson sang, but her efforts went unrewarded with applause. Bernie Sanders passionately declared that while "Nero fiddled" as Rome burned, "Trump golfs"; D.C. Mayor Muriel Bowser accused the President of plotting to defeat democracy while the people "peacefully protested" in Lafayette Square; and the President's opponent described a Manichean struggle, wherein "the current president has cloaked America in darkness for much too long," and yet barely a hurrah was to be heard.[1] When pondering what Steve Peoples of *The Chicago Tribune* said was "one of the most urgent questions heading into a virtual convention"—that is, "whether the format could generate enthusiasm"—he noted that the answer, "charitably, is that it remains a tall order."[2]

When the Republicans' turn came, the contrast couldn't have been starker. The primary stage was pleasing to the eye, people were actually in attendance, applause was modest yet steady, and the speakers were dynamic and well-rehearsed. Girl Next Door Kim Klacik noted the Democrats' failure to accomplish anything in Baltimore for 70 years other than ruin the city; Richard Grennell credited President Trump with ending the endless wars waged by Bush and Obama; NFL players Jack Brewer and Herschel Walker wondered how the President could be called a racist; and the President's lesser known daughter—a recent law school graduate—presented a thoughtful mediation on the power of propaganda and the duty of free thinkers to resist it. Between the speeches, the President issued a pardon and swore in new citizen

[1] Annie Linskey, Matt Viser, Bolby Itkowitz, Felicia Sonmez and John Wagner, "Joe Biden Accepts Democratic Presidential Nomination, with a call for Optimism at a Time of Fear," www.washingtonpost.com, August 21, 2020.

[2] Steve Peoples, "5 Takeaways from the first night of the Democratic Convention, including Michelle Obama's Dominant Moment," www.chicagotribune.com, August 17, 2020.

immigrants from Africa, and survivors of communist regimes called on America to reject the rise of radical socialism and fight to preserve American liberty. The event ended with a fire-works display to end all such displays and a live concert from the White House's external mezzanine by the highly competent Christopher Macchio and his orchestra. "From start to finish," observed *The New York Post's* Michael Goodwin, "Donald Trump's Republican convention team…unveiled a smart program that skillfully stitched together people, policies and politics."[3]

Democrats and their friends in the media, of course, hated it. Attempts to find an objective metric for adjudging the Republican effort wanting fizzled after early announcements that the DNC won the television ratings war lost their resonance upon the discovery that on-line viewership tilted in the other direction and victory in the convention fundraising battle was awarded to team Trump.[4] The Republican effort was probably best summed up by Bill Maher in an interview with Joy Reid on MSNBC. "It was very effective…. I feel very nervous; the same way I did four years ago at this time."[5]

The real dilemma for the Democrats was this: there were far too many faces of color speaking at the RNC to declare it racist and too many women who addressed the convention to call it sexist. Immigrants were seen being sworn in as new citizens and a black man received a pardon. The clear superiority of the quality of the presentation, its success in generating enthusiasm and the absence of a hook on which to hang the typical Democrat caricatures of Republicans forced a shift of criticism to an entirely novel ground, considerably more lacking in emotional resonance with the general public. The appearance during the convention via video of Secretary of State Mike Pompeo while on a diplomatic mission to Israel and the attendance on the White House lawn of hundreds of White House employees provided the much-needed opening. In a tone of disgust, Biden-loving television commentators denounced the Secretary and everyone present at the fire-works show as violators of the Hatch Act. Joining in the criticism almost

---

[3] Michael Goodwin, "At RNC Trump is Putting on Greatest Reality Show on Earth," *The New York Post*, August 26, 2020.

[4] Matt Margolis, "Sorry Libs, the GOP Convention Had Better Viewership Than the Democrat Convention," https://pjmedia.com, August 29, 2020.

[5] "Bill Maher: I'm nervous about election day, 'the same way I was Feeling Four Years Ago,'" www.msn.com, August 28, 2020.

simultaneously were the President's leading foes in the Congress. "Far from normal," tweeted Congressman Jerry Nadler, "this is just the latest example of the Trump Administration's clear disregard for the Hatch Act: using an official government position for partisan political activity."[6] Representative Raja Krishnamoorthi agreed, noting that "the Special Counsel needs to address what we've been witnessing this week from the Trump Administration."[7] Congressman Eliot Engel condemned Pompeo in particular as someone who "seems to think the office he holds, the Department he runs, the personnel he oversees, and the taxpayer dollars that pay for all of it are there for his personal and political benefit," and promised to commence a contempt action in the committee he chairs.[8] Speaker Pelosi presumed to speak for the American people as a whole, saying they "know these people are unethical and illegal and doing things outside the law."[9] A former "director of the Office of Government Ethics tweeted that "short of bribery or other serious criminality, I cannot recall anything remotely close to this.'"[10] One commentator concluded that the Trump Administration's conduct at the RNC is yet "another warning that this President does not respect the need to maintain a wall between governance and partisan politics," and that if he wasn't defeated in November, "that wall is likely to crumble even more than it already has."[11]

The arcane Hatch Act is not particularly well-known among those not employed by either the State or federal governments. The Act generally prohibits a range of political activities by government officials, including using one's "authority or influence for the purpose of interfering with or affecting the result of an election," soliciting, accepting or receiving "a political contribution," seeking political contributions from subordinates, running for the nomination or as a

---

[6] Jeanine Santucci, Savannah Behrmann and William Cummings, "'The Rules Go Out the Window': Democrats Deride RNC Over Hatch Act, Coronavirus and Transgender issues," www.usatoday.com, August 26, 2020.

[7] Id.

[8] Morgan Phillips, "House Foreign Affairs Committee announces Contempt Proceedings Against Pompeo," foxnews.com, August 28, 2020.

[9] Santucci, et al., op. cit.

[10] Melisa Gomez, "Federal Ethics Breaches at the RUNC Warrant Hatch Act Inquiries, Experts Say," *The Los Angeles Times*, August 26, 2020.

[11] Ian Millhiser, "The Hatch Act, the Law Trump Flouted at the RNC, Explained," www.vox.com, August 26, 2020.

candidate for election to a partisan political office, soliciting or discouraging subordinates from participation in any political activity of any person who has an application for any compensation, grant, contract, ruling license, permit or certificate pending before the employing office of "such employee," engaging in political activity while in any room or building occupied in the discharge of official duties while wearing a uniform or official insignia identifying the office or position of the employee, or using any vehicle owned or leased by the government of the United States or any agency for political purposes.

Passed in 1939, it has withstood nearly every legal challenge. Its place in the constitutional scheme governing public employment was confirmed in the case of *United States Civil Service Commission v. National Association of Letter Carriers*. Speaking for the majority, Justice Byron White said it was the judgment of Congress that partisan political activities of federal employees needed to be limited if the government was "to operate effectively and fairly," elections were "to play their proper part in representative government," and employees themselves were "to be sufficiently free from improper influences."[12] The law, said White, was supported by four significant governmental interests: a generalized interest in ensuring that federal employees administer the law "in accordance with the will of Congress" rather than in accordance with the "will of a particular political party"; avoidance of a perception by the public of a partisan bureaucracy that would undermine public confidence in the fairness of the administration of government; the prevention of political parties from using and thus misusing "the thousands or hundreds of thousands of federal employees, paid for at public expense, to man its political structure and political campaigns"; and ensuring that federal employees did not feel pressured or coerced "to vote in a certain way or perform political chores in order to curry favor with their superiors rather than to act out of their own beliefs."[13]

There can be little dispute that the interests of the government in limiting the political activity of its personnel while on duty are legitimate. How far the Congress might trench upon the ability of government employees to express their political preferences, however, remains at issue. Though employed by the government, federal officials

[12] *United States Civil Service Commission v. National Association of Letter Carriers* (1973) 413 U.S. 548, 564, 93 S.Ct. 2880.

[13] Id., at 564-566.

retain First Amendment rights, including the right to speak about and financially support candidates for elected office. For the reason that no right is absolute, there is a permissible zone of regulatory power Congress may exercise over federal employees, even in the area of expressive liberty, so long as the regulation aims to ensure that speech rights don't undermine the ability of employees to fulfill the purpose of their employment. Whether the government might bar the Secretary of State from addressing words about the President's foreign policy successes to a political convention via video, or veto the choice by political appointees working for the President in the White House to attend an after-hours political event on the White House lawn, are questions that can only be answered by history itself in light of Congress's constitutional powers.

The Framers were silent on the matter, though some hint of their worry over the proclivity of the public work force to advance particular political interests is evident in Madison's characterization of federalism and the separation of powers as mechanisms to check partisanship within government.[14] Congress, too, they authorized to create terms of employment, including, by inference, a requirement that the officials it creates refrain from certain types of conduct harmful to the agencies employing them and the nation as a whole. Likewise, the President, as chief of the executive branch, might impose standards upon employees consistent with the purposes of government.

If the worry over a partisan bureaucracy was scant at the time of the Founding, it certainly grew during the first decade of the Republic. As early as the year 1801, President Jefferson observed "with dissatisfaction officers of the General Government taking on various occasions active parts in the elections of public functionaries, whether of the General or State Governments."[15] Though he urged employees to exercise the franchise in a manner consistent with their conscience, he admonished that agents of the government were expected not to "attempt to influence the votes of others nor take any part in the business of electioneering, that being deemed inconsistent with the spirit of the Constitution and [their] duties to it.'"[16]

---

[14] See Federalist No. 9.

[15] Scott J. Bloch, "The Judgement of History: Faction, Political Machines, and the Hatch Act," 7 U.Pa. J. Lab. & Emp. L. 225 (2005), at p. 229.

[16] Id.

This admonition did little to deter the spirit of faction and the temptation of public employees to engage in partisan activity, or of the government itself to coerce its employees to serve as partisan agents. Andrew Jackson's election created the spectacle of what was perceived to be a mad rush to staff the ranks of the civil service with loyal party functionaries in a manner reminiscent of what had already happened in New York City under the dominance of Tammany Hall. Federal workers from this time onward "were progressively brought under the dominion of the...party machine and subjected to various party requirements as a condition of continuing their employment," including the "obligations to pay party assessments, to do party work at election time, and to 'vote right.'"[17] To combat this development, Senator John C. Calhoun of South Carolina sponsored a bill requiring the President to explain his discharge of any federal official.[18] Calhoun's unsuccessful attempt to rein in the politicization of the bureaucracy was followed by Representative John Bell's similar attempt in 1840 to restrict the power of the executive to remove inferior officials of the executive branch for reasons that had nothing to do with merit and everything to do with patronage. To allow the executive absolute discretion over the termination of rank and file employees, Bell said, constituted "manifestly a violation of the freedom of elections; an attack upon the public liberty; and a high misdemeanor."[19] When a man is not left free to vote as he pleased, Bell noted, the man is made to understand that the office or employment which gives him bread, or supplies his family with the comforts of life, will be taken from him if he doesn't vote for a particular candidate.[20] Bell's failed effort to defeat partisan misuse of the federal work force soon yielded to rather more enthusiasm for self-restraint on the part of the executive itself. In his inaugural address, President William Henry Harrison vowed that "never with my consent shall an officer of the people, compensated for his services out of their pockets, become the pliant instrument of Executive will."[21] His sudden death a month later quickly ended his government, along with the nascent effort to prevent the use of federal employees in a manner that brought the government

---

[17] David P. Currie, "President Harrison & the Hatch Act," 6 Green Bag 2d 7 (2002), at p. 8.

[18] Id.

[19] Id., at p. 10.

[20] Id.

[21] Id., at pp. 12-13.

"into conflict with the freedom of election."

Civil service reform of any meaningful type did not occur until after the Civil War. The exponential growth of the federal government during the war accompanied the expansion of government's mandate, and though Congress scaled back government's scope following the Confederate surrender, the federal work force remained much larger than it had been prior to secession and the attack on Fort Sumter. Perhaps anticipating the day when the formerly disloyal Democrats would gain control of the legislature, the Republican Congress enacted a law in 1876 to bar any exchange of items by federal employees for political purposes. In an 1882 opinion upholding the law, Chief Justice Morrison Waite noted that the apparent purpose of the law—"to promote efficiency and integrity in the discharge of official duties"—easily fell within the scope of Congress's power.[22] Disregarding Justice Bradley's dissenting view that the law impermissibly denied to federal workers "the privilege of associating and making joint contributions with such other citizens as he may choose" and constituted "an unjust restraint to propagate and promote his views on public affairs" in clear violation of the First Amendment, the Congress soon contemplated a much broader remedy in the form of the Pendleton Act. On one side of the debate over the Act's merits "were the politicians who, in the tradition of Andrew Jackson saw government primarily as a vehicle for responding to the political choices of the electorate."[23] For them, "it simply would not do...to make the supporters of defeated policy the administrators of a new regime. When the people speak on election day, the entire government should change according to their wishes."[24] On the other side "were the reformers, who brought a dramatically different view of government to the debate," emphasizing "the inefficiency of frequent overhauls of the federal services, and the political corruption that was likely to follow when a ward heeler took control of a federal agency."[25] Government, they insisted, "could not afford the incompetence of the federal employee whose only job qualification was her ability to mobilize her precinct on election day."[26]

---

[22] *Ex Parte Curtis* (1882) 106 U.S. 371, 1 S.Ct. 381.

[23] William L. Magness, "'Un-hatching' Federal Employee Political Endorsements," 134 U. Pa. L. Rev. 1497 (1986), at p. 1511.

[24] Id.

[25] Id.

[26] Id.

Aided by the shocking assassination of President Garfield by a disappointed office seeker, the reformers prevailed and the Pendleton Act became law. In addition to creating a merit-based hiring process, what the Act did was empower the executive to empanel a Civil Service Commission, charged with promulgating and enforcing a set of administrative rules designed to prevent the politicization of the federal bureaucracy.[27] The first rule it issued, and the focus of much of its subsequent enforcement efforts, was a prohibition on "preventing coercion by government employees" aimed at obtaining campaign contributions, endorsements and electioneering services.[28]

The Civil Service Commission soldiered on reasonably well up until the 1930s, when the Roosevelt Administration and a sympathetic Congress undertook the most unprecedented expansion of government and the federal work force in American history. Within three months of taking office, Roosevelt signed into law bills creating the Agricultural Adjustment Administration, the Civil Conservation Corps, the Civil Works Administration, the Subsistence Homesteads Division, the Farm Credit Administration, the Federal Deposit Insurance Corporation, the Federal Emergency Relief Administration, the Federal Surplus Relief Corporation, the Home Owner's Loan Corporation, the National Recovery Administration, the Public Works Administration, and the Tennessee Valley Authority. Within a matter of years, Congress would follow the achievements of the first hundred days with the creation of the Civil Aeronautics Authority (later the FAA), the Drought Relief Service, the Federal Art Project, the Federal Communications Commission, the Federal Housing Administration, the Farm Security Administration, the Federal Works Agency, the National Labor Relations Board, the National Youth Administration, the Resettlement Administration, the Rural Electrification Administration, the Securities and Exchange Commission, the Social Security Administration, the United States Housing Authority, the United States Maritime Commission and the Works Progress Administration, or WPA. The result of all this legislating was what historian William Leuchtenburg called "an unprecedented program of government-industry co-operation," promising, if not delivering, the distribution of "stupendous sums to millions of staple farmers"; acceptance of responsibility for the

---

[27] Id., at pp. 1501-1502.
[28] Bloch, op. cit., at p. 230.

welfare of millions of unemployed; engagement in far reaching experimentation in regional planning; the dedication of billions of dollars to save homes and farms from foreclosure; the undertaking of huge public works spending; the protection of small bank deposits of the country; and the establishment of the federal regulation of Wall Street.[29] It resulted, too, in the opportunity to staff all of the relevant agencies and the expanded existing federal departments with men and women eager for work and so grateful for the job that they'd do whatever it took to keep the Roosevelt Administration in power.

If suspicions that the Roosevelt Administration desired to use the horde of new federal workers as a political army were based on nothing more than partisan bias and fear, they were soon enough confirmed by experience. With so much patronage at his disposal and with the full support of strong majorities in both houses of Congress, FDR was quick in realizing the utility of "the creating and the manipulating of federal jobs to strengthen his political support."[30] Persistent unemployment and misery nearly four years into the New Deal shook FDR's confidence in his reelection and gave Republicans plausible hope that they might turn Roosevelt and the Democrats out of power in the fall of 1936. To counter popular dissatisfaction over the deepening of the Depression, the Roosevelt Administration adopted a very calculated use of the patronage power, primarily through the WPA. WPA supervisors throughout the country "routinely checked on the political leanings of relief workers, demanded they switch parties on pain of termination, and required them to wear partisan buttons."[31] Administration officials were dispatched to "key states to do polls, distribute questionnaires, and solicit support for Roosevelt."[32] On occasion, "those working in the WPA or other programs had to kick back part of their salaries to support Roosevelt, or other Democrat candidates."[33] PWA surveys, WPA projects, and CCC camps "became campaign tools that Roosevelt" and

---

[29] William E. Leuchtenburg, *Franklin Roosevelt and the New Deal: 1932-1940* (New York: Harper & Row, 1963), at p. 61.

[30] Burton Folsom, Jr., *New Deal or Raw Deal? How FDR's Economic Legacy Has Damaged America* (New York: Threshold Editions, 2008), at p. 169.

[31] John T. Flynn, *The Roosevelt Myth*, rev. ed. (New York: Devin-Adair Company, 1956), at p. 134.

[32] Folsom, op. cit., at p. 182.

[33] Id.

his underlings "used for Roosevelt's reelection."[34]

The magnitude of the abuse was stunning. In the four months before the 1936 election, the federal government hired 300,000 men, a third of whom were laid off a month after the polls closed.[35] Nowhere was the abuse of patronage authority and the coercion of the federal workforce more obnoxious than in Kentucky in 1938, where the fate of an important senate seat lay in the balance. One anti-New Dealer complained that "every agency of the federal government dispensing relief is resorting to methods and policies that are crudely reprehensible to force the citizens of the great commonwealth to support" the Democrat side.[36] An investigative reporter employed by the Scripps-Howard Syndicate found massive evidence that the WPA was being deployed to aid FDR's favored candidate, and wrote that "it was a keen disappointment to find that the WPA was being exploited for politics and to ponder the ultimate effect to our democracy if such a large group, dependent upon the administration in power, should be hereafter utilized and organized politically."[37]

The abuse in Kentucky wasn't an anomaly. Complaints of political deployment of public funds and the use of WPA workers to advance the Administration's fortunes arose in no less than nine states, including Tennessee, Oklahoma, North Dakota, Indiana and Illinois.[38] In West Virginia, junior Senator Rush Holt denounced the Administration for discharging workers for political reasons, depriving others of relief jobs until someone in the Democrat Party could vouch for their loyalty, using workers during working hours to participate in political conventions and meetings, denying projects to communities that opposed the Democrats, paying high salaries to politically influential people, and issuing raises to workers who took part in political campaigns.[39] WPA chief Harry Hopkins denied all of the charges during a Senate hearing, but the scope of the abuse was so broad that few gave his purportedly exculpatory testimony any credence.[40]

---

34 Id., at p. 181.
35 Id., at p. 182.
36 Id., at p. 200.
37 Id., at p. 201.
38 "Hopkins' Remark Will Be Ignored by Senate Probe," *The Evening Star*, July 27, 1938.
39 "Holt's Charges," *The Times-News*, July 18, 1938.
40 Edward W. Pickard, "Politics in Relief," *Midland Journal*, July 15, 1938.

The result of the scandal wasn't anything so dramatic as the prevention of the grand misuse of the federal workforce for political ends. Rather, it was a series of hearings "detailing a sordid debauchery of the ballot hitherto unknown in this country," and the consolidation of majorities in both houses of Congress in favor of Senator Carl Hatch's proposed reform bill, soon to be known as the Hatch Act.[41] Initially opposed by FDR, but reluctantly signed by him into law, the Act codified the administrative directives generated by claims under the Pendleton Act and all but barred any on-duty and much off-duty politicking by federal employees. The right to vote was unimpaired, as was the right to speak about the issues of the day, but for the purpose of protecting the massive bureaucracy from use as campaign foot soldiers and to prevent the forced enlistment of public servants in partisan crusades contrary to their own preferences, no one employed by the federal government would be permitted to work for a campaign, speak on behalf of a candidate, or even run for partisan office.

In reviewing the history informing the enactment of the Hatch Act, it seems that the primary if not exclusive purpose of the law was to prevent a President from using his status as chief of the executive branch to transform the federal workforce into a political machine to advance his purely political interests, primarily at election time. The Congress was obviously concerned that coercion of federal employees to perform political functions in return for obtaining or preserving their jobs be prevented as well. In the wake of the Hatch Act, the federal civil service would not become as it did in the 1930s: either willing or unwilling agents of partisan political interests. The events at the RNC recently complained of by Democrats and hostile media don't really fall within the scope of these concerns. Secretary Pompeo wasn't on duty when he addressed the Convention; he was taking time away from his diplomatic responsibilities to express himself on the foreign policy successes of the government that would soon be subject to electoral judgment. His role as a senate-confirmed principle officer of the United States, too, probably exempts him from the power of Congress to regulate his use of his time. He certainly cannot be removed from office by anyone save the President or by Congress exercising its power of impeachment, hence any censure of him under the Act is effectively toothless. The much-

[41] Bloch, op. cit., at pp. 231-232.

derided swearing in of new citizens wasn't a partisan activity at all: it was a function of government that citizens of the United States have every right to observe, even during a political convention. There was nothing overtly partisan about the ceremony, though, of course, the logical inference to be drawn was that the President, while much criticized by his partisan opponents for his supposed opposition to immigration from non-white nations, is actually highly supportive of such immigrants and desires them to enter the pathway to citizenship provided for in our laws.

The inclusion of White House employees in the convention audience while on federal property as the President delivered his partisan acceptance speech is probably the most troubling of the actions criticized in the media, but in the end it isn't problematic at all. The Hatch Act only prohibits employees from engaging in political activity *inside* government buildings, not outside, and *only during working hours.* Though within the curtilage of the government structure in which they work, White House employees present at the final event of the convention were outside of the building itself, hence not in violation of the law.[42] They also appear to have been off duty. Even had they been inside the White House and on the clock, awkward would be any effort to charge persons who work for the President in the President's home with the crime of engaging in partisan activity. Such people are undoubtedly avid supporters of the President, unlikely to feel coerced when engaging in the promotion of his interests. The mere act of sitting in a chair pales in comparison to the actions they take every day to promote the President's political agenda, which cannot really be distinguished from what the President believes is in the best interests of the nation. The White House isn't the IRS or the FBI or any other federal work site: it's the President's home and the political and administrative nerve center of the President's government, staffed (primarily) with people who are political appointees, not civil servants. The critics ought to worry more about the 1993 reforms that permitted the federal civil service to mobilize in favor of Democrat politicians who support pay raises and generous retirement benefits, or the holdovers from the previous administration who used their investigative power to illegally surveille the President and his campaign and make false claims about

[42] Bloch, op. cit., at p. 244.

crimes supposedly committed by him and his supporters. Compared to these actions and offenses, sitting in a chair after hours and applauding one's boss who lawfully employs them for political purposes is hardly a crisis justifying all the hysterics.

The Vote is in the Mail

IT was not, some said, the Lincoln-Douglas Debate. Nor even Nixon v. Kennedy. The august trappings of the venue suggested a serious tone would be maintained; the actual event itself revealed the formalities to be naught but evidence of a grand mockery. On stage stood two men whose histories as politicians justly earned them the title of the two biggest a-holes who ever ran for or held political office. Joe Biden's long claim on the title had been solidified during his brutal beat down of a hapless Paul Ryan eight years earlier during the 2012 Vice Presidential Debate, and further confirmed since then via the many times on camera when he'd berated members of the public for being stupid, overweight, and dog faced pony soldiers. Having only entered politics very recently, the President's own claim probably dated back to the moment he shattered all debate conventions by responding to Hillary Clinton's expression of worrisome dismay over Donald Trump heading the Justice Department with the ultimate come-back insult: "because you'd be in jail."

Within a few minutes of this most recent debate, the uncertainly as to who the true champion was resolved in the incumbent's favor. From the moment the former Vice President uttered his first words, the self-styled tough guy who once said he'd like to take the President out behind the gym and teach him a lesson, found himself overwhelmed verbally and psychologically by the master troller-in-chief's running, single-word objections to just about everything he said. The inability of the former Vice President either to concentrate or take control was so obvious that the moderator stepped in and all but assumed the role of the President's debate opponent. Biden regained some composure after the moderator managed to establish some firmer limits on the freedom of the participants to interject, but still found himself in a position the media for the most part had spared him: being forced to address issues of substance and explain what his actual policies if elected might be, such as whether he supported the riots that have raged in many of our cities for months, endorsed the communist BLM and Green New Deal, assisted his drug addicted son in getting lucrative jobs with foreign entities with close ties to tyrannical regimes, and if he planned to pack the Supreme Court of the United States to offset the President's entirely lawful success in filling vacant judicial positions.

For those who understood the President to be the least "presidential" figure to ever hold the office, they weren't disappointed. He was rudely assertive, bombastic, insulting, and direct. And yet he also presented his agenda, warts and all, with no effort to hide it. His opponent, however, couldn't make up his mind where he stood, denied he supported the Green New Deal one moment and touted it the next, laughably refused to identify a single person he'd appoint to the Supreme Court due to the lack of time available to utter a single name, accused the President of racism despite his own history as the primary champion of a crime bill rightly hated by African Americans since the day it was signed into law by President Clinton more than two decades ago, blamed the President for a destructive COVID-related shut-down of the economy yet vowing when he's president that he'll lock us down more firmly, condemned the President's lack of support for small business while promising to restore the small-business crushing taxes of the Obama-Biden Administration, and claimed to be the more presidential of the two even as he called the sitting President of the United States a "clown" and told him repeatedly to "shut up." And that was when he was at his own eloquent and coherent. As a friend of mine said, "Trump is a dick and Biden is an idiot." True enough, but who wants an idiot for President?

Depending on one's perspective, there are apparently many who actually do. And this election won't be any different, despite the fact that the largest percentage of voters ever will be voting by mail. COVID-fears remain significant among the population, stoked in part by a Democrat Party that insists on the extreme lethality of the coronavirus and the need to shift voting away from methods that might more easily spread it to ones that promise to limit its currency. The enthusiasm for mail-in voting in fact has been marked, notwithstanding legitimate concerns that absentee voting has always entailed a degree of risk of fraud and is all the more likely to occur with the lifting of many of the historical restrictions on voting absentee designed to protect the integrity of the vote. In California, Oregon, Nevada and elsewhere, Democrat controlled state governments have dispensed with the need for anyone to formally request a vote-by-mail ballot and have permitted so-called harvesters to pick up completed ballots from voters in order to deliver them to the polls. Democrat resistance to the purging of voting rolls of long-inactive and deceased voters, combined with the extreme hostility of the postal service rank-and-file to the sitting President give rise to obvious fears that mail-in voting might permit abuse on a scale never witnessed in history. At the debate itself, when the issue came up, the President echoed these fears, saying that so far, voting by mail has been "a disaster." A mail-in ballot requested by the voter, he said was okay. But now, "they're sending millions of ballots all over the country. There's fraud. They found them in creeks. They found some…in a wastepaper basket." In some instances, more than one ballot had been sent to the same voter. Worse, he noted, was the potential for chicanery after all the votes were in. Some States, he said, were prepared to receive mail-in ballots a week after the election. "That's seven days after the election [results] should have been announced. We have major States…all run by Democrats" prepared to do just that. If that wasn't an opportunity for ballot fraud, it's hard to conceive what is.

Though the President's articulation of the problem was neither ideal nor artful, the concern he expressed was legitimate. Throughout the late summer and early fall, ballots have been prepared and millions and millions have been mailed out, many to people who never requested them and might not be aware they are coming to an address from which they long ago moved away. Teams of paid ballot harvesters have moved into place, ready to knock on the doors of complete strangers in order to solicit their completed or near completed ballots to deliver to polling places. And in every battleground State, lawyers employed by the Democrat National Committee file legal actions seeking judicial modification of express statutory deadlines for the mailing and receipt of mail-in ballots. In some States, the efforts have failed right out of the gate. Challenges to firm vote reception deadlines reached the courts in Arizona, Ohio, Maine, and New Hampshire, but failed to gain traction. Even in Arizona, where the Ninth Circuit Court of Appeals found that the State's requirement that ballots be received only in the precincts where voters were registered to vote adversely impacted African

Americans and other non-white peoples, a request for an injunction barring its operation while the current election was pending was refused.[1] Only in Wisconsin, Michigan, Pennsylvania and Georgia has any success been had, at least temporarily, but that success could well be enough to alter the outcome of the election in favor of Democrats in States the Democrats need to win this time around if their ticket is to prevail over the much-reviled incumbent.

The cases are similar in that each focuses primarily on the deadline for the receipt of mail-in ballots. The Democrat National Committee and others sued the Secretaries of State in these States and alleged that because of the impact that fears surrounding COVID-19 will likely have on the numbers of persons voting by mail, the deadline had to change. If the experience during the recent primaries was to be a guide, many mail-in votes simply wouldn't make it through the post in time to be counted. In Wisconsin, Federal District Court Judge William M. Conley explained that fear of contracting the virus kept many from voting in person in April and caused a run on mail-in ballots, which in turn gave rise to shortages of ballot materials and an overwhelming of personnel unused to so large a work load.[2] During the April primary, "clerks received a flood of absentee ballot requests" that swamped inadequately staffed election offices, absentee certificate envelope supplies became exhausted, many ballots were never received by voters, or were received too late, and many that were placed in the mail never made it back in time for tallying. Of the ballots that actually were returned to the clerk's offices, "more than 14,000…were rejected due to an 'insufficient' witness certification and 'thousands' were rejected for other reasons." In-person voting was hardly an adequate substitute due to popular fears that the disease might be spread in that manner and the likelihood that many election judges would decline to serve due to their own concerns over becoming infected through contact with so many people. The experience during the primary would likely recur on November 3: long waits at polling places that were short-staffed and incapable of providing proper sanitizing procedures. Because the turn-out for the November election is expected to be higher than in the primary, Judge Conley could little doubt that the Wisconsin Election Commission, clerks and voters "will

---

[1] Robert Barnes, "Supreme Court to Hear Arizona Voting Rights Case Next Year," www.thewashingtonpost.com, October 2, 2020.

[2] *Democratic National Committee v. Bostelmann*, Case No. 20-cv-249-wmc.

again face unique challenges in the upcoming election" and that many will follow the Commission's advice to vote via absentee ballot. The result would surely be an even greater bottleneck in the processing of those ballots by the postal service and election officials, a large number of ballots not being received before the deadline expired, and the effective disenfranchisement of thousands of voters.

In Michigan, Judge Cynthia Stephens of the Court of Claims considered evidence that "in light of delays attributable to the COVID-19 pandemic, mail delivery has become significantly compromised, and the risk for disenfranchisement when a voter returns an absentee voter ballot by mail is very real."[3] Significant mail delays since the onset of the pandemic, particularly in the Detroit area, "major operational changes" within the Postal Service—such as elimination of overtime hours—leading to a slow-down in mail delivery, and the recent experience of absentee ballots arriving after the primary election deadline had passed all contributed to an entirely foreseeable election day disaster. As in Wisconsin, in-person voting was hardly a reasonable option in the midst of a pandemic, particularly for the elderly and those whose health was already compromised. Such persons were equally in need of assistance in delivering their ballots once they'd been completed, but current law permitted only a narrow class of persons to handle delivery of someone else's vote.

In Pennsylvania, the analysis was similar.[4] The State's Supreme Court noted that county election boards in the recent primary "were inundated with over 1.8 million requests for mail-in ballots, rather than the expected 80,000-100,000, due in large part to the COVID-19 pandemic, which caused many voters to be wary of congregating in polling places." The massive increase in demand for mail-in ballots prevented election boards from providing "electors with ballots in time for the electors to return their ballot in accord with the statutory deadline."

In each of these cases, the courts considered whether irreparable harm would result in the absence of a change in the voting deadline, the inadequacies of legal remedies and the likelihood of the challengers' success on the merits of their claims once full and proper evidentiary hearings could occur. As the right of citizens to vote was at issue, the

---

[3] *Michigan Alliance for Retired Americans v. Benson*, Case No. 20-000108-MM.

[4] *Pennsylvania Democratic Party et al. v. Kathy Boockvar*, Case No. 133 MM 2020.

courts also weighed "the character and magnitude of the asserted injury" against "the precise interests put forward by the State as justifications for the burden imposed by its rule." Upon considering these various factors, Judge Conley in Wisconsin accepted as fact the Wisconsin Election Commission's projection that "1.8 to 2 million individuals will vote via absentee ballot, exceeding the number of absentees by a factor of three for any prior general, presidential election and exceeding by as much as a million the number of absentee voters that overwhelmed election officials during the April 2020 election." He concluded that the statutory deadline for the fall election "is likely to disenfranchise a significant number of voters…given the projected, record volume of absentee ballots." Combined with the likely impact of the massive volume of mail the Postal Service will be faced with processing, delays were inevitable. In Michigan, Judge Stephens held that despite that lack of ambiguity in the text of the law mandating the deadline for the receipt of mail-in votes, it was appropriate in light of the impact of the coronavirus on voting and the mail system "to extend the received-by deadline for mail-in ballots to prevent the disenfranchisement of voters." Pennsylvania's Supreme Court reached a similar conclusion.

The specific remedy the three courts fashioned was essentially the same: extension beyond election day for as many as 14 days of the statutory deadline for the receipt of mail-in ballots. While the rest of the nation had shut the door on voting, these three battleground States would, at the behest of the Democrat Party, keep it open longer so that additional votes might be cast. That the majority of these votes would be Democrat cannot be doubted.

The problems with these decisions are myriad. The election is not merely a state activity. It is state-run to be sure, but it is for the purpose of permitting the peoples in the States to vote for representatives in the federal government. For that reason, federal interests are implicated. The Congress has made it clear through various statutes that federal elections are to occur throughout the nation on a single day.[5] What these courts have done is to deviate from the will of Congress without specifically addressing Congress's public policy concerns and have created the beginnings of a patchwork of deadlines for what was

[5] 2 U.S.C. § 1; 2 U.S.C. § 7; and 3 U.S.C. § 1.

intended to be a single day of reckoning for the entire nation. A similar concern for uniformity motivated the Supreme Court of the United States in the year 2000 when it accepted jurisdiction over the controversy between the candidates for the office of President arising out of a state court interpretation of election standards. The Supreme Court ultimately overruled the High Court of Florida that had permitted four counties to adopt whatever standards they wished for discerning voter intent from imperfectly marked ballots and authorized the setting aside of election day deadlines intended to conform with federal mandates related to the certification of state-wide ballot counts.[6] The people of Florida were entitled to a single standard and a single deadline for the completion of the voting. Analogously, the people of all the States are entitled to a single election day, a single deadline for receipt and counting of the ballots, and a single date on which the election conclusively ends. Otherwise, the people of some States receive benefits that others don't, and a troubling degree of uncertainty remains at a time when the people as a whole really ought to be putting the election behind them.

The Wisconsin, Michigan and Pennsylvania decisions, of course, involve the right of people to vote and address the impact on the ability to vote the coronavirus may have come November 3. The concern is a legitimate one, not to be dismissed as unimportant. However, the right to vote is not something so vital that long-established rules governing its exercise ought to be set aside by the extraordinary powers of judicial bodies. Legislatures came up with these rules through a process of deliberation, and modified them over time based in part on actual experience. The coronavirus undoubtedly has created burdens on election officials, postal workers and voters themselves. These burdens are not so great that they cannot be overcome within the context of existing rules. As with other rights, the principle burden of casting a vote rightfully belongs to the holder of the right. As with any person enjoying a legally sanctioned benefit, the law favors the vigilant. Those who fail to act reasonably and in a timely fashion in the wake of receiving notice of the relevant rules often find themselves quite justly bereft of what was rightfully theirs. The coronavirus is no secret kept from the masses. It is the single greatest topic of discussion in our time. We've suffered a tremendous loss of liberty as a result of government action supposedly

[6] *Bush v. Gore* (2000) 531 U.S. 98, 121 S.Ct. 525.

designed to keep us safe, and no remedy is available for it in the eyes of some officeholders and courts. We lose what we cherish because the greater good demands it. That position, of course, is unfounded, at least in its most extreme version, and yet there is a lesson to be learned from it—that the emergency asks much from everyone, and if it is true that the emergency is lawfully imposed, it ought to demand a higher degree of care by those who desire not to suffer a loss of what the law and the Constitution guarantee. Vote early then, not late, and don't expect that a court will extend the time for you when others must be bound by the original deadline.

That some courts actually are coming to the rescue of those sleeping on their rights is utterly dismaying. The regulation of elections is within the peculiar purlieu of State legislatures. Indeed, the Constitution itself indicates that "the times, places and manners of holding Elections for Senators and Representatives, shall be prescribed in each State by the Legislature thereof," not the Courts.[7] Judicial modification of the date set for an election, the time when all votes must be received, and the manner in which elections are to be conducted is an obvious trespass upon a field expressly reserved to the legislatures of the States. As this upcoming election includes voting for the President—or more properly for electors who shall in turn chose the President—the intervention by the courts is equally offensive; for the Constitution provides that it is for the Congress, not the Courts, to "determine the time of chusing the Electors, and the Day on which they shall give their votes," and that whatever day Congress selects "shall be the same throughout the United States."[8]

The infamous Florida election of the year 2000 owes much of the distaste with which it is viewed to the cynicism of those who sought to alter the apparent outcome. Though they alleged violation of rights of voters throughout the State, the partisans of the defeated Democrat candidate sought relief only in the most Democrat of strongholds: Volusia, Palm Beach, Broward and Miami-Dade Counties. The thinking apparently was that with more Democrats voting in those counties, the risk during a recount of uncovering un-tabulated Republican votes to add to the victor's tallies was lower. Here, the zeal by which the Democrats on the eve of the election are seeking extension of time to send in ballots, and other changes to legislatively established voting

---

[7] *Constitution of the United States*, Article I, Section 4.
[8] Id., at Article II, Section 1.

laws, is highly suspicious of an unsavory motive. The heavy focus on States the incumbent president unexpectedly won in 2016 and which the Democrats must prevail in if they are to unseat him only deepens the suspicion. Covid has already provided a justification for the legislative scaping of many of the vote integrity provisions of State election codes in order to facilitate voting in a manner supposedly less likely to spread the incidence of the disease. The remainder of the Democrat strategy appears to be to get mail-in ballots to as many people as possible, encourage them to vote if they are Democrats and facilitate delivery by third parties; and if election day doesn't go as they hope, to compare the list of returned ballots with those that were distributed to voters and make up the needed difference. Evidence of this has already emerged: video of a car load of absentee ballots that may have been harvested contrary to Minnesota law; an elaborate vote faking effort in the State of New York; and the illegal use of business addresses on absentee ballots in Nevada.[9] Extended deadlines to present such ballots to voting authorities is essential to this plan, hence the enormous amount of effort the Party has made to change what courts really have no authority to alter, and yet have altered anyway in a number of States.

Each of the judicial decisions discussed above is undoubtedly headed to the Supreme Court for expedited hearing prior to election day. How those decisions will fare is subject to some degree of predictably that has only been enhanced by the departure from the bench of Ruth Bader Ginsburg. The tell-tale authority to heed is one of recent vintage, arising from the same pandemic that has given birth to the pending controversies. In April of this year, the Supreme Court reviewed a decision of the Seventh Circuit Court of Appeals that had upheld a lower court ruling allowing for extended voting deadlines. In that case, the lower court had continued the day for receipt of mail-in votes by a week. No one disputed the extension, hence it wasn't actually reviewed by the Court. What was reviewed was the issue of whether any votes received after the original deadline must be postmarked no later than that date. Though the Supreme Court felt that failure by the moving party to even

---

[9] Miranda Devine, "Project Veritas Uncovers 'Ballot Harvesting Fraud' in Minnesota," https://nypost.com, September 27, 2020; Jon Levine, "Confessions of a Voter Fraud: I was a master at Fixing Mail-In Ballots," https://nypost.com, August 29, 2020; and Video: Visiting Nevada Voters Registered at Commercial Addresses," https://publicinterestlegal.org, October 5, 2020.

have asked for the requested relief from the district court was dispositive of the case, it nevertheless expressed the view that the lower court's subsequent granting of relief not originally asked for "so close to the election date...contravened this Court's precedents."[10] The Supreme Court, it said, "has repeatedly emphasized that lower federal courts should ordinarily not alter the election rules on the eve of an election," and that "when a lower court intervenes and alters the election rules so close to the election date, our precedents indicate that this Court, as appropriate, should correct that error."

The decision might not be entirely on point. It can't be certain that the Supreme Court would rule in a similar fashion where the lower courts had actually granted relief expressly requested by the moving party. Nor does the decision of the Supreme Court consider the many problems facing voters that occurred after it issued its opinion and which informed the more recent rulings of the courts in Wisconsin, Michigan and Pennsylvania. Consequently, the better guidance is to be sought from appellate courts that have had an opportunity to consider the issue in light of our most recent experience. The first court to issue such an opinion was the Court of Appeals for the Eleventh Circuit, led by two recent front runners for the vacant Supreme Court seat, Brit Grant and Barbara Lagoa. In that case, the Circuit Court considered a recent decision by a Georgia Federal District Court that had, like the courts discussed above, extended the date for receipt of mail-in ballots. Instead of adhering to the State's unambiguous deadline of 7 p.m. on Election Day, the lower court "manufactured its own ballot deadline so that the State is now required to count any ballot that was both postmarked by and received within three days of Election Day."[11] The case, said Judge Grant, turned on application of the so-called Anderson-Burdick Test, and a weighing of the "character and magnitude of the burden the State's rule imposes" on the right to vote "against the interests the State contends justify that burden," as well as consideration of "the extent to which the State's concerns make the burden necessary." Under that test, a rule imposing a "severe burden" on the right to vote will survive only if it is narrowly tailored and advances a compelling interest. If the rule imposes only "'reasonable, nondiscriminatory

---

10 *Republican National Committee v. Democratic National Committee* (2020) 589 U.S. __.

11 *The New Georgia Project, et al. v. Raffensperger et al.*, Case No. 20-13360-D.

restrictions,' then 'a State's important regulatory interests will usually be enough' to justify it."

A skeptical Judge Grant noted that the lower court "offered only a few paragraphs of light analysis before concluding that the Election Day receipt deadline for absentee ballots places a severe burden on voters," and focused exclusively on problems experienced by voters outside of Georgia itself. The lower court merely assumed, as in other States, that "a high number of absentee ballot requests due to COVID-19 'will lead to a potentially substantial backlog, increasing the possibility that voters will receive their ballots on a later date,'" assumed that any ballot rejected on account of the deadline would constitute a severe burden on voting rights as opposed to being the result of voter negligence, and ignored the fact that the percentage of absentee ballots rejected in the Georgia primary was actually smaller than usual. A review of the evidence, she said, revealed no impact on the right to vote of any great significance. Georgia, in fact, had "provided numerous avenues to mitigate chances that voters will be unable to cast their ballots." They could "request absentee ballots as early as 180 days before the election and may receive the ballots as early as 49 days before the election, or return their ballots through the mail, hand-delivery, or a drop box," or "participate in early in-person voting," or simply show up to vote on election day to vote in-person." Faced with these various options, it remained for voters simply to make a timely choice between them. Any disenfranchising occurring in this environment was due not to a catastrophe caused by the collision of a disease with an inadequate voting system, but a voter's own lack of diligence. And since it was on voters to avail themselves of the available options in voting, there wasn't much of a burden at all imposed by the rules, hence the rules themselves need only be reasonable to pass Constitutional muster. The reasons given, including "conducting an efficient election, maintaining order, quickly certifying election results, and preventing voter fraud," were sufficient, she concluded, to support the State's contention that no change in the deadline to submit a mail-in vote was merited.

The second decision followed close on the heels of the first, overturning the Wisconsin ruling discussed above. Instead of focusing of the factual basis for the lower court's decision, the Court for the Seventh Circuit considered two crucial jurisdictional issues: whether federal courts were permitted to alter election rules so close to an election, and whether such changes are properly made by the courts rather than legislatures. In considering the first issue, Judges Frank Esterbrook and Trump-appointee Amy St. Eve noted that while courts have deprecated changes in election laws close to Election Day, they have not completely forbidden them. "A last-minute event may require a last-minute reaction."[12] The reason given for making the change in Wisconsin, however, could not be described as a last-minute event. "The World Health Organization declared a pandemic seven months ago, the State of Wisconsin closed many businesses and required social distancing last March, and the State has conducted two elections (April and August) during the pandemic." A decision altering election deadlines issued in May based on April experience would not have been untimely; waiting until September definitely was. And this assumes a court is the proper body to make such a change. The Circuit Court reminded the parties that the Supreme Court, in the century-old case of *Jacobson v. Massachusetts*, acknowledged that it was within the peculiar prerogatives of legislatures to address social needs in time of pandemic. The demands of individuals complaining their rights had been violated by legislatures acting in accordance with their lawful police powers simply had to give way to the greater good. That general proposition, of course, is subject to limitation and exception, but not in the circumstances evident here. Voters, after all, "have had many months since March to register or obtain absentee ballots." Social distancing by voters, too, has long been known as a recommended way to avoid catching or transmitting the disease. Voters could easily overcome the problems contemplated by the lower court simply "by planning ahead and taking advantage of the opportunities allowed by State law."

The election will be on us soon enough. The voting has already commenced. The question of the date by which mail-in ballots in Wisconsin, Michigan, Pennsylvania and elsewhere must be received will undoubtedly be resolved before November 3, by a Court perhaps containing a justice that Joe Biden and his supporters absurdly contend the current President and Senate have no right to nominate and confirm. For those who wish to vote by mail, nothing is stopping them now from consigning their votes to the postal service and trusting in the agents of that much maligned bureau to deliver them in time to be counted. For

[12] *DNC v. Bostelmann*, Case No. 20-2835.

the timorous who prefer to remain at home, they have the additional option of summoning the courage to venture into a world they imagine to be swarming with the molecule that comprises the coronavirus, don their mask and make their way to their designated polling place, to take up a disinfected stylus or pen and proceed to their socially distanced booth to mark their ballot cards. Even now some of these terrified souls contemplate doing so, but they tremble at the thought, convinced by endless messaging in the traditional press and hipper social media that they are but a hair's breadth away from a fatal illness that only perpetual lock-down can contain. The God we in California and elsewhere in the Union acknowledge in our very Constitutions as the author of our liberties is the same God who admonishes us to be not afraid. The President echoed this same admonishment. Some mocked him for it, and did so while failing to comprehend the irony that it was he of all people who offered them the best advice for unseating him. They might actually succeed in doing so, but reliance on mail-in ballots to achieve that end, absent fraud, seems an awfully desperate measure, unlikely to deliver them what they desire, and more likely than not to leave them, as they were four years ago, baying in the streets to a heaven whose shuttered windows leave no opening for entreaties to pass.

Amy Decisis

IN a law review article published four years before she took her seat on the bench of the Seventh Circuit Court of Appeals, Amy Coney Barrett observed that "nominees to the Supreme Court are routinely asked to describe their judicial philosophies, reflecting the public's expectation that they have one and keen interest in what it is."[13] She described the hypothetically cagey nominee who avoids revelation of her judicial philosophy and any and all questions about how she might go about drawing conclusions in particular cases. At her own hearing of her nomination as an Associate Justice of the Supreme Court, the now Justice Barrett had ample opportunities to discuss both her view of the

[13] Amy Coney Barrett, "Precedent and Jurisprudential Disagreement," 91 Tex. L. Rev. 1711 (2013), at p. 1717.

law and her likely approach to particular issues that might come before her as a member of the high bench, and managed to avoid any disclosures beyond affirming that she was indeed an adherent to the judicial philosophy of Originalism that was popularized by her mentor, the late Justice Antonin Scalia. Her caginess, however, didn't fool anyone, particularly members of the Senate minority who were well aware of her academic credentials, scholarly writings and her judicial output during her nearly three years on the Seventh Circuit. And when the moment for the final vote came, they were unequivocal in their opinions about her elevation to the highest court in the land. Charles Schumer said it was "one of the darkest days in the 231-year history of the United States Senate," a day on which "the Republican Senate majority decided to thwart the will of the people and confirm a lifetime appointment to the Supreme Court in the middle of a presidential election after more than 60 million Americans have voted."[14] The ever-strident Elizabeth Warren called Barrett's nomination "illegitimate," and said the rush to get her on the Court was due to the majority's knowledge that "the American people are not on their side."[15] Peaking out from his basement during what for him appears to be a physically taxing election campaign, Joe Biden condemned the "unprecedented" haste in confirming her to the Court, and called on Americans to rectify the error by voting his opponent out of office.[16] His running mate, who questioned the nominee via zoom, also used the word "illegitimate" to describe the proceedings, and vowed that her party and the American people will not forget this latest Republican outrage.[17] The most execrable comment came from Senator Ed Markey of Massachusetts, who scurrilously condemned Justice Barrett's judicial philosophy as fundamentally racist, sexist and homophobic.[18] He later called on Democrats to retake control of the federal government on November 3

[14] Nick Visser, "Schumer Issues Warning to GOP: You May Regret This For 'A Lot Longer' Than You Think," www.huffpost.com, October 26, 2020.

[15] John Nichols, "Make McConnell Pay for Amy Coney Barrett," www.thenation.com, October 28, 2020.

[16] Kenneth Garger, "Biden Slams 'Rushed and Unprecedented' Amy Coney Barret Confirmation," https://nypost.com, October 27, 2020.

[17] Dominick Mastrangelo, "Harris Blasts GOP for Confirming Amy Coney Barrett: 'We Won't Forget This,'" https://thehill.com, October 26, 2020.

[18] "Senator Ed Markey Slams Judicial Originalism' as 'Racist,' 'Sexist,' and 'Homophobic,'" https://news.yahoo.com, October 26, 2020.

and quickly expand the membership of the Supreme Court in order to cancel out the effect of the President's success in placing conservative justices onto the federal bench.

The great fear, of course, is not so much that Justice Barrett will rule conservatively, but that her originalist attitudes and Christian values will specifically compel her to contribute to the reversal of that landmark of progressive jurisprudence, *Roe v. Wade*, and thereby end the constitutional protection for the destruction of unborn human life. For those opposed to Barrett's inclusion on the Court, *Roe* is a super-precedent, a foundational decision of American jurisprudence, and essential to the liberty said to be protected by the Due Process Clauses of the Fifth and Fourteenth Amendments. Some super-precedents, however, are more super than others in that they never seem to generate a single challenge. Since *Roe* was decided in 1973, there have been a half dozen challenges to its holding that abortion is a constitutional right as certain as freedom of speech and the equal protection of law. The most notable of the challenges came a year after the consolidation of the Reagan Era Court with the addition of Clarence Thomas in 1991. The argument presented by the challengers was that *Roe* was incorrectly decided, that no right to an abortion existed in the Constitution, that abortion itself is contrary to the traditions and collective conscience of the American People and was utterly absent from the minds of citizens living at the time of the framing of the Fourteenth Amendment. The Court's majority was painfully aware of the merits of the argument. But error in judicial decision-making wasn't the only or even the most important factor it believed governed its task. Error was regrettable, but so too was the disruption that reversal might have, both with regard to the public's confidence in the Court and in the lives of people who had come to rely on the Court's earlier pronouncement.[19] How reliance entered into the Court's calculus is anyone's guess. It's a principle drawn from the commercial context, justifying the inference of a basis for recovering damages from one who wrongfully induced it. Reliance in the context of abortion came in the form of the organization of "intimate relationships" and "the availability of abortion in the event that contraception should fail." Because the majority believed that many people presently relied on abortion as Plan B in the event of a broken

[19] *Planned Parenthood of Southeastern Pennsylvania v. Casey* (1992) 505 U.S. 833, 854, 112 S.Ct. 2791.

condom or a lapse in diligence in ingesting the pill, abortion would be available indefinitely. It would be available even after those seeking it might otherwise have become aware of a judicial decision overturning *Roe* and had time to alter their reliance accordingly.

Other than *Dred Scott v. Sandford, Roe* is the worst decision ever reached by the Supreme Court of the United States, and the 1992 decision affirming it did little to obviate the error.[20] In fact, by injecting the odd principle of reliance into its calculus, the Court actually made the decision even more objectionable. If a judicial decision is wrong, it is illegal. Ordinarily, an illegal act is null and void. But in modern constitutional jurisprudence, error alone isn't sufficient to eliminate erroneous interpretations of the higher law. The mere fact that people might follow a law or its judicial gloss appears to justify retaining it, as repugnant as it might be to the true meaning of the Constitution. Many don't see the harm, of course, when they benefit from a harmful act, but few who merely watch the benefits accrue from the sidelines could deny that if a court held that the government could, say, eliminate all opportunities by people to protest its policies, a violation of the First Amendment had been erroneously confirmed.

The opinion that Amy Coney Barrett could see the harm in adhering to *Roe* without due consideration of so-called reliance interests is based almost exclusively on the fact that she's a Catholic and that she subscribes to a judicial philosophy that has long criticized the so-called Right to Privacy as an illegitimate graft onto the Constitution. That she is actually prepared to overrule *Roe* and strike it from the liberty guarantees of our great charter is not entirely clear, and a review of her limited judicial output on the Seventh Circuit hardly clarifies the matter. The better source for information that might inform our predictions regarding her response to a challenge to *Roe* is her abundant scholarly writing that focuses on the proper limits of judicial action, the role and strength of Stare Decisis and how the Court ought to act when recognizing a deviation of prior judicial decisions from the Constitution's text.

The most striking thing about Justice Barrett's scholarly writing is not her originalist philosophy, which is striking enough. What

---

[20] See Rex Grady, "Abortion & the Conscience of the Court," in *What is This Freedom? Law, Faith & History in the Time of Trump* (Santa Rosa: Lilburne & Company, LLC, 2019), at pp. 423-437.

dominates her thinking is a strong skepticism about power generally and doubt over the comfort with which any judge should take when exercising the power allotted to her by law. The judicial system is a coordinate branch of government in the federal scheme, and yet its job is not to rule *sua sponte* on legal controversies. Its authority to issue enforceable rulings is dependent on the existence of actual legal disputes that have come before it either through its original jurisdiction or on appeal. Appeals themselves depend upon the existence of inferior courts, which is largely in the hands of Congress. When a case finally comes before it, what's at issue is a law, often enacted by Congress. Though a particular judge might favor a strong presumption against legislative action, the Constitution itself does not generally support this. From a purely prudential standpoint, Justice Barrett thinks the courts to be poorly qualified to engage in anything other than the barest review of Congress's handiwork. Congress is the best judge of the meaning of the laws it enacts, and the meaning itself is best discerned from the language of the law itself. A generally deferential approach to reviewing statutes she believes is respectful of the Framers' allocation of legislative power to the Congress, and tends to avoid the potential for harm flowing from an erroneous decision. When the Supreme Court makes a mistake, it is "extremely difficult to correct."[21] Justice Barrett is open, too, to the possibility that the Supreme Court might not be the sole judge of what is constitutional and what isn't. State resistance to the Court's authority, she notes, was common in the early Republic. On at least thirty-two occasions States refused to obey Court rulings and orders. Presidents have also defied the Court. She wonders about the limits of the Supreme Court's power to bind non-judicial actors, whether its judgments should be obeyed without question, whether "attempts to create test cases through a sort of 'civil disobedience' to Supreme Court opinions" is proper, and if we might safely become less fearful over "institutional attacks on the Court in an attempt to engineer substantive results."[22] Now that she herself has joined the Supreme Court, she might be a bit less skeptical about judicial power than she once was, but her willingness to question the Court's competence and authority suggests

[21] Amy Coney Barrett, "Countering the Majoritarian Difficulty," 32 Const. Comment. 61 (2017), at p. 78.

[22] Amy Coney Barrett, "Introduction: Stare Decisis and Nonjudicial Actors," 83 Notre Dame L. Rev. 1147 (2008), at p. 1172.

a mind open to the idea that the Court is hardly the ultimate or even the best arbiter of our rights and privileges.

Barrett's general skepticism about judicial power is evident in her concern over the role of the Supreme Court as the head of the judicial branch of government. As the President is chief of the executive branch and the Congress is solely vested with power over legislation, there are many who consider the Supreme Court as not merely the court of final instance, empowered to determine whether the inferior courts ruled correctly on issues of law, but as the regulator of the procedures of those courts as well. The power is one that is often ascribed to Article III's general delegation of the judicial authority to the judicial branch, inherent in the nature of the judiciary and the implied hierarchy of courts that are said to be inferior to the one-and-only "Supreme" Court. Justice Barrett notes the arguments in favor of the Court's broad regulatory authority. One is that "judicial power encompasses those prerogatives and obligations that have customarily attended the judicial function, particularly the Anglo-American common law courts at the time of the framing," and these included the power of a superior court to supervise inferior ones.[23] Another argument is that the Constitution "implicitly grants each branch the incidental authority it needs to get its job done."[24]

These arguments, though advanced by their proponents with confidence, suffer from the common flaw of being of recent vintage. They weren't formulated and embraced by the Court until after its transformation by FDR from a body committed to a classically liberal outlook into a dynamo of progressive change. The arch-progressive Felix Frankfurter first asserted the Court's supervisory authority in the 1942 case of *McNabb v. United States*. In reviewing the evidentiary rules relied on by a federal district court in a criminal proceeding, Frankfurter asserted that the scope of the High Court's "reviewing power over convictions brought here from the federal courts is not confined to ascertainment of constitutional validity."[25] Supervision by the High Court "of the administration of criminal justice in the federal courts," he said, "implied the duty of establishing and maintaining civilized

---

[23] Amy Coney Barrett, "Procedural Common Law," 94 Va. L. Rev. 813 (2008), at p. 847, quoting Saikrishna Prakash and Michael Ramsey.

[24] Id., at pp. 847-48.

[25] *McNabb v. United States* (1943) 318 U.S. 332, 63 S.Ct. 608.

standards of procedure and evidence."[26] This authority, he asserted, was evident "from the very beginning of its history," and was manifest, among other things, in "rules of evidence to be applied in federal criminal prosecutions."[27]

Barrett, however, was unable find anything that indicates the Court was understood from the earliest days to possess such power. The Constitution's Article III does grant some power to courts, but until the coming of the New Deal the power was considered by legal scholars to be merely "a grant of authority over local procedure."[28] Prior to Frankfurter's assertion of the Supreme Court's supervisory power over all inferior Article III tribunals, "the Supreme Court had openly claimed such a direct power over inferior court procedure only when it promulgated court rules pursuant to congressional authorization—for example, when it promulgated the Federal Equity Rules, the Federal Admiralty Rules, and the Federal Rules of Civil Procedure."[29] Frankfurter's claim of broad regulatory authority was an obvious breach with this earlier tradition and constitutes a power grab analogous to those undertaken by the other branches of government during the same era.

Some have justified the power as one implied by the reference to the highest court as "supreme." Barrett finds that implication suspect. Merely because the Supreme Court is referred to as "supreme" doesn't necessarily grant it any authority over the other courts. "Founding-era evidence," she says, "suggests that the terms 'supreme' and 'inferior' may well describe the differing geographic and subject matter jurisdictions of various courts rather than their respective places in a pyramid of authority."[30] The debates at the Philadelphia Convention and over ratification in the States were silent on the point, and no evidence from English, colonial, or Founding-era history has been discovered that establishes an explicit link between a "supreme court" and "superintendence of procedure."[31] The more definitive source of an answer to the question is the text of the Constitution itself, which

---

[26] Id.
[27] Id.
[28] Amy Coney Barrett, "The Supervisory Power of the Supreme Court," 106 Colum. L. Rev. 324 (2006), at p. 325.
[29] Id., at p. 329.
[30] Id., at p. 327.
[31] Id.

explicitly provides that Congress, not the Supreme Court, possessed the power to prescribe procedural rules applicable in all federal courts.

Barrett points out that if the Supreme Court's power over inferior court procedure was one granted by the Constitution, it would have been superfluous for the Framers to have granted the power to regulate court procedures to Congress. Such a power, too, if granted, would have been exercised early on. The evidence for it, Barrett says, is weak. Indeed, it was Congress who acted in the first days of the Republic, not the Court. In Section 17 of the Judiciary Act of 1789, Congress granted all federal courts the power to "make and establish all necessary rules for the orderly conduction of business in the said courts."[32] Its Process Act of the same year directed all federal courts to follow the modes of proceeding prescribed by the civil law in equity and admiralty suits, and in common law suits to follow the modes of process used in the supreme court of the state in which the federal court sat.[33] These powers, flowing from laws prescribed by Congress, were happily executed by the courts without any complaint that they violated any principle of the separation of powers or intruded on the Supreme Court's inherent authority to prescribe uniform procedural rules applicable in inferior courts and across all jurisdictional lines. That the authority to do so was lacking is evident from Attorney General Edmund Randolph's recommendation to Congress that it vest the Supreme Court with it, and Justice Story's contention that the only inherent power the Supreme Court had was the same one it shared with all other courts: the power to regulate its own officers and to protect them in the performance of their functions.[34]

A cautious view of the matter, Barrett says, "would consider Article III's silence regarding the means by which the Supreme Court might control its inferiors (particularly in contrast to Article II) or the means by which members of the judiciary might control one another (particularly in contrast to Article I) to counsel against implying any powers in that regard."[35] Early case law has been pointed to by some scholars as evidence of early support for the Court's supervisory role in prescribing lower court procedure, but Barrett discounts this as an example of the

---

[32] Amy Coney Barrett, "Procedural Common Law," op. cit., at p. 856.

[33] Id., at p. 856.

[34] Id., at pp. 860 and 863.

[35] Amy Coney Barrett, "The Supervisory Power of the Supreme Court," op. cit., at p. 361.

Court merely acting on a statutory grant by Congress to follow procedures in accordance with existing common law principles. What the Court was doing was drawing from the common law, which was understood to be a source of fixed principles applicable in all situations, in all courts. The Court was not inventing new law and imposing it—the law it applied already bound the lower courts. The Court merely declared what the law was; it didn't create it.[36]

The consequence of this insight, Barrett says, is "potentially far-reaching. If the authority to impose procedural rules on the lower courts is lacking, an entire body of legal principles binding the lower courts—rules of statutory construction, claim preclusion and even stare decisis"—would evaporate and leave the lower courts free to fashion their own rules and ascribe whatever value to precedent they thought appropriate.[37] The power to regulate procedure would be confined to the regulating court itself. The power would permit "a court to regulate its own proceedings, but [wouldn't] empower a reviewing court to supervise the proceedings of a lower court by prescribing procedures that the lower court must follow."[38] Consequently, inherent procedural authority wouldn't "enable the development of procedural doctrines that are uniform across jurisdictions."[39] To the extent that the Supreme Court possessed any power over procedure, its power would extend only to itself and would be subject to revision by Congress if and when that body determines intervention is necessary.[40]

The Supreme Court, of course, is known for its development of substantive law. Historically, its power was seen in such things as interpreting the Constitution. It's rulings in such instances are considered final until amended by the people at large. It is also seen in the construction of statutes, where its decisions are merely tentative and subject to revision by the legislature. In the process of construing statutory language and determining the meaning of provisions of the positive law, the Supreme Court and lower courts are often guided by common law principles thought to be of general application. Among these common law principles are what are known as substantive canons

---

[36] Id., at p. 377.
[37] Id., p. 387.
[38] Any Coney Barrett, "Procedural Common Law," op. cit., at p. 817.
[39] p. 817.
[40] Id., at 888.

of construction. Justice Barrett finds these legal principles to be of special concern for those sharing her jurisprudential outlook. Strict consideration of legal language, whether in the Constitution or in a statute, mandates a search for the drafter's intent—a search that often necessitates exploration beyond legislative materials and entails the mining in diverse sources for evidence of the original public meaning of operative terms. To the extent a substantive canon of construction applied in similar cases causes a deviation from the more obvious or suspected meaning of statutory language, the textualist judge of originalist leanings finds herself in a dilemma. For Justice Barrett, the only justification for deviation is the demand of the Constitution itself. And yet many textualists who share her originalist principles appear to have no difficulty in applying the canons even in situations where they alter the more likely meaning of the law they are deployed to interpret. If it is actually true that any of the canons permit "a departure from a text's most natural meaning, that departure," she insists, "must be reconciled with the constitutional structure."[41]

Reviewing the history of some of the more notable canons, Justice Barrett found that many appear from the earliest date in the record of the Supreme Court's decisions. John Marshall, among others, viewed them with favor and even developed a few of his own that subsequently became lodestars for courts at all levels of the federal judiciary. The early use of canons, however, appears in the view of Justice Barrett to have been rather modest. The courts that employed them were undoubtedly aware of an earlier English tradition that permitted judges to inject equity into the work of interpreting positive law and to bend legislative language in ways that a judge believed was preferable to any legislative choice that might have inspired the language in the first place. This tradition of equitable interpretation by judges appears to have been a feature of the judiciary intimately connected to the judiciary's relationship with the sovereign monarch. Barrett agrees with the historian John Manning that this historic prerogative of the judge was self-consciously abandoned during the early Republic on account of its inconsistency with the Constitution's indenture to the People and the explicit vesting of legislative power in the Congress.[42] An example of the

---

[41] Amy Coney Barrett, "Substantive Canons and Faithful Agency," 90 B.U.L. Rev. 109 (2010), at p. 111.

[42] Id., at pp. 115-116.

restraint typical of the early bench is found in the application of the Rule of Lenity—the presumption that a penal statute be construed in favor of the accused. In discussing the rule, John Marshall reminded the parties that the rule itself didn't "imply that the intention of the legislature, as manifested by their words, is to be overruled; but that in cases where the intention is not distinctly perceived, where, without violence to the words or apparent meaning of the act, it may be construed to embrace or exclude a particular case, where the mind balances and hesitates between the two constructions, the more restricted construction ought to prevail; especially in cases where the act to be punished is in itself indifferent, and is rendered culpable only by positive law."[43] This insistence on a limited scope for the canon and the supremacy of the legislature, says Barrett, "is a constant refrain in the case law." Courts, she notes, "repeatedly emphasized that lenity could never overcome the ordinary meaning of a statute; on the contrary, the principle applied only in the event of ambiguity."[44] The same was true of other canons, whether devised by the early Supreme Court to deal with novel problems arising in American law or received into its body with the English common law.

Barrett has few qualms about the use of canons to aid in the determination of meaning when statutory language is ambiguous, perhaps in part because the statutes against which the canons apply have been drafted against a common law body of principles within the implicit knowledge of the drafters. The better use of the canons, however, comes in the context of construing Congress's acts with the dictates of the Constitution. When used in this way, substantive canons protect larger constitutional interests from legislative overreaching and cannot be said to invade any legitimate legislative policy choices. This is especially true when the canon at issue is constitutionally inspired. Such canons, she says, "have the virtue of promoting an identifiable (and short of constitutional amendment, closed) set of norms that have been sanctioned by a super-majority as higher law. They do less violence to the legislative bargain because legislators can anticipate their potential effect on statutory interpretations and modify their language accordingly."[45] When a judge acts to apply a canon to advance constitutional priorities, the separation of powers dilemma that arises

[43] Id., at pp. 130-131, quoting Marshall.
[44] Id., at p. 131.
[45] Id., at p. 168.

from lethal employment of judicial review is not merely blunted; it's entirely justified.[46]

Barrett's skepticism of judicial power is most significant in the area of precedent and the enduring authoritative value of judicial decisions. Respect for prior decisions of the court on points of law is embodied in the principle of Stare Decisis. Generally speaking, she considers it to be "a sensible rule because, among other things, it protects the reliance interests of those who have structured their affairs in accordance with the Court's existing cases."[47] Some decisions she recognizes as beyond question, whether consistent with the Framers' Constitution or not: *Marbury v. Madison, Martin v. Hunter's Lessee, Helvering v. Davis, The Legal Tender Cases, Mapp v. Ohio, Brown v. Board of Education* and *The Civil Rights Cases.* "The force of these cases," she says," derives from the People, who have taken their validity off the Court's agenda." No serious litigant ever challenges the bedrock vitality of the points of law embodied in these cases (that is, that the Court possesses the power of judicial review, or that the Supreme Court's review of state court interpretations of the Constitution is both permissible and good policy, or that Social Security is within the power of Congress to provide, or that the government is permitted to issue paper money, and that racial segregation violates the Fourteenth Amendment's Equal Protection Clause), and if any ever did, "no inferior…or state court would take them seriously, at least in the absence of any indicia that the broad consensus supporting a precedent was crumbling."[48] Widespread support by the public "does not immunize these cases from overruling; it immunizes them from being challenged in the first place."[49] Originalists such as herself might have taken a different approach with some of these so-called super-precedents in the first instance, even if they might agree with the essential holding of some or all of them, but they don't question their validity, and likely would never have the opportunity to do so because of the simple fact that the Court will probably never be presented with a request that they be overruled.[50]

---

46 Id., at p. 181.

47 Amy Coney Barrett, "Originalism and Stare Decisis," 92 Notre Dame L. Rev. 1921 (2017), at p. 1921.

48 Amy Coney Barrett, "Precedent and Jurisprudential Disagreement," op. cit., at p. 1735.

49 Id., at p. 1736.

50 Amy Coney Barrett, "Originalism and Stare Decisis," op. cit., at p. 1929.

The fear that Barrett the originalist is poised to disrupt long accepted constitutional doctrine being unfounded, there is nonetheless the strong possibility that Barrett will question the soundness of doctrine that remains controversial. Like other jurists, she understands that in the hierarchy of precedent, Stare Decisis in constitutional cases is protected by the weakest of presumptions. This hardly translates into instability in the settled law, nor routine upheaval of decisional authority. What it means, instead, is that while constitutional decisions are not usually set in stone, modifying or overruling them is dependent on a number of factors, the most prominent one being the need for a majority on the Court to agree upon an outcome that is based on more than a naked expression of power. Justices, she observes, "do not all share the same interpretive methodology," hence they "do not have an agreed-upon standard for identifying 'error' in constitutional cases."[51] In reaching a decision to overturn a precedent, justices of diverse interpretive outlooks need to agree. Even a new majority prepared to reverse existing precedent must still "defend its approach to the Constitution and be sure enough of that approach to warrant unsettling reliance interests."[52] Precedent—even precedent enjoying a weak presumption of validity—demands that a new majority bear "the weight of explaining why the constitutional vision of their predecessors was flawed and of making the case as to why their's better captures the meaning of our fundamental law."[53] It is an obligation that requires both an explanation on the merits and "an explanation of why its view is so compelling as to warrant reversal."[54] This is not always an easy task, even for a justice convinced that constitutional doctrine is inconsistent with what the Constitution actually demands.

Perhaps the most positive aspect of a weak presumption of validity for constitutional decisions is that it allows disputes about the precedent to be aired at all, and makes possible the correction of errors even of long-standing duration. When that actually occurs, there is always the fear that the public would lose confidence in the court. That was certainly a consideration in the mind of the majority in *Casey* back in

---

[51] Amy Coney Barrett, "Precedent and Jurisprudential Disagreement," op. cit., at p. 1711.

[52] Id.

[53] Id., at p. 1722.

[54] Id.

1992. Barrett herself is not one to fret over this potentiality. In rejecting precedent, she says there is little reason to think that reversal would do the Court much harm. "Stare Decisis is not a hard-and-fast rule in the Court's constitutional cases, and the Court has not been afraid to exercise its prerogative to overrule precedent" from time-to-time.[55] Americans, she says, are hardly unaware that justices on the court view the law differently from one another, approach its interpretation in ways peculiar to the particular justice, and urge in accordance with that approach either the continuity of existing interpretations, or a break with the past.[56] That justices do this very thing is what the people expect, as is the occasional rejection of old orthodoxies. Even a future rejection of *Roe* and its progeny would come as no surprise to the American People given the decades-long controversy surrounding it. The ability of the Court to utilize Stare Decisis to "declare a permanent victor in a divisive constitutional struggle" is a function that history, the Court and the People alike reject.[57]

Doubting the necessity of Stare Decisis as a mechanism to preserve institutional integrity and public confidence, Barrett also doubts the need for inferior courts to respect Stare Decisis in many matters before them. Her writing on this topic has been confined to the issue of the strength of the presumption favoring existing authority in statutory matters, but the outlook revealed there might well shed light on her willingness to allow lower courts far greater leeway to consider the prospect of overruling all manner of cases so long as it isn't approached cavalierly and without due consideration of the text of the relevant law and its intended meaning. The rationale for the strong presumption favoring prior interpretations of statutes is that it respects the legislature's prerogative as the originator of the law. It is a court, of course, that interprets the law as drafted by Congress and perhaps modifies its intended meaning, yet had the court truly deviated from Congress's intent, the assumption is that Congress would quickly revisit the statute and amend it so as to overcome the court's erroneous interpretation. "By failing to amend the statute, Congress signals its

[55] Id., at p. 1726.
[56] Id., at p. 1728.
[57] Id., at p. 1727.

acquiescence" to the court's conclusion as to its meaning.[58]

For Barrett, this theory of acquiescence makes far more sense when the decision is issued by the Supreme Court. The Supreme Court is a single body, and the preeminent one in the country, and its decisions are more easily tracked by the legislature, hence more likely to generate interest in a legislative corrective. For courts of appeal to insist that their own prior decisions and the decisions of district courts are guarded by a super strong presumption of correctness doesn't make much sense at all. With thirteen separate appellate circuits, the possibility of discordant interpretations grows, as does the difficulty of tracking them all. "It is both impractical and inconsistent with the system of appellate review that Congress has designed for the inferior courts "to assume that Congress will respond to them in the same way."[59] The institutional barriers to Congress actually correcting a mistaken decision, whether by the Supreme Court or one of the various courts of appeals, are high. While a court that makes an erroneous decision can actually easily reconsider the prior record and identify the error and correct it, the process of legislatively correcting a mistaken judicial interpretation of a law entails drafting an amendment acceptable to a majority of hundreds of members of Congress, reconciliation of all differences of opinion between Congress's two chambers, and the assent of the President.[60] Better that the courts of appeal drop any overwhelming commitment to their prior determination of the meaning of statutes than to require of Congress the equivalent of the labors of Hercules to overcome erroneous judicial interpretations.

One final objection to courts of appeal adopting a super strong presumption favoring judicial interpretations of statutes is constitutional and applies as much to the Supreme Court as it does to inferior tribunals. When courts interpret a statute, they potentially alter the intended meaning of the text and thereby impose a de facto amendment. Amending a statute is fundamentally a legislative task, not judicial. To effect such a change, bicameral action is typically necessary, and the finished product must be presented to the President for his or her consideration. Even if it were true that Congress's failure to take

---

[58] Amy Coney Barrett, "Statutory Stare Decisis in the Courts of Appeal," 73 Geo. Wash. L. Rev. 317 (2005), at p. 317.

[59] Id., at p. 318.

[60] Id., at p. 324.

action in the wake of an erroneous interpretation represented congressional acquiescence, Congress "is not the only body with a role in making or amending statutes."[61] Omitted from the calculus of acquiescence is "the executive's role in the legislative process."[62] In Barrett's view, it would be better for the health of the constitutional balance among the branches of government for all courts, including the Supreme Court, to consider their statutory decisions to be only weakly presumptive, instead of "super strong" in their precedential effect.

That Stare Decisis is even a legitimate principle Justice Barret finds questionable. As noted earlier, Barrett considered the power of the Supreme Court either to adopt procedural rules or to impose them uniformly upon the inferior courts. In doing so, she expressed doubt that the Constitution authorized or permitted it. In an article from 2003, she wondered whether Stare Decisis actually violated the principle of Due Process itself. Courts, she noted, honor precedent as a self-imposed restriction upon themselves. Stare Decisis is a prudential doctrine, not a constitutionally mandated one. It bears some similarity to the preclusive doctrines of Res Judicata and Collateral Estoppel. Both Preclusion and Stare Decisis result in the refusal by a court to hear the merits of a claim. The difference between the two is how exactly they do so. Preclusion applies against a party to a matter involving an issue that the party previously litigated. On the earlier occasion, the party effected by the doctrine had an opportunity to be heard, to present evidence in support of his or her position, and to challenge both the position of the opponent and the conclusion of the court. In this sense, preclusion honors Due Process, for it cannot apply unless a prior adjudication on the same point has already occurred. In contrast, Stare Decisis entails no consideration of the rights of the party bound by it. The party never had an opportunity to raise his or her case before hand, nor to address the merits of the ultimate ruling of fact or law, or to challenge the court on appeal. A claimant subject to Stare Decisis can certainly attempt to make persuasive arguments for overruling precedent, but the court hearing the matter "is obligated…to ignore them."[63] Barrett argued that in its "rigid application—when it effectively forecloses a litigant from

---

61 Id., at p. 339.

62 Id.

63 Amy Coney Barrett, "Stare Decisis and Due Process," 74 U. Colo. L. Rev. 1011 (2003), at p. 1018.

meaningfully urging error-correction—Stare Decisis unconstitutionally deprives a litigant of the right to a hearing on the merits of her claims."[64]

Barrett identified judicial preoccupation with reliance interests protected by Stare Decisis as the primary obstacle to permitting more flexible review of legal precedent. In allowing real and alleged social reliance on past decisions, even when a decision is of questionable constitutional merit, courts have effectively flipped the priorities that the law ought to embrace. When individual liberties are at stake, Due Process ordinarily is demanded, "and, when precedent clearly exceeds the bounds of statutory or constitutional text, reliance interests should figure far less prominently in a court's overruling calculus."[65] Reliance, she acknowledged is important. When a litigant alleges an error in a prior decision "that falls within what we might think of as the courts' 'policy making' authority, reliance interests ought to weigh heavily in a court's decision regarding whether to change course."[66] She agreed that reliance "ought to weigh heavily if the issue is whether the previous court should have chosen one reasonable interpretation of a text rather than another, or decided differently a matter within its federal common law authority. A court possesses discretion in these matters, and frank consideration of policy appropriately guides its exercise of discretion."[67] However, when "a litigant demonstrates that precedent demonstrably conflicts with the statutory or constitutional provision it purports to interpret, the role of reliance is significantly diminished, and possibly eliminated."[68] The Constitution, she noted, does not clearly grant the judicial department the power to consider societal reliance as a reason not to overturn an erroneous judicial decision, and the judicial oath, Article V, and separation-of-powers principles cut against it."[69] Moreover, "a broad power to trump constitutional text with erroneous gloss would remove the lien between judicial interpretation and constitutional amendment. A broad power to trump statutory text with erroneous gloss would remove the line between judicial interpretation and legislation. And, importantly, broad power in either circumstance would remove the Due Process limit on the judiciary's exercise of power

[64] Id., at p. 1013.
[65] Id., at p. 1015.
[66] Id., at p. 1061.
[67] Id., at pp. 1061-1062.
[68] Id., at p. 1062.
[69] Id.

over an individual."[70] If the courts "are willing to claim the power to adhere to clear error, they ought to at least be cognizant of the Due Process effect on individual litigants before they do so."[71]

Her final objection to too strong a commitment to precedent is the fact that, as a historical reality, Stare Decisis is a doctrine of relatively recent origin. "The notion that courts have any sort of obligation to follow precedent did not surface," she said, "until the time of Blackstone, and even Blackstone's concept of precedent was relatively soft."[72] Indeed, it wasn't until the middle of the Nineteenth Century that American lawyers began to conceive "of precedent as a binding force."[73] Even after that time, the doctrine wasn't "as rigid as the version of Stare Decisis employed today. The rules that give modern Stare Decisis doctrine much of its rigor are decidedly modern."[74] This is hardly a reason to reject precedent, but it is a reason for considering how much weight precedent ought to be given.

Barrett's skepticism of judicial power and the ability of judges to always correctly decide controversies, her doubt that the Supreme Court is vested with special authority to prescribe rules for all inferior courts (including rules mandating Stare Decisis), her reservations about the sanctity of precedent generally and highly disputed ones specifically, her distrust of reliance as an important consideration weighing against reversing existing authority, her belief that due process is more important than doctrinal stability, and her commitment to an originalist approach to interpreting the Constitution all suggest that when the time comes for the consideration of *Roe* and the constitutional right to an abortion, she will not hesitate to contemplate reversing it. However, her understanding that the judicial process is imperfect and often marked by compromise and that much uncertainty exists regarding the true meaning of the law probably means she's more than willing to accept an outcome less perfect than the one she believes is mandated by the Framers' intent and perhaps her own conscience. Her own mentor Justice Scalia was often willing to accept past error, so long as he could improve if not cure it with a decision far truer to the Constitution he was

---

[70] Id., at p. 1063.
[71] Id., at p. 1063.
[72] Id., at p. 1065.
[73] Id.
[74] Id.

sworn to defend.[75] *Roe* may survive Justice Barrett, but if it does its constitutional prominence will likely be drastically reduced.

In the evening ceremony that almost immediately followed the vote to confirm her nomination, Justice Barrett pointed out the fundamentally political nature of the process she had just endured. "It is the job of a senator," she observed, "to pursue her policy preferences."[76] Putting such preferences aside would, in fact, constitute "a dereliction of duty" to the people who elected her.[77] This, however, was not the duty of a judge. Elections are not something a federal judge is required to endure in order to take her seat. Judges, therefore, "have no basis for claiming that their preferences reflect those of the people."[78] A Judge is instead guided by a single principle: is the law valid or not? Absent from her consideration are the objections of Congress, the President, the People, and her own "private beliefs that might otherwise move her."[79]

Justice Barrett's critics, of course, don't believe it. They believe, instead, that she is a creature of her private beliefs and that she will not hesitate to impose them using the power vested in her as a member of the Supreme Court. This is the very reason they've been so harsh in their opposition, and why not a single Democrat in the Senate voted to confirm this highly qualified, brilliant and exceptional person to one of most important posts in our government. To the extent that Justice Barrett's private beliefs embrace conclusions of law reflective of her sincere understanding of the nature of the Constitution, the critics are correct. Her personal objection to abortion as violative of church doctrine and the will of God, however, is of no matter; for there has never been a right to an abortion protected and promoted by the Constitution, regardless of what a majority of justices on the Supreme Court have said. The decision to protect that so-called right is as offensive to the Constitution as any other terrible decision one could name in the Court's long history. No reliance by Americans on that decision can ever justify an erroneous interpretation of the Constitution, and Justice Barrett,

[75] Amy Coney Barrett, "Originalism and Stare Decisis," op. cit., at pp. 1938-1939.

[76] Devin Dwyer, Ben Gittleson & Trish Turner, "Following Confirmation to Supreme Court, Barrett Takes 1st Oath at White House," https.//abcnews.go.com, October 26, 2020.

[77] Id.

[78] Id.

[79] Id.

though she holds abortion to be a moral abomination and sin against the Creator, very well may consider it to be a decision that Stare Decisis ought to protect no longer. If she does and *Roe* falls, those who object will have to do what the Framers' always intended: vote in their home States, amend their State Constitutions, and perhaps even work to amend the Constitution of the United States. That they will do these things and cease doing harm to the Constitution by insisting that justices on the Court provide them with relief their own membership in the minority bars them from accomplishing politically we can only hope.

A Dark Winter

WHEN the exercise of virtue becomes manifest in material success, the experience of man instructs us that the inevitable consequence is virtue's destruction by those sentiments, greed and glory, that such success so naturally breeds. In the wake of the reduction of Carthage and the subjugation of Hispania and the Hellenistic nations in the east, the virtue that made the expansion of the Roman Republic possible gradually succumbed to the corrosive effects of the children its expansive policies spawned. Men in authority, guiding the defense of the nation and leading its citizen armies in the field, saw in the midst of their triumph opportunities crying out for their indulgence. Defeated realms the world over presented their own citizens as tribute when treasures of gold and silver became exhausted and bade them farewell as triremes shipped the unfortunates to the Italian homeland to till the soil that fed the peoples of the growing municipalities of empire.

With riches derived from the spoils of war, men already wealthy and influential expanded their domestic domains, and employing a captive and servile population of immigrants, steadily undermined the ability of free citizens and free labor to compete in the market place. The value of gold diminished with a glut of the metal circulating through the exchanges and debts grew as small farmers found themselves in need of capital to pay free labor that the larger, wealthier landowners no longer found necessary to employ. "Wherever the eye turned," said the historian Mommsen, "it encountered abuses and decay," and these twin banes in time became so pronounced that "the question could not but force itself on every sagacious and well-disposed man, whether this state of things were not capable of remedy or amendment."[1]

Travelling through the Tuscan countryside, a young veteran of noble family named Tiberius Gracchus "found the country almost depopulated, there being hardly any free husbandmen or shepherds, but for the most part only barbarian, imported slaves."[2] When he won popular election to the high office of Tribune, Gracchus undertook an effort to remedy the situation by delivering land, and with it jobs and industry, back to the free population that had been displaced and impoverished through the introduction of cheap foreign labor.

Being a veritable declaration of war on those who had exploited the advantage abroad into power at home, "the moneyed men, and those of great estates," became "exasperated, through their covetous feelings…through anger and party spirit," and undertook a campaign "to seduce the people, declaring that Tiberius was designing a general redivision of lands, to overthrow the government, and put all things into confusion."[3] As Gracchus worked to correct the corruption of the constitutional system that favored slavery over free labor, non-citizen over citizen, and an elite whose ambition and outlook was international not national, the various branches of the government his opponents controlled sought to undermine him at every turn. The feud, said Mommsen, "spread daily more and more, and became more envenomed, and more personal."[4] Every word the reformer uttered, every gesture he made, even the most innocuous and routine, came to be interpreted by his enemies as indicia of a malicious design he had on the powers of state.[5] Before his term in office was over, an enraged host of enemies hunted him throughout the City, overcame him in flight and slaughtered him in the street. Such hatred and malice they had for him, they heaped the cruelest and most unnatural of insults upon his dead body, refused it a proper burial and dragged it out through the night before dumping it into the Tiber, where what didn't decompose in the waters was consumed by beasts once it found its way in the river's

---

[1] Theodor Mommsen, *The History of Rome*, Volume III (London: J.M. Dent & Sons, Ltp., 1911), at p. 80

[2] Lucius Mestrius Plutarchus, *Plutarch's Lives*, Volume IV (New York: The Athenaeum Society, 1905), at p. 514

[3] Id., at p. 515

[4] Mommsen, op. cit., at p. 87.

[5] Id., at 88.

current to the sea beyond Ostia. The purge that followed against the partisans of the overthrown leader hardly ended the threat his movement posed, for "the people...showed evident marks of their anger...and were clearly waiting only for the opportunity to be revenged."[6]

So began the great civil war that waged intermittently for the next century, and did not end until a tyrant of Gracchus' party, possessing uncommon genius in conceiving strategy and executing it, defeated all rivals and eliminated all but the form of the Constitution by filling nearly every office of public trust not with a loyal adherent, but with himself. By then the people had forgotten their former leader and his populist impulses and contentedly made sacrifice to his successor who had decreed his divine status and the eternity of his imperium as fitting compensation for his triumph over his many jealous and rancorous rivals. To the extent that history remembers Gracchus at all, it is as "a tolerably able, thoroughly well-meaning, conservative patriot, who simply did not know what he was doing; who in the fullest belief that he was calling the people evoked the rabble, and grasped at the crown without being himself aware of it, till the inexorable concatenation of events urged him irresistibly into the career of the demagogue-tyrant."[7]

The same might one day be said of Donald Trump, who came to power most unexpectedly at the head of a movement of citizens discontented over the influx of illegal, foreign and highly discounted labor, the export of domestic industry abroad through the opening of virtually unrestricted access to the goods of nations that permitted slave labor, the promotion of anti-American fanaticism all over the globe and particularly the volatile Middle East, and the embrace of partisan policies passed off as science that tended to further degrade the nation's economic profile and the happiness of its people. The success he achieved in righting the economic wrongs, stemming the tide of illegal immigration and slave-manufactured goods, and bringing an end to conflicts abroad might have earned him a historic place in the annals of the American presidency, but for the introduction early in his final, fateful year in office of a disease originating in the heart (and perhaps brain) of the nation's most significant competitor and led to increasingly feverish calls for the literal ending of business as usual. The forced

[6] Plutarchus, op. cit., at p. 529.
[7] Mommsen, op. cit., at p. 94.

closure of schools, businesses and government operations by state and local officials were said to be for the sake of protecting the people from the spread of a disease so dangerous that all of humanity was threatened with destruction. An unrelenting torrent of news from the four quarters of creation reaffirmed the danger and terrified a good segment of the population into taking refuge in homes they dared not leave without first covering their faces almost completely, donning masks and saturating themselves with sanitizing chemicals. The interests that opposed the President, in the media, in state government and the Congress, in academia, social media and information oriented corporations, global enterprise generally and the opposition political party spoke in many voices a uniform condemnation of the President's alleged ineptitude in responding to the "crisis," and then blamed him for the physical destruction that followed the economic ruin when radical and radicalized foot soldiers of the progressive movement revolted in city after city, ostensibly in protest over several instances of police brutality, real or alleged, but in truth as part of a concerted strategy to discredit the man whose very existence was an affront to the decades-long effort to transform the United States from a constitutional republic in substance, to one in mere name, operated for the benefit of globalists intent on organizing markets for their own benefit and reorganizing humanity itself as if to prove they, not the Creator, are the true masters of the universe.

Nevertheless, as the election of November 3 approached, many factors favored the President's reelection and the continuation of policies that had proven highly salutary to the health of the nation. Unlike many politicians successful in winning election on the strength of their promises, the President had actually delivered on his. The base of his support, thus, was prepared to cast their vote for him a second time and even donate cash to his campaign and the war chest of the party he headed. Notwithstanding the deleterious impact of the coronavirus, the number of jobs had grown, whole industries had returned to American shores, cash that had been locked away in offshore banks beyond the reach of tax authorities now flowed into the national economy, growing it all the more. The stock market operated at record highs, and the nation as a whole prospered. Long a critic of foreign wars, the President made history in ending them, not only ones in which the United States was a party, but others in which the country had been a mere bystander or an ally of one side or another. As the President's critics in the military fumed over the fading justifications for large budget appropriations, and foreign-based industry gnashed its teeth over greater challenges to competing with American concerns, poorly governed nations fretted over the inability to dump their surplus populations on the United States, and assorted Marxists, progressives, Democrats and media talking heads employed by media subsidiaries of global corporate entities reflexively predicted doom for the President, nothing but doom. As the people grew tired of lock downs supposedly designed to prevent the spread of a virus that came to increasingly resemble the flu, restrictions on economic life eased. The hypocrisy of progressive governors who called for the strongest strictures on liberty to fight the disease while they happily and secretly attended large dinner parties with friends and allies and lent their tacit support to progressive rioters who decried the lack of compliance with social distancing rules except when they were busy burning down police stations and private businesses, only expedited the emergence of a consensus favoring a return to normalcy. The President's support in his own party was substantially greater than four years before, the cash his campaign had raised was greater than anything ever seen, and his party's success in registering new voters exceeded that of the Democrats in every State where it counted.

The quality of the President's opponents only increased the likelihood of reelection. When the campaign season began, few persons of national stature were in the running, and several who were lacked cross party appeal or had expiration dates long since passed. Senators Bernie Sanders, Elizabeth Warren and Kamala Harris offered variations on the theme of condescending Marxism and were virtually tied in the repulsive charmlessness of their personalities. Entrepreneurs Andrew Yang and Tom Steyer represented the yin and yang of human personality types: one amiable and unassumingly smart, the other overbearing and entitled, yet both equally committed to policies that would have precluded their own dizzying success had they been in place during their rise to the top. Julian Castro, Cory Booker, Amy Klobuchar and Mayor Pete were garden variety progressives of differing temperaments yet united in their scorn for Trump. With the exception of Senator Sanders, only former Vice President Joseph Biden approached anything resembling a household name, but his nearly fifty years in public service, confused presentation in debate, and his virtual absence from the campaign trail did little to recommend him to the Democrat voting block beyond support for his retirement to a senior assisted living community. Numerous debate faux pas and a dismal fourth and fifth place finish in the Iowa and New Hampshire primaries notwithstanding, Biden's persistence finally won him the confidence of party elders none too impressed with the few virtues and many vices of his intra-party competitors, and they in turn convinced the field to retire in Biden's favor. With Biden unwilling to meet with the press or voters, his son's laptop contents revealing the candidate's involvement in what appeared to be an international influence peddling and money laundering operation, and the President himself generating a tidal wave of support manifest in massive rallies every few days, the President's re-election seemed all but certain.

The only obstacle in the President's way was the effectiveness of his opponents in altering the rules governing elections in key jurisdictions. The threat posed by the virus, at least as presented in the media and vouched for by the Governors of New York, California and Michigan, generated fear among voters that casting a ballot in person posed potentially fatal consequences and justified lawsuits to relax voting rules long on the books as safeguards against fraud and abuse that might unlawfully alter the outcome of elections and deliver political power to candidates and parties that lacked actual popular support. Despite the constitutional mandate that legislatures exercise sole authority over rules governing the time, place and manner of federal elections, Democrat legal teams persuaded courts in numerous States to issue orders extending voting deadlines well beyond election day, relaxing vote delivery requirements and permitting near universal voting by mail without the traditional protections against vote fraud that applied when voting absentee. Where courts were slow to act, agreements were reached with governors and election official even in Republican States, permitting voting contrary to clear legislative mandates. Inexplicably, the Supreme Court of the United States declined to hear even a single appeal of any of these results before the election and not a single legislature in an effected State, despite most being controlled by Republican majorities, bothered to take corrective action in defense of their right as the authorized maker of rules for federal elections.

Come election night, the polls favored Biden, as did most of the media, but no evidence existed that they were correct. All other indicators pointed to Trump. The early counting of the votes appeared to bear this out. Several hours into the count, Trump led in all the predicable locales, and had leads in all of the so-called battleground States, including a seemingly insurmountable 800,000-vote advantage in Pennsylvania, where he had added 200,000 new voters to the Republican rolls since 2017 and championed the cause of the State's industrial work-force. With most of the vote in, the inexplicable suddenly occurred: voting suddenly stopped in a half dozen counties in the key states of Wisconsin, Michigan, Minnesota, Pennsylvania, Nevada, Arizona and Georgia. The simultaneous stoppage in so many jurisdictions, apparently coordinated, was utterly unprecedented. Only in Atlanta was even a reason given: a burst water pipe in the civic center had caused a flood and required the evacuation of the venue. And yet the count didn't actually cease. It continued, and the margins now favoring Biden defied any known rules of statistics and all historical experience in vote counting. In some places, the spike in votes for Biden came in the tens, even hundreds of thousands of votes, with few additional votes being recorded for Trump. In other places, the numbers being fed to the news media and reported live on cable television revealed actual reduction in the number of votes previously counted for the President. The most obnoxious situation occurred in Atlanta where video cameras recorded the departure of everyone from the counting room except four or five election officials. As soon as everyone else was gone, these workers produced a set of boxes hidden in a draped dresser-like object, pulled pristine ballots from inside them and started running them through the vote counting scanners that were supposed to be dormant until morning due to a flood that never actually occurred. One of the workers was filmed running the same stack of creaseless ballots through the scanner multiple times. In all, approximately 18,000 votes were likely counted in Fulton County in those fateful hours, which was more than Biden's ultimate margin of victory in Georgia.

The simultaneous stopping of ballot counting signaled an irregularity so great that Trump's defeat at that moment appeared inevitable. It took nearly a week for the vote to be fully counted. The process actually seemed to slow to a standstill the nearer the process came to its end. In every place it mattered, with the exception of North Carolina, Biden crept ahead in the count and ultimately prevailed. The inevitable recounts changed nothing. When signature verification of mail-in ballots occurred, no outside observers were allowed and virtually no irregularities were discovered—an impossibility given the historic rate of error in absentee ballots and the tens of millions of ballots that were cast by mail this time around. Democrat election officials mocked the challengers; even their Republican counterparts denied any wrongdoing. When suits were filed in courts in a half dozen jurisdictions nearly every single one was dismissed for lack of standing or lack of justiciability. The media began sounding a uniform mantra: it was a free and fair election, the most secure in history, and Joe Biden was President-elect. Even Trump nominees on the bench—in District Courts, Circuit Courts and the Supreme Court—refused to hear the cases. When a lone Judge in Pennsylvania granted an injunction in favor of a challenge to the illegal changes made to the State's election laws on the eve of the election, the Supreme Court of the State took it upon itself within hours to issue an order dismissing the case with prejudice. No one had asked it to do so. No hearing was actually held. Equally bizarre was the refusal by Republican majorities in the senate and assemblies of six states that had flipped from Trump to Biden to formally investigate obvious voting irregularities and the many changes to their laws the executive and the judiciary had improperly affected shortly before the voting commenced. The fix, so it seemed, was in.

If Joe Biden actually won the election and didn't prevail simply because his party had perfected the art of the steal, it's a victory that continues to defy logic and all of the historic indicia of electoral success. The man himself is 78 years old—older by far than any man ever elected to the job. He's rude, crude and obnoxious, and while he bears some resemblance to his opponent in this respect, he lacks any originality, flare or charisma. When every other candidate in modern history has felt the need to be seen and heard among the people, if only to show them that they are physically up to the demands of the job and can relate to real people and think on their feet when asked a tough question, Joe Biden hid from the voters, and when he was rarely asked a question by an unfriendly citizen, he invariably insulted them. While his opponent generated massive displays of enthusiasm, Joe Biden attracted almost no one other than press to his own campaign events. When the votes were counted, he'd lost all but one of the bell-weather counties that victorious candidates for the office invariably win, and won the fewest number of counties nation-wide that any candidate has ever won and still won the election. He won States that his opponent managed to take from the Democrats four years before and helped restore to prosperity, despite saying he was going to double down on the unpopular coronavirus shutdowns and permanently dismantle the fossil fuel-related industries those States depend on for jobs, income and income taxes. He won the States of Georgia and Arizona that are solid red, where enthusiasm for the President was high. Such massive popular support as Biden supposedly registered on Election Day ordinarily would yield considerable coattails, pulling less popular down-ballot candidates to victory along with him. Bizarrely, Biden had no coattails. Instead, it was his losing competitor whose popularity contributed to the expansion of the number of state houses controlled by Republicans, added a governor to the Republican tally and narrowly missed retaking control of the House. Biden also achieved something most astounding of all: he managed to beat a President who grew his base of support by nearly ten million votes and drew percentage points away from the Democrats in key Democrat constituencies. Indeed, Biden scored the greatest popular vote total in history: greater than the first woman candidate Hillary Clinton; more even than the god-man idol of the Progressives, Barack Obama. What makes this accomplishment so stunningly improbable is that when Joe Biden ran against Clinton and Obama back in 2007 and 2008, he got creamed so badly that he never registered more than a single percentage point of support among Democrats and dropped out of the race even before the first primary. As Biden was already past his prime in 2008 and generated zero enthusiasm among voters in 2020, who really believes he won so resoundingly while promising "a dark winter" and a return to the policies that delivered the country to Trump four years earlier?

With his own judicial nominees and legislatures controlled by his own party refusing to intervene to address the many open and obvious irregularities, the only hope for Trump and his seventy-four million supporters lay in a challenge to the count of the electoral college votes by Vice President Pence and the Congress on January 6. With numerous Trump electors sending their own certificates to be considered by the Vice President and numerous Republicans in both houses prepared to object to the tallying for Biden of electors from the disputed States, it seemed not totally unreasonable to expect the election might be decided by the Congress voting as an assembly of States -- a prospect that favored the Republicans due to the fact that the congressional delegations of thirty States contained more Republicans than Democrats. Hoping to show congressional Republicans the support for this gambit that existed among the constituents who had placed them all in power, the President encouraged the gathering of the MAGA nation on the National Mall while Congress met to certify the election results. Standing before a crowd of several hundred thousand, he outlined his case for disregarding the official count and favorably acknowledged the plan of many of the participants to march toward the capitol itself to engage in peaceful demonstrations.

What happened next was dubbed a riot, an insurrection and an attempted coup, incited by the President and aiming to terrorize the Congress into disregarding their oaths to defend the Constitution and place Trump illegitimately on the throne. In truth, the so-called insurrection was but a mere handful of unruly people, and a large number of others who were permitted to walk into the building, take photographs and even enter the House Chamber that had been evacuated in haste by the members of Congress and pose for photographs snapped by their fellow protestors and members of the media. A large line of people was filmed walking a gauntlet of numerous capital police officers who gestured to them in friendly fashion, and some even took selfies with one of the officers. One man walked around with a lectern from the well of the House, while one especially minacious protestor crept into Nancy Pelosi's office and left a nasty note on her desk. Elsewhere on the premises, violence erupted. A window was broken and people wearing helmets climbed through. Scuffles between some police and protestors broke out. At one point, a plain cloths officer walked up to an unarmed demonstrator in the middle of a crowd and shot her point blank, killing her nearly instantly. Later, it was learned that Steve Sund, the head of the Capitol Police had asked days in advance for a larger security task force, but his supervisors, the Sergeants of Arms of the House and Senate, declined. Sund is an expert in crowd control and knew the capital well. A few more officers would easily have prevented entry of the Capitol building and diffused any commotion. It was as if an incident was desired by those inside the building, and once it happened, all but the screaming was over.

When the counting resumed later the same day, the wind from the sails of those who favored objecting to the vote had died. The media outcry became deafening in its uniformity. Anyone who objected to the count must be with the insurgents and an enemy of the nation and Constitution, a co-conspirator in the plot to steal the election from the freely and fairly elected President-elect. Many in the President's party now denounced and abandoned him. Members of his cabinet resigned. Twitter and Facebook banned him from their forums, and many who spoke in favor of the President or justified or defended the events at the Capitol or claimed Biden and the Democrats stole the election were banned as well. Hugely popular and lucratively monetized commentators who used the YouTube platform suddenly disappeared. The largest information technology company in the world, well known for its anti-Trump biases, excluded the primary (and conservative) competitor of Twitter from its servers and people identified in the many videos of the events at the Capitol were harassed at home, fired from their jobs, or arrested. The House passed a Resolution demanding the Vice President invoke the Twenty-Fifth Amendment, and then summarily impeached the President on a nearly party-line vote for doing nothing more than exercising his First Amendment Rights. Having spent much of the year reviling the national guard and calling for the disarming and defunding of the police, the progressive left now hailed law enforcement and the guard as the saviors of the nation. What was black was now white. What was bad was now the height of virtue. What was execrable when others even thought it was now the most necessary of all measures. Everyone knew it wasn't merely Trump who was to blame; it was his supporters as well, and if the country was to be safe from their evil, the Constitution itself would have to yield. Burn the cities down when the police shoot a man reaching into a car after having been told repeatedly to halt during an attempted arrest for domestic violence; but break a window in the Capitol building and pose for a photo in the well of the House flexing a bicep and wearing a ridiculous Buffalo hat and see how fast the national guard shows up with orders to shoot to kill.

These past four years might have prepared us better for this outcome, but the general outline was certainly predictable from the first. Donald J. Trump not only spoke about putting the nation and its people first; he actually succeeded in doing it. His success came at the expense of all those who had planned so long to integrate the country into a global system controlled by the self-styled best and brightest, who would insulate their own lives and fortunes from the policies they would impose on everyone else. For years, these types engaged in massive resistance to the President, even from within his administration, spied on him illegally and released confidential and classified material in the hopes of embarrassing him, or simply made it up when nothing better was available. They decried him as a racist, a hater of Muslims and Jews and the best friend the rich ever had, even as their own partisans oversaw the decay of communities where African Americans lived, welcomed monetary support from the super-rich, denied Jews had a right to a nation of their own, and scoffed at the existence of the God revered and worshiped by Muslim, Jew and Christian alike. In power in the nation's capital, they now promise, through the dying hand of their withered leader, to be guided by a "science" that conveniently supports a command economy that big government fascists, new age progressives and neo-Marxists have ever hungered for. They expect to secure the direct public funding for the slaughter of innocents in the womb, launch renewed legal assaults on religious liberty in the name of Covid, and provide massive bail outs of Blue States and cities whose Democrat governors ravaged their own citizens in order to wreck the economy Trump's policies revived after nearly a decade of stagnation under Bush and Obama. They vow to revive the Iran Deal that will unleash Iranian nuclear might, to restore a trade regime that formerly led to the divesting by American industry from America and its migration abroad, and to open the borders to allow the colonization of the United States by foreign nationals with no heed of any governing law. They promise to "build back better," to initiate the "great reset," pack the federal judiciary including the Supreme Court with enough progressive justices to radically alter the jurisprudence and meaning of the Constitution and turn the federal city that the Constitution requires be subject to the power of Congress into the Fifty-First State.

There is no real limit to what progressives aim to do with their new-found power. Dissatisfied with the status quo, they will continue to tinker with reality in the hopes of making something even God Himself apparently was not talented enough to conceive. For those who understand that the Constitution was designed to prevent such unhinged experimentation, to limit the power available to the government, and permit the people to find their happiness in the great common market the Constitution makes possible, the days ahead look to be a dark winter indeed. Whether there will be a spring to follow it only the passage of time and the unrolling of the scroll of our destiny as a people will tell.

INDEX

ABOUT THE AUTHOR

Rex Grady is a native of California and a graduate of the University of California at San Diego, the University of New Brunswick (Canada), and Empire College School of Law in Santa Rosa, California. He possesses B.A., M.A., M.A. and J.D. degrees from those institutions. He is a trial lawyer and, since the year 2007, Professor of Constitutional Law and Legal History at Empire College. In addition to this book, he is the author of *Oromocto Adieu: Four Decades on the River and the Origins of North Lake Parish*, *Let Ocean Seethe and Terra Slide: A History of the Sonoma Coast and the State Park that Shares its Name*, the two volume *Cases & Controversies: A Student's Guide to Law School Exams in Constitutional Law*, and the prequal to the instant volume, *What is this Freedom?: Law, Faith and History in the Time of Trump*. He lives in Santa Rosa, California with his wife and children.

Made in the USA
Monee, IL
04 November 2026

67385951R10295